THE *unofficial* GUIDE®
TO Walt Disney World® with Kids

2023

COME CHECK US OUT!

Supplement your valuable guidebook with tips, news, and deals by visiting our websites:

theunofficialguides.com

touringplans.com

Also, while there, sign up for The Unofficial Guide newsletter for even more travel tips and special offers.

Join the conversation on social media:

@theUGSeries   theUnofficialGuides

theUnofficialGuides   theUnofficialGuides

TheUnofficialGuideSeries

Other Unofficial Guides

The Disneyland Story: The Unofficial Guide to the Evolution of Walt Disney's Dream

Universal vs. Disney: The Unofficial Guide to American Theme Parks' Greatest Rivalry

The Unofficial Guide to Disney Cruise Line

The Unofficial Guide to Disneyland

The Unofficial Guide to Las Vegas

The Unofficial Guide to Universal Orlando

The Unofficial Guide to Walt Disney World

The Unofficial Guide to Washington, D.C.

THE *unofficial* GUIDE®
TO Walt Disney World® with Kids

2023

BOB SEHLINGER *and* LILIANE J. OPSOMER
with LEN TESTA

(Walt Disney World® is officially known as Walt Disney World® Resort.)

Please note that prices fluctuate in the course of time and that travel information changes under the impact of many factors that influence the travel industry. We therefore suggest that you write or call ahead for confirmation when making your travel plans. Every effort has been made to ensure the accuracy of information throughout this book, and the contents of this publication are believed to be correct at the time of printing. Nevertheless, the publishers cannot accept responsibility for errors or omissions, for changes in details given in this guide, or for the consequences of any reliance on the information provided by the same. Assessments of attractions and so forth are based upon the authors' own experiences; therefore, descriptions given in this guide necessarily contain an element of subjective opinion, which may not reflect the publisher's opinion or dictate a reader's own experience on another occasion. Readers are invited to write the publisher with ideas, comments, and suggestions for future editions.

Published by:
AdventureKEEN
2204 First Ave. S, Ste. 102
Birmingham, AL 35233

Cover design by Scott McGrew

Text design by Vertigo Design with modifications by Annie Long

For information on our other products and services or to obtain technical support, please contact us from within the United States at 800-678-7006 or by fax at 877-374-9016.

AdventureKEEN also publishes its books in a variety of electronic formats. Some content that appears in print may not be available in electronic formats.

ISBN 978-1-62809-131-1 (pbk.); ISBN 978-1-62809-132-8 (ebook)

Distributed by Publishers Group West

Manufactured in the United States of America

5 4 3 2 1

CONTENTS

LIST *of* MAPS

ACKNOWLEDGMENTS

THANKS TO OUR TEAM OF YOUNG PUNDITS—Lucy Bravo, A. J. Kwiatkowski, Sabrina Martins, Felicity Pipe, Isabelle Sanders, and Brendan Reilly—for their unique wisdom and fun-loving attitude (gotta have attitude, right?).

The cartoons were drawn by Tami Knight, possibly the nuttiest artist in Canada, and Chris Eliopoulos, a talented illustrator/Disney fanatic based in New Jersey.

For research and contributions concerning family dynamics and child behavior, thanks to psychologist Karen Turnbow. Kudos also to *Unofficial Guide* Research Director Len Testa and his team for the data collection and programming behind the touring plans in this guide.

Thanks also to Kate Johnson for her editorial and production work on this book. Steve Jones and Cassandra Poertner created the maps, Potomac Indexing prepared the index, and Annie Long did the layout. Also, thank you to Scott McGrew for patiently helping us find the best cover.

Much appreciation also goes to our publisher and chief operating officer, Molly Merkle, for encouraging Liliane to undertake this revision after two years of so many changes.

Last but certainly not least, we want to dedicate this edition to the hard work and courage of the cast members in all the theme parks. You continued to create magic under the most difficult of circumstances, and are still doing so.

To our readers, thank you for purchasing our book. When you visit, have a magical time and tell the cast members how much you appreciate their work. Brendan, one of our young contributors, advises: "Be nice to the cast members." We could not agree more.

—*Bob Sehlinger, Liliane Opsomer,*
and Len Testa

INTRODUCTION

WHY "UNOFFICIAL"?

DECLARATION OF INDEPENDENCE

THE AUTHORS AND RESEARCHERS OF THIS GUIDE specifically and categorically declare that they are and always have been totally independent of the Walt Disney Company Inc.; of Disneyland Inc.; of Walt Disney World Inc.; and of any and all other members of the Disney corporate family not listed.

The authors believe in the wondrous variety, joy, and excitement of the Walt Disney World attractions. At the same time, we recognize that Walt Disney World is a business. In this guide, we represent and serve you, the consumer. If a restaurant serves bad food, a gift item is overpriced, or a certain ride isn't worth the wait, we can say so, and in the process we hope to make your visit more fun, efficient, and economical.

YOUR UNOFFICIAL TOOLBOX

WHEN IT COMES TO WALT DISNEY WORLD, a couple with kids needs different advice than a party of seniors going to the EPCOT International Flower & Garden Festival. Likewise, adults touring without children and honeymooners all require their own special guidance.

To meet the varying needs of our readers, we created *The Unofficial Guide to Walt Disney World,* or what we call the Big Book. At 759 pages, it contains all the information that anyone traveling to Walt Disney World needs to have a super vacation. It's our cornerstone.

As thorough as we try to make the main guide, though, there just isn't sufficient space for all the tips and resources that may be useful to certain readers. Therefore, we've developed additional guides that provide information tailored to specific visitors. Though some advice from the Big Book, such as arriving early at the theme parks, is echoed in these guides, most of the information is unique.

Here's what's in the toolbox:

The guide you're reading now presents detailed planning and touring tips for a family vacation, along with special touring plans for families that you won't find in any other book. *The Unofficial Guide to Walt Disney World with Kids* is the only Unofficial Guide created with the guidance of a panel of kids, all of varying ages and backgrounds.

The Unofficial Guide to Universal Orlando, by Seth Kubersky with Bob Sehlinger and Len Testa, is a comprehensive guide to Universal Orlando. At 398 pages, it's the perfect tool for understanding and enjoying Universal's ever-expanding complex, consisting of theme parks, a water park, eight resort hotels, nightclubs, and restaurants. The guide includes field-tested touring plans that will save you hours of standing in line.

THE MUSIC OF LIFE

THOUGH IT'S COMMON in our culture to see life as a journey from cradle to grave, Alan Watts, a noted late-20th-century philosopher, saw it differently. He viewed life not as a journey but as a dance. In a journey, he said, you are trying to get somewhere and are consequently always looking ahead, anticipating the way stations and thinking about the end. Though the journey metaphor is popular, particularly in the West, it is generally characterized by a driven, goal-oriented mentality: a way of living and being that often inhibits those who subscribe to the journey metaphor from savoring each moment of life.

When you dance, by contrast, you hear the music and move in harmony with the rhythm. Like life, a dance has a beginning and an end. But unlike a journey, your objective is not to get to the end but to enjoy the dance while the music plays. You are totally in the moment and care nothing about where on the floor you stop when the dance is done.

As you begin to contemplate your Walt Disney World vacation, you may not have much patience for a philosophical discussion about journeys and dancing. But you see, it is relevant. If you are like most travel guide readers, you are apt to plan and organize and to anticipate and control, and you like things to go smoothly. And truth be told, this leads us to suspect that you are a person who looks ahead and is outcome-oriented. You may even feel a bit of pressure concerning your vacation. Vacations, after all, are special events and expensive ones as well. So you work hard to make the most of your experience.

We also believe that work, planning, and organization are important, and at Walt Disney World they are essential. But if they become your focus, you won't be able to hear the music and enjoy the dance. Though a lot of dancing these days resembles highly individualized seizures, there was a time when each dance involved specific steps, which you committed to memory. At first you were tentative and awkward, but eventually the steps became second nature and you didn't think about them anymore.

Metaphorically, this is what we want for you and your children or grandchildren as you embark on your Walt Disney World vacation. We want you to learn the steps ahead of time, so that when you're on your vacation and the music plays, you will be able to hear it, and you and your children will dance with grace and ease.

YOUR PERSONAL TRAINERS

WE'RE HERE TO WHIP YOU INTO SHAPE by helping you plan and enjoy your Walt Disney World vacation. Together we'll make sure that it really *is* a vacation, as opposed to, say, an ordeal or an expensive way to experience heatstroke. Our objective, simply put, is to ensure that you and your children have fun.

Because this book is specifically for adults traveling with children, we'll concentrate on your special needs and challenges. We'll share our most useful tips, as well as the travel secrets of more than 500,000 families interviewed.

So who *are* we? There's a bunch of us, actually. Your primary personal trainers are Liliane and Bob. Helping out big time are Felicity, Isabelle, Lucy, Sabrina, A. J., and Brendan.

Felicity is 11 years old and lives in the United Kingdom. Also known as Tink, she fancies all things Disney and enjoys singing, drawing, and making new friends. Tink adores meeting all the princesses and, like Princess Ariel, loves playing in the water. She

Felicity always looks forward to her next Florida vacation.

Felicity returned to Walt Disney World this summer and has some wise advice for all of us regarding COVID: Use lots of hand sanitizer when you've been on a ride, and wash your hands regularly, especially before eating. Wear a mask if you're on a ride and close to other people. Bring plenty of masks in case you misplace one. Ask a cast member to change their gloves if you are buying food from a cart. Avoid really crowded areas. Way to go, Felicity!

Our observer on the ground is 15-year-old Isabelle. She began visiting the parks when she was just 6 months old and has been an Annual Pass holder since the age of 3. She enjoys reading, especially the Harry Potter books, and plays soccer and the saxophone. She has been on more than 20 cruises and is a frequent contributor to the Disney Cruise Line blog podcast. Her favorite ride is Rock 'n' Roller Coaster Starring Aerosmith, and her favorite restaurant is Chef Art Smith's Homecomin'. Isabelle lives in Orlando and dislikes busy, crowded days at the parks.

Isabelle

Fifteen-year-old Lucy spends her time swimming, reading, and crafting, but most of all she loves to travel. She dotes on all animals, but her favorites are dogs. Lucy even has her own YouTube channel, where she shares all her hobbies. She lives in Rogers, Arkansas, though she wishes it were Orlando. She visits her pal

Lucy Mickey several times a year.

Sabrina is 11 years old and loves all things Disney. She's very active and plays softball, hockey, and basketball. Her favorite rides are Journey into Imagination with Figment and Space Mountain. She goes to Les Halles Boulangerie–Patisserie in EPCOT every chance she gets.

Sabrina

A. J., a 15-year-old black belt from Fanwood, New Jersey, participates in basketball and soccer, plays video games, and writes. His hamster, Nacho, also gets lots of playtime and attention. Together with his family, he visits Walt Disney World regularly, and when it's time to start planning, A. J. is hands-on. He is thrilled to share his tips with our readers.

A. J.

LILIANE

Twelve-year-old Brendan resides in Trophy Club, Texas. Some of his hobbies are playing tennis and golf, acting, and watching theme park videos. His favorite experience in the Disney parks is Star Wars: Galactic Starcruiser. His favorite park in Disney World is Disney's Hollywood Studios, but he also loves EPCOT!

Brendan

Liliane, a native of Belgium, moved to Birmingham, Alabama, in 2014 after 25 years in New York City. She's funny and very charming in the best European tradition, and she puts more energy into being a mom than you would think possible without performance-enhancing drugs. Optimistic and happy, she loves the sweet and sentimental side of Walt Disney World. You might find her whooping it up at the *Hoop-Dee-Doo Musical Revue,* but she dreads riding a roller coaster with Bob.

Speak of the devil, Bob isn't a curmudgeon exactly, but he likes to unearth Disney's secrets and show readers how to beat the system. His idea of a warm fuzzy might be the Rock 'n' Roller Coaster, but he'll help you save lots of money, find the best hotels and restaurants, and return home less than terminally exhausted. These caricatures pretty much sum up the essence of Bob and Liliane.

BOB

If you're thinking that the cartoons paint a somewhat conflicted picture of your personal trainers, well, you're right. Admittedly, Bob and Liliane have been known to disagree on a thing or two. Together, however, they make a good team. You can count on them to give you both sides of every story. Let's put it this way: Liliane will encourage you to bask in the universal-brotherhood theme of It's a Small World. Bob will show up later to help you get the darned song out of your head.

Len is our research dude. His really complicated scientific wizardry will help you save a bundle of time—would you believe 4 hours in a single day?—by staying out of those pesky lines.

Oops, almost forgot: There's another team member you need to meet. Called a Wuffo, she's our very own character. She'll warn you when rides are too scary, too dark, too wet, or too rough, and she'll tell you which rides to avoid if you have motion sickness. You'll bump into her throughout the book doing, well, what characters do.

ABOUT *This* GUIDE

DISNEY WORLD HAS BEEN OUR BEAT for more than three decades, and we know it inside out. During those years, we've observed many thousands of parents and grandparents trying—some successfully, others less so—to have a good time at Walt Disney World. Some of these, owing to unfortunate dynamics within the family, were handicapped right from the start. Others were simply overwhelmed by the size and complexity of Walt Disney World; still others fell victim to a lack of foresight, planning, and organization.

Disney World is a better destination for some families than for others. Likewise, some families are more compatible on vacation than others. The likelihood of experiencing a truly wonderful Disney World vacation transcends the theme parks and attractions offered. In fact, the theme parks and attractions are the only constants in the equation. The variables that will define the experience and determine its success are intrinsic to your family: things like attitude, sense of humor, cohesiveness, stamina, flexibility, and conflict resolution.

The simple truth is that Disney World can test you as a family. It will overwhelm you with choices and force you to make decisions about how to spend your time and money. It will challenge you physically as you cover miles on foot and wait in lines touring the theme parks. You will have to respond to surprises (both good and bad) and deal with hyperstimulation.

This guide will forewarn and forearm you. It will help you decide whether a Disney World vacation is a good idea for you and your family at this particular time. It will help you sort out and address the attitudes and family dynamics that can affect your experience. Most important, it will provide the confidence that comes with good planning and realistic expectations.

LETTERS AND COMMENTS FROM READERS

MANY WHO USE *The Unofficial Guide to Walt Disney World with Kids* write us to comment or share their own touring strategies. We appreciate all such input, both positive and critical, and encourage our readers to continue writing. Their comments and observations are frequently incorporated into revised editions of the guide and have contributed immeasurably to its improvement.

BOB In this book, you'll read experienced Disney World visitors' opinions of the parks that you can apply to your own travel circumstances.

Privacy Policy

If you write us or complete our reader survey, rest assured that we won't release your name and address to any mailing-list companies, direct mail advertisers, or other third parties. Unless you instruct us otherwise, we'll assume that you don't object to being quoted in the guide.

How to Contact the Authors

Bob, Liliane, and Len
The Unofficial Guide to Walt Disney World with Kids
2204 First Ave. S, Ste. 102
Birmingham, AL 35233
info@theunofficialguides.com
Facebook: TheUnofficialGuideToWaltDisneyWorldWithKids
Twitter: @TheUGSeries

When emailing us, please tell us where you're from. If you snail mail us, put your address on both your letter and envelope; the two sometimes get separated. It's also a good idea to include your phone number. Because we're travel writers, we're often out of the office for long periods of time, so forgive us if our response is slow. Unofficial Guide email isn't forwarded to us when we're traveling, but we'll respond as soon as possible after we return.

Online Reader Survey

Express your opinions about your Walt Disney World visit at touring plans.com/walt-disney-world/survey. This online questionnaire lets every member of your party, regardless of age, tell us what he or she thinks about attractions, hotels, restaurants, and more.

If you'd rather print out and mail us the survey, send it to the address above. In any case, let us know what you think!

A QUICK TOUR *of a* BIG WORLD

WALT DISNEY WORLD COMPRISES more than 40 square miles, an area twice as large as Manhattan. Situated strategically in this vast expanse are the **Magic Kingdom, EPCOT, Disney's Animal Kingdom,** and **Disney's Hollywood Studios** theme parks. Walt Disney World also contains two water parks, **Blizzard Beach** and **Typhoon Lagoon.** But there's more: over three dozen hotels and a campground; more than 100 restaurants; a massive year-round sports center; a shopping and entertainment complex, **Disney Springs;** four interconnected lakes; six convention centers; four golf courses; and an array of spas, recreation options, and other activities.

The transportation system consists of four-lane highways, elevated **monorails,** a network of **canals,** and the **Skyliner** gondola system. There is also a point-to-point transportation service connecting the theme parks and the resorts. The **Minnie Van** service works with the Lyft app to get from resort to resort, or from the resort to a park and back. It is also available for transportation to and from Orlando International Airport. And if this weren't enough, there is also a 11,500-acre **Wilderness Preserve,** established in partnership with The Nature Conservancy and funded by Disney to help mitigate impacts on wetlands caused by its theme park developments. More on this on page 457.

THE MAJOR THEME PARKS

The Magic Kingdom

When people think of Walt Disney World, most think of the Magic Kingdom, opened in 1971. It consists of adventures, rides, and shows featuring Disney cartoon characters, as well as Cinderella Castle. It's only one element of Disney World, but it remains the heart.

The Magic Kingdom is divided into six "lands," with five arranged around a central hub. First you come to **Main Street, U.S.A.,** which connects the Magic Kingdom entrance with the hub. Clockwise around the hub are **Adventureland, Frontierland, Liberty Square, Fantasyland,** and **Tomorrowland.** The Magic Kingdom has more rides, shows, and entertainment than any other WDW theme park. A comprehensive tour takes two days; a tour of the highlights can be done in one full day.

Four hotels (**Contemporary Resort** and **Bay Lake Tower, Polynesian Village & Villas,** and **Grand Floridian Resort & Villas**) are connected to the Magic Kingdom by monorail and boat. Two other hotels—**Shades of Green** (operated by the US Department of Defense, for service members) and **Wilderness Lodge** (including its adjacent time-share permutations, **Boulder Ridge Villas** and **Copper Creek Villas & Cabins**)—are nearby but aren't served by the monorail. Also nearby and served by boat and bus is **Fort Wilderness Resort & Campground.**

EPCOT

Opened in October 1982, EPCOT is twice as big as the Magic Kingdom and comparable in scope. As of 2019, the "front" (southern) part of EPCOT, formerly known as Future World, now consists of three areas (**World Discovery, World Celebration,** and **World Nature**) holding giant pavilions dedicated to human creativity, technological advancement, the natural world, and—increasingly—cartoon characters. **World Showcase,** the "back" (northern) part of EPCOT, is arranged around a 40-acre lagoon and presents the architectural, social, and cultural heritages of almost a dozen nations; each country is represented by replicas of famous landmarks and settings familiar to world travelers.

The EPCOT resort hotels—the **BoardWalk Inn & Villas, Dolphin, Swan, Swan Reserve,** and **Yacht & Beach Club Resorts and Beach Club Villas**—are within a 5- to 15-minute walk of the International Gateway, the World Showcase entrance to the theme park. The hotels are also linked to EPCOT and Disney's Hollywood Studios by canal and walkway. EPCOT is connected to the Magic Kingdom and its hotels by monorail. An elevated gondola system called the Skyliner links EPCOT and Disney's Hollywood Studios to Disney's Pop Century, Art of Animation, Caribbean Beach, and Riviera Resorts.

continued on page 12

South Orlando

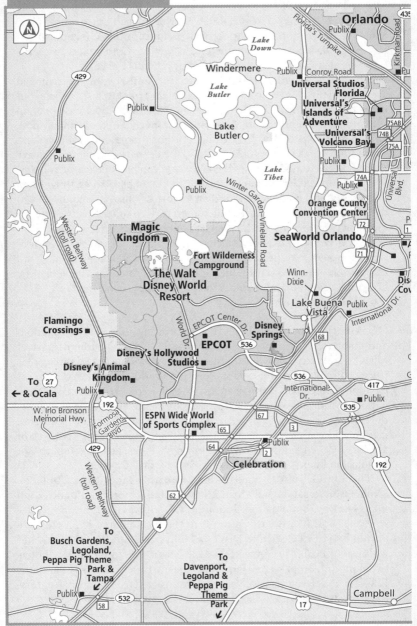

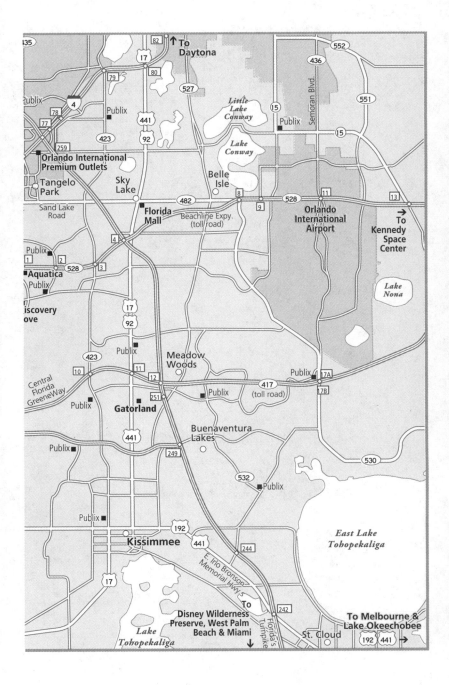

Walt Disney World

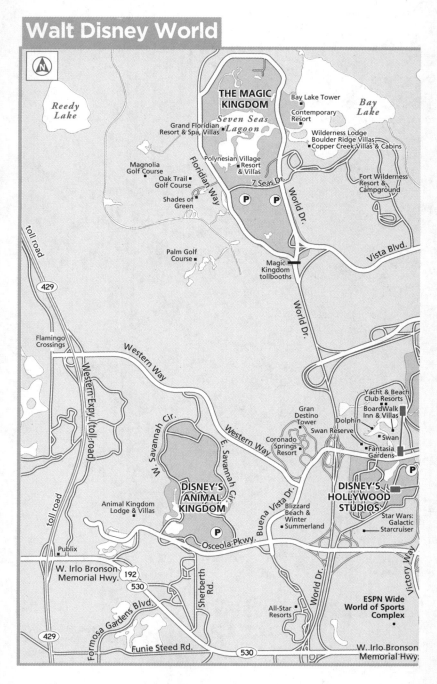

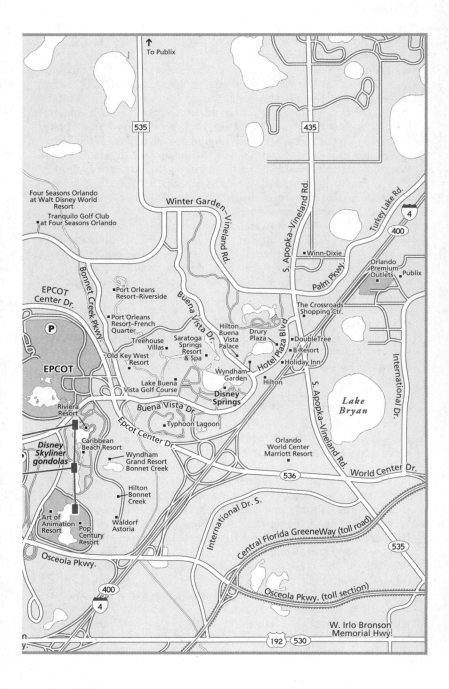

continued from page 7

Disney's Animal Kingdom

About five times the size of the Magic Kingdom, Disney's Animal Kingdom combines zoological exhibits with rides, shows, and live entertainment. The park is arranged in a hub-and-spoke configuration somewhat like the Magic Kingdom. A lush tropical rainforest serves as Main Street, funneling visitors to **Discovery Island,** the park's hub. Dominated by the park's central icon, the 14-story-tall, hand-carved **Tree of Life,** Discovery Island offers services, shopping, and dining. From there, guests can access the themed areas: **Pandora, Africa, Rafiki's Planet Watch, Asia,** and **DinoLand U.S.A.** Discovery Island, Africa, Rafiki's Planet Watch, and DinoLand U.S.A. opened in 1998, followed by Asia in 1999. Africa, the largest themed area at 100 acres, features free-roaming herds in a re-creation of the Serengeti Plain.

Pandora: The World of Avatar, a 12-acre extension, opened to much fanfare in 2017. Based on James Cameron's *Avatar* film, Pandora includes two headliner rides and one restaurant. The big draw, however, is Pandora's scenery—including "floating mountains" and glow-in-the-dark plants—which Disney has replicated here. See page 355 for more details.

Disney's Animal Kingdom has its own parking lot and is connected to other Walt Disney World destinations by the Disney bus system. No hotels are located within Animal Kingdom proper. The **All-Star Resorts, Animal Kingdom Lodge & Villas, Art of Animation Resort, Coronado Springs Resort** and **Gran Destino Tower,** and **Pop Century Resort** are all nearby.

Disney's Hollywood Studios

Opened in 1989 as Disney-MGM Studios in an area a little larger than the Magic Kingdom, Disney's Hollywood Studios (DHS) consists of two areas. One, occupying about 50% of the Studios, is a theme park focused on movies, music, and TV. Park highlights include a re-creation of **Hollywood and Sunset Boulevards** from Hollywood's Golden Age, several rides and musical shows, and a movie stunt show. **Mickey & Minnie's Runaway Railway,** replacing The Great Movie Ride inside the replica of Grauman's Chinese Theatre, opened in 2020. The other half of DHS consists of two immersive lands based on popular Disney film franchises. **Toy Story Land** opened in 2018 with three highly themed rides for children. **Star Wars: Galaxy's Edge,** opened in 2019, has two state-of-the-art, large rides for older children, teens, and adults.

On March 1, 2022, the eagerly awaited **Star Wars: Galactic Starcruiser,** a two-night, immersive, *Star Wars*–themed hotel, opened adjacent to Disney's Hollywood Studios and close to the Star Wars: Galaxy's Edge part of the park (though not connected to it).

Transportation from the hotel to the land is completely separate from regular transportation to the Studios and is available only to guests staying at Star Wars: Galactic Starcruiser.

DHS is connected to other Walt Disney World areas by highway, canal, and gondola but not by monorail. Guests can park in the Studios' parking lot or commute by bus. Guests at most EPCOT resort hotels can reach the Studios by boat, on foot, or by gondola. The new Skyliner gondola system connects DHS with EPCOT, as well as the Art of Animation, Pop Century, Caribbean Beach, and Riviera Resorts.

THE WATER PARKS

DISNEY WORLD HAS TWO MAJOR water parks: **Typhoon Lagoon** and **Blizzard Beach.** Opened in 1989, Typhoon Lagoon is distinguished by a wave pool capable of making 6-foot waves. Blizzard Beach (*temporarily closed*) opened in 1995 and features more slides. Both parks are beautifully landscaped and pay great attention to atmosphere and aesthetics. Typhoon Lagoon and Blizzard Beach have their own adjacent parking lots and can be reached by Disney bus.

OTHER WALT DISNEY WORLD VENUES

Disney Springs

Themed to evoke a Florida waterfront town, Disney Springs encompasses the **Marketplace,** on the east; the **West Side; The Landing,** on the waterfront; and **Town Center,** in the middle, all featuring shops and restaurants and a Florida–meets–Spanish Colonial architectural theme.

Multistory parking garages (Orange, Lime, and Grapefruit) and two surface lots (Strawberry and Watermelon) serve the area. There are two additional lots: Lemon, which is for valet parking ($20 plus tax and gratuity), and Mango, which is a preferred lot, meaning that for a fee of $10 you can park closer to the entrance of Disney Springs' West Side (this is the closest parking for attending a Cirque du Soleil show). Parking spaces for guests with disabilities are available in all lots and garages; a valid disability parking permit is required.

Disney Springs is accessed via Disney transportation from Disney resorts. Bus service from the four Disney theme parks to Disney Springs operates daily, 4–11 p.m., or until 2 hours after theme parks close, whichever is earlier. There is no transportation from Disney Springs to the theme parks.

Disney's BoardWalk

Near EPCOT, the BoardWalk is an idealized replication of an East Coast 1930s waterfront resort. Open all day, the BoardWalk features upscale restaurants, shops and galleries, and a brewpub. In the evening, a nightclub with dueling pianos and a DJ dance club join the lineup;

both are for guests age 21 and up only. There's no admission fee for the BoardWalk, but the piano bar levies a cover charge at night. This area is anchored by the **BoardWalk Inn & Villas,** along with its adjacent convention center. The BoardWalk is within walking distance of the EPCOT resorts, EPCOT's International Gateway entrance, and Disney's Hollywood Studios. Boat transportation is available to and from EPCOT and Disney's Hollywood Studios, the Skyliner gondolas connect the BoardWalk to the Studios and the hotels on its route, and buses serve other Disney World locations.

ESPN Wide World of Sports Complex

The 220-acre Wide World of Sports is a state-of-the-art competition and training facility consisting of a 9,500-seat ballpark; an 8,000-seat arena; a field house; and venues for baseball, softball, tennis, track and field, volleyball, and dozens of other sports. The complex also hosts a mind-boggling calendar of professional and amateur competitions. Walt Disney World guests not participating in events may pay admission to watch any of the scheduled competitions.

Disney Cruise Line: The Mouse at Sea

Disney launched its own cruise line in 1998 with the 2,400-passenger *Disney Magic.* Four more ships were added, and two more will join the fleet in a few years. Most cruises depart from Port Canaveral, Florida (about 90 minutes from Walt Disney World), or from Miami, with three-, four-, and seven-night itineraries. Bahamian and Caribbean cruises include a day at Castaway Cay, Disney's 1,000-acre private island, or Lighthouse Point, a new, 750-acre private resort for Disney cruise guests scheduled to open in 2024. Find out more on the Lighthouse Point website Disney launched early 2020, lighthousepointbahamas.com. Cruises can be packaged with a stay at Disney World. Disney offers a free online video at disney cruiseline.com to help familiarize you with Disney Cruise Line cruises.

LILIANE Board the ship as early as possible. Check on your dining rotation, and reserve Enchanté (on the *Disney Wish*), Palo, or Remy; shore excursions if you haven't done so; spa treatments; and kids' programs. Relax and get ready for the departure party.

Disney cruises are perfect for families and for kids of all ages. Though the cruises are family-oriented, extensive children's programs and elaborate child-care facilities allow grown-ups plenty of opportunities to relax and have some time to themselves. The ships are modern ocean liners with classic steamship lines. The cabins are among the most spacious in the industry, and the staff is attentive and accommodating. From the waitstaff at breakfast, lunch, and dinner to the cabin stewards, we have not experienced any better.

SABRINA Bring lots of magnets to decorate the door of your cabin, and put your room key on a lanyard around your neck, so you don't lose it.

Cabin design reveals Disney's finely tuned sense of the needs of families and offers a cruise-industry first: a split bathroom with a bathtub/shower combo and sink in one room, and a toilet, sink, and vanity in another. This configuration, found in all but standard inside cabins, allows any family member to use the bathroom without monopolizing it.

A big party with appearances by Mickey and Minnie marks departures, when the ship's horn toots "When You Wish Upon a Star." Halfway through your voyage, Disney throws a deck party, where Mickey saves all passengers from Captain Hook and his evil plans.

Dining is a true pleasure. Each night, passengers move to a different family restaurant—each with its own unique theme and menu—and take their table companions and waitstaff with them. In addition to the family restaurants, the ships have a range of cafés offering pizza, burgers, sandwiches, and ice-cream bars. Room service is available 24-7.

LILIANE Disney strictly enforces a minimum age limit (18) for dining at Enchanté, Palo, and Remy.

For a night out without kids, Palo, which offers tables with a view, is a must. Reservations are also a must, and a surcharge of $45 per person is added for this service to your onboard bill. The food is excellent, the ambience sophisticated.

SABRINA Don't eat too much ice cream just because it's free. You may end up feeling sick.

In addition to Palo on the *Disney Magic* and *Wonder*, the *Dream* and the *Fantasy* crank it up a notch with Remy. Chefs Scott Hunnel of Victoria & Albert's and Arnaud Lallement from L'Assiette Champenoise (a Michelin three-star restaurant outside Reims, France) created the French-inspired menu, served in an Art Nouveau–style dining room. This upscale dining experience on the high seas costs $125 per person. If you think this is a little over the top, we completely agree. Whatever happened to the no-frills, great-food philosophy we learned from Remy in *Ratatouille*?

Lallement also created a French-influenced menu for the *Disney Wish*'s new, adults-only restaurant, Enchanté, inspired by Disney's *Beauty and the Beast*. Dinner is $125 per person. On the same ship, Palo Steakhouse strikes a balance between Italian fare and modern steakhouse dining, with decor inspired by Cogsworth from *Beauty and the Beast*. Prix fixe lunch or dinner is $45 per person.

The Disney ships offer 15,000-plus square feet of playrooms and other kids' facilities. Programs include interactive activities, play areas supervised by trained counselors, and a children's drop-off service in the evening. Passengers can register their children for the nursery, and group babysitting is available for select hours every day.

ISABELLE The Oceaneer Club has interactive activities and lots of arts and crafts. If you leave the crafts you make behind, there is a chance they will be tossed. Bring a small bag with you to save your masterpieces!

Big with kids of all ages are the pools and the nightly entertainment on board, which show Disney at its best. The theaters stage several musical productions each cruise, and with full-screen cinemas, show first-run movies as well as classic Disney films. Movies are also played poolside on a screen affixed to the forward funnel in the ships' family-pool areas.

Shore excursions depend on the itinerary, but all Caribbean and Bahamian cruises make at least one call at **Castaway Cay.** The best way to enjoy the island is to disembark first thing in the morning and secure a prime spot at the beach, complete with hammock and shade. **Castaway Family Beach** is served by a tram running every 5 minutes (or it's a 0.25-mile walk). **Cookie's BBQ** and **Cookie's Too** serve an array of food that is included in the price of your cruise. Programs for kids on Castaway Cay give parents a chance to enjoy **Serenity Bay,** the adults-only beach.

ISABELLE On Castaway Cay get two cookies from Cookie's BBQ or Cookie's Too and put ice cream in between to make your own ice cream sandwich.

Liliane sailed the *Disney Wish* just recently. Read about her three-night voyage at tinyurl.com/wishreview.

To get the most out of your cruise, we recommend *The Unofficial Guide to Disney Cruise Line,* by Erin Foster with Len Testa and Ritchey Halphen, which presents advice for first-time cruisers; money-saving tips for booking your cruise; and detailed profiles for restaurants, shows, and nightclubs, along with deck plans and thorough coverage of the ports visited by DCL.

DISNEY-SPEAK POCKET TRANSLATOR

THOUGH IT MAY COME AS A SURPRISE to many, Walt Disney World has its own somewhat peculiar language. Here are some terms you're likely to bump into.

DISNEY-SPEAK	ENGLISH DEFINITION
ADVENTURE	Ride
ATTRACTION	Ride or theater show
ATTRACTION HOST	Ride operator
BACKSTAGE	Behind the scenes, out of view of customers
CAST MEMBER	Employee
CHARACTER	Disney character impersonated by an employee
COSTUME	Work attire or uniform
DARK RIDE	Indoor ride
DAY GUEST	Any customer not staying at a Disney resort
FACE CHARACTER	A character who does not wear a head-covering costume (Snow White, Cinderella, Jasmine, and the like)
GENERAL PUBLIC	Same as day guest
GENIE+/ LIGHTNING LANE	New ride-reservation system that replaced FastPass+
GREETER	Employee positioned at an attraction entrance
GUEST	Customer
HIDDEN MICKEYS	Frontal silhouette of Mickey's head worked subtly into the design of buildings, railings, vehicles, golf greens, attractions, and just about anything else
OFF-SITE	A hotel located outside Walt Disney World's boundaries
ON-SITE	A hotel located inside Walt Disney World's boundaries and served by Disney's transportation network
ONSTAGE	In full view of customers
PRESHOW	Entertainment at an attraction prior to the feature presentation
RESORT GUEST	A customer staying at a Disney resort
SECURITY HOST	Security guard
SOFT OPENING	Opening a park or attraction before its stated opening date
TRANSITIONAL EXPERIENCE	An element of the queuing area and/or preshow that provides a story line or information essential to understanding the attraction

PART 1

BASIC CONSIDERATIONS

IS WALT DISNEY WORLD *for* EVERYONE?

ALMOST ALL VISITORS ENJOY WALT DISNEY WORLD on some level and find things to see and do that they like. In fact, for many, the theme park attractions are just the tip of the iceberg. The more salient question, then—this is a family vacation, after all—is whether the members of your family basically like the same things. If you do, fine. If not, how will you handle the differing agendas?

A mother from Toronto described her husband's aversion to Disney's (in his terms) "phony, plastic, and idealized version of life." As they toured the parks, he was a real cynic and managed to diminish the experience for the rest of the family. As it happened, however, Dad's pejorative point of view didn't extend to the Disney golf courses. So Mom packed him up and sent him golfing while the family enjoyed the parks.

If you have someone in your family who doesn't like theme parks or, for whatever reason, doesn't care for Disney's brand of entertainment, it helps to get that attitude out in the open. Our recommendation is to deal with the person up front. Glossing over or ignoring the contrary opinion and hoping that "Tom will like it once he gets there" is naive and unrealistic. Either leave Tom at home or help him discover and plan activities that he will enjoy, resigning yourself in the process to the fact that the family won't be together at all times.

KNOW THYSELF, AND NOTHING TO EXCESS

THIS GOOD ADVICE WAS MADE AVAILABLE to ancient Greeks courtesy of the oracle of Apollo at Delphi. First, concerning the "know thyself" part, we want you to do some serious thinking about what you want in a vacation. We also want you to entertain the notion that having fun on your vacation may be different from doing and seeing as much as possible. Because Walt Disney World is expensive, many families confuse "seeing everything" to "get our money's worth" with having a great time. Sometimes the two are compatible, but more often they are not. So if sleeping in late, sunbathing by the pool, or taking a nap ranks high on your vacation hit parade, you need to accord them due emphasis on your Disney visit, even if it means you see less of the theme parks.

Which brings us to the "nothing to excess" part. At Walt Disney World, especially if you are touring with children, less is definitely

 LILIANE You can enjoy a perfectly wonderful time in the World if you're realistic, organized, and prepared.

more. Trust us—you cannot go full tilt dawn to dark in the theme parks day after day. First you'll get tired, then you'll get cranky, and then you'll adopt a production mentality ("We have three more rides, and then we can go back to the hotel"). Finally, you'll hit the wall because you just can't maintain the pace.

Plan on seeing Walt Disney World in bite-size chunks with plenty of sleeping, swimming, napping, and relaxing in between. Ask yourself over and over in both the planning stage and while you are at Walt Disney World: What will contribute the greatest contentedness, satisfaction, and harmony? Trust your instincts. If stopping for ice cream or returning to the hotel for a swim feels like more fun than seeing another attraction, do it— even if it means wasting the remaining hours of an admissions pass.

BOB Determine your needs and preferences before you leave home, and develop an itinerary that incorporates all the things that make you happiest.

The **AGE THING**

THERE IS A LOT OF SERIOUS REFLECTION among parents and grandparents in regard to how old a child should be before embarking on a trip to Walt Disney World. The answer, not always obvious, stems from the personalities and maturity of the children, as well as the personalities and parenting style of the adults.

WALT DISNEY WORLD FOR INFANTS AND TODDLERS

WE BELIEVE THAT TRAVELING with infants and toddlers is a great idea. Developmentally, travel is a stimulating learning experience for even the youngest of children. Infants, of course,

 BOB Sehlinger's Law postulates that the number of adults required to take care of an active toddler is equal to the number of adults present, plus one.

will not know Mickey Mouse from a draft horse but will respond to sun and shade, music, bright colors, and the extra attention they receive from you. From first steps to full mobility, toddlers respond to the excitement and spectacle of Disney World, though of course in a much different way than you do. Your toddler will prefer splashing in fountains and clambering over curbs and benches to experiencing most attractions, but no matter: He or she will still have a great time.

Somewhere between 4 and 6 years old, your child will experience the first vacation that he or she will remember as an adult. Though more likely to remember the coziness of the hotel room than the theme parks, the child will be able to experience and comprehend many attractions and will be a much fuller participant in your vacation. Even so, his or her favorite activity is likely to be swimming in the hotel pool.

LILIANE Traveling with infants and toddlers sharpens parenting skills and makes the entire family more mobile and flexible, resulting in a richer, fuller life for all.

As concerns infants and toddlers, there are good reasons and bad reasons for vacationing at Walt Disney World. A good reason for taking your little one to Disney World is that you want to go and there's no one available to care for your child during your absence. Philosophically, we are very much against putting your life (including your vacations) on hold until your children are older. Especially if you have children of varying ages (or plan to, for that matter), it's better to take the show on the road than to wait until the youngest child reaches the perceived ideal age.

An illogical reason, however, for taking an infant or toddler to Disney World is that you think it's the perfect vacation destination for babies. It's not. For starters, the attractions are geared more toward older children and adults. Even play areas such as Tom Sawyer Island in the Magic Kingdom are developed with older children in mind.

LILIANE Baby supplies, including disposable diapers, formula, and baby food, are for sale, and there are rockers and special chairs for nursing mothers.

That said, let us stress that, for the well prepared, taking a toddler to Disney World can be a glorious experience. There's truly nothing like watching your child respond to the colors, the sounds, the festivity, and, most of all, the characters. You'll return home with scrapbooks of photos that you will treasure forever. Your little one won't remember much, but your memories will be unforgettable.

If you elect to take your infant or toddler to Disney World, rest assured that their needs have been anticipated by Disney. The major theme parks have centralized facilities for infant and toddler care. Everything necessary for changing diapers, preparing formula, and warming bottles and food is available. Dads in charge of little ones are welcome at the centers and can use most services offered. In addition, men's rooms in the major theme parks have changing tables.

Infants and toddlers are allowed to experience any attraction that doesn't have minimum height or age restrictions. A Minneapolis mom suggests using a baby sling:

The baby sling was great when standing in lines—much better than a stroller, which you have to park before getting in line (and navigate through crowds). My baby was still nursing when we went to Disney World. The only really great place I found to nurse in the Magic Kingdom was a hidden bench in the shade in Adventureland between the snack stand (next to the Enchanted Tiki Room*) and the small shops. It is impractical to go to the baby station every time, so a nursing mom should be comfortable about nursing in very public situations.*

Two points in our reader's comment warrant elaboration. First, the rental strollers at all of the major theme parks are designed for toddlers and children up to 3 and 4 years old but are definitely not for infants. If you bring pillows and padding, the rental strollers can be made to work. We recommend you bring or rent a collapsible stroller. The park strollers cannot leave the parks, and there will be many instances when you will have to walk, whether it's to and from your hotel room to the Disney transportation or from and to your car in the parking lot at the end of your park visit.

Even if you opt for a stroller (your own or a rental), we nevertheless recommend that you also bring a baby sling or baby/child backpack. There will be many times when you will have to park the stroller and carry your child.

 LILIANE In addition to providing an alternative to carrying your child, a stroller serves as a handy cart for diaper bags, water bottles, and other items you deem necessary.

The second point that needs addressing is our reader's perception that there are not many good places in the theme parks for breastfeeding unless you are accustomed to nursing in public. Many nursing moms recommend breastfeeding during a dark Disney theater presentation. This works only if the presentation is long enough for the baby to finish nursing. *The Hall of Presidents* at the Magic Kingdom and *The American Adventure* at EPCOT will afford you about 23 and 29 minutes, respectively.

Many Disney shows run back-to-back, with only 1 or 2 minutes in between to change the audience. If you want to breastfeed and require more time than the length of the show, tell the cast member on entering that you want to breastfeed and ask if you can remain in the theater and watch a second showing while your baby finishes. Keep in mind that many shows may have special effects or loud soundtracks that may make children even as old as 7 uncomfortable.

If you can adjust to nursing in more public places with your breast and the baby's head covered with a shawl or some such, nursing will not be a problem at all. Even on the most crowded days, you can always find a corner of a restaurant or a comparatively secluded bench or garden spot to nurse. Finally, the Baby Care Centers, with their private nursing rooms, are centrally located in all of the parks except the Studios.

A mom from Georgia wrote to us, and we totally agree with her:

Many women have no problem nursing uncovered, and they have the right to do so in public without being criticized. Even women who want to cover up may have a baby who won't cooperate and flings off the cover; plus, it's not necessary to sit through all of The Hall of Presidents *to feed your child. Babies will eat almost anywhere, and mothers shouldn't feel pressured to sneak off when a baby is hungry.*

WALT DISNEY WORLD FOR 4- TO 6-YEAR-OLDS

CHILDREN AGES 4–6 VARY immensely in their capacity to comprehend and enjoy Walt Disney World. With this age group, the go/no-go decision is a judgment call. If your child is sturdy, easygoing, and fairly adventuresome, and demonstrates a high degree of independence, the trip will probably work. On the other hand, if your child tires easily, is temperamental, or is a bit timid or reticent in embracing new experiences, you're much better off waiting a few years. Whereas the travel and sensory-overload problems of infants and toddlers can be addressed and (usually) remedied on the go, discontented 4- to 6-year-olds have the ability to stop a family dead in its tracks, as this mother of three from Cape May, New Jersey, attests:

> My 5-year-old was scared pretty badly on a dark ride our first day at Disney World. For the rest of the trip, we had to reassure her before each and every ride before she would go.

If you have a tiring, clinging, and/or difficult 4- to 6-year-old who, for whatever circumstances, will be part of your group, you can sidestep or diminish potential problems with a bit of pretrip preparation. Even if your preschooler is plucky and game, the same prep measures (described later in this section) will enhance his or her experience and make life easier for the rest of the family.

Parents who understand that a visit with 4- to 6-year-old children is going to be more about the cumulative experience than it is about seeing it all will have a blast, as well as wonderful memories of their children's amazement.

THE IDEAL AGE

THOUGH OUR READERS REPORT both successful trips and disasters with children of all ages, the consensus is that the ideal children's ages for family compatibility and togetherness at Walt Disney World are 8–12 years. This age group is old enough, tall enough, and sufficiently stalwart to experience, understand, and appreciate practically all Disney attractions. Moreover, they are developed to the extent that they can get around the parks on their own steam without being carried or collapsing. Best of all, they're still young enough to enjoy being with Mom and Dad. From our experience, ages 10–12 are better than 8 and 9, though what you gain in maturity is at the cost of that irrepressible, wide-eyed wonder so prevalent in the 8- and 9-year-olds.

WALT DISNEY WORLD FOR TEENS

TEENS LOVE WALT DISNEY WORLD, and for parents of teens, the World is a nearly perfect, albeit expensive, vacation choice. Though your teens might not be as wide-eyed and impressionable as their younger sibs, they are at an age where they can sample, understand, and enjoy practically everything Disney World has to offer.

For parents, Walt Disney World is a vacation destination where you can permit your teens an extraordinary amount of freedom. The entertainment is wholesome; the venues are safe; and the entire complex of hotels, theme parks, restaurants, and shopping centers is accessible via the Disney World transportation system. The transportation system allows you, for example, to enjoy a romantic dinner and an early bedtime while your teens take in the late-night fireworks at the theme parks. After the fireworks, Disney transportation will deposit them safely back at the hotel.

Because most adolescents relish freedom, you may have difficulty keeping your teens with the rest of the family. Thus, if one of your objectives is to spend time with your teenage children during your Disney World vacation, you will need to establish some clear-cut guidelines regarding togetherness and separateness before you leave home. Make your teens part of the discussion and try to meet them halfway in crafting a decision everyone can live with. For your teens, touring on their own at Walt Disney World is tantamount to being independent in a large city. It's intoxicating, to say the least, and can be an excellent learning experience, if not a rite of passage. In any event, we're not suggesting that you just turn them loose. Rather, we are just attempting to sensitize you to the fact that, for your teens, there are some transcendent issues involved.

Most teens crave the company of other teens. If you have a solitary teen in your family, do not be surprised if he or she wants to invite a friend on your vacation. If you are invested in sharing intimate, quality time with your teen, the presence of a friend will make this difficult, if not impossible. However, if you turn down the request to bring a friend, be prepared to go the extra mile to be a companion to your teen at Disney World. Expressed differently, if you're a teen, it's not much fun to ride Space Mountain by yourself.

One specific issue that absolutely should be addressed before you leave home is what assistance (if any) you expect from your teen in regard to helping with younger children in the family. Once again, try to carve out a win-win compromise. Consider the case of the mother from Indiana who had a teenage daughter from an earlier marriage and two children under age 10 from a second marriage. After a couple of vacations where she thrust the unwilling teen into the position of being a surrogate parent to her half-sisters, the teen declined henceforth to participate in family vacations.

Many parents have written *The Unofficial Guide* asking if there are unsafe places at Walt Disney World or places where teens simply should not be allowed to go. Though the answer depends more on your family values and the relative maturity of your teens than on Disney World, the basic answer is no. Though it's true that teens (or adults, for that matter) who are looking for trouble can find it anywhere, there is absolutely nothing at Disney World that could be construed as a precipitant or a catalyst.

As a final aside, if you allow your teens some independence and they are getting around on the Walt Disney World transportation system, expect some schedule slippage. If your teen happens to just miss the bus, he or she might have to wait 15–45 minutes (more often 15–20 minutes) for the next one. If punctuality is essential, advise your independent teens to arrive at a transportation station an hour before they are expected somewhere, to allow sufficient time for the commute. Also set clear rules on how often your teen should check in with you. When using a smartphone, we recommend texting versus calling when it comes to simple check-ins, as the noise in the theme parks might prevent you from hearing them, and vice versa.

About INVITING *Your* CHILDREN'S FRIENDS

IF YOUR CHILDREN WANT TO INVITE FRIENDS on your Walt Disney World vacation, give your decision careful thought. There is more involved here than might be apparent. First, consider the logistics of numbers. Is there room in the car? Will you have to leave something at home that you had planned on taking to make room in the trunk for the friend's luggage? Will additional hotel rooms or a larger condo be required? Will the increased number of people in your group make it hard to get a table at a restaurant?

If you determine that you can logistically accommodate one or more friends, the next step is to consider how the inclusion of the friend will affect your group's dynamics. Generally speaking, the presence of a friend will make it harder to really connect with your own children. So if one of your vacation goals is an intimate bonding experience with your children, the addition of friends will probably frustrate your attempts to realize that objective.

If family relationship building is not necessarily a primary objective of your vacation, it's quite possible that the inclusion of a friend will make life easier for you. This is especially true in the case of only children, who may otherwise depend exclusively on you to keep them happy and occupied. Having a friend along can take the pressure off and give you some much-needed breathing room.

If you decide to allow a friend to accompany you, limit the selection to children you know really well and whose parents you also know. Your Disney World vacation is not the time to include "my friend Eddie from school" whom you've never met. Your children's friends who have spent time in your home will have a sense of your parenting style, and you will have a sense of their personality, behavior, and compatibility with your family. Assess the prospective child's potential to fit in well on a long trip. Is he or she polite, personable, fun to be with, and reasonably mature? Does he or she relate well to you and to the other members of your family?

Because a Disney World vacation is not, for most of us, a spur-of-the-moment thing, you should have adequate time to evaluate potential candidate friends. A trip to the mall, including a meal in a sit-down restaurant, will tell you volumes about the friend. Likewise, inviting the friend to share dinner with the family and then spend the night will provide a lot of relevant information. Ideally this type of evaluation should take place early on in the normal course of family events, before you discuss the possibility of a friend joining you on your vacation. This will allow you to size things up without your child (or the friend) realizing that an evaluation is taking place.

By seizing the initiative, you can guide the outcome. Ann, a Springfield, Ohio, mom, for example, anticipated that her 12-year-old son would ask to take a friend on their vacation. As she pondered the various friends her son might propose, she came up with four names. One, an otherwise sweet child, had a medical condition that Ann felt unqualified to monitor or treat. A second friend was overly aggressive with younger children and was often socially inappropriate for his age. Two other friends, Chuck and Marty, with whom she'd had a generally positive experience, were good candidates for the trip. After orchestrating some opportunities to spend time with each of the boys, she made her decision and asked her son, "Would you like to take Marty with us to Disney World?" Her son was delighted, and Ann had diplomatically preempted having to turn down friends her son might have proposed.

We recommend that you do the inviting instead of your child and that you extend the invitation to the parent (to avoid disappointment, you might want to sound out the friend's parent before broaching the issue with your child). Observing this recommendation will allow you to query the friend's parents concerning food preferences, any medical conditions, how discipline is administered in the friend's family, and how the friend's parents feel about the way you administer discipline.

Before you extend the invitation, give some serious thought to who pays for what. Make a specific proposal for financing the trip a part of your invitation. For example: "There's room for Marty in the hotel room, and transportation's no problem because we're driving. So we'll just need you to pick up Marty's meals, theme park admissions, and spending money."

Additionally, make sure the friend's parents agree with whatever COVID precautions you expect your family and the friend you bring along to follow.

Considerations for
SINGLE PARENTS

BECAUSE SINGLE PARENTS GENERALLY are also working parents, planning a special getaway with your children can be the best way to spend some quality time together. But remember, the vacation is not just for your child—it's for you too. You might invite a grandparent or a favorite aunt or uncle along; the other adult provides company for you, and your child will benefit from the time with family members. You might likewise consider inviting an adult friend.

Though bringing along an adult friend or family member is the best option, the reality is that many single parents don't have friends, grandparents, or favorite aunts or uncles who can make the trip. And while spending time with your child is wonderful, it is very difficult to match the energy level of your child if you are the sole focus of his or her world.

One alternative: Try to meet other single parents at Walt Disney World. It may seem odd, but most of them are in the same boat as you; besides, all you have to do is ask. Another option, albeit expensive, is to take along a trustworthy babysitter (18 or up) to travel with you.

The easiest way to meet other single parents at the World is to hang out at the hotel pool. Make your way there on the day you arrive, after traveling by car or plane and without enough time to blow a full admission ticket at a theme park. In any event, a couple of hours spent poolside is a relaxing way to start your vacation.

If you visit Walt Disney World with another single parent, get adjoining rooms; take turns watching all the kids; and, on at least one night, get a sitter and enjoy an evening out.

Throughout this book we mention the importance of good planning and touring. For a single parent, this is an absolute must. In addition, make sure you set aside some downtime at the hotel every day.

Finally, don't try to spend every moment with your children on vacation. Instead, plan some activities for your children with other children. Disney programs for children, for example, are worth considering. Then take advantage of your free time to do what you want to do: Read a book, have a massage, take a long walk, or enjoy a catnap.

While pricey, one of the best ways for single parents to relax is to add a three- or four-night cruise to their Disney stay. Onboard activities will keep your child occupied and give you time to relax.

"He Who Hesitates Is Launched!": TIPS *and* WARNINGS *for* GRANDPARENTS

SENIORS OFTEN GET INTO PREDICAMENTS caused by touring with grandchildren. Run ragged and pressured to endure a blistering pace, many seniors just concentrate on surviving Walt Disney World rather than enjoying it. The theme parks have as much to offer older visitors as they do children, and seniors must either set the pace or dispatch the young folks to tour on their own.

An older reader from Alabaster, Alabama, writes:

Being a senior is not for wusses. At Disney World particularly, it requires courage and pluck. Things that used to be easy take a lot of effort, and sometimes your brain has to wait for your body to catch up. Half the time, your grandchildren treat you like a crumbling ruin and then turn around and trick you into getting on a roller coaster in the dark. Seniors have to be alert and not trust anyone—not their children or even the Disney people, and especially not their grandchildren. When your grandchildren want you to go on a ride, don't follow along blindly like a lamb to the slaughter. Make sure you know what the ride is all about. Stand your ground and do not waffle. He who hesitates is launched!

If you don't get to see much of your grandchildren, you might think that Walt Disney World is the perfect place for a little bonding and togetherness. Wrong! Disney World can potentially send children into system overload and can precipitate behaviors that pose a challenge even to adoring parents, never mind grandparents. You don't take your grandchildren straight to Disney World for the same reason you don't buy your 16-year-old son a Ferrari: Handling it safely and well requires some experience.

Begin by spending time with your grandchildren in an environment that you can control. Have them over one at a time for dinner and to spend the night. Check out how they respond to your oversight and discipline. Determine that you can set limits and that they will accept those limits. When you reach this stage, you can contemplate some outings to the zoo, the movies, the mall, or the state fair. Gauge how demanding your grandchildren are when you are out of the house. Eat a meal or two in a full-service restaurant to get a sense of their social skills and their ability to behave appropriately. Don't expect perfection, and be prepared to modify your own behavior a little too. As a senior friend of ours told her husband, "You can't see Walt Disney World sitting on your butt."

If you have a good relationship with your grandchildren and have had a positive one-on-one experience taking care of them, you might consider a trip to Disney World. If you do, we have two recommendations. First, visit Disney World without them to get an idea of what you're getting into. A scouting trip will also provide you with an opportunity to enjoy some of the attractions that won't be on the itinerary when you return with the grandkids. Second, if you are considering a trip of a week's duration, you might think about buying a Disney package that combines four days at Disney World with a three-day cruise. In addition to being a memorable experience for your grandchildren, the cruise provides plenty of structure for children of almost every age, thus allowing you to be with them but also to have some time off. Call Disney Cruise Line at ☎ 800-951-3532 or visit disneycruise.com.

Tips for Grandparents

1. It's best to take one grandchild at a time, two at the most. Cousins can be better than siblings because they don't fight as much. To preclude sibling jealousy, try connecting the trip to a child's milestone, such as finishing the sixth grade.

2. Let your grandchildren help plan the vacation, and keep the first one short. Be flexible and don't overplan. Take a break in the afternoon.

3. Discuss mealtimes and bedtime. Fortunately, many grandparents are on an early dinner schedule, which works nicely with younger children. Plan your evening meal early to avoid long waits. And make Advance Reservations if you're dining in a popular spot, even if it's early. Take some crayons and paper to keep younger kids occupied.

4. Gear plans to your grandchildren's age levels because if they're not happy, you won't be happy. Take a day off between visits to the parks.

5. Create an itinerary that offers some supervised activities for children in case you need a rest.

6. If you're traveling by car, this is the one time we highly recommend earbuds. Kids' musical tastes are vastly different from most grandparents'. It's simply more enjoyable when everyone can listen to their own preferred style of music, at least for some portion of the trip.

7. Take along a night-light.

8. Carry a notarized statement from parents for permission for medical care in case of an emergency. Also be sure you have insurance information and copies of any prescriptions for medicines the kids may take. Bring a backup pair of any prescription eyeglasses in case one gets lost or broken.

9. Tell your grandchildren about any medical problems you may have, so they can be prepared if there's an emergency.

10. Many attractions and hotels offer discounts for seniors, so check ahead of time for bargains.

11. Make sure you and your teens get to know the ins and outs of the new Disney Genie+ system long before you arrive at Walt Disney World.

12. Lay down the rules when it comes to the time you are OK with your grandchildren being on their cellphones; you did not come to Walt Disney World to watch your grandkid spending a huge amount of time on social media. And do lead by example. Disney, especially with the new Genie+ system, already requires you to spend a lot of time on your phone. There is a time where the cellphone does not need to be part of the vacation, especially during dinnertime.

ORDER *and* DISCIPLINE *on the* ROAD

OK, OK, WIPE THAT SMIRK OFF YOUR FACE. Order and discipline on the road may seem like an oxymoron to you, but you won't be hooting when your 5-year-old launches a screaming stem-winder in the middle of Fantasyland. Your willingness to give this subject serious consideration before you leave home may well be the most important element of your pretrip preparation.

Discipline and maintaining order are more difficult when traveling because everyone is, as a Boston mom put it, "in and out" (in strange surroundings and out of the normal routine). For children, it's hard to contain the excitement and anticipation that bubble to the surface in the form of fidgety hyperactivity, nervous energy, and, sometimes, acting out. Confinement in a car, plane, or hotel room only exacerbates the situation, and kids are often louder than normal, more aggressive with siblings, and more inclined to push the envelope of parental patience and control. It doesn't get much better in the theme parks;

there's more elbow room, but there's also overstimulation, crowds, heat, and miles of walking. All this, coupled with marginal or inadequate rest, can lead to meltdown in the most harmonious of families.

The following discussion was developed by leading child psychologist Dr. Karen Turnbow, who has contributed to The Unofficial Guides for years and who has spent many days at Walt Disney World conducting research and observing families.

Sound parenting and standards of discipline practiced at home, applied consistently, will suffice to handle most situations on vacation. Still, it's instructive to study the hand you're dealt when traveling. For starters, aside from being ablaze with adrenaline, your kids may believe that rules followed at home are suspended when traveling. Parents reinforce this notion by being inordinately lenient in the interest of maintaining peace in the family. While some of your home protocols (such as going to bed at a set time) might be relaxed to good effect on vacation, differing from your normal approach to discipline can precipitate major misunderstandings.

Children, not unexpectedly, are likely to believe that a vacation (especially a vacation to Walt Disney World) is expressly for them. This reinforces their focus on their own needs and largely erases any consideration of yours. Such a mind-set dramatically increases their sense of hurt and disappointment when you correct them or deny them something they want. An incident that would hardly elicit a pouty lip at home could well escalate to tears or defiance when traveling.

 LILIANE Discuss your vacation needs with your children and explore their wants and expectations well before you depart on your trip.

The stakes are high for everyone on a vacation— for you because of the cost in time and dollars but also because your vacation represents a rare opportunity for rejuvenation and renewal. The stakes are high for your children too. Children tend to romanticize travel, building anticipation to an almost unbearable level. Discussing the trip in advance can ground expectations to a certain extent, but a child's imagination will, in the end, trump reality every time. The good news is that you can take advantage of your children's emotional state to preestablish rules and conditions for their conduct while on vacation. Because your children want what's being offered *sooooo* badly, they will be unusually accepting and conscientious regarding whatever rules are agreed upon.

According to Dr. Turnbow, successful response to (or avoidance of) behavioral problems on the road begins with a clear-cut disciplinary policy at home. Both at home and on vacation, the approach should be the same and should be based on the following key concepts:

1. LET EXPECTATIONS BE KNOWN. Discuss what you expect from your children, but don't try to cover every imaginable situation. Cover expectations in regard to compliance with parental directives, treatment of siblings, resolution of disputes, schedule (including wake-up and bedtimes), courtesy and manners, staying together, and who pays for what.

2. EXPLAIN THE CONSEQUENCES OF NONCOMPLIANCE. Detail very clearly and firmly the consequences of unmet expectations. This should be very straightforward and unambiguous. If you do (or don't do) X, this is what will happen.

3. WARN YOUR KIDS. You're dealing with excited children, not machines, so it's important to issue a warning before meting out discipline. It's critical to understand that we're talking about one unequivocal warning rather than multiple warnings or nagging. These undermine your credibility and make your expectations appear relative or less than serious. They also effectively pass control of the situation from you to your child (who may continue to act out as an attention-getting strategy).

4. FOLLOW THROUGH. If you say that you are going to do something, do it. Period. Children must understand that you are absolutely serious and committed.

5. BE CONSISTENT. Inconsistency makes discipline random in the eyes of your children. Random discipline encourages random behavior, which translates to a near-total loss of parental control. Both at home and on the road, your response to a given situation or transgression must be perfectly predictable. Structure and repetition, essential for effective learning, cannot be achieved in the absence of consistency.

6. BE IN THE MOMENT The latest technological innovations are not in sync with manners and etiquette, and it's important that you address this issue. Decisions need to be made about the usage of smartphones, and it's best to establish the rules prior to leaving on your vacation. Be sure that all family members know what's expected when it comes to the use of cell phones and time spent on social media. Emphasize the importance of being in the moment. Agree on what is acceptable, when, and where. Most of all, lead by example. It's OK to take pictures, but there comes a time when capturing an image is not worth the commotion. Cyber values such as sharing your experiences on social media cannot and should not supersede the simple value of family togetherness (not to mention the security risks of broadcasting that you're not home).

ACTIVE LISTENING AND A FEELING VOCABULARY

THOUGH THE PREVIOUS SIX are the biggies, several other corollary concepts and techniques are worthy of consideration.

First, understand that whining, tantrums, defiance, sibling friction, and even holding the group up are ways in which children communicate with parents. Frequently, the object or precipitant of a situation has little or no relation to the unacceptable behavior. On the surface, a fit may appear to be about the ice cream you refused to buy little Robby, but there's almost always something deeper, a subtext that is closer to the truth (this is the reason why ill behavior often persists after you give in to a child's demands). As often as not, the real cause is a need for attention. This need is so powerful in some children that they will subject themselves to certain punishment and parental displeasure to garner the attention they crave.

To get at the root cause of the behavior in question requires both active listening and empowering your child with a "feeling vocabulary." Active listening is a concept that's been around for a long time. It involves being alert not only to what a child says but also to the context in which it is said, to the language used and possible subtext, to the child's emotional state and body language, and even to what's *not* said. Sounds complicated, but it's basically being attentive to the larger picture and, more to the point, being aware that there is a larger picture.

Helping your child to develop a feeling vocabulary consists of teaching your child to use words to describe what's going on. The idea is to teach the child to articulate what's really troubling him, to be able to identify and express emotions and mood states in language.

It all begins with convincing your child that you're willing to listen attentively and take what he's saying seriously. Listening to your child, you help him transcend the topical by reframing the conversation to address the underlying emotional state(s). That his brother hit him may have precipitated the mood, but the act is topical and of secondary importance. What you want is for your child to be able to communicate how that makes him feel and to get in touch with those emotions. When you reduce an incident (hitting) to the emotions triggered (anger, hurt, rejection, and so on), you have the foundation for helping him to develop constructive coping strategies. A child who can tell his mother why he is distressed is a child who has discovered a coping strategy far more effective (not to mention easier for all concerned) than a tantrum.

Until you get the active listening and feeling vocabulary going, be careful not to become part of the problem. There's a whole laundry list of adult responses to bad behavior that only make things worse. Hitting, swatting, yelling, name-calling, insulting, belittling, using sarcasm, pleading, nagging, and inducing guilt ("We've spent thousands of dollars to bring you to Disney World and now you're spoiling the trip for everyone!") figure prominently on the list.

DEALING WITH UNWANTED BEHAVIORS

RESPONDING TO A CHILD appropriately in a disciplinary situation requires thought and preparation. Following are key things to keep in mind and techniques to try when your world blows up while waiting in line for Dumbo.

1. BE THE ADULT. Children can push their parents' buttons faster and more lethally than just about anyone or anything else. They've got your number, know precisely how to elicit a response, and are not reluctant to go for the jugular. Fortunately (or unfortunately), you're the adult, and you must act like one. If your kids get you ranting and caterwauling, you effectively abdicate your adult status. Worse, you suggest by way of example that being out of control is an acceptable expression of hurt or anger. No matter what happens, repeat the mantra, "I am the adult in this relationship."

2. FREEZE THE ACTION. Being the adult and maintaining control almost always translates to freezing the action. Instead of a knee-jerk response, freeze the action by disengaging. Wherever you are or whatever the family is doing, stop in place and concentrate on one thing and one thing only: getting all involved to calm down. Practically speaking, this usually means initiating a time-out. It's essential that you take this action immediately. Grabbing your child by the arm or collar and dragging him toward the car or hotel room only escalates the turmoil by prolonging the confrontation and by adding a coercive physical dimension to an already volatile emotional event. If, for the sake of people around you (as when a toddler throws a tantrum in church), it's essential to retreat to a more private place, choose the first place available. Firmly sit the child down and refrain from talking to him until you've both cooled off. This might take a little time, but the investment is worthwhile.

3. ISOLATE THE CHILD. You'll be able to deal with the situation more effectively and expeditiously if the child is isolated with one parent. Dispatch the uninvolved members of your party for a break or have them go on with the activity or itinerary without you (if possible) and arrange to rendezvous later at an agreed time and place. In addition to letting the others get on with their day, isolating the offending child with one parent relieves him of the pressure of being the group's focus of attention and object of anger. Equally important, isolation frees you from the scrutiny and expectations of the others in regard to how to handle the situation.

4. REVIEW THE SITUATION WITH THE CHILD. If, as discussed previously, you've made your expectations clear, stated the consequences of failing those expectations, and administered a warning, review the situation with the child and follow through with the discipline warranted. If, as often occurs, things are not so black-and-white, encourage the child to communicate his feelings. Try to uncover what occasioned the acting out. Lecturing and accusatory language don't work well here, nor do threats. Dr. Turnbow suggests that a better approach (after the child is calm) is to ask, "What can we do to make this a better day for you?"

5. FREQUENT TANTRUMS OR ACTING OUT. The preceding four points relate to dealing with an incident as opposed to a chronic condition. If a child frequently acts out or throws tantrums, you'll need to employ a somewhat different strategy.

Tantrums are cyclical events evolved from learned behavior. A child learns that he can get your undivided attention by acting out. When you respond, whether by scolding, admonishing, threatening, or negotiating, your response further draws you into the cycle and prolongs the behavior. When you accede to the child's demands, you reinforce the effectiveness of the tantrum and raise the cost of capitulation next time around. When a child thus succeeds in monopolizing your attention, he effectively becomes the person in charge.

To break this cycle, you must disengage from the child. The object is to demonstrate that the cause-and-effect relationship (that is, a tantrum elicits parental attention) is no longer operative. This can be accomplished by refusing to interact with the child as long as the untoward behavior continues. Tell the child that you are unwilling to discuss his problem until he calms down. You can ignore the behavior, remove yourself from the child's presence (or vice versa), or isolate the child with a time-out. The important thing is to disengage quickly and decisively with no discussion or negotiation.

LILIANE Tantrums are about getting attention. Giving your child attention when things are on an even keel often preempts acting out.

Most children don't pick the family vacation as the time to start throwing tantrums. The behavior will be evident before you leave home, and home is the best place to deal with it. Be forewarned, however, that bad habits die hard, and a child accustomed to getting attention by throwing tantrums will not simply give up after a single instance of disengagement. More likely, the child will at first escalate the intensity and length of his tantrums. By your consistent refusal over several weeks (or even months) to respond to his behavior, however, he will finally adjust to the new paradigm.

Children are cunning as well as observant. Many understand that a tantrum in public is embarrassing to you and that you're more likely to cave in than you would at home. Once again, consistency is the key, along with a bit of anticipation. When traveling, it's not necessary to retreat to the privacy of a hotel room to isolate your child. You can carve out space for time-out almost anywhere: on a theme park bench, in your car, in a restroom, even on a sidewalk. You can often spot the warning signs of an impending tantrum and head it off by talking to the child before he reaches an explosive emotional pitch.

6. SALVAGE OPERATIONS. Children are full of surprises, and sometimes the surprises are not good. If your sweet child manages to make a mistake of mammoth proportions, what do you do? This happened to an Ohio couple, resulting in the offending kid pretty much being grounded for life. Fortunately there were no injuries or lives lost, but the parents had to determine what to do for the remainder of the vacation. For starters, they split the group. One parent escorted the offending child back to the hotel, where he was effectively confined to his room for the duration of the trip. That evening, the parents arranged for in-room sitters for the rest of the stay. Expensive? You bet, but better than watching your whole vacation go down the tubes.

A family at the Magic Kingdom had a similar experience, though the offense was of a more modest order of magnitude. Because it was their last day of vacation, they elected to place the child in time-out, in the theme park, for the rest of the day. One parent monitored the culprit while the other parent and the siblings enjoyed the attractions. At agreed times, the parents would switch places. Once again, not ideal, but preferable to stopping the vacation.

PART 2

GETTING *Your* ACT TOGETHER

Visiting Walt Disney World is a bit like childbirth—you never really believe what people tell you, but once you've been through it yourself, you know exactly what they were saying!

—Hilary Wolfe, a mother and *Unofficial Guide* reader from Swansea, Wales, United Kingdom

GATHERING INFORMATION

IN ADDITION TO USING THIS GUIDE, we recommend that you visit our sister website, TouringPlans.com. It complements and augments the information in our books and provides real-time personal services that are impossible to build into a book. The book is your comprehensive reference source; TouringPlans.com is your personal concierge. Sign up for free at touringplans.com/walt-disney-world/join/basic.

With that free access, you'll be able to create custom touring plans, follow them in the parks, and update them if conditions change while you're there. You'll also find tools for saving money on tickets, plus up-to-the-minute information on rides, restaurants, crowds, park hours and operations, and more.

A few parts of the site require a small subscription fee to access: a detailed, day-by-day crowd calendar, for example, or a service that sends your hotel-room request directly to Disney. That subscription covers the costs of the extra people, technology, and external companies that it takes to provide them, beyond what's needed for the books.

Here's a brief rundown of some of the things you'll find on the site:

CUSTOM TOURING PLANS *Our best and most efficient touring plans are those provided in this guide.* For families with unique circumstances, we provide custom touring plans online. You can also customize the plans in this book by simply skipping any attractions that don't interest you.

Like the plans in this book, the free online plans will also identify which Genie+ reservations to obtain, and when, to minimize your waits in line throughout the day. Online plans also work with Disney's Disability Access Service.

DETAILED 365-DAY CROWD CALENDAR FOR EACH THEME PARK Subscribers can see which parks will be the least crowded every day of their trip, using a 1-to-10 scale.

GENIE+/INDIVIDUAL LIGHTNING LANE INFORMATION The site shows which Genie+ and Individual Lightning Lane reservations are the most useful to obtain and will automatically suggest the best ones for your touring plans.

ANSWERS TO YOUR TRIP-PLANNING QUESTIONS Our online community includes tens of thousands of Disney experts and fans willing to help with your vacation plans. Ask questions and offer your own helpful tips.

HOTEL ROOM VIEWS AND ONLINE FAX SERVICE We have photos of the views from every hotel room in Walt Disney World—more than 35,000 images—and we'll give you the exact wording to use with Disney to request a specific room. For subscribers, we'll even automatically fax your room request to Disney 30 days before you arrive. Disney will try to accommodate your request, but its ability to do so depends on a number of variables that we can't control. The majority of the faxed requests we send on behalf of readers are honored in full or partially, but sometimes Disney just can't make it work.

TICKET DISCOUNTS A customizable search helps you find the cheapest tickets for your specific needs. The average family can save $20–$80 by purchasing admission from one of our recommended ticket wholesalers.

LINES APP Our in-park app, Lines, is available on the Apple App Store and Google Play. It has lots of interesting, free features designed to accompany you in the parks. It provides ride and park information that Disney doesn't, including

- **Posted and actual wait times at attractions** Lines is the only Disney-parks app that displays both posted wait times and the actual times you'll wait in line. The wait time posted outside of a ride is often much longer than the real wait time, often because Disney is trying to do crowd control. With Lines, you can make better decisions about what to see. Seeing actual wait times can also help set kids' expectations about how long they'll be in line.

- **"Ride now or wait" recommendations** Lines shows you whether ride wait times are likely to get longer or shorter. If you find a long line at a particular attraction, Lines tells you the best time to come back.

- **Real-time touring plan updates while you're in a park** Lines automatically updates your custom touring plan to reflect actual crowd conditions at a given moment. You can also restart your plan and add or change attractions, breaks, meals, and more.

- **In-park chat feature with our Lines community** Have a quick question while you're in the parks? Ask our community of thousands of Liners and get a response within seconds.

The Unofficial Guide and **TouringPlans.com,** along with the Lines app, are designed to work together as a comprehensive planning and touring resource.

Our other website, **TheUnofficialGuides.com,** is dedicated to news about our guidebooks and features a blog with posts from *Unofficial Guide* authors. You can also sign up for the **"Unofficial Guides News-letter,"** which contains even more travel tips and special offers.

We invite you to follow us on Facebook at facebook.com/theun officialguides and facebook.com/theunofficialguidetowaltdisneyworld withkids), Instagram (@theunofficialguides), Twitter (@theugseries), and YouTube (@theunofficialguideseries). You can also follow Liliane on Twitter (@lilianeopsomer).

Next, we recommend the following:

1. **WALT DISNEY WORLD RESORT VACATION-PLANNING VIDEOS** Disney has videos advertising Walt Disney World's offerings, Disney Cruise Line, and other Disney destinations at disneyplanning.com.

2. **GUIDE FOR GUESTS WITH DISABILITIES** An overview of services and options for guests with disabilities is available at Guest Relations when entering the parks; at resort front desks; at wheelchair-rental areas (locations are listed in each theme park chapter); and at disneyworld .disney.go.com/guest-services/guests-with-disabilities.

3. **VISIT ORLANDO DEALS** If you're considering staying outside the World or patronizing out-of-the-World attractions and restaurants, check out Visit Orlando (visitorlando.com), where you'll find discounts on hotels, restau-rants, ground transportation, shopping malls, dinner theaters, and Disney and non-Disney theme parks and attractions. To view the deals, click on "Offers." You can also call 407-363-5872 (8 a.m.–8 p.m. Eastern time), down-load the Visit Orlando app, or sign up for emails via the website.

IMPORTANT WALT DISNEY WORLD TELEPHONE NUMBERS

WHEN YOU CALL the main information number, you'll be offered a menu of options for recorded information on operating hours, recreation areas, shopping, entertainment, tickets, reservations, and driving direc-tions. See the table on page 38 for a list of phone numbers.

DISNEY ONLINE: OFFICIAL AND OTHERWISE

THE WALT DISNEY COMPANY features a set of high-tech enhance-ments in its theme parks and hotels. Known as **MyMagic+,** the technology includes rubber wristbands (**MagicBands**) with embedded computer chips that function as admission tickets, hotel keys, and more.

MyMagic+ requires you to make detailed decisions about every day of your trip, sometimes months in advance, if you want to visit popular parks and avoid long waits in line. Disney's requirement that you make park reservations means you must decide in advance which theme park you want to visit on each day of your trip, and restaurant reservations require you to know the exact time you want to eat, and where, two months before you arrive. The My Disney Experience section of the Walt Disney World website (disneyworld.disney.go.com/plan) and the My Disney Experience mobile app are the glue that binds it all together. Because you must plan so much before you leave home, we cover the basics of both the website and the app in the next section. While we provide navigational instructions here, note that Disney's web design-ers move things around all the time, so you may have to hunt around to find some features.

More information about theme park reservations is on page 39; MagicBands are on page 68; details on Disney's new ride reservation systems—Genie+, Lightning Lane, and Individual Lightning Lane—start on page 262. Disney's other new way of waiting in lines, called virtual queues or boarding groups, is described on page 263. Finally, Disney's Genie itinerary-planning service, which you absolutely should not use, is profiled on page 258.

My Disney Experience Online

At disneyworld.disney.go.com/plan, you can make park, hotel, dining, and some recreation reservations; buy admission; and get park hours, attraction information, and much more.

TECHNICAL PROBLEMS Disney World's website is so unreliable that a Google search for "My Disney Experience issues" returns around 72 million results (not kidding). Likewise, Disney's mobile app frequently doesn't work as intended. If you run into technical issues on the website, the first thing to do is to use your browser's "private" or "incognito" mode to do what you want. Disney's website often places so many cook-ies on your computer that it appears to break its own system.

If that doesn't work and human interaction is required, call ☎ 407-939-4357 in the US or ☎ 0800 16 90 749 in the UK for help. Set aside a full day to get these issues resolved. You read that right: Disney's phone systems have been understaffed since the start of the pandemic, and stories abound of multihour waits for support, only for the call to be disconnected when the caller hits a certain number of hours on hold.

BEFORE YOU BEGIN Set aside *at least* 30–40 minutes to complete this process. Make sure you have the following items on hand:

- A valid admission ticket or confirmation number for everyone in your group
- Your hotel-reservation number if you're staying on-site
- A computer, smartphone, or tablet connected to the internet
- An email account that you can access easily while traveling
- A schedule of the parks you'll be visiting each day, including arrival and departure times and the times of any midday breaks
- The dates, times, and confirmation numbers of any dining or recreation reservations you've made

If you're coordinating travel plans with friends or family who live elsewhere, you'll also need the following information:

- The names and (optional) email addresses of the people you're traveling with
- A schedule of the parks they are visiting on each day of their trip, including their arrival, departure, and break times
- The dates and times of any dining or recreation reservations they have made

GETTING STARTED Go to disneyworld.disney.go.com/plan and click "Create Account." You'll be asked for your email address, name, billing

IMPORTANT WDW TELEPHONE NUMBERS

General Information ☎ 407-824-4321 or ☎ 407-824-2222	
General Information for Deaf or Hard-of-Hearing Guests (TTY) ☎ 407-827-5141	
General Information for Guests with Disabilities ☎ 407-939-7807	
Accommodations/Reservations ☎ 407-W-DISNEY (934-7639) • **UK** 0800 028 0778	
Advent Health Centra Care • **Kissimmee** ☎ 407-390-1888 • **Lake Buena Vista** ☎ 407-934-2273 • **Universal-Dr. Phillips** ☎ 407-291-8975	
Blizzard Beach Information ☎ 407-560-3400	
Dining Advance Reservations and **Resort Dining and Information** ☎ 407-WDW-DINE (939-3463)	
ESPN Wide World of Sports Complex ☎ 407-939-4263 or 407-939-1500	
Golf Reservations and Information ☎ 407-WDW-GOLF (939-4653)	
Guided-Tour Information ☎ 407-WDW-TOUR (939-8687)	
Lost and Found • **Today:** Visit Guest Relations in the park. • **Yesterday or before (all Disney parks)** ☎ 407-824-4245 • **Yesterday or before (Disney Springs)** ☎ 407-828-3150	
Outdoor Recreation Reservations and Information ☎ 407-WDW-PLAY (939-7529)	
Security ☎ 407-560-7959 (routine) or ☎ 407-560-1990 (urgent)	
Tennis Lessons ☎ 321-228-1146	
Ticket Inquiries ☎ 407-939-7679	
Typhoon Lagoon Information ☎ 407-560-4120	
Walt Disney Travel Company ☎ 407-939-6244	
Weather Information ☎ 407-827-4545	
Wrecker Service ☎ 407-824-0976 (or call **Security** after hours; see above)	

address, and birth date. (Disney uses your billing address to send your hotel-reservation information, if applicable, and to charge your credit card for anything you purchase.)

Once you've created an account, the website will display a page with links to other steps in the planning process. These steps are described next. The steps apply only to the first time you sign in; the website shows you different screens and options when you sign in after that. In those cases, click the "My Disney Experience" icon in the upper-right corner of the page, and look for wording like that below.

DISNEY HOTEL INFORMATION If you're staying at a Disney hotel, select "Resort Hotel" and then "Link Reservation." Enter your reservation number. This associates your My Disney Experience (MDE) account with your hotel stay in Disney's computer system. If you've booked a travel package that includes theme park admission, Disney computers will automatically link the admission to your MDE account, allowing you to skip the "Linking Tickets" step below. If you've booked a Disney hotel through a third-party site like Expedia, that site should send you a Disney reservation number to use here. Note that it can take up to a week for third-party sites to send Disney your booking information, so plan accordingly.

REGISTER FRIENDS AND FAMILY Click the "Family & Friends" icon; then enter the names and ages of everyone traveling with you. You can do this later, but you'll need the information when you make your park and dining reservations.

LINKING TICKETS You will need to have purchased theme park tickets for each member of your group and linked them to each member's MDE profile before making some reservations.

If you haven't purchased your tickets, do so now. Disney's website doesn't have the cheapest prices for theme park tickets of three or more days. See pages 65–67 for where to find better deals. Once your third-party tickets have been purchased, you can add them to MDE just like tickets bought directly from Disney.

If you have already purchased tickets but have not linked them, click the "Park Tickets" widget, then click on "Link Tickets" and follow the instructions.

MAKING THEME PARK RESERVATIONS After you've purchased and linked park tickets to your family's MDE account, click the "Park Reservations" icon to get started. If you're buying 1- to 10-day tickets, you'll be able to make park reservations for as many days as you have park admission (e.g., five days of reservations if you have a 5-day ticket). Annual Pass holders who are booked at a Disney hotel can make reservations for each day of their hotel stay, while pass holders staying off-site can make three at a time. Annual Pass holders can make an additional reservation once an existing reservation's day is done.

MAKING DINING RESERVATIONS Click the "Dining" icon, then the "Make a Reservation" link to get started. (You may have to reenter your travel dates.) A list of every Walt Disney World eatery will be displayed. Use the filtering criteria at the top of the page to narrow the list.

Once you've settled on a restaurant, click the restaurant's name to check availability for your preferred time and the number of people in your party. If space is available, you'll need to indicate which members of your party will be joining you. You'll also need to enter a credit card number to hold your reservation. If you want to make other dining reservations, you'll need to repeat this process for each reservation. Guests staying on-site can make dining reservations 60 days before their arrival. See page 163 for more on making dining reservations.

My Disney Experience Mobile App

In addition to its website, Disney offers a companion app called **My Disney Experience,** available on Apple's App Store and the Google Play Store. It includes park hours, attraction operating hours and descriptions, wait times for buses, restaurant hours with descriptions and menus, the ability to make dining and ride reservations online, GPS-based directions, counter-service meal ordering, the locations of park photographers, and more. Note that My Disney Experience is optimized for the latest phones and tablets, so some features, including mobile ordering, may not be available on all devices.

Our Recommended Websites

Searching online for Disney information is like navigating an immense maze for a very small piece of cheese: There's a lot of information available, but you may find a lot of dead-ends before getting what you want. Our picks follow.

BEST Q&A SITE Walt Disney World has a **Mom's Panel,** chosen from among 10,000-plus applicants. The panelists have a website, disney worldmoms.com, where they offer tips and discuss how to plan a Disney World vacation. Several moms have specialized experience in areas such as Disney Cruise Line; some speak Spanish too.

BEST GENERAL UNOFFICIAL WALT DISNEY WORLD WEBSITE Besides TouringPlans.com, **AllEars.net** is the first website we recommend to friends who want to make a trip to Disney World. Updated several times a week, the site includes breaking news, tons of photos, Disney restaurant menus, resort and ticket information, tips for guests with special needs, and more. We also check **wdwmagic.com** for news and happenings around Walt Disney World.

BEST MONEY-SAVING SITE **MouseSavers** (mousesavers.com) keeps an updated list of discounts for use at Disney resorts. Discounts are separated into categories such as "For the general public" and "For residents of certain states." Anyone who calls or books online can use a current discount. Savings can be considerable—up to 40% in some cases. MouseSavers also has discounts for rental cars and non-Disney hotels in the area.

BEST WALT DISNEY WORLD PREVIEW SITE If you want to see what a particular attraction is like, **TouringPlans.com** offers free videos or photos of every attraction. Videos of indoor (dark) rides are sometimes inferior to those of outdoor rides due to poor lighting, but even the videos and photos of indoor rides generally provide a good sense of what the attraction is about. **YouTube** is also an excellent place to find videos of Disney and other Central Florida attractions.

SOCIAL MEDIA **Facebook, Twitter,** and **Instagram** are popular places for Disney fans to post comments, tips, and photos. Following fellow Disneyphiles as they share their in-park experiences can make you feel like you're there, even as you're stuck at work. Disney World's official social media handles are facebook.com/waltdisneyworld, twitter.com /waltdisneyworld, and instagram.com/waltdisneyworld. You can also join more than 10,600 fans for news and insights on our own Facebook page, facebook.com/theunofficialguidetowaltdisneyworldwithkids.

BEST DISNEY DISCUSSION BOARDS There are tons of these; among the most active are **disboards.com, forums.wdwmagic.com, forum.touring plans.com,** and, for Brits, **thedibb.co.uk** (*DIBB* stands for Disney Information Bulletin Board).

BEST SITES FOR TRAFFIC, ROADWORK, CONSTRUCTION, AND SAFETY INFORMATION Visit cfxway.com for the latest information on roadwork in the Orlando and Orange County areas. The site also has detailed maps, directions, and toll information for the most popular tourist destinations. Important I-4 construction updates can be found at i4ultimate.com and i4byond.com. Visit flhsmv.gov/safety-center/child-safety/safety-belts-child -restraints to learn about state child-restraint requirements. For driving directions, we like Google Maps.

Liliane's Favorite Podcasts

If you just can't make it through the year without the Mouse, don't despair. Sounds, images, and news from the World are available in abundance online. Here are some of my favorites.

BE OUR GUEST A fun, high-energy, Disney-related podcast. Visit beour guestpodcast.podbean.com for more info.

THE DISNEY DISH Join theme park historian Jim Hill and TouringPlans. com's Len Testa at podcasts.jimhillmedia.com/show/the-disney-dish -with-jim-hill for insightful and fun shows filled with theme park news, rumors, and history.

DISNEY DREAM GIRLS Recorded in the UK, this all-female podcast pro- motes Disney girl power. Visit disneydreamgirlspodcast.blogspot.co.uk.

GEEKIN' ON WDW All Disney geeks will enjoy this passionate and enthu- siastic podcast at geekinonwdw.com, hosted by a father–daughter team.

ORLANDO TOURISM REPORT A weekly show covering Central Florida hospitality news: orlandotourismreport.com/category/podcast. It's also live on Friday, 10 a.m.–noon, on 91.5 FM WPRK (Winter Park) radio.

ROPE DROP RADIO Derek and Doug are two dads who love Disney. Their podcast is fun and provides tips for all things Walt Disney World and Disney Cruise Line: wdwropedroppers.com/podcast-2.

THE PARKSCOPE UNPROFESSIONAL PODCAST Sit back and listen to six dudes talk about their love of theme parks: parkscope.simplecast.com.

SOUNDS OF DISNEY Join Jeff Davis, also known as The Sorcerer, as he delights his audience with music, news, and Disney songs from the parks. In addition to the podcast, Davis's website, srsounds.com, pro- vides music, videos, pictures, and a message board.

THE UNOFFICIAL UNIVERSAL ORLANDO PODCAST This biweekly pod- cast highlights news, interviews, and discussions about the Universal Orlando Resort: uuopodcast.com.

◀▮ ALLOCATING TIME

YOU SHOULD ALLOCATE 6 days for a whirl- wind tour (7–10 days if you're old-fashioned and insist on some relaxation during your vaca- tion). If you don't have 6-plus days, then you need to be prepared to make some hard choices.

BOB If you must visit during the busy summer season, cut your visit short by one or two days so that you will have the weekend or a couple of vacation days remaining to recuperate when you get home.

A seemingly obvious point lost on many families is that Walt Disney World is not going anywhere. There's no danger that it will be packed up and shipped to Iceland anytime soon. This means that you can come back if you don't see everything this year. Disney has planned it this way, of course, but that doesn't matter. It's infinitely more sane to resign yourself to the reality that seeing everything during one visit is impossible. We recommend, therefore, that you approach Walt Disney World the same way you would an eight-course French dinner: leisurely, with plenty of time between courses.

WHEN TO GO TO WALT DISNEY WORLD

LET'S CUT TO THE ESSENCE: Disney World between mid-June and mid-August is rough. You can count on large summer crowds as well as Florida's trademark heat and humidity. Avoid these dates if you can. Ditto for Memorial Day and Labor Day weekends. Other holiday periods (such as Easter, spring break, Halloween, Thanksgiving, Christmas, and so on) are very crowded, but the heat is not as bad.

BOB Though crowds have grown in September and October as a result of promotions aimed at families without school-age children and the international market, these months continue to be good for touring.

The least busy time *historically* is from Labor Day in September through the beginning of October—but see our caveat below. Next slowest are the weeks in mid-January after the Martin Luther King Jr. holiday weekend up to Presidents' Day in February (except when the Walt Disney World Marathon runs after MLK Day). The weeks after Thanksgiving and before Christmas are less crowded than average, as is mid-April–mid-May, after spring break and before Memorial Day.

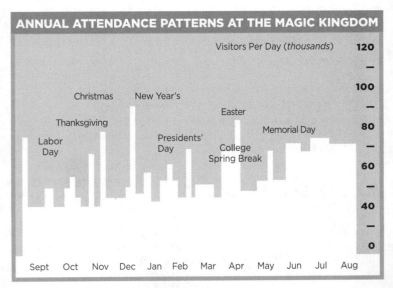

ANNUAL ATTENDANCE PATTERNS AT THE MAGIC KINGDOM

Visitors Per Day (*thousands*)

Late February, March, and early April are dicey. Crowds ebb and flow according to spring break schedules and the timing of Mardi Gras and Presidents' Day weekend. Besides being asphalt-melting hot, July brings throngs of South American tourists on their winter holiday.

The basic rule of thumb is that Disney World is more crowded when school is out and less crowded when kids are in school. However, Disney has become adept at loading slow periods of the year with special events, conventions, food festivals, and the like. Discounts on rooms and dining during slower periods also figure in.

In short: The World can be packed at any time, and you need to dig a little deeper than merely the time of year to pinpoint the least crowded dates. For a calendar of scheduled Disney events, see touringplans.com /walt-disney-world/events#. Huge conventions at the Orange County Convention Center also contribute to the problem (see page 44).

Other factors affecting crowding and long lines include a combination of closed rides and the number of employees Disney decides to use in the parks. As a result, we've added more data about ride closures to our Crowd Calendar forecasts. Last but certainly not least, Disney, in an effort to save money, reduces ride capacity and schedules fewer cast members to work the rides during slower periods of the year, resulting in longer wait times even when the parks are not crowded.

So, parents, what to do? If your children are of preschool age, definitely go during a cooler, less-crowded time. If you have school-age children, look first for an anomaly in your school-year schedule: in other words, a time when your kids will be out of school when most schools elsewhere are in session. Anomalies are most often found at the beginning or end of the school year (for example, school starts late or lets out early), at Christmas, or at spring break. In the event that no such anomalies exist, and provided that your kids are good students, our recommendation is to ask permission to take your children out of school either just before or after the Thanksgiving holiday. Teachers may be willing to assign lessons that can be made up at home over the Thanksgiving holiday, before or after your Disney World vacation.

If none of these options are workable for your family, consider visiting Disney World the week immediately before school starts (excluding Labor Day weekend) or the week immediately after school lets out (excluding Memorial Day weekend). This strategy should remove you from the really big mob scenes by about a week or more.

The time that works best for families with kids is the week before school ends. Because grades must be finalized earlier, there is often little going on at school during that week. Check far in advance with your child's teacher to determine if any special exams or projects will occur in that last week. If no major assignments are on the child's schedule, then go for it.

Incidentally, taking your kids out of school for more than a few days is problematic. We have received well-considered letters from parents and teachers who don't think taking kids out of school is such a hot idea. A Fairfax, Virginia, dad put it thus:

My wife and I do not encourage families to take their children out of school. My wife is an eighth-grade science teacher. She has parents pull their children, some honor roll students, out of school for vacations, only to discover when they return that the students are unable to comprehend the material. Several students have been so thoroughly lost in their assignments that they ask if they can be excused from the tests. Parental suspicions about the quality of their children's education should be raised when children go to school for 6 hours a day yet supposedly can complete this same instruction with less than an hour of homework each night.

A Martinez, California, teacher offers this compelling analogy:

There are a precious 180 days for us as teachers to instruct our students, and there are 185 days during the year for Disney World. I have seen countless students struggle to catch up the rest of the year due to a week of vacation during critical instructional periods. It's like walking out of a movie after watching the first 5 minutes, and then returning for the last 5 minutes and trying to figure out what happened.

But a schoolteacher from Penn Yan, New York, expresses a different opinion:

As a teacher and a parent, I disagree with the comments from teachers saying that it's horrible for a parent to take a child out for a vacation. If a parent takes the time to let us know that a child is going to be out, we help them get ready for upcoming homework the best we can. If the child is a good student, why shouldn't they go have a wonderful experience with their family? I also don't understand when teachers say they can't get something together for the time the student will be out. We all have to plan ahead, and we know what we are teaching days, if not weeks, in advance. Take 20 minutes out of your day and set something up. Learn to be flexible!

If possible, ask your child's teacher for a list of topics they'll be covering while you're away. Have your child study these on the plane or in the car, during midday breaks, and at night before bed.

BE UNCONVENTIONAL The Orange County Convention Center in Orlando hosts some of the largest conventions and trade shows in the world. Hotel rooms anywhere near Walt Disney World are hard to find when there's a big convention—rooms less than $75 or more than $200 a night (that is, budget and upscale) go quickly. Check the convention schedule for the next seven months at calendar.occc.net/calendar; click on any meeting during your Disney dates to view the expected attendance. (Don't worry about conventions with fewer than 10,000 attendees unless you want to book a hotel in the International Drive area.)

DON'T FORGET AUGUST Kids go back to school pretty early in Florida (and in a lot of other places). This makes mid- to late August a good time to visit for families who can't vacation during the off-season. A New Jersey mother of two school-age children spells it out:

Walt Disney World Climate

	JAN	FEB	MAR	APR	MAY	JUN	JUL	AUG	SEP	OCT	NOV	DEC
AVERAGE DAILY HIGH												
	71°F	73°F	78°F	83°F	89°F	91°F	92°F	92°F	90°F	84°F	78°F	72°F
AVERAGE DAILY HEAT INDEX (TEMPERATURE + HUMIDITY)												
	76°F	75°F	80°F	88°F	104°F	109°F	116°F	117°F	110°F	92°F	80°F	74°F
AVERAGE DAILY TEMPERATURE												
	60°F	61°F	67°F	71°F	77°F	81°F	82°F	83°F	81°F	75°F	68°F	62°F
AVERAGE DAILY HUMIDITY												
	62%	73%	71%	70%	71%	70%	74%	76%	76%	75%	74%	73%
AVERAGE RAINFALL PER MONTH												
	2.9"	2.7"	4.0"	2.3"	3.1"	8.3"	7.0"	7.7"	5.1"	2.5"	2.1"	2.9"
NUMBER OF DAYS OF RAIN PER MONTH												
	6	6	7	5	8	14	16	16	13	8	5	6

The end of August is the PERFECT time to go. There were virtually no wait times, 20 minutes at the most.

JUNE AND THE EARLY BIRD It's not an easy turnaround, but heading for Walt Disney World in late May or early June as soon as school is out will net big rewards. Late May through about June 12 is still considered shoulder season, so the crowds will not have spiked to summer levels. Also the weather is usually cooler than in late August. An exception to the above is Memorial Day weekend, though the week following the holiday is one of the best of the whole summer, crowdwise.

High-Low, High-Low, It's Off to Disney We Go

We strongly recommend going to Disney World in the fall, winter, or spring because of the milder weather, generally smaller crowds, and deeper discounts. However, these benefits come with some trade-offs. The parks often close early during the off-season, either because of low crowds or special events, and even when crowds are small, it's difficult to see big parks such as the Magic Kingdom between 9 a.m. and 7 p.m. Early closing also usually means no evening parades or fireworks. And because these are slow times, some rides and attractions may be closed. Finally, Central Florida temperatures fluctuate wildly during late fall, winter, and early spring; daytime highs in the 40s and 50s aren't uncommon.

On the other hand, Disney generally has the best lodging offers during these times of the year, including the Free Dining plans, if offered. If you plan to stay on-site, this could represent some serious savings. Disney announced in June 2022 that no dining plan, free or otherwise, will be offered for the foreseeable future. This may change, but for now, that's all we know!

We realize that off-season touring isn't possible for many families. We want to make it clear, therefore, that you can have a wonderful experience regardless of when you go. Our advice, irrespective of season, is to arrive early at the parks and avoid the crowds by using one of our touring plans. If attendance is light, kick back and forget the touring plans.

Holidays and Special Events at Walt Disney World

You can't beat the holidays for live entertainment, special events, parades, fireworks, and elaborate decorations at the theme parks and resort hotels. Unfortunately, you also can't beat holiday periods for crowds. A mom from Ogden, Utah, puts it this way:

> *We know the lines will be outrageous, but the special shows, parades, and decorations more than make up for it. For first-timers who want to see the rides, Christmas is not ideal, but for us it's the most colorful and exciting time to go.*

Here's a look at the larger special events and major holidays at Walt Disney World.

SABRINA There are lots of marathons every year, and you can sign up for cool races and get different medals.

JANUARY To be held January 1–5, 2023, the **Walt Disney World Marathon** pulls in 60,000 runners and their families—enough people to affect crowd conditions and pedestrian traffic throughout the World. Information on all Disney running events can be found at rundisney.com.

Each year the China Pavilion in EPCOT has a **Chinese New Year** celebration (usually late January or early February), typically with Chinese acrobats and special activities for kids.

The **EPCOT International Festival of the Arts,** a celebration of art, food, and entertainment, takes place daily from mid-January to mid-February, with Disney on Broadway performances held at the America Gardens Theatre.

FEBRUARY **Black History Month** is celebrated throughout Walt Disney World with displays, artisans, storytellers, and entertainers.

In 2023, **Presidents' Day** is February 20, and **Mardi Gras** is February 21, bringing increases in attendance starting the weekend before. The **Princess Half-Marathon** schedule (February 23–26, 2023) includes a health expo, kids' races, a family 5K, a 10K, and the big race. The event draws more than 30,000 runners, enough to increase park attendance and affect vehicular and pedestrian traffic.

MARCH Most of March and early April are peak spring break season. The **EPCOT International Flower & Garden Festival** runs from early March through early July. The 30 million blooms from some 1,200 species will make your eyes pop, and best of all, the event doesn't seem to affect crowd levels at EPCOT. Food and beverage kiosks at the festival make it more like fall's International Food & Wine Festival (see page 47), only with flowers. Check out Liliane's 2022 review and how the festival can be fun for kids at tinyurl.com/flowergardenfestkids. Spike's Pollen Nation Exploration (map and stickers are $9.99

ISABELLE EPCOT's Festival of the Arts is my favorite festival! There is art everywhere!

plus tax) is a great way to occupy children during the festival. Spike the honeybee has pollinated the different festival gardens, and the task is to find Spike and apply corresponding stickers on the map. Once finished, kids can claim a prize.

In Disney Springs, the **Mighty St. Patrick's Day Festival,** a weeklong celebration culminating on St. Patrick's Day (March 17), pays tribute to Irish music, dance, and food.

Springtime Surprise Weekend, held from the end of March through early April, is a new event replacing the Star Wars Rival Run half-marathon. The 2022 races included an Expedition Everest 5K, Race for the Taste 10K, and The Twilight Zone Tower of Terror 10-Miler. Held at the same time as the EPCOT International Flower & Garden Festival, the race is sure to bring lots of crowds to all parks. For more information on this new race, check rundisney.com.

APRIL The Magic Kingdom showcases Mickey, Minnie, and the gang, all dressed in their Sunday best, in the **Easter Parade** (April 9, 2023), which takes place prior to the Festival of Fantasy Parade that makes its way down Main Street, U.S.A. The merriment includes Mr. and Mrs. Easter Bunny, Daisy Duck, Thumper and Ms. Bunny, Rabbit from Winnie the Pooh, White Rabbit, Clara Cluck, and the Azalea Trail Maids from Mobile, Alabama. About 10 days prior to Easter, guests can meet the Easter Bunny in the Town Square courtyard. Ask at the front desk about activities (such as egg hunts) at your hotel and other Disney resorts.

At EPCOT, kids will love the **Egg-stravaganza** (map and stickers are $9.99 plus tax). Be on the lookout for a dozen hidden Disney character–themed eggs. The eggs are 1.5 feet tall! Upon completion of the game, kids can choose one Disney character–themed egg as a prize. In 2022 the game was offered March 31–July 4.

A fan-organized event, **Dapper Day,** when guests visit the parks wearing period costumes from the 1920s to 1950s, occurs in April and November. Visit dapperday.com for more information.

JUNE Since 1991, LGBTQ people from around the world have been converging on and around the World for **Gay Days,** a week of events centered on the theme parks. Gay Days attracts more than 160,000 LGBTQ visitors and their families and friends. For additional information, visit gaydays.com.

JULY Independence Day at Disney World basically means crowds and more crowds. All parks are in a festive and patriotic mood, and the fireworks are incredible. A very special place to visit is *The Hall of Presidents* at the Magic Kingdom. We recommend watching the evening fireworks from the Polynesian Village Resort instead of from the parks. Most parks will reach full capacity by 10 a.m., and no advance reservations will get you into a park once it has closed. So pick your park and be prepared to stay there all day.

Those who say Christmas is the most wonderful time of year have never been to the **EPCOT International Food & Wine Festival.** Held in World Showcase from mid-July through mid-November, the celebration represents 25 nations and cuisines, including demonstrations, wine seminars, and tastings. Though many activities are included in EPCOT admission, some workshops and tastings are by reservation only and cost more than $100. Call ☎ 407-WDW-DINE (939-3463) starting around the beginning of August for more information. We think the culinary demos and the wine-and-beverage seminars are the best values at the festival. Because most of the food kiosks are set up around World Showcase, it can be difficult to walk through the crowds at some of the popular spots. Wait times at EPCOT's attractions, however, are affected only slightly.

Mickey's Not-So-Scary Halloween Party takes place at the Magic Kingdom from 7 p.m. to midnight on select days mid-August–October. The festivities include trick-or-treating, character sightings (some rare), parades, live music, occasional light retheming of a few attractions, and the *Disney's Not-So-Spooky Spectacular* fireworks show. In 2022, prices were $109–$199 for adults and $99–$189 for kids, depending on the day. Also see page 315.

Most Disney resorts have some complimentary activities on Halloween, ranging from Halloween movies under the stars to trick-or-treating, costume parades, and contests. Check at the reception desk for a detailed schedule of events happening during your stay.

Teens and young adults looking for a non-Disney Halloween happening should check out the party at **Universal CityWalk.** And if you'd rather have a monster with a chain saw running after you, consider attending Universal theme parks' **Halloween Horror Nights.** (*Note:* No costumes are allowed at the parks on these special nights.) For more information, visit halloweenhorrornights.com.

NOVEMBER The **Wine and Dine Half-Marathon** weekend (usually the first weekend in November) includes a 5K and 10K race in addition to the half-marathon. The number of runners and their cheer squads, combined with the guests who descend on EPCOT for the food festival alone, blow up crowd levels like a puffer fish. Vehicular and pedestrian traffic is disturbed by the running courses throughout Disney property.

There are no special Thanksgiving events or decorations in the parks, so if you're looking for the equivalent of the Macy's Thanksgiving Parade, you're out of luck, though many of the Christmas decorations are normally in place the day after Thanksgiving. But the kids are out of school, and this is the busiest travel weekend of the year. Your best bet for the least-crowded park will be EPCOT.

Remember to make your dining arrangements long before your visit, especially if you want a traditional Thanksgiving meal. While there is plenty of food at the World, note that not all restaurants offer turkey with all the trimmings. Some that do include **Liberty Tree Tavern** at the Magic Kingdom, **50's Prime Time Café** at Disney's Hollywood Studios, **Cítricos** at the Grand Floridian, and **Garden Grill Restaurant** at EPCOT. For information and reservations, call ☎ 407-WDW-DINE (939-3463). Disney changes its food offerings faster than lightning, so to avoid disappointment, call the restaurant and ask about its Thanksgiving menu prior to making reservations.

The annual **Disney Parks Magical Christmas Day Parade,** televised on December 25, is taped mid- to late November or the first week of December. The parade and musical performances are taped at Walt Disney World and Disneyland. The filming of the musical segments at Walt Disney World ties up pedestrian traffic on these days.

LILIANE Did I mention it'll be packed? This is not a good time for first-time visitors, but fun can be had even at peak times. (I stayed at Disney World on Christmas Eve and Christmas Day and loved it.)

DECEMBER During Christmas week, don't expect to see all the attractions in a single day of touring at any park. All parks, especially the Magic Kingdom, will be filled to capacity, and Disney stops admitting guests as early as 10 a.m. (not to mention that women will have to wait up to 20 minutes to use the restrooms in the Magic Kingdom). As you might have guessed by now, your only way in is getting there early. Be at the gates with admission passes in hand at least 1 hour before scheduled opening time. Most of all, bring along a humongous dose of patience and humor. The daily tree-lighting ceremonies and the parades are wonderful. Again, most parks will reach capacity by 10 a.m., and no reservation will get you into a park once it's closed. So *pick your park* and be prepared to stay there all day.

Also, be sure to make dinner reservations long before your visit, especially if you're spending Christmas Eve and Christmas Day at the parks. Christmas festivities at Disney World usually run November 24– December 30. From the Monday following Thanksgiving weekend until December 20 or so, you can enjoy the decorations and holiday events without the crowds. This between-holidays period is one of our favorite times of year at Disney World.

The **Magic Kingdom** is home to a stunning display of holiday decorations, a **tree-lighting ceremony,** and **Mickey's Once Upon a Christmastime Parade.** It's also where **Mickey's Very Merry Christmas Party** happens. This event takes place 7 p.m.–midnight (after regular hours; guests can get into the park starting at 4 p.m.) on 20-plus evenings in November and December. It includes holiday-themed stage shows featuring Disney characters, an unlimited supply of complimentary snacks and drinks, Mickey's Once Upon a Christmastime Parade, a special holiday-themed fireworks show, carolers, "a magical snowfall on Main Street," and meet and greets with Disney characters in their holiday best. Cinderella Castle is decked in thousands of lights, and holiday-themed live performances are held throughout the park. Prices are $159–$199 for adults and $149–$189 for kids (plus tax). We don't recommend this party for first-time visitors.

With about twice the land of the Magic Kingdom, **EPCOT** is a good option on Christmas Day, but that doesn't mean it's a ghost town, just somewhat less crowded than the Magic Kingdom. Again, if your heart is set on touring a park on Christmas Day, you'll have to get up early.

EPCOT's **International Festival of the Holidays** takes place from the end of November through December 30. Don't miss the park's

Candlelight Processional, featuring a celebrity narrator accompanied by a huge live choir and a full orchestra. (Check closer to the opening of the festival for exact dates and daily performance times. You can also find out who the celebrity narrator is.) The show takes place daily at the America Gardens Theatre and is included with regular EPCOT admission. Special lunch and dinner packages are available for an additional charge and include preferred seating for the processional (call ☎ 407-939-3463 for reservations). If you don't want to spring for one of the packages, we recommend lining up at least 1 hour prior to the show of your choice. Guests with preferred seating should arrive at the reserved-seating entrance 30 minutes before the beginning of the show. Seats in this section are available on a first-come, first-served basis and are opened to general admission 15 minutes before the beginning of the show.

Holiday Kitchens features booths scattered around World Showcase, offering festive holiday-themed tasting portions of food and drink. The new nightly fireworks show, *Harmonious,* is a great way to end the night.

A new scavenger hunt, **Olaf's Holiday Tradition Expedition!**, replaces Chip & Dale's Christmas Tree Spree (map and stickers are $9.99 plus tax). Search for Olaf in each pavilion, and then match the tradition on his sleigh to the location sticker on the scavenger hunt map.

At the **United Kingdom Pavilion,** Father Christmas tells of his country's holiday customs. The **France Pavilion** is home to Père Noël. In **Japan,** the *Daruma* seller tells how the Japanese celebrate the New Year. (*Daruma* dolls symbolize the New Year and are said to bring good luck.) In **Italy,** meet La Befana, the good witch who brings gifts to children on the Epiphany.

Visit **China** and make sure to see the Chinese Lion Dancers, a typical part of any Chinese New Year celebration. In **Norway,** meet the Christmas elf Julenisse, who represents simplicity and peace. In **Mexico,** Fiesta de Navidad includes dancers and the Mariachi Cobre band.

At the **United States Pavilion,** Santa and Mrs. Claus meet with guests, and the Voices of Liberty, clad in Dickensian costumes, bring joy with their Christmas carols. The professional and moving performance is a most appropriate show for the season.

Disney's Animal Kingdom has a gigantic Christmas tree and holiday entertainment throughout the park. Check out the holiday decorations in Pandora, DinoLand U.S.A., and elsewhere around the park.

Disney's Hollywood Studios is also dressed for the season. The *Sunset Seasons Greetings* sound-and-light show projected on The Twilight Zone Tower of Terror, complete with snow falling on Sunset Boulevard, runs several times per hour. The *Jingle Bell, Jingle BAM!* nighttime show is projected on the Grauman's Chinese Theatre. Echo Lake gets a holiday overhaul, and even Gertie the giant dinosaur wears a Santa hat.

Minnie's Holiday Dine at Hollywood & Vine is another nice way to celebrate the season at Hollywood Studios. Minnie, joined by Mickey, Donald, Daisy, and Santa Goofy, meets with guests as they dine on holiday-themed menu items. The event costs $55 per adult and $36 per child, plus tax and gratuity, and includes table activities and souvenir party gifts. The dinner is offered early November through the first week of January.

You thought we were done? No way. There's much more to see outside the parks. The **holiday decorations** at the Walt Disney World resorts are attractions in their own right. Generally speaking, each resort incorporates its theme into its holiday finery. At **Port Orleans Resort,** for example, expect Mardi Gras colors in the trees, while the **Yacht Club** has trees adorned with miniature sailboats. Also make sure to visit the **Grand Floridian,** where the mother of all Christmas trees—five stories tall!—dominates the lobby, along with a gingerbread house. At the **Beach Club,** poinsettias and a gingerbread carousel are the big draw. For a more natural approach, visit **Wilderness Lodge** and **Animal Kingdom Lodge.**

If you're staying at a Disney resort over Christmas, check with the concierge to see what holiday events might be going on. Happenings can range from carolers, brass bands, and country singers to Christmas-cookie decorating, visits with Santa, and readings of "The Night Before Christmas."

During December, Disney offers 25-minute **"sleigh" rides** through the woods from the Fort Wilderness Campground. The horse-drawn vehicle is wheeled but made to look like a red sleigh, complete with sleigh bells. Each sleigh can accommodate up to four adults or two adults plus up to three children age 9 and under.) *Note:* At press time, sleigh rides had not yet returned; check disneyworld.disney.go.com/recreation/holiday-sleigh-rides for updates. Historically, prices were $75–$84 per sleigh.

In addition to a nightly tree-lighting ceremony, lots of live entertainment occurs at **Disney Springs** for the holidays. The atmosphere is festive, and shops and restaurants have special window dressings. If you're looking for the perfect Christmas card, this is the place to get it. Santa appears in his chalet, and you can take pictures with your own camera or use Disney's Memory Maker service. For a less classical picture, Santa Goofy appears in the chalet December 25–January 3. Ask at Guest Relations for the daily schedule.

Ring in the New Year with Mickey and friends. If you're in the mood for a night of partying and live entertainment, there's no better place than Disney Springs or **Universal CityWalk.** Both offer a choice of parties and midnight fireworks. The Magic Kingdom shows fireworks on both December 30 and December 31 for those who either wish to see fireworks in multiple parks or don't wish to be caught in the largest crowds of the year on New Year's Eve.

Though all parks, with the exception of Animal Kingdom, have spectacular fireworks at midnight, here are a few different options for the last night of the year:

- If culinary delights are your thing and money is no object, this would be a good night for dinner at Victoria & Albert's. The restaurant, inside Disney's Grand Floridian Resort, features modern American cuisine with exquisite ingredients sourced from around the world. A 10-course dinner, eclectic wines, and live harp music are all part of the experience!

- Forget the rides—the lines will be looong. Relax at your hotel pool and go out for a great dinner that night. If you have little children, get a babysitter (see page 69). The trick is to arrive a day before New Year's, settle in, go to a water park, and start the touring after January 2, when crowds thin out.

- At EPCOT, welcome the New Year several times. Have a drink before 6 p.m. (midnight in Germany) at the Biergarten in Germany. Then go to the Rose & Crown Pub in the United Kingdom and repeat the celebration at 7 p.m. Best of all, you get to start all over again a few hours later when the clock finally strikes midnight at EPCOT.

In the past two years, due to COVID, holiday activities took place in a modified form. We hope that for the upcoming season they will be back in their former glory. Always confirm events with your resort.

Selecting the Day of the Week for Your Visit

We receive thousands of emails and letters from readers each year asking which park is the best bet on a particular day. To make things easier for you (and us!), TouringPlans.com provides a calendar covering the next year (click "Crowd Calendar" on the home page). For each date, we offer a crowd-level index based on a scale of 1–10, with 1 being least crowded and 10 being most crowded. The calendar also lists the best and worst park(s) to visit in terms of crowd conditions on any given day.

EARLY THEME PARK ENTRY
(FORMERLY MORNING EXTRA MAGIC HOURS)

EARLY THEME PARK ENTRY (EARLY ENTRY) is a perk for families staying at Walt Disney World resort hotels, including the Dolphin, Swan, and Swan Reserve; Shades of Green; the Four Seasons; the Disney Springs hotels (including the newly opened Drury Plaza Hotel); and the Hilton hotels in Bonnet Creek. Guests at those resorts can enter any of Disney's four theme parks 30 minutes earlier than official park opening on any day of the week. This perk replaced the Extra Magic Hours (EMH) program that ran until 2020.

WHAT'S REQUIRED? A valid ticket or MagicBand and a reservation for that theme park on that day are required to enter the park. If you haven't yet checked into your Disney hotel, make sure you have your reservation linked to your My Disney Experience account.

WHEN IS EARLY ENTRY OFFERED? Early Entry is offered every day at all four Disney theme parks.

HOW DOES EARLY ENTRY WORK? Eligible resort guests (see above) are invited to enter any theme park 30 minutes before the general public. During this time, guests can enjoy select attractions. In the Magic Kingdom, for example, you should find attractions open in Fantasyland and Tomorrowland at least.

In practice, we think on-site guests should arrive at their chosen park's entrance about an hour before official opening. That gets you at the front of the crowd, ready to go to your first attraction as soon as the park opens. On days of high attendance, Disney might open the park a bit earlier than 30 minutes in advance, giving you even more of a bonus.

During holidays and other busy times, the Magic Kingdom opens to regular guests at 8 a.m., and Early Entry begins at 7:30 a.m., so you'll need to be at the entrance no later than 7 a.m. You won't be alone, but because relatively few people are willing to get up that early for a theme park, your first few hours in the parks will be (pardon us) magical.

Early Entry affects theme park attendance much less than the previous EMH program because EMH was offered only at one or two parks per day. When Animal Kingdom offered morning EMH on Monday, for example, rides at that park had longer waits throughout the day because of the additional guests who arrived early to take advantage of their perk and stayed all day.

With Early Entry, that incentive to visit a specific park on a specific day is removed because Early Entry is offered at every park every day. That spreads out Disney resort guests more evenly among the parks, while still providing an on-site benefit for Disney to dangle in front of potential hotel customers.

If you're staying at a Disney resort, remember these three things about Early Entry:

1. The Magic Kingdom has more attractions open for Early Entry than any other park. We think the Magic Kingdom's Early Entry, coupled with a good touring plan, is the most worthwhile of any park.

2. Early Entry is especially useful when Disney opens new rides, such as Tron Lightcycle/Run at the Magic Kingdom.

3. Early Entry is a big advantage when using the standby line at popular attractions, such as Star Wars: Rise of the Resistance at Disney's Hollywood Studios, and EPCOT's Guardians of the Galaxy: Cosmic Rewind.

WHAT'S THE CATCH? The primary disadvantage of Early Entry for on-site guests is that they must now get up an extra half-hour early to beat the crowds. That's mitigated somewhat (for now) by the staggered park opening times.

Off-site guests are considerably disadvantaged by the Early Entry program. With the old EMH schedule, off-site guests could level the playing field by simply avoiding the park that offered morning EMH. If that park was EPCOT, then it was still possible to stay at an inexpensive hotel, get up early, and be at the front of the pack when the Magic Kingdom's rides opened.

With Early Entry, off-site guests are guaranteed to have thousands of on-site guests already in front of them at any theme park they visit on any day. When the Magic Kingdom opens a new ride, such as Tron Lightcycle/Run, it's a safe bet that its line will be hours long well before the first off-site guest even sets foot inside the park.

When planning your vacation, be sure to regularly check the theme parks' opening hours. They change often and can affect your itinerary; be prepared to alter your plans. Also important is to confirm that you have transportation from your resort at least 1 hour prior to Early Entry. We recommend checking both park hours and transportation the night before your visit to the parks. You can do so online (disney world.disney.go.com/calendars/park-hours), but checking (or double-checking) at the concierge desk is not a bad idea either.

All the resorts that are served by the new Skyliner have reduced bus service. So, if you do not want to use the gondola, plan ahead or use a ride service, such as Uber, Lyft, or the Minnie Van.

EXTENDED EVENING THEME PARK HOURS (FORMERLY EVENING EXTRA MAGIC HOURS)

EXTENDED EVENING THEME PARK HOURS (EETPH) is the limited revival of the former Evening Extra Magic Hours program, which was discontinued in 2020. Typically held on one night per week and (for now) only for certain parks, Extended Evening Theme Park Hours allows guests staying at Disney's Deluxe and DVC resorts—and only those guests—two extra hours in that park after official closing. Thus, if the Magic Kingdom closes at 9 p.m. to regular guests, the park will operate EETPH from 9 to 11 p.m. for guests at Disney Deluxe or DVC resorts only.

During EETPH, Disney sets up checkpoints throughout the park, such as the entrance to each land, to verify that guests entering the area are eligible for the program. Disney scans your MagicBand or plastic ticket to verify your resort.

Most theme park attractions are open during EETPH, although brand-new rides are often excluded, for maintenance.

The advantage to EETPH is that so few guests qualify that those lines are exceptionally short. In late December 2021, we managed to see 10 attractions in the Magic Kingdom during EETPH, waiting a total of 31 minutes in line. For comparison, those same 10 attractions would've taken almost 7 hours to see during that day. At EPCOT, the lines are so short that the limiting factor to "how many rides can I ride" is the walking distance between them.

BUT WAIT, THERE'S MORE—FOR A PRICE, OF COURSE

DISNEY AFTER HOURS AT MAGIC KINGDOM (not offered at press time; Magic Kingdom; 3 hours after regular park closing; select days; was $137 per person in 2019). Yes, it's $137 for 3 hours in the park, but the high cost keeps crowds low. Most rides will have wait times of 5 minutes or less, meaning that the number of rides you can visit depends largely on how fast you can walk between them and how long the rides last. Admission price includes unlimited ice cream, popcorn, and select non-alcoholic beverages.

ANIMAL KINGDOM AFTER HOURS (not offered at press time; Animal Kingdom; 3 hours after regular park closing; days of week vary; was $137 per person in 2019). If you can't get up early for Avatar Flight of

Passage and you're visiting during a busy time of year, this is the most direct way to experience the ride (multiple times!) with short waits. Plus, nighttime rides on Kilimanjaro Safaris (if offered) and Expedition Everest are vastly different than during the day. Ice-cream novelties, popcorn, and select bottled beverages are included.

EARLY MORNING MAGIC HOURS are not offered at any park, at this time.

DISNEY H2O GLOW AFTER HOURS AT DISNEY'S TYPHOON LAGOON takes place on select days from the end of May through the end of August, from 8 p.m. to 11 p.m. Guests can get a head start on the fun by entering the park at 6 p.m. and riding many of the favorite attractions and dancing to the beat of a DJ. Prices are $75 for adults and $70 for children ages 3–9 (tax not included). Ice-cream novelties, popcorn, and select fountain beverages are included in the cost of this ticketed event and are available at carts stationed throughout the park.

PLANNING *Your* WALT DISNEY WORLD VACATION BUDGET

HOW MUCH YOU SPEND DEPENDS on when you visit and how long you stay. But even if you stop by only for an afternoon, be prepared to drop a bundle. Later we'll show you how to save money on lodging. This section will give you some sense of what you can expect to pay for admissions and food. And we'll help you decide which admission option will best meet your needs.

HOW MUCH DOES A DISNEY VACATION COST?

EVERY YEAR, WE HEAR FROM tens of thousands of families who are either planning or just back from a Disney vacation, and we talk with travel agents who hear from thousands more. The thing that surprises these families the most is how expensive their trip turned out to be.

So that you know what you're dealing with up front, we've created the table on pages 58–61. It shows how much Disney vacation you get for $1,500, $2,000, $3,000, and $4,000, for families of various sizes. Most cells in the table contain a list of options, such as the type of hotel or restaurant you choose. These options illustrate the trade-offs you should consider when planning your trip—and there will be trade-offs. Here's an example for a family of two adults and one child with a $2,000 budget, excluding transportation:

OPTION A Two full days at a Disney theme park, two counter-service meals and one sit-down meal each day, and one night at a Disney Deluxe resort

OPTION B Three days at Disney's theme parks, three counter-service meals each day, and three nights at a budget off-site motel

In this case (and in general), your choice is between (1) a nicer hotel or (2) a longer trip, which allows more days in the parks and more nights in a cheaper hotel. You may also get more table-service meals each day. If you'd like to plug in your own numbers, you can download TouringPlans.com's auto-updating spreadsheet at tinyurl .com/wdwyouget2023. Ticket prices are based on Disney's March 2022 costs and include tax. All hotel prices are quoted for summer nights in 2022 and include tax. These prices are likely 15%–20% higher than what you'll pay later in the year—at press time, Disney had not released discounts for late 2022 or 2023.

Here are the assumptions we made to go along with actual prices from Disney's website:

- Children are ages 3–9; adults are age 10 and up.
- The cost of Base Tickets comes from Disney's website, reflects the average of the minimum and maximum price, and includes tax.
- One night at a non-Disney budget hotel—the Rodeway Inn Maingate West— booked through the hotel, costs $65.49.
- One night at Disney's All-Star Music Resort (the cheapest Disney Value resort at the time) costs $185.38 on the WDW website.
- One night at Disney's Coronado Springs Resort (the cheapest Disney Moderate resort at the time) costs $290.26 using Disney's website.
- One night at Disney's Animal Kingdom Lodge (the cheapest Disney Deluxe/ DVC resort at the time) costs $518.07 using Disney's website.
- A day's worth of counter-service meals, plus one snack, costs $56.06 for adults and $41.36 for kids.
- A counter-service breakfast and lunch, a snack, and a table-service meal costs $88.05 per adult and $55.63 per child.

In most places in the table, theme park admission ranges from 35% to 60% of the cost of a trip, regardless of family size. If you're not staying at a Deluxe resort, it's safe to assume that ticket costs will take half of your budget (again, excluding transportation).

It's a different story for off-site hotels, which lack services like free shuttles and extra time in the theme parks. Excellent third-party resorts, such as the **Sheraton Vistana** and the **Marriott Harbour Lake,** offer two-bedroom rates that are up to 65% less than those of Disney's cheapest one-bedroom Deluxe hotels. It helps considerably if you have a car, even if you factor in the cost of gas.

The Unofficial No-Frills Guide to Walt Disney World

With even a bare-bones visit to the World now out of reach of many families, frugality is becoming ever more necessary. These tips can help.

1. Buy your admission online from one of the sellers on page 64. Get tickets only for the number of days you plan to visit, and skip all add-on options. Disney adds a $21.30 surcharge to every ticket of three days or longer that is bought at its theme parks. Why? Because it can; it knows that you're not likely to turn the kids around and leave once you're that close.

2. Book a hotel outside of Walt Disney World. Hotels on US 192 (Irlo Bronson Memorial Highway) are usually the least expensive. Also, consider renting a vacation home (see discussion starting on page 128) if you have four or more people in your group.

3. Eat breakfast in your hotel room from a cooler; take lunch, snacks, and drinks to the park; and eat dinner outside the World using discount coupons. A ziplock bag filled with cereal bars, granola, raisins, and crackers goes a long way toward staving off hunger. Also, all Disney restaurants will give you a free cup of ice water. Instead of wasting money and calories on sugary drinks, this is an easy way to save some cash. Eat dinner outside the World using discount coupons. Trust us, this will save you not only a small fortune but also time.

4. Avoid parking fees by using your hotel's shuttle service or by taking a Disney bus from the water parks or Disney Springs (where—for the moment— parking is free) to a Disney hotel, then to a theme park. This suggestion takes a lot of time, so do it only if you're budgeting to the penny. If you are staying at a Disney property and are trying to avoid resort parking fees, do not park overnight at Disney Springs; your car will be towed!

5. Buy discounted Disney merchandise from one of Orlando's two **Disney's Character Warehouse** outlets (4951 International Dr., ☎ 407-354-3255; 8200 Vineland Ave., ☎ 407-477-0222; tinyurl.com/disneyoutlets).

6. Bring your own stroller. It's handy to have it for the airport and resort areas as well. Remember that most airlines will gate-check your stroller for free.

WALT DISNEY WORLD ADMISSION OPTIONS

DISNEY OFFERS MORE THAN 7,000 theme park ticket options, ranging from the humble **1-Day Base Ticket,** which is good for a single day's entry into one Disney theme park, to the blinged-out **Incredi-Pass,** good for 365 days of admission to every Disney theme park and more attractions. See the table on pages 62–63 for a summary of the most common admission types.

A theme park reservation is required for each day you plan to use your theme park tickets. Make reservations as far in advance as possible. Capacity is limited, and buying park tickets, even directly from Disney and for specific dates, doesn't guarantee that you'll get a park reservation. Thus, there's a risk that you could purchase tickets that cannot be used, especially during busier times of the year.

If you purchased tickets and were not able to use them, call Disney about your specific situation at ☎ 407-939-1289. Set aside at least 4 hours to wait on hold for this call.

Date-Based Pricing and Other Surcharges

Disney introduced date-based pricing for all theme park tickets in late 2018. The price of the ticket changes based on the days of the year you're traveling.

Tickets are now generally most expensive when children are out of school: Christmas and other holidays, spring break, and summer vacation. Less-expensive tickets are generally available during non-holiday periods when children are in school and during months subject to inclement weather: January and February, for example, and peak hurricane season in September.

To avoid additional surcharges when buying tickets, you must tell Disney the first date on which you plan to visit a theme park or water

continued on page 61

WHAT YOU PAY AND WHAT YOU GET AT WDW

• 2 ADULTS/$4,000

BUDGET OPTION ($3,873)
• 10 days theme park admission, parking
• 10 sit-down dinners
• 10 nights at a budget off-site motel

VALUE OPTION ($3,762)
• 8 days theme park admission
• 8 counter-service meals
• 9 nights at a Disney Value resort

MODERATE OPTION ($3,970)
• 7 days theme park admission
• 7 counter-service meals
• 7 nights at a Disney Moderate resort

DELUXE OPTION ($3,919)
• 5 days theme park admission
• 2 counter-service meals, 3 sit-down dinners
• 4 nights at a Disney Deluxe resort

• 2 ADULTS, 2 KIDS/$4,000

BUDGET OPTION ($4,073
• 6 days theme park admission, parking
• 4 counter-service meals, 2 sit-down dinners
• 6 nights at a budget off-site motel

VALUE OPTION ($4,050)
• 5 days theme park admission
• 5 sit-down meals
• 5 nights at a Disney Value resort

MODERATE OPTION ($3,966)
• 4 days theme park admission
• 4 counter-service meals
• 4 nights at a Disney Moderate resort

DELUXE OPTION ($3,918)
• 3 days theme park admission
• 1 counter-service meal, 2 sit-down dinners
• 3 nights at a Disney Deluxe resort

• 2 ADULTS, 1 KID/$4,000

BUDGET OPTION ($3.969)
• 9 days theme park admission, parking
• 9 counter-service meals
• 9 nights at a budget off-site motel

VALUE OPTION ($3,883)
• 6 days theme park admission
• 6 counter-service meals
• 7 nights at a Disney Value resort

MODERATE OPTION ($4,037)
• 6 days theme park admission
• 6 counter-service meals
• 5 nights at a Disney Moderate resort

DELUXE OPTION ($4,010)
• 4 days theme park admission
• 4 sit-down dinners
• 3 nights at a Disney Deluxe resort

• 3 ADULTS/$4,000

BUDGET OPTION ($3,825)
• 8 days theme park admission, parking
• 8 counter-service meals
• 8 nights at a budget off-site motel

VALUE OPTION ($3,807)
• 6 days theme park admission
• 6 counter-service meals
• 6 nights at a Disney Value resort

MODERATE OPTION ($4,126)
• 5 days theme park admission
• 3 counter-service meals, 2 sit-down dinners
• 5 nights at a Disney Moderate resort

DELUXE OPTION ($3,896)
• 3 days theme park admission
• 1 counter-service meal, 2 sit-down dinners
• 3 nights at a Disney Deluxe resort

• 3 ADULTS, 1 KID/$4,000

BUDGET OPTION ($3,997)
• 6 days theme park admission, parking
• 6 counter-service meals
• 6 nights at a budget off-site motel

VALUE OPTION ($3,955)
• 4 days theme park admission
• 1 counter-service meal, 3 sit-down dinners
• 4 nights at a Disney Value resort

MODERATE OPTION ($4,044)
• 4 days theme park admission
• 4 counter-service meals
• 4 nights at a Disney Moderate resort

DELUXE OPTION ($4,012)
• 3 days theme park admission
• 1 counter-service meal, 2 sit-down dinners
• 3 nights at a Disney Deluxe resort

• 2 ADULTS/$3,000

BUDGET OPTION ($3,006)
• 9 days theme park admission, parking
• 9 counter-service meals
• 9 nights at a budget off-site motel

VALUE OPTION ($2,973)
• 6 days theme park admission
• 5 counter-service meals, 1 sit-down dinner
• 6 nights at a Disney Value resort

MODERATE OPTION ($3,106)
• 5 days theme park admission
• 5 counter-service meals
• 5 nights at a Disney Moderate resort

• 2 ADULTS, 1 KID/$3,000

BUDGET OPTION ($3,098)
• 6 days theme park admission, parking
• 6 counter-service meals
• 6 nights at a budget off-site motel

VALUE OPTION ($2,962)
• 4 days theme park admission
• 3 counter-service meals; 1 sit-down dinner
• 4 nights at a Disney Value resort

MODERATE OPTION ($3,013)
• 4 days theme park admission
• 4 counter-service meals
• 3 nights at a Disney Moderate resort

WHAT YOU PAY AND WHAT YOU GET AT WDW *(continued)*

2 ADULTS/$3,000 *(continued)*

DELUXE OPTION ($3,034)
- 4 days theme park admission
- 4 counter-service meals
- 3 nights at a Disney Deluxe resort

2 ADULTS, 2 KIDS/$3,000

BUDGET OPTION ($3,141)
- 4 days theme park admission, parking
- 4 counter-service meals
- 4 nights at a budget off-site motel

VALUE OPTION ($3,012)
- 3 days theme park admission
- 3 sit-down dinners
- 3 nights at a Disney Value resort

MODERATE OPTION ($3,142)
- 3 days theme park admission
- 2 counter-service meals, 1 sit-down dinner
- 3 nights at a Disney Moderate resort

DELUXE OPTION ($3,035)
- 2 days theme park admission
- 2 counter-service meals
- 3 nights at a Disney Deluxe resort

3 ADULTS, 1 KID/$3,000

BUDGET OPTION ($2,825)
- 3 days theme park admission, 3 days parking
- 4 counter-service meals
- 3 nights at a budget off-site motel

VALUE OPTION ($3,124)
- 3 days theme park admission
- 3 sit-down dinners
- 3 nights at a Disney Value resort

MODERATE OPTION ($3,108)
- 3 days theme park admission
- 3 counter-service meals
- 3 nights at a Disney Moderate resort

DELUXE OPTION ($3,075)
- 2 days theme park admission
- 2 counter-service meals
- 3 nights at a Disney Deluxe resort

2 ADULTS, 2 KIDS/$2,000

BUDGET OPTION ($1,902)
- 2 days theme park admission, parking
- 2 sit-down dinners
- 3 nights at a budget off-site motel

VALUE OPTION ($2,037)
- 2 days theme park admission
- 2 counter-service meals
- 3 nights at a Disney Value resort

MODERATE OPTION ($2,061)
- 2 days theme park admission
- 2 counter-service meals
- 2 nights at a Disney Moderate resort

DELUXE OPTION ($1,999)
- 2 days theme park admission
- 2 counter-service meals
- 1 night at a Disney Deluxe resort

2 ADULTS, 1 KID/$3,000 *(continued)*

DELUXE OPTION ($2,934)
- 3 days theme park admission
- 3 sit-down dinners
- 2 nights at a Disney Deluxe resort

3 ADULTS/$3,000

BUDGET OPTION ($3,006)
- 5 days theme park admission, parking
- 4 counter-service meals, 1 sit-down dinner
- 5 nights at a budget off-site motel

VALUE OPTION ($2,962)
- 4 days theme park admission
- 4 counter-service meals
- 4 nights at a Disney Value resort

MODERATE OPTION ($3,091)
- 4 days theme park admission
- 4 counter-service meals
- 3 nights at a Disney Moderate resort

DELUXE OPTION ($2,759)
- 3 days theme park admission
- 3 counter-service meals
- 2 nights at a Disney Deluxe resort

3 ADULTS, 1 KID/$2,000

BUDGET OPTION ($1,978)
- 2 days theme park admission, parking
- 2 sit-down dinners
- 3 nights at a budget off-site motel

VALUE OPTION ($2,002)
- 2 days theme park admission
- 1 counter-service meal, 1 sit-down dinner
- 2 nights at a Disney Value resort

MODERATE OPTION ($2,101)
- 2 days theme park admission
- 2 counter-service meals
- 2 nights at a Disney Moderate resort

DELUXE OPTION ($2,039)
- 2 days theme park admission
- 2 counter-service meals
- 1 night at a Disney Deluxe resort

3 ADULTS/$2,000

BUDGET OPTION ($1,979)
- 3 days theme park admission, parking
- 3 counter-service meals
- 3 nights at a budget off-site motel

VALUE OPTION ($2,093)
- 3 days theme park admission
- 2 counter-service meals
- 2 nights at a Disney Value resort

MODERATE OPTION ($2,041)
- 2 days theme park admission
- 2 counter-service meals
- 3 nights at a Disney Moderate resort

DELUXE OPTION ($1,880)
- 2 days theme park admission
- 2 sit-down dinners
- 1 night at a Disney Deluxe resort

continued on next page

continued from previous page

WHAT YOU PAY AND WHAT YOU GET AT WDW *(continued)*

• 2 ADULTS/$2,000

BUDGET OPTION ($2,082)
- 5 days theme park admission, parking
- 5 counter-service meals
- 5 nights at a budget off-site motel

VALUE OPTION ($1,890)
- 3 days theme park admission
- 3 counter-service meals
- 4 nights at a Disney Value resort

MODERATE OPTION ($2,019)
- 3 days theme park admission
- 3 counter-service meals
- 3 nights at a Disney Moderate resort

DELUXE OPTION ($1,944)
- 2 days theme park admission
- 2 sit-down meals
- 2 nights at a Disney Deluxe resort

• 2 ADULTS, 1 KID/$2,000

BUDGET OPTION ($1,985)
- 3 days theme park admission, parking
- 3 counter-service meals
- 4 nights at a budget off-site motel

VALUE OPTION ($1,843)
- 2 days theme park admission
- 2 sit-down dinners
- 3 nights at a Disney Value resort

MODERATE OPTION ($2,001)
- 2 days theme park admission
- 2 counter-service meals
- 3 nights at a Disney Moderate resort

DELUXE OPTION ($1,805)
- 2 days theme park admission
- 2 sit-down dinners
- 1 night at a Disney Deluxe resort

• 2 ADULTS/$1,500

BUDGET OPTION ($1,470)
- 3 days theme park admission, parking
- 3 counter-service meals
- 4 nights at a budget off-site motel

VALUE OPTION ($1,519)
- 3 days theme park admission
- 3 counter-service meals
- 2 nights at a Disney Value resort

MODERATE OPTION ($1,489)
- 2 days theme park admission
- 2 sit-down dinners
- 2 nights at a Disney Moderate resort

DELUXE OPTION ($1,426)
- 2 days theme park admission
- 2 sit-down dinners
- 1 night at a Disney Deluxe resort

• 2 ADULTS, 1 KID/$1,500

BUDGET OPTION ($1,445)
- 2 days theme park admission, parking
- 1 counter-service meal, 1 sit-down dinner
- 3 nights at a budget off-site motel

VALUE OPTION ($1,501)
- 2 days theme park admission
- 2 counter-service meals
- 2 nights at a Disney Value resort

MODERATE OPTION ($1,499)
- 2 days theme park admission
- 1 counter-service meal, 1 sit-down dinner
- 1 night at a Disney Moderate resort

DELUXE OPTION ($1,094)
- 1 day theme park admission
- 1 counter-service meal
- 1 night at a Disney Deluxe resort

• 2 ADULTS, 2 KIDS/$1,500

BUDGET OPTION ($906)
- 1 day theme park admission, parking
- 1 counter-service meal
- 2 nights at a budget off-site motel

VALUE OPTION ($1,033)
- 1 day theme park admission
- 1 sit-down dinner
- 1 night at a Disney Value resort

MODERATE OPTION ($1,530)
- 1 day theme park admission
- 2 counter-service meals
- 2 nights at a Disney Moderate resort

DELUXE OPTION ($1,273)
- 1 day theme park admission
- 1 counter-service meal
- 1 night at a Disney Deluxe resort

• 3 ADULTS/$1,500

BUDGET OPTION ($1,407)
- 2 days theme park admission, parking
- 2 counter-service meals
- 3 nights at a budget off-site motel

VALUE OPTION ($1,452)
- 2 days theme park admission
- 1 counter-service meal, 1 sit-down dinner
- 1 night at a Disney Value resort

MODERATE OPTION ($1,461)
- 2 days theme park admission
- 2 counter-service meals
- 1 night at a Disney Moderate resort

DELUXE OPTION ($1,114)
- 1 day theme park admission
- 1 counter-service meal
- 1 night at a Disney Deluxe resort

• 3 ADULTS, 1 KID/$1,500

BUDGET OPTION ($1,036)
- 1 day theme park admission, parking
- 1 sit-down dinner
- 2 nights at a budget off-site motel

MODERATE OPTION ($1,466)
- 1 day theme park admission
- 1 sit-down dinner
- 2 nights at a Disney Moderate resort

WHAT YOU PAY AND WHAT YOU GET AT WDW *(continued)*

• 3 ADULTS, 1 KID/$1,500 *(continued)*

VALUE OPTION ($1,466)	DELUXE OPTION ($1,293)
• 1 day theme park admission	• 1 day theme park admission
• 1 counter-service meal, 1 sit-down dinner	• 1 counter-service meal
• 2 nights at a Disney Value resort	• 1 night at a Disney Deluxe resort

continued from page 57

park. Your ticket price will be based on that starting date, the number of days you plan to visit the theme parks or water parks, and whether you plan to visit more than one theme park per day. See the table on page 62–63 for more details.

If you need to move your vacation dates from more-expensive to less-expensive days, Disney will not refund the difference in ticket prices—but they will charge you the incremental cost if you need to move from less-expensive to more-expensive days.

When Tickets Expire

Along with implementing date-based pricing, Disney has shortened the amount of time you have to use your tickets. Whereas previously all tickets expired 14 days from the date of first use, ticket expiration is now based on how many days you're visiting the theme parks and water parks, as shown in the table on page 63–63.

Example: If you purchase a basic 4-Day Base Ticket and specify that you'll start using it on June 1, 2023, you must complete your four theme park visits by midnight June 7, 2023. Once you start using your ticket, any unused admissions expire even if you don't use them.

If you purchase a ticket and don't use any of it before it expires, you can apply the amount paid for that ticket toward the purchase of a new ticket at current prices, provided the new ticket's price is the same cost (or more) of the expired ticket.

TICKET ADD-ONS

THREE TICKET ADD-ON OPTIONS are available with your park admission, each at an additional cost:

PARK HOPPER Unless you visit more than one theme park per day, the cost is about $69–$91 (including tax) on top of the ticket price. The longer your stay, the more affordable it is: As an add-on to a 7-Day Base Ticket, for example, the flat fee works out to $13 a day for park-hopping privileges; as an add-on to a 2-Day Base Ticket, the fee works out to $40 a day. If you want to visit the Magic Kingdom in the morning and eat at EPCOT in the evening, this is the feature to request. At press time, guests must make a reservation for the first park they wish to visit, and they must enter that park first. Guests will not be allowed to hop to the second park until 2 p.m., though that is subject to change. At press time, the 2 p.m. time was strictly enforced.

WDW THEME PARK TICKET OPTIONS

	1-DAY	2-DAY	3-DAY	4-DAY	5-DAY	
USE WITHIN: 1 DAY	4 DAYS	5 DAYS	7 DAYS	8 DAYS	
BASE TICKET AGES 3–9						
ALL PARKS: $111–$164	$216–$319	$321–$461	$419–$578	$446–$611	
—	($108–$160/day)	($107–$154/day)	($105–$144/day)	($89–$122/day)	
BASE TICKET AGE 10+						
ALL PARKS: $116–$169	$226–$330	$336–$476	$437–$597	$466–$631	
—	($113–$165/day)	($112–$159/day)	($109–$149/day)	($93–$126/day)	

Base Ticket admits guest to one theme park each day of use. Tickets must be used within the number of days shown in the "Use Within" row above.

FLEXIBLE DATES *(add-on)*					
AGES 3–9: $0–$53 AGE 10+: $0–$53	$5–$109 $6–$109	$4–$144 $5–$145	$4–$163 $6–$165	$5–$170 $6–$171	

Flexible Dates allows you to start using your ticket on any day of the year, through December 31, 2021. Tickets expire 14 days after first use.

PARK HOPPER					
AGES 3–9: $180–$233 AGE 10+: $185–$239	$296–$399 $306–$410	$401–$541 $416–$556	$509–$669 $528–$687	$536–$701 $557–$721	

Park Hopper option entitles guest to visit more than one theme park on each day of use. See page 61 for details.

WATER PARK AND SPORTS					
AGES 3–9: $185–$224 AGE 10+: $191–$244	$296–$368 $306–$378	$406–$505 $421–$520	$492–$625 $511–$644	$520–$671 $540–$691	

Water Park and Sports entitles you to a specified number of visits (between 1 and 10) to a choice of entertainment and recreation venues. It's a flat $75 fee to add to any ticket for any age and any ticket length.

PARK HOPPER PLUS					
AGES 3–9: $201–$255 AGE 10+: $207–$260	$335–$421 $345–$431	$443–$562 $458–$577	$535–$685 $554–$704	$562–$722 $582–$742	
1 visit	2 visits	3 visits	4 visits	5 visits	

Park Hopper Plus option entitles guest to a specified number of visits (1–10) to a choice of entertainment and recreation venues, plus the Park Hopper option above. PHP tickets expire 1 day later than the "Use Within" days above.

Also at press time, Disney required you to enter the park for which you made your reservation before entering a second park. Thus, if you made your park reservation for the Magic Kingdom but did not go, you have two options:

- Cancel your Magic Kingdom park reservation and obtain a day-of park reservation for EPCOT.
- Go to the Magic Kingdom and tap in to enter. Then turn around and go to EPCOT.

On days of limited park-reservation availability, you may be forced to visit your first park before entering a second.

NOTE: ALL TICKET AND ADD-ON PRICES INCLUDE 6.5% SALES TAX.				
6-DAY	**7-DAY**	**8-DAY**	**9-DAY**	**10-DAY**
9 DAYS	10 DAYS	12 DAYS	13 DAYS	14 DAYS
BASE TICKET AGES 3-9				
$459-$625	$473-$640	$496-$656	$513-$669	$530-$680
($77-$104/day)	($68-$91/day)	($62-$82/day)	($57-$74/day)	($53-$68/day)
BASE TICKET AGE 10+				
$480-$646	$494-$662	$518-$679	$536-$692	$554-$704
($80-$108/day)	($71-$95/day)	($65-$85/day)	($60-$77/day)	($55-$70/day)
Park choices are Magic Kingdom, EPCOT, Disney's Hollywood Studios, or Disney's Animal Kingdom.				
FLEXIBLE DATES *(add-on)*				
$5-$171 $6-$172	$7-$174 $6-$174	$8-$169 $7-$168	$11-$165 $9-$163	$12-$162 $10-$160
In essence, the Flexible Dates option prices your ticket as the most expensive possible under Disney's pricing scheme, plus a small surcharge.				
PARK HOPPER				
$550-$716 $571-$736	$563-$730 $585-$752	$586-$747 $609-$769	$603-$759 $627-$782	$620-$770 $644-$794
Park choices are any combination of Magic Kingdom, EPCOT, Disney's Hollywood Studios, or Disney's Animal Kingdom on each day of use.				
WATER PARK AND SPORTS				
$575-$740 $596-$761	$593-$756 $615-$778	$624-$777 $647-$799	$635-$788 $658-$811	$644-$798 $668-$822
Choices are Disney's Blizzard Beach water park, Disney's Typhoon Lagoon water park, Oak Trail Golf Course, ESPN Wide World of Sports Complex (if open), and Fantasia or Winter Summerland minigolf.				
PARK HOPPER PLUS				
$575-$740 $596-$761	$593-$756 $647-$799	$624-$777 $630-$791	$635-$788 $658-$811	$644-$798 $668-$822
6 visits	7 visits	8 visits	9 visits	10 visits
Choices are Disney's Blizzard Beach water park, Disney's Typhoon Lagoon water park, Oak Trail Golf Course, ESPN Wide World of Sports Complex (if open), or Fantasia Gardens or Winter Summerland minigolf.				

WATER PARK AND SPORTS This $75 (including tax) option provides daily entry to Disney's two water parks (Blizzard Beach and Typhoon Lagoon), the Oak Trail Golf Course, Fantasia Gardens and Winter Summerland minigolf, and the ESPN Wide World of Sports Complex.

PARK HOPPER PLUS The Park Hopper Plus (PHP) option combines the Park Hopper and Water Park and Sports add-ons. This option costs $91–$112 more than a Base Ticket, including tax, which is cheaper than the combined cost of the two options purchased separately.

You can't change how many Park Hopper/Water Park/PHP admissions you can buy with either option; the number is fixed, and unused days aren't refundable. You can, however, skip Park Hopper/Water Park/PHP entirely and buy an individual admission to any of the venues above—that's frequently the best deal if you're not park-hopping and want to visit just Typhoon Lagoon and/or Blizzard Beach once.

If you buy a ticket but then decide later that you want to add the Park Hopper/PHP option, you can do so. Disney doesn't prorate the cost: If you add Park Hopper/PHP on the last day of your trip, you'll pay the same price as if you'd bought it before you left home.

ANNUAL PASSES

NOTE: At press time, sales of all versions of Annual Passes except the Pixie Dust Pass were paused. A theme park reservation is required for each day you plan to use your theme park tickets. Purchasing an Annual Pass doesn't guarantee you a theme park reservation.

LILIANE I keep my Annual Passes in the same place as my passport, insurance papers, and other travel documents. And I always keep a copy of my receipt documenting the purchase.

Annual Passes provide unlimited use of the major theme parks for one year. Pass holders can add on a year of water park access for an additional $99 (plus tax) on top of the prices shown. Four versions are available (prices are for age 3 and up and include tax):

- The **Pixie Dust Pass** ($399 plus tax; Florida residents only) allows for holding up to three simultaneous park reservations. The Pixie Dust Pass has the most blockout dates—dates when the pass cannot be used: almost all weekends are off-limits, plus a week or two around every major holiday and chunks of time around minor holidays.

- The **Pirate Pass** ($699 plus tax; Florida residents only) includes four simultaneous park reservations. It has fewer blockout dates on weekends than the Pixie Dust Pass but retains the blockout dates for holidays.

- The **Sorcerer Pass** ($899 plus tax; Florida residents and Disney Vacation Club members only) includes five simultaneous park reservations. The only blockout dates in 2021 were the Wednesday to Sunday around Thanksgiving, and December 17–31.

- The **Incredi-Pass** ($1,299 plus tax; available to everyone) includes five simultaneous park reservations and has no blockout dates.

Holders of all Annual Passes get additional perks, including free parking; hotel, dining, and merchandise discounts; and seasonal offers such as a dedicated entrance line at the parks. The passes are not valid for special events. See disneyworld.com/passes for more information about all Annual Pass options.

WHERE TO PURCHASE TICKETS

YOU CAN BUY YOUR ADMISSION on arrival at Walt Disney World (and pay a $21.30 per-ticket surcharge for 3-Day tickets and up) or buy them in advance to avoid that fee.

If you're trying to keep costs to an absolute minimum, consider using an online ticket wholesaler, such as **Tripster** (☎ 888-590-5910; tripster .com) or **Boardwalk Ticketing** (boardwalkticketing.com), especially for trips of three or more days in the parks. All tickets are brand new, and the savings can easily exceed $200 for a family of four. Vendors will provide you with electronic tickets just like Disney does, so you'll be able to make park reservations immediately through My Disney Experience online. Tripster offers discount tickets for almost all Central Florida attractions, including Disney, Universal, and SeaWorld. Boardwalk Ticketing offers them only for Disney. Discounts for the major theme parks range from about 6% to 12%. Tickets for other attractions are more deeply discounted.

Finally, tickets are available at some non-Disney hotels and shopping centers, and through independent ticket brokers. Because Disney admissions are only marginally discounted in the Walt Disney World–Orlando area, the chief reason for you to buy from an independent broker is convenience. Offers of free or heavily discounted tickets abound, but the catch is that they generally require you to attend a time-share sales presentation.

FOR ADDITIONAL INFORMATION ON ADMISSION

LILIANE Steer clear of passes offered on eBay, Craigslist, and the like.

IF YOU HAVE A QUESTION OR CONCERN regarding admissions that can be addressed only through a person-to-person conversation, contact **Disney Ticket Inquiries** at ☎ 407-566-4985 or ticket.inquiries@disneyworld.com. If you call, be aware that you may spend considerable time on hold; if you email, be aware that it can take up to three days to get a response. In contrast, the ticket section of the Disney World website—disneyworld.disney.go.com/tickets—is surprisingly straightforward in showing how ticket prices break down.

HOW TO SAVE MONEY ON DISNEY WORLD TICKETS

DISNEY'S DATE-BASED PRICING SCHEME is the most complicated system it has ever used for ticket purchases—so complicated, in fact, that we wrote a computer program to analyze all the options and to look for loopholes in the new pricing rules. Visit **TouringPlans.com** and try our **Ticket Price Comparison Tool** (tinyurl.com/ug-ticketcalculator). It aggregates ticket prices from Disney and a number of online ticket vendors. Answer a few questions related to the size of your party and the parks you intend to visit, and the calculator will identify your four cheapest ticket options. It will also show you how much you'll save versus buying at the gate.

The program will also make recommendations for considerations other than price. For example, Annual Passes might cost more, but Disney often offers substantial resort discounts and other deals to Annual Pass holders. These resort discounts, especially during the off-season, can more than offset the price of the pass.

Our Ticket Price Comparison Tool will automatically use all of the tips below and more. If you'd rather do the heavy lifting yourself (please don't), here's what you'll need to consider:

1. BUY PARK TICKETS BEFORE YOU GET TO THE PARKS. As mentioned previously, if you buy at the theme parks, Disney adds a surcharge of $21.30 per ticket to park tickets with three or more days of admission.

2. BUY FROM A THIRD-PARTY WHOLESALER. As we've noted, Disney contracts with third-party ticket vendors to offer discounts to price-sensitive consumers who'll visit only if they are able to get a deal. By using other companies, Disney doesn't have to offer those discounts directly to people who'd visit anyway. These vendors sign contracts with Disney and provide the same tickets you'd purchase at Walt Disney World. See "Where to Purchase Disney World Tickets," page 64, for vendors we recommend.

3. MEMBERS OF THE US MILITARY AND FLORIDA RESIDENTS GET SPECIAL DISCOUNTS. Disney's recent deal for US military personnel included a 4-Day Park Hopper for $350, substantially less than the regular price. Florida resident discounts aren't as steep, but they're better than anything the general public gets.

4. SET YOUR TICKET'S START DATE EARLIER THAN YOUR ARRIVAL DATE. Suppose you're visiting for a long weekend (Thursday–Sunday) and you're buying 4-Day tickets. You'd naturally pick Thursday as your ticket's start date. But remember that 4-Day park tickets are valid for seven days. If you're visiting at the start of a busy (expensive) season, setting your ticket start date to Monday or Tuesday can save around $8 per ticket.

5. BUY A SEPARATE WATER PARK TICKET INSTEAD OF THE WATER PARK AND SPORTS ADD-ON IF YOU PLAN TO VISIT ONLY ONE WATER PARK. The break-even point on the Water Park and Sports option is two water-park visits.

6. VISIT A WATER PARK ON YOUR FIRST OR LAST DAY. Let's say your Disney World trip starts at the end of a busy period and you're already planning one water park visit. Visiting the water park on your first day allows you to set your theme park start date one day later, saving around $3 per ticket. The same advice works in reverse: If your trip ends at the beginning of a busy season, plan to visit the water park on the last day.

Ticket Deals for Canada Residents

Disney often discounts theme park admission for Canada residents by setting the Canadian dollar at par with the United States dollar. The exchange rate as of this writing is $1 CAD equals $0.78 USD, so this deal effectively boosts the value of the loonie by around 25%. Visit disneyworld.disney.go.com/en_CA/special-offers to see the latest offers.

Ticket Deals for United Kingdom Residents

In the UK, Disney offers advance-purchase tickets that aren't available in the United States. As we went to press, you can get **14-Day Ultimate Tickets** for £469 for adults and £449 for kids—the same price as a 7-Day Ultimate Ticket. Ultimate Tickets provide unlimited admission to major and minor parks along with park-hopping privileges to the major parks. They expire 14 days after first use. To find out more, call ☎ 0800-169-0730 in the UK or ☎ 407-566-4985 in the US (Monday–Friday, 9 a.m.–8 p.m. Eastern time; Saturday, 9 a.m.–7 p.m.; and Sunday, 10 a.m.–4 p.m.), or go to disneyholidays.co.uk/walt-disney-world or the **Disney Information Bulletin Board** at thedibb.co.uk.

Discounts Available to Certain Groups and Individuals

DISNEY VACATION CLUB Members get a discount on Annual Passes.

CONVENTION-GOERS Disney World, Universal Orlando, SeaWorld, and other Orlando-area parks sometimes set up a web link, cited in your convention materials, where you can purchase discounted afternoon and evening admissions.

DISNEY CORPORATE SPONSORS If you work for one of these, you may be eligible for discounted admissions or perks at the parks. Check with your workplace's employee-benefits office.

FLORIDA RESIDENTS get substantial savings on virtually all tickets. You'll need to prove Florida residency with a valid driver's license or state identification card.

MILITARY, DEPARTMENT OF DEFENSE, AND CIVIL-SERVICE EMPLOY-EES Active-duty and retired military, Department of Defense (DOD) civilian employees, some civil-service employees, and dependents of these groups can buy Disney multiday admissions at a 9%–10% discount. Military personnel can buy discounted admission for nonmilitary guests if the military member accompanies the nonmilitary guest. If a group seeks the discount, at least half of the members of the group must be eligible for the military discount.

DISNEY YOUTH EDUCATION SERIES Disney runs daily educational programs for K–12 students; these programs also offer substantial ticket discounts (but with substantial restrictions). See disneyyouth.com.

Special Passes

Go to **MouseSavers.com** for information on passes that are not known to the general public and are not sold at any Walt Disney World ticket booth. For details, see tinyurl.com/wdwdiscounttix.

ANTICIPATING DISNEY TICKET PRICE INCREASES

DISNEY USUALLY RAISES PRICES once or twice a year. Hikes were announced in February 2022 and 2020, March 2019, February and September 2018, February 2014–2017, June 2011–2013, and August 2006–2010. We expect the next increase in early 2023.

BOB Save money on tickets by planning ahead—buy them before the next price increase.

Prices on all tickets went up an average of almost 5% in 2022, 6% in 2020, 4% in 2019, 9% in 2018, and 7% in 2017. Year-over-year hikes averaged around 5% earlier in this decade. For budgeting purposes, assume an increase of around 8% per year to be safe.

TICKETS, BIOMETRICS, WRISTBANDS, AND RFID

ONE ADMISSION MEDIUM is a rubber wristband about the size and shape of a small wristwatch. Called a **MagicBand,** it contains a tiny radio frequency identification (RFID) chip, which stores a link to the record of your admission purchase in Disney's computers. Your MagicBand also functions as your Disney hotel-room key, and it can (optionally) work as a credit card for most food and merchandise purchases. Note that MagicBands are no longer complimentary; see pages 93–94 for pricing information.

Each member of your family gets their own MagicBand, each with a unique serial number. The wristbands are removable, resizable, and waterproof, and they have ventilation holes for cooling. Eleven colors are available: black, blue, green, mint green, orange, pink, purple, red, yellow, dark gray, and gray (the default). You can choose your colors and personalize your bands when you order them at the Disney World website. More customized bands are available throughout the parks.

BOB You can create stickers of almost any color or design for your MagicBand at magicyourband.com.

Some guests, particularly those with hand- or wrist-mobility issues, find using the MagicBand physically challenging. To help with this, the center portion of the band (essentially a puck the size of a quarter) is removable. The puck can then be placed on a lanyard, making it easier to maneuver.

Along with the wristband, each family member will be asked to select a four-digit personal-identification number (PIN) for purchases. See below for details.

If you don't want a MagicBand, you're staying off-property, or you bought your admission from a third-party vendor, your second "ticket" option is a Key to the World (KTTW) Card, which is a flexible, credit card–size piece of plastic with an embedded RFID chip.

Your third option is to use the My Disney Experience (MDE) app on your Bluetooth-enabled smartphone. This option allows you to "tap" your smartphone for admission at park entrances, in the same way you tap your phone for payments at stores and restaurants.

Of these options, we think the MagicBands and KTTW Cards are the fastest and easiest to use. The main problem with using the MDE app is that it's far slower to take out your phone, open the app, and find the right screen to do what you want. And that's assuming you don't have to connect to Wi-Fi, log into the app, or remember the password you used.

RFID for Payment, Genie+, Hotel-Room Access, and Photos

Disney's hotel-room doors have RFID readers, allowing you to enter your room either by tapping your wristband or KTTW Card against the reader or by telling the MDE app to open the door. RFID readers are also installed at virtually every Disney cash register on-property, allowing you to pay for food, drinks, Genie+ and Individual Lightning Lane reservations, and souvenirs by tapping your MagicBand/KTTW Card against the reader. For in-person purchases, you'll be asked to verify your identity by entering your PIN on a small keypad.

The MDE app requires that you enable Bluetooth for tickets, photos, ride reservations, and payments. Doing so will allow your location to be tracked while you're using the app.

If you're using Disney's Memory Maker service, your MagicBand/KTTW Card serves as the link between your photos and your family. Each photographer carries a small RFID reader, against which you tap your MagicBand, KTTW Card, or (eventually) phone after having your photo taken. The computers that run the Memory Maker system will link your photos to you, and you'll be able to view them on the Disney World website.

BOB Disney strongly encourages guests to use contactless methods of payment throughout the World. These include MagicBands, ApplePay, Google Pay, credit cards, and debit cards.

Disney's onboard ride-photo computers incorporate RFID technology too. As you begin down the big drop near the finale of Splash Mountain, for example, sensors read the serial number on your MagicBand (or detect the Bluetooth signal sent from the MDE app on your phone) and pass it to Splash Mountain's cameras. When those cameras snap your family plunging into the briar patch, they attach your MagicBands' serial numbers to the photo, allowing you to see the ride photos together after you've returned home. Because ride sensors may not pick up the signal from an RFID card or a phone sitting in a wallet or purse, we think onboard ride photos require MagicBands.

Many people are understandably wary of multinational corporations tracking their movements. As noted earlier, guests who prefer not to wear MagicBands or download the MDE app can instead obtain KTTW Cards, which are somewhat harder to track (RFID-blocking wallets are available online). Disney says guests who opt out of MagicBands and the MDE app don't get the full range of ride experiences, though, so there's a trade-off.

BABYSITTING

CHILDCARE CENTERS Childcare isn't available inside the theme parks, and in early 2018 Disney closed all of its childcare centers. The only one still available is **Camp Dolphin** at the Dolphin and Swan hotels. Camp Dolphin is a fun-filled club exclusively for kids ages 5–12. Hours are 4–8 p.m. Reservations are required, and the price is $65 per child; a choice of a kid's meal and soda is included. Receive up to 2 hours of complimentary time at Camp Dolphin by getting a treatment at Mandara Spa (treatment of $75 and up) or by dining at Shula's Steak House, Todd English's bluezoo, or Il Mulino New York Trattoria. Simply present your receipt as proof of purchase when you pick up your child.

IN-ROOM BABYSITTING Two companies currently provide in-room sitting in Walt Disney World and surrounding areas: **Kid's Nite Out** and

Sunshine Babysitting. Both companies provide sitters older than age 18 who are screened, reference-checked, police-checked, and trained in CPR. See table below for details. A bilingual sitter may be available but is not guaranteed.

BABYSITTING SERVICES

KID'S NITE OUT	SUNSHINE BABYSITTING
☎ 407-828-0920 or 800-696-8105 kidsniteout.com	☎ 407-421-6505 sunshinebabysitting.com Email: resortchildcare@gmail.com
HOTELS SERVED All WDW and Orlando-area hotels	**HOTELS SERVED** All WDW and Orlando-area hotels
MINIMUM CHARGES 4 hours	**MINIMUM CHARGES** 4 hours
BASE HOURLY RATES • 1 child, $25 • 2 children, $28 • 3 children, $31 • 4 children, $34	**BASE HOURLY RATES** • 1 child, $18; each additional child, $2 more
EXTRA CHARGES Transportation fee, $12; before 8 a.m. or after 9 p.m., +$5 per hour. Additional fees apply during holidays.	**EXTRA CHARGES** Transportation fee, $12; before 8 a.m. and after 9 p.m., + $2 per hour; + $2 per hour during bank-holiday weekends and from October 1 through the first week of January; +$4 per hour for major holidays and weekends. $10 per meal for services of 6 hours or more.
CANCELLATION DEADLINE 24 hours before service (48 hours for holidays)	**CANCELLATION DEADLINE** 24 hours before service
FORM OF PAYMENT AE, D, MC, V; tips in cash	**FORM OF PAYMENT** Cash, AE, D, MC, V; tips in cash
THINGS SITTERS WON'T DO Transport children in private vehicle, take children swimming or boating, give baths	**THINGS SITTERS WON'T DO** Transport children in private vehicles, take children swimming, boating, give baths

SPECIAL PROGRAMS
for CHILDREN

LILIANE Disney is tinkering with prices and availability of packages now more than ever. Check ahead of time before promising your kids any activity.

SEVERAL CHILDREN'S PROGRAMS are available at Disney World parks and resorts. Many of Disney's Deluxe and Disney Vacation Club resorts offer a continuous slate of free children's activities from early morning through the evening, from storytelling and cookie decorating to hands-on activities themed to the resort.

BEHIND THE SEEDS AT EPCOT (*temporarily unavailable*) This 1-hour walking tour of The Land greenhouses and labs at EPCOT has plenty of interaction for the kids, such as playing guessing games and feeding fish at the fish farm. The greenhouses are home to more than 60 crops from around the world. Did you know that the food grown in The Land is used at restaurants throughout EPCOT? The price is $25 per adult and $20 per child (ages 3–9). Call ☎ 407-938-1373 for additional information and reservations.

CAPTAIN HOOK'S PIRATE CREW (*temporarily unavailable*) This kids' program is offered nightly at Disney's Beach Club, transporting kids ages 4–12 to an environment full of excitement and adventure with Captain Hook himself in attendance! Activities include a treasure hunt, a sailing excursion on Crescent Lake, and dinner. Check-in begins at 4:30 p.m., and programing runs 5–8 p.m. for a fee of $55 plus tax. Children must be fully toilet-trained, and parents must be physically present to check children in and out of the program. To book this tour, call ☎ 407-938-1373.

CARING FOR GIANTS This family-friendly, 1-hour backstage experience at the Animal Kingdom gives guests the opportunity to meet dedicated animal-care experts who provide for the care and wellness of the elephant herd. African cultural representatives share stories of Disney's conservation efforts. Tours are offered throughout the day, 9:30 a.m.–4 p.m. Pricing for all ages is $35 and does not include park admission. Children must be at least 4 years old to attend; children age 17 or under must be accompanied by an adult. To book, call ☎ 407-938-1373.

DINE WITH AN ANIMAL SPECIALIST (*temporarily unavailable*) We highly recommend this experience at Sanaa, one of the restaurants at Animal Kingdom Lodge. Not only will you and your family be treated to a fabulous African-inspired lunch, but you'll also get to spend time with a caretaker who shares fun facts about his or her work with the animals. After lunch, guests are taken outside and behind the gates to meet an endangered animal.

Limited to 12 participants, the lunch is offered Wednesdays and Saturdays at 11 a.m. The price—$60 for adults and $35 for kids ages 3–9 (it's best suited for age 8 and up)—includes tax and tip. At the end of the meal, guests are invited to make a voluntary $5 donation to the Disney Conservation Fund. It's educational, fun, and a great value.

DISNEY'S FAMILY MAGIC TOUR (*temporarily unavailable*) This is an approximately 2-hour guided tour of the Magic Kingdom for the entire family. Even children in strollers are welcome. The tour combines information about the Magic Kingdom with a guided scavenger hunt with riddles. There's usually a marginal plot such as saving Wendy from Captain Hook, in which case the character at the end of the tour is Wendy. The tour departs Monday, Tuesday, Friday, and Saturday at 10 a.m. The cost is about $39 per person plus tax and a valid Magic Kingdom admission. Reservations can be made by calling ☎ 407-WDW-TOUR (939-8687).

DISNEY'S PERFECTLY PRINCESS TEA PARTY (*temporarily unavailable*) It certainly takes a princely sum to cover the tab on this Grand Floridian shindig, hosted by Rose Petal, an enchanted storytelling rose. Your little princess gets to sip tea with Princess Aurora. Girls receive an 18-inch My Disney Girl Princess Aurora doll dressed in a gown and accessories. Other loot includes a tiara, silver bracelet, fresh rose, "Best Friend" certificate for the doll, and cinch bag. Princes who attend the tea party will receive a sword and shield, souvenir pin, Disney plush, and "Best Friend" certificate. The cost is about $334, including tax and gratuity, for one adult and one child ages 3–9; add an additional guest age 10 and up for $99 or an additional child for $235 (adults-only bookings not available). Call ☎ 407-939-6983 for availability.

DISNEY'S THE MAGIC BEHIND OUR STEAM TRAINS (*temporarily unavailable*) Kids must be age 10 or older for this 3-hour tour, presented Sunday–Thursday. At the 7:30 a.m. start time, join the crew of the Walt Disney World Railroad as they prepare their steam locomotives for the day. Cost is $54 per person, plus tax and a valid Magic Kingdom admission. Call ☎ 407-WDW-TOUR (939-8687) for information and reservations. Check in at the Main Entrance of Magic Kingdom 15 minutes prior to the start of your tour. If you must cancel, please do so at least 48 hours in advance.

FORT WILDERNESS ARCHERY EXPERIENCE Fans of Princess Merida, this is your activity! Guests age 7 and up can learn how to hold and fire a compound bow in this 75-minute archery program. With class sizes limited to 10 guests, this is a wonderful experience held at the campsites at Fort Wilderness Resort. The fee for the program is $47.93, including tax. The archery experience is available on select days, 2:45–4:15 p.m. For reservations, call ☎ 407-WDW-PLAY (939-7529).

UP CLOSE WITH RHINOS This 1-hour tour is offered daily at 11 a.m. at the Animal Kingdom. The tour discusses the behavior and biology of the park's white rhinos, as well as the challenges that threaten the animals in the wild. Participants must be 4 years of age or older; guests under age 18 must be accompanied by a paying adult. No cameras, video equipment, or cell phones may be used while on this backstage tour. The price for all ages is $45 plus tax. To book this tour, call ☎ 407-938-1373.

WILD AFRICA TREK This backstage tour of the Animal Kingdom is not for the faint of heart, but you, and especially your kids, will get a real sense of adventure. On this 3-hour walking and driving tour, you will visit Harambe Wildlife Reserve and the savanna for up-close encounters with giraffes, rhinos, tigers, and lions. At some point in the tour, secured to an overhead track with a safety harness, you will walk a wobbly bridge and get incredible views of hippos and crocodiles. Halfway through the tour, guests will indulge in gourmet eats in an outdoor setting on the savanna. Foods offered include chicken curry salad, marinated tandoori shrimp, smoked salmon roulade with dill, and fresh fruit. (Menu items are subject to change without notice.) Your encounters with the animals will be captured by a professional photographer, and at the end of the tour, you'll receive a photo code to access and download the images. You can bring your own camera or smartphone too, but only if you have a strap that can be attached to the provided vest or can hang the camera securely around your neck.

LILIANE I love, love, love this tour. I wish I could go on it every time I visit and capture tigers and lions and more with my camera.

Wear comfortable clothes and sneakers, and bring a strap for your glasses or sunglasses. Participants also receive a complimentary souvenir, which currently is a water bottle that clips to your vest. For anything you cannot attach to your vest, Disney provides lockers. The guides are incredibly knowledgeable, and a wireless headset allows you to hear the guide at all times. The price is $199, plus tax and gratuity, and varies during peak seasons such as December and Easter. Participants must be 8 years of age or older, at least 48 inches tall, and 45–300 pounds with the harness gear on. The trek is available multiple times daily. Call ☎ 407-938-1373 for reservations.

WONDERLAND TEA PARTY (*temporarily unavailable*) This event is held Monday–Friday, 2–3 p.m., at 1900 Park Fare restaurant at the Grand Floridian. The price is $52.19, including tax (ages 4–12). The program consists of decorating and eating cupcakes and having "tea" with characters from *Alice in Wonderland*. Small children might get scared meeting the White Rabbit or Mad Hatter. Reservations can be made by calling ☎ 407-824-1391.

BIRTHDAYS AND SPECIAL OCCASIONS

GUESTS WHO ARE CELEBRATING A BIRTHDAY or visiting Walt Disney World for the first time can pick up a button corresponding to the celebration at Guest Relations when entering any of the parks. Often upon check-in, clerks at the Disney resorts will ask if any member of your party is celebrating a special event. It's especially fun for birthday kids, as cast members will congratulate your child throughout the day in the hotel, on the bus, in the park, and at restaurants throughout the World. A Lombard, Illinois, mom put the word out and was glad she did:

> My daughter turned 5 while we were there, and I asked about special things that could be done. Our hotel asked me who her favorite character was and did the rest. We came back to our room on her birthday and there were balloons, a card, and an autographed Cinderella 5-by-7-inch photo! When we entered the Magic Kingdom, we received an It's My Birthday Today pin (FREE!), and at the restaurant she got a huge cupcake with whipped cream, sprinkles, and a candle. IT PAYS TO ASK!!

Another great and reasonably priced treat is to have your child's first haircut at the **Harmony Barber Shop** on Main Street, U.S.A. at the Magic Kingdom. Rest assured that your kid will walk away with a good haircut, and you may even be treated to a song by the Dapper Dans, Disney's famous barbershop quartet. The best time to go is during a parade. You get a good view, and the staff sings along with the parade music. It's a great photo op. An Ohio mom celebrated her child's first haircut at the barber shop:

> The barbershop makes a big deal with baby's first haircut—pixie dust, photos, a certificate, and a "free" mouse ears hat!

Don't fret—children of any age and adults, girls included, will be served at the Harmony Barber Shop.

PART 3

WHERE *to* STAY

WHEN TRAVELING WITH CHILDREN, your hotel is your home away from home, your safe harbor, and your sanctuary. Staying in a hotel is in itself a great adventure for children. They take in every detail and delight in such things as having a pool at their disposal and obtaining ice from a noisy machine. Of course, it's critical that your children feel safe and secure, but it adds immeasurably to the success of the vacation if they really like the hotel.

BOB In our opinion, if you're traveling with a child age 12 or younger, one of your top priorities should be to book a hotel within easy striking distance of the parks.

In truth, because of their youth and limited experience, children are far less particular about hotels than adults, but kids' memories are like little steel traps, so once you establish a lodging standard, that's pretty much what they'll expect every time. A couple from Gary, Indiana, stayed at the pricey Yacht Club Resort at Walt Disney World because they heard that it offered a knock-out swimming area (which it does). When they returned 2 years later and stayed at one of Disney's All-Star Resorts for about a third of the price, their 10-year-old carped all week. If you're on a budget, it's better to begin with modest accommodations and move up to better digs on subsequent trips as finances permit.

"YOU CAN'T ROLLER-SKATE IN A BUFFALO HERD"

THIS WAS A SONG TITLE FROM THE 1960S. If we wrote that song today, we'd call it "You Can't Have Fun at Disney World if You're Drop-Dead Tired." Believe us, Disney World is an easy place to be penny-wise and pound-foolish. Many families who cut lodging expenses by booking a budget hotel end up so far away from Disney World that it's a major hassle to return to the hotel in the middle of the day for swimming and a nap. By trying to spend the whole day at the theme parks, however, they wear themselves out quickly, and the dream vacation suddenly disintegrates into short tempers and exhaustion. And don't confuse this advice with a sales pitch for Disney hotels. You will find dozens of hotels outside

Disney World that are as close or closer to certain Disney parks than some of the resorts inside the World. Our main point—our only point, really—is that you should be able to return to your hotel easily when the need arises.

LODGING CONSIDERATIONS

COST

AT WALT DISNEY WORLD, standard hotel-room rates range from about $118 to more than $2,100 per night. Outside, rooms are as low as $80 a night. Clearly, if you are willing to sacrifice some luxury and don't mind a 10- to 25-minute commute, you can really cut your lodging costs by staying outside Walt Disney World. Hotels in the World tend to be the most expensive, but they also offer some of the highest quality, as well as a number of perks not enjoyed by guests who stay outside the World. The costs shown in the Hotel Information Table on pages 114–116 are rounded to the nearest $50.

Disney's cheapest hotel rooms compare favorably with non-Disney rooms within this price range. Rooms at the **Pop Century Resort,** for example, cost $162–$361 (before discounts) throughout the year, plus they have convenient transportation and perks such as separate park reservations. In addition, Pop Century has completed a major, stylish refurbishment. For an incremental cost of around $66–$129 per night (again, before discounts), we think Pop Century is the best Value choice for most readers.

Off-site hotels and homes are often better deals for families looking for more space, or high-end lodging and service, for the same money. For instance, Disney's cheapest family suite, at the **Art of Animation Resort,** sleeps six and costs $428–$764 per night. A comparable room at the **Sonesta ES Suites Lake Buena Vista** costs around $170–$305 per night, depending on the time of year. Renting a three-bedroom condo in Kissimmee is even cheaper: around $150–$250 per night. You can afford a longer trip with those savings—a fact that more than offsets the advantage of park reservations.

Similarly, the cheapest room at Disney's flagship **Grand Floridian Resort & Spa** costs between about $737 and $1,080, depending on the date of stay. The cheapest room at the **Four Seasons Resort Orlando** (adjacent to Walt Disney World) is at the upper end of that range. But the Four Seasons room is larger and better in every way, with restaurants generally as good as or better than the Grand Flo's, along with superior customer service.

LOCATION AND TRANSPORTATION OPTIONS

ONCE YOU'VE DETERMINED YOUR BUDGET, think about what you want to do at Walt Disney World. Will you go to all four theme parks, or will you concentrate on one or two? If you'll be driving a car, the location of your Disney hotel isn't especially important unless you plan to spend most of your time at the Magic Kingdom. (Disney transportation is always more efficient than your car in this case because it deposits you right at the theme park entrance.)

Most convenient to the Magic Kingdom are the three resorts linked by monorail: the **Grand Floridian** and its **Villas,** the **Contemporary** and **Bay Lake Tower,** and the **Polynesian Village.**

Wilderness Lodge, Boulder Ridge Villas, and **Copper Creek Villas & Cabins,** along with **Fort Wilderness Resort & Campground,** are linked to the Magic Kingdom by boat and to everywhere else in the World by bus. **Shades of Green** only has bus service.

The most centrally located resorts in Walt Disney World are the EPCOT hotels—**BoardWalk Inn & Villas, Yacht & Beach Club Resorts, Beach Club Villas, Riviera Resort, Swan,** and **Dolphin**—and **Coronado Springs** (including the new **Gran Destino Tower**), near the Animal Kingdom. The EPCOT hotels are within easy walking distance of Disney's Hollywood Studios (DHS) and EPCOT's International Gateway. Except at Coronado Springs, boat service is also available at these resorts, with vessels connecting to DHS.

LILIANE Just for the record, the EPCOT resorts within walking distance of the International Gateway are a long, long walk from Future World, the section of EPCOT where families tend to spend most of their time.

Caribbean Beach, Riviera, Pop Century, and **Art of Animation Resorts** are just south and east of EPCOT and DHS. They are connected to EPCOT and DHS by the Skyliner gondola and to everything else by bus. All resorts on the new Skyliner line have seen their bus transportation options to DHS and EPCOT reduced. Instead of every 20 minutes, buses to these two resorts now leave approximately once per hour. What makes it worse is that there is no official schedule for the buses to EPCOT and DHS, so you can't plan properly. If you are set on not using the gondola, we strongly recommend you stay at a hotel that is not along the Skyliner route. If that is not possible, use your car or a ride service. Along Bonnet Creek, **Old Key West** and **Port Orleans Resorts** also offer quick access to those parks. **Saratoga Springs** is connected to Disney Springs via a pedestrian bridge; boat and bus service are available.

BOB If you plan to use Disney transportation to visit all four major parks and the water parks, book a centrally located resort that has good transportation connections, such as the EPCOT resorts: the **Polynesian Village, Caribbean Beach, Art of Animation, Pop Century, Coronado Springs, Port Orleans,** or **Riviera Resorts.**

Though not centrally located, the **All-Star Resorts** and **Animal Kingdom Lodge & Villas** have good bus service to all Disney World destinations and are closest to Animal Kingdom.

Wilderness Lodge and **Fort Wilderness** have the most inconvenient transportation service of the Disney hotels. Spotty bus service is also a drawback shared by **Saratoga Springs** and **Treehouse Villas.**

Disney Skyliner, a new aerial tramway gondola system, connects the **Art of Animation, Pop Century,** and **Caribbean Beach Resorts,** as well as other locations, with DHS and the International Gateway entrance at

COSTS PER NIGHT OF DISNEY HOTEL ROOMS, 2022 *(rack rate)*	
Rates are for standard rooms except as noted.	
ALL-STAR RESORTS	$150–$236
ALL-STAR MUSIC RESORT FAMILY SUITES	$300–$581
ANIMAL KINGDOM LODGE	$411–$701
ANIMAL KINGDOM VILLAS *(studio, Jambo House/Kidani Village)*	$411–$825
ART OF ANIMATION FAMILY SUITES	$428–$764
ART OF ANIMATION RESORT	$228–$336
BAY LAKE TOWER AT CONTEMPORARY RESORT *(studio)*	$554–$923
BEACH CLUB RESORT	$464–$846
BEACH CLUB VILLAS *(studio)*	$464–$821
BOARDWALK INN	$519–$870
BOARDWALK VILLAS *(studio)*	$519–$870
BOULDER RIDGE VILLAS *(studio)*	$392–$785
CARIBBEAN BEACH RESORT	$285–$411
CONTEMPORARY RESORT *(Garden Wing)*	$482–$846
COPPER CREEK VILLAS & CASCADE CABINS *(studio)*	$392–$760
CORONADO SPRINGS RESORT	$253–$381
DOLPHIN *(Sheraton)*	$264–$427
FORT WILDERNESS RESORT & CAMPGROUND *(cabins)*	$450–$725
GRAN DESTINO TOWER	$371–$500
GRAND FLORIDIAN RESORT & SPA	$773–$1,083
GRAND FLORIDIAN VILLAS *(studio)*	$757–$1,200
OLD KEY WEST RESORT *(studio)*	$393–$647
POLYNESIAN VILLAGE RESORT	$921–$1,185
POLYNESIAN VILLAS & BUNGALOWS *(studio)*	$579–$1,012
POP CENTURY RESORT	$191–$314
PORT ORLEANS RESORT *(French Quarter & Riverside)*	$278–$386
RIVIERA RESORT *(studio)*	$445–$699
SARATOGA SPRINGS RESORT & SPA *(studio)*	$389–$663
STAR WARS: GALACTIC STARCRUISER *(rate is for a 2-night stay)*	$5,000+
SWAN *(Westin)*	$307–$445
SWAN RESERVE *(Autograph Collection)*	$325–$504
TREEHOUSE VILLAS	$1,079–$2,000
WILDERNESS LODGE	$648–$790
YACHT CLUB RESORT	$591–$846

EPCOT. Disney has also started a point-to-point transportation system called the **Minnie Van** service. The Minnie Mouse–themed midsize SUVs transport guests, on demand, throughout Walt Disney World. The SUVs accommodate up to eight passengers.

Open the Lyft app from anywhere within Walt Disney World Resort to access the Minnie Van service to request a ride, or call ☎ 407-828-3500. Prices vary based on distance traveled. The service is available

6:30 a.m.–12:30 a.m. for transportation on Disney property only, which includes the four main theme parks, all Disney-owned resorts, Disney's two water parks, and Disney Springs. The Minnie Van service is more expensive than Uber.

A Minnie Van airport shuttle is available 6 a.m.–11:59 p.m. for a flat rate of $155, gratuity not included. The pick-up location at the airport is by the baggage claim escalators. The Minnie Van is pet-friendly and the service can be added to a Walt Disney World package. The Minnie Van airport shuttle is now also available for the Swan and Dolphin hotels, the Four Seasons Resort Orlando at Walt Disney World Resort, Shades of Green, the Disney Springs Resort Area hotels, Hilton Orlando Bonnet Creek, Waldorf Astoria Orlando, Wyndham Grand Orlando Resort Bonnet Creek, Wyndham Bonnet Creek Resort, SpringHill Suites Orlando at Flamingo Crossings and TownePlace Suites Orlando at Flamingo Crossings.

To reserve an accessible vehicle that accommodates a wheelchair or electronic convenience vehicle, call ☎ 407-828-3500. Vans accommodate up to six guests and six medium-size suitcases, and they can be equipped with up to three complimentary car seats.

Last but not least, you can book a Minnie Van transfer between a Walt Disney World resort and Port Canaveral. The transfer from the port to a Disney resort at the end of your cruise is also available. The transfer is a flat fee of $249, one way, gratuity not included, and must be booked by calling the Disney Cruise Line embarkation services at ☎ 800-395-9374.

COMMUTING TO AND FROM THE THEME PARKS

FOR VISITORS LODGING INSIDE WALT DISNEY WORLD With three important exceptions, the fastest way to commute from your hotel to the theme parks and back is in your own car. And though many guests use the Disney transportation system and appreciate not having to drive, based on timed comparisons, it's almost always less time-consuming to drive. The exceptions are these: (1) commuting to the Magic Kingdom from the hotels on the monorail (Grand Floridian, Polynesian Village, and Contemporary Resort and Bay Lake Tower); (2) commuting to the Magic Kingdom from any Disney hotel by bus or boat; and (3) commuting to EPCOT on the monorail from the Polynesian Village Resort via the Transportation and Ticket Center (TTC).

If you stay at the Polynesian, you can catch a direct monorail to the Magic Kingdom, and by walking 100 yards or so to the TTC, you can catch a direct monorail to EPCOT. At the nexus of the monorail system, the Polynesian is certainly the most convenient resort. From either the Magic Kingdom or EPCOT, you can return to your hotel quickly and easily whenever you want.

Second to the Polynesian in terms of convenience are the Grand Floridian and Contemporary, also on the Magic Kingdom monorail, but they cost as much as or more than the Polynesian. Less expensive

Disney hotels transport you to the Magic Kingdom by bus or boat. For reasons described below, this is more efficient than driving a car.

DRIVING TIME TO THE THEME PARKS FOR VISITORS LODGING OUTSIDE WALT DISNEY WORLD For vacationers staying outside Walt Disney World, we've calculated the approximate commuting time to the major theme parks' parking lots from several off-World lodging areas. Add a few minutes to our times to pay your parking fee and to park. Once parked at the TTC (Magic Kingdom parking lot), it takes an average of 20–30 more minutes to reach the Magic Kingdom. At EPCOT and Animal Kingdom, the lot-to-gate transit time is 10–15 minutes; at Disney's Hollywood Studios (DHS), it's 8–12 minutes. If you haven't purchased your theme park admission in advance, tack on another 10–20 minutes.

DRIVING TIME TO THE THEME PARKS				
MINUTES TO: **FROM:**	**MAGIC KINGDOM PARKING LOT**	**EPCOT PARKING LOT**	**DISNEY'S ANIMAL KINGDOM PARKING LOT**	**DISNEY'S HOLLYWOOD STUDIOS PARKING LOT**
Downtown Orlando	35	31	37	33
North International Drive and Universal Orlando	24	21	26	22
Central International Drive and Sand Lake Road	26	23	27	24
South International Drive and SeaWorld	18	15	20	16
FL 535	12	9	13	10
US 192, west of I-4	10–15	7–12	5–10	5–10
US 192, east of I-4	10–18	7–15	5–12	5–13

Our Hotel Information Table on pages 114–116 shows the commuting time, not including getting to and from the parking lot to the turnstiles, to the Disney theme parks from each hotel listed. Those commuting times represent an average of several test runs. Your actual time may be shorter or longer depending on many variables.

SHUTTLE SERVICE FROM HOTELS OUTSIDE WALT DISNEY WORLD Many hotels in the Walt Disney World area provide shuttle service to the theme parks. They represent a fairly carefree alternative for getting to and from the parks, letting you off near the entrance (except at the Magic Kingdom) and saving you the cost of parking. The rub is that they might not get you there as early as you desire (a critical point if you are using our touring plans) or be available at the time you wish to return to your lodging. Also, be forewarned that most shuttle services do not add vehicles at park opening or closing times. In the morning, your biggest problem is that you might not get a seat. At closing time, however, and sometimes following a hard rain, you can expect a lot of competition for standing space on the bus. If there is no room, you might have to wait 30 minutes to an hour for the next shuttle.

CONVENIENCE, CONVENIENTLY DEFINED Conceptually, it's easy to grasp that a hotel that is closer is more convenient than one that is far away. But nothing is that simple at Walt Disney World, so we'd better tell you exactly what you're in for. If you stay at a Walt Disney World resort and use the Disney transportation system, you'll have a 5- to 10-minute walk to the bus stop, monorail station, or dock (whichever applies). Once there, buses, trains, or boats generally run about every 15–25 minutes, so you might have to wait a short time for your transportation to arrive. Once you're on board, most conveyances make additional stops en route to your destination, and many take a less-than-direct route. Upon arrival, however, they deposit you fairly close to the entrance of the theme park. Returning to your hotel is the same process in reverse and takes about the same amount of time.

Regardless of whether you stay in Walt Disney World, if you use your own car, here's how your commute shakes out: After a 1- to 5-minute walk from your room to your car, you drive to the theme park, stopping to pay a parking fee or showing your MagicBand for free parking (if you're a Disney resort guest). Disney cast members then direct you to a parking space. If you arrive early, your space may be close enough to the park entrance (Magic Kingdom excepted) to walk. If you park farther afield, a Disney tram will come along every 5 minutes to collect you and transport you to the entrance.

At the Magic Kingdom, the entrance to the park is separated from the parking lot by the TTC and the Seven Seas Lagoon. After parking at the Magic Kingdom lot, you take a tram to the TTC and then board a ferry or monorail (your choice) for the trip across the lagoon to the park. This process is fairly time-consuming and is to be avoided if possible. The only way around it, however, is to stay at a Disney resort and commute directly to the Magic Kingdom entrance via Disney bus, boat, or monorail. Happily, all the other theme parks are situated adjacent to their parking lots.

Because families with children tend to spend more time on average at the Magic Kingdom than at the other parks, and because it's so important to return to your hotel for rest, the business of getting around the lagoon can be a major consideration when choosing a place to stay; the extra hassle of crossing the lagoon (to get back to your car) makes coming and going much more difficult. The half hour it takes to commute to your hotel via car from the Animal Kingdom, DHS, or EPCOT takes an hour or longer from the Magic Kingdom. If you stay at a Disney hotel and use the Disney transportation system, you may have to wait 5–25 minutes for your bus, boat, or monorail, but it will take you directly from the Magic Kingdom entrance to your hotel, bypassing the lagoon and the TTC.

DINING

DINING FIGURES INTO THE LODGING DISCUSSION only if you don't plan to have a car at your disposal. If you plan on using the Disney transportation system (for Disney hotel guests) or the courtesy shuttle of your non-Disney hotel, you will either have to dine at the theme parks or near your hotel. If your hotel offers a lot of choices or if other restaurants are within walking distance, then there's no problem. If your hotel is somewhat isolated and offers limited selections, you'll feel like Bob did on a canoe trip once when he ate northern pike at every meal for a week because that's all he could catch.

At Disney World, though it's relatively quick and efficient to commute from your Disney hotel or campground to the theme parks, it's a long, arduous process requiring transfers to travel from hotel to hotel. Disney hotels that are somewhat isolated and that offer limited dining choices include the All-Stars, Art of Animation, Caribbean Beach, Coronado Springs, Old Key West, Pop Century, and Wilderness Lodge Resorts, as well as the Fort Wilderness Campground.

The best resorts for dining quality are **Animal Kingdom Lodge & Villas** and the **Grand Floridian Resort & Villas.** Three of Walt Disney World's top 10 sit-down restaurants are found at Animal Kingdom Lodge: **Jiko—The Cooking Place, Sanaa,** and **Boma—Flavors of Africa.** The Grand Floridian holds Walt Disney World's very best restaurant, **Victoria & Albert's,** and readers rank five of its other restaurants in the top 25. The Grand Floridian is also a short monorail ride from the **California Grill** at the Contemporary Resort, another top venue. If high-quality dining is a top priority for you and these two resorts fit in your budget, we think they're excellent choices.

The best resorts for dining quality and selection are the EPCOT resorts: the **Beach Club Villas, BoardWalk Inn & Villas, Dolphin, Swan,** and **Yacht and Beach Club Resorts.** (Not included is the Swan Reserve, which has one restaurant for the entire hotel.) Each has good sit-down restaurants, and each is within easy walking distance of the others, as well as the dining options available in EPCOT's **World Showcase.** However, on-site quick-service options are limited for all but the BoardWalk Inn & Villas, and readers rate these hotels below average for quick-service options. If quick, simple breakfasts and lunches are what you're after, stay elsewhere.

The only other hotels in Disney World with similar access to a concentrated area of good restaurants are those in the **Disney Springs Resort Area** (B Resort & Spa, DoubleTree Suites, Hilton Orlando Buena Vista Palace, Hilton Orlando Lake Buena Vista, Holiday Inn Orlando, Saratoga Springs Resort & Spa, and Wyndham Garden Lake Buena Vista). In addition to the hotels' own restaurants, all are within walking distance of restaurants in **Disney Springs.** As with the EPCOT resorts, though, many readers complain about the difficulty in finding quick, tasty breakfast and lunch options at these hotels.

LILIANE If you share a room with your children, you all should hit the sack at the same time. Establish a single compromise bedtime, probably a little early for you and a bit later than the children's usual weekend bedtime. Observe any nightly rituals you practice at home, such as reading a book before lights-out.

If you want a condo-type accommodation so you have more flex-ibility for meal preparation than eating out of a cooler, the best deals in Disney World are the prefab log cabins at **Fort Wilderness Resort & Campground.** Other Disney lodgings with kitchens are available at **all of the villas,** plus **Bay Lake Tower, Old Key West, Riviera Resort,** and **Saratoga Springs,** but all are much more expensive than the cabins at the campground. Outside Disney World, an ever-increasing number of condos are available, and some are very good deals. See our discussion of lodging outside Disney World starting on page 130.

THE SIZE OF YOUR GROUP

LARGER FAMILIES AND GROUPS may be interested in how many people can stay in a Disney resort room, but only Lilliputians would be comfortable in a room filled to capacity. Groups requiring two or more rooms should consider condo, suite, or villa accommodations, either in or out of Disney World. If there are more than six in your party, you will need either two hotel rooms, a suite (see Wilderness Lodge), a villa, or a condo.

STAYING IN OR OUT OF THE WORLD: WEIGHING THE PROS AND CONS

1. COST If cost is your primary consideration, you'll lodge much less expensively outside Walt Disney World.

2. EASE OF ACCESS Even if you stay in Disney World, you're dependent on some mode of transportation. It may be less stressful to use the Disney transportation system, but with the exception of commuting to the Magic Kingdom, the fastest, most efficient, and most flexible way to get around is usually a car. If you're at EPCOT, for example, and want to take the kids back to the Contemporary Resort for a nap, forget the monorail. You'll get back much faster by car.

Readers complain about problems with the Disney transportation system more than most topics. These comments from a Columbus, Ohio, reader are typical:

It sometimes felt like we were visiting Mass Transit World instead of Walt Disney World. More and more [of our] energy was devoted to planning and getting from point A to point B than in the past. I've never rented a car on property, but after this trip I will consider it.

Though it's only for the use and benefit of Disney guests, the Dis-ney transportation system is nonetheless public, and users must expect inconveniences: conveyances that arrive and depart on their sched-ule, not yours; the occasional need to transfer; multiple stops; time lost loading and unloading passengers; and, generally, the challenge of understanding and using a large, complex transportation network.

Traffic on I-4 is the largest potential problem with staying at an off-site hotel, especially if you're coming or going during rush hours. Thus, the closer your off-site hotel is to Disney property, the less risk there is of being stuck in I-4 traffic.

HOTEL | MAXIMUM OCCUPANCY PER ROOM

ALL-STAR RESORTS | Standard room: 4 plus child under age 3 in crib; Family Suite: 6 people plus child in crib

ANIMAL KINGDOM LODGE | 4 plus child under age 3 in crib

ANIMAL KINGDOM VILLAS: JAMBO HOUSE | Studio: 4; 1 bedroom: 4 or 5; 2 bedroom: 8 or 9; Grand Villa: 12; all plus child in crib

ANIMAL KINGDOM VILLAS: KIDANI VILLAGE | Studio: 4; 1 bedroom: 5; 2 bedroom: 9; Grand Villa: 12; all plus child in crib

ART OF ANIMATION | Little Mermaid buildings: 4; Cars, Finding Nemo, and Lion King buildings: 6; all plus child in crib

BAY LAKE TOWER AT THE CONTEMPORARY RESORT | Studio: 4; 1 bedroom: 5; 2 bedroom: 9; Grand Villa: 12; all plus child in crib

BEACH CLUB RESORT | 5 plus child under age 3 in crib

BEACH CLUB VILLAS | Studio and 1 bedroom: 4; 2 bedroom: 8; Grand Villa: 12; all plus child in crib

BOARDWALK INN | 5 plus child under age 3 in crib

BOARDWALK VILLAS | Studio and 1 bedroom: 4; 2 bedroom: 9; Grand Villa: 12; all plus child in crib

BOULDER RIDGE VILLAS AND COPPER CREEK VILLAS & CABINS AT WILDERNESS LODGE | Boulder Ridge studio: 5; Copper Creek studio: 4; 1 bedroom: 4; 2 bedroom: 8; Copper Creek 3 bedroom: 12; all plus child in crib

CARIBBEAN BEACH RESORT | 4 plus child under age 3 in crib; 5 in rooms with Murphy bed

CONTEMPORARY RESORT | 5 plus child under age 3 in crib

CORONADO SPRINGS RESORT | 4 plus child under age 3 in crib

DOLPHIN | 5

FORT WILDERNESS CABINS | 6 plus child under age 3 in crib

GRAN DESTINO TOWER AT CORONADO SPRINGS RESORT | Standard and executive rooms: 4; 1 bedroom: 5; presidential suites: 8; all plus a child in crib

GRAND FLORIDIAN RESORT | 5 plus child under age 3 in crib

OLD KEY WEST RESORT | Studio: 4; 1 bedroom: 5; 2 bedroom: 9; Grand Villa: 12; all plus child in crib

POLYNESIAN VILLAGE RESORT | 5 plus child under age 3 in crib

POLYNESIAN VILLAS & BUNGALOWS | Studio: 5 plus child in crib; 2 bedroom bungalow: 8 plus child in crib

POP CENTURY RESORT | 4 plus child under age 3 in crib

PORT ORLEANS–FRENCH QUARTER | 4 plus child under age 3 in crib

PORT ORLEANS–RIVERSIDE | 4 plus child under age 3 in crib or trundle bed; 5 in rooms with Murphy bed

RIVIERA RESORT | Tower Studio: 2; Deluxe Studio and 1 bedroom: 5; 2 bedroom: 9; Grand Villa: 12; all plus a child in crib

SARATOGA SPRINGS RESORT | Studio and 1 bedroom: 4; 2 bedroom: 8; Grand Villa: 12; all plus child in crib

STAR WARS: GALACTIC STARCRUISER | Standard Cabin: 5; Galaxy Class Suite: 4; Grand Captain Suite: 8

SWAN | 4

SWAN RESERVE | 8

TREEHOUSE VILLAS AT SARATOGA SPRINGS RESORT | 9 plus child in crib

THE VILLAS AT GRAND FLORIDIAN RESORT | Studio and 1 bedroom: 5; 2 bedroom: 9 or 10; Grand Villa: 12; all plus child in crib

WILDERNESS LODGE | Standard room: 4 plus child under age 3 in crib; Deluxe room with sleeper sofa: 6

YACHT CLUB RESORT | 5 plus child under age 3 in crib

3. YOUNG CHILDREN Though the hassle of commuting to most non-Disney hotels is only slightly (if at all) greater than that of commuting to Disney hotels, a definite peace of mind results from staying in the World. Regardless of where you stay, make sure you get your young children back to the hotel for a nap each day.

4. SPLITTING UP If your party will likely split up to tour (as frequently happens in families with children of widely varying ages), staying in Walt Disney World offers more transportation options, and therefore more independence.

5. SLOPPIN' THE HOGS If you have a large crew that chows down like pigs at the trough, you may do better staying outside the World, where food is far less expensive. Also, many off-site hotels' prices include some sort of complimentary breakfast.

6. VISITING OTHER ATTRACTIONS If you plan to visit SeaWorld, Legoland, the newly opened Peppa Pig Theme Park, the Kennedy Space Center, the Universal theme parks, or other area attractions, it may be more convenient to stay outside the World. Remember the number one rule, though: Stay close enough to return to your hotel for rest in the middle of the day.

WALT DISNEY WORLD LODGING

BENEFITS OF STAYING IN WALT DISNEY WORLD

IN ADDITION TO PROXIMITY—especially easy access to the Magic Kingdom—Walt Disney World resort hotel and campground guests are accorded other privileges and amenities unavailable to those staying outside the World. Though some of these perks are only advertising gimmicks, others are potentially quite valuable. Here are the benefits and what they mean:

1. CONVENIENCE Commuting to the theme parks using the Disney transportation system is easy, especially if you stay in a hotel connected by monorail, boat, or Skyliner.

2. EARLY ACCESS TO ATTRACTION AND RESTAURANT RESERVATIONS Guests at Disney resorts can make Genie+ reservations (see page 258) starting at 7 a.m.; off-site guests must wait until the park opens. Guests staying on-property can also make dining reservations 60 days before they arrive and then an additional 10 days into their trip.

3. EARLY THEME PARK ENTRY Disney resort guests—along with guests of the Swan, Dolphin, and Swan Reserve; Shades of Green; Signia by Hilton Orlando Bonnet Creek; Waldorf Astoria Orlando; the Four Seasons; and the Disney Springs Resort Area hotels—enjoy extra time in the theme parks not available to the general public. In many cases, this means shorter waits in line for Disney's most popular rides. See page 52 for details.

4. EXTENDED EVENING THEME PARK HOURS Guests staying at Disney Deluxe resorts and Disney Vacation Club (DVC) properties, plus the Dolphin, Swan, and Swan Reserve and Shades of Green, get two extra hours in the theme parks after they close to regular guests. At the time of this writing, Extended Evening Hours were offered one day per week at the Magic Kingdom and EPCOT only. See page 54 for details.

5. SEPARATE POOL OF PARK RESERVATIONS The Disney Park Pass reservation system holds a certain number of reservation slots to be used only by Disney resort guests. Thus, even if no park reservations remain for (off-site) Annual Pass holders or (off-site) guests with dated tickets, Disney resort guests might still be able to get reservations. This is a big advantage, especially if you're trying to get into Disney's Hollywood Studios during busier times of the year.

6. FREE PARKING AT THE THEME PARKS Disney resort guests with cars pay nothing to park in theme park lots—this saves you $25 per day. Be aware, though, that Disney charges for overnight parking at its hotels.

7. GOLFING PRIVILEGES Disney guests get priority tee times at the on-property golf courses.

8. NO RESORT FEES Unlike most hotels outside of Walt Disney World, the on-site hotels don't charge a nebulous nightly resort fee (versus a parking fee) on top of their advertised rates.

9. THEME All of the Disney hotels are themed, in pointed contrast to non-Disney hotels, which are, well, mostly just hotels. Each Disney hotel is designed to make you feel that you're in a special place or period of history. See the table on page 86 that lists the hotels and their themes.

Themed rooms are a huge attraction for children, firing their imaginations and really making the hotel an adventure and a memorable place. Some resorts carry off their themes better than others, and some themes are more exciting. **Wilderness Lodge,** for example, is extraordinary. The lobby opens eight stories to a timbered ceiling supported by giant columns of bundled logs. One look eases you into the Northwest wilderness theme. The isolated lodge is heaven for kids.

Animal Kingdom Lodge & Villas replicate the grand safari lodges of Kenya and Tanzania and overlook their own African-inspired game preserve. By far the most exotic of the Disney resorts, they're made for families with children.

Another favorite of kids is **Treehouse Villas at Saratoga Springs Resort.** Designed in the adventurous image of their 1970s predecessors, the tree houses are nestled in the woods alongside the Lake Buena Vista Golf Course.

The **Polynesian Village Resort & Villas** convey the feeling of the Pacific Islands. It's great for families. Most kids don't know Polynesia from amnesia, but they like those cool "lodge" buildings and all the torches at night. Many waterfront rooms on upper floors offer perfect

WALT DISNEY WORLD RESORT HOTEL THEMES	
**HOTEL	THEME**	
ALL-STAR RESORTS	Sports, movies, and music
ANIMAL KINGDOM LODGE & VILLAS	African game preserve
ART OF ANIMATION RESORT	Disney's animated films
BAY LAKE TOWER AT THE CONTEMPORARY	Ultramodern high-rise
BEACH CLUB RESORT & VILLAS	New England beach club of the 1870s
BOARDWALK INN	East Coast boardwalk hotel of the early 1900s
BOARDWALK VILLAS	East Coast beach cottages of the early 1900s
CARIBBEAN BEACH RESORT	Caribbean islands
CONTEMPORARY RESORT	The future as envisioned by past and present generations
CORONADO SPRINGS RESORT	Northern Mexico and the American Southwest
DOLPHIN	"Modern" (read: early-1990s-vintage) Florida resort
GRAN DESTINO TOWER	Spanish/Moorish influences
GRAND FLORIDIAN RESORT & VILLAS	Turn-of-the-20th-century luxury hotel
OLD KEY WEST RESORT	Relaxed Florida Keys vibe
POLYNESIAN VILLAGE RESORT & VILLAS	Hawaii and South Seas islands
POP CENTURY	Popular-culture icons from various decades of the 20th century
PORT ORLEANS–FRENCH QUARTER	Turn-of-the-19th-century New Orleans
PORT ORLEANS–RIVERSIDE	Old Louisiana bayou-side retreat
RIVIERA RESORT	Mediterranean beach resort in the South of France
SARATOGA SPRINGS RESORT	1880s Victorian lake
STAR WARS: GALACTIC STARCRUISER	*Star Wars*–themed adventure
SWAN	What modern looked like 30 years ago
SWAN	Brand-new resort with a true 21st-century design aesthetic
TREEHOUSE VILLAS	Rustic vacation homes with modern amenities
WILDERNESS LODGE, BOULDER RIDGE VILLAS, AND COPPER CREEK VILLAS & CABINS	Grand national park lodge of the early 1900s
YACHT CLUB RESORT	New England seashore hotel of the 1880s

views of Cinderella Castle and the Magic Kingdom fireworks across the Seven Seas Lagoon.

LILIANE Old Key West, Coronado Springs, and the Port Orleans resorts are among my favorites.

Grandeur, nostalgia, and privilege are central to the **BoardWalk Inn & Villas, Grand Floridian Resort & Villas, Saratoga Springs Resort,** and **Yacht and Beach Club Resorts and Beach Club Villas.** Kids appreciate the creative swimming facilities of these resorts but are relatively neutral toward their shared Eastern Seaboard theme.

Port Orleans Resorts lack the mystery and sultriness of New Orleans's French Quarter, but it's hard to replicate the Big Easy in a sanitized Disney version. The Riverside section of Port Orleans, however, hits the mark with its antebellum Mississippi River theme, as does **Old Key West Resort** with its Florida Keys theme. Children like each of these resorts, even though the themes are a bit removed from their frame of reference. The **Caribbean Beach Resort**'s theme is much more effective at night, thanks to creative lighting. By day, the resort looks like a Miami condo development. Its pirate-themed suites are a big hit with little buccaneers, and the playground and swimming pool fit in nicely with the pirate theme.

Riviera Resort, the 15th Disney Vacation Club property, opened December 2019. Built on several acres of land that were previously part of the Caribbean Beach Resort, the resort is designed to capture the magic of Europe. Lush landscaping, beautiful gardens, and fountains enhance its waterfront setting. The pools and the S'il Vous Play interactive water play area are sure to impress kids.

LILIANE Just in case your luggage is delayed or your room isn't ready, always pack a change of clothes and bathing suits for all family members in your carry-on luggage. While you wait, enjoy the resort pool!

Coronado Springs Resort offers several styles of Mexican and Southwestern American architecture. Though the lake setting is lovely and the resort is attractive, the theme (with the exception of the main swimming area) isn't especially stimulating for kids. But like the Caribbean, it's beautiful at night.

The **All-Star Resorts** comprise almost 35 three-story, T-shaped hotels with almost 6,000 guest rooms. There are 15 themed areas: 5 celebrate sports (surfing, basketball, tennis, football, and baseball), 5 recall Hollywood movies, and 5 have musical motifs. The resort's design—with entrances shaped like giant Dalmatians, Coke cups, footballs, and the like—is pretty adolescent, sacrificing grace and beauty for energy and novelty. **Pop Century Resort** is pretty much a clone of All-Star Resorts, only here the giant icons symbolize decades of the 20th century (Big Wheels, 45-rpm records, silhouettes of people doing period dances, and such), and period memorabilia decorates the rooms. Across the lake from Pop Century is **Art of Animation Resort,** with icons and decor based on *Cars, Finding Nemo, The Lion King,* and *The Little Mermaid.*

BOB Alligators can be found in almost all bodies of water in Florida, including those at Disney World. Though alligator-related deaths are rare, people can be attacked near the water's edge. Alligators are most active in the late afternoon and at dark. Give them a wide berth (they can run faster than you) and do NOT feed them.

Pretense aside, the **Contemporary, Bay Lake Tower, Swan,** and **Dolphin** are essentially themeless but architecturally interesting. The Contemporary is a 15-story, A-frame building with monorails running through the middle. Views from guest rooms in the Contemporary are among the best at Walt Disney World. Bay Lake Tower at the Contemporary Resort is a sleek, curvilinear high-rise offering bird's-eye views of Bay Lake. The Swan and Dolphin hotels are massive yet whimsical.

10. GREAT SWIMMING AREAS Disney World resorts offer some of the most imaginative swimming facilities that you are likely to find anywhere. Exotically themed; beautifully landscaped; and equipped with slides, fountains, and smaller pools for toddlers, Disney resort swimming complexes are a quantum leap removed from the typical

DISNEY WORLD RESORT POOLS: RATED AND RANKED FOR KIDS

RANK/HOTEL	POOL RATING
1. Yacht & Beach Club Resorts and Beach Club Villas *(shared complex)*	★★★★★
2. Grand Floridian Resort & Villas	★★★★½
3. Animal Kingdom Villas *(Kidani Village)*	★★★★½
4. Saratoga Springs and Treehouse Villas	★★★★½
5. Wilderness Lodge and Boulder Ridge & Copper Creek Villas	★★★★½
6. Animal Kingdom Lodge & Villas *(Jambo House)*	★★★★
7. Port Orleans Resorts	★★★★
8. Coronado Springs Resort and Gran Destino Tower	★★★★
9. Dolphin	★★★★
10. Swan	★★★★
11. Polynesian Village, Villas, & Bungalows	★★★★
12. Bay Lake Tower	★★★★
13. Caribbean Beach Resort	★★★★
14. Riviera Resort	★★★★
15. BoardWalk Inn & Villas	★★★½
16. Contemporary Resort	★★★½
17. Swan Reserve	★★★½
18. All-Star Resorts	★★★
19. Art of Animation Resort	★★★
20. Old Key West Resort	★★★
21. Fort Wilderness Resort & Campground	★★★
22. Pop Century Resort	★★★
23. Shades of Green	★★★

Note: Star Wars: Galactic Starcruiser does not have a pool.

rectangular hotel pool. The **Grand Floridian** and the **Polynesian** also offer a sand beach on Seven Seas Lagoon. Others, such as the **Caribbean Beach, Riviera Resort,** and **Port Orleans** resorts, have elaborately themed playgrounds near their swimming areas.

The DISNEY RESORTS

DISNEY RESORTS 101

BEFORE YOU MAKE ANY DECISIONS, it's helpful to understand these basics regarding Disney resorts.

Disney groups its resorts into four main categories: **Value, Moderate, Deluxe, and Deluxe Villa.** It's a handy system that we'll use in discussing both Disney and off-site hotels. A fifth category, **Campground,** is exclusive to **Fort Wilderness Resort**'s campsites. (**Star Wars: Galactic Starcruiser** isn't yet classified as a hotel; Disney calls it an "experience.")

Value resorts have the lowest rates of any Disney-owned hotels, along with the smallest rooms and most limited amenities.

Moderate resorts are a step up from the Values in guest-room quality, amenities, and cost. Disney also classifies **The Cabins at Fort Wilderness Resort** as a Moderate resort.

Deluxe resorts are Disney's top-of-the-line hotels, boasting extensive theming, luxurious rooms, and superior on-site dining, recreation, and services.

Disney Deluxe Villa (DDV) resorts, also known as **Disney Vacation Club (DVC) resorts,** offer suites, some with full kitchens. DDV/DVC resorts, several of which are attached to Deluxe resorts, equal or surpass Deluxe resorts in quality. They can also be a better value.

MAKING RESERVATIONS Whether you book your hotel room through Disney, a travel agent, the internet, a tour operator, or an organization like AAA, you can frequently save by reserving the room exclusive of any vacation package. This is known as a **room-only reservation.**

We recommend booking your trip at the Walt Disney World website (disneyworld.com) instead of calling the Disney Reservation Center (DRC) at ☎ 407-W-DISNEY (934-7639). Not only is booking online much faster than booking by phone, but DRC reservationists are also focused on selling you a Walt Disney Travel Company package. Even if you insist that all you want is the room, they'll try to persuade you to bundle it with some small extra, like a minigolf pass, so that your purchase can be counted as a package—this lets Disney apply various restrictions and cancellation policies that you wouldn't be saddled with if you bought just the room by itself. If you must book by phone, call before 11 a.m. or after 3 p.m. Eastern time.

CANCELLATION POLICIES Regarding cancellation, know that there are some trade-offs. If you book a package and then cancel 2–29 days before arrival, you lose your $200 deposit. If you cancel a day or less before arrival, you lose the entire package cost, including your airfare and insurance. If you reserve only a room and cancel fewer than five days before arrival (six days if you booked through Disney's website), you lose your deposit of one night's room charge, which can easily be more than $200 if you booked at a Moderate, Deluxe, or DDV resort. Further, Disney imposes a $50 fee, plus a $15 processing fee, for changing your package's details—including adjusting travel dates, moving to a cheaper resort, or adding a discount code—30 days or fewer before your trip.

If you must book by phone rather than online, tell the agent up front what you want in terms of lodging, and make sure to get a room-only rate quote. Then tell the agent what you're looking for in terms of park admissions. When you've pinned down your room selection and lodging costs, ask the agent if he or she can offer you any deals that beat the à la carte prices. But don't be swayed by little sweeteners included in a package unless they have real value for you. If the first agent you speak to isn't accommodating, hang up and call back—DRC has hundreds of agents, some more helpful than others.

If you need specific information, call the resort directly, ask for the front desk, and pose your question before phoning the DRC (the person who answers your call almost certainly won't be at the hotel's front desk, but they'll know who to ask). If your desired dates aren't available, keep calling back or checking online. Something might open up.

YOUR HOTEL-ROOM VIEW Rates at Disney hotels vary from season to season and from room to room according to view. Furthermore, each Disney resort has its own seasonal calendar that varies depending on the resort instead of that tired old 12-months-of-the-year thing that the rest of us use. But as confusing as Disney seasons can be, they're logic personified compared with the panoply of guest-room views that the resorts offer. Depending on the resort, you can choose standard views, courtyard views, water views, pool views, lagoon views, nature views, garden views, theme park views, or savanna views, among others.

Standard view, the most ambiguous category, crops up at about three-fourths of Disney resorts. It's usually interpreted as a view of infrastructure or unremarkable scenery. At Animal Kingdom Lodge, for example, you have savanna views, pool views, and standard views. Savanna views overlook the replicated African veldt, pool views overlook the swimming pool, and value and standard views offer stunning vistas of . . . rooftops and parking lots.

With a standard view, however, you can at least pinpoint what you won't be seeing. Every resort defines views of water differently. At the Grand Floridian Resort & Spa, for example, rooms with views of Seven Seas Lagoon are sensibly called lagoon-view rooms, while those with views of the marina or pools are known as garden-view rooms.

Zip over to the Yacht Club Resort, another Deluxe property. Like the Grand Floridian, the Yacht Club is on a lake and has a pool and a marina. Views of all three are lumped into one big "water" category—anything wet counts! But wait, what's the view of the lake, pool, or waterfall called at the Wilderness Lodge? You guessed it: courtyard.

Our favorite water views are at the Contemporary Resort's South Garden Wing, which extends toward Bay Lake to the east of the giant A-frame. Rooms in this three-story structure, such as room 6109, afford some of the best lake vistas in Disney World. Many rooms are so near the water, in fact, that you could spit a prune pit into the lake from your window. And their category? Garden view.

For many readers, a good view is essential to enjoying their hotel room. Getting the view you want, however, doesn't necessarily mean that you'll have the experience you want, as a Rochester, New York, couple points out:

> *We stayed in the Conch Key building at the Grand Floridian. The view was lovely, but we could hear the boat's horn blasting every 20 minutes, 7 a.m.–midnight. It was obnoxious and kept us up.*

It's worth noting that scoring a Grand Floridian room with a view of the Magic Kingdom can require excruciatingly specific verbiage, as a mom from Pontefract, England, attests:

We stayed at the Grand Floridian and paid extra for a Magic Kingdom view. I was soooo disappointed when all I could see from the balcony was Space Mountain. I was so looking forward to sitting on the balcony with a glass of wine and watching the fireworks. Next time I'll ask for a view of Cinderella Castle—not just a Magic Kingdom view.

TouringPlans.com's **Hotel Room Views** project uses more than 35,000 photos to show the view you get from every Disney-owned hotel room in Walt Disney World, plus instructions on how to request each specific room. It uses interactive maps for every building in every resort, so you can search for rooms by cost, view, walking distance, noise, wheelchair accessibility, and more. As you read this chapter, visit touringplans.com/walt-disney-world/hotels to see photos of the rooms we recommend. Disney won't guarantee a specific room when you book but will post your request on your reservation record. The easiest way to make a request is to use our Hotel Room Views tool, described above. Select the room you want, and we'll automatically email your request to Disney 30 days before you arrive.

Our experience indicates that making a request with just a single room number confuses Disney's reservationists; as a result, they're unsure where to place you if the room you've asked for is unavailable. To increase your odds of getting the room you want, tell the reservationist (or your travel agent) to the letter what characteristics and amenities you desire. A week or two before you arrive, call your resort's front desk. Call late in the evening when they're not so busy and reconfirm the requests that by now should be appearing in their computer system.

Be politely assertive when speaking to the Disney agent. At Port Orleans Riverside, for example, rooms with king beds have options for standard-, garden-, pool-, preferred-, and river-view rooms. If you want to overlook the river, say so; likewise, if you want a pool view, speak up. Similarly, state clearly such preferences as a particular floor, a room near restaurants, or a room away from elevators and ice machines. If you have a long list of preferences, type it in order of importance and email, fax, or snail-mail it to the hotel. Include your contact information and your reservation-confirmation number. Be brief, though: We're told that Disney's reservation system has a limited amount of space to store what you write.

It will be someone from Disney's Centralized Inventory Management team, or the resort itself, who assigns your room. Call back in a few days to make sure your preferences were posted to your record.

CHECK-IN AND CHECKOUT PROCEDURES AT WALT DISNEY WORLD RESORTS

UP TO 60 DAYS BEFORE your arrival, you can log on to mydisney experience.com to complete the check-in process, make room requests and dining reservations, and note events such as birthdays and anniversaries that you're celebrating during your trip. Depending on how much information you provide to the site before your trip, your resort check-in can be eliminated or streamlined considerably in a variety of ways.

DIRECT-TO-ROOM CHECK-IN If you provide the website with a credit card number, a PIN for purchases, and your arrival and departure times, Disney will send you an email or text confirmation that your check-in is complete. Next, Disney will email or text you with your room number a few hours before you arrive at your resort, allowing you to go straight to your room without stopping at the front desk.

ONLINE CHECK-IN If you have checked in online but haven't added a credit card or PIN to your account, you'll still be able to bypass the regular check-in desk and head for the Online Check-In Desk to finish the check-in process. Note that online check-in should be completed at least 24 hours before you arrive.

AT THE FRONT DESK At the Value resorts, such as All-Star Sports, which get lots of tour and sports-team traffic, Disney has separate check-in areas for those groups, leaving the huge main check-in desk free for regular travelers. A cast member also roams the lobby and can issue an "all hands-on deck" alert when lines develop.

The arrival of a busload of guests can sometimes overwhelm the front desk at Deluxe resorts, which have smaller front desks and fewer agents, but this is the exception rather than the rule.

If your room is unavailable when you arrive, Disney will either give you a phone number to call to check on the room or will offer to call or send a text message to your cell phone when it's ready.

Checkout is a snap. Your bill will be prepared and emailed, affixed to your doorknob, or slipped under your door the night before you leave. If everything is in order, you have only to pack up and depart.

EARLY CHECK-IN Official check-in time is 3 p.m. at Disney hotels and 4 p.m. for DVC time-shares. Note that if you check in early and you ask for a room that's ready, that request will cancel out any previous one you've made.

HOUSEKEEPING SERVICE As of summer 2021, Disney's housekeeping service visits rooms every other day.

OVERNIGHT PARKING FEES Disney charges resort guests a fee to park overnight. Each resort category has a different pricing structure:

- **Value:** $15 per night
- **Moderate:** $20 per night
- **Deluxe and DVC:** $25 per night for non-DVC members

Guests staying at the campground section of Disney's Fort Wilderness Resort still get free standard parking, with each campsite providing a parking space for one vehicle.

DVC members aren't charged for overnight parking if they're staying at a DVC property. Members also get to park free when they use vacation points to stay at a non-DVC Disney resort hotel.

Day guests who visit the Disney resorts to eat, shop, use recreational facilities, and the like can still park free (again, valet parking costs extra). Day parking in the theme parks also remains free for guests staying on-property.

Complimentary overnight self-parking is available for

- Guests with disabilities
- Cast members staying as guests
- Guests traveling as part of some groups or conventions

WALT DISNEY WORLD HOTELS:
Strengths and Weaknesses for Families

WE'VE GROUPED THE DISNEY RESORTS by location. Closest to the Magic Kingdom are the **Contemporary Resort** and **Bay Lake Tower, Grand Floridian Resort & Villas,** and **Polynesian Village Resort, Villas, & Bungalows,** all on the monorail; **Fort Wilderness Resort & Campground** and the **Wilderness Lodge, Boulder Ridge Villas,** and **Copper Creek Villas & Cabins,** which are connected to the Magic Kingdom by boat; and the US military resort, **Shades of Green,** served by bus.

Close to EPCOT are the **BoardWalk Inn & Villas, Caribbean Beach, Riviera,** the non-Disney-owned **Swan** and **Dolphin,** the **Yacht & Beach Club Resorts,** and the **Beach Club Villas.** These are also the closest hotels to Disney's Hollywood Studios (DHS).

The **All-Star, Art of Animation, Coronado Springs,** and **Pop Century Resorts** are near both DHS and Animal Kingdom. Closest to the Animal Kingdom is **Animal Kingdom Lodge & Villas.**

Closer to Disney Springs and Bonnet Creek are **Old Key West, Port Orleans,** and **Saratoga Springs Resorts.** Also nearby are the seven independent hotels of the **Disney Springs Resort Area (DSRA).**

Guests can now use a smartphone as a room key at all Disney resorts. The digital key also unlocks common area doors or gates—including pools, arcades, fitness centers, elevators, and Club Level lounges.

Here is how to use your smartphone to unlock your resort door:

1. If Bluetooth on your mobile device is turned off, turn it on.
2. Download and open the My Disney Experience app.
3. If the app asks for permission to use Bluetooth, allow it to do so.
4. Link your Disney Resort hotel reservation to your Disney account.
5. View your Disney Resort hotel reservation.
6. Select "Unlock Door."
7. Agree to use your device to unlock your door.
8. Hold your mobile device against the door lock.

Note that MagicBands are no longer complimentary. Guests residing in the United States and Canada can order them up to 10 days prior to arrival. MagicBands can also be bought upon arrival at your resort.

The basic solid-colored bands are $19.99, themed bands are $29.99, and limited-release bands are $34.99 and up.

MAGIC KINGDOM RESORTS

Disney's Contemporary Resort & Bay Lake Tower

STRENGTHS	WEAKNESSES
• On the Magic Kingdom monorail	• Most expensive resort at WDW
• Easy walk to the Magic Kingdom	• Monorail aside, the theme leaves children cold
• Iconic architecture; the only hotel that the monorail goes *through*	• Magic Kingdom–view rooms mostly look out at parking lots and are overpriced
• Large, very attractive guest rooms with nice views of Bay Lake	
• Excellent children's pool	• Very small studios in Bay Lake Tower sleep no more than 2 people comfortably
• Convenient parking ($25/night)	
• Marina	• Bus transportation to DHS, Animal Kingdom, water parks, and Disney Springs are shared with other resorts
• Recreational options, including super games arcade	
• Excellent dining options on-site and via monorail	

THE CONTEMPORARY RESORT has a sleek, ultramodern look, with an A-frame design that allows the monorail to pass through. And it has lots to offer the active family: six lighted tennis courts, three swimming pools, a health club, volleyball courts, a beach, and a marina that rents boats of various sizes—you must be at least 18 years old, which helps limit the traffic a little. Guest rooms are quite stunning and, in our opinion, the nicest to be found at Walt Disney World. There's no compelling theme, but then show us a child who isn't wowed by monorails tearing though the inside of a hotel.

Bay Lake Tower is a high-rise DVC property situated on Bay Lake between the Contemporary Resort and the Magic Kingdom. Like other DVC developments, it offers studios and one-, two-, and three-bedroom suites. Features include a fireworks-viewing deck, a rooftop lounge (for DVC owners only), a lakeside pool, and a sky bridge linking the tower to the Contemporary Resort's monorail station. Bay Lake Tower has its own check-in desk, as well as its own private pool and pool bar, plus a small fire pit on the beach.

Disney's Fort Wilderness Resort & Campground

DISNEY'S FORT WILDERNESS RESORT & CAMPGROUND is a spacious area for tent and RV camping. Fully equipped, air-conditioned prefabricated log cabins are also available for rent.

Tent/Pop-Up campsites provide water, electricity, and cable TV and run $89–$179 a night depending on season. **Full Hook-Up** campsites have all the amenities above, accommodate large RVs, and run $118–$219 per night. **Preferred** campsites for tents and RVs add sewer connections and run $126–$242 per night. **Premium** campsites add an

DISNEY'S FORT WILDERNESS RESORT & CAMPGROUND

STRENGTHS	WEAKNESSES
• Informality	• Isolated location
• Children's play areas	• Complicated bus service
• Best recreational options at WDW	• Confusing campground layout
• Special day and evening programs	• Lack of privacy
• Campsite amenities	• Very limited on-site dining options
• Plentiful showers and toilets	• Extreme distance to store and restaurant facilities from many campsites
• *Hoop-Dee-Doo Musical Revue* dinner show	• Crowding at beaches and pools
• Off-site dining options via boat at the Magic Kingdom	• Small baths in cabins

extra-large concrete parking pad and run $137–$250 a night. Disney says all campsites accommodate up to 10 people. Free parking for one vehicle is included in the nightly rate.

Sites are level and provide picnic tables, waste containers, grills, and free Wi-Fi. Fires are prohibited except in grills. Pets are permitted in some loops for a $5 fee per night but aren't allowed in tents or pop-up trailers.

Fort Wilderness offers arguably the widest variety of recreational facilities and activities of any Disney resort. Among them are nightly campfire programs; Disney movies; a dinner theater; two swimming pools; a beach; walking paths; bike, boat, canoe, golf-cart, and kayak rentals; horseback riding; wagon rides; and tennis, basketball, and volleyball courts. There are multiple dining options, including a full-service restaurant, a food truck, and a tavern. Comfort stations with toilets, showers, pay phones, an ice machine, and laundry facilities are within walking distance of all campsites.

A path near **Pioneer Hall** leads to the Wilderness Lodge area. This flat, paved walkway is about 0.75 mile long and is a great place to see deer and other woodland creatures. It also provides easy access to the restaurants at Wilderness Lodge.

Access to the Magic Kingdom is by boat from Fort Wilderness Landing and to EPCOT by bus, with a transfer at the Transportation and Ticket Center (TTC) to the EPCOT monorail. Boat service may be suspended during thunderstorms, in which case Disney will provide buses. An alternative route to the Magic Kingdom is by internal bus to the TTC, then by monorail or ferry to the park. Transportation to all other Disney destinations is by bus.

Complimentary standard parking is available to guests staying at The Campsites at Disney's Fort Wilderness Resort.

Here's what you *can't* do: drive anywhere *within* the campground (of course, you can drive to enter or exit the campground), not even from your campsite back to the trading post. You must take the bus, rent a bike or golf cart, or walk. Bus or boat transportation to the theme parks can be laborious.

Obviously, Fort Wilderness draws a lot of families (did we mention the wagon rides?) and, in hot weather, a lot of bugs and thunderstorms. If you want things a little more comfortable, ask for a full-service hookup and get water, electricity, an outdoor grill, sanitary disposal, and even a cable-TV connection. If you want extra privacy and even more amenities, rent one of the prefab log cabins, which get you a full bathroom, a full kitchen, a living room, a patio and grill, housekeeping services, air-conditioning, and, yes, cable TV.

If you rent a cabin or camp in a tent or RV, particularly in fall or spring, keep abreast of local severe-weather conditions.

Several independent campgrounds and RV parks are convenient to Walt Disney World. See **Camp Florida** (campflorida.com/regions/central-florida) for listings.

Disney's Grand Floridian Resort & Spa, Grand Floridian Villas

STRENGTHS	WEAKNESSES
• Boat and monorail transportation to the Magic Kingdom	• Very expensive resort
• Large rooms with daybeds	• Children don't get the theme
• Character meals	• Dining more adult-oriented than at other resorts
• Fantastic *Alice in Wonderland*-themed splash area for kids	• Self-parking across the street ($25/night)
• Diverse recreational options	• Bus transportation to DHS, Animal Kingdom, water parks, and Disney Springs shared with other resorts
• Good restaurant selection via monorail	
• Brand-new Bibbidi Bobbidi Boutique (currently unavailable)	• Noise from Magic Kingdom and boat horns and whistles

THE GRAND FLORIDIAN HAS A LOT TO OFFER: a white-sand beach, a spa and fitness center, tennis courts, elaborate dining (from high tea to personal butler service), and so on. But the tone strikes some people as rather hoity-toity, the music in the lobby can be disconcertingly loud, the rooms are not as expansive or good-looking as the public spaces, and the complex is frequently crowded with sightseers. Also, because a wedding chapel is on the grounds, there are frequently receptions, photo sessions, and bridezilla fits—which, depending on your outlook, add charm or are inconveniences. The Villas at the Grand Floridian, a DVC property situated between the main building and the Polynesian Village Resort, along Seven Seas Lagoon, has 200 rooms in studio, one-, two-, and three-bedroom configurations, along with a 0.25-acre kids' pool.

Disney's Polynesian Village Resort, Villas, & Bungalows

THE POLYNESIAN IS ARRAYED along the Seven Seas Lagoon facing the Magic Kingdom. It's a huge complex, but the hotel buildings, laid out like a South Seas–island village around a ceremonial house, are of a decidedly human scale compared with the hulking Grand Floridian and Contemporary Resorts. From the tiki torches at night to the bleached-sand beach, kids love the Polynesian.

DISNEY'S POLYNESIAN VILLAGE RESORT, VILLAS & BUNGALOWS

STRENGTHS	WEAKNESSES
• Most family-friendly dining on the monorail loop	• Excellent swimming complex and recreational options
• Fun South Seas theme that kids love	**WEAKNESSES**
• Boat and monorail transportation to the Magic Kingdom; walking distance to EPCOT monorail	• Bungalows obstruct the view of some buildings
• Rooms among the nicest at WDW	• Noise from boat horns and whistles
• Character meals	• Inadequate self-parking ($25/night)
• Beach and marina	• Bus transportation to DHS, Animal Kingdom, water parks, and Disney Springs shared with other resorts

The villas and bungalows are part of DVC. The bungalows, built on stilts on the Seven Seas Lagoon, offer spectacular views of the Magic Kingdom fireworks and the Electrical Water Pageant on the Seven Seas Lagoon but obstruct the view for some buildings that previously had it. The noise level at the bungalows is terrible. Every time a ferry leaves the dock, which is about every 12 minutes from about an hour before the parks open until an hour after they close, the ferry sounds a warning horn. It's so loud and frequent that we don't recommend staying there if you want to relax during the day, get a baby to nap, or have a good night's sleep. The resort's location at WDW's transportation nexus makes it the most convenient resort for those without a car.

In early 2022, Disney announced construction of a large new DVC building for the Polynesian. This tower, which concept art suggests is at least eight stories high, will sit on the northwest side of the Polynesian's land, between the existing Aotearoa and Fiji buildings and Disney's Wedding Pavilion at the Grand Floridian. A new pool complex is also planned between those existing buildings and the new tower.

This project has an aggressive construction schedule with an opening in 2024. Just based on proximity, we expect construction noise to significantly impact the Aotearoa and Fiji buildings, as well as Tuvalu and Tonga, at least. The walkway between the Polynesian and the Grand Floridian (and, thus, the Magic Kingdom) may be closed for parts of this construction, though plans show the walkway again once work is complete.

Shades of Green

THIS DELUXE RESORT IS OWNED and operated by the US Armed Forces and is open only to US military personnel (including members of the National Guard and reserves, retired military, employees of the US Public Health Service and the Department of Defense, and their families, as well as foreign military personnel attached to US units and some civilian contractors). Shades of Green consists of one three-story building nestled among three golf courses that are open to all Disney guests. Tastefully nondescript, Shades of Green is at the same time pure peace and quiet. There's no beach or lake, but there are two pools. If you qualify

SHADES OF GREEN

STRENGTHS	WEAKNESSES
• Large guest rooms	• Video arcade and game room with pool tables
• Discount tickets for military personnel	**WEAKNESSES**
• Views of golf course from guest rooms	• No interesting theme
• Convenient self-parking	• Limited on-site dining
• Swimming complex, fitness center	• Limited bus service
• On-site car rental in the mornings (Alamo and National)	• No free parking at the theme parks
	• $15/night parking fee

to stay here, don't even think about staying anywhere else. Shades of Green has its own website, shadesofgreen.org.

Disney's Wilderness Lodge, Boulder Ridge Villas, and Copper Creek Villas & Cascade Cabins

STRENGTHS	WEAKNESSES
• Along with Animal Kingdom Lodge, it's the least expensive Deluxe resort	• $25/night parking fee
• Magnificently rendered theme that children can't get enough of	• Transportation to Magic Kingdom is by bus or boat only
• Good on-site dining	• Bus transportation to the Magic Kingdom sometimes shared with Fort Wilderness
• Great views from guest rooms	• Smallest rooms and baths of Disney's Deluxe resorts
• Close to recreational options at Fort Wilderness	• Noise from main building's lobby can be heard inside nearby rooms
• Elaborate swimming complex	• Rooms in main lodge sleep only 4 people (plus child in crib)
• Convenient self-parking	
• Character meal	

THIS DELUXE RESORT IS INSPIRED by national-park lodges of the early 20th century. The Wilderness Lodge complex, which includes the DVC properties Boulder Ridge Villas and Copper Creek Villas & Cascade Cabins, ranks with Animal Kingdom Lodge & Villas as one of the most impressively themed and meticulously detailed Disney resorts. It's also the hands-down favorite of children. You won't have any trouble convincing the kids to abandon the theme parks for rest and a swim if you stay at Wilderness Lodge.

Disney's Wilderness Lodge refers to the hotel (that is, the non-timeshare) component of the main building (the lodge), which opened in 1994. **Boulder Ridge Villas** refers to time-share rooms in an adjacent building that opened in 2000. **Copper Creek Villas & Cascade Cabins** refers to DVC time-share rooms in the main building (Copper Creek Villas) and the lakeside Cascade Cabins, both opened in 2017.

On the shore of Bay Lake, the lodge consists of an eight-story central building flanked by two seven-story guest wings and a wing of studio and one- and two-bedroom condominiums. The hotel features exposed timber columns, log cabin–style facades, and dormer windows. The grounds are landscaped with evergreen pines and pampas grass. The lobby boasts an 82-foot-tall stone fireplace and two 55-foot Pacific Northwest totem poles. Timber pillars, giant tepee chandeliers, and stone- and wood-inlaid floors accentuate the lobby's rustic luxury. Though the resort isn't on vast acreage, it does have a beach, a children's water-play area, and a delightful pool modeled on a mountain stream, complete with waterfall and geyser.

Kids will enjoy the new Story Book Dining at Artist Point, where a forestlike environment inspired by *Snow White and the Seven Dwarfs* awaits. Snow White, a few of her forest-dwelling friends, and the Evil Queen are your hosts.

While prohibitively expensive for most (more than $4,400 per night in peak season), the luxurious two-bedroom, two-bathroom lakefront Cascade Cabins are absolutely breathtaking. They come with a fully equipped kitchen, a washer and dryer, a fireplace, and a screened-in wraparound porch with a built-in hot tub. The peaceful, quiet setting is perfect after a busy day in the parks.

EPCOT RESORTS

Disney's BoardWalk Inn & Villas

STRENGTHS	WEAKNESSES
• Lively seaside and amusement-pier theme	• $25/night self-parking
• Within walking distance of EPCOT's International Gateway and DHS	• Limited quick-service dining options suitable for kids; no character meals
• Boat service to EPCOT and DHS	• Limited children's activities
• Modest but well-themed swimming complex	• No transportation to EPCOT main entrance
• Health and fitness center	• Bus service to the Magic Kingdom, Animal Kingdom, water parks, and Disney Springs shared with other EPCOT resorts
• Views from waterside guest rooms	
• 3-minute walk to BoardWalk midway and dining options	

ON CRESCENT LAKE, the BoardWalk Inn is a Deluxe resort. The complex is a detailed replica of an early 20th-century Atlantic coast boardwalk. Facades of hotels, diners, and shops create an inviting and exciting waterfront skyline. In reality, behind the facades, the BoardWalk Inn & Villas are a single integrated structure. Restaurants and shops occupy the boardwalk level, while accommodations rise up to six stories above. The inn and villas share one pool with an old-fashioned amusement park theme and have two quiet pools.

It is a 5-minute walk to the Skyliner's International Gateway station at EPCOT if you wish to take this transportation to Disney's Hollywood Studios.

Disney's Caribbean Beach Resort

THE CARIBBEAN BEACH RESORT CONSISTS of two dozen colorful, two-story, motel-style buildings separated into five areas named for Caribbean islands: **Aruba, Barbados, Jamaica, Martinique,** and **Trinidad.**

DISNEY'S CARIBBEAN BEACH RESORT

STRENGTHS	
• Colorful Caribbean theme	• Skyliner service to EPCOT and DHS
• Children's play areas	• Convenient self-parking ($20/night)
• Rooms with *Pirates of the Caribbean* and *Finding Nemo* themes	**WEAKNESSES**
	• Lackluster on-site dining
• Lakefront setting	• No character meals
• Large food court	• Check-in far from rest of resort
• One of two Moderate resorts that can sleep five (with a Murphy bed)	• Multiple bus stops
	• Dining gets low marks from readers
• Five pools and children's activities	• Some "villages" a good distance from restaurants and shops

Decor is distinguished by neutral beach tones, bright tropical accent colors, and furnishings of dark wood and rattan.

The refurbished **Old Port Royale** building houses the check-in desk, restaurants, and shops. A food court has counter-service and grab-and-go options; **Sebastian's Bistro** is a sit-down restaurant with waterfront tables. In addition to the five village pools, the resort's main pool is themed as an old Spanish fort, complete with slides and water cannons.

Each day from 9:30 a.m. to 11:30 a.m., the kids-only **Islands of the Caribbean Pirate Cruise** (*temporarily unavailable*) sets sail from Caribbean Cay, a tropical island located in the middle of Barefoot Bay. The adventure is for kids ages 4–12 and the cost is $39–$49 per child. Call ☎ 407-WDW-PLAY (939-7529) for pricing and reservations. The new gondola system connects the resort to DHS and EPCOT. Bus service to EPCOT and DHS is approximately once an hour.

Disney's Riviera Resort

STRENGTHS	WEAKNESSES
• Character breakfast	• Self-parking fee $25/night
• Pool with interactive water play area for children	• Theme meaningless to children
	• Except for character breakfast, dining more adult-oriented than at other resorts
• Skyliner service to EPCOT and DHS	

DISNEY'S NEWEST, DELUXE French Riviera–themed DVC is located next to the Caribbean Beach Resort. In addition to deluxe studios and one-, two-, and three-bedroom villas, the resort offers tower studios designed for two guests. The Tower studios are small and dark.

The Riviera's restaurants include the quick-service Primo Piatto with grab-and-go options; Le Petit Café, a lobby coffee bar that turns into a wine bar in the evening; and the Bar Riva pool bar serving European- and Mediterranean-style fare. The rooftop Topolino's Terrace is a Signature restaurant, with great views of the nightly fireworks at EPCOT and Disney's Hollywood Studios and a prix fixe character breakfast. Did you know that in Italy Mickey Mouse is called Topolino?

The main pool includes S'il Vous Play, an interactive water play area for children. For a more relaxing experience, guests retreat to the Beau Soleil quiet pool. Bus service to EPCOT and DHS is approximately once an hour.

The Skyliner gondola system connects the resort to EPCOT and Hollywood Studios, and the rest of Disney World is accessed via bus.

Walt Disney World Swan, Dolphin & Swan Reserve

STRENGTHS	
• Best-priced location on Crescent Lake	• Within walking distance of EPCOT's International Gateway and DHS
• Extremely nice guest rooms	**WEAKNESSES**
• Good on-site and nearby dining	• Tiny bathrooms at the Swan
• Very nice swimming complex	• Spotty front desk service and housekeeping at the Swan
• Only hotel with on-site childcare	• Primarily adult convention and business clientele
• Children's programs, character meals	
• Only hotels within walking distance of minigolf (Fantasia Gardens)	• Distant guest self-parking ($35/night); daily resort fee ($35/night)
• On-site car rental (National and Alamo)	• No Disney Dining Plan
• Participates in Early Theme Park Entry	• Bus service no longer by Disney

OPENED IN 1990, the Swan and Dolphin face each other on either side of an inlet of Crescent Lake. The Swan Reserve is located across the street. Although they're in Walt Disney World and Disney handles their reservations, they're managed by Sheraton (Dolphin) and Westin (Swan), and the Swan Reserve is part of the Autograph Collection. As such, they can be booked directly through Marriott as well as through Disney.

All three resorts are served by Disney transportation to the theme parks and participate in Early Theme Park Entry, but they don't participate in the Disney Dining Plan (even when it is available).

Swan and Dolphin collectively house more than a dozen restaurants and lounges and are within easy walking distance of EPCOT and the BoardWalk.

Be aware that the hotels no longer use Disney bus transportation between their hotels and Disney's theme parks and water parks. Buses going to the Magic Kingdom will drop you off at the Transportation and Ticket Center, where you'll have to take a boat, monorail, or bus to get to the Magic Kingdom (Disney buses will drop you off right at the park entrance.) Likewise, bus service between the Swan/Dolphin and Disney Springs has changed.

The Swan and Dolphin are patronized by business types and adult travelers rather than families, and their theme is more surrealistic than whimsical. That said, a quick glance at the Swan and Dolphin's strengths will verify that they have as much or more to offer families than the Disney resorts. Multiple pools, a sandy beach, swan boats, the Grotto Pool's waterfall, and a waterslide are sure to wow kids.

SWAN RESERVE This 14-story hotel opened in 2021 and is adjacent to Disney's Fantasia Gardens minigolf course. The resort has 349 guest rooms and suites, some with views of either EPCOT or Hollywood Studios. Standard rooms sleep four and are around 330 square feet, 16 square feet larger than a Disney Moderate.

Our stay at the Swan Reserve had mixed results. The beds are comfortable; the bathrooms are functional, with good water pressure; and it's possible to see theme park fireworks from some of the rooms. However, we could hear normal-volume conversations from a room next door, indicating the soundproofing isn't great.

As a smaller resort, the Swan Reserve has just one full-service restaurant, **Amare.** That can be a problem on busy nights, since Amare handles its own restaurant orders, plus those from the bar, pool, and room service.

The Swan Reserve has a stylish pool and a fitness center. Bus service is provided to Disney's theme parks, water parks, and Disney Springs, and the Swan and Dolphin are a short walk across the street. But the lack of amenities, coupled with the soundproofing issues, means you should consider another hotel for your vacation.

Disney's Yacht & Beach Club Resorts and Beach Club Villas

STRENGTHS	
• Fun nautical New England theme	• Best pool complex of any WDW resort
• Attractive guest rooms	• Convenient self-parking ($25/night)
• Children's programs, character meals	• View from waterside guest rooms
• Boat and Skyliner service to EPCOT and DHS	**WEAKNESSES**
• Within walking distance of EPCOT's International Gateway	• Bus service to the Magic Kingdom, Animal Kingdom, water parks, and Disney Springs shared with other EPCOT resorts
• Close to many BoardWalk and EPCOT dining options	• No convenient counter-service food
	• Views and balcony size are hit-or-miss

SITUATED ON CRESCENT LAKE across from Disney's BoardWalk, the Yacht & Beach Club Resorts are connected and share a boardwalk, marina, and swimming complex. The Yacht Club Resort has a breezy Nantucket and Cape Cod atmosphere with its own lighthouse, lots of polished wood, and burnished brass. Its sibling resort, the Beach Club, shares most of the facilities but is a little sportier and more casual in atmosphere. The DVC Villas at the Beach Club are available for rent, have their own small pool, and may offer more privacy. The resorts offer a shared mini–water park, Stormalong Bay, with a white-sand beach and marina, as well as an unusual number of facilities for sports, such as tennis and volleyball, plus fitness rooms and more. Many of the guest rooms have balconies, though a relatively small percentage look across the lake toward the BoardWalk. Pirates ages 4–12 can embark on the Albatross Treasure Cruise sailing

SABRINA I love the pool at the Beach Club because it has sand and you can use a pail and shovel to build things.

around Crescent Lake and EPCOT's Showcase Lagoon. The 2-hour, kids only treasure hunt (*temporarily unavailable*) costs $39–$49 per child.

ANIMAL KINGDOM RESORTS

Disney's All-Star Resorts: Movies, Music & Sports

STRENGTHS	WEAKNESSES
• Least expensive of the Disney resorts	• Older rooms (Sports and Music) feel small and in need of an update
• Very kid-friendly theme	• No full-service dining; food courts often overwhelmed at mealtimes
• Lots of pools	
• Food courts and in-room pizza delivery	• No character meals
• Family Suites at All-Star Music are less expensive than those at Art of Animation	• All three resorts share buses during slower times of year; bus stops often crowded
	• Limited recreation options
• Convenient parking	• $15 parking fee

DISNEY'S VERSION OF A BUDGET RESORT features three distinct themes executed in the same hyperbolic style. Spread over a vast expanse, the resorts comprise 30 three-story motel-style guest room buildings. Each resort has its own lobby, food court, and registration area. All-Star Sports features huge sports equipment: bright football helmets, tennis rackets, and baseball bats, all taller than the buildings they adorn. Similarly, All-Star Music features 40-foot guitars, maracas, and saxophones, while All-Star Movies showcases giant popcorn boxes and icons from Disney films. Lobbies of all are loud (in both decibels and brightness) and cartoonish, with checkerboard walls and photographs of famous athletes, musicians, or film stars, and they also have a dedicated area for kids to watch Disney shows and movies while parents are checking in.

At 260 square feet, guest rooms are very small—so small, in fact, that a family of four attempting to stay in one room might redefine *family values* by week's end. The All-Stars are the noisiest Disney resorts, though guest rooms are well soundproofed and quiet. Each resort has two main pools, all featuring replicas of Disney characters.

All-Star Music has 192 Family Suites in the Jazz and Calypso Buildings. Suites measure roughly 520 square feet, slightly larger than the cabins at Fort Wilderness but slightly smaller than Art of Animation's Family Suites. Each suite, formed from the combination of two formerly separate rooms, includes a kitchenette with minifridge, microwave, and coffee maker. Sleeping accommodations include a queen bed in the bedroom, plus a pullout sleeper sofa, a chair bed, and an ottoman bed. A hefty door separates the two rooms.

All of the All-Star Movies' buildings have been refurbished. These rooms include vinyl "hardwood" floors, sleek modern storage units, queen beds, 10 USB outlets, and a coffee maker. One of the beds folds into the wall when not being used, converting into a table; two chairs are included. Space has been freed under the fixed bed for storage. The bathroom remodel swaps out plastic shower curtains for sliding glass doors, new showerheads, and tile walls. The grooming area is vastly improved, with modular shelving, better lighting, and increased counter space. Another sliding door separates the bath from the main living space, allowing three people to get ready at the same time.

Older rooms are found throughout All-Star Sports and All-Star Music. That said, a turnaround is also underway in these two properties. The pandemic disrupted that work.

We receive a lot of letters commenting on the All-Star Resorts. From a Massachusetts family of four:

I would never recommend the All-Star for a family. It was like dormitory living. Our room was about 1 mile from the bus stop, and the room was tiny—you needed to step into the bathroom, shut the door, and then step around the toilet that blocked half the tub.

But a Baltimore family had a positive experience:

Yes, the rooms are small, but the overall magic there is amazing. The lobby played Disney movies, which is perfect if you get up early and the buses aren't running yet. Customer service was impeccable.

Disney's Animal Kingdom Lodge/ Jambo House and Kidani Village Villas

STRENGTHS	WEAKNESSES
• Exotic theme	• On-site nature programs and storytelling
• Most rooms have private balconies	• Remote location
• View of savanna and animals from guest rooms	• $25/night parking fee
• Creatively themed swimming areas	• Savanna views can be hit-or-miss
• Excellent on-site dining, including a buffet	• Limited counter-service dining
• Proximity to non-Disney restaurants on US 192	• Erratic bus service
	• Jambo House villas are smaller than those at Kidani Village

TAILOR-MADE FOR FAMILIES, Animal Kingdom Lodge is a snazzy take on safari chic, with balcony views of wildlife that alone may be worth the tab. Its distance from the other parks may be a drawback for those planning to explore all of Disney World, but on the other hand, if you have a car, it's the closest resort to the affordable family restaurants lining US 192 (Irlo Bronson Memorial Highway).

The lodge fuses African tribal architecture with the rugged style of grand East African national park lodges. Five-story thatched-roofed wings fan out from a vast central rotunda that houses the lobby and features a huge mud fireplace. Public areas and many rooms offer panoramic views of a private 21-acre wildlife preserve punctuated with streams and elevated *kopjes* (rock outcrops) and populated with some 200 free-roaming hoofed animals and birds. Most of the lodge's guest rooms boast hand-carved furnishings and richly colored upholstery. Almost all rooms have full balconies.

Studio and one-, two-, and three-bedroom villa accommodations are available at Jambo House (the main building) and adjacent Kidani Village, a DVC property. Having stayed at Kidani Village, we think it's a quieter, more relaxed experience. The lobby and rooms have a more personal feel than Jambo House's, and Kidani's distance from Jambo House makes it feel remote. The bus stops are a fair distance from the main building too, and it's easy to head in the wrong direction when you're coming back from the parks at night.

Except for the three-bedroom units, most rooms at Kidani are larger than their counterparts at Jambo House, anywhere from 50 square feet for a studio to more than 200 square feet for a two-bedroom unit. Kidani's villas also have one more bathroom for one-, two-, and three-bedroom units. Kidani's rooms should be due for refurbishment in 2023 (the last soft-goods update happened in 2016).

Besides theming, Jambo House's strength is its upscale dining options: Readers place all three sit-down restaurants at Animal Kingdom Lodge among Walt Disney World's top 10. At the top of the list is **Jiko—The Cooking Place.** Twin wood-burning ovens are the focal point of the restaurant, which serves meals inspired by the myriad cuisines of Africa. **Boma—Flavors of Africa,** the family restaurant, serves a buffet breakfast and dinner, with food prepared in an exhibition kitchen featuring a wood-burning grill and rotisserie. Tables are under thatched roofs. **Sanaa,** the third restaurant, at Kidani Village, offers African cooking with Indian flavors. **Victoria Falls,** a delightful mezzanine lounge overlooking Boma, rounds out the hotel's sit-down service. **The Mara,** the lone quick-service place, can get crowded, even with extended hours.

Other amenities include a village marketplace, outdoor movies, and a nightly campfire hosted by cast members.

A Starlight Safari tour is offered to guests age 8 and up. The tour costs $95 (tax included) and leaves nightly (weather permitting) at 8:30 p.m. and 10 p.m. Cast members meet participants at Sanaa, and, equipped with night-vision goggles, they board a safari truck for their 1-hour trip through the savanna.

Disney's Art of Animation Resort

ART OF ANIMATION RESORT draws its inspiration from four Disney animated films: *The Lion King* and *The Little Mermaid,* as well as Disney-Pixar's *Finding Nemo* and *Cars.*

The Value resort, located across Hour Glass Lake from Pop Century, has 864 rooms and 1,120 Family Suites. The latter have two separate bathrooms, a master bedroom, three separate sleeping areas within the living space, and a kitchenette. The resort consists of four-story buildings and a series of themed swimming pools, including a large feature pool at the *Finding Nemo* courtyard. A water-play area, as well as a 68,800-square-foot commercial building with shopping and dining space, completes the picture. As at Pop Century, large, colorful icons stand in the middle of each group of buildings; here, though, they represent film characters rather than pop-culture touchstones.

DISNEY'S ART OF ANIMATION RESORT

STRENGTHS	• Skyliner service to EPCOT and DHS
• Exceptional theming	**WEAKNESSES**
• Family Suites are well designed	• Most expensive Value resort
• Best pool of the Value resorts	• No full-service dining or character meals
• Food court	
• Some buildings offer interior hallways	• Rooms not as nice as new rooms at Pop Century and All-Star Movies
• One bus stop	• $15/night parking fee

Three of the four sets of themed buildings have pools; the *Lion King* complex has a playground instead. Like the other Value resorts, Art of Animation has a central building—here called Animation Hall—for check-in and bus transportation; it also holds the food court, Landscape of Flavors; a gift shop; and a video arcade.

Reader reports on Art of Animation have mostly been positive. A mom from Blountville, Tennessee, says:

The Art of Animation Resort was the highlight of our trip! Our daughter loves The Little Mermaid, *and the rooms, while small and basic, were adorable. The courtyards, the pools, the main lobby areas, etc.— Disney is fantastic at attention to detail. Our daughter loved pointing out* Lion King, Finding Nemo, *and* Little Mermaid *characters.*

As at Pop Century, the Skyliner is the main Disney transportation option from Art of Animation to EPCOT and Disney's Hollywood Studios, and in the morning lines form to get to Hollywood Studios starting around 90 minutes to 2 hours before park opening. (Disney adds bus service to EPCOT and DHS during busy times.) Your best bet is to drive or take a ride service or taxi to the Studios. Access to the rest of Walt Disney World is on buses.

Another issue specific to Art of Animation is slow Wi-Fi speeds, as network speed and reliability are absolutely critical when you're competing with thousands of other guests to make Genie+ and Individual Lighting Lane reservations exactly at 7 a.m.

Noise and soundproofing are likewise issues. A Guyton, Georgia, mom comments:

The room was very poorly soundproofed. I heard snoring and bathroom noises from other rooms that I should not have been able to hear. One afternoon my toddler and I returned to the room for a nap—I suppose housekeeping was cleaning the room above ours, but it sounded like someone was bowling up there.

Disney's Coronado Springs Resort & Gran Destino Tower

NEAR ANIMAL KINGDOM, Coronado Springs Resort is Disney's only midpriced convention property. Inspired by northern Mexico and the American Southwest, the resort is divided into four separately themed areas. The two- and three-story **Ranchos** call to mind Southwestern cattle ranches, while the two-story **Cabanas** are modeled after Mexican

DISNEY'S CORONADO SPRINGS RESORT & GRAN DESTINO TOWER

STRENGTHS	WEAKNESSES
• Nice renovated guest rooms; beautiful guest rooms at Gran Destino Tower	• Conventioneers may be off-putting to vacationing families
• Food court	• No character meals
• Mayan-themed swimming area with waterslides	• Multiple bus stops
	• Many rooms far from dining and services
• Setting beautiful at night	• Theme at Gran Destino Tower meaningless to children
• Rooftop dining at Gran Destino Tower	
• Plenty of on-site dining at Gran Destino Tower	• Dining more adult-oriented at Gran Destino Tower than at other resorts
	• $20/night parking fee

beach resorts. The multistory **Casitas** embody elements of Spanish architecture found in Mexico's great cities.

This vast resort surrounding a 22-acre lake has three small pools and one large swimming complex. The main pool features a reproduction of a Mayan step pyramid with a waterfall cascading down its side.

In July 2019 the 15-story Gran Destino Tower opened. The tower is now the main lobby for the entire resort. Toledo offers tapas, steak, and seafood in a rooftop setting overlooking Lago Dorado and the fireworks from nearby parks.

LILIANE I enjoy dining at the brand-new Toledo rooftop restaurant at the Gran Destino Tower while watching the nighttime fireworks.

The decor of Gran Destino Tower is inspired by Spanish architecture. The new tower has 545 rooms, including standard rooms and executive, one-bedroom, and presidential suites.

Nestled in the middle of the lake is Three Bridges Bar & Grill. The eatery is connected to the resorts by three walkways across the lake.

Disney's Pop Century Resort

STRENGTHS	WEAKNESSES
• Large swimming pools	• Theming geared more toward adults than kids and teens
• Food court	
• Convenient self-parking	• Small rooms are the same size as All-Stars' but slightly more expensive
• Stylish new room design	• No full-service dining or character meals
• One bus stop	• Limited recreation options
• Skyliner service to EPCOT and DHS	• $15/night parking fee

ON VICTORY WAY near the ESPN Wide World of Sports Complex is Pop Century Resort, an economy resort and a near-clone of the All-Star Resorts (that is, four-story, motel-style buildings around a central pool, food court, and registration area). Decorative touches make the difference. Where the All-Stars display larger-than-life icons from sports, music, and movies, Pop Century draws its icons from decades of the 20th century. Look for such oddities as building-size Big Wheels and Hula-Hoops, punctuated by silhouettes of people dancing the decade's fad dance.

The public areas are marginally more sophisticated than the ones at the All-Star Resorts, with 20th-century period furniture and decor rolled up in a saccharine, those-were-the-days theme. The food court, bar, playground, pools, and so on emulate the All-Star model in size and location, but a Pop Century departure from the All-Star precedent has merchandise retailers thrown in with the fast-food concessions in a combination dining-and-shopping area. The resort is connected to EPCOT and DHS by the Skyliner gondola and to the rest of Walt Disney World by bus, but because of the limited dining options, we recommend having a car.

Readers rate Pop's bus service relatively low. Pop Century shares a Skyliner station with the Art of Animation (AOA) Resort. The Skyliner connects Pop and AOA with the Caribbean Beach and Riviera Resorts, and it's the main Disney transportation to Hollywood Studios and EPCOT. (Disney adds bus service to EPCOT and DHS during busy times.) On average, the Skyliner is more efficient than the bus system for getting between these resorts and the theme parks. However, lines can form at Pop's Skyliner station anywhere from 90 minutes to 2 hours before opening at Hollywood Studios. We think it's far less of a hassle to drive, take a ride service, or call a taxi.

After a major refurbishment in 2018, we think Pop Century has the best rooms of any Disney Value resort. The carpet has been replaced with a modern hardwood-floor look, and space-saving storage areas, including built-in shelving, are everywhere. The second bed in the room is a fold-down option, as at AOA. When the bed isn't in use, it disappears into the wall, freeing up floor space (and turning into a desk). The bathroom overhaul is stylish and efficient, with lots more shelf space, plenty of storage, and a modern shower. A lake separating Pop Century from AOA offers water views not available at the All-Star Resorts.

A reader from Dublin, Georgia, likes Pop Century for several reasons:

(1) It's far superior to the All-Star Resorts. (2) There's a lake and a view of fireworks. (3) The courtyards have Twister games and neat pools for children. (4) The memorabilia is interesting to us of a certain age. (5) I love the gift shop, food court, and bar combo. The [dinner entrées are among] the best bargains and the best food anywhere. (6) Bus transportation is better than anywhere else, including Grand Floridian! (7) The layout is more convenient to the food court. (8) The noise from neighbors is not worse than anywhere else. (9) Where else do the cast members do the shag to oldies?

From a Jackson, Mississippi, family:

We loved the newly remodeled rooms at Pop Century—they are very modern-looking and have loads of storage space. But while there was no noise from rooms next to or above us, the noise directly outside was disturbing.

THE BONNET CREEK RESORTS

Disney's Old Key West Resort

STRENGTHS	WEAKNESSES
• Largest villas of the DVC/DDV resorts, with full kitchens	• Boat service to Disney Springs
• Quiet, lushly landscaped setting	• Theme meaningless to children
• Convenient self-parking	• $25/night parking fee
• Small, more private swimming pools in each accommodations cluster	• Multiple bus stops
• Nice family pool with waterslide and free sauna for parents inside lighthouse	• Mediocre on-site dining, no character meals
• Recreation options	• No easily accessible off-site dining
	• Extreme distance of many guest rooms from dining and services

THIS WAS THE FIRST DVC PROPERTY. Though the resort is a time-share property, units not being used by owners are rented on a nightly basis. It's a favorite among readers and *Unofficial Guide* staff for its room quality and quiet surroundings. An Erie, Pennsylvania, reader thinks it's Walt Disney World's best-kept secret:

> *Old Key West has the most spacious rooms and the easiest access to your car—right outside your door! There are a number of small, almost private pools, so you don't have to go to the main pool to swim.*

Old Key West is a large aggregation of two- to three-story buildings modeled after Caribbean-style residences and guesthouses of the Florida Keys. Arranged subdivision-style around a golf course and along Bonnet Creek, the buildings are in small neighborhood-like clusters and feature pastel facades, white trim, and shuttered windows. The registration area—along with a full-service restaurant, modest fitness center, marina, and sundries shop—is in Conch Flats Community Hall. Each cluster of accommodations has a quiet pool; a larger pool is at the community hall. A waterslide in the shape of a giant sandcastle is the primary kid pleaser at the main pool.

Each villa has a private balcony with views of the golf course, the landscape, or a waterway; the waterway views are among the best of any Walt Disney World resort.

Old Key West is connected by boat to Disney Springs (and by bus when the boat isn't running). Transportation to other Disney destinations is by bus. Walking time to the transportation loading areas from the most remote rooms is about 6 minutes.

Disney's Port Orleans Resorts–French Quarter and Riverside

THE PORT ORLEANS RESORTS are good-looking, lower-cost hotel alternatives with fairly easy access to Disney Springs, and they're pretty popular among families too.

The 1,008-room French Quarter section is a sanitized Disney version of the New Orleans French Quarter. Consisting of seven

DISNEY'S PORT ORLEANS RESORTS–FRENCH QUARTER AND RIVERSIDE

STRENGTHS	• Varied recreational offerings
• Aquatic play area and creative pool	• Boat service to Disney Springs
• Riverside is one of two Moderate resorts that can sleep 5 (with a Murphy bed at Alligator Bayou)	**WEAKNESSES**
	• No full-service dining at French Quarter; no character meals
• Disney princess–themed rooms at Magnolia Bend (Riverside)	• Extreme distance of many guest rooms from dining and services
• Food courts	• French Quarter and Riverside may share bus service during slower times of year
• Convenient self-parking	
• Children's play areas	• $20/night parking fee

three-story buildings next to the Sassagoula River, the resort suggests what New Orleans would look like if its buildings were painted every year and its garbage collectors never went on strike. Wrought iron filigree, shuttered windows, and old-fashioned iron lampposts festoon prim pink-and-blue guest buildings. In keeping with the Crescent City theme, French Quarter is landscaped with magnolia trees and overgrown vines. The centrally located Mint, containing the registration area and food court, is a reproduction of a turn-of-the-19th-century building where Mississippi Delta farmers sold their harvests; the registration desk features a vibrant Mardi Gras mural and old-fashioned bank-teller windows. The Doubloon Lagoon swimming complex surrounds a colorful fiberglass creation depicting Neptune riding a sea serpent. We think French Quarter has the most attractive and tasteful rooms of any of the Disney Moderate resorts. If your visit falls on Mardi Gras, be sure to watch the annual cast member parade and enjoy free activities at the courtyard party at French Quarter.

Port Orleans Resort–Riverside draws on the lifestyle and architecture of Mississippi River communities in antebellum Louisiana. Spread along the Sassagoula River, which encircles Ol' Man Island (the section's main swimming area), Riverside is subdivided into two more themed areas: the "mansion" area, featuring plantation-style architecture, and the "bayou" area, with tin-roofed rustic-looking wooden buildings. Mansions are three stories tall, while bayou guest-houses are a story shorter. A set of 512 rooms is themed to Disney's *The Princess and the Frog.* Rooms in Alligator Bayou underwent a refurbishment in 2019. Riverside's food court is a working cotton press powered by a 35-foot waterwheel. The table-service Boatwright's Dining Hall is located inside the main Sassagoula Steamboat Company building, between the River Roost Lounge and the Riverside Mill food court. The restaurant is open for dinner only and serves Southern fare. The main reader gripes about Riverside are its food options and its bus service.

Disney's Saratoga Springs Resort & Spa/
Treehouse Villas at Disney's Saratoga Springs Resort & Spa

STRENGTHS	
• Lushly landscaped setting	• No character meals
• Very nice spa and fitness center	• Theme and atmosphere not very kid-friendly
• Convenient self-parking	
• Closest resort to Disney Springs and Typhoon Lagoon	• Limited number of units makes the Treehouses among the most difficult accommodations to book at WDW
• Nice themed swimming complex	
• Hiking, jogging, and water recreation	• Bus service takes some time to get out of the (huge) resort; internal bus service slow and inconvenient
WEAKNESSES	
• Limited dining options	• $25/night self-parking fee

THE MAIN POOL IS THIS RESORT'S FOCAL POINT. Called High Rock Spring, it tumbles over boulders into a clear, free-form heated pool. The area offers a waterslide that winds among the rocks, two hot tubs, and an interactive water-play area for children. Saratoga Springs is the largest DVC resort, with a path and a pedestrian bridge connecting it to the Disney Springs shopping area (across the lake). There is boat and bus service, though the boats don't run if lightning threatens. The resort's decor plays on the history and retro-Victorian style of the upstate New York racing resort, with traditional horse-country prints and drawings, stable-boy uniforms for the bellhops, and so on. The spa has a fitness center attached.

Favorites of kids are the Treehouse Villas, nestled in a pinewood bordering the golf course. With the living and sleeping areas about 10 feet off the ground, you really do feel like you're in a tree house. There are only 60 three-bedroom units, so if you want to reserve one, book well in advance. Bus travelers connect via Saratoga Springs, a major hassle.

Star Wars: Galactic Starcruiser

STRENGTHS	WEAKNESSES
• The absolute best themed entertainment and storytelling available anywhere	• Expensive
	• No time for relaxation
• Good food on board	• Standard cabins aren't particularly comfortable

BOTH A RESORT AND AN EXPERIENCE, the Galactic Starcruiser, unlike other Disney properties, welcomes guests for two-night stays only. As on cruise ships, everyone checks into and out of the starcruiser, named the *Halcyon*, on the same days, for the same two-day itinerary. Likewise, a daily schedule shows what you'll be doing at any given time, including assigned seating times for meals.

The Galactic Starcruiser has just 100 rooms: 94 standard cabins, 4 Galaxy Class suites, and 2

BRENDAN I used my datapad for the itinerary and on the second day, which is when you find out what meetings you've been invited to.

Grand Captain suites. Stays include all meals, snacks, and nonalcoholic beverages, with plenty of upsell options.

Standard rooms include a queen bed and two bunk beds; a walk-in shower, one sink, and a separate water closet. With doors separating the sink area from the rest of the room, and another door for the toilet, it's possible for three people to get ready at the same time. There's also a minifridge, hair dryer, and wall-mounted television, but no coffee maker or microwave. There's plenty of storage space for your luggage and costumes. Air-conditioning is controlled through a digital thermostat. And there's an Alexa-like video-chat terminal in your room.

There are no windows aboard the *Halycon*. Instead, a video screen embedded in the wall emulates the view you'd see from space. Disney has taken this an extra step forward by syncing the video on your screen to the video that's displayed from other "windows" around the ship. So, for example, if a group of people launch the *Halcyon* into hyperspace during bridge training, your stateroom's video screen will also show the jump to light speed.

For *Star Wars* fans, the story is set in the timeline of the last set of *Star Wars* movies (*Episodes VII, VIII,* and *IX*). Characters referenced include Rey, Kylo Ren, Chewbacca, and Yoda, but not Luke Skywalker or Darth Vader.

Transportation to and from the *Halcyon* (named after a Corellian star) is achieved via a launch pod courtesy of Chandrilla Star Line. The name of the airline and the starcruiser are taken out of the *Star Wars* canon. According to Wookieepedia, Chandrilla is the name of the planet where Ben Solo (aka Kylo Ren) was born. It is also the home planet of Mon Mothma, the first Chancellor of the New Republic.

Aboard the *Halcyon*, a set of seven live actors explain the plot and, in one-on-one conversations, ask you to perform tasks to help them and their cause. The actors who play the main characters are the heart and soul of the experience.

Disney encourages guests to dress in *Star Wars*–appropriate clothing and to develop a backstory (before you arrive) that ties in, even tangentially, to the *Star Wars* universe. Your backstory does not have to be extensive, but it shows that you want to participate actively in the game instead of just observing and helps the characters improvise dialog for you and determine which side you're supporting.

BRENDAN Have fun, dress up, let loose, engage in the story. Even if you don't like character interactions, talk to the characters on board to set up your allegiance.

For example, if you're approached by a character who asks where you're from and you say, "Pittsburgh," that might be taken as a sign that you're not willing to play along. If, however, your answer starts with something like "I was born to poor spice miners on the third moon of Endor," they know you're up for an adventure. All Disney cast members—not just the main actors—will remember your backstory throughout the voyage.

In addition to role-playing, lightsaber training sessions are available, and guests can visit the bridge and engine room for more activities. The second day of your Starcruiser experience includes a visit to the Galaxy's Edge land in Disney's Hollywood Studios. You might be tempted to skip this part of the cruise, especially if you've already experienced the land. However, we think visiting is mandatory, along with riding both rides and completing all the tasks you're asked to do. Doing these unlocks special events for you to participate in back on the ship. To get the most out of the experience, we strongly recommend you participate in all activities.

BRENDAN
You can get unlimited blue milk on the *Halcyon.*

DINING The Starcruiser has one dining location: the Crown of Corellia Dining Room, open for breakfast from 7 to 11 a.m. on Day 2 and until checkout on Day 3. Lunch is served from 1 to 4 p.m. on Day 2 and is available immediately after you board on Day 1. Both breakfast and lunch are served cafeteria-style, where you walk through the kitchen and grab small plates of whatever strikes your fancy. Be forewarned that most food items come in unexpected or unusual shapes, and sometimes in exotic colors, which may be off-putting to picky eaters. For example, the waffles are round on the *Halcyon,* and the sliced fruit is amazingly translucent. It's all good—some of it is quite good—and you can eat as much as you like.

Dinner each night is a full-blown, multicourse production, with live entertainment accompanying the food. If you're familiar with how other Disney World restaurants serve family-style meals, that's how dinner is run: Each night's dinner features a fixed menu. Unless you request otherwise, small plates of every item offered in every course are brought to your table. Eat as much as you like, and you're encouraged to ask for more of anything you particularly enjoyed. Like other cruises, the cost of meals is included in your fare; the cost of alcoholic beverages is not.

We found the dinner fare to be comparable in quality to the popular African-themed buffet Boma at Disney's Animal Kingdom Lodge. There's plenty of food, and it's tasty and visually appealing. An optional $30 upcharge gets you seating at the Captain's Table for dinner. The primary benefit of this is that part of the story unfolds at that table, giving you a front-row seat for the action. We recommend booking the Captain's Table, preferably for dinner on Day 2.

IS IT WORTH THE MONEY? At just under $5,000 for two adults for two days (and $6,000 for a family of four), the experience makes sense only if you're willing to go all-in and play the game as it's intended. That means that for around 42 hours, you must believe that the events in *Star Wars* actually happened, that The Force is real, and that you'll do absolutely anything anyone asks of you to further your cause.

The two-day voyage is worthwhile only to well-off, experienced travelers who enjoy both *Star Wars* and days-long role-playing. If

continued on page 117

HOTEL INFORMATION TABLE

All-Star Movies Resort
★★★★
1901 W. Buena Vista Drive
Lake Buena Vista, FL 32830
☎ 407-939-7000
tinyurl.com/allstarmovies

LOCATION	WDW
ROOM RATING	84
COST ($ = $50)	$$$$
DAILY RESORT FEE	None

COMMUTING TIMES TO PARKS
(in minutes):

MAGIC KINGDOM	6:15
EPCOT	5:45
ANIMAL KINGDOM	4:15
DHS	5:15

All-Star Music Resort
★★★★
1801 W. Buena Vista Drive
Lake Buena Vista, FL 32830
☎ 407-939-6000
tinyurl.com/allstarmusicresort

LOCATION	WDW
ROOM RATING	88
COST ($ = $50)	$$$$+
DAILY RESORT FEE	None

COMMUTING TIMES TO PARKS
(in minutes):

MAGIC KINGDOM	6:15
EPCOT	5:45
ANIMAL KINGDOM	4:15
DHS	5:15

All-Star Sports Resort
★★★★
1701 W. Buena Vista Drive
Lake Buena Vista, FL 32830
☎ 407-939-5000
tinyurl.com/allstarsports

LOCATION	WDW
ROOM RATING	87
COST ($ = $50)	$$$$+
DAILY RESORT FEE	None

COMMUTING TIMES TO PARKS
(in minutes):

MAGIC KINGDOM	6:15
EPCOT	5:45
ANIMAL KINGDOM	4:15
DHS	5:15

Art of Animation Resort
★★★½
1850 Animation Way
Lake Buena Vista, FL 32830
☎ 407-938-7000
tinyurl.com/artofanimationresort

LOCATION	WDW
ROOM RATING	82
COST ($ = $50)	$$$$$$–
DAILY RESORT FEE	None

COMMUTING TIMES TO PARKS
(in minutes):

MAGIC KINGDOM	12:00
EPCOT	10:00
ANIMAL KINGDOM	12:00
DHS	3:00

Bay Lake Tower at Disney's Contemporary Resort *(studios)*
★★★★½
4600 N. World Drive
Lake Buena Vista, FL 32830
☎ 407-824-1000
tinyurl.com/baylaketower

LOCATION	WDW
ROOM RATING	90
COST ($ = $50)	$– x 17
DAILY RESORT FEE	None

COMMUTING TIMES TO PARKS
(in minutes):

MAGIC KINGDOM	on monorail
EPCOT	11:00
ANIMAL KINGDOM	17:15
DHS	14:15

Beach Club Resort
★★★★
1800 EPCOT Resorts Blvd.
Lake Buena Vista, FL 32830
☎ 407-934-8000
tinyurl.com/disneybeachclub

LOCATION	WDW
ROOM RATING	87
COST ($ = $50)	$ x 14
DAILY RESORT FEE	None

COMMUTING TIMES TO PARKS
(in minutes):

MAGIC KINGDOM	7:15
EPCOT	5:15
ANIMAL KINGDOM	6:45
DHS	4:00

Boulder Ridge Villas at Disney's Wilderness Lodge *(studios)*
★★★★
901 Timberline Drive
Lake Buena Vista, FL 32830
☎ 407-824-3200
tinyurl.com/wlvillas

LOCATION	WDW
ROOM RATING	83
COST ($ = $50)	$– x 12
DAILY RESORT FEE	None

COMMUTING TIMES TO PARKS
(in minutes):

MAGIC KINGDOM	By ferry
EPCOT	10:00
ANIMAL KINGDOM	15:15
DHS	13:30

Caribbean Beach Resort
★★★★
1114 Cayman Way
Lake Buena Vista, FL 32830
☎ 407-934-3400
tinyurl.com/caribbeanbeachresort

LOCATION	WDW
ROOM RATING	83
COST ($ = $50)	$ x 7
DAILY RESORT FEE	None

COMMUTING TIMES TO PARKS
(in minutes):

MAGIC KINGDOM	8:00
EPCOT	6:00
ANIMAL KINGDOM	7:15
DHS	4:15

Contemporary Resort
★★★★
4600 N. World Drive
Lake Buena Vista, FL 32830
☎ 407-824-1000
tinyurl.com/contemporarywdw

LOCATION	WDW
ROOM RATING	88
COST ($ = $50)	$ x 14
DAILY RESORT FEE	None

COMMUTING TIMES TO PARKS
(in minutes):

MAGIC KINGDOM	On monorail
EPCOT	11:00
ANIMAL KINGDOM	17:15
DHS	14:15

Fort Wilderness Resort *(cabins)*
★★★★
4510 N. Fort Wilderness Trl.
Lake Buena Vista, FL 32830
☎ 407-824-2900
tinyurl.com/ftwilderness

LOCATION	WDW
ROOM RATING	88
COST ($ = $50)	$– x 12
DAILY RESORT FEE	None

COMMUTING TIMES TO PARKS
(in minutes):

MAGIC KINGDOM	13:15
EPCOT	8:30
ANIMAL KINGDOM	20:00
DHS	14:00

Grand Floridian Resort & Spa
★★★★½
4401 Floridian Way
Lake Buena Vista, FL 32830
☎ 407-824-3000
tinyurl.com/grandflresort

LOCATION	WDW
ROOM RATING	90
COST ($ = $50)	$ x 19
DAILY RESORT FEE	None

COMMUTING TIMES TO PARKS
(in minutes):

MAGIC KINGDOM	On monorail
EPCOT	4:45
ANIMAL KINGDOM	11:45
DHS	6:45

Old Key West Resort
★★★★½
1510 North Cove Rd.
Lake Buena Vista, FL 32830
☎ 407-827-7700
tinyurl.com/oldkeywest

LOCATION	WDW
ROOM RATING	91
COST ($ = $50)	$+ x 11
DAILY RESORT FEE	None

COMMUTING TIMES TO PARKS
(in minutes):

MAGIC KINGDOM	10:45
EPCOT	6:00
ANIMAL KINGDOM	14:30
DHS	10:30

Animal Kingdom Lodge
★★★★
2901 W. Osceola Pkwy.
Lake Buena Vista, FL 32830
☎ 407-938-3000
tinyurl.com/aklodge

LOCATION	WDW
ROOM RATING	88
COST ($ = $50)	$+ x 11
DAILY RESORT FEE	None

COMMUTING TIMES TO PARKS
(in minutes):

MAGIC KINGDOM	8:15
EPCOT	6:15
ANIMAL KINGDOM	2:15
DHS	6:00

Animal Kingdom Villas (*Jambo House, studios*) ★★★★
2901 W. Osceola Pkwy.
Lake Buena Vista, FL 32830
☎ 407-938-3000
tinyurl.com/akjambo

LOCATION	WDW
ROOM RATING	85
COST ($ = $50)	$ x 12
DAILY RESORT FEE	None

COMMUTING TIMES TO PARKS
(in minutes):

MAGIC KINGDOM	8:15
EPCOT	6:15
ANIMAL KINGDOM	2:15
DHS	6:00

Animal Kingdom Villas (*Kidani Village, studios*) ★★★★
3701 W. Osceola Pkwy.
Lake Buena Vista, FL 32830
☎ 407-938-7400
tinyurl.com/akkidani

LOCATION	WDW
ROOM RATING	89
COST ($ = $50)	$- x 13
DAILY RESORT FEE	None

COMMUTING TIMES TO PARKS
(in minutes):

MAGIC KINGDOM	8:15
EPCOT	6:15
ANIMAL KINGDOM	2:15
DHS	6:00

Beach Club Villas (*studios*)
★★★★
1800 EPCOT Resorts Blvd.
Lake Buena Vista, FL 32830
☎ 407-934-8000
tinyurl.com/beachclubvillas

LOCATION	WDW
ROOM RATING	86
COST ($ = $50)	$ x 14
DAILY RESORT FEE	None

COMMUTING TIMES TO PARKS
(in minutes):

MAGIC KINGDOM	7:15
EPCOT	5:15
ANIMAL KINGDOM	6:45
DHS	4:00

BoardWalk Inn ★★★★½
2101 N. EPCOT Resorts Blvd.
Lake Buena Vista, FL 32830
☎ 407-939-6200
tinyurl.com/boardwalkinn

LOCATION	WDW
ROOM RATING	90
COST ($ = $50)	$ x 14
DAILY RESORT FEE	None

COMMUTING TIMES TO PARKS
(in minutes):

MAGIC KINGDOM	7:15
EPCOT	5:30
ANIMAL KINGDOM	7:00
DHS	3:00

BoardWalk Villas
★★★★
2101 N. EPCOT Resorts Blvd.
Lake Buena Vista, FL 32830
☎ 407-939-6200
tinyurl.com/boardwalkvillas

LOCATION	WDW
ROOM RATING	89
COST ($ = $50)	$- x 15
DAILY RESORT FEE	None

COMMUTING TIMES TO PARKS
(in minutes):

MAGIC KINGDOM	7:15
EPCOT	5:30
ANIMAL KINGDOM	7:00
DHS	3:00

Copper Creek Villas & Cabins at Disney's Wilderness Lodge
(*studios*) ★★★★
901 Timberline Drive
Lake Buena Vista, FL 32830
☎ 407-824-3200
tinyurl.com/wdwcoppercreek

LOCATION	WDW
ROOM RATING	88
COST ($ = $50)	$+ x 12
DAILY RESORT FEE	None

COMMUTING TIMES TO PARKS
(in minutes):

MAGIC KINGDOM	By ferry
EPCOT	10:00
ANIMAL KINGDOM	15:15
DHS	13:30

Coronado Springs Resort
★★★★½
1000 W. Buena Vista Drive
Lake Buena Vista, FL 32830
☎ 407-939-1000
tinyurl.com/coronadosprings

LOCATION	WDW
ROOM RATING	90
COST ($ = $50)	$- x 8
DAILY RESORT FEE	None

COMMUTING TIMES TO PARKS
(in minutes):

MAGIC KINGDOM	5:30
EPCOT	4:00
ANIMAL KINGDOM	4:45
DHS	4:45

Dolphin ★★★★
1500 EPCOT Resorts Blvd.
Lake Buena Vista, FL 32830
☎ 407-934-4000
swandolphin.com

LOCATION	WDW
ROOM RATING	85
COST ($ = $50)	$$$$$
DAILY RESORT FEE	$35

COMMUTING TIMES TO PARKS
(in minutes):

MAGIC KINGDOM	6:45
EPCOT	5:00
ANIMAL KINGDOM	6:15
DHS	4:00

Polynesian Village Resort
★★★★½
1600 Seven Seas Drive
Lake Buena Vista, FL 32830
☎ 407-824-2000
tinyurl.com/wdwpolyvillage

LOCATION	WDW
ROOM RATING	90
COST ($ = $50)	$- x 17
DAILY RESORT FEE	None

COMMUTING TIMES TO PARKS
(in minutes):

MAGIC KINGDOM	On monorail
EPCOT	8:00
ANIMAL KINGDOM	16:15
DHS	12:30

Polynesian Villas & Bungalows (*studios*) ★★★★½
1600 Seven Seas Drive
Lake Buena Vista, FL 32830
☎ 407-824-2000
tinyurl.com/wdwpolyvillage

LOCATION	WDW
ROOM RATING	91
COST ($ = $50)	$- x 17
DAILY RESORT FEE	None

COMMUTING TIMES TO PARKS
(in minutes):

MAGIC KINGDOM	On monorail
EPCOT	8:00
ANIMAL KINGDOM	16:15
DHS	12:30

Pop Century Resort
★★★★
1050 Century Drive
Lake Buena Vista, FL 32830
☎ 407-938-4000
tinyurl.com/popcenturywdw

LOCATION	WDW
ROOM RATING	87
COST ($ = $50)	$$$$$$-
DAILY RESORT FEE	None

COMMUTING TIMES TO PARKS
(in minutes):

MAGIC KINGDOM	8:30
EPCOT	6:30
ANIMAL KINGDOM	6:15
DHS	5:00

HOTEL INFORMATION TABLE *(continued)*

Port Orleans Resort–French Quarter ★★★★
2201 Orleans Drive
Lake Buena Vista, FL 32830
☎ 407-934-5000
tinyurl.com/portorleansfq

LOCATION	WDW
ROOM RATING	85
COST ($ = $50)	$+ x 7
DAILY RESORT FEE	None

COMMUTING TIMES TO PARKS
(in minutes):

MAGIC KINGDOM	12:00
EPCOT	8:00
ANIMAL KINGDOM	16:15
DHS	12:30

Port Orleans Resort–Riverside ★★★★
1251 Riverside Drive
Lake Buena Vista, FL 32830
☎ 407-934-6000
tinyurl.com/portorleansriverside

LOCATION	WDW
ROOM RATING	84
COST ($ = $50)	$+ x 7
DAILY RESORT FEE	None

COMMUTING TIMES TO PARKS
(in minutes):

MAGIC KINGDOM	12:00
EPCOT	8:00
ANIMAL KINGDOM	16:15
DHS	12:30

Riviera Resort ★★★★½
1080 Esplanade Ave.
Lake Buena Vista, FL 32830
☎ 407-828-7030
tinyurl.com/disneyriviera

LOCATION	WDW
ROOM RATING	93
COST ($ = $50)	$- x 12
DAILY RESORT FEE	None

COMMUTING TIMES TO PARKS
(in minutes):

MAGIC KINGDOM	8:00
EPCOT	6:00
ANIMAL KINGDOM	7:15
DHS	4:15

Saratoga Springs Resort & Spa ★★★★½
1960 Broadway
Lake Buena Vista, FL 32830
☎ 407-827-1100
tinyurl.com/saratogawdw

LOCATION	WDW
ROOM RATING	92
COST ($ = $50)	$+ x 11
DAILY RESORT FEE	None

COMMUTING TIMES TO PARKS
(in minutes):

MAGIC KINGDOM	14:45
EPCOT	8:45
ANIMAL KINGDOM	18:15
DHS	14:30

Shades of Green ★★★★½
1950 W. Magnolia Palm Drive
Lake Buena Vista, FL 32830
☎ 407-824-3400
shadesofgreen.org

LOCATION	WDW
ROOM RATING	92
COST ($ = $50)	$$+
DAILY RESORT FEE	None

COMMUTING TIMES TO PARKS
(in minutes):

MAGIC KINGDOM	3:30
EPCOT	4:45
ANIMAL KINGDOM	9:30
DHS	6:15

Star Wars: Galactic Starcruiser
201 S. Studio Drive
Lake Buena Vista, FL 32836
☎ 407-939-5277
tinyurl.com/galacticstarcruiser

LOCATION	WDW
ROOM RATING	83
COST ($ = $50)	$ x 80
DAILY RESORT FEE	None

COMMUTING TIMES TO PARKS
(in minutes):

MAGIC KINGDOM	12:00
EPCOT	11:00
ANIMAL KINGDOM	12:00
DHS	8:00

Swan ★★★★
1200 EPCOT Resorts Blvd.
Lake Buena Vista, FL 32830
☎ 407-934-3000
swandolphin.com

LOCATION	WDW
ROOM RATING	86
COST ($ = $50)	$$$$$
DAILY RESORT FEE	$35.00

COMMUTING TIMES TO PARKS
(in minutes):

MAGIC KINGDOM	6:30
EPCOT	4:45
ANIMAL KINGDOM	6:15
DHS	4:00

Swan Reserve
1500 EPCOT Resorts Blvd.
Lake Buena Vista, FL 32830
☎ 407-934-3000
swandolphin.com

LOCATION	WDW
ROOM RATING	–
COST ($ = $50)	$+ x 8
DAILY RESORT FEE	$35.00

COMMUTING TIMES TO PARKS
(in minutes):

MAGIC KINGDOM	6:30
EPCOT	4:45
ANIMAL KINGDOM	6:15
DHS	4:00

Treehouse Villas at Disney's Saratoga Springs Resort & Spa ★★★★
1960 Broadway
Lake Buena Vista, FL 32830
☎ 407-827-1100
tinyurl.com/saratogawdw

LOCATION	WDW
ROOM RATING	89
COST ($ = $50)	$+ x 10
DAILY RESORT FEE	None

COMMUTING TIMES TO PARKS
(in minutes):

MAGIC KINGDOM	12:45
EPCOT	7:15
ANIMAL KINGDOM	16:45
DHS	12:30

The Villas at Disney's Grand Floridian Resort & Spa ★★★★½
4401 Floridian Way
Lake Buena Vista, FL 32830
☎ 407-824-3000
tinyurl.com/grandfloridianvillas

LOCATION	WDW
ROOM RATING	93
COST ($ = $50)	$ x 19
DAILY RESORT FEE	None

COMMUTING TIMES TO PARKS
(in minutes):

MAGIC KINGDOM	on monorail
EPCOT	4:45
ANIMAL KINGDOM	11:45
DHS	6:45

Wilderness Lodge ★★★★
901 Timberline Drive
Lake Buena Vista, FL 32830
☎ 407-824-3200
tinyurl.com/wildernesslodge

LOCATION	WDW
ROOM RATING	88
COST ($ = $50)	$- x 13
DAILY RESORT FEE	None

COMMUTING TIMES TO PARKS
(in minutes):

MAGIC KINGDOM	By ferry
EPCOT	10:00
ANIMAL KINGDOM	15:15
DHS	13:30

Yacht Club Resort ★★★★
1700 EPCOT Resorts Blvd.
Lake Buena Vista, FL 32830
☎ 407-934-7000
tinyurl.com/yachtclubwdw

LOCATION	WDW
ROOM RATING	88
COST ($ = $50)	$ x 14
DAILY RESORT FEE	None

COMMUTING TIMES TO PARKS
(in minutes):

MAGIC KINGDOM	7:15
EPCOT	5:15
ANIMAL KINGDOM	6:45
DHS	4:00

continued from page 113

that's you, then this is a chance to create your own *Star Wars* story that stays with you for the rest of your life.

Before you shell out the astronomical amount for the two days on the Galactic Starcruiser, though, make sure you've seen much of the US—and that means Alaska, Hawaii, the Rocky Mountains, the Great Plains, and the Pacific Northwest. If you haven't been to Europe, do that next. If your family history is from another part of the world—Africa, Asia, South America, the North Pole—go see the homeland.

After you've done all that, we would absolutely recommend spending $5,000 on the Starcruiser. It's a chance for your family to have two intense days together doing things that aren't possible anywhere else in the world.

INDEPENDENT HOTELS OF THE DISNEY SPRINGS RESORT AREA

THE SEVEN HOTELS of the Disney Springs Resort Area (DSRA) were created in the days when Disney had far fewer of its own resorts. The hotels—**B Resort & Spa, DoubleTree Suites by Hilton Orlando Lake Buena Vista–Disney Springs Area, Hilton Orlando Buena Vista Palace, Hilton Orlando Lake Buena Vista, Holiday Inn Orlando–Disney Springs Area,** and **Wyndham Garden Lake Buena Vista**—are chain properties with minimal or nonexistent theming, though the Hilton Orlando Buena Vista Palace, especially, is pretty upscale. The **Drury Plaza Hotel Orlando** is scheduled to open in late 2022 at Disney Springs.

The main advantage to staying in the DSRA is being in Disney World and near Disney Springs. Guests at the two Hiltons, Wyndham Garden, and Holiday Inn are an easy 5- to 15-minute walk from the Marketplace on the east side of Disney Springs. Guests at Best Western, B Resort, and DoubleTree are about 10 minutes farther by foot. Disney transportation can be accessed at Disney Springs, though the Disney buses take a notoriously long time to leave due to the number of stops throughout the shopping and entertainment complex. Though all DSRA hotels offer shuttle buses to the theme parks, the service is provided by private contractors and is somewhat inferior to Disney transportation in frequency of service, number of buses, and hours of operation. All these hotels are easily accessible by car and are only marginally farther from the Disney parks than several of the Disney resorts (and DSRA hotels are quite close to Typhoon Lagoon).

Free parking at the theme parks isn't offered, but guests staying at a DSRA hotel can enjoy Early Theme Park Entry.

DSRA hotels, even the ones focused on business and convention travelers, try to appeal to families. Some have pool complexes rivaling the ones at the Disney resorts, while others offer a food court or all-suite rooms. A few sponsor character meals and organized kids' activities; all have counters for buying Disney tickets, and most have Disney gift shops. On the downside, the rooms in many hotels are outdated.

When you're looking at room rates on the DSRA website, note that they don't include nightly self-parking, resort fees, or taxes. These can add $48–$64 per night to the cost of your room, as shown in the following table.

ADDITIONAL FEES AT THE DSRA RESORTS *(includes tax)*				
HOTEL	**SELF-PARKING**	**RESORT FEE**	**INTERNET**	**TOTAL PER DAY**
B Resort & Spa	$23	$32	Free	$55
DoubleTree Suites	$23	$23	Free*	$45
Drury Plaza Hotel Orlando	$25	None	Free	$22
Hilton Orlando BV Palace	$22	$35	Free*	$57
Hilton Orlando LBV—Disney Springs Area	$22	$35	Free*	$57
Hilton Orlando LBV	$22	$35	Free*	$57
Holiday Inn Orlando—Disney Springs Area	$20	$33	Free	$53
Wyndham Garden LBV	$20	$24	Free	$44

After joining free Hilton Honors program

Take a peek at the combined website for the DSRA hotels at disney springshotels.com. The hotels we recommend in this area are profiled starting on page 140.

HOW *to* GET DISCOUNTS *on* LODGING *at* WALT DISNEY WORLD

THERE ARE SO MANY GUEST ROOMS in and around Walt Disney World that competition is brisk, and everyone, including Disney, wheels and deals to fill them. Here are some tips for getting price breaks at Disney properties:

1. SEASONAL SAVINGS You can save 15%–35% or more per night on a Walt Disney World hotel room by scheduling your visit during the slower times of the year. However, Disney has so many seasons in its calendar that it's hard to keep up; plus, the dates for each "season" vary among resorts. Disney also changes the price of its hotel rooms with the day of the week, charging more for the same room on Friday and Saturday nights. The rate hikes can range from $36 to more than $100 or more per room, per night.

2. ASK ABOUT SPECIALS Disney's website will display discounts available to the general public for your dates. Look for the words "special offer" near the top of the page, in the section that asks whether you're booking a room-only or package deal. You must click on the particular special to get the discount; otherwise, you may be charged the full rack rate. If you're calling Disney, ask the reservationist specifically about specials. For example, "What special rates or discounts are available at Disney hotels during the time of our visit?"

3. CHECK MOUSESAVERS The folks at **MouseSavers** (mousesavers.com) maintain a list of discounts for Disney resorts. The discounts are separated into categories such as "for anyone," "for Annual Pass holders," and "for residents of certain states." Anyone calling ☎ 407-W-DISNEY (934-7639) can use a current discount. Discounts for the general public also appear on Disney's website (see "Ask About Specials" above); however, MouseSavers shows you targeted discounts that Disney's website may not.

MouseSavers has a great historical list of when discounts were released and what they encompassed at mousesavers.com/historical wdwdiscounts.html. You can also sign up for the MouseSavers newsletter, with discount announcements, Disney news, and exclusive offers not available to the general public.

4. INTERNET SELLERS Expedia (expedia.com), **Hotels.com, Hotwire** (hotwire.com), **One Travel** (onetravel.com), **Priceline** (priceline.com), and **Travelocity** (travelocity.com) offer discounted rooms at Disney hotels, but usually at a price approximating the going rate obtainable from the Walt Disney Travel Company or Walt Disney World Central Reservations. Most breaks are in the 7%–25% range. Always check these websites' prices against Disney's. Hotels.com offers a point system, where you earn one point for each night you book. Ten points will give you one free night at any hotel you choose. The value of the free reward night is based on the average value of the total reward nights accrued.

5. RENTING DISNEY VACATION CLUB POINTS The Disney Vacation Club (DVC) is Disney's time-share condominium program. DVC resorts, also known as Disney Deluxe Villa (DDV) resorts, at Disney World are **Animal Kingdom Villas, Bay Lake Tower** at the Contemporary, **Beach Club Villas, BoardWalk Villas, Boulder Ridge Villas** and **Copper Creek Villas & Cabins** at Wilderness Lodge, **Old Key West Resort, Polynesian Villas & Bungalows, Riviera Resort, Saratoga Springs Resort & Spa, Treehouse Villas** at Saratoga Springs, and **The Villas at Grand Floridian Resort.** Construction on a new DVC resort, **Reflections—A Disney Lakeside Lodge,** started but was suspended during the pandemic. It looks like the project has been abandoned. Each DVC resort offers studios and one and two-bedroom villas (some resorts also offer three-bedroom villas; the Polynesian only has studios and two-bedroom bungalows). Studios have kitchenettes, wet bars, and fridges; villas come with full kitchens. Most accommodations have patios or balconies.

DVC members receive a number of points annually that they use to pay for their Disney accommodations. Sometimes members elect to "rent" (sell) their points instead of using them in a given year. Though Disney is not involved in the transaction, it allows DVC members to make these points available to the general public. The going rental rate is $13–$18 per point when you deal with members directly; third-party brokers often charge more for acting as middleman.

You have two options when renting points: go through a company that specializes in DVC points rental, or locate and deal directly with the selling DVC member. For a fixed rate of around $20 per point, **David's Vacation Club Rentals** (dvcrequest.com) will match your request for a specific resort and dates to its available supply. The per-point rate is a bit higher than if you did the legwork yourself, but David's takes requests months in advance and notifies you as soon as something becomes available; plus, it takes credit cards. We've used David's for huge New Year's Eve events and last-minute trips, and it's tops. In addition to David's, some readers have had good results with **The DVC Rental Store** (dvcrentalstore.com). **DVCReservations.com** emails a newsletter roughly every week with steeply discounted DVC rooms available within the next 90 days. These discounts are by far the best generally available deals you can find on Disney hotel rooms: typically, 35%–60% off Disney's rates. For example, we've seen $251 per night for a 465-square-foot studio villa at Polynesian Village Resort, while Disney's website quoted $711. For reference, that $251 per night was just $50 more than Disney was charging for a 260-square-foot room at its Pop Century Value resort the same nights.

You're most likely to find these last-minute rentals for stays of one to four nights. If you're willing to switch resorts every couple of nights, though, you can easily make a week of it.

When you deal directly with the selling DVC member, you pay him or her directly, such as by certified check (few members take credit cards). The DVC member makes a reservation in your name and pays Disney the requisite number of points. Usually your reservation is documented by a confirmation sent from Disney to the owner and then passed along to you. Though the deal you cut is strictly up to you and the owner, you should always insist on receiving the aforementioned confirmation before making more than a one-night deposit.

We suggest checking online at one of the various Disney discussion boards, such as **MouseOwners.com** or **Disboards.com,** if you're not picky about where you stay and when you go and are willing to put in the effort to ask around. If you're trying to book a particular resort, especially during a busy time of year, there's something to be said for the low-hassle approach of a points broker.

6. CRACK THE (PIN) CODE Disney maintains a list of recent Disney World visitors and those who have inquired about a Disney World vacation. During slow times of the year, Disney will send these folks direct mail and emails with personalized discounts. Each offer is uniquely identified by a long string of letters and numbers, called a PIN code.

The PIN code is required to get the discount (thus, it can't be shared), and Disney will verify the street or email address to which the code was sent is yours.

To get your name in the Disney system for a PIN code, call ☎ 407-W-DISNEY (934-7639) and request written information. If you've been to Walt Disney World before, your name and address will, of course, already be on record, but you won't be as likely to receive a PIN-code offer as you would by calling and requesting to be sent information. Go to disneyworld.com and sign up to automatically receive offers and news via email. You might also consider getting a **Disney Rewards Visa Card,** which entitles you to around two days' advance notice when a discount is released (visit disney.go.com/visa for details).

7. TRAVEL AGENTS We believe a good travel agent is the best friend a traveler can have. And though we at *The Unofficial Guide* know a thing or two about the travel industry, we always give our agent a chance to beat any deal we find. If she can't beat it, we let her book it anyway if she can get commission from it, thus nurturing the relationship.

Magical Vacations Travel (MVT) is a travel agency with a unique approach. It commits to Disney to sell a certain number of rooms (for example, 10 rooms at three nights each) during a certain time period, and it can't return any unsold rooms. In return, Disney sells MVT those hotel rooms at rates below what's offered to the general public.

MVT also lets clients cancel, with refunds, using Disney's standard cancellation policy—that is, up to 5 or 6 days in advance rather than the 30-day policy it's held to in its contract. That's part of the risk that MVT accepts in return for being able to offer less-expensive rooms. If you can work with the available dates, the savings can be amazing.

At the time of this writing, MVT's rates seem to be at least 10% lower than the cheapest discounted rate Disney is offering to the general public.

A disclaimer: We have no relationship of any kind with MVT. Rather, we just think they have an interesting, innovative business model. If you try MVT, let us know how it worked for you.

Three obvious situations where it makes sense to engage a travel agent are as follows:

1. This is one of your first trips to Walt Disney World and you'd like to talk to someone objective in person.

2. You're looking to save time in evaluating several different what-if scenarios, such as which of two discounts saves the most money.

3. You want someone else to keep checking if a better deal than what you already have comes along.

We can't emphasize enough how much time (and money) a travel agent will save you in those last two scenarios. If you're trying to compare, say, the cost difference between a Value and a Moderate resort with a particular discount that may not be available at all resorts on all dates, you could easily spend an hour working through different combinations to find the best deal. We think most people give up far before finishing, potentially wasting a lot of money. Good travel agents will do this for you at no charge (because they'll earn a commission from Disney when you book through them).

Each year we ask our readers to rate the travel agents who helped plan their Disney trip. So who are the best Disney-specialist travel agents? Each year we ask our readers to rate the travel agents who helped them plan their Disney vacations. Our survey asks two questions:

1. Is this agent an expert on Walt Disney World?
2. Would you use this agent again?

For this edition, we received surveys about more than 1,750 agents. The top 11 agents for 2023 are listed below. None of them charge a fee for their services.

- **SUE PISATURO** of **Small World Vacations** (sue@smallworldvacations.com) is our Empress of Travel and a longtime friend of and contributor to this guide.
- **Darren Wittko** (darren@magicalvacationstravel.com) made our readers' list for the ninth year in a row.
- **Mike Rahlmann** (mike.rahlmann@themagicforless.com) appears on the list for the seventh straight time.
- **Holly Biss** (holly@magicalvacationstravel.com) makes her fourth appearance on our list.
- **Sharon Iocono** (sharon@magicalvacationstravel.com) made the list for the third time.
- **Gina Akin** (gina@touringplans.com) and **Michelle McKnight** (michelle@touringplans.com) made the list for the second time.
- **Joe Cheung** (josephpcheung@gmail.com), **Sarah Goff** (sarah@touringplans.com), **Alex Cenac** (alex@touringplans.com), and **Missy Blair** (missy@touringplans.com) all made the list for the first time.

8. OTHER AVAILABLE DISCOUNTS If you're a member of AARP, AAA, or any travel or auto club, ask whether the group has a discounts program before shopping elsewhere.

9. MILITARY DISCOUNTS The Shades of Green Armed Forces Recreation Center offers luxury accommodations at rates based on a service member's rank, as well as tickets to the theme parks. For rates and other information, call ☎ 888-593-2242 or visit shadesofgreen.org.

10. YEAR-ROUND DISCOUNTS AT THE SWAN AND DOLPHIN RESORTS Government workers, teachers, nurses, the military, and AAA and *Entertainment Coupon Book* members can save on rooms at the Dolphin or Swan (when space is available, of course). Call 888-828-8850, or visit swandolphin.com and click on "Special Offers."

11. ROOM UPGRADES Sometimes a room upgrade is as good as a discount. If you're visiting Disney World during a slower time, book the least-expensive room your discounts will allow. Checking in, ask very politely about being upgraded to a water-view or pool-view room. A fair percentage of the time, you'll get one at no additional charge or at a deep discount. Understand, however, that a room upgrade should be considered a favor. Hotels are under no obligation to upgrade you, so if your request is not met, accept the decision graciously. Also, note that suites at Deluxe resorts are exempt from discount offers.

HOW *to* EVALUATE *a* WALT DISNEY WORLD TRAVEL PACKAGE

HUNDREDS OF WALT DISNEY WORLD package vacations are offered each year. Some are created by the Walt Disney Travel Company, others by airlines, independent travel agents, and wholesalers. Almost all include lodging at or near Disney World, plus theme park admissions. Packages offered by airlines include air transportation.

Prices vary seasonally; mid-March–Easter, summer, and holiday periods are the most expensive. Off-season, you can negotiate great discounts, especially at non-Disney properties. Airfares and car rentals are cheaper off-peak too.

Almost all package ads are headlined something to the effect of "Five Days at Walt Disney World from $645." The keyword is *from:* The rock-bottom price includes the least desirable hotels; if you want better or more-convenient digs, you'll pay more—often much more.

Packages offer a wide selection of hotels. Some, like the Disney resorts, are very dependable. Others run the gamut of quality. Checking two or three independent sources is best. Also, before you book, ask how old the hotel is and when the guest rooms were last refurbished. Locate the hotel on a map to verify its proximity to Disney World. If you won't be driving a car, make sure the hotel has adequate shuttle service.

Packages with non-Disney lodging are much less expensive. But guests at Disney-owned properties (and several third-party hotels that operate inside Disney World's boundaries) get free parking, extra time at the parks, and access to Disney transportation.

Packages should be a win–win proposition for both the buyer and the seller. The buyer makes just one phone call and deals with one salesperson to set up the whole vacation. The seller, likewise, deals with the buyer only once.

Because selling packages is efficient and the packager can often buy package components in bulk at a discount, the seller's savings in operating expenses are sometimes passed on to the buyer. In practice, however, the seller may not pass on those savings: Packages are sometimes loaded with extras that cost the packager almost nothing but run the package's price sky-high.

Choose a package that includes features you're sure to use—you'll pay for all of them, whether you use them or not. If price is more important than convenience, call around to see what the package would cost if you booked its components on your own. If the package price is less than the à la carte cost, the package is a good deal. If costs are about equal, the package is probably worth it for the convenience.

Much of the time, however, you'll find you save significantly by buying the components individually.

It's much faster to book a Disney Resort room online than it is to call Disney reservations (☎ 407-W-DISNEY [934-7639]). If you call, you'll be subjected to a minute or so of recordings covering recent park announcements—press 0 to skip this. Next, you'll go through about 5–10 minutes of answering more than a dozen recorded questions, asking you everything from your name and home address to the salutation you prefer. Slog on through if you actually want to make a reservation. (When the question "How many times have you been to Walt Disney World?" pops up, answering "zero" may route you to an additional survey for "first-timers.") Unfortunately, there doesn't seem to be a way to bypass these questions by pressing 0.

WALT DISNEY TRAVEL COMPANY PACKAGES

DISNEY'S TRAVEL-PACKAGE PROGRAM mirrors the admission-ticket program. Here's how it works: You begin with a base-package room and tickets. Tickets can be customized to match the number of days you intend to tour the theme parks and range in length from 2 to 10 days. (The 1-Day Base Ticket isn't eligible for packages.) As with theme park admissions, the package program offers strong financial incentives to book a longer stay. "The longer you play, the less you pay per day," is the way Disney puts it, borrowing a page from Sam Walton's concept of the universe. An adult 1-Day Base Ticket costs $116–$169 (including tax), depending on the day of your visit, whereas if you buy a 7-Day Base Ticket, the average cost per day drops to $70–$95. You can purchase options to add on to your Base Tickets, such as hopping between theme parks or visiting the water parks or ESPN Wide World of Sports. (See page 57 for more details on ticket pricing.)

With Disney travel packages, you can avoid paying for features you don't intend to use—you need not purchase a package with theme park tickets for the entire length of your stay. Rather, you can choose to purchase as many days of admission as you intend to use. On a one-week vacation, for example, you might want to spend only 5 days in the Disney parks, saving 1 day each for Universal Orlando and SeaWorld. (That is, even if your Disney hotel stay is 7 days, you can buy admission tickets lasting anywhere from 2 to 10 days; the ticket length doesn't need to match your hotel-stay length.) Likewise, if you don't normally park-hop, you can purchase multiday admissions that don't include the Park Hopper add-on. Best of all, you can buy the various add-ons at any time during your vacation.

Before we inundate you with a boxcar of options and add-ons, let's begin by defining the basic components of a Disney travel package:

- One or more nights of accommodations at your choice of any Disney resort. Rates vary with lodging choice: The Grand Floridian is usually the most expensive, and the All-Star, Pop Century, and Art of Animation Resorts are the least expensive.

- Base ticket for the number of days you tour the theme parks (must be at least 2-Day Base Tickets)
- Unlimited use of the Disney transportation system
- Free day parking at the theme parks
- Official Walt Disney Travel Company luggage tag (one per person)

MORE TIPS FOR BOOKING DISNEY LODGING FOR LESS

SARAH STONE, WEBMASTER for MouseSavers (mousesavers.com), has the following money-saving suggestions:

BOOK ROOM-ONLY. It's frequently a better deal to book a room-only reservation than to buy a package. Disney likes to sell packages because they're easy and profitable. When you buy one, you're typically paying a premium for the convenience, but you can often save money by putting together your own package. It's not hard—just book room-only at a resort and buy your passes, meals, and extras separately.

Disney doesn't break down the individual prices of the components of its packages, but direct comparison shows that Disney prices these components the same as if you'd purchased them separately at full price, plus a small extra "package fee." What Disney doesn't tell you, though, is that these components can often be purchased separately at a discount—and those discounts aren't always reflected in the prices of Disney's package. (Sometimes Disney does offer package-only discounts, but those are relatively rare, with the exception of Free Dining).

Disney's packages often include coupons and sometimes small bits of merchandise like luggage tags, but the cash value of those extras is minimal. Also, packages require a $200 deposit and full payment 30 days in advance, and they have stringent change and cancellation policies. In contrast, booking room-only requires a deposit of one night's room rate with the remainder due at check-in. Your reservation can be changed or canceled for any reason until six days before check-in.

USE DISNEY'S DISCOUNTS TO REDUCE YOUR ROOM-ONLY OR PACKAGE RATE. Disney uses discount programs to push unsold rooms at certain times of year and occasionally offers packages that include resort discounts or value-added features. Check a website like MouseSavers to learn about discounts that may be available for your vacation dates. Some discounts are available to anyone, while others are just for Florida residents, Annual Pass holders, and so on.

Discounts aren't always available from Disney for every hotel or every date, and they typically don't appear until two to six months in advance. The good news is that you can usually apply a discount to an existing reservation. Just call the Disney Reservation Center at ☎ 407-W-DISNEY (934-7639) or contact a Disney-savvy travel agent, and ask whether any rooms are available at your preferred hotel for your preferred dates using the discount.

In addition, other travel sellers sometimes tack on an additional discount on top of Disney's or offer a small discount on rooms that Disney doesn't typically discount. These discounts vary constantly, but you can check MouseSavers for the latest ways to score additional stackable discounts.

BE FLEXIBLE. Finding a discount on a room or package is a little like shopping for clothes at a discount store: If you wear a size extra-small or extra-large, or you like green when everyone else is wearing pink, you're a lot more likely to score a bargain. Likewise, resort discounts are available only when Disney has excess rooms to fill.

You're more likely to get a discount during less popular times (such as value season) and at larger or less popular resorts—Animal Kingdom Lodge and Old Key West Resort, for instance, seem to have discounted rooms available more often than the other Disney resorts do. On the other hand, really popular resorts and room types, like the Little Mermaid rooms at Art of Animation and the Royal Rooms at Port Orleans Riverside, are often excluded from discounts because Disney can fill them at full price.

BE PERSISTENT. This is the most important tip. Disney allots a certain number of rooms to each discount. Once the discounted rooms are gone, you won't get that rate unless someone cancels. Fortunately, people change and cancel reservations all the time. If you can't get your preferred dates or hotel with one discount, try another one (if available) or keep checking back first thing in the morning to check for cancellations—the system resets overnight, and any reservations with unpaid deposits are automatically released for resale.

KEEP AN EYE OUT FOR FREE DINING. (*Note:* Disney Dining Plans, including Free Dining, are temporarily unavailable.) One of Disney's most popular package bargains, the Free Dining promotion has been offered since 2005 during less busy times of year. When you purchase a full-price room and full-price tickets for each person in the room, you get a Disney Dining Plan for your entire stay. The trick is choosing one of Disney's cheapest rooms and enjoying all that free food.

If you choose a Value resort, you get the Quick-Service Dining Plan; if you choose a Deluxe resort, you get the standard plan. The plan included with a Moderate resort varies from year to year depending on how many rooms Disney must fill. You can always pay the difference to upgrade, say, from quick-service to standard or from standard to deluxe, but you don't get a discount on the upgrade charge.

Free Dining is usually offered September–November (a slow time due to heat, humidity, hurricane season, and kids going back to school), with blackouts for holidays; sometimes it's also offered in late August, early December, or other times during the year.

Some years Disney has offered a similar discount, usually called Stay, Play & Dine, which requires buying a full package with a dining plan. As with other package discounts, Disney doesn't tell you which components it's discounting, but our analysis shows that Stay, Play &

Dine is primarily a discount on the dining plan (usually 40%–60% off) combined with an otherwise-full-price hotel room and tickets. Sometimes there is also a very small discount on the hotel rate for some room types. This discount has typically been offered February– May, with blackouts for holidays and spring-break season.

Of course, Free Dining isn't free—you still have to pay full price for your tickets and your room(s), and you could possibly get a better deal by taking advantage of other discounts. For example, where a family of three or four staying in a Value resort will usually find Free Dining to be the best deal available, a couple staying in a Deluxe resort will often do better with a hotel discount instead. Bottom line: Check out a variety of discount options to make sure you're getting the best deal.

Finally, if you're not a fan of the regimented nature of Disney's dining plans, Free Dining may not hold much appeal, so consider how much it's worth to have the freedom to eat the way you want.

Note: Again, at the time of this writing, dining plans were still suspended at Walt Disney World, and obviously Free Dining and other packages with dining discounts aren't going to be offered until the plans return. We feel confident that dining plans will, in fact, return; they're far too popular for Disney to eliminate. The various plans are covered in detail beginning on page 157.

PURCHASING ROOM-ONLY PLUS PASSES VERSUS A PACKAGE

SUE PISATURO of Small World Vacations (smallworldvacations.com), a travel agency that specializes in Walt Disney World, also thinks there's more involved in a package-purchase decision than money.

Should you purchase a Walt Disney World package or buy all the components of the package separately? There's no single answer to this confusing question.

A Walt Disney World package is like a store-bought prepackaged kids' meal, the kind with compartments for meat, cheese, crackers, drink, and dessert: You just grab the package and go. It's easy, and if it's on sale, why bother doing it yourself? If it's not on sale, it still may be worth the extra money for convenience.

Purchasing the components of your vacation separately is like buying each of the meal's ingredients, cutting them up into neat piles, and packaging the lunch yourself. Is it worth the extra time and effort to do it this way? Will you save money if you do it this way?

You have two budgets to balance when you plan your Disney World vacation: time and money. Satisfying both is your ultimate goal. Research and planning are paramount to realizing your Disney vacation dreams. Create your touring plans before making a final decision regarding the number of days and options on your theme park passes. Create your dining itinerary (and make Advance Reservations, if possible) to determine if the Disney Dining Plan can save you some money.

CONDOMINIUMS AND VACATION HOMES

BECAUSE CONDOS TEND to be part of large developments (frequently time-shares), amenities such as swimming pools, playgrounds, and fitness centers often rival those found in the best hotels. Generally speaking, condo developments don't have restaurants, lounges, or spas. In a condo, if something goes wrong, someone will be on hand to fix the problem. Vacation homes rented from a property-management company likewise will have someone to come to the rescue, although responsiveness tends to vary vastly from company to company. If you rent directly from an owner, correcting problems is often more difficult, particularly when the owner doesn't live in the same area as the rental home.

In a vacation home, all the amenities are self-contained (in planned developments, there may be community amenities as well). Depending on the home, you might find a small swimming pool, a hot tub, a two-car garage, a family room, a game room, or even a home theater. Features found in both condos and vacation homes include full kitchens, laundry rooms, TVs, and DVD players. Interestingly, though almost all freestanding vacation homes have private pools, very few have backyards. This means that, except for swimming, the kids are pretty much relegated to playing in the house.

Time-share condos are clones when it comes to furniture and decor, but single-owner condos and vacation homes are furnished and decorated in a style that reflects the owner's taste. Vacation homes, usually one- to two-story houses in a subdivision, very rarely afford interesting views (though some overlook lakes or natural areas), while condos, especially the high-rise variety, sometimes offer exceptional ones.

Here are the vacation home companies we recommend:

Florida Dream Homes (floridadreamhomes.com) has a good reputation for customer service and has photos of and information about the homes in its online inventory.

Vrbo (Vacation Rentals by Owner; vrbo.com) is a nationwide listing service that puts prospective vacation-home renters in direct contact with owners. The site is straightforward and always lists a large number of rental properties in Celebration, Disney's planned community situated about 8–10 minutes from the theme parks. Two similar listing services with good websites are **Vacation Rentals 411** (vacationrentals411.com) and **Last Minute Villas** (lastminutevillas.net).

Visit Orlando (visitorlando.com) is the website to check if you're interested in renting a condominium at one of the many time-share developments (click on "Places to Stay" at the site's home page). You can call the developments directly, but going through this site allows you to bypass sales departments and escape their high-pressure invitations to sit through sales presentations. The site also lists hotels, vacation homes, and campgrounds.

BE CAREFUL OUT THERE: HOTEL SCAMS

IN A VERY PERSUASIVE SCAM that's been metastasizing to hotels all over the country, a guest receives a phone call, purportedly from the front desk, explaining that a computer glitch has occurred and that the hotel needs the guest's credit card information again to expedite checkout.

Here's what you need to know: (1) A legitimate hotel won't ask you to provide sensitive information over the phone, and (2) a legitimate hotel especially won't call you in the middle of the night to get it out of you. If this happens to you, hang up and contact hotel security.

Another scam involves websites that look very polished and official and may even include the logos of well-known hotel brands. The scammers will happily sell you a room, paid for in advance with your credit card, and then email you credible-looking confirmation documents. Problem is, they never contacted the hotel to make the booking, or they made the booking but failed to pay the hotel.

Number-Crunching

Comparing a Disney Travel Company package with purchasing the package components separately is a breeze.

1. Pick a Disney resort and decide how many nights you want to stay.
2. Work out a rough plan of what you want to do and see so you can determine the admission passes you'll require.
3. When you're ready, call the Disney Reservation Center (DRC) at ☎ 407-W-DISNEY (934-7639) and price a package, including tax, for your selected resort and dates. The package will include both admissions and lodging. It's also a good idea to get a quote from a Disney-savvy travel agent (see pages 121–122).
4. To calculate the costs of buying accommodations and admission separately, call the DRC a second time. This time, price a room-only rate for the same resort and dates. Be sure to ask about the availability of any special deals. While you're still on the line, obtain the prices, including tax, for the admissions you require. If you're not sure which of the various admission options will best serve you, consult the free Ticket Calculator at TouringPlans.com.
5. Add the room-only rates and the admission prices. Compare this sum to the DRC quote for the package.
6. Check for deals and discounts on packages, room-only rates, and theme park admission.

Throw Me a Line!

If you buy a package from Disney, don't expect reservationists to offer suggestions or help you sort out your options. Generally, they respond only to your specific questions, ducking queries that require an opinion. A reader from North Riverside, Illinois, complains:

> *The representatives from WDW were very courteous, but they only answered the questions posed and were not eager to give advice on what might be most cost-effective. I feel a person could spend 8 hours on the phone with WDW reps and not have any more input than you get from reading the website.*

If you can't get the information you need from a Disney reservationist, get in touch with a good travel agent.

LODGING *Outside*
WALT DISNEY WORLD

AT THIS POINT YOU'RE PROBABLY WONDERING how a hotel outside Walt Disney World could be as convenient as one inside. Well, Mabel, Disney World is a *muy largo* place, but like any city or state, it has borders.

Just south of Walt Disney World on US 192 are a bunch of hotels and condos—some great bargains—that are closer to Animal Kingdom and Disney's Hollywood Studios than are many hotels in Disney World. Similarly, there are hotels along Disney's east border, FL 535, that are exceptionally convenient if you plan to use your own car.

Lodging costs outside of Walt Disney World vary incredibly. If you shop around, you can find a clean motel with a pool within a few minutes of Disney World for as low as $80 a night. You can also find luxurious, expensive hotels. Because of hot competition, discounts abound.

GOOD NEIGHBOR HOTELS

SOME HOTELS PAY DISNEY a marketing fee to display a GOOD NEIGHBOR designation. Usually a ticket shop in the lobby sells full-price Disney tickets. Other than that, the designation means nothing for the consumer. It doesn't guarantee quality—some Good Neighbor hotels are very nice; others, not so much. Some are close to Disney World, while others are quite far away. Disney requires Good Neighbor hotels to provide shuttle service to Walt Disney World.

SELECTING AND BOOKING A HOTEL
OUTSIDE WALT DISNEY WORLD

THERE ARE FOUR PRIMARY out-of-the-World areas to consider.

1. INTERNATIONAL DRIVE AREA This area, about 15–25 minutes northeast of Walt Disney World, parallels I-4 on its eastern side and offers a wide selection of both hotels and restaurants. Accommodations range from about $50 to $500 per night. The chief drawbacks are terribly congested roads, countless traffic signals, and inadequate access to westbound I-4. While I-Drive's biggest bottleneck is its intersection with Sand Lake Road, the mile between Kirkman and Sand Lake Roads is almost always gridlocked. This increases the odds that you'll hit traffic going to a theme park in the morning, returning in the evening, or both.

2. LAKE BUENA VISTA AND THE I-4 CORRIDOR A number of hotels are situated along FL 535 and west of I-4 between Walt Disney World and I-4's intersection with the Florida Turnpike. These properties are easily reached from the interstate and are near a large number of restaurants, including those on I-Drive. The Visit Orlando website lists most of them (visitorlando.com/places-to-stay; click "International Drive Area").

Hotel Concentrations Around Walt Disney World

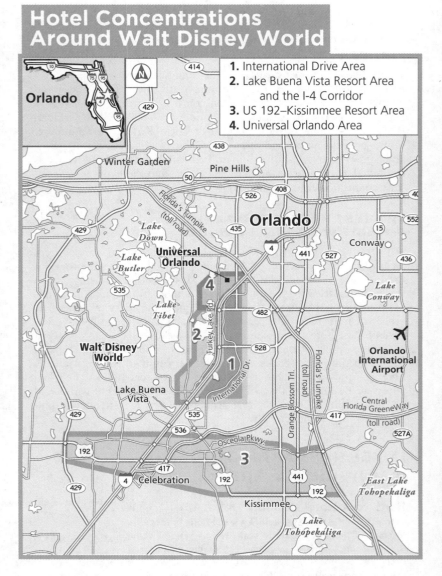

Orlando

1. International Drive Area
2. Lake Buena Vista Resort Area and the I-4 Corridor
3. US 192–Kissimmee Resort Area
4. Universal Orlando Area

3. US 192/IRLO BRONSON MEMORIAL HIGHWAY This is the highway to Kissimmee, southeast of Walt Disney World. In addition to a number of large, full-service hotels, some small, privately owned motels often offer a good value. Several dozen properties on US 192 are closer to the Disney theme parks than the more expensive hotels in the Disney Springs Resort Area are. A variety of restaurants are located along US 192. Hotels on US 192 and in Kissimmee can be found at experience kissimmee.com; you can also order a copy of Experience Kissimmee's newsletter by calling ☎ 407-569-4800. Though traffic is heavy on Irlo Bronson west of the Maingate, it doesn't compare with the congestion found east of the Maingate and I-4.

4. UNIVERSAL ORLANDO AREA In the triangular area bordered by I-4 on the southeast, Vineland Road on the north, and Turkey Lake Road on the west are Universal Orlando and the hotels most convenient to it. Running north–south through the middle of the triangle is Kirkman Road, which connects to I-4. On the east side of Kirkman are a number of independent hotels and restaurants. Universal hotels, theme parks, and CityWalk are west of Kirkman. Traffic in this area is not nearly as congested as on nearby International Drive, and there are good inter-state connections in both directions.

THE BEST HOTELS FOR FAMILIES OUTSIDE WALT DISNEY WORLD

WHAT MAKES A SUPER FAMILY HOTEL? Roomy accommodations, an in-room fridge, a great pool, complimentary breakfast, and programs for kids are a few of the things *The Unofficial Guide* hotel team researched in selecting the top hotels for families from among hundreds of properties in the Disney World area. Some of our picks are expensive, others are more reasonable, and some are a bargain. Regardless of price, each of these hotels understands a family's needs.

Though most of the hotels in the next section offer some type of shuttle to the theme parks, some offer very limited service. Call the hotel before you book and ask what the shuttle schedule will be when you visit. Because families, like individuals, have different wants and needs, we haven't ranked these properties; they're listed geographi-cally and then alphabetically.

INTERNATIONAL DRIVE & UNIVERSAL AREAS

Hard Rock Hotel Orlando   ★★★★½

Rate per night $362–$603. **Pool** ★★★★. **Fridge in room** Yes (microwave $15/day). **Shuttle to parks** Yes (Universal, Volcano Bay, SeaWorld, Discovery Cove, Aquatica). **Maximum number of occupants per room** 5 (2 queens plus rollaway)/3 (king plus rollaway). **Comments** Pets welcome ($100/night flat fee, 2 max). $28/night self-parking.

5800 Universal Blvd. Orlando
☎ 407-503-2000 or 888-464-3617
hardrockhotelorlando.com

THE HARD ROCK HOTEL is the closest resort to Universal's theme parks. The exterior has white stucco walls, arched entryways, and rust-colored roof tiles. Inside, the lobby is a tribute to rock-and-roll style, with marble, chrome, and stage lighting.

International Drive & Universal Hotels

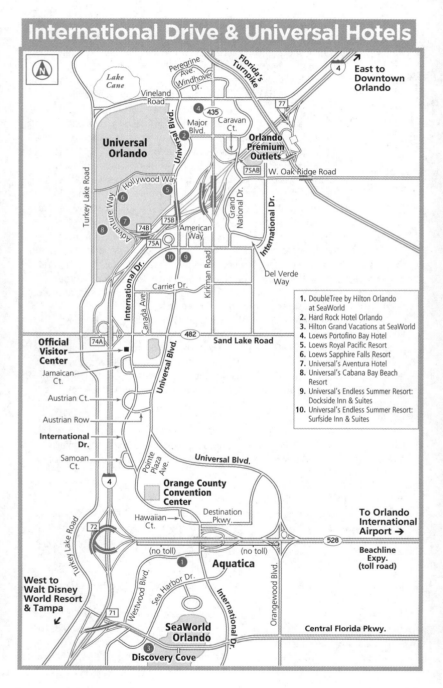

1. DoubleTree by Hilton Orlando at SeaWorld
2. Hard Rock Hotel Orlando
3. Hilton Grand Vacations at SeaWorld
4. Loews Portofino Bay Hotel
5. Loews Royal Pacific Resort
6. Loews Sapphire Falls Resort
7. Universal's Aventura Hotel
8. Universal's Cabana Bay Beach Resort
9. Universal's Endless Summer Resort: Dockside Inn & Suites
10. Universal's Endless Summer Resort: Surfside Inn & Suites

The hotel's eight floors hold 650 rooms and 29 suites, with the rooms categorized into standard, deluxe, and club-level tiers. Standard rooms measure 375 square feet and are furnished with two queen beds, a TV, a refrigerator, a coffee maker, and an alarm clock with a 30-pin iPhone docking port.

LILIANE The Rock Star Suites in the Hard Rock Hotel are for tweens, teens, and anyone who ever dreamed of performing onstage. Sign me up anytime!

A six-drawer dresser and separate closet with sliding doors ensure plenty of storage space. In addition, most rooms have a reading chair and a small desk with two chairs. An optional rollaway bed, available for an extra charge, allows standard rooms to sleep up to five people.

Each room's dressing area features a sink and hair dryer. The bathroom is probably large enough for most adults to get ready in the morning while another person gets ready in the dressing area. We rate the rooms at Hard Rock slightly ahead of the more expensive Portofino Bay.

In 2018 the hotel added newly redesigned Rock Star Suites, complete with an in-room stage, lights, a selection of Fender guitars, and priceless memorabilia in each room, sure to make the heart of any rock fan beat faster. Every one-of-a-kind Rock Star Suite consists of a king room that connects through a "stage door" to a room with two twin beds and roadie case–inspired furniture. You can also listen to some records on a Crosley turntable.

Situated in the middle of the resort's C-shaped main building, the 12,000-square-foot pool includes a 250-foot waterslide, a sand beach, and underwater speakers so you can hear the music while you swim. Adjacent to the pool are a fountain play area for small children, a sand-volleyball court, hot tubs, and a poolside bar. The Hard Rock also has a small, functional fitness center. Like all Universal Orlando Resort hotels, the Hard Rock has a business center and video arcade.

On-site dining includes The Kitchen—a casual full-service restaurant open for breakfast, lunch, and dinner—featuring American food such as burgers, steaks, and salads. The Palm Restaurant is an upscale steak house available for dinner only. And, of course, the Hard Rock Café is just a short distance away at Universal CityWalk.

Hilton Grand Vacations at SeaWorld ★★★★

6924 Grand Vacations Way
Orlando
☎ 407-239-0100
tinyurl.com/seaworldhgv

Rate per night $170–$492. **Pool** ★★★★. **Fridge in room** Yes (full kitchen in suites). **Shuttle to parks** Yes (Universal, Sea-World). **Maximum number of occupants per room** 2 (studio)/8 (3-bedroom suite). **Comments** Guests get front-of-line access to some SeaWorld rides.

ACROSS THE STREET FROM SEAWORLD, Hilton Grand Vacations is within a 15-minute drive of both Walt Disney World and Universal Orlando. While that means spending more time in a car, you get a lot more room for your money: one-bedroom suites are 878 square feet, compared to around 520 for Disney's Value Family Suites and Fort Wilderness Cabins, and they cost less than those at Disney. Plus Grand Vacations has free parking.

Unofficial Guide readers give this Hilton an A for room quality and a solid B for room quietness. Studios have kitchenettes. Suites come equipped with a washer and dryer, kitchen with utensils, dishwasher, oven/range, microwave, coffee maker, and TVs. One-bedroom suites have a sofa bed and one bathroom; two-bedroom suites have two baths, and three-bedroom suites have three. Decor isn't the most modern, but it is bright, clean, functional, and comfortable.

Amenities include three pools with cabanas, a fitness center, a kids' playground, basketball and tennis courts, and a business center. One sit-down and one counter-service/grab-and-go restaurant serve 6:30 a.m.–11 p.m.

Loews Portofino Bay Hotel ★★★★½

5601 Universal Blvd. Orlando
☎ 407-503-1000 or 888-464-3617
loewshotels.com /portofino-bay-hotel

Rate per night $389–$618. **Pool ★★★★. Fridge in room** Yes. **Shuttle to parks** Yes (Universal, Volcano Bay, SeaWorld, Discovery Cove, Aquatica). **Maximum number of occupants per room** 5 (2 queens plus rollaway)/3 (king plus rollaway). **Comments** Pets welcome ($100/night flat fee, 2 max). $28/night self-parking.

UNIVERSAL'S TOP-OF-THE-LINE HOTEL evokes the Italian seaside city of Portofino, complete with a man-made bay past the lobby. To Universal's credit, the layout, color, and theming of the guest-room buildings are a good approximation of the architecture around the harbor in the real Portofino (Universal's version has fewer yachts, though).

Inside, the lobby is decorated with pink-marble floors, white wood columns, and arches. The space is airy and comfortable, with side rooms featuring seats and couches done in bold reds and deep blues.

Most guest rooms are 450 square feet, larger than most at Disney's Deluxe resorts, and have either one king bed or two queens. King rooms sleep up to three people with an optional rollaway bed; the same option allows queen rooms to sleep up to five. Two room-view options are available: Garden rooms look out over the landscaping and trees (many of these are the east-facing rooms in the resort's east wing, while others face one of the three pools); bay-view rooms face either west or south and overlook Portofino Bay.

Rooms come furnished with a flat-panel LCD TV, a minifridge, an alarm clock with USB charging ports, and a coffee maker. Other amenities include a small desk with two chairs, a comfortable reading chair with lamp, a chest of drawers, and a standing closet. As at all Universal on-site hotels, Wi-Fi is free in guest rooms and the lobby, though you can pay $15 per day for higher speeds. Beds are large, plush, and comfortable.

The guest bathrooms are the best on Universal property. The shower has enough water pressure to strip the paint from old furniture, not to mention an adjustable spray nozzle that varies the water pulses to simulate everything from monsoon season in the tropics to the rhythmic thumps of wildebeest hooves during migrating season.

Kids love the Despicable Me Kids' Suites. The two-bedroom suites (connected via a door to the adults' room) offer privacy for Mom and Dad and a kids' room with two twin beds or a bunk bed designed to capture the excitement of Gru's Lab.

Portofino Bay has three pools, the largest of which is the Beach Pool, on the west side of the resort. Two smaller quiet pools sit at the far end of the east wing and to the west of the main lobby. The Beach Pool has a zero-entry design and a waterslide themed after a Roman aqueduct, plus a children's play area, hot tubs, and a poolside bar and grill. The Villa Pool has private cabana rentals for that Italian Riviera feeling. Rounding out the luxuries are the full-service Mandara Spa; a complete fitness center with weight machines, treadmills, and more; a business center; and a video arcade. On-site dining includes three sit-down restaurants serving Italian cuisine; a deli; and a café serving coffee and gelato.

Loews Royal Pacific Resort ★★★★½

Rate per night $327–$545. **Pool ★★★★. Fridge in room** Yes. **Shuttle to parks** Yes (Universal, Volcano Bay, SeaWorld, Discovery Cove, Aquatica). **Maximum number of occupants per room** 5 (2 queens plus rollaway)/3 (king plus rollaway). **Comments** Saturday character breakfast. Pets welcome ($100/night flat fee; 2 max). $28/night self-parking.

6300 Hollywood Way
Orlando
☎ 407-503-3000 or
888-464-3617
loewshotels.com
/royal-pacific-resort

THE SOUTH SEAS–INSPIRED theming at Royal Pacific Resort is both relaxing and structured. Guests enter the lobby from a walkway two stories above an artificial stream that surrounds the resort. Once you're inside, the lobby's dark teakwood accents contrast nicely with the enormous amount of light coming in from the windows and three-story A-frame roof. Palms line the walkway through the lobby, and through these you see that the whole lobby surrounds an enormous outdoor fountain.

The 1,000 guest rooms are spread among three Y-shaped wings attached to the main building. Standard rooms are 335 square feet and feature one king or two queen beds, fitted with 300-thread-count sheets. Rooms have modern monochrome wall treatments and carpets accented with boldly colored floral graphics and include a flat-panel TV, a minifridge, a coffee maker, an alarm clock, and several USB-equipped power outlets. Other amenities include a small desk with two chairs, a comfortable reading chair, a chest of drawers, and a large closet. A dressing area with sink is separated from the rest of the room by a wall. Next to the dressing area is the bathroom, with a tub, shower, and toilet. While they're acceptable, the bathroom and dressing areas at the Royal Pacific are our least favorite in the upscale Universal resorts. Kids brave enough will want to stay in the Jurassic World suites.

The Royal Pacific's zero-entry pool includes a sand beach, a volleyball court, a play area for kids, a hot tub, and cabanas for rent, plus a poolside bar and grill.

Amenities include a 5,000-square-foot fitness facility, a business center, a video arcade, a full-service restaurant, a sushi bar, two bars, and a weekly luau (*temporarily suspended*). Islands Dining Room, serving Pacific Rim and traditional fare, is open for breakfast and dinner and has a play area for kids. Jake's American Bar is open for lunch, dinner, and late-night eats, while the poolside Bula Bar & Grille offers wraps, sandwiches, burgers, salads, and fruity drinks.

Loews Sapphire Falls Resort ★★★★

Rate per night $2326–$350. **Pool** ★★★★. **Fridge in room** Yes.
Shuttle to parks Yes (Universal, Volcano Bay, SeaWorld, Discovery
Cove, Aquatica). **Maximum number of occupants per room** 5 (2
queens plus rollaway)/3 (king plus rollaway). **Comments** Pets welcome ($100/stay). $26/night self-parking.

6601 Adventure Way
Orlando
☎ 407-503-5000 or
888-464-3617
loewshotels.com
/sapphire-falls-resort

WITH 1,000 ROOMS, Sapphire Falls Resort brings a sunny Caribbean island
vibe to the moderate-price market. Sandwiched between Loews Royal Pacific
Resort and Universal's Cabana Bay Beach Resort, both physically and price-
wise, Sapphire Falls sports all the amenities of Universal's three Deluxe hotels,
including water taxi transportation to the parks, with the crucial exception of
complimentary Express Passes.

Water figures heavily at Sapphire Falls, whose namesake waterfalls form
the scenic centerpiece of the resort. The 16,000-square-foot zero-entry main
pool features a white-sand beach, a waterslide, children's play areas, a fire pit,
and cabanas for rent. A fitness room holds a sauna and hot tub. For dinner,
Amatista Cookhouse offers table-service Caribbean dining, with an open
kitchen and waterfront views. Drhum Club Kantine serves small plates near the
pool bar's fire pit. New Dutch Trading Co. is an island-inspired grab-and-go marketplace, and Strong Water Tavern in the lobby specializes in rum and serves
tasty, island-inspired tapas from a menu longer than you'd expect. It's one of our
favorite on-site restaurants and a great way to end your night. Try the ceviche.

Sapphire Falls also contains 131,000 square feet of meeting space and a
business center. Covered walkways connect to a parking structure, which in
turn connects to the meeting facilities at Royal Pacific, making the sister properties ideal for conventions.

The rooms range from 321 square feet in a standard queen or king to 529
square feet in the 36 Kids' Suites to 1,353 square feet in the 15 Hospitality Suites.
The standard rooms have separate bath and vanity areas. The Kids' Suites
include a king bed and sofa, with two twin beds in a separate bedroom that
connects only to the adults' room. A sliding panel separates the vanity from the
tub and toilet. All rooms have a TV, minifridge, and coffee maker.

Universal's Aventura Hotel ★★★★½

Rate per night $164–$278. **Pool** ★★★½. **Fridge in room** Yes
(microwave $15/day). **Shuttle to parks** Yes (Universal, Sea-
World, Discovery Cove, Aquatica). **Maximum number of occupants per room** 4 (standard)/6 (Kids' Suites). **Comment**
Walking distance to Volcano Bay. $18/night self-parking.

6725 Adventure Way
Orlando
☎ 407-503-6000 or
888-464-3617
loewshotels.com/universals
-aventura-hotel

THE ROOMS OF THIS relatively small, boutique-style modern resort are
cleanly designed and are similar in size to Disney's Moderate resorts. The prices,
however, are much more in line with a Value resort.

The 575-square-foot suites feature three separate sleeping areas, each
with floor-to-ceiling, wall-to-wall windows. Suites in the top floors have sweeping views of Universal Orlando's theme parks and Volcano Bay. The largest
room comes with a king bed, minifridge, TV, desk, and chairs. Separated by a
three-quarter wall and a curtain is the children's sleeping area, with two twin

beds and a TV. Right next to it is a separate space with a pullout sofa, a table, and a third TV mounted on the wall. Here, kids can hang out, play, and watch TV without messing up the bedrooms. The bathroom has a tub, a separate shower, toilet, and a double vanity. Several family members can get ready at the same time in this space, which is an added bonus.

The 600-room, 17-story glass tower is located across from Cabana Bay Beach Resort southwest of Sapphire Falls. Amenities include early park admission to Universal's theme parks, complimentary transportation around the resort, a pool, a hot tub, a kids' splash pad, a food hall with five different cuisines, and the rooftop bar and grill Bar 17. Aventura also has on-site car rental, a gift shop, and a fitness center. A stay at the resort does *not* include complimentary Express Passes. Aventura Hotel is a prime location for visiting Volcano Bay.

During inclement weather, the lifeguards entertain kids on the covered bar patio with games. Here, kids can also enjoy a game of table tennis, pool, or Foosball. The second floor of the hotel contains a fitness center and a virtual reality game room; the six different games (Snowball, Longbow, Vortex, Fruit Ninja, Space Pirates, and Zombie Training Center) cost $10 each to play.

Universal's Cabana Bay Beach Resort ★★★★

6550 Adventure Way
Orlando
☎ 407-503-4000 or
888-464-3617
loewshotels.com
/cabana-bay-hotel

Rate per night $164–$278 standard, $214–$358 suites. **Pool ★★★★**. **Fridge in room** Yes. **Shuttle to parks** Yes (Universal, SeaWorld, Discovery Cove, Aquatica). **Maximum number of occupants per room** 4 (standard)/6 (suites). **Comment** Character greeting on Friday evenings. $18/night self-parking.

CABANA BAY WAS UNIVERSAL'S first on-site hotel aimed at the value and moderate markets. The theme is midcentury modern, with lots of windows, bright colors, and period-appropriate lighting and furniture.

Kids love the two large and well-themed pools (one with a lazy river), the amount of space they have to run around in, the video arcade, and the vintage cars parked outside the hotel lobby. Adults appreciate the sophisticated kitsch of the decor, the multiple lounges, the business center, and the on-site Starbucks. We think Cabana Bay is an excellent choice for price- and/or space-conscious families visiting Universal.

LILIANE Lock me up in a volcano-view tower room anytime. Did you know that Krakatau erupts once in a while? It's a sight to behold by day or by night!

Each family suite has a small bedroom with two queen beds, separated from the living area and kitchenette by a sliding screen; a pullout sofa in the living area offers additional sleeping space. (Standard rooms also have two queen beds.) The bath is divided into three sections: toilet, sink area, and shower room with additional sink. The kitchenette has a microwave, coffee maker, and minifridge. A bar area allows extra seating for quick meals, and a large closet has enough space to store everyone's luggage. Built-in USB charging outlets for your devices are a thoughtful touch.

Recreational options include the 10-lane Galaxy Bowl (about $12.99 per person with shoe rental), poolside table tennis and billiards, and a large Jack LaLanne fitness center. Outdoor movies are shown nightly near the pool.

In addition to Starbucks, a food court with seating area shows 1950s TV clips. Swizzle Lounge in the lobby, two pool bars, in-room pizza delivery, and the Galaxy Bowl round out the on-site dining options. You'll find more restaurants and clubs nearby at the Royal Pacific Resort and Universal CityWalk.

Unlike the other Universal resorts, Cabana Bay offers no watercraft service to the parks—it's either take the bus or walk. A pedestrian bridge connects Cabana Bay to CityWalk and the rest of Universal Orlando, but we recommend the bus service for most people. Bus service from Cabana Bay to the parks is superior to any bus transportation from Disney hotels to Disney parks. Cabana Bay guests are eligible for early entry at Universal and Volcano Bay but do not get complimentary Universal Express Passes.

Universal added two towers that enlarged the resort by 360 more standard guest rooms and 40 suites. Half of those rooms overlook the lush, 28-acre Volcano Bay water park, with amazing views of the rides and the 200-foot-high Krakatau volcano.

Universal's Endless Summer Resort
★★★½

Rate per night $113–$223 standard; $168–$278 suites. **Pool** ★★★. **Fridge in room** Yes. **Shuttle to parks** Yes (Universal, Volcano Bay, SeaWorld, Discovery Cove, Aquatica). **Maximum number of occupants per room** 4 (standard)/6 (suites). **Comment** $15/night self-parking.

Surfside: 7000 Universal Blvd. Orlando; loewshotels.com /surfside-inn-and-suites
Dockside: 7125 Universal Blvd. Orlando; loewshotels.com /dockside-inn-and-suites
☎ 407-503-7000 or 888-273-1311

AS UNIVERSAL'S LATEST HOTEL COMPLEX, Endless Summer Resort features two hotel towers: Surfside Inn & Suites opened in 2019, and Dockside Inn & Suites opened in 2020. Surfside Inn has 360 standard rooms and 390 two-bedroom suites, while Dockside has 577 standard rooms and 723 two-bedroom suites. With both hotels open, Universal has almost doubled the number of its on-site value rooms. Both resorts' color schemes include pale blues and greens, with lots of white. Bright ocean- and surf-themed art hangs on the walls. Room soundproofing is excellent, which is a surprise at this price, and there are plenty of under-shelf hooks on which to hang things, though only a handful of drawers for stowing your clothes. Our biggest nitpick is the poor quality of the soft goods—foam pillows and polyester-blend bath towels should be illegal.

Standard rooms are around 313 square feet and have vinyl "hardwood" floors, two queen beds, a chair, a minifridge, a coffee maker, an iron, and an ironing board. They're about the size of a Disney Moderate room at Disney Value prices: about $100–$145 per night cheaper than a Moderate. That's quite a savings.

Two-bedroom suites are 440 square feet and include a kitchenette with picnic-style table and microwave, plus one bathroom. Two-bedroom is a misnomer, though: The suite comprises one main room with two beds and a separate room with another bed. That's about 65–80 square feet smaller—and one less bathroom than—Disney's Family Suites. Universal's suites, however, are roughly $150–$240 cheaper per night.

The pools are unusually shallow (maximum depth 4 feet) and lack waterslides. Unfortunately, Endless Summer guests are forbidden to crash the pools at the non-Value resorts. Each hotel includes a well-stocked free fitness room, plus a Universal Studios Store and a video arcade. Full-service dining isn't offered, but cafeteria-style food courts, lobby and pool bars, Starbucks cafés, and pizza delivery are all available. Between the two hotels, we think Surfside has a slight edge due to its smaller, more manageable size, but Dockside has a few improved amenities and food options.

Because Endless Summer is on the opposite side of International Drive and I-4 from the rest of Universal Orlando, walking to the parks from the resort isn't practical, so a fleet of free buses is provided, servicing both the parking hub (from which you walk to CityWalk and the theme parks) and direct to Volcano Bay. The ride from here is actually slightly shorter than the one from Cabana Bay; travel time is barely 5 minutes each way, and the entire trip (including walking and waiting to depart) takes about 15 minutes.

As at Cabana Bay, guests at Endless Summer get free early admission to Universal's theme parks but not free Universal Express.

LAKE BUENA VISTA & I-4 CORRIDOR

B Resort ★★★½

1905 Hotel Plaza Blvd.
Lake Buena Vista
☎ 407-828-2828 or
866-759-6832
bhotelsandresorts
.com/b-resort-and-spa

Rate per night $129–$199. **Pool** ★★★½. **Fridge in room** Yes. **Shuttle to parks** Yes (Disney). **Maximum number of occupants per room** 4 plus child in crib. **Comments** $32/night resort fee. $22/night self-parking fee. Guests are eligible for Early Theme Park Entry benefits.

LOCATED WITHIN WALKING DISTANCE of shops and restaurants and situated 5 miles or less from the Disney parks, the 394-room B Resort targets couples, families, groups, and business travelers.

Decorated in cool blues, whites, and grays, guest rooms and suites afford views of downtown Orlando, area lakes, and theme parks. Along with B Resort–exclusive Blissful Beds, each room is outfitted with sleek modern furnishings and a large interactive TV. Additional touches include a minifridge, in-room snacks, and gaming consoles (available on request). Some rooms are also equipped with bunk beds, kitchenettes, or wet bars.

The bathroom is spacious, with plenty of storage. The glass shower is well-designed and has good water pressure. There's absolutely nothing wrong with this hotel at this price point, except for the terrible traffic you have to endure every night because of Disney Springs.

Amenities include free Wi-Fi, a spa, a beauty salon, and a fitness center. The main restaurant, American Kitchen Bar & Grill, serves comfort food made with contemporary ingredients. Hungry guests can also choose from a poolside bar and grill; The Pickup, a grab-and-go shop just off the lobby that serves quick breakfasts, snacks, picnic lunches, and ice cream; and in-room dining 6–11 a.m. and 5 p.m.–midnight. (*Note:* Spa and salon services and in-room dining are all temporarily unavailable.)

Other perks: a zero-entry pool with interactive water features, a kids' area, and more than 25,000 square feet of meeting and multiuse space.

Lake Buena Vista, I-4 Corridor, and US 192 Hotels

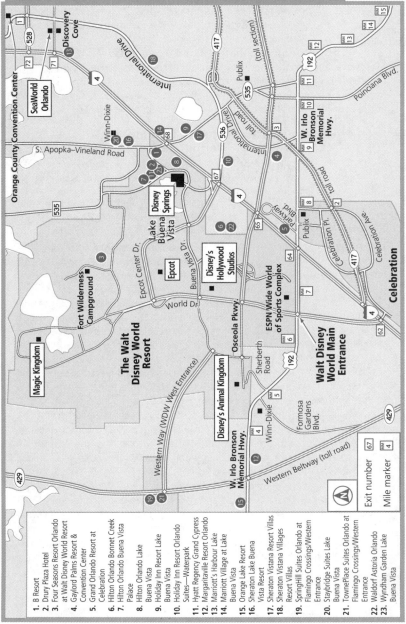

1. B Resort
2. Drury Plaza Hotel
3. Four Seasons Resort Orlando at Walt Disney World Resort
4. Gaylord Palms Resort & Convention Center
5. Grand Orlando Resort at Celebration
6. Hilton Orlando Bonnet Creek
7. Hilton Orlando Buena Vista Palace
8. Hilton Orlando Lake Buena Vista
9. Holiday Inn Resort Lake Buena Vista
10. Holiday Inn Resort Orlando Suites—Waterpark
11. Hyatt Regency Grand Cypress
12. Margaritaville Resort Orlando
13. Marriott's Harbour Lake
14. Marriott Village at Lake Buena Vista
15. Orange Lake Resort
16. Sheraton Lake Buena Vista Resort
17. Sheraton Vistana Resort Villas
18. Sheraton Vistana Villages Resort Villas
19. SpringHill Suites Orlando at Flamingo Crossings/Western Entrance
20. Staybridge Suites Lake Buena Vista
21. TownePlace Suites Orlando at Flamingo Crossings/Western Entrance
22. Waldorf Astoria Orlando
23. Wyndham Garden Lake Buena Vista

Drury Plaza Hotel Orlando—Disney Springs Area
(too new to rate)

2000 Hotel Plaza Blvd.
Lake Buena Vista
☎ 407-560-6111
druryplazahotel
orlando.com

DRURY PLAZA is the newest hotel in the DSRA. It opened the first 264 of a planned 602 hotel rooms in October, and the rest will follow in the first half of 2023. Amenities include a large pool area, two restaurants and a grab-and-go store, and 24-hour fitness and business centers. Room types include king beds, queen beds, and two-room suites. All rooms have a microwave, a minifridge, a coffeemaker, and an iron and ironing board.

The Drury is around a half-mile walk to Disney Springs and offers complimentary transportation to the Disney parks and Disney Springs. Guests staying at the Drury are also eligible for Early Theme Park Entry benefits.

Four Seasons Resort Orlando at Walt Disney World Resort ★★★★★

10100 Dream Tree Blvd.
Golden Oak
☎ 407-313-7777
or 800-267-3046
fourseasons.com/
orlando

Rate per night $613–$1,355. **Pool** ★★★★★. **Fridge in room** Yes. **Shuttle to parks** Yes (Disney). **Maximum number of occupants per room** 4 (3 adults or 2 adults and 2 children). **Comments** The best pool complex in Disney World. Character breakfast Thursdays, Saturdays, and select Tuesdays, 7-10 a.m. (reservations required; call ☎ 407-313-7777). Guests are eligible for Early Theme Park Entry benefits.

THE PLUSH FOUR SEASONS is the best deluxe resort in the area, with comfort, amenities, and personal service that far surpass anything Disney's Deluxes offer. The Spanish Revival–inspired architecture calls to mind Florida's grand resorts of the early 20th century.

Most of the 444 guest rooms have an 80-square-foot balcony with a table and chairs. Standard guest rooms average around 500 square feet and feature either one king bed with a sleeper sofa or two double beds (a crib is available in double rooms). Amenities include two TVs (one in the mirror above the bathroom sink), a coffee maker, a minifridge, a work desk with two chairs, and Bluetooth speakers for your personal audio. Each nightstand has four electrical outlets and two USB ports. Bathrooms have glass-walled showers, a separate tub, marble vanities with two sinks, mosaic-tile floors, hair dryers, and lighted mirrors.

If you're looking for family activities, the Four Seasons Resort has them. Explorer Island comprises an adult pool, a family pool, a 242-foot waterslide, a children's splash zone, a playground, and a lazy river. The free Kids for All Seasons program runs daily, 10 a.m.–noon and 1–5 p.m. Other amenities include a full-service spa and fitness center.

Capa, a Spanish-themed rooftop restaurant, serves seafood and steaks. Ravello serves American breakfasts and upscale Italian dishes for dinner. PB&G (Pool Bar and Grill) serves sandwiches, seafood, and salads by the main pool.

The shuttle service to the parks is free and by luxury coach, but the schedule is not as frequent as the Disney buses. Guests staying at the resort are better off having a car or taking a ride service.

Hilton Orlando Buena Vista Palace ★★★

Rate per night $192–$296. **Pool** ★★★½. **Fridge in room** Yes. **Shuttle to parks** Yes (Disney). **Maximum number of occupants per room** 4. **Comments** $35/night resort fee. $22/night self-parking. Sunday character breakfast. Guests are eligible for Early Theme Park Entry benefits.

THIS UPSCALE, CONVENIENT HOTEL is surrounded by an artificial lake and plenty of palms. Hilton has invested substantially in renovations since 2016, but more improvements are needed to bring the property up to par with the Hilton image. The spacious pool area comprises three heated pools, the largest of which is partially covered; a hot tub and sauna; a basketball court; and a sand volleyball court. A pool concierge will fetch your favorite magazine or fruity drink, and there is a Sunday character breakfast with Disney friends (*temporarily unavailable*). The 897 guest rooms are posh and spacious; each comes with a desk, a coffee maker, a hair dryer, satellite TV with pay-per-view movies, an iron and board, and a minifridge. There are also 117 suites. In-room babysitting is available. One lighted tennis court, a fitness center, an arcade, and a playground round out the recreation options. Two restaurants and a mini-market are on-site, and if you aren't wiped out after the parks, drop by the lobby lounge for a nightcap.

1900 E. Buena Vista Dr.
Lake Buena Vista
☎ 407-827-2727
buenavistapalace.com

Hilton Orlando Lake Buena Vista ★★★★

Rate per night $266–$315. **Pool** ★★★½. **Fridge in room** Yes. **Shuttle to parks** Yes (Disney). **Maximum number of occupants per room** 4. **Comments** $35/night resort fee. $22/night self-parking fee. Sunday character breakfast. Guests are eligible for Early Theme Park Entry benefits.

1751 Hotel Plaza Blvd.
Lake Buena Vista
☎ 407-827-4000
hilton-wdwv.com

THOUGH THE DECOR IS DATED, the rooms are comfortable and nicer than some others in the DSRA. On-site dining includes Covington Mill Restaurant, offering a breakfast buffet and sandwiches and salads for lunch; Andiamo, an Italian bistro; and Benihana, a Japanese steak house and sushi bar. The two pools are matched with a children's spray pool and a 24-hour fitness center. A game room and 24-hour market are on-site. Babysitting is available.

Holiday Inn Resort Lake Buena Vista ★★★½

Rate per night $110–$148. **Pool** ★★★. **Fridge in room** Yes. **Shuttle to parks** Yes (Disney, Universal, Aquatica, and SeaWorld). **Maximum number of occupants per room** 4–6. **Comments** $24.95/night resort fee. Pets welcome (2 max, 75-pound limit; for pets 50 pounds or less, $50 per pet for the first 4 nights and $10 per pet, per night after that; for pets over 50 pounds, $75 per pet for the first 4 nights and $10 per pet, per night after that; service animals are exempt from the fee.)

13351 FL 535
Orlando
☎ 407-239-4500
hiresortlbv.com

THE BIG LURE HERE IS KIDSUITES—405-square-foot rooms, each with a separate children's area that sleeps two to four kids in one or two bunk beds. The adult area has its own TV, a safe, a hair dryer, and a kitchenette with fridge, microwave, sink, and coffee maker (as do standard guest rooms). Kid-friendly perks include the tiny Kids' Movie Theater, which shows movies all day, every day; a splash pad; and an arcade with video games and air hockey. Other amenities include a fitness center for the grown-ups and a large pool with a kiddie pool and two hot tubs. Applebee's serves breakfast, lunch, and dinner; there's also a minimart. Kids age 12 and younger eat free at breakfast and dinner from a special menu when dining with a paying adult (maximum four kids per adult), and dive-in movies are shown at the pool seasonally on Saturday nights.

Holiday Inn Resort Orlando Suites—Waterpark ★★★½

14500 Continental Gateway, Orlando
☎ 407-387-5437
hisuitesorlando.com

Rate per night $153–$250. **Pool** ★★★★. **Fridge in room** Yes (microwave). **Shuttle to parks** Yes (Disney [TTC], Disney Springs, Universal, Volcano Bay, SeaWorld). **Comments** $49/night resort fee plus tax. **Maximum number of occupants per room** 8.

AFTER A $30 MILLION RENOVATION in 2016, the hotel once known as Nickelodeon Suites became the Holiday Inn Resort Orlando Suites—Waterpark.

The suites come in one-, two-, and three-bedroom varieties, and each suite contains a minifridge, a microwave, a TV, and high-speed internet. The resort also boasts a water park with seven slides, a 4-D Experience, Laser Challenge, and a 3,000-square-foot arcade. Kids will love the many free activities at the main pool.

The resort is huge, and the layout of the hotel is somewhat confusing. Unless you prefer the more remote, quiet pool area, we suggest that you request a room close to the main pool and The Market Place, the shopping and dining area of the complex. The shuttles to the parks depart from The Market Place.

Hyatt Regency Grand Cypress ★★★★½

1 Grand Cypress Blvd. Orlando
☎ 407-239-1234
grandcypress.hyatt.com

Rate per night $159–$329. **Pool** ★★★★★. **Fridge in room** Yes, plus minibar. **Shuttle to parks** Yes (Disney, Universal, Volcano Bay, SeaWorld). **Maximum number of occupants per room** 4. **Comments** $40/night resort fee. Pets welcome (up to 6 nights, $150 per stay; 7–30 nights, additional $150 deep-cleaning fee; more than 30 nights, fee based on resort's discretion. Weight limits: 1 dog, 50 pounds or lighter; 2 dogs, 75 pounds or lighter combined). $22/night self-parking.

THERE ARE MYRIAD REASONS to stay at the 1,500-acre Grand Cypress, but the pool ranks as number one. The 800,000-gallon tropical paradise has waterfalls and a suspension bridge, along with a 124-foot waterslide, a splash zone, a pool bar, and kids' rock-climbing facilities.

The 767 standard guest rooms are 360 square feet and have a Florida ambience, with green and reddish hues, touches of rattan, and private balconies. Amenities include a minibar, an iron and board, a safe, a hair dryer, a ceiling fan, and cable/satellite TV with pay-per-view movies and video games. Suite and villa accommodations offer even more amenities. Two restaurants offer dining options, and three lounges provide nighttime entertainment.

Marriott's Harbour Lake ★★★★

7102 Grand Horizons Blvd. Orlando
☎ 407-465-6100
tinyurl.com/harbourlake

Rate per night $229–$469 (1 bedroom)/$259–$499 (2 bedroom). **Pool** ★★★★. **Fridge in room** Yes. **Shuttle to parks** No. **Maximum number of occupants per room** 4 (1 bedroom)/8 (2 bedroom).

THE RESORT FEATURES STUDIOS and one- and two-bedroom villas with fully equipped kitchens, separate living and dining areas, and a washer and dryer. Most rooms have balconies.

Kids will love the Florida Falls pool complex, with its water playground and waterslide. The larger Shipwreck Landing pool area contains a pirate ship, complete with waterslides and water cannons. The on-site fitness center and Key Lime Greens, an 18-hole minigolf course, are also sure to please.

The only drawback is the very limited on-site dining. The Outpost offers grab-and-go food, while The Patio Bar and Grill serves breakfast, lunch, and dinner. Note that the grill closes during inclement weather.

Sheraton Vistana Resort Villas ★★★★

Rate per night $147–$327. **Pool** ★★★½. **Fridge in room** Yes (full kitchen). **Shuttle to parks** Yes (Disney, for a fee). **Maximum number of occupants per room** 4 (1 bedroom)/8 (2 bedroom). **Comments** These time-share villas are also rented nightly.

8800 Vistana Centre Dr. Orlando
☎ 407-239-3100 or 866-208-0003
tinyurl.com/vistana resortvillas

IF YOU WANT A SERENE RETREAT from the theme parks, this is an excellent base. The Sheraton Vistana is deceptively large, stretching across both sides of Vistana Centre Drive. The spacious villas come in one-bedroom and two-bedroom layouts. Each villa has a full kitchen (including fridge/freezer, microwave, oven/range, dishwasher, toaster, and coffee maker, with an option to prestock with groceries and laundry products), a washer and dryer, TVs in the living room and each bedroom (one with DVD player), a stereo with CD player in some villas, a separate dining area, and a private patio or balcony in most. The grounds offer seven swimming pools (three with bars), four playgrounds, two restaurants, game rooms, fitness centers, a minigolf course, and sports equipment rental (including bikes), as well as courts for basketball, volleyball, tennis, and shuffleboard. The mind-boggling array of activities for kids (and adults) ranges from crafts to games and sports tournaments. Of special note: Vistana is highly secure, with locked gates bordering all guest areas, so children can have the run of the place without parents worrying about them wandering off. The one downside: noise, both above (from being on the flight path of a helicopter tour company) and below (from International Drive).

Sheraton Vistana Villages Resort Villas ★★★★

Rate per night $179–$359. **Pool** ★★★★. **Fridge in room** Yes (full kitchen). **Shuttle to parks** No. **Maximum number of occupants per room** 6 (2 bedroom).

12401 International Dr. Orlando
☎ 407-238-5000
tinyurl.com/vistana villagesresort

THIS IS ONE OF TWO Sheraton Vistana properties in Orlando that are favorites of *Unofficial Guide* readers (the other is the Vistana Resort Villas in Lake Buena Vista, profiled above). The 1,100-square-foot, two-bedroom villas are the rooms to get. While that's double the size of a Disney one-bedroom Family Suite, rack rates are much less than Disney's.

Suites have fully equipped kitchens and a washer and dryer. All rooms have a private balcony or patio. The resort has two pools, including one zero-entry for kids; a fitness center; and a business center.

This family from Bedford, Texas, really enjoyed their stay:

> I highly recommend Vistana Villages—it's the best value for the money. Plenty of space for everyone to spread out, great pools, and fantastic location. It was 10 minutes to EPCOT and Hollywood Studios and 5 minutes to Disney Springs, and lots of restaurants were nearby.

The Vistana Villages are about a 15-minute drive from Walt Disney World (and you don't have to take I-4!) and 20 minutes to Universal Orlando.

Signia by Hilton Orlando Bonnet Creek ★★★★

Rate per night $250–$385. **Pool** ★★★★½. **Fridge in room** Yes. **Shuttle to parks** Yes (Disney). **Maximum number of occupants per room** 4. **Comments** $45/night resort fee. $30/night self-parking. Guests are eligible for Early Theme Park Entry benefits.

14100 Bonnet Creek
Resort Lane
Orlando
☎ 407-597-3600
hiltonbonnetcreek.com

THIS IS ONE OF OUR FAVORITE non-Disney hotels in Lake Buena Vista, and the value for the money beats anything in Disney's Deluxe category. Located behind Disney's Caribbean Beach and Pop Century Resorts, this Hilton is much nicer than the ones in the Disney Springs Resort Area.

Standard rooms are around 414 square feet and have either one king bed or two queens. The mattresses and linens are very comfortable. Other features include a 37-inch TV, a spacious work desk, a small reading chair with floor lamp, a nightstand, and a digital clock. A coffee maker, a minifridge, a hair dryer, and an iron and board are all standard, along with free wired and free wireless internet. Bathrooms include tile floors, and some have glass showers. Unfortunately, the layout isn't as up-to-date as other hotels'—where many upscale hotel bathrooms have two sinks (so two people can primp at once), the Hilton's bathrooms have only one.

Families will enjoy the huge zero-entry pool, complete with waterslide, as well as the 3-acre lazy river. Even better, the Hilton staff runs arts-and-crafts activities poolside during the day, allowing parents to grab a quick swim and a cocktail. Pool-facing cabanas are available for rent. A nice fitness center sits on the ground floor.

The Signia participates in the neighboring Waldorf Astoria's WA Kids Club (*temporarily closed*) for children ages 5–12. When available, the daytime program runs daily, 10:30 a.m.–2:30 p.m., and an evening program is available on Friday and Saturday, 6–10 p.m. Price is $75 for the first child, $25 for each additional child. To make reservations, call ☎ 407-597-5388.

More than a dozen restaurants and lounges are between the Hilton and the Waldorf Astoria, with cuisine including steak, Italian, sushi, and tapas. A coffee bar, an American bistro, and a breakfast buffet round out the choices. Reservations are recommended for the fancy places.

Sonesta ES Suites Lake Buena Vista ★★★★½

8751 Suiteside Dr.
Lake Buena Vista
☎ 407-238-0777
tinyurl.com
/sonestalbv

Rate per night $169–$259. **Pool** ★★★. **Fridge in room** Yes (full kitchen). **Shuttle to parks** Yes (Disney, Universal). **Maximum number of occupants per room** 4 (1 bedroom)/8 (2 bedroom). **Comments** Free grab-and-go breakfast.

WE FOUND THIS GEM through our reader surveys, which named this Staybridge Suites the best off-site hotel near Walt Disney World in 2016. Having stayed there, we agree. The best value is the two-bedroom suite: one bedroom has a king bed; the other, two doubles (a sleeper sofa is standard in both the one- and two-bedroom suites). Each bedroom has its own full bathroom. In between the bedrooms are a living room; small dining area; and full kitchen with dishwasher, range, microwave, and refrigerator. The suite also contains plates, cups, glasses, and cutlery, plus basic pots and pans. A large-screen TV in the living room is matched by smaller TVs in each bedroom. Other amenities include free Wi-Fi and a free grab-and-go breakfast. Service is excellent. Be aware that the Sonesta is so popular that it's unlikely your room will be ready much before the 4 p.m. check-in time.

The hotel is about 0.5 mile from the Disney Springs Resort Area, just around the corner on South Apopka–Vineland Road. Nearby are two small shopping centers, both in easy walking distance.

Waldorf Astoria Orlando   ★★★★½

14200 Bonnet Creek Resort Lane, Orlando
☎ 407-597-5500
waldorfastoriaorlando.com

Rate per night $353–$735. **Pool ★★★★. Fridge in room** Yes. **Shuttle to parks** Yes (Disney). **Maximum number of occupants per room** 4 plus child in crib. **Comments** Good alternative to Disney Deluxe resorts; $45/night resort fee. Guests are eligible for Early Theme Park Entry benefits.

BEAUTIFULLY DECORATED AND WELL MANICURED, the Waldorf Astoria is more elegant than any Disney resort. Service is excellent, and the staff-to-guest ratio is far higher than at Disney properties. It's located between I-4 and Disney's Pop Century Resort, near the Hilton Orlando at the back of the Bonnet Creek Resort property.

At just under 450 square feet, standard rooms feature either two queen beds or one king. A full-size desk allows you to get work done if necessary, and rooms also have TVs, high-speed internet, and Wi-Fi. The bathrooms are spacious and gorgeous, with marble floors, glass-walled showers, separate tubs, and enough counter space for a Broadway makeup artist.

Amenities include a fitness center, a spa, a golf course, six restaurants, and two pools (including a zero-entry pool for kids). Poolside cabanas are available for rent.

Waldorf Astoria's WA Kids Club (*temporarily unavailable*) is for children ages 5–12. When available, the daytime program runs daily, 10:30 a.m.–2:30 p.m., and an evening program is available on Friday and Saturday, 6–10 p.m. Price is $75 for the first child, $25 for each additional child.

Wyndham Garden Lake Buena Vista
★★★½

1850 Hotel Plaza Blvd. Lake Buena Vista
☎ 407-842-6644
wyndhamlake buenavista.com

Rate per night $110–$150. **Pool ★★★★. Fridge in room** Yes. **Shuttle to parks** Yes (Disney). **Maximum number of occupants per room** 4. **Comment** Character breakfast Tuesday, Thursday, and Saturday. $35/night resort fee. $22/night parking. Guests are eligible for Early Theme Park Entry benefits.

THE MAIN REASON TO STAY at the Wyndham is the short walk to Disney Springs. The lobby is bright and airy, and check-in service is friendly. Rooms are larger than most and have full refrigerators. Pool-facing rooms in the hotel's wings have exterior hallways that overlook the pool and center courtyard; these hallways can be noisy during summer months. The elevators are unusually slow—it's probably faster to walk to the second and third floors, assuming you're up for the exercise.

US 192 AREA

Gaylord Palms Resort & Convention Center ★★★★½

Rate per night $352–$409. **Pool** ★★★★. **Fridge in room** Yes.
Shuttle to parks Yes (Disney: free; Universal, Volcano Bay, Sea-World: $21/person round-trip). **Maximum number of occupants per room** 4. **Comments** $30/night resort fee. $28/night parking.

6000 W. Osceola Pkwy.
Kissimmee
☎ 407-586-0000
gaylordpalms.com

THIS UPSCALE RESORT has a colossal convention facility and caters to business clientele, but it's still a nice (if pricey) family resort. Hotel wings are defined by the three themed glass-roofed atria they overlook: Key West's design is reminiscent of island life in the Florida Keys; Everglades is an overgrown spectacle of shabby swamp chic, complete with piped-in cricket noise and a robotic alligator; and the immense, central St. Augustine harks back to Spanish Colonial Florida. Lagoons, streams, and waterfalls connect all three, and walkways and bridges abound. A fourth wing, Emerald Bay Tower, overlooks the Emerald Plaza shopping and dining area of the St. Augustine atrium. These rooms are the nicest and the most expensive, and they're mostly used by conventioneers. The rooms (with perks such as high-speed internet) work better as retreats for adults than for kids. However, children will enjoy wandering the themed areas and playing in the family pool (with water-squirting octopus). In-room childcare is provided by Kid's Nite Out (see page 69).

Holiday Inn Club Vacations at Orange Lake Resort ★★★★

Rate per night $132–$175. **Pools** ★★★★. **Fridge in room** Yes. **Shuttle to parks** Yes, for a fee (varies based on your destination). **Maximum number of occupants per room** Varies. **Comments** This is a time-share property, but if you rent directly through the resort instead of the sales office, you won't have to listen to any sales pitches. $15/night resort fee. 6–10 minutes from the Disney theme parks.

8505 W. Irlo
Bronson Memorial
Hwy., Kissimmee
☎ 407-477-7025
or 888-465-4329
tinyurl.com/holiday
innorangelake

FROM ITS SEVEN POOLS AND MINI WATER PARK to its golfing opportunities (36 holes of championship greens plus two 9-hole executive courses), Orange Lake offers an extensive menu of amenities and recreational opportunities. If you tire of lazing by the pool, try waterskiing, wakeboarding, tubing, fishing, or other activities on the 80-acre lake. There are also exercise programs, organized competitive sports and games, arts-and-crafts sessions, and minigolf. Karaoke, live music, a Hawaiian luau, and movies at the resort cinema are some of the evening options.

The 2,412 units, ranging from suites and studios to three-bedroom villas, are tastefully decorated and comfortably furnished; all have fully equipped kitchens. These rooms are massive and cheap: The 1,700-square-foot, three-bedroom villa sleeps 11 people and goes for as little as $255 a night. That's about the same as five—five!—Disney Moderate rooms, for less money.

If you'd rather not cook on vacation, try one of the seven restaurants scattered across the resort: two cafés, three grills, one pizzeria, and a fast-food place.

We reevaluated the resort after a reader noticed several negative reviews of the property on TripAdvisor, most mentioning room cleanliness. Our test room—a one-bedroom villa with washer and dryer and full kitchen for $136 per night with tax—was spotless, as were the rooms we got to peek into around the resort.

Lake Buena Vista, I-4 Corridor, and US 192 Hotels

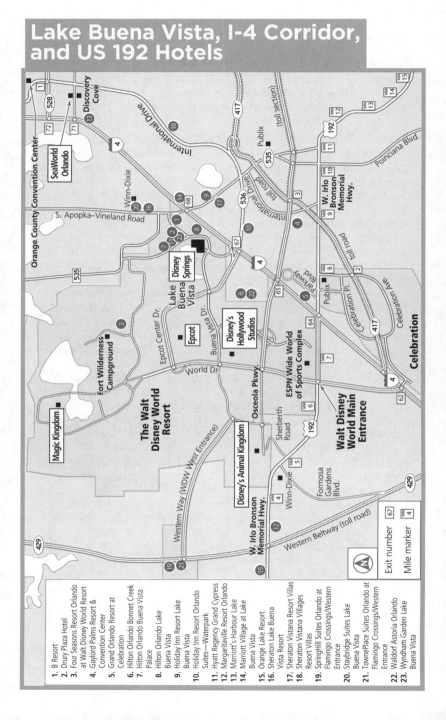

As far as suites go, we like the **Sonesta ES Suites Lake Buena Vista** a bit better, but we'd stay at Orange Lake again.

Margaritaville Resort Orlando ★★★★

8000 Fins Up Circle
Kissimmee
☎ 407-479-0950
or 855-995-9099
tinyurl.com
/margaritaville-fl

Rate per night $230–$440 hotel rooms, $229–$2,120 cottages (1–8 bedrooms). **Pool ★★★★. Fridge in room** Yes (full kitchen). **Shuttle to parks** No. **Maximum number of occupants per room** 2 (standard room)/18 (8-bedroom cottage).

BEYOND OUR ABSOLUTE CERTAINTY that Margaritaville's restaurant would serve a Cheeseburger in Paradise, Jimmy Buffett's lyrics reveal few thoughts about hotel management. We were skeptical that this was going to be anything other than a standard hotel with some tropical prints and parrots. But Margaritaville is a well-designed, reasonably priced resort that's worth considering for large families and groups, especially those who aren't going to Walt Disney World every day.

Sitting on an impressive 300 acres of land, Margaritaville has two kinds of accommodations: The main building holds 186 standard rooms and suites, and another 187 one- to eight-bedroom vacation cottages sit around a central lake. (Construction of additional accommodations is planned.)

An island/beach theme is consistent across the resort. Standard hotel rooms are 470 square feet, larger than any standard Disney Deluxe room. Amenities include vinyl floors, a microwave and coffee maker, and good lighting. Bathrooms are well lit and spacious, with walk-in glass showers and good water pressure.

Vacation cottages are freestanding homes, ranging from one-story, one-bedroom bungalows to three-story, eight-bedroom buildings that sleep up to 18 guests. The most notable thing about these cottages is that nothing feels cheap or underbuilt. The kitchen layout makes it easy to cook for large groups. The couches, chairs, and beds are comfortable. Bathrooms have good water pressure. The AC blows cold. The lights and appliances work the way they're supposed to. And the homes we've stayed in have been spotlessly clean.

A 5-minute walk from the hotel lobby puts you in the middle of Sunset Walk, Margaritaville's dining and entertainment district consisting of 15 restaurants and bars with cuisines ranging from sushi to British pub to Memphis barbecue. We think it's worth visiting.

There's also an on-site water park—Island H2O Water Park—but we consider Universal's Volcano Bay a better value. For more information, visit Island H2O's website: islandh2owaterpark.com.

A Publix supermarket is half a mile away. A free internal shuttle service links the hotel, cottages, and Sunset Walk. If you're headed to Disney property from Margaritaville, you can avoid almost all of the US 192 traffic by taking Inspiration Drive to Black Lake Road to Osceola Parkway. That half-mile, traffic-free stretch of road puts you smack-dab between Animal Kingdom and Animal Kingdom Lodge, with clear, easy access to the rest of Walt Disney World.

Polynesian Isles Resort (Diamond Resorts) ★★★★½

Rate per night $112–$298 1-bedroom villas, $170–$355 2-bedroom villas. **Pool ★★★½. Fridge in room** Yes (full kitchen). **Shuttle to parks** No. **Maximum number of occupants per room** 4 (1-bedroom)/6 (2-bedroom), plus child in crib.

LET'S START BY SAYING that the Polynesian Isles' rooms aren't the most modern and could use a good interior decorator. And the location, a few miles east of I-4 in Kissimmee, isn't the most upscale. But there are few other places in Orlando where you can get 1,500–1,600 square feet of space for less than $200 a night including tax. (Quantity, as they say, has a quality all its own.)

3045 Polynesian Isles Blvd. Kissimmee ☎ 407-396-1622 or 800-925-3673 polynesianisle.com

One-bedroom villas are 1,500 square feet and have one king bed and one sofa bed; two-bedroom villas are 1,600 square feet and have king, queen, and sofa beds. Both villa types are outfitted with a full kitchen, a dining room table with seating for six, upholstered chairs, and a TV. Bathrooms are large and clean, with decent water pressure and so-so lighting.

The resort's Polynesian theme is pulled off well for something not in a theme park. Other amenities include tennis courts, a basketball half-court, a very small fitness room, a playground, and a pool.

FLAMINGO CROSSINGS

FLAMINGO CROSSINGS IS LOCATED at the intersection of US 429 and Western Way—we're not exaggerating when we say it's less than 60 seconds from Disney property by car. Follow Western Way for a bit, and you'll end up at Coronado Springs Resort.

Five hotels are located here. Three are Marriott brands: Residence Inn; SpringHill Suites; and TownePlace Suites, an extended-stay hotel. Two are Hilton properties: Home2 Suites and Homewood Suites. All have 220–300 rooms. In terms of value, we'd rate them in this order:

1. SpringHill Suites   2. Residence Inn   3. Homewood Suites
4. TownePlace Suites   5. Home2 Suites

The related hotels are adjacent and share parking, a huge pool complex, and gyms. Other amenities include practice fields and facilities—a nod to the sports groups that participate in events at the ESPN Wide World of Sports Complex. The lobbies are constantly abuzz with color-coordinated teens either preparing for or unwinding from some event.

Despite the potential for noise, our rooms were very quiet. They were also spotless. Our two-bedroom suite had a small, full kitchen, while our studio had a microwave and coffee maker. Both had only one bathroom, and we think the two-bedroom units could have used a second. Water pressure was better at the Marriott properties than the Hiltons.

In addition to being close to Disney property, the Flamingo Crossings hotels are about a 10-minute drive to a wide variety of suburban retailers on US 192, including Publix, Super Target, and tons of restaurants. That said, if you have a car or you aren't participating in anything at the Wide World of Sports Complex, we think any of the other resorts in the preceding section offer better value for the money.

Home2 Suites by Hilton   ★★★½

Rate per night $140–$250. **Pool** ★★★★. **Fridge in room** Yes. **Shuttle to parks** Yes (Magic Kingdom only; $5). **Maximum number of occupants per room** 6, plus child in crib.

341 Flagler Ave. ☎ 407-993-3999 tinyurl.com /fc-home2suites

THE HOTEL OFFERS studios with either one king bed or two queen beds, plus one- and two-bedroom suites. One-bedroom suites have a king bed. Two-bedroom suites have one king bed and one queen bed. Studios have a TV, full-size refrigerator, microwave, sink, and dishwasher. Suites have a separate living area, a sofa bed, two TVs, a microwave, a full-size refrigerator, a sink, and a dishwasher. Free hot breakfast is served daily. There is no fee for parking or Wi-Fi.

Homewood Suites by Hilton ★★★★

Rate per night $150–$250. **Pool** ★★★★. **Fridge in room** Yes. **Shuttle to parks** Yes (Magic Kingdom only; $5). **Maximum number of occupants per room** 4 (1-bedroom suite with king and pullout beds)/5 (1-bedroom suite with 2 queen and pullout beds), plus child in crib.

411 Flagler Ave.
☎ 407-993-3011
tinyurl.com/fc
-homewoodsuites

THE 229 AIR-CONDITIONED ROOMS feature kitchenettes with full-size refrigerators and stovetops, as well as 49-inch LED TVs. Other conveniences include microwaves and coffee/tea makers. A complimentary buffet breakfast is served on weekdays, 6–9 a.m., and on weekends, 7–10 a.m. There is no fee for parking or WiFi.

Residence Inn *(too new to rate)*

Rate per night $211–$280 studio, $220–$303 1-bedroom suite, $331–$421 2-bedroom suite. **Pool** ★★★★. **Fridge in room** Yes. **Shuttle to parks** No. **Maximum number of occupants per room** 2 (studio)/6 (1-bedroom suite with pull-out sofa)/8 (2-bedroom suite with pull-out sofa).

2111 Flagler Ave.
Kissimmee
☎ 407-993-3233
tinyurl.com/fc
-residenceinn

THIS RESIDENCE INN has studios and one and two-bedroom suites, along with a fitness center and free hot breakfast. Those amenities, along with Disney-competitive peak-season rates for the two-bedroom suites, make this a good option for large families. And while we're not fans of the foam pillows here, you can ask for feather pillows, which is a nice plus.

SpringHill Suites ★★★★

Rate per night $149–$199. **Pool** ★★★★. **Fridge in room** Yes. **Shuttle to parks** Yes (Magic Kingdom only; $5). **Maximum number of occupants per room** 6, plus child in crib.

13279 Hartzog Rd.
☎ 407-507-1200
tinyurl.com
/fc-springhill

THE ROOMY SUITES at SpringHill include a minifridge, a microwave, a sofa bed, and a coffee maker.

TownePlace Suites ★★★★

Rate per night $146–$199. **Pool** ★★★★. **Fridge in room** Yes. **Shuttle to parks** Yes (Magic Kingdom only; $5). **Maximum number of occupants per room** 3 (1-bedroom suite)/5 (2-bedroom suite with 2 queen and pullout beds), plus child in crib.

13295 Hartzog Rd.
Kissimmee
☎ 407-507-1300
tinyurl.com/fc
-towneplace

THIS EXTENDED-STAY HOTEL offers spacious one- and two-bedroom suites with fully equipped kitchens.

GETTING A GOOD DEAL ON A ROOM OUTSIDE WALT DISNEY WORLD

UNABLE TO COMPETE WITH Disney resorts for convenience or perks, out-of-World hotels lure patrons with bargain rates. The extent of the bargain depends on the season, day of the week, and local events. Here are tips and strategies for getting a good deal on a room outside Walt Disney World.

1. VISIT ORLANDO HOTEL DEALS This discount program sponsored by Visit Orlando offers discounts of up to 25% at Orlando hotels. The program also offers discounts at some area attractions, dinner theaters, museums, performing-arts venues, restaurants, shops, and more. Go to visitorlando.com and click on "Deals."

2. HOTEL SHOPPING ONLINE When we're really looking for a deal, we scour sites such as the ones below for unusually juicy deals that meet our criteria (location, quality, price, amenities).

OUR FAVORITE ONLINE HOTEL RESOURCES
mousesavers.com Best site for hotels in Disney World
hotelcoupons.com Self-explanatory
experiencekissimmee.com Primarily US 192-Kissimmee area hotels
visitorlando.com Good info; not user-friendly for booking
orlandovacation.com Great rates for condos and home rentals

If we find a hotel that fills the bill, we check it out at other websites and comparative travel search engines such as **Kayak** (kayak .com), **Hotels.com,** and **Mobissimo** (mobissimo.com) to see who has the best rate. (As an aside, Kayak sells travel products, raising the issue of whether products not sold by Kayak are equally likely to come up in a search. Mobissimo, on the other hand, only links potential buyers to provider websites.) Hotels.com is a booking engine that lets you earn points toward a future free stay. Another site is **Trivago** (trivago.com). Your initial shopping effort should take about 15–20 minutes, faster if you can zero in quickly on a particular hotel.

 BOB Always call the specific hotel, not the hotel chain's national 800 number.

Next, call the hotel or have your travel agent call. Start by asking about specials. If there are none, or if the hotel can't beat the best price you've found on the internet, share your findings and ask if the hotel can do better. Sometimes you'll be asked for proof of the rate you've discovered online—to be prepared for this, go to the site and enter the dates of your stay, and make sure the rate you've found is available. If it is, print the page or take a screenshot of this information and have it handy for your travel agent or for when you call the hotel.

3. IF YOU MAKE YOUR OWN RESERVATION Call and ask about specials before you inquire about corporate rates. Don't hesitate to bargain, but do it before you check in. If you're buying a weekend package, for example, and want to extend your stay, you can often obtain at least the corporate rate for the extra days.

HOW *to* CHILDPROOF
a HOTEL ROOM

SMALL CHILDREN UP TO 3 YEARS OLD (and sometimes older) can wreak mayhem—if not outright disaster—in a hotel room. Chances are that you're pretty experienced when it comes to spotting potential dangers, but just in case you need a refresher course, here's what to look for.

Begin by checking for hazards that you can't fix yourself: balconies, chipping paint, cracked walls, sharp surfaces, shag carpeting, and windows that can't be secured shut. If you encounter anything that you don't like or is too much of a hassle to fix, ask for another room.

If you use a crib supplied by the hotel, make sure that the mattress is firm and covers the entire bottom of the crib. The mattress cover, if there is one, should fit tightly. Slats should be 2.5 inches (about the width of a soda can) or less apart. Make sure the drop sides work properly. Check for sharp edges and potentially toxic substances. Wipe down surfaces with disinfectant. Finally, position the crib away from drapery cords, heaters, wall sockets, and air conditioners.

A Manteno, Illinois, mom offers this suggestion:

> *You can request bed rails at the Disney resorts. Our 2½-year-old was too big for the Pack 'n Play; the bed rails worked perfectly for us.*

If your infant can turn over, we recommend changing him or her on a pad on the floor. Likewise, if you have a child seat of any sort, place it where it cannot be knocked over, and always strap your child in.

If your child can roll, crawl, or walk, you should bring about eight electrical outlet covers and some cord to tie cabinets shut and to bind drapery cords and the like out of reach. Check for appliances, lamps, ice buckets, and anything else that your child might pull down on him- or herself. Have the hotel remove coffee tables with sharp edges, as well as both real and artificial plants that are within your child's reach. Round up items from tables and countertops, such as courtesy toiletries and drinking glasses, and store them out of reach.

If the bathroom door can be accidentally locked, cover the locking mechanism with duct tape or a doorknob cover. Use the security chain or upper latch on the room's entrance door to ensure that your child doesn't open it without your knowledge.

Inspect the floor and remove pins, coins, and other foreign objects that your child might find. Don't forget to check under beds and furniture. *Tip:* Crawl around the room on your hands and knees to see possible hazards from your child's perspective.

If you rent a suite or a condo, you'll have more territory to childproof and will have to deal with things such as cleaning supplies, a stove, a refrigerator, cooking utensils, and low cabinet doors. Sometimes the best option is to seal off the kitchen with a safety gate. Access to a private pool should be locked at all times.

PART 4

DINING

DINING OPTIONS ABOUND BOTH IN AND OUT of Walt Disney World, and if you're so inclined, there are a lot of ways to save big bucks while keeping your crew nourished and happy.

▌ DINING *in* WALT DISNEY WORLD

IF THE AVERAGE PARENTS roaming Walt Disney World were primarily concerned with pleasing their palates, the hottest dinner ticket in the parks wouldn't be the *Hoop-Dee-Doo Musical Revue.* In fact, if you want to know what Disney visitors really like, look at the numbers: Every year, they consume 10 million hamburgers, 6 million hot dogs, 75 million sodas, and 150 tons of popcorn.

So, for many families, food is a secondary consideration, but if you *do* care about dining out on your vacation or you'd like to experiment with different cuisines, *The Unofficial Guide to Walt Disney World* includes detailed reviews of the sit-down establishments in Disney World.

 LILIANE Parents should be aware that both full- and counter-service restaurants at Disney World serve very substantial portions. You can easily split an entrée, put aside parts of dinners for lunch the next day (if you have an in-room fridge), or load up at lunch and go light on dinner.

WALT DISNEY WORLD RESTAURANT CATEGORIES

IN GENERAL, FOOD AND BEVERAGE offerings at Walt Disney World are defined by service, price, and convenience.

FULL-SERVICE RESTAURANTS Full-service restaurants are located in all Disney resorts (except the Value resorts and Port Orleans French Quarter), all major theme parks, and Disney Springs. Disney operates most of the restaurants in the theme parks and its hotels, while contractors or franchisees operate the rest. Advance Reservations (see page 163) are recommended for most full-service restaurants except those in the Disney Springs Resort Area. The restaurants accept American Express,

WALT DISNEY WORLD BUFFETS & FAMILY-STYLE RESTAURANTS

RESTAURANT	LOCATION	CUISINE	MEALS SERVED	CHARACTERS
AKERSHUS ROYAL BANQUET HALL (temporarily closed)	EPCOT	American (B), Norwegian (L, D)	B, L, D	Yes
BIERGARTEN RESTAURANT	EPCOT	German	L, D	No
BOMA—FLAVORS OF AFRICA	Animal Kingdom Lodge	American (B), African (D)	B, D	No
CAPE MAY CAFE	Beach Club Resort	American	B, D	Yes (B)
THE CRYSTAL PALACE	Magic Kingdom	American	L, D	Yes
THE DIAMOND HORSESHOE	Magic Kingdom	American	L, D*	No
FRESH MEDITERRANEAN MARKET	Dolphin Hotel	Mediterranean/ American	B, L	No
GARDEN GRILL RESTAURANT	EPCOT	American	L, D	Yes
GARDEN GROVE	Swan Hotel	American	B, Br	No
HOLLYWOOD & VINE	Disney's Hollywood Studios	American	B, L, D	Yes
HOOP-DEE-DOO MUSICAL REVUE	Fort Wilderness	American	D	No
LIBERTY TREE TAVERN	Magic Kingdom	American	L, D	No
1900 PARK FARE	Grand Floridian	American	B, D	Yes
'OHANA	Polynesian Village	American/Polynesian	B, D	Yes (B)**
TRAIL'S END RESTAURANT	Fort Wilderness	American	B, Br, D	No
TUSKER HOUSE RESTAURANT	Animal Kingdom	American (B), African (L, D)	B, L, D	Yes
WHISPERING CANYON CAFE	Wilderness Lodge	American	B, L, D	No

* Serves family-style meals only at the meal(s) indicated. *Note:* The Diamond Horseshoe is open seasonally.

** Character-breakfast buffet served only on weekends

*** Serves buffet-style meals only at the meal(s) indicated

MasterCard, Visa, Discover Card, Diners Club, Disney gift cards, Disney Dream Reward Dollars, and Japan Credit Bureau.

BUFFETS AND FAMILY-STYLE RESTAURANTS Many of these have Disney characters in attendance, and most have a separate children's menu with dishes such as hot dogs, burgers, chicken nuggets, pizza, macaroni and cheese, and spaghetti and meatballs. In addition to the buffets, several restaurants serve a family-style, all-you-can-eat, fixed-price meal.

Advance Reservations are required for character buffets and recommended for all other buffets and family-style restaurants. Most major credit cards are accepted.

If you want to eat a lot but don't feel like standing in yet another line, then consider one of the all-you-can-eat family-style restaurants. These feature platters of food brought to your table in courses. You can eat as much as you like—even go back to a favorite appetizer after you finish the main course. The food tends to be a little better than what you'd find on a buffet line.

The table on the opposite page lists buffets and family-style restaurants where you can belly up for bulk loading at Walt Disney World.

FOOD COURTS Featuring a collection of counter-service eateries under one roof, food courts can be found at Disney's Moderate and Value resorts. (The closest thing to a food court at the theme parks is EPCOT's **Sunshine Seasons**.) Advance Reservations are not available.

COUNTER SERVICE Counter-service fast food is plentiful in all the theme parks and at the BoardWalk and Disney Springs. You'll find hot dogs, burgers, chicken sandwiches, salads, and pizza almost everywhere.

Ordering meals ahead of time through the My Disney Experience app is strongly suggested for all counter-service restaurants.

- Place your counter-service restaurant order 30–45 minutes before you want to eat; that will allow the restaurant enough time to prepare your food before you arrive, and it will reduce your wait. During busier times of the year, you may need to submit those orders 1–2 hours in advance, to be safe.

- Consider eating before noon or after 1 p.m., when it will be easier to find open tables at counter-service restaurants.

FAST CASUAL Somewhere between hamburgers and formal dining are the establishments in this category, including three in the theme parks: **Satu'li Canteen** at the Animal Kingdom and **Sunshine Seasons** and **Les Halles Boulangerie–Patisserie**, both at EPCOT. The menu choices are a cut above what you'd typically see at a counter-service location. At Sunshine Seasons, for

LILIANE Les Halles Boulangerie–Patisserie has amazing sandwiches, cheese platters, and quiches and the best sweets ever.

example, chefs prepare grilled salmon on an open cooking surface while you watch, or you can choose from rotisserie chicken or pork, tasty noodle bowls, or large sandwiches made with artisanal breads. Entrées cost about $1–$2 more on average than traditional counter service, but the variety and food quality more than make up for the difference.

VENDOR FOOD Vendors abound at the theme parks, Disney Springs, and the BoardWalk. Offerings include popcorn, ice-cream bars, churros (Mexican pastries), soft drinks, bottled water, and (in theme parks) fresh fruit. Prices include tax; many vendors accept credit cards, charges to your room at a Disney resort, and the Disney Dining Plan (when it's offered). Others take only cash (look for a sign near the register).

DISNEY DINING PLANS

NOTE: AT PRESS TIME, dining plans, including Free Dining, remained temporarily suspended, but Disney says they'll return.

Disney offers prepaid dining plans to accompany its lodging packages (see page 123). They are available to guests at all Disney resorts except the Swan, the Dolphin, the hotels of the Disney Springs Resort Area, and Shades of Green. If you want to sign up for one of Disney's prepaid dining plans, you must do so when you book your Disney resort room or package vacation from Disney or an authorized Disney travel agent (not through an online reseller), have Annual Passes, or be members of the Disney Vacation Club (DVC). Except for DVC members, a three-night minimum stay is typically also required. Overall cost is determined by the number of nights you stay at a Disney resort.

Before you make any dining reservations, you must obtain a theme park reservation. Having a dining reservation inside a theme park doesn't provide access to that park—you still need a park reservation to get in.

Disney's most popular restaurants can run out of reservations months in advance. Also, most Disney restaurants hold no tables at all—none—for walk-in guests. That means it's important to book your dining reservations as soon as you're able (60 days before your visit).

Things to Consider When Evaluating a Disney Dining Plan

Disney offers three dining plans. The standard Disney Dining Plan provides, for each member of your group (age 3 and up) and for each night of your stay, one counter-service meal, one full-service meal, and two snacks at participating Disney dining locations and restaurants, including room service at some Disney resorts (type "Disney Dining Plan locations" into your favorite search engine to find websites listing them all). The plan also includes one refillable drink mug per person, per package, but it can be filled only at Disney-resort counter-service restaurants. For guests age 10 and up, the price for 2020 was $78, including tax; for guests ages 3–9, the price was $30.50 per night. Children younger than age 3 eat free from an adult's plate.

For instance, if you're staying for three nights, you'll be credited with three counter-service meals, three full-service meals, and six snacks for each member of your party. All these meals are placed in a group account. The meals in your account can be used by anyone in your group, on any combination of days, so you're not required to eat every meal every day. This means that, for example, you can skip a full-service meal one day and have two on another day.

The counter-service meal includes

- An entrée (a sandwich, dinner salad, pizza, or the like) or a complete combo meal (such as a burger and fries), plus drink; breakfast is typically a combo platter with eggs, bacon or sausage, potatoes, a biscuit, and a drink.

The full-service sit-down meals include

- An entrée or a complete combo meal, plus drink
- A dessert (except breakfast)

If you're dining at a buffet, the full-service meal includes the food and beverages. Tax is included in the dining plan, but tips are not. Beverage choices include soda, coffee, or tea; one milkshake, smoothie, or specialty hot chocolate; or, for guests age 21 and older, one beer, glass of wine, or cocktail from a predetermined list.

A snack can be any of several single-serving items such as a pretzel or bottle of water. They are often specifically marked as dining plan snacks on menus and may include the following:

- A frozen ice-cream novelty, ice pop, or fruit bar
- A scoop of popcorn
- A 12-ounce coffee, hot chocolate, or hot tea
- A prepackaged container of milk or juice
- A piece of whole fruit
- A bag of snacks
- A 20-ounce bottle of Coca-Cola, Sprite, or Dasani water
- A 20-ounce fountain soft drink

Disney's top-of-the-line restaurants (aka Disney Signature Restaurants), along with Cinderella's Royal Table, the dinner shows, regular room service, and in-room pizza delivery, count as two full-service meals on the standard dining plan.

In addition to the preceding, the following rules apply:

- Everyone staying in the same resort room must participate in the Disney Dining Plan.
- Children ages 3–9 must order from the kids' menu, if available. This rule is occasionally relaxed at Disney's counter-service restaurants, enabling older kids (age 10 and up) to order from the adult menu.
- Alcoholic and specialty beverages are included in the plan.
- A full-service meal can be breakfast, lunch, or dinner. The greatest savings occur when you use your full-service-meal credits for dinner.
- The dining plan expires at midnight on the day you check out of your Disney resort. Unused meals are nonrefundable.
- Neither the Disney Dining Plan nor Disney's Free Dining promotion can be added to a discounted room-only reservation.

QUICK-SERVICE DINING PLAN This plan includes meals, snacks, and drinks at most counter-service eateries and outdoor carts in Walt Disney World. In 2020 the cost was $55.01 per day for guests age 10 and up, and $26 per day for kids ages 3–9. The plan includes two counter-service meals and two snacks per day, in addition to one refillable drink mug per person, per package (eligible for refills only at counter-service locations in your Disney resort).

DISNEY DINING PLAN PLUS This plan offers a choice of two full- or counter-service meals per day at any participating restaurant. It also includes two snacks per day and a refillable drink mug. In 2020 the Plus Plan was $94.60 (including tax) for adults and children age 10 and up, and $35 for children ages 3–9 for each night of your stay.

DISNEY DELUXE DINING PLAN This plan offers a choice of full- or counter-service meals for three meals a day at any participating restaurant. In addition to the three meals a day, the plan also includes two snacks per day and a refillable drink mug. In 2020 the Deluxe Plan was $119 (including tax) for adults and children age 10 and up, and $47.50 for children ages 3–9 for each night of your stay.

In addition to dining plans, the vacation packages include sweeteners, such as a free round of minigolf and discounts on spa treatments, salon services, and recreational activities like water sports.

Disney ceaselessly tinkers with the dining plans' rules, meal definitions, and participating restaurants. Here are some recent examples:

- You can exchange a sit-down meal credit for a counter-service meal, though doing this even once can negate any savings you get from using a plan in the first place.

- At sit-down restaurants, you can substitute dessert for a side salad, cup of soup, or fruit plate.

- You can exchange one sit-down or counter-service meal credit for three snacks at a counter-service location, if you do so within the same transaction. (This is not a good deal.)

- Some counter-service restaurants don't differentiate between adult and child meal credits. If you have two adult credits and two child credits, you can purchase four adult counter-service meals with the credits.

Finally, you can usually use your credits to pay for the meals of people who are not on any dining plan. We've heard of sporadic instances of Disney not allowing this, but we think they're instances of confusion about what the dining-plan rules actually say: The rules say that meals can't be transferred, but they say nothing about meals being shared—as if that could even be enforced.

To ensure that everybody knows the rules, it might help to carry a printout of them with you—see disneyworld.disney.go.com/guest -services/disney-dining-plan. As long as someone enrolled in the dining plan tells the server in advance that he or she plans to redeem the appropriate number of credits and then orders the meals for the diners who aren't enrolled, everything should be on the up and up. Should a server or manager tell you that the rules prohibit meal sharing, just point out that your copy of the rules doesn't say that.

The plan has been one of the most requested of Disney's package add-ons since its introduction; families report that their favorite aspect is the peace of mind that comes from knowing their meals are paid for ahead of time, rather than having to keep track of a budget while they're in the parks. Families also enjoy the communal aspect of sitting down together for a full meal, without having to worry about who's picking up the food or doing the dishes.

Costwise, however, it's difficult for many families to justify using the plan. If you prefer to always eat at counter-service restaurants, you'll be better off with the Quick-Service Plan. You should also avoid the Disney Dining Plan if you have finicky eaters, are visiting during holidays or summer, or can't get reservations at your first- or second-choice sit-down restaurants. In addition, if you have children age 10 and up, be sure they can eat an adult-size dinner at a sit-down restaurant every night; if not, you'd probably come out ahead just paying for everyone's meals without the plan.

If you opt for the plan, skipping one full-service meal during a visit of five or fewer days can mean the difference between saving and losing money. In our experience, having a scheduled sit-down meal for every day of a weeklong vacation can be mentally exhausting, especially for kids. One option might be to schedule a meal at a Disney Signature Restaurant, which requires two full-service credits, and have no scheduled sit-down meal on another night in the middle of your trip, allowing everyone to decide on the spot if they're up for something formal.

As already noted, many of the most popular restaurants are fully booked as soon as their reservation windows open. If you're still interested in the Disney Dining Plan, book your restaurants as soon as possible, typically 60 days before you visit. Then decide whether the plan makes economic sense. For more on Advance Reservations, see page 163.

If you're making reservations to eat at Disney hotels other than your own, having a car allows you to easily access all the participating restaurants. When you use the Disney transportation system, dining at the various resorts can be a logistical nightmare. Those without a car may want to weigh the immediate services of a taxi or ride-hailing service—typically $16–$33 each way across Disney property—against a 50- to 75-minute trip (each way) using Disney transportation.

When Disney offers Free Dining discounts, typically in September, it generally charges rack rate for the hotel. (*Note:* Free Dining was unavailable as we went to press). Room-only discounts are often available at these times, too, meaning you should work out the math to see which discount works best for you, or have a travel agent do it for you.

In most cases we examined, Free Dining was a better deal for families of two adults and up to two kids under age 10 staying at a Value or Moderate resort. The break-even point at a Deluxe resort depended on whether the kids ate like adults.

Readers who try the Disney dining plans have varying experiences. A St. Louis family of three comments:

> *We got the dining plan and would* never *do it again. Far too expensive, far too much food, and then you have to tip on top of the expense. Much easier to buy what you want, where and when you want.*

A Belmont, Massachusetts, dad likes the Quick-Service Plan:

> *If you intend to eat Disney food, the counter-service meal plan is a good option. We didn't want the full plan because the restaurants seemed overpriced, and the necessity of reservations months in advance seemed crazy and a bar to flexibility.*

But a reader from The Woodlands, Texas, laments that the plan has altered the focus of her vacation:

> *For me, the dining plan has taken a lot of the fun out of going to Disney World. Now, dining for each day must be planned months in*

advance unless one is to eat just hot dogs, pizza, and other walk-up items. I want to have fun. I don't want to be locked into a tight schedule, always worrying about where we need to be when it's time to eat, and I don't want to eat when I'm not hungry just because I have a reservation somewhere.

A mom from Orland Park, Illinois, comments on the difficulty of getting Advance Reservations:

It's next to impossible to get table reservations anywhere good. I don't enjoy planning my day exclusively around eating at a certain restaurant at a certain time—but that is what you must do months in advance if you want to eat at a good sit-down restaurant in Disney. That is ridiculous.

On a positive note, many readers report that Disney cast members are much more knowledgeable about the dining plan these days than in the past. A Washington, D.C.–area couple writes:

The kinks are worked out, and everyone at the parks we talked to seemed to get it, but we still spent $40 or more at most sit-down dinners on [additional] drinks and tips.

A Land O' Lakes, Florida, dad bumped into this problem:

We had some trouble with our dining plan being invalidated after checkout, though it was supposed to be valid until midnight of our checkout date. That was annoying because calls to the resort were needed to verify the meals left on our passes for The Crystal Palace and for some snacks later.

The dining plan left a family of five from Nashville, Tennessee, similarly dazed and confused:

What was annoying was the inconsistency. You can get a 16-ounce chocolate milk on the kids' plan, but only 8 ounces of white milk at many places. At Earl of Sandwich, you can get 16 ounces of either kind. A pint of milk would count as a snack (price $1.79), but they wouldn't count a quart of milk (price $2.39) because it wasn't a single serving. However, in Animal Kingdom, my husband bought a water-bottle holder (price $3.75) and used a snack credit.

Reader Tips for Getting the Most Out of a Dining Plan

A mom from Radford, Virginia, shares the following:

Warn people to eat lunch early if they have dinner reservations before 7 p.m. Disney doesn't skimp on food—if you eat a late lunch, you WILL NOT be hungry for dinner.

A mom from Brick Township, New Jersey, found that the dining plan streamlined her touring:

This was great for the kids because we did a character-dining experience every day. This helped us in the parks because we didn't have to wait in line to see the characters. Instead, we got all of our autographs during our meals.

A Saskatoon, Saskatchewan, father of three says it's important to be vigilant when it comes to the outdoor food vendors:

> We had a problem with a vendor who charged us meal service for each of the ice-cream bars we purchased. This became evident at our final sit-down meal, when we didn't have any meal vouchers left. Check the receipts after every purchase!

ADVANCE RESERVATIONS: WHAT'S IN A NAME?

THOUGH THEY'RE CALLED ADVANCE RESERVATIONS, most dining reservations at Disney World don't guarantee you a table at a specific time, as they would at your typical hometown restaurant. Instead, reservations fill time slots. The number of slots available is based on the average length of time that guests occupy a table at a particular restaurant, adjusted for seasonality. When you arrive at a restaurant having made Advance Reservations, your wait to be seated will usually be less than 20 minutes during peak hours, and often less than 10 minutes. If you're a walk-in, especially during busier seasons, expect to either wait 40–75 minutes or be told that no tables are available.

GETTING ADVANCE RESERVATIONS AT POPULAR RESTAURANTS

TWO OF THE HARDEST RESERVATIONS to get in Walt Disney World these days are at EPCOT's **Space 220** and Hollywood Studios' **Oga's Cantina.** Why? The Studios is very popular because of the *Star Wars* and *Toy Story* attractions, and Oga's capacity is very limited. Likewise, Space 220 is, along with **Coral Reef Restaurant,** one of the most picturesque dining locations in the park. You'll have to put in some effort to secure Advance Reservations at these places, especially during busier times of year.

The easiest and fastest way to get a reservation is to go to disney world.disney.go.com/dining starting at 5:45 a.m. Eastern time, a full hour before phone reservations open. To familiarize yourself with how the site works, try it out a couple of days before you actually make reservations. You'll also save time by setting up a **My Disney Experience** account online before your 60-day booking window (see page 37), making sure to enter any credit card information needed to guarantee your reservations.

If you live in California and you have to get up at 2:45 a.m. Pacific time to make a reservation, Disney couldn't care less: There's no limit to the number of hoops they can make you jump through if demand exceeds supply.

Disney's website is usually within a few seconds of the official time as determined by the federal government, accessible online at time.gov. Using this site, synchronize your computer to the second the night before your 60-day window opens if your computer hasn't synchronized automatically already.

Early on the morning on which you want to make reservations, take a few moments to type the date of your visit into a word processor in

MM/DD/YYYY format—for example, 11/16/2023 for November 16, 2023. Select the date, and type **Ctrl-C** (Windows) or **Cmd-C** (Mac) to copy it to your computer's clipboard. This will save you from having to retype the date when the site comes online.

Next, start trying the Disney website about 3 minutes before 5:45 a.m. You'll see a text box where you can specify the date of your visit: Click in the text box; select it (**Ctrl-A** on Windows or **Cmd-A** on Mac); paste in the date you copied earlier (**Ctrl-V** on Windows or **Cmd-V** on Mac; don't right-click to paste—every millisecond counts!); then press the **Tab** key. You'll also see a place to specify the location (such as Magic Kingdom), the time of your meal, and your party size; you can fill in this information ahead of time too. Then click "search times."

If your date isn't yet available, a message will appear saying, "There is a problem searching for reservations at this time" or something similar. If this happens, refresh the browser page and start over. If you don't see an error message, however, the results returned will tell you whether your restaurant has a table available.

Note that while you're typing, other guests are trying to make Advance Reservations, too, so you want the transaction to happen as quickly as possible. Flexibility on your part counts—it's much harder to get seating for a large group, so give some thought to breaking your group into numbers that can be accommodated at tables for four. Also make sure you have your credit card out where you can read it.

Advance Reservations for **Cinderella's Royal Table,** character meals, the *Fantasmic!* and *Harmonious* **Dining Packages, Victoria & Albert's,** and the *Hoop-Dee-Doo Musical Revue* are actual reservations—that is, they require complete prepayment with a credit card at the time of the booking. The name on the booking can't be changed after the reservation is made. Reservations may be canceled, with the deposit refunded in full, by calling 407-WDW-DINE (939-3463) at least 48 hours before seating for these shows (versus 24 hours ahead for regular Advance Reservations). Disney will work with you in the event of an emergency.

If you don't have access to a computer at 5:45 a.m. on the morning you need to make reservations, be ready to call 407-WDW-DINE at 6:45 a.m. Eastern time and follow the prompts to speak to a live person. You may still get placed on hold if call volume is higher than usual, and you'll be an hour behind the early birds with computers. Still, you'll be well ahead of those who didn't make it up before sunrise.

Note that when the Disney Dining Plan returns and you want to book a *Harmonious* or *Fantasmic!* package, Cinderella's Royal Table, or *Hoop-Dee-Doo Musical Revue,* you may be better off reserving by phone anyway. The online system may not recognize your table-service credits, but you can book and pay with a credit card, then call 407-WDW-DINE after 6:45 a.m. and have them credit the charge for the meal back to your card; be aware that this can be a potential hassle if you get an uncooperative cast member. When you get to Walt Disney World, you'll use credits from your dining plan to "pay" for the meal. (Sometimes the online system has glitches and shows no availability; in this case, call after 6:45 a.m. to confirm if the online system is correct.)

NEVER, NEVER, NEVER, NEVER GIVE UP Not getting what you want the first time you try doesn't mean the end of the story. A mom from Cincinnati advises persistence in securing Advance Reservations:

> I was crushed when I called and tried to reserve Chef Mickey's and couldn't. I decided not to give up and would go online once or twice a day to check reservations for Chef Mickey's and the other restaurants I wanted. It took me about a week, but sooner or later I ended up booking every single reservation I wanted except one.

A woman from Franklin, Tennessee, agrees:

> I started trying to get a reservation at Be Our Guest Restaurant about a month out from our vacation. By checking the website whenever I thought of it—morning, noon, and night—I ended up getting not only a lunch reservation but a dinner reservation!

Last-Minute Dining Reservations

Because a fee is charged for failing to cancel an Advance Reservation in time (see page 166), you can often score a last-minute reservation: as long as the reservation holder calls to cancel before midnight the day before, he or she won't be charged, so your best shot at picking up a canceled reservation is to repeatedly call 407-WDW-DINE (939-3463) or visit disneyworld.disney.go.com/dining as often as possible between 10 and 11 p.m.

If you still can't get an Advance Reservation, go to the restaurant on the day you wish to dine, and try for a table as a walk-in. Yes, we've already told you this is a long shot—that said, you may be able to swing it between 2:30 and 4:30 p.m., the hours when most full-service restaurants are most likely to take walk-ins, if they do at all. Your chances of success increase during less-busy times of year or on cold or rainy days during busier seasons. If you don't mind eating late, see if you can get a table during the restaurant's last hour of serving. Disney full-service restaurants in the theme parks can be very hard-nosed about walk-ins: Even if you walk up and see that the restaurant isn't busy, you may still need to visit Guest Services to make a reservation, as a Fayetteville, Georgia, reader relates:

> We went to the Hollywood & Vine check-in podium at DHS to try for walk-in seating because it was an off time—3:30 p.m.—and we could see that the restaurant was virtually empty. But we were turned away for lack of availability. So we walked to Guest Services, obtained a reservation there, walked back to the podium, and were immediately checked in.

Landing an Advance Reservation for Cinderella's Royal Table at dinner is somewhat easier than at lunch (or at breakfast, when offered), but the price is $62 for adults and $37 for children ages 3–9 during peak times of year (prices may vary seasonally by as much as $15–$20). Throw in tax and gratuity, and you're looking at around $260 for one meal for a family of four. But if you're unable to lock up a table for breakfast or lunch, a dinner reservation will at least get your kids inside the castle.

No-Show Penalties

Disney restaurants charge a no-show fee of $10–$25 per person (at Victoria & Albert's, you'll be charged $100 per person if you cancel less than five days before the reservation; if you don't show up or if you cancel within 24 hours of the reservation, the full price will be charged); this has reduced the no-show rate to virtually zero, and these restaurants are booked every day according to their actual capacity. Only one person needs to dine at the restaurant for Disney to consider your reservation fulfilled, even if you have a reservation for more people. Some restaurants booked through OpenTable.com do not have no-show penalties. While Disney says it requires 24 hours' notice, you can cancel up until midnight of the day before your meal in many instances.

THEME PARK RESTAURANTS AND ADMISSION

MANY FIRST-TIME VISITORS to Disney World are surprised to learn that admission to a theme park is required to eat at that park's restaurants. The lone exception is **Rainforest Cafe** at Animal Kingdom, which can be entered from the parking lot just outside the theme park; you must have admission, however, if you want to enter Animal Kingdom after you eat.

If you're booking a meal for a day when you weren't expecting to visit the parks, you'll need to check the restaurant's location to make sure it isn't in a theme park. Also, if you've visited a theme park earlier in the day that's different from the one where your restaurant is located, you'll need the **Park Hopper** option (see page 61) to dine inside the second theme park. Currently, park hopping is allowed only after 2 p.m.

DRESS

DRESS IS INFORMAL at most theme park restaurants, but Disney has a business-casual dress code for some of its resort restaurants: khakis, dress slacks, jeans, or dress shorts with a collared shirt for men and capris, skirts, dresses, jeans, or dress shorts for women. Restaurants with this dress code are **Jiko—The Cooking Place** at Animal Kingdom Lodge, the **Flying Fish** at the BoardWalk, **California Grill** at the Contemporary Resort, **Monsieur Paul** at EPCOT's France Pavilion, **Cítricos** and **Narcoossee's** at the Grand Floridian Resort, **Yachtsman Steakhouse** at the Yacht Club Resort, **Il Mulino** at the Swan hotel, and **Todd English's bluezoo** and **Shula's Steak House** at the Dolphin. **The Edison** at Disney Springs prohibits shorts and worn jeans, in addition to the rules above. **Victoria & Albert's** at the Grand Floridian is the only Disney restaurant that requires men to wear a jacket to dinner (they'll provide one if needed).

THE REALITY OF GETTING LAST-MINUTE DINING RESERVATIONS

IF YOUR VACATION is more than 60 days out and you want to dine at a popular venue such as Be Our Guest Restaurant, following our advice below will get you the table you want more than 80% of the time.

The longer you wait, the more effort you'll have to put in to find a reservation. For example, if you're trying for an early breakfast at Be Our Guest within the next seven days, your chance of finding any table the first time you check is less than 3%, based on our tests. But if you have the time and patience to visit Disney's website around 30 times over the next week—nope, not a typo—you have a 50-50 shot at snapping up a last-minute cancellation.

Besides Be Our Guest, the list below shows the restaurants where capacity and demand make finding a last-minute reservation more difficult. If you're planning a trip within the next 30 days, you'll probably need to seek out alternatives.

- **CHEF MICKEY'S** *(Contemporary Resort)* The food isn't anything special, and neither is the venue. But the draws are the Disney characters and the service, both of which are great.
- **CINDERELLA'S ROYAL TABLE** *(Magic Kingdom)* Reservations are somewhat easier to get for dinner than for lunch.
- **50'S PRIME TIME CAFE** *(Disney's Hollywood Studios)* Although the food is lackluster, 50's Prime Time is entertaining for kids and highly rated by readers.
- **OGA'S CANTINA** *(Disney's Hollywood Studios)* Tiny capacity and photogenic drinks make this the hardest place to get into at the Studios.
- **RAGLAN ROAD** *(Disney Springs)* Long regarded as one of Disney Springs' best restaurants, Raglan Road is tough to book for dinner.
- **SPACE 220** *(EPCOT)* The draw here is the setting, inside a simulated space station, rather than the food.
- **T-REX** *(Disney Springs)* A popular venue for kids because of the theming and dinosaurs. If you can't get a reservation here, join Landry's Select Club (landrysselect .com) to get priority access to T-REX instead.

Also, be aware that smoking is prohibited at all restaurants and lounges on Walt Disney World property. Diners who puff must get their nicotine fix outdoors—and in the theme parks, that also means going to a designated smoking area outside the parks.

FOOD ALLERGIES AND DIETARY NEEDS

IF YOU HAVE FOOD ALLERGIES or observe a specific type of diet (such as eating kosher), make this known when you make your Advance Reservations, and alert your server when you arrive at the restaurant. Be aware that for kosher or other special diets, there is a cancellation charge, to cover the cost of special-ordering individual meal components. Almost all Walt Disney World restaurants have dedicated allergy-friendly menus available upon request. Also, many Disney sit-down restaurants have adapted their dishes so that almost anyone with a common allergy can order off the standard menu. Chefs at sit-down and quick-service locations will go out of their way to accommodate you. If you have any doubts, a chef or cast member trained in special diets will discuss your needs with you before your order is placed. For more details, visit disneyworld.disney.go.com/guest-services/special-dietary -requests, or email specialdiets@disneyworld.com.

A Phillipsburg, New Jersey, mom reports her family's experience:

My 6-year-old has many food allergies. When making my Advance Reservations, I indicated these to the clerk. When we arrived at the restaurants, the staff was already aware of my child's allergies and assigned our table a chef who double-checked the list of allergies with us. The chefs were very nice and made my son feel very special.

To request kosher or halal meals at table-service restaurants, call ☎ 407-WDW-DINE (939-3463) 24 hours in advance. All Disney menus have vegetarian options; vegans may have to talk to the chef.

A FEW CAVEATS

BEFORE YOU BEGIN EATING your way through the World, here's what you need to know:

1. Theme park restaurants rush their customers to make room for the next group of diners. Dining at high speed may appeal to a family with young, restless children, but for people wanting to relax, it's more like eating in a pressure chamber than fine dining.

2. Disney restaurants have comparatively few tables for parties of two, and servers are generally disinclined to seat two guests at larger tables. If you're a duo, you might have to wait longer—sometimes much longer—to be seated.

3. At full-service Disney restaurants, an automatic gratuity of 18% is added to your tab—even at buffets where you serve yourself.

"WAITER, THESE PRICES ARE GIVING ME HEARTBURN!"

INCREASES IN DISNEY'S TICKET COSTS are always sure to grab headlines, but most people don't notice that Disney's restaurant prices rise about as fast. For example, while the inflation-adjusted cost of a 1-day theme park ticket has increased about 73% since 2010, the average lunch entrée price at Le Cellier has gone from around $22 to just under $50—an increase of 109%. For reference, the average meal cost in a US restaurant went up 32% during the same time, according to the Federal Reserve.

You might need a stiff drink after seeing those prices, but alcohol is no bargain either. While the average bottle of wine in WDW costs three times as much as retail, some wines have much higher markups. For example, a $9 bottle of Placido Pinot Grigio costs $45 in EPCOT and various Disney resort lounges—five times as much as the retail price. If you rent a car and eat dinner each day at non-Disney restaurants, you'll save enough to more than pay for the rental cost.

This comment from a New Orleans mom spells it out:

Disney keeps pushing prices up and up. For us, the sky is NOT the limit. We won't be back.

MOBILE ORDERING

THE MY DISNEY EXPERIENCE APP offers this time-saving perk at almost all of Disney's counter-service restaurants. Using the app, you place an order, pay for your meal online, and notify the restaurant when you've arrived for pickup. You'll be directed to a separate window or line to pick up your food, bypassing the regular line. Be sure to keep your app updated to see the latest participating restaurants.

Beyond Mobile Ordering: Tips for Saving Time and Money

Even if you confine your meals to counter-service fare, you lose a lot of time getting food in the theme parks. Not to mention that every time you buy a soda, it's going to set you back more than $4, and everything else from hot dogs to salad is high. You can say, "Oh, well, we're on vacation" and pay the exorbitant prices, or you can plan ahead and save big bucks.

LILIANE All quick-service restaurants will give you free ice water; just ask!

You could rent a condo and prepare your own meals, but you didn't travel all the way to Disney World to cook. So let's be realistic and assume that you'll eat your evening meals out— which is what most families do because, among other reasons, they're too tired to think about cooking. That leaves breakfast and lunch. Here are some ways to minimize the time and money you spend hunting and gathering:

1. Eat breakfast before you arrive. Restaurants outside the World offer some outstanding breakfast specials. Plus, some hotels have small refrigerators in guest rooms, or you can rent a fridge or bring a cooler. If you can get by on cold cereal, pastries, fruit, and juice, this will save a ton of time and money.

2. Prepare sandwiches and snacks to take to the theme parks in hip packs; carry water bottles or rely on drinking fountains. Alternatively, after a good breakfast, buy snacks from vendors instead of eating lunch.

3. All theme park restaurants are busiest between 11:30 a.m. and 2:15 p.m. for lunch and 6 and 9 p.m. for dinner. For shorter lines and faster service, don't eat during these hours, especially 12:30–1:30 p.m.

4. Many counter-service restaurants sell cold sandwiches. Buy a cold lunch minus drinks before 11:30 a.m., and carry it in a small plastic bag until you're ready to eat (within an hour or so of purchase for food-safety reasons). Ditto for dinner. Buy drinks at the appropriate time from any convenient vendor.

5. Most fast-food eateries have more than one service window. Regardless of the time of day, check the lines at all windows before queuing. Sometimes a window that's staffed but out of the way will have a much shorter line or none at all. Note, however, that some windows may offer only certain items.

6. If you're short on time and the park closes early, stay until closing and eat dinner outside Disney World before returning to your hotel. If the park stays open late, eat dinner about 4 or 4:30 p.m. at the restaurant of your choice. You should sneak in just ahead of the dinner crowd.

If you opt to buy groceries, you can stock up at Publix (14928 E. Orange Lake Blvd. and 3221 Vineland Road, both in Kissimmee). There's also a Winn-Dixie on Apopka–Vineland Road, about a mile north of Crossroads Shopping Center. The Super Target on Rolling Oaks Boulevard is the closest to the Western Way entrance. The closest Costco, at 4696 Gardens Park Blvd., is near Universal Orlando.

THE COST OF COUNTER-SERVICE FOOD

Bagel or muffin	$4.50
Brownie	$4.50
Burrito	$11.75–$12.29
Cake or pie	$3.99–$8.00
Cereal with milk	$6–$9
Cheeseburger with fries	$5–$6
Chicken breast sandwich	$11–$14
Chicken nuggets with fries	$10–$11
Children's meal (various)	$7–$9
Chips	$4
Cookie	$3–$8
Fried fish basket with fries	$12–$16
Fries	$5–$7
Fruit (whole)	$2.30–$4.20
Fruit cup / fruit salad	$4–$6
Hot dog	$7–$14
Ice cream / frozen novelties	$6–$13
Nachos with cheese	$6–$12
PB&J sandwich	$7 (kids' meal)–$11
Pizza (personal)	$11–$12
Popcorn	$4–$9
Pretzel	$6–$8
Salad (entrée)	$11–$15
Salad (side)	$4–$10
Smoked turkey leg	$13–$16
Soup / chili	$5–$7
Sub / deli sandwich	$8–$13
Veggie burger	$12–$14

THE COST OF COUNTER-SERVICE DRINKS

DRINK	SMALL	LARGE
Beer	$8	$14
Bottled water	$3.50	$5.50
Coffee	$3.50	$5.75
Latte	$4.25	$5.75
Float, milkshake, or sundae	$4.50	$5.50
Fruit juice	$5	$7
Hot tea and cocoa	$3.50	$5.50
Milk	$2	$3.60
Soft drinks, iced tea, and lemonade	$4	$6

Each person on a Disney Dining Plan (when it's available) gets a free mug, refillable at any Disney resort. There is a short wait between refills: a screen on the soda fountain shows the exact amount of time until guests can fill up their mug again. If you're not on a dining plan and wish to purchase a refillable mug, the cost is $19.99 for the length of your stay at Disney resorts and around $11.99 at the water parks.

FAST FOOD IN THE THEME PARKS

BECAUSE MOST MEALS during a Disney World vacation are consumed on the run while touring, we'll tackle counter-service and vendor foods first. Plentiful in all theme parks are hot dogs, hamburgers, chicken sandwiches, salads, and pizza. They're augmented by special items that relate to the park's theme or the part of the park you're touring. In EPCOT's Germany, for example, counter-service bratwurst and beer are sold. At Liberty Square Market and Prince Eric's Village Market (Fantasyland), vendors sell smoked turkey legs. Counter-service prices are fairly consistent from park to park.

Getting your act together at counter-service restaurants is more a matter of courtesy than necessity. Rude guests rank fifth among reader complaints. A mother from Fort Wayne, Indiana, points out that indecision can be as maddening as outright discourtesy, especially when you're hungry:

Every fast-food restaurant has menu signs the size of billboards, but do you think anybody reads them? People still don't have a clue what they want when they finally get to the counter. If by some miracle they've managed to choose between the hot dog and the hamburger, they then fiddle around another 10 minutes deciding what size Coke to order. Folks, PULEEEZ get your orders together ahead of time!

A North Carolina reader on counter-service food lines:

Many counter-service registers serve two queues each, one to the left and one to the right of each register. People are not used to this and will instinctively line up in one queue per register, typically on the right side, leaving the left vacant. We had register operators wave us

*up to the front several times to start a left queue instead of waiting
behind others on the right.*

Healthful Food at Walt Disney World

Most fast-food counters and even vendors offer health-conscious
choices. All of the major theme parks have fruit stands. See page 199.

HARD CHOICES

DINING DECISIONS WILL DEFINITELY affect your Walt Disney
World experience. If you're short on time and you want to see the theme
parks, avoid full service. Ditto if you're short on funds. If you do want
full service, arrange Advance Reservations—as mentioned above, they
won't actually reserve you a table, but they can minimize your wait.

Integrating Meals into the Unofficial Guide Touring Plans

Arrive before the park of your choice opens. Tour expeditiously, using
your chosen plan (taking as few breaks as possible), until about 11 or
11:30 a.m. Disney World's restaurants are busiest at 12:30 p.m. and
6:30 p.m. Once the park becomes crowded around midday, meals and
other breaks won't affect the plan's efficiency. If you intend to stay in
the park for evening parades, fireworks, or other events, eat dinner early
enough to be finished in time for the festivities.

Character Dining

A number of restaurants, primarily those with
all-you-can-eat buffets and family-style meals,
offer character dining. At character meals, you
pay a fixed price and dine in the presence of one
to five Disney characters who circulate throughout the restaurant, hugging children (and sometimes adults), posing for photos, and signing
autographs. They are served at restaurants in
and out of the theme parks. See page 263 for
more information.

A. J. I don't recommend
getting autographs
during the character din-
ing meals unless
your heart is
really set on it. I
found it stressful
to run to the
buffet, shovel food onto
my plate, and run back to
the table, hoping I didn't
miss a character.

DISNEY DINING SUGGESTIONS

FOLLOWING ARE SUGGESTIONS for dining at each of the major
theme parks. If you want to try a theme-park full-service restaurant, be
aware that the restaurants continue to serve after the park's official
closing time. Don't worry if you're depending on Disney transportation:
Buses, boats, and monorails run 1–2 hours after the parks close.

The Magic Kingdom

Be Our Guest in Fantasyland, **Liberty Tree Tavern** in Liberty Square, and
Jungle Navigation Co. Ltd. Skipper Canteen in Adventureland are the
park's best full-service restaurants. **The Crystal Palace** on Main Street
serves a decent but expensive character buffet. Avoid **Tony's Town**

Square Restaurant on Main Street and **The Diamond Horseshoe** (open seasonally) in Frontierland.

AUTHORS' FAVORITE COUNTER-SERVICE RESTAURANTS
- Columbia Harbour House *Liberty Square*
- Pecos Bill Tall Tale Inn and Café *Frontierland*

These two restaurants offer the most variety within the Magic Kingdom. **Columbia Harbour House**'s offerings include lobster rolls and chicken potpie. **Pecos Bill Tall Tale Inn and Café** serves fabulous tacos and beef nachos and has plenty of seating. Our favorite is the three soft-shell tacos with a selection of ground beef, chicken, spicy beef, or spicy breaded cauliflower (the latter topped with five-spice yogurt and pineapple salsa). Otherwise, the Magic Kingdom's fast-food eateries are undistinguished. They're also about twice as expensive as McDonald's, for about the same quality. On the positive side, portions are large, sometimes large enough for children to share.

Be Our Guest no longer serves breakfast, and the counter-service lunch has also been discontinued. Instead, you can reserve a table for lunch or dinner. It is a prix-fixe menu consisting of an appetizer, a main course, and a trio of desserts. Currently the menu is the same at lunch and dinner, and both are $62 (plus tax and gratuity) for adults. Children (ages 3–9) choose from a separate menu priced at $37.

EPCOT

Since the beginning, dining has been an integral component of EPCOT's entertainment product. World Showcase has many more restaurants than attractions, and EPCOT has added bars, tapas-style eateries, and full-service restaurants faster than any park in memory.

SABRINA I like the mac and cheese at Chefs de France.

For the most part, EPCOT's restaurants have always served decent food, though the World Showcase restaurants have occasionally been timid about delivering honest representations of their host nations' cuisine. While it's true that the less adventuresome diner can find steak and potatoes on virtually every menu, the same kitchens will serve up the real thing for anyone willing to ask.

Many EPCOT restaurants are overpriced, most conspicuously **Chefs de France** (Sabrina's recommendation gives an indication as to why), **Coral Reef Restaurant** (The Seas), and **Monsieur Paul** (France). EPCOT restaurants that combine attractive ambience and well-prepared food with good value are **Biergarten** (Germany), **Rose & Crown** (United Kingdom), **Spice Road Table** (Morocco), **Teppan Edo** (Japan), and **Via Napoli** (Italy). Biergarten also features live entertainment.

In September 2021, **Space 220** opened adjacent to Mission: Space. The "interstellar" restaurant mimics dining in orbit. A special elevator transports you to and from the restaurant, where you dine in front of large "windows" (250-foot digital screens) that show the Earth, moon, and stars. Reservations are hard to get, and the food is good but overpriced. At the France Pavilion, the new addition is **La Crêperie de Paris,**

LILIANE'S TOP 10 DISNEY WORLD SNACKS

FOLLOWING IS A LIST of particularly decadent or unusual snacks available at WDW. These are the goodies worth scouring the parks and resorts for. We've omitted the usual funnel cakes, popcorn, and ice cream available anywhere. Also absent are the truly bizarre snacks, such as the squid treats sold at the Mitsukoshi Department Store in the Japan Pavilion at EPCOT's World Showcase.

10. MILKSHAKES from Beaches & Cream Soda Shop at the Beach Club Resort Hand-dipped, thick, and creamy. When was the last time you sported a milkshake mustache? For large crowds, or large appetites, try the Kitchen Sink: a huge sundae consisting of mountains of ice cream and toppings that is actually served in a kitchen sink.

9. KAKIGŌRI at the Japan Pavilion, EPCOT's World Showcase A little on the sweet side but lighter than ice cream, the shaved ice at this small stand comes in unique flavors, such as honeydew melon, strawberry, and tangerine.

8. GHIRARDELLI SODA FOUNTAIN AND CHOCOLATE SHOP at Disney Springs Marketplace Everything is good, and the atmosphere has a sophisticated ice-cream-shop-plus-coffee-bar vibe. Very San Fran.

7. TURKEY LEGS Available at the Magic Kingdom and EPCOT, these must come from 85-pound turkeys because they're huge, not to mention extra juicy and flavorful. Grab some napkins and go primal on one of these bad boys, and don't worry about the stares you might attract—they're all just jealous.

6. FROZEN CHOCOLATE-COVERED BANANA This treat is available in all the parks and is Liliane's idea of a healthy snack!

5. RONTO WRAP at Disney's Hollywood Studios Available at Ronto Roasters in Star Wars: Galaxy's Edge, a Ronto Wrap consists of roasted pork and grilled pork sausage, topped with peppercorn sauce and tangy slaw and wrapped in a pita. Like the turkey leg, this is a filling snack and a good breakfast, lunch, or dinner!

4. ZEBRA DOMES at Animal Kingdom Lodge Offered as a dessert on the Boma—Flavors of Africa buffet. They consist of a layer of sponge cake topped with cream liqueur mousse and then covered in white chocolate and drizzled with dark chocolate ganache. Fun and yum rolled into one!

3. CHOCOLATE-COVERED PINEAPPLE SPEARS at Big Top Treats in Fantasyland at the Magic Kingdom At EPCOT's Karamell-Küche, the chocolate-covered spears come with caramel and chocolate drizzled on top!.

2. LES HALLES BOULANGERIE–PATISSERIE at the France Pavilion, EPCOT's World Showcase There are simply no words to adequately describe the pastries at this bakery. Try the frangipane or the napoleon. Oh, did we mention the flan tart, the crème brûlée, and the chocolate mousse?

But the number one snack at Walt Disney World is . . .

1. Two words: DOLE WHIP! Available in Adventureland at the Magic Kingdom, Dole Whip is a soft-serve pineapple–ice cream dream. Liliane prefers her Dole Whip with rum, available at Animal Kingdom's Tamu Tamu Refreshments.

Brendan

I love Mickey ice-cream bars. They're a delicious snack!

which offers both sit-down dining and a take-away window (with a smaller snack menu).

Throughout the year EPCOT runs food festivals. Its annual **Food & Wine Festival** runs mid-July–late November; the **International Festival of the Holidays** begins a few days later. **Festival of the Arts** follows that and lasts through late February, and then it's time for **Flower & Garden** from March through July.

While it's not the same as sitting inside a well-themed World Showcase pavilion, food booths have their pluses: There's a lot of variety, the food quality can be quite good, and it's generally faster than a full sit-down meal.

AUTHORS' FAVORITE COUNTER-SERVICE RESTAURANTS

- Les Halles Boulangerie-Patisserie *France*
- Sommerfest *Germany*
- Sunshine Seasons *The Land*
- Tangierine Café *Morocco*

Les Halles Boulangerie–Patisserie sells pastries, sandwiches, and quiche. The pastries are made on-site, and the sandwiches are as close to actual French street food—in taste, size, and price—as you'll get anywhere in EPCOT. Another favorite is the chicken-and-lamb shawarma platter at Morocco's **Tangierine Café.** Besides juicy lamb, it comes with some of the best tabbouleh we've tasted in Florida.

Disney's Animal Kingdom

We recommend that you tour early after a good breakfast, and then graze on vendor food until dinner. Then try **Yak & Yeti** for a moderately priced (for Disney), moderately paced meal, or **Tiffins** if you have a little more time and money.

Animal Kingdom offers a lot of counter-service fast food, along with **Tusker House,** a buffet-style restaurant in Africa, and **Yak & Yeti,** a table-service restaurant in Asia. You'll find plenty of traditional Disney theme park food—hot dogs, hamburgers, and the like—but even the fast food is superior to typical Disney fare. A third full-service restaurant inside the Animal Kingdom, **Tiffins** (an upscale place featuring international cuisine), is located on Discovery Island. **Rainforest Cafe** has entrances both inside and outside the theme park, meaning that you don't have to buy park admission to eat there.

FELICITY The food at the Tusker House buffet is different from all other buffets. I know because I ate at all of them. I love the chicken, mashed potatoes, and gravy; I had three servings.

AUTHORS' FAVORITE COUNTER-SERVICE RESTAURANTS

- Flame Tree Barbecue *Discovery Island*
- Harambe Market *Africa*
- Satu'li Canteen *Pandora*
- Yak & Yeti Local Food Cafes *Asia*

We like **Flame Tree Barbecue** for its waterfront dining pavilions and **Yak & Yeti Local Food Cafes** (just outside the full-service Yak & Yeti) for casual Asian dishes, from egg rolls to crispy honey chicken. **Harambe Market** has several smaller food windows. The park's *Avatar*-themed **Satu'li Canteen** is Pandora's answer to Chipotle's rice bowls. You pick a base of starch, grain, or lettuce; a protein; and garnishes.

Disney's Hollywood Studios

Dining at Disney's Hollywood Studios is less ethnic than at EPCOT and possibly less interesting than at any other park. The Studios has five restaurants for which Advance Reservations are recommended: The

Hollywood Brown Derby, 50's Prime Time Café, Sci-Fi Dine-In Theater, Mama Melrose's Ristorante Italiano, and the Hollywood & Vine buffet.

 FELICITY Mama Melrose's is a very dark restaurant and not that much fun for kids. The upscale **Hollywood Brown Derby** is by far the best restaurant at the Studios. For simple Italian food, including pizza, **Mama Melrose's** is fine; just don't expect anything fancy. At the **Sci-Fi Dine-In Theater,** you eat in little cars at a simulated drive-in movie from the 1950s; you won't find a more entertaining restaurant in Walt Disney World. The food is somewhat better at the **50's Prime Time Café,** where you sit in Mom's time-warp kitchen and scarf down meat loaf while watching clips of vintage TV sitcoms. **Hollywood & Vine** features characters from the Disney Channel during breakfast and lunch, while Minnie and friends have seasonal-themed dinners.

A new sit-down restaurant, **Roundup Rodeo BBQ,** will open in the Studios' Toy Story Land in 2022.

AUTHORS' FAVORITE COUNTER-SERVICE RESTAURANTS

- ABC Commissary *Commissary Lane*
- Backlot Express *Echo Lake*
- Docking Bay 7 Food and Cargo *Star Wars: Galaxy's Edge*

Several restaurants opened with the debut of Star Wars: Galaxy's Edge. **Docking Bay 7 Food and Cargo** is the main eatery of the land. For a quick bite, visit **Ronto Roasters.** Stop at the **Milk Stand** to try the famous blue or green milk. Even though both milks are vegan, neither one is very good. We recommend you try one and share with the family before you spring for buying one for each member of your party. **Oga's Cantina** is the land's main watering hole, where guests enjoy exotic beverages and small plates. At **Kat Saka's Kettle,** go for some colorful kettle-cooked popcorn with sweet, spicy, and savory seasoning. Liliane's favorite brewpub, **BaseLine Tap House,** offers a very limited food selection. Try the cheese and charcuterie platter; at $10, it's a bargain.

READERS' COMMENTS ABOUT DISNEY DINING

EATING IS A POPULAR TOPIC among our readers. In addition to participating in our restaurant survey, they like to share their thoughts with us. The following comments are representative of those we receive.

A reader from Glendale, Illinois, had a positive experience:

> *In general, we were pleasantly surprised. I expected it to be over-priced, generally bad, and certainly unhealthy. There were a lot of options, and almost all restaurants (including counter service) had generally good food and some healthy options. It's not the place to expect fine cuisine—and it's certainly overpriced—but if you understand the parameters, you can eat quite well.*

Here's a 13-year-old girl from Omaha, Nebraska, who doesn't get bent out of shape over one bad meal:

> *Honestly, when was the last time you came home from Disney World and said, "Gosh, my vacation really sucked because I ate at a bad restaurant?"*

From a reader in the United Kingdom:

We had the most fantastic meal at California Grill. Being Central London–living, foodie types, we're very hard to please, but the meal there really was second to none.

We've received consistent raves for Boma—Flavors of Africa:

Please stop telling everyone how wonderful Boma is. I love it so much there, and I don't want everyone to know the secret—it's already difficult to get a table!

A Laurel, Maryland, couple rave about Tiffins:

Tiffins is one of the best restaurants in all of Disney World. It's pricey, but the food is spectacular, and the setting is very quiet and relaxing.

Sanaa, in the Kidani Village section of Animal Kingdom Lodge, impressed an Ellicott City, Maryland, family:

Sanaa is a beautiful restaurant with delicious and inexpensive (for Disney) food that you can't find anywhere else in Walt Disney World. We had a fabulous adults-only evening here, but I would bring children too, for an early dinner overlooking the savanna.

One reader tried three character meals and shared the following:

The Crystal Palace [Magic Kingdom]: *HUGE hit with my kids! We met Eeyore, Pooh, Tigger, and Piglet. The food was great too—lots of choices, and all done very well.*

Chef Mickey's [Contemporary Resort]: *By far the best dining experience we had. And with it being Chef Mickey's, we of course got to meet Mickey, Minnie, Pluto, Goofy, and Donald. A must-do!*

Hollywood & Vine [Hollywood Studios]: *We didn't care for this one at all—if it hadn't been for meeting the Disney Junior characters, we probably wouldn't have picked it. The food was subpar, but the worst was the seating and organization of the characters; most of the tables were booths, which made it very hard for children to get in and out. There was no rhyme or reason to which way the characters were going, and the handlers were nowhere to be found.*

One mom in Columbia, South Carolina, was unimpressed with the character dinners:

Walt Disney World is becoming grossly overpriced. Major piece of advice: Unless your kids love character dining, skip ALL the sit-down restaurants.

A Lombard, Illinois, mom underscores the need to make Advance Reservations:

Please stress that if you want a "normal" dining hour at a specific restaurant, call them as far in advance as possible—IT IS WORTH IT! I wanted to change one reservation about two weeks before our arrival date, and I had a choice of either 7:45 or 9 p.m. for dinner (not feasible with little ones).

COUNTER-SERVICE RESTAURANT MINI-PROFILES

NOTE: MOST, BUT NOT ALL, counter-service restaurants are on the Disney Dining Plan (when it returns). Those *not* on the plan are noted in the blue ratings bar.

To help you find palatable fast food that suits your taste, we provide thumbnail profiles of the theme park counter-service restaurants, listed alphabetically by park. They're rated for quality, portion size, and value. The value rating ranges A–F as follows:

A = Exceptional value, a real bargain	**D** = Somewhat overpriced
B = Good value	**F** = Significantly overpriced
C = Fair value, you get exactly what you pay for	

In addition, we list reader-survey results for each restaurant, expressed as a percentage of positive (👍) responses. We use the following categories to provide context for the percentages:

DINING SURVEY RATINGS SYSTEM		
LABEL	**COUNTER-SERVICE RESTAURANTS**	**SIT-DOWN RESTAURANTS**
Exceptional	Rating of 94% or higher	
Much Above Average	Rating of 91%–94%	
Above Average	Rating of 89%–91%	Rating of 88.5%–91%
Average	Rating of 88%–89%	Rating of 87%–88.5%
Below Average	Rating of 85%–88%	Rating of 84%–87%
Much Below Average	Rating of 80%–85%	Rating of 80%–84%
Do Not Visit	Rating of 79% or lower	

THE MAGIC KINGDOM

Aloha Isle

QUALITY Excellent   **VALUE** B+   **PORTION** Medium   **LOCATION** Adventureland
READER-SURVEY RESPONSES 98% 👍 (Exceptional)

SELECTIONS Dole Whip floats and cups, pineapple upside-down cake, juice, and bottled water.

COMMENTS Located next door to *Walt Disney's Enchanted Tiki Room*. The pineapple Dole Whip soft-serve is a world-famous Disney treat.

Casey's Corner

QUALITY Good   **VALUE** C   **PORTION** Medium   **LOCATION** Main Street, U.S.A.
READER-SURVEY RESPONSES 91% 👍 (Much Above Average)

SELECTIONS Hot dogs, corn dog nuggets, fries, and brownies.

COMMENTS Best to stop at Casey's when it's extra-busy—that's the best guarantee of a fresh bun and hot fries.

Columbia Harbour House

QUALITY Good   VALUE B+   PORTION Medium   LOCATION Liberty Square
READER-SURVEY RESPONSES   91% 👍 (Much Above Average)

SELECTIONS Grilled salmon with vegetable rice, lobster roll, New England clam chowder, and grilled shrimp skewer. Yogurt for dessert. For kids: shrimp skewers, grilled salmon, PB&J Uncrustables sandwich, or chicken strips served with a choice of sides and a choice of a small low-fat milk or a small bottle of Dasani water.

COMMENTS Liliane's favorite is the lobster roll. The upstairs seating is far more quiet than downstairs and has tables near electric outlets, good for recharging your phone.

Cosmic Ray's Starlight Cafe

QUALITY Fair–poor   VALUE C–   PORTION Large   LOCATION Tomorrowland
READER-SURVEY RESPONSES   79% 👍 (Do Not Visit)

SELECTIONS Greek salad, barbecue chicken sandwich, chicken strips, or Angus bacon cheeseburger. Chocolate Bundt cake for dessert. For kids: chicken strips or macaroni & cheese.

COMMENTS Cosmic Ray's is a crowded, high-volume restaurant where you sacrifice food quality and ambience in the name of just getting something to eat.

Friar's Nook

QUALITY Good   VALUE B   PORTION Medium–large   LOCATION Fantasyland
READER-SURVEY RESPONSES   86% 👍 (Below Average)

SELECTIONS Hot dogs and bratwurst with tots.
COMMENTS Unless you're desperate, skip it!

Gaston's Tavern

QUALITY Good   VALUE C   PORTION Medium   LOCATION Fantasyland   READER-SURVEY RESPONSES   93% 👍 (Much Above Average) NOT ON DISNEY DINING PLAN

SELECTIONS Ham-and-Brie sandwich with chips, warm cinnamon roll, and LeFou's Brew (frozen apple juice flavored with toasted marshmallow).

COMMENTS Clever setting, limited menu. The supersweet LeFou's Brew is basically expensive apple juice.

Golden Oak Outpost *(seasonal)*

QUALITY Fair   VALUE C   PORTION Medium   LOCATION Frontierland
READER-SURVEY RESPONSES   77% 👍 (Do Not Visit)

SELECTIONS Fried fish sandwich, French fries topped with chili and cheese, or chicken strips. Chocolate cookie for dessert.
COMMENTS Many better quick-service options are available.

Liberty Square Market

QUALITY Good   VALUE C   PORTION Medium   LOCATION Liberty Square   READER-SURVEY RESPONSES   91% 👍 (Much Above Average) NOT ON DISNEY DINING PLAN

SELECTIONS Turkey legs, pretzel with cheese dip, fruits, and assorted candy.
COMMENTS There's seating nearby, but none of it is covered.

The Lunching Pad

QUALITY Fair   VALUE C   PORTION Medium   LOCATION Tomorrowland
READER-SURVEY RESPONSES 85% 👍 (Below Average)

SELECTIONS Cheese-stuffed pretzel, frozen sodas, classic hot dog.
COMMENTS The frozen carbonated drinks—cola or blue raspberry—are a treat in summer's heat.

Main Street Bakery

QUALITY Good   VALUE B   PORTION Medium   LOCATION Main Street, U.S.A.
READER-SURVEY RESPONSES 92% 👍 (Much Above Average)

SELECTIONS Coffee drinks and teas; breakfast sandwiches and pastries.
COMMENTS Disney-themed Starbucks, with the same food and drinks you'd find in any other. Very crowded at park opening and mealtimes.

Pecos Bill Tall Tale Inn and Cafe

QUALITY Good   VALUE C   PORTION Medium-large   LOCATION Frontierland
READER-SURVEY RESPONSES 86% 👍 (Below Average)

SELECTIONS Pork fajita platter with rice and beans, beef nachos, and cheeseburger. For kids: cheeseburger, mac and cheese, beef or chicken taco, or chicken rice bowl. Greek yogurt or nugget churros for dessert.
COMMENTS These items are an improvement over the old burgers.

Pinocchio Village Haus

QUALITY Fair-poor   VALUE D   PORTION Medium   LOCATION Fantasyland
READER-SURVEY RESPONSES 81% 👍 (Much Below Average)

SELECTIONS Flatbreads, tomato-basil soup. For kids: flatbreads; chicken strips, or PB&J Uncrustables sandwich.
COMMENTS An easy stop for families in Fantasyland, but it's usually crowded. Consider Columbia Harbour House, only a few minutes' walk away (it's tastier, too).

Tomorrowland Terrace Restaurant *(seasonal)*

QUALITY Fair   VALUE C-   PORTION Medium-large   LOCATION Tomorrowland
READER-SURVEY RESPONSES 87% 👍 (Below Average)

SELECTIONS Chicken and shrimp platter, lobster roll. For kids: PB&J Uncrustables sandwich.
COMMENTS Ratings have improved over the past year, probably because the Terrace was serving the menu from Columbia Harbour House. Grab an outdoor table and watch the castle lit by fireworks.

Tortuga Tavern *(seasonal)*

QUALITY Fair   VALUE B   PORTION Medium-large   LOCATION Adventureland
READER-SURVEY RESPONSES 75% 👍 (Do Not Visit)

SELECTIONS Hot dogs; sandwich with peanut butter, chocolate-hazelnut spread, and banana.
COMMENTS Large, shaded eating area.

EPCOT

L'Artisan des Glaces

QUALITY Excellent   VALUE C   PORTION Large   LOCATION France   READER-SURVEY RESPONSES 97% 👍 (Exceptional)   NOT ON DISNEY DINING PLAN

SELECTIONS Flavors change but can include vanilla, chocolate, mint choco-late, salted caramel, and coffee ice creams. Sorbet flavors can include strawberry, mango, lemon, and mixed berry. Over-21s can enjoy two scoops in a martini glass, topped with a shot of Grand Marnier, rum, or whipped cream–flavored vodka.

COMMENTS Hands down, the best ice cream at Disney World, freshly made on the spot. Our white chocolate–coconut had shaved fresh coconut in it. The chocolate macaron ice-cream sandwich is worth every calorie.

La Cantina de San Angel

QUALITY Good **VALUE** B **PORTION** Medium-large **LOCATION** Mexico
READER-SURVEY RESPONSES 89% 👍 (Above Average)

SELECTIONS Tacos with seasoned beef, chicken, or shrimp; fried cheese empanadas; grilled chicken with Mexican rice, corn, guacamole, and torti-llas; churros and margaritas. For kids, empanadas, chicken tenders, or mac and cheese.

COMMENTS The cantina is a popular spot for a quick meal, with 150 covered outdoor seats. When it's extra-busy, the back of La Hacienda's dining room is opened for air-conditioned seating.

Connections Cafe and Eatery

QUALITY Good **VALUE** B **PORTION** Medium **LOCATION** World Celebration
READER-SURVEY RESPONSES 90% 👍 (Above Average)

SELECTIONS The extensive Eatery menu features French bistro, Mediterra-nean, Southwestern, and banh mi burgers. General Tso chicken salad and Niçoise-style salad are also on the menu. Kids will enjoy pizza or chicken breast nuggets. There is also a Starbucks inside Connection Café with the usual brand offerings. We recommend the Liège waffle for dessert.

COMMENTS The Eatery replaced the demolished Electric Umbrella.

Crêpes Á Emporter by La Crêperie de Paris

QUALITY Good **VALUE** B **PORTION** Medium **LOCATION** France
READER-SURVEY RESPONSES 78% 👍 (Do Not Visit)

SELECTIONS At this spot just outside the sit-down restau-rant La Crêperie de Paris, guests can order either sweet crepes (topped with vanilla or chocolate ice cream, hazel-nut-chocolate spread, red berries, or butter and sugar) or savory galettes (cream of Brie; ratatouille; or béchamel, cheese, and ham).

COMMENTS Liliane thinks that, if you want to enjoy great crepes, pick the least "loaded" one and enjoy!

BRENDAN Each member of your party should try a different crepe at La Crepêrie de Paris so you can taste-test all of them.

Fife & Drum Tavern

QUALITY Fair **VALUE** C **PORTION** Large **LOCATION** United States
READER-SURVEY RESPONSES 87% 👍 (Below Average)

SELECTIONS Turkey legs, popcorn, ice cream, frozen slushes, wine, beer, alcoholic lemonade, and root beer.

COMMENTS Great place to grab a drink before a show at American Gardens Theatre. Seating is also available in and around the Regal Eagle Smoke-house, behind the Fife & Drum.

Les Halles Boulangerie–Patisserie

QUALITY Good   **VALUE** A   **PORTION** Small-medium   **LOCATION** France
READER-SURVEY RESPONSES   95% 👍 (Exceptional)

SELECTIONS Sandwiches (ham and cheese; turkey BLT; chicken breast; Brie, cranberry, and apple); imported-cheese plates; quiches; soups; pastries.

COMMENTS Les Halles is a wonderful spot for a quiet breakfast. Usually crowded starting at lunch and stays that way throughout the day. One of Liliane's favorite counter-service restaurants in all of Disney World.

Kabuki Cafe

QUALITY Good   **VALUE** B   **PORTION** Small   **LOCATION** Japan
READER-SURVEY RESPONSES   95% 👍 (Exceptional)

SELECTIONS Sushi, including California roll with cucumber, crab, and avocado; Nigiri combo with with salmon, tuna, and shrimp; edamame; shaved ice flavored with fruit or milk, such as strawberry, melon, cherry, or tangerine; Japanese beer, including a frozen Kirin, slushie style; wine and sake; sodas.

COMMENTS The sushi is frequently premade and comes as four bite-size pieces, small enough to be a snack without ruining your appetite for something else later in World Showcase. Share a frozen Kirin.

Katsura Grill

QUALITY Good   **VALUE** B   **PORTION** Small-medium   **LOCATION** Japan
READER-SURVEY RESPONSES   85% 👍 (Below Average)

SELECTIONS Sushi; udon noodle bowls; chicken and beef teriyaki; chicken-cutlet curry; edamame; miso soup; cheesecake; teriyaki chicken kid's plate; Kirin beer, sake, and plum wine.

COMMENTS Great spot to grab some sushi and sit outside.

Kringla Bakeri Og Kafe

QUALITY Good-excellent   **VALUE** B   **PORTION** Small-medium   **LOCATION** Norway
READER-SURVEY RESPONSES   94% 👍 (Exceptional)

SELECTIONS Pastries and desserts; imported beer.

COMMENTS Try the school bread or the rice cream (not a typo). Shaded outdoor seating.

Lotus Blossom Café

QUALITY Fair   **VALUE** C   **PORTION** Medium   **LOCATION** China
READER-SURVEY RESPONSES   81% 👍 (Much Below Average)

SELECTIONS Pork egg rolls, pot stickers, orange chicken, caramel-ginger or lychee ice cream, plum wine, T-Cha Jasmine draft beer.

COMMENTS The food is mediocre.

Refreshment Outpost

QUALITY Good   **VALUE** B-   **PORTION** Small   **LOCATION** Between Germany and China
READER-SURVEY RESPONSES   89% 👍 (Above Average)

SELECTIONS Hot dogs, frozen slushes, ice-cream floats, seasonal draft beer, and Mango Starr (mango purée and Starr African rum).

COMMENTS The hot dogs here aren't bad at all, but there are plenty of better dining options within a few minutes' walk. Often serves African dishes during the Food & Wine festival.

Refreshment Port

QUALITY Good **VALUE** B– **PORTION** Medium **LOCATION** Near Canada
READER-SURVEY RESPONSES 92% 👍 (Much Above Average)

SELECTIONS Poutine (fries, brisket, beef gravy, cheese curds) and ice cream.
COMMENTS Almost everyone in line is here for the ice cream. For the poutine, it helps to be Canadian.

Regal Eagle Smokehouse: Craft Drafts & Barbecue

QUALITY Good **VALUE** B **PORTION** Large **LOCATION** United States
READER-SURVEY RESPONSES 92% 👍 (Much Above Average)

SELECTIONS Craft beer and barbecue, of course! Kiddos can enjoy a burger, barbecue chicken leg or chicken salad, and even a barbecue rib platter, all served with their choice of two sides. Banana pudding or s'mores brownie for dessert. Beer and cider from around the United States is served, as well as wines from the West Coast. An outdoor bar has craft brews on draft, and the outdoor seating area is a great place to relax.
COMMENTS A huge improvement over what was here before, Regal Eagle serves passable barbecue in hearty portions, with the Texas brisket (on garlic toast) being our favorite. If you're craving more, **The Polite Pig** at Disney Springs sets the standard in Walt Disney World.

Rose & Crown Pub

QUALITY Good **VALUE** C+ **PORTION** Medium **LOCATION** United Kingdom **READER-SURVEY RESPONSES** 95% 👍 (Exceptional) **NOT ON DISNEY DINING PLAN**

SELECTIONS Fish-and-chips; Scotch egg (hard-boiled, wrapped in sausage, and deep-fried); Guinness, Harp, and Bass beers, as well as other spirits.
COMMENTS Most of the crowd is here to drink in an authentic British pub. Outside the pub is **Yorkshire County Fish Shop** (see page 184), which serves food to go. Liliane thinks there's nothing better than fish-and-chips with a cold Harp.

Sommerfest

QUALITY Fair **VALUE** C **PORTION** Medium **LOCATION** Germany
READER-SURVEY RESPONSES 86% 👍 (Below Average)

SELECTIONS Bratwurst with sauerkraut, pretzel bread pudding, and German wine and beer.
COMMENTS Grab a spot in the courtyard to indulge in a hearty sausage and a cold Pilsner. Skip the pretzel bread pudding.

Sunshine Seasons

QUALITY Excellent **VALUE** A **PORTION** Medium **LOCATION** The Land
READER-SURVEY RESPONSES 86% 👍 (Below Average)

SELECTIONS Sunshine Seasons, a food court–like counter-service venue, consists of food stations. The Grill offers wood-fired rotisserie chicken and grilled fish with seasonal vegetables. At the sandwich station, go for the

Mediterranean vegetable sandwich; meat lovers will enjoy the roast beef. At the Asian shop, go for the Mongolian beef or the stir-fried shrimp dish. The soup-and-salad station offers soups made daily and unusual creations such as the Power Salad (quinoa, almonds, and chicken). In addition to these, Sunshine Seasons also has several grab-and-go stations where you can get prepackaged food. On the kids' menu are pizza rolls (cheese or pepperoni) and mac and cheese. Currently open for lunch and dinner.

COMMENTS We think the low reader ratings are due to the long lines to get food and pay, not the quality of the food.

Tangierine Café

QUALITY Good **VALUE** B **PORTION** Medium **LOCATION** Morocco
READER-SURVEY RESPONSES 92% 👍 (Much Above Average)

SELECTIONS Grilled chicken, lamb, or beef kebabs with couscous, tomato-onion salad, and aioli; stone-baked Moroccan bread served with hummus and dips.

COMMENTS Tangierine Café was one of the highest-rated quick-service eateries in EPCOT before the pandemic. It was run by a third party that pulled out during the pandemic. Disney now runs the place and has drastically shrunk the menu. But the food remains much better than average, and it's a lovely spot to dine.

Yorkshire County Fish Shop

QUALITY Good **VALUE** B+ **PORTION** Medium **LOCATION** United Kingdom
READER-SURVEY RESPONSES 97% 👍 (Exceptional)

SELECTIONS Fish-and-chips, Bass ale draft, Harp lager.

COMMENTS There's usually a line for the crisp, hot fish-and-chips at this convenient fast-food window attached to the Rose & Crown Pub. Outdoor seating overlooks the lagoon.

DISNEY'S ANIMAL KINGDOM

Creature Comforts

QUALITY Good **VALUE** C **PORTION** Small **LOCATION** Discovery Island near Africa
READER-SURVEY RESPONSES 96% 👍 (Exceptional)

SELECTIONS Coffee drinks and teas; sandwiches and pastries.

COMMENTS Disney-themed Starbucks. The fare is largely the same as you'd find at any other, plus the occasional Animal Kingdom–themed treat.

Flame Tree Barbecue

QUALITY Excellent **VALUE** B- **PORTION** Large **LOCATION** Discovery Island
READER-SURVEY RESPONSES 96% 👍 (Exceptional)

SELECTIONS St. Louis–style ribs; smoked half-chicken; pulled-pork sandwich; pulled-chicken salad; ribs-and-chicken combo served with baked beans and coleslaw; sausage, egg, and cheese biscuit; spinach and feta quiche; child's plate of baked chicken drumstick, hot dog, or PB&J sandwich; pulled pork platter; Safari Amber and Bud Light beer; wine. For desert, cupcake or frozen mango slushie.

COMMENTS One of our favorites for lunch. Shaded outdoor seating overlooks the water. Offers a huge allergy-friendly menu.

Harambe Market

QUALITY Good	VALUE B	PORTION Large	LOCATION Africa
READER-SURVEY RESPONSES 95% 👍 (Exceptional)			

SELECTIONS Ribs or chicken bowl or a combo thereof, salad with or without chicken. Beer and Leopard's Eye (Snow Leopard vodka blended with kiwi-and-mango-flavored Bibo). The kids' menu includes a chicken bowl and chicken nuggets.

COMMENTS Plenty of shaded seating. Modeled after a typical real-life market in an African nation during the 1960s colonial era. The spice-rubbed ribs and chicken bowl are our favorites.

Kusafiri Coffee Shop and Bakery

QUALITY Good	VALUE B	PORTION Medium	LOCATION Africa	READER-SURVEY RESPONSES 94% 👍 (Exceptional) NOT ON DISNEY DINING PLAN

SELECTIONS Sausage, egg, and cheese biscuit and assorted muffins for breakfast. Chicken or pork flatbread for lunch.

COMMENTS The colossal cinnamon roll is a favorite anytime.

Pizzafari

QUALITY Fair	VALUE C	PORTION Medium	LOCATION Discovery Island
READER-SURVEY RESPONSES 73% 👍 (Do Not Visit)			

SELECTIONS Cheese or pepperoni personal pizzas; Caesar salad with or without chicken. Plant-based Greens and Grains Salad. Kids' choices: mac and cheese, cheese pizza, or PB&J. Cupcake for desert. Beer available.

COMMENTS Hectic at peak mealtimes, but there's lots of seating. The pizza is unimpressive but popular. Better options are at **Harambe Market.**

Restaurantosaurus

QUALITY Fair	VALUE C	PORTION Medium-large	LOCATION DinoLand U.S.A.
READER-SURVEY RESPONSES 87% 👍 (Below Average)			

SELECTIONS Angus bacon cheeseburger; chicken nuggets; Cobb salad with chicken; hot dogs; kids grilled chicken strips, mac and cheese, cheeseburger.

COMMENTS Plenty of seating.

Satu'li Canteen

QUALITY Good	VALUE A	PORTION Medium	LOCATION Pandora
READER-SURVEY RESPONSES 96% 👍 (Exceptional)			

SELECTIONS Beef, chicken, shrimp, or tofu bowls served over a base of grains or vegetables with sauce. For dessert try the blueberry cream cheese mousse served with passion fruit curd or the chocolate cake served on a cookie layer and topped with banana cream.

COMMENTS Most meals are also available as kids' meals, with only a few non-Pandora-inspired offerings for children. The food is a welcome departure from regular park fare but doesn't work for unadventurous or picky eaters. Breakfast is offered seasonally. Has a huge allergy-friendly menu.

Yak & Yeti Local Food Cafes

QUALITY Fair	VALUE C	PORTION Large	LOCATION Asia
READER-SURVEY RESPONSES 91% 👍 (Much Above Average)			

SELECTIONS At breakfast: breakfast bowls with scrambled eggs, potatoes, peppers, onions, and cheese; sausage and egg English muffins; yogurt; fruit salad; French toast for kids. At lunch: honey chicken, Korean fried chicken sandwich or teriyaki chicken salad. Kids menu is the usual cheeseburger, chicken strips, or PB&J.

COMMENTS For filling up when you're in a hurry.

DISNEY'S HOLLYWOOD STUDIOS

ABC Commissary

QUALITY Fair   VALUE D   PORTION Medium-large   LOCATION Commissary Lane
READER-SURVEY RESPONSES   86% 👍 (Below Average)

SELECTIONS Shrimp tacos, pork carnitas served on flour tortillas, Mediterranean salad, chicken club sandwich. For the kids: turkey sandwich, pork taco, or grilled ham and cheese sandwich. For dessert: mint–chocolate chip cheesecake or tropical tart. Has plenty of gluten-free and allergy-free menu items.

COMMENTS One of the few places that has made substantial improvements in food quality.

Backlot Express

QUALITY Fair   VALUE C   PORTION Medium-large   LOCATION Echo Lake
READER-SURVEY RESPONSES   88% 👍 (Average)

SELECTIONS One-third-pound Angus cheeseburger; Southwest chicken salad; Cuban sandwich. For kids: chicken strips, mac and cheese; Wookie cookie for dessert.

COMMENTS BB-8's stein with unlimited refills is Liliane's favorite. The seating areas have fun movie props. Indoor and outdoor seating available. Huge allergy-friendly menus.

Catalina Eddie's

QUALITY Fair   VALUE C   PORTION Medium-large   LOCATION Sunset Boulevard
READER-SURVEY RESPONSES   67% 👍 (Do Not Visit)

SELECTIONS Cheese and pepperoni pizzas, Caesar salad with chicken, and chocolate mousse. For kids: cheese or pepperoni pizza.

COMMENTS Seldom crowded. Nothing to write home about.

Docking Bay 7 Food and Cargo

QUALITY Excellent   VALUE A   PORTION Medium   LOCATION Galaxy's Edge
READER-SURVEY RESPONSES   92% 👍 (Much Above Average)

SELECTIONS Smoked Kaadu ribs—named after the creature Jar Jar rode in *Episode I* but actually pork—are cut vertically to give them an alien appearance, then glazed with a sticky-sweet sauce and served with down-home blueberry corn muffins. Endorian Tip Yip (chicken) is roasted on a quinoa-curry salad or compressed into cubes, deep-fried, and served with a roasted vegetable-potato mash and herb gravy. Vegans will enjoy the Felucian Kefta (plant-based meatballs) with hummus, cucumber relish, and pita. While pescatarians can try the chilled Peka Tuna Poke. For dessert, Outpost Puff (a chocolate pastry filled with guajillo chocolate mousse and finished with Thai tea panna cotta and spiced pineapple). Kids' offerings include a version of the fried chicken Tip Yip and Ithorian Pasta Rings (a plant-based "meat" marinara sauce with a side of vegetables). This counter-service eatery is currently closed for breakfast. Once it becomes available again, and we are sure it will, try the overnight oats—they are delicious!

COMMENTS Most items are above average in terms of quality. The Tip Yip chicken is moist and flavorful, as is the plant-based kefta. Note that the kids' menu isn't particularly child-friendly. In keeping with the idea that you're on an alien plant, most of the food isn't in recognizable shapes or colors.

Dockside Diner

QUALITY Fair   VALUE C   PORTION Small-medium   LOCATION Echo Lake
READER-SURVEY RESPONSES 80% 👍 (Much Below Average)

SELECTIONS Shrimp salad roll; chipotle chicken salad roll; PB&J or macaroni and cheese for kids.

COMMENTS Limited seating at nearby picnic tables.

Fairfax Fare

QUALITY Fair   VALUE B   PORTION Medium-large   LOCATION Sunset Boulevard
READER-SURVEY RESPONSES 81% 👍 (Much Below Average)

SELECTIONS Pretzel dog, all-beef quarter-pound hot dog, all-beef quarter-pound dog with bacon and mac-and-cheese topping.

COMMENTS There are much better options in the park.

PizzeRizzo

QUALITY Poor   VALUE D   PORTION Large   LOCATION Grand Avenue
READER-SURVEY RESPONSES 81% 👍 (Much Below Average)

SELECTIONS Personal pizzas, meatball subs, antipasto salad, cannoli.

COMMENTS Unmemorable pizza. Umbrella-shaded tables outdoors.

Ronto Roasters

QUALITY Good   VALUE B   PORTION Medium   LOCATION Galaxy's Edge
READER-SURVEY RESPONSES 95% 👍 (Exceptional)

SELECTIONS Ronto Wrap (flatbread sandwich filled with roast pork and grilled sausage) and grilled zucchini wrap. Breakfast options available.

COMMENTS A disgruntled smelting droid named 8D-J8 does the cooking here, turning mysterious alien meats on a rotating spit beneath a recycled pod-racing engine. The sandwiches are delicious. Wash it down with a nonalcoholic Tatooine Sunset (unsweetened tea with melon and blueberry lemonade) or a Surly Sarlacc (grapefruit and rose vodka, raspberry lemonade, and spicy mango flowers).

Rosie's All-American Café

QUALITY Fair   VALUE C   PORTION Medium   LOCATION Sunset Boulevard
READER-SURVEY RESPONSES 82% 👍 (Much Below Average)

SELECTIONS Cheeseburgers; chicken nuggets; fries; foot-long all-beef hot dog; salad with pulled pork. The kids' menu is bare: cheeseburgers and chicken breast nuggets. S'mores cupcake for dessert.

COMMENTS A quick stop on the way to Tower of Terror or Rock 'n' Roller Coaster. Plenty of shaded seating.

The Trolley Car Cafe

QUALITY Good VALUE B PORTION Small LOCATION Hollywood Boulevard
READER-SURVEY RESPONSES 91% 👍 (Much Above Average)

SELECTIONS Coffee drinks and teas; sandwiches and pastries.

COMMENTS The pink-stucco Spanish Colonial facade of this Disney-themed Starbucks calls to mind Old Hollywood, while the industrial-style interior is themed to evoke a trolley-car switching station. The fare is largely the same as you'd find at any other Starbucks.

Woody's Lunch Box

QUALITY Excellent VALUE A– PORTION Medium-large LOCATION Toy Story Land
READER-SURVEY RESPONSES 90% 👍 (Above Average)

SELECTIONS Breakfast: breakfast bowl with scrambled eggs, potato barrels (tater tots), and country gravy. Lunch and dinner: sandwiches (barbecue brisket, smoked turkey, grilled three-cheese); tomato-basil soup; "totchos" (potato barrels smothered with chili, queso, and corn chips). Grilled cheese and turkey sandwiches are available for kids, but they will eagerly eat from the adult menu, especially the totchos!

COMMENTS Health alert: The potato barrels and lunch box tarts are not what you want for your child; healthier options are available elsewhere. There is limited seating at nearby picnic tables with umbrellas. Use mobile ordering here to avoid long waits in line.

DISNEY'S FULL-SERVICE RESTAURANTS

LILIANE Young children are the rule, not the exception, at Disney restaurants.

DISNEY RESTAURANTS offer excellent opportunities to introduce kids to the variety and excitement of ethnic food. No matter how formal a restaurant appears, the staff is accustomed to wiggling, impatient, and often boisterous children. **Chefs de France** at EPCOT, for example, may be the only French restaurant where most patrons wear shorts and T-shirts and at least two dozen young diners are attired in basic black . . . mouse ears.

Almost all Disney restaurants offer children's menus, and all have booster seats and high chairs. They understand how tough it may be for kids to sit for an extended period of time, and waiters will supply little ones with crackers and rolls and serve your dinner much faster than in comparable restaurants elsewhere. In fact, we have received lots of complaints from guests who felt rushed through their meals. At restaurants with prix fixe menus, such as **'Ohana** at the Polynesian, Disney seems to bring your food out at warp speed. Unless you have little children and welcome the quick turnaround, we say take your time and eat at your own pace.

EPCOT

Kids most enjoy Biergarten in Germany, San Angel Inn in Mexico, Coral Reef Restaurant at World Nature, and the character meals at Akershus

Royal Banquet Hall at the Norway Pavilion. **Biergarten** combines a rollicking and noisy atmosphere with good basic food, including pork roast and German sausages. A German oompah band entertains, and kids can often participate in Bavarian dancing. **San Angel Inn** is in the Mexican village marketplace. From the table, children can watch boats on the Gran Fiesta Tour drift beneath a smoking volcano. With a choice of tacos and other familiar items, picky children usually have no difficulty finding something to eat. (Be aware, though, that the service here is sometimes glacially slow.) **Coral Reef,** with tables beside windows looking into The Seas' aquarium, offers a colorful meal-time diversion for all ages. If your kids don't eat fish, Coral Reef also serves beef and chicken. The downside is that the food is extremely expensive. **Akershus Royal Banquet Hall** (*temporarily closed*) offers breakfast (smorgasbord of dilled salmon, mackerel, and goat cheese), as well as lunch and dinner (smorgasbord of meats, cheeses, seafood, and salads; herb-roasted chicken with potatoes; grilled salmon; cheese-and-spinach-stuffed pasta; and kjottkake—beef-and-pork meatballs served with mashed potatoes, vegetables, and lingonberry sauce). For kids: mac and cheese, grilled chicken, cheese pizza, salmon, and meatballs. The character meal is super expensive, but you pay for face time with the princesses.

FELICITY The San Angel Inn is really dark, making it difficult to eat. It was hard to sit through dinner knowing that the Gran Fiesta Tour boats were nearby. I just wanted to get up and ride it over and over again.

As mentioned on page 173, **Space 220** is an overpriced, outer space–themed restaurant at World Discovery. Will the kids like the views from the restaurant, the "Stellarvator" ride, and the trading cards that come with all kids' drinks? Yes! Is it worth your money? Absolutely not! Read Liliane's review here: theunofficialguides.com/2022/06/02/space-220-interstellar-dining-at-epcot.

While certainly not cheap, **Spice Road Table** provides the added value of a great location. Situated along the edge of World Showcase Lagoon in the Morocco Pavilion, it serves Mediterranean-inspired small plates similar to Spanish tapas, and its outdoor terrace provides views for fireworks at night. Kids will like sitting outside, and the small plates can be shared. The entire family will enjoy the fireworks while Mom and Dad have a nice glass of wine.

The Magic Kingdom

Be Our Guest Restaurant and **Cinderella's Royal Table,** both in Fantasyland, are the hot tickets here, but reservations are often well-nigh impossible to get. For the best combination of food and entertainment, book a character meal at **The Crystal Palace.**

In Adventureland **Jungle Navigation Co. Ltd. Skipper Canteen** offers extensive, exciting, and very pricey choices—including char siu pork and Kungaloosh! dessert (chocolate cake with caramelized bananas and cashew-caramel ice cream).

FELICITY The Crystal Palace is amazing. The breakfast lasagna is yummy, and the fluffy characters are super nice to cuddle.

Disney's Hollywood Studios

All ages enjoy the atmosphere and entertainment at the **Sci-Fi Dine-In Theater Restaurant** and the **50's Prime Time Café.** Unfortunately, the Sci-Fi's food is close to dismal, with the exception of dessert. Theme aside, children enjoy the character meals at **Hollywood & Vine,** and the pizza at **Mama Melrose's** never fails to please. **The Hollywood Brown Derby** offers fine dining in the park. **Roundup Rodeo BBQ,** a much-needed new table-service restaurant inside Toy Story Land, is set to open sometime in 2022. No opening date has been announced, but you can be certain it will be very popular.

A. J. The Sci-Fi Dine-In Theater is the best themed restaurant. You sit in a convertible booth, watch old sci-fi movie trailers and cartoons, and drink milkshakes. What's better than that?

FELICITY I knew you had to watch your manners and eat all your food, including the vegetables, at 50's Prime Time. This made me pretty nervous. Our server was nice and friendly, but I kept wondering if she was going to tell me off.

Disney's Animal Kingdom

The four full-service restaurants here are **Tusker House Restaurant** (a character buffet); **Rainforest Cafe,** a favorite of children; **Yak & Yeti Restaurant;** and **Tiffins.** Both Bob and Liliane agree that Tiffins is the best restaurant inside the theme parks.

FAVORITE EATS AT DISNEY SPRINGS

MARKETPLACE

Earl of Sandwich | Sandwich paradise

Ghirardelli Soda Fountain & Chocolate Shop | Ice cream and chocolate treats

T-REX | Burgers, ribs, pasta, and kids' menu in a Jurassic setting with animatronic dinosaurs

WEST SIDE

Food Trucks at Exposition Park | A world of choices, including macaroni and cheese and tacos

House of Blues | Cajun food and kids' menu. For shows in the music hall next door, check out hob.com. | *Table service only*

Jaleo | Authentic Spanish cuisine, including tapas, paella, and Serrano and Ibérico ham by celebrity chef José Andrés. | *Table service only*

Pepe by José Andrés | A grab-and-go dining spot in front of Jaleo with sandwiches and sangria

Starbucks | Bistro boxes, coffee and tea, croissants, pastries, and salads

THE LANDING AND TOWN CENTER

Amorette's Patisserie | Mini cakes

Blaze Fast-Fire'd Pizza | Best pizza ever. Lines are out the door—that should tell you enough!

Cookes of Dublin | Next to Raglan's Irish Pub and Restaurant. Serves fish-and-chips (also available as a kids' portion) and much more!

Morimoto Asia | Pan-Asian food. Inside is table service only, but Morimoto Street Food, a window on the outdoor patio, serves octopus fritters, baby ribs, pork egg rolls, and noodles at a reasonable price.

Raglan Road Irish Pub and Restaurant | Irish food and live music | *Table service only*

Specialty Restaurants

As you've undoubtedly noticed by now, Disney World is trend-savvy, and every market share has its niche. So if you've become accustomed to oak-fired filet of beef, the **California Grill** atop the Contemporary Resort will oblige. Great sushi can be had at **Teppan Edo** at Japan in EPCOT and at **Kimonos** in the Swan hotel. The best and biggest, though way overpriced, steaks are at **Shula's Steak House** in the Dolphin, **Le Cellier Steakhouse** at the Canada Pavilion, and **Yachtsman Steakhouse** at the Yacht Club. At EPCOT's Italy, **Via Napoli,** an authentic Neapolitan pizzeria, features wood-burning ovens and imports water from a source that most resembles the water in Naples, home of some of the world's best pizza dough. The 300-seat pizzeria has both indoor and outdoor dining. In Mexico, the counter-service **La Cantina de San Angel** and the full-service **La Hacienda de San Angel** (dinner only) offer a combined 400 seats with alfresco seating for lunch and a perfect place for viewing EPCOT's nightly fireworks.

Food aficionados will want to try the classic-Continental prix-fixe **Victoria & Albert's** at the Grand Floridian, where you pay $425 per person (chef's table), plus wine pairings; the **Flying Fish** (at the Board-Walk); **Jiko—The Cooking Place** and **Sanaa,** both at Animal Kingdom Lodge; and the ultra-chic **California Grill.**

Disney Springs

Disney Springs has an amazing array of dining venues. The West Side has three food trucks featuring a variety of dishes that may include tacos, steak, chicken, fish, and vegetarian bowls, along with macaroni and cheese topped with either crunchy cheese puffs, lobster and shrimp, bacon, chicken, or barbecue brisket. Food truck offerings and schedules change often.

House of Blues, part of the chain of New Orleans–style music halls/restaurants once partly owned by Blues Brother Dan Aykroyd, has done well with its Louisiana-inspired fare. **The Smokehouse** is a quick-service barbecue joint operated by the House of Blues. **City Works Eatery & Pour House,** opened in February 2020, is only a skip away from Cirque du Soleil. The menu features American classics with a modern twist and a huge selection of craft beers on tap. There is plenty of indoor and outdoor seating, and sports fans will be able to watch the game of their choice on one of the 17 massive HDTVs.

Jaleo, a concept by world-renowned chef José Andrés, opened in 2019. It features an extensive menu of tapas reflecting the rich regional diversity of traditional and contemporary Spanish cuisine. Jaleo is Liliane's favorite restaurant at Disney Springs.

At The Landing, **Jock Lindsey's Hangar Bar,** an aviation-themed lounge located between Paradiso 37 and The Boathouse, is named after the pilot from the *Indiana Jones* films. The lounge features unique cocktails, such as Reggie's Revenge and the Fountain of Youth, both containing Florida vodkas; and Hovito Mojito. Other drinks worth trying are the Cool-headed Monkey, made with African rum, and The Scottish Professor. This family-friendly, 150-seat waterfront lounge serves little plates, such as spiced meatballs on mini buns with yogurt sauce. Check out the memorabilia in the bar's indoor seating area.

Iron Chef Masaharu Morimoto brought prestige to Disney Springs, when he opened its first pan-Asian restaurant: **Morimoto Asia** highlights foods from around the continent. Bob and Liliane love dining there. Guests can pick from several dining lounges or the coveted spot in the show kitchen. Items on the menu include Peking duck, orange chicken, ramen with roasted duck and pork, and a large selection of sushi rolls. And kids (age 9 and under) don't need to feel left out: kid-friendly dishes such as lo mein with Cantonese noodles, mini ramen with pork or chicken, and egg fried rice are also available.

The Edison, an industrial Gothic restaurant and bar serving American food and craft cocktails, opened in early 2018. With multiple themed areas (such as The Lab, The Ember Parlour, The Tesla Lounge, and the Waterfront Patio) and a steady lineup of unique acts (DJs, dancers, and even palm readers have been spotted), it is sure to keep you entertained. The Edison is a lot of fun, especially for Mom and Dad on a night out. The food is decent and nicely presented, but overpriced. We recommend you dine elsewhere and enjoy the atmosphere and entertainment of The Edison past 9 p.m. at one of its bars.

Stay away from **Maria and Enzo's Ristorante.** The food is adequate Italian fare in a very noisy setting. **Pizza Ponte** is a quick-service eatery that's connected to Maria and Enzo's. If money isn't an issue, we recommend **Enzo's Hideaway.** The setting is a speakeasy-inspired tunnel serving Italian dishes and the largest selection of aged rums and scotches in Disney Springs.

At **The Boathouse,** an upscale seafood restaurant on the waterfront, kids enjoy watching the amphibious cars drive by. One of Liliane's

LILIANE Get a grip, people! It's cookies, and they're not given away for free!

favorites is **Erin McKenna's Bakery NYC,** the world's premier vegan and gluten-free bakery. **Vivoli il Gelato** serves gelato made with fresh, seasonal ingredients. The newest sweet addition to The Landing is **Gideon's Bakehouse.** The store offers cookies and slices of cake. The line is out the door, even though the offerings are pricey.

Family-friendly restaurants include **Raglan Road,** an Irish pub and restaurant featuring live Celtic music and several outdoor food-and-beverage locations. **Paradiso 37** highlights the cuisines of the Americas (North, Central, and South) served both indoors and out. **STK Orlando** is a high-end steakhouse with a rooftop terrace. The steaks are great, but Bob and Liliane are not fans. The restaurant is extremely noisy, to the point that one cannot have a conversation with anyone across the table. **Chef Art Smith's Homecomin'** has become a favorite among Disney Springs visitors; it offers local farm-to-table ingredients and traditional Southern cooking. **Terralina Crafted Italian** offers dishes curated by James Beard award–winning chef Tony Mantuano.

Board a stationary "steamship" to eat at **Paddlefish,** where the menu consists of seafood, sandwiches, and salads. Did you know that what is today known as Paddlefish at Disney Springs started out as the *Empress Lily* riverboat? The riverboat restaurant was named after Walt Disney's wife, Lillian, and on May 1, 1977, she attended the dedication, together with five of the Disney grandchildren. Moored at Pleasure Island, the *Empress Lily* contained a jazz lounge and three restaurants, the Empress Room being the most elegant dining experience at Walt Disney World until the opening of Victoria & Albert's in 1988. A character breakfast was held on the riverboat, which at the time was very rare at Walt Disney World.

Town Center is home to lots of eateries, such as **Blaze Fast-Fire'd Pizza; D-Luxe Burger;** the table-service restaurant **Frontera Cocina** by celebrity chef Rick Bayless; and **Amorette's Patisserie. The Polite Pig,** with the same owners as The Ravenous Pig, serves wood-fired fare and beer, wine, and cocktails.

Planet Hollywood Observatory has an outdoor terrace and bar called Stargazers, which features live entertainment. The menu lacks a lot when it comes to quality and taste; however, the restaurant is a favorite among teens. Planet Hollywood added an outdoor quick-service spot called **Chicken Guy,** brought to life by Planet Hollywood founder Robert Earl and celebrity chef Guy Fieri, hoping to draw in the next-door movie theater crowd and those still hungry on their way to the nearby parking garage. There are so many great offerings now at Disney Springs that we recommend you skip Planet Hollywood.

For parents' night out, try **Wine Bar George,** featuring recommendations by Master Sommelier George Miliotes. The lounge also serves small plates designed to complement the wine list. **The Basket** (The Landing) brings a counter-service component to Wine Bar George, serving sandwiches, cookies, and wine. **Wolfgang Puck Bar & Grill** (Town Center) offers the best of the chef's signature dishes.

Kid-Friendly Spots

If your kids haven't had their fill of robotic crocodiles, singing parrots, and the like, T-REX and Rainforest Cafe will serve up all they can handle. There are two **Rainforest Cafe** branches, one at Disney Springs Marketplace and a super-theatrical version at the entrance to Animal Kingdom, where the decor and animatronic elephants make it fit right in. Not surprisingly in a place where the sky "rains" and the stars flicker overhead, more thought went into naming the dishes than perfecting the recipes. Note that the Animal Kingdom location serves breakfast.

If your kids prefer dinosaurs to pachyderms, try **T-REX,** which is located within spitting distance of the Rainforest Cafe at Disney Springs and is operated by the same folks. The food is better than Rainforest, and children go nuts about being surrounded by a life-size animatronic brontosaurus, triceratops, and such.

continued on page 198

WALT DISNEY WORLD RESTAURANTS BY CUISINE

CUISINE	LOCATION	OVERALL RATING	COST	QUALITY RATING	VALUE RATING
AFRICAN					
BOMA—FLAVORS OF AFRICA	Animal Kingdom Lodge-Jambo House	★★★★½	Exp	★★★★	★★★★
JIKO—THE COOKING PLACE	Animal Kingdom Lodge-Jambo House	★★★★½	Exp	★★★★	★★★½
SANAA	Animal Kingdom Villas-Kidani Village	★★★★	Exp	★★★★	★★★★
JUNGLE NAVIGATION CO. LTD. SKIPPER CANTEEN	Magic Kingdom	★★★½	Exp	★★★	★★★
TUSKER HOUSE RESTAURANT	Animal Kingdom	★★★	Exp	★★★	★★★
AMERICAN					
CALIFORNIA GRILL	Contemporary	★★★★	Exp	★★★★★	★★★
CHEF ART SMITH'S HOMECOMIN'	Disney Springs	★★★★	Mod	★★★★	★★★½
THE HOLLYWOOD BROWN DERBY	DHS	★★★★	Exp	★★★★	★★★
TIFFINS	Animal Kingdom	★★★★	Exp	★★★★	★★★
GEYSER POINT BAR & GRILL	Wilderness Lodge	★★★½	Mod	★★★½	★★★
GRAND FLORIDIAN CAFE	Grand Floridian	★★★½	Mod-Exp	★★★½	★★★½
LIBERTY TREE TAVERN	Magic Kingdom	★★★½	Exp	★★★	★★★
STORY BOOK DINING WITH SNOW WHITE AT ARTIST POINT	Wilderness Lodge	★★★½	Exp	★★★★	★★★½
WOLFGANG PUCK BAR & GRILL	Disney Springs	★★★½	Exp	★★★★	★★★½
ALE & COMPASS	Yacht Club	★★★	Mod	★★★	★★★
BOATWRIGHT'S DINING HALL	Port Orleans Riverside	★★★	Mod-Exp	★★★	★★
CAPE MAY CAFÉ	Beach Club	★★★	Exp	★★★	★★★
CINDERELLA'S ROYAL TABLE	Magic Kingdom	★★★	Exp	★★★	★★
CITY WORKS EATERY AND POUR HOUSE	Disney Springs	★★★	Mod	★★★	★★★
THE EDISON	Disney Springs	★★★	Exp	★★★½	★★★
50'S PRIME TIME CAFE	DHS	★★★	Mod	★★★	★★★
GARDEN GRILL RESTAURANT	EPCOT	★★★	Exp	★★★	★★★
HOUSE OF BLUES	Disney Springs	★★★	Mod	★★★½	★★★
OLIVIA'S CAFE	Old Key West	★★★	Exp	★★★	★★
THREE BRIDGES BAR & GRILL	Coronado Springs	★★★	Exp	★★★	★★½
T-REX	Disney Springs	★★★	Exp	★★	★★

* Closed at press time.

WDW RESTAURANTS BY CUISINE (continued)

CUISINE	LOCATION	OVERALL RATING	COST	QUALITY RATING	VALUE RATING
AMERICAN (continued)					
TUSKER HOUSE RESTAURANT	Animal Kingdom	★★★	Exp	★★★	★★★
WHISPERING CANYON CAFE	Wilderness Lodge	★★★	Exp	★★★½	★★★★
BE OUR GUEST RESTAURANT	Magic Kingdom	★★½	Exp	★★★★	★★
BEACHES & CREAM SODA SHOP	Beach Club	★★½	Mod	★★½	★★
CHEF MICKEY'S	Contemporary	★★½	Exp	★★★	★★★
THE CRYSTAL PALACE	Magic Kingdom	★★½	Exp	★★½	★★★
FRESH MEDITERRANEAN MARKET	Dolphin	★★½	Mod	★★½	★★
HOLLYWOOD & VINE	DHS	★★½	Exp	★★★	★★★
PADDLEFISH	Disney Springs	★★½	Exp	★★★½	★★½
RAINFOREST CAFE	Animal Kingdom and Disney Springs	★★½	Mod	★★	★★
SPACE 220	EPCOT	★★½	Exp	★★★	★★
SPLITSVILLE	Disney Springs	★★½	Mod	★★½	★★
BIG RIVER GRILLE & BREWING WORKS	BoardWalk	★★	Mod	★★	★★
THE FOUNTAIN	Dolphin	★★	Mod	★★	★★
GARDEN GROVE	Swan	★★	Mod	★★★	★★
THE PLAZA RESTAURANT	Magic Kingdom	★★	Mod	★★	★★
SCI-FI DINE-IN THEATER RESTAURANT	DHS	★★	Mod	★★½	★★
TRAIL'S END RESTAURANT	Fort Wilderness Resort	★★	Exp	★★	★★
TURF CLUB BAR & GRILL	Saratoga Springs	★★	Exp	★★★	★★
PLANET HOLLYWOOD	Disney Springs	★½	Mod	★★	★★
MAYA GRILL	Coronado Springs	★	Exp	★	★
BRITISH					
ROSE & CROWN DINING ROOM	EPCOT	★★★	Mod	★★★½	★★
BUFFET					
BOMA—FLAVORS OF AFRICA	Animal Kingdom Lodge-Jambo House	★★★★½	Exp	★★★★	★★★★
THE CRYSTAL PALACE	Magic Kingdom	★★½	Exp	★★½	★★★
1900 PARK FARE*	Grand Floridian	★★½	Exp	★★★	★★★
AKERSHUS ROYAL BANQUET HALL*	EPCOT	★★	Exp	★★	★★★★
BIERGARTEN	EPCOT	★★	Exp	★★	★★★★

* Closed at press time.

WDW RESTAURANTS BY CUISINE *(continued)*

CUISINE	LOCATION	OVERALL RATING	COST	QUALITY RATING	VALUE RATING
CAJUN					
BOATWRIGHT'S DINING HALL	Port Orleans Riverside	★★★	Mod–Exp	★★★	★★
CHINESE					
NINE DRAGONS RESTAURANT	EPCOT	★★★	Mod	★★★½	★★½
COCKTAILS AND BAR BITES					
JOCK LINDSEY'S HANGAR BAR	Disney Springs	★★	Inexp	★★	★★
FRENCH					
MONSIEUR PAUL*	EPCOT	★★★★	Exp	★★★★½	★★★
TOPOLINO'S TERRACE	Riviera	★★★★	Exp	★★★★	★★★
LA CRÊPERIE DE PARIS	EPCOT	★★★½	Mod	★★★½	★★★★
CHEFS DE FRANCE	EPCOT	★★★	Exp	★★★	★★★
BE OUR GUEST RESTAURANT	Magic Kingdom	★★½	Exp	★★★★	★★
GERMAN					
BIERGARTEN	EPCOT	★★	Exp	★★	★★★★
GLOBAL					
PARADISO 37	Disney Springs	★★½	Exp	★★★	★★★
GOURMET					
VICTORIA & ALBERT'S	Grand Floridian	★★★★★	Exp	★★★★★	★★★★
INDIAN/AFRICAN					
SANAA	Animal Kingdom Villas–Kidani Village	★★★★	Exp	★★★★	★★★★
IRISH					
RAGLAN ROAD	Disney Springs	★★★★	Exp	★★★★	★★★
ITALIAN					
TOPOLINO'S TERRACE	Riviera	★★★★	Exp	★★★★	★★★
VIA NAPOLI	EPCOT	★★★★	Exp	★★★½	★★★
TUTTO GUSTO WINE CELLAR	EPCOT	★★★½	Exp	★★★★	★★★
MARIA & ENZO'S RISTORANTE	Disney Springs	★★★½	Exp	★★★½	★★★
TERRALINA CRAFTED ITALIAN	Disney Springs	★★★½	Exp	★★★	★★★
IL MULINO NEW YORK	Swan	★★★	Exp	★★★	★★
TRATTORIA AL FORNO	BoardWalk	★★★	Mod	★★★½	★★
TUTTO ITALIA	EPCOT	★★★	Exp	★★★★	★★
MAMA MELROSE'S	DHS	★★½	Exp	★★★	★★
TONY'S TOWN SQUARE RESTAURANT	Magic Kingdom	★★½	Exp	★★★	★★

* Closed at press time

WDW RESTAURANTS BY CUISINE (continued)

CUISINE	LOCATION	OVERALL RATING	COST	QUALITY RATING	VALUE RATING
JAPANESE/SUSHI					
TAKUMI-TEI*	EPCOT	★★★★½	Exp	★★★★★	★★★½
KIMONOS	Swan	★★★★	Mod	★★★★	★★★
MORIMOTO ASIA	Disney Springs	★★★★	Exp	★★★★	★★★★
TEPPAN EDO	EPCOT	★★★½	Exp	★★★★	★★★
TOKYO DINING	EPCOT	★★★	Mod	★★★★	★★★
MEDITERRANEAN					
CÍTRICOS	Grand Floridian	★★★★	Exp	★★★★½	★★★
FRESH MEDITERRANEAN MARKET	Dolphin	★★½	Mod	★★½	★★
MEXICAN					
LA HACIENDA DE SAN ANGEL	EPCOT	★★★★	Exp	★★★★	★★★½
FRONTERA COCINA	Disney Springs	★★★½	Exp	★★★½	★★★
SAN ANGEL INN RESTAURANTE	EPCOT	★★★	Exp	★★★	★★
MAYA GRILL	Coronado Springs	★	Exp	★	★
MOROCCAN					
SPICE ROAD TABLE	EPCOT	★★★★	Inexp	★★★★	★★★
RESTAURANT MARRAKESH*	EPCOT	★★★	Exp	★★½	★★
NORWEGIAN					
AKERSHUS ROYAL BANQUET HALL*	EPCOT	★★	Exp	★★	★★★★
PAN-ASIAN/POLYNESIAN					
TIFFINS	Animal Kingdom	★★★★	Exp	★★★★	★★★
MORIMOTO ASIA	Disney Springs	★★★★	Exp	★★★★	★★★★
'OHANA	Polynesian Village	★★★	Exp	★★★½	★★★
KONA CAFE	Polynesian Village	★★★	Mod	★★★	★★★★
TRADER SAM'S GROG GROTTO	Polynesian Village	★★★	Inexp	★★★	★★★
YAK & YETI RESTAURANT	Animal Kingdom	★★★	Exp	★★½	★★
SEAFOOD					
NARCOOSSEE'S	Grand Floridian	★★★★½	Exp	★★★½	★★
FLYING FISH	BoardWalk	★★★★	Exp	★★★★	★★★
TODD ENGLISH'S BLUEZOO	Dolphin	★★★★	Exp	★★★★	★★★
THE BOATHOUSE	Disney Springs	★★★½	Exp	★★★	★★
CORAL REEF	EPCOT	★★½	Exp	★★	★★
PADDLEFISH	Disney Springs	★★½	Exp	★★★½	★★½
SEBASTIAN'S BISTRO	Caribbean Beach	★★	Exp	★★	★★★

* Closed at press time

WDW RESTAURANTS BY CUISINE (continued)

CUISINE	LOCATION	OVERALL RATING	COST	QUALITY RATING	VALUE RATING
SPANISH/TAPAS					
JALEO	Disney Springs	★★★★	Mod	★★★★	★★★★
TOLEDO	Coronado Springs	★★★½	Exp	★★★	★★½
THREE BRIDGES BAR & GRILL	Coronado Springs	★★★	Mod	★★★	★★½
STEAK					
SHULA'S STEAK HOUSE	Dolphin	★★★★	Exp	★★★★	★★
STEAKHOUSE 71	Contemporary Resort	★★★★	Exp	★★★★	★★★½
STK ORLANDO	Disney Springs	★★★½	Exp	★★★★	★★½
LE CELLIER STEAKHOUSE	EPCOT	★★★½	Exp	★★★½	★★★
YACHTSMAN STEAKHOUSE	Yacht Club	★★½	Exp	★★★½	★★
WINE/SMALL PLATES					
WINE BAR GEORGE	Disney Springs	★★★★	Mod–Exp	★★★★	★★★★

continued from page 193

Celebrity Chefs

Film and sports stars, as well as Food Network and food-magazine stars, have been enlisted in the Disney World parade. Along with Gaston Lenôtre and Roger Vergé, Paul Bocuse was one of the eponymous **Chefs de France** who designed the menu for that restaurant and for **Monsieur Paul** (*temporarily closed*) in EPCOT. Paul's son, Jérôme, heads **La Crêperie de Paris** in the France Pavilion. Boston star chef Todd English created **bluezoo** for the Dolphin hotel.

Ethnic Food

Although the official guides to Walt Disney World describe various restaurants as "delicious," "delectable," and "delightful," the truth is that only perhaps a dozen of the nearly 100 full-service establishments are first-rate. And some of the most disappointing restaurants, in general, are the often attractive but commissary-bland ethnic kitchens.

A blessing in disguise to many children and picky eaters of all ages, most of the "ethnic" food at Walt Disney World is Americanized—or, rather, homogenized—especially at EPCOT, where visitors from so many countries, including the US, tend to have preconceived notions of egg rolls and enchiladas. **Teppan Edo** in the Japan Pavilion happens to be one of the better restaurants in the World, with pretty good teppanyaki (and good tempura next door), but it specializes in a particularly Westernized form of Japanese cuisine. **Takumi-Tei** (*temporarily closed*) is a Signature Dining Restaurant serving maki sushi, roasted bone marrow, marinated duck, misoyaki sea bass, and more. A seven-course tasting menu is available for $150. **Nine Dragons Restaurant** in the China Pavilion serves satisfying appetizers, such as crispy duck bao buns, salt-and-pepper shrimp with spinach noodles, and honey-sesame chicken. The **San Angel Inn** in the Mexico Pavilion is associated with the famous Debler family of Mexico City.

Liliane loves meeting the princesses at Norway's **Akershus Royal Banquet Hall** (*temporarily closed*), but Bob finds the buffet stodgy, smoky, and cheese- and mayonnaise-heavy.

Healthy Choices

A lot of the food at Disney World, particularly the fast food, isn't exactly healthy. But healthy options do exist. **Sunshine Seasons** in The Land Pavilion at EPCOT is a fast-casual spot where the food is freshly prepared, often when you order it. Healthy options include rotisserie chicken, oak-grilled salmon, and Caesar salad with oak-fired chicken.

Beyond that, fruit stands and juice bars are scattered around, and healthier food options include veggie sandwiches, wraps, rotisserie chicken, soft pretzels, popcorn, and baked potatoes (not, frankly, prepared with the apparent care of the turkey legs but with about a tenth of the calories and salt), as well as frozen fruit bars in the ice-cream freezers and frozen yogurt or smoothies at the ice-cream shops. Look for the fruit markets in Liberty Square in the Magic Kingdom, at The Land Pavilion in EPCOT, on Sunset Boulevard in Disney's Hollywood Studios, and at the Harambe Village marketplace in Animal Kingdom.

WALT DISNEY WORLD RESTAURANTS: RATED AND RANKED

THE TABLE ON PAGES 194–198 lists all of Walt Disney World's full-service restaurants, categorized by cuisine. Within each category, they are ordered first by overall star rating and then alphabetically. The table also notes each restaurant's cost range, along with its quality and value ratings, described below and on the next page.

OVERALL RATING This represents the entire dining experience: style, service, ambience, and food quality. Five stars is the highest rating attainable. Four-star restaurants are above average, and three-star restaurants offer good, though not necessarily memorable, meals. Two-star restaurants serve mediocre fare, and one-star restaurants are below average. Our star ratings don't correspond to ratings awarded by AAA, Forbes, Zagat, or other restaurant reviewers.

★★★★★	Exceptional value, a real bargain
★★★★	Good value
★★★	Fair value, you get exactly what you pay for
★★	Somewhat overpriced
★	Significantly overpriced

COST RANGE The next rating tells you how much you'll spend on a full-service entrée. Appetizers, sides, soups/salads, desserts, drinks, and tips aren't included. Costs are categorized as inexpensive ($13 or less), moderate ($13–$24), or expensive ($24 and up).

QUALITY RATING The food quality is rated on a scale of one to five stars, five being the best. The criteria are taste, freshness of ingredients, preparation, presentation, and creativity of food served. Price is not a factor.

VALUE RATING If you are looking for both quality and value, then you should check the value rating, expressed as stars.

◖ DINNER THEATERS

THE BELOVED *Hoop-Dee-Doo Musical Revue* is back, but Disney has announced the permanent closure of the *Spirit of Aloha* dinner show.

Like other Disney restaurant reservations, when you make a reservation for *Hoop-Dee-Doo*, you'll receive a confirmation number and be told to pick up your tickets at a Disney-hotel Guest Relations desk. Unlike regular Advance Reservations, your seating times for dinner shows are guaranteed. If you fail to cancel your tickets at least 48 hours before your reservation time, your credit card will still be charged the full amount. Reservations can be made 60 days in advance at ☎ 407-939-3463.

Hoop-Dee-Doo Musical Revue at Pioneer Hall, Fort Wilderness Resort & Campground

Showtimes 4, 6:15, and 8:30 p.m. nightly. **Cost** *Category 1:* $72 adults, $43 children ages 3–9. *Category 2:* $67 adults, $39 children. *Category 3:* $64 adults, $38 children. Prices include tax and gratuity. **Discounts** Seasonal. **Type of seating** Tables of various sizes to fit the number in each party, set in an Old West–style dance hall. **Menu** All-you-can-eat barbecue ribs, fried chicken, salad, baked beans, and corn bread. Vegetarian, vegan, and gluten-free options are available; make sure to mention dietary needs when making your reservations. **Beverages** Unlimited beer, wine, sangria, and soft drinks. **Comments** Disney Dining Plan (when available) credits can be used for Category 2 and 3 seats but not Category 1.

HOOP-DEE-DOO IS THE LONGEST-RUNNING SHOW at Disney World and a nostalgic favorite for many. If you've ever thought *Country Bear Jamboree* would benefit from free-flowing beer and wine and barbecue, this is the show for you.

Audience participation includes sing-alongs, hand-clapping, and a finale where you may find yourself onstage. During the meal, the music continues (softly). The food itself isn't bad, and you can't complain about the portion size.

Give special consideration to transportation when planning your evening at Fort Wilderness. There is no parking at Pioneer Hall, which is accessible only by boat (Magic Kingdom and the loop between Fort Wilderness, Wilderness Lodge, and the Contemporary) and the Fort Wilderness internal bus system. After shows, buses at the Pioneer Hall stop take you to the Magic Kingdom bus depot. If driving, allow plenty of time (about an hour) to get there. The fastest option may be to take a ride-hailing service, which will drop you off as close as possible to the venue. Or do as this California dad suggests:

Take the boat from the Magic Kingdom rather than a bus. The dock is a short walk from Pioneer Hall in Fort Wilderness, while the bus goes to the main Fort Wilderness parking lot, where you transfer to another bus to Pioneer Hall.

Boat service may be suspended during thunderstorms, so if it's raining or looks like it's about to rain, Disney will provide bus service from the parks.

DINING *Outside*
WALT DISNEY WORLD

UNOFFICIAL GUIDE RESEARCHERS LOVE good food and invest a fair amount of time scouting new places to eat. Access to restaurants outside of Walt Disney World can really cut the costs of your overall vacation, but you need to have wheels. If you eat only your evening meals outside the World, the savings will more than pay for a rental car.

There are plenty of choices outside Walt Disney World. The range is quite broad and includes elegant dining options, as well as familiar chain restaurants and local family eateries.

Our recommendations for specialty and ethnic fare served outside the World are summarized in the table that starts on page 202.

BUFFETS AND MEAL DEALS OUTSIDE WALT DISNEY WORLD

BUFFETS, RESTAURANT SPECIALS, and discount dining abound in the area surrounding Walt Disney World, especially along US 192 (Irlo Bronson Memorial Highway) and International Drive. The local visitor magazines, distributed free at non-Disney hotels, among other places, are packed with advertisements and discount coupons for seafood feasts, Chinese buffets, Indian buffets, and breakfast buffets, as well as specials for everything from lobster to barbecue. For a family trying to economize, some of the come-ons are mighty sweet. But are these places any good? Is the food fresh, tasty, and appealing? Are the restaurants clean and inviting? Armed with little more than a roll of Tums, the *Unofficial* research team tried all the eateries that advertise heavily in the free tourist magazines. Here's what we discovered.

CHINESE SUPER BUFFETS If you've ever prepared Chinese food, especially a stir-fry, you know that split-second timing is required to avoid overcooking. So it should come as no big surprise that Chinese dishes languishing on a buffet lose their freshness, texture, and flavor in a hurry.

In the past, we were able to find several Chinese buffets we felt comfortable recommending; unfortunately, we would return the next year only to discover that their quality had slipped. We then searched for new buffets to replace the ones we removed from the book, and we can tell you that wasn't fun work. At the end of the day, **Ichiban Buffet** (5269 W. Irlo Bronson Memorial Hwy., ☎ 407-396-6668;

continued on page 204

Where to Eat Outside Walt Disney World

AMERICAN

- **THE RAVENOUS PIG** 565 W. Fairbanks Ave., Winter Park; ☎ 407-628-2333; theravenouspig.com; moderate–expensive. Closed Mondays. New American cuisine; an award-winning menu changes seasonally. Online ordering and curbside pickup.

- **SEASONS 52** 7700 W. Sand Lake Rd., Orlando; ☎ 407-354-5212; seasons52.com; moderate–expensive. Delicious, creative New American food that's low in fat and calories. Extensive wine list. Online ordering and curbside pickup.

- **SLATE** 8323 W. Sand Lake Rd., Orlando; ☎ 407-500-7528; slateorlando.com; moderate–expensive. Combines intimacy and casual dining with greater success than many Restaurant Row establishments. Grab a quick bite from the extensive menu or try heartier fare from the copper-clad wood oven. Delivery via Grubhub.

BARBECUE

- **BUBBALOU'S BODACIOUS BAR-B-QUE** 5818 Conroy Rd., Orlando (near Universal Orlando); ☎ 407-295-1212; bubbalous.com; inexpensive. Tender, smoky barbecue; tomato-based Killer Sauce. Online ordering. Delivery via DoorDash, Grubhub, and Uber Eats.

- **4 RIVERS SMOKEHOUSE** 874 W. Osceola Pkwy., Kissimmee, and six area locations; ☎ 844-474-8377; 4rsmokehouse.com; inexpensive. Closed Sundays. Award-winning brisket, plus fried okra, cheese grits, and collards. Outdoor seating available. Online ordering, curbside pickup, and drive-thru.

CARIBBEAN

- **BAHAMA BREEZE** 8849 International Dr., Orlando; ☎ 407-248-2499; 8735 Vineland Ave.; ☎ 407-938-9010; bahamabreeze.com; moderate. A creative and tasty take on Caribbean cuisine from the owners of Olive Garden and LongHorn Steakhouse. Patio seating available. Use call-ahead seating to check wait time. Online ordering.

CUBAN/SPANISH

- **COLUMBIA** 649 Front St., Celebration; ☎ 407-566-1505; columbiarestaurant.com; moderate/expensive. Authentic Cuban and Spanish creations, including paella and the famous 1905 Salad. One of our favorite places in Celebration. Outdoor seating available.

- **CUBA LIBRE** 9101 International Dr. at Pointe Orlando; ☎ 407-226-1600; cubalibre restaurant.com; moderate. Upscale, like Columbia above, it specializes in ceviches, tapas, and classic Cuban main courses ranging from $20 to $32. Salsa dancing until 2 a.m. on Fridays and 2:30 a.m. on Saturdays.

- **HAVANA'S CAFÉ** 8544 Palm Pkwy., Orlando; ☎ 407-238-5333, havanascubancuisine .com; moderate. Authentic homemade Cuban cuisine and Bob and Len's personal favorite. We've had several Orlando-area Cubans email us to say "There's a hole-in-the-wall place on Palm Parkway you need to try," and they always mean Havana's. Reservations recommended. Outdoor seating available. Takeout available. Delivery via Uber Eats and Grubhub.

ETHIOPIAN

- **NILE ETHIOPIAN RESTAURANT** 7048 International Dr., Orlando; ☎ 407-354-0026; nileorlando.com; inexpensive–moderate. Authentic stews and delicious vegetarian dishes. Bob's favorite Orlando/WDW-area restaurant. Curbside pickup available. Delivery via Grubhub.

- **SELAM ETHIOPIAN & ERITREAN CUISINE** 5494 Central Florida Pkwy., Orlando; ☎ 407-778-3119; ethiopianrestaurantorlando.com; inexpensive–moderate. Closed on Tuesdays. The dishes here are a little spicier than the ones at Nile (see above). Specialties from Eritrea (Ethiopia's neighbor to the north) provide some nice variety. Outdoor seating available. Delivery via Grubhub, Uber Eats, and DoorDash.

GREEK

- **TAVERNA OPA ORLANDO** 9101 International Dr., Orlando; ☎ 407-351-8660; opaorlando.com; moderate. Try traditional Greek standouts like pastitsio, boureki, and moussaka, along with kebabs and seafood specialties cooked on a wood fire. Live entertainment many nights. Reservations available online or via OpenTable. Delivery via DoorDash and Uber Eats.

*20 minutes or more from Walt Disney World

Where to Eat Outside Walt Disney World *(continued)*

INDIAN

- **TABLA CUISINE** 5847 Grand National Dr., Orlando; ☎ 407-248-9400; tablacuisine
.com; moderate. Within the Clarion Inn on I-Drive, but don't let that keep you away from one of the better Indian restaurants in the area. The menu also includes Chinese and Thai dishes. Online ordering, curbside pickup, and delivery available.

ITALIAN

- **ANTHONY'S COAL FIRED PIZZA AND WINGS** 8031 Turkey Lake Rd., Orlando; ☎ 407-363-9466; acfp.com; inexpensive. Pizzas, wings, sandwiches, beer, wine. Online wait list and ordering. Delivery via Uber Eats, but coal-fired pizza doesn't travel well.

- **BICE RISTORANTE ORLANDO** (94%/Exceptional) Loews Portofino Bay Hotel, Universal Orlando Resort, 5601 Universal Blvd., Orlando; ☎ 407-503-1415; bice
-orlando.com; expensive. Authentic Italian and great wines. Excellent service—we've never had a bad meal here. Reservations required. Outdoor seating available.

- **PEPERONCINO CUCINA** 7988 Via Dellagio Way, Orlando; ☎ 407-440-2856; facebook.com/peperoncinoorlando; moderate. Calabrian chef Barbara Alfano runs a tight and authentic kitchen, creating pastas and wood-fired pizza worthy of the name. Reservations available. Outdoor seating available. Delivery via Uber Eats.

JAPANESE/SUSHI

- **AKASAKA** 7786 W. Sand Lake Rd., Orlando; ☎ 407-370-0007; akasaka-sushi.com; moderate. A favorite sushi bar for locals. The tempura is popular too. Takeout available. Delivery via DoorDash and Uber Eats.

- **HANAMIZUKI** 8255 International Dr., Orlando; ☎ 407-363-7200; hanamizuki.us; moderate-expensive. Pricey but authentic. Takeout available. Delivery via DoorDash, Grubhub, and Uber Eats.

- **NAGOYA SUSHI** 7600 Dr. Phillips Blvd., Ste. 66, in the very rear of The Marketplace at Dr. Phillips; ☎ 407-248-8558; nagoyasushi.com; moderate. Closed Mondays; open for lunch Tuesday–Sunday, noon–3 p.m.; for dinner Sunday and Tuesday–Thursday, 4:30–9:30 p.m. and Friday–Saturday, 4:30–10 p.m. Small, intimate restaurant with great sushi and an extensive menu. Reservations available by phone or online. Takeout available. Delivery via DoorDash and Uber Eats.

- **SUSHI TOMI** 8463 S. John Young Pkwy., Orlando; ☎ 407-352-8635; sushitomi orlando.com; moderate. Monday–Friday, 11:30 a.m.–2:30 p.m.; Monday–Saturday, 5:30–9:30 p.m. Reservations available by phone or online. Takeout available.

LATIN

- **SOFRITO LATIN CAFE** 8607 Palm Pkwy., Orlando; ☎ 407-778-4205; sofritocafe
.com; inexpensive. Located near the corner of FL 535 and Palm Parkway, Sofrito specializes in comfort foods from Cuba, Colombia, Argentina, Chile, Puerto Rico, Peru, Dominican Republic, Brazil, and Venezuela. The restaurant is modern but sterile. The best play is to order takeout for pickup. Outdoor seating available. Delivery via DoorDash.

MEXICAN

- **EL PATRON** 12167 S. Apopka-Vineland Rd., Orlando; ☎ 407-238-5300; elpatron orlando.com; moderate. Family-owned restaurant serving freshly prepared Mexican dishes. Full bar. Weekend brunch buffet and weekday lunch buffet, with the buffet now served by staff. Outdoor seating available. Online reservations, takeout, and delivery available. The all-you-can-eat Taco Tuesdays should be a national holiday.

- **EL TENAMPA MEXICAN RESTAURANT** 4565 W. Irlo Bronson Memorial Hwy., Kissimmee; ☎ 407-397-1981; inexpensive. Family-owned, with an extensive menu of authentic Mexican regional fare in a small, colorful room. Try their steak dish called Arrachera el Tenampa. Outdoor seating available. Takeout and delivery available. Delivery also via DoorDash and Grubhub.

MOROCCAN

- **MERGUEZ** 11951 International Dr., Orlando; ☎ 407-778-4343; merguez.restaurant; inexpensive. Bright, informal setting with adjacent alfresco option. Excellent and representative Moroccan specialties. Awesome bastillas and tagines. Couscous, following the Moroccan custom, is served on Friday only. No alcohol sold. Outdoor seating available. Takeout available. Delivery via Uber Eats.

continued on next page

Where to Eat Outside Walt Disney World *(continued)*

NEW WORLD

• **KNIFE AND SPOON** 4012 Central Florida Pkwy., in the Ritz-Carlton; ☎ 407-393-4333; grandelakes.com/dining/knife-and-spoon; expensive. Open Wednesday–Saturday, 5:30–10 p.m. Serves seafood, dry-aged steak, and pasta. Reserve online or via OpenTable.

PERUVIAN

• **EL INKA GRILL** 7600 Dr. Phillips Blvd., Orlando; ☎ 407-930-2810; elinkagrill.com; moderate. El Inka Grill features numerous ceviche and tiradito (thin raw fish marinated in citrus juice) preparations, including three ceviches that are grilled. Traditional Peruvian beef, fish, and chicken entrées run $17–$24 and most come with several sides. Portions are generous. Outdoor seating available. Takeout available. Delivery via DoorDash.

SEAFOOD

• **CELEBRATION TOWN TAVERN** 721 Front St., Celebration; ☎ 407-566-2526; thecelebrationtowntavern.com; moderate. Popular hangout for locals, featuring New England–style seafood. Clam chowder and lobster rolls are big hits. Outdoor seating available. Takeout available.

STEAK

• **BULL & BEAR** Waldorf Astoria Orlando, 14200 Bonnet Creek Resort Ln.; ☎ 407-597-5413; bullandbearorlando.com; expensive. Closed Mondays; open Tuesday–Sunday, 6–10 p.m. Classic steakhouse with a clubby ambience. The fried chicken is life-affirming. Reservations via phone, website, or OpenTable.

• **THE CAPITAL GRILLE** Pointe Orlando, 9101 International Dr., Orlando; ☎ 407-370-4392; thecapitalgrille.com; expensive. Dinner only. Dry-aged steaks, good wine list, and classic decor. Curbside pickup 5–9 p.m.

• **TEXAS DE BRAZIL** 5259 International Dr., Orlando; ☎ 407-355-0355; texasdebrazil.com; expensive. All you can eat in a Brazilian-style *churrascaria*. Filet mignon, sausage, pork, chicken, lamb, and more. Age 2 and under are free, ages 3–5 are $5, and ages 6–12 are half-price. Salad bar with 40-plus options temporarily unavailable, but salads are available to order. Takeout and delivery via website.

• **VITO'S CHOP HOUSE** (*dinner only*) 8633 International Dr., Orlando; ☎ 407-354-2467; vitoschophouse.com; moderate. Sunday–Thursday, 5–9 p.m.; Friday–Saturday: 5–9:30 p.m. Upscale meatery with a taste of Tuscany. Specialty martini list, 850 wine selections, and a variety of cigars.

THAI

• **THAI SILK** 5532 International Dr., Orlando; ☎ 407-226-8997; thaisilkorlando.com; moderate. Acclaimed by Orlando dining critics for its authentic Thai dishes. Delicious vegetarian options; vegan and gluten-friendly options; impressive wine list. Takeout available. Delivery via DoorDash, Grubhub, Postmates, or Uber Eats.

• **THAI THANI** 11025 International Dr., Orlando; ☎ 407-239-9733; thaithani.net; moderate. Specializes in Thai duck dishes.

continued from page 201

5529 International Dr., ☎ 407-930-8889; ichibanbuffet.com) and **Hokkaido Chinese & Japanese Buffet** (12173 S. Apopka–Vineland Road, ☎ 407-778-5188; 5737 W. Irlo Bronson Memorial Hwy., ☎ 407-396-0669; hokkaidobuffetorlando.com) are the best choices in their genre. Ichiban is our pick, with Japanese hibachi and sushi, plus traditional and American-style Chinese dishes. Its I-Drive location is our favorite. Hokkaido buffets are comparable, so select whichever is most convenient to you. Selections dry out on buffets, so seek out a popular one, where dishes are replenished frequently.

INDIAN BUFFETS Indian food works better on a buffet than Chinese food; in fact, it actually improves as the flavors marry. In the Disney

World area, most Indian restaurants offer a buffet at lunch only—not too convenient if you're spending your day at the theme parks. If you're out shopping or taking a day off, these Indian buffets are worth trying: **Aashirwad Indian Cuisine** (7000 S. Kirkman Road, ☎ 407-370-9830, aashirwadrestaurant.com); **Ahmed Indian Restaurant** (11301 S. Orange Blossom Trl., Ste. 104; ☎ 407-856-5970; ahmedrestaurant.com); and **Woodlands Pure Vegetarian Indian Cuisine** (6040 S. Orange Blossom Trl., ☎ 407-854-3330, woodlandsusa.com).

CHURRASCARIAS A number of these South American–style meat emporiums have sprung up along International Drive. Our picks are **Café Mineiro** (6432 International Dr., ☎ 407-248-2932, cafemineirosteak house.com), north of Sand Lake Road, and **Boi Brazil Steakhouse** (5668 International Dr., ☎ 407-354-0260, boibrazil.com). Both offer good value. More expensive are the Argentinean churrasco specialties at **The Knife** (12501 FL 535, ☎ 321-395-4892, thekniferestaurant.com); be sure to try the sweetbreads, an Argentine specialty. If you prefer chain restaurants, the pricey **Texas de Brazil** and **Fogo de Chão** also have locations in Orlando.

SEAFOOD AND LOBSTER BUFFETS These affairs don't exactly fall under the category of inexpensive dining. The main draw is all the lobster you can eat. The problem is that lobsters, like Chinese food, don't wear well on a steam table. After a few minutes on the buffet line, they make better tennis balls than dinner, so try to grab yours immediately after a fresh batch has been brought out. There are several lobster buffets in the area, and all do a reasonable job, but we prefer **Boston Lobster Feast** (7702 W. Irlo Bronson Memorial Hwy., ☎ 407-768-1166, bostonlobsterfeast.com). This is the place where you can actually have a conversation over dinner.

BREAKFAST AND ENTRÉE BUFFETS Most chain steakhouses in the area, including **Ponderosa** and **Golden Corral**, offer entrée buffets. All serve breakfast, lunch, and dinner. At lunch and dinner, you get the buffet when you buy an entrée, usually a steak; breakfast is a straightforward buffet (that is, you don't have to buy an entrée). As for the food, it's chain-restaurant quality but pretty good all the same. The prices are a bargain, and you can get in and out at lightning speed—important at breakfast when you're trying to get to the parks early. Some locations offer lunch and dinner buffets at a set price without your having to buy an entrée. In addition to the steakhouses, the WDW-area **Shoney's** also offers breakfast, lunch, and dinner buffets. Local freebie visitor magazines are full of discount coupons for all of the previous restaurants.

A New Hampshire reader notes:

> *You mention quite a few buffets for off-site dining, but it would have been nice to know their normal morning business hours. Some buffets (like Ponderosa) didn't open until 8 a.m. for breakfast. This is way too late if you're trying to get to the park [for a 9 a.m.] opening time.*

DISNEY BUFFETS VS. OFF-SITE BUFFETS Most off-site buffets are long on selection but don't compare favorably to Disney's in terms of quality; likewise, the setting and ambience of Disney buffets is generally superior. An exception is **Café Osceola** (9939 Universal Blvd., Orlando; ☎ 407-996-9939; rosenshinglecreek.com/dining) at the Rosen Shingle Creek Resort. The restaurant specializes in carved meats.

MEAL DEALS Discount coupons are available for a wide range of restaurants. **Sonny's Real Pit Bar-B-Q** is a meat eater's delight. Among its offerings, the Family Feast ($57 per family of four) includes pulled pork, plus chicken, ribs, barbecue beans, slaw, fries, corn bread, and tea. The closest location to Walt Disney World and Universal is at 7423 S. Orange Blossom Trail in Orlando (☎ 407-859-7197, sonnysbbq.com). No coupons are available (or needed) for Sonny's, but they're available for other "meateries."

COUPONS Find discounts and two-for-one coupons for many of the restaurants mentioned in freebie visitor guides, available at most hotels outside Walt Disney World. **Visit Orlando** (☎ 407-363-5800, visit orlando.com) offers discounts and information on its website and via phone. In Kissimmee, visit the **Osceola County Welcome Center and History Museum** (4155 W. Vine St.; ☎ 407-396-8644; osceolahistory .org; open Wednesday–Sunday, 10 a.m.–4 p.m.).

THE GREAT ORLANDO PIZZA SCAM Plenty of reputable local pizza joints deliver to hotels in and around the theme parks; many Disney and Universal resorts offer pizza delivery as well. But for a few years now, con artists have been distributing fliers advertising delivery to hotel guests—they ask for your credit card number over the phone, but the pizza never arrives. Disregard any such fliers you find.

PART 5

KNOW *Before* YOU GO

The **BRUTAL TRUTH** *About* **FAMILY VACATIONS**

IT HAS BEEN SUGGESTED THAT THE PHRASE *family vacation* is a bit of an oxymoron. This is because you can never take a vacation from the responsibilities of parenting if your children are traveling with you. Though you leave your work and normal routine far behind, your children require as much attention, if not more, when traveling as they do at home.

Parenting on the road is an art. It requires imagination and organization. Think about it: You have to do all the usual stuff (feed, dress, bathe, supervise, teach, comfort, discipline, put to bed, and so on) in an atmosphere where your children are hyperstimulated, without the familiarity of place and the resources you take for granted at home. Though it's not impossible—and can even be fun—parenting on the road is not something you want to learn on the fly, particularly at Walt Disney World.

The point we want to drive home is that preparation, or the lack thereof, can make or break your Walt Disney World vacation. Believe us—you do *not* want to leave the success of your expensive Disney vacation to chance. But don't confuse chance with good luck. Chance is what happens when you fail to prepare. Good luck is when preparation meets opportunity.

Your preparation can be organized into several categories, all of which we will help you undertake. Broadly speaking, you need to prepare yourself and your children mentally, emotionally, physically, organizationally, and logistically. You also need a basic understanding of Walt Disney World and a well-considered plan for how to go about seeing it.

MENTAL *and* EMOTIONAL PREPARATION

MENTAL PREPARATION BEGINS with realistic expectations about your Disney vacation and consideration of what each adult and child in your party most wants and needs from their Walt Disney World experience. Getting in touch with this aspect of planning requires a lot of introspection and good, open family communication.

DIVISION OF LABOR

TALK ABOUT WHAT YOU and your partner need and what you expect to happen on the vacation. This discussion alone can preempt some unpleasant surprises mid-trip. If you are a two-parent family, do you have a clear understanding of how the parenting workload is to be distributed? We've seen some distinctly disruptive misunderstandings in two-parent households where one parent is (pardon the legalese) the primary caregiver. Often, the other parent expects the primary caregiver to function on vacation as he or she does at home. The primary caregiver, on the other hand, is ready for a break. He or she expects the partner to either shoulder the load equally or perhaps even assume the lion's share so he or she can have a *real* vacation. However you divide the responsibility, of course, is up to you. Just make sure you negotiate a clear understanding *before* you leave home.

TOGETHERNESS

ANOTHER DIMENSION TO CONSIDER is how much togetherness seems appropriate to you. For some parents, a vacation represents a rare opportunity to really connect with their children—to talk, exchange ideas, and get reacquainted. For others, a vacation affords the time to get a little distance, to enjoy a round of golf while the kids are participating in a program organized by the resort.

At Walt Disney World you can orchestrate your vacation to spend as much or as little time with your children as you desire, but more about that later. The point here is to think about both your own and your children's preferences and needs concerning your time together. A typical day at a Disney theme park provides the structure of experiencing attractions together, punctuated by periods of waiting in line, eating, and so on, which facilitate conversation and sharing. Most attractions can be enjoyed together by the whole family, regardless of age. This allows for more consensus and less dissent when it comes to deciding what to see and do. For many parents and children, however, the rhythms of a Walt Disney World day seem to consist of passive entertainment experiences alternated with endless discussions of where to go and what to do next. As a mother from Winston-Salem, North Carolina, reported:

Our family mostly talked about what to do next with very little sharing or discussion about what we had seen. The conversation was pretty task-oriented.

Two observations: First, fighting the crowds and keeping the family moving along can easily escalate into a pressure-driven outing. Having an advance plan or itinerary eliminates moment-to-moment guesswork and decision-making, thus creating more time for savoring and connecting. Second, external variables such as crowd size, noise, and heat can be so distracting as to preclude any meaningful togetherness. These negative impacts can be moderated, as previously discussed, by your being selective concerning the time of year, day of the week, and time of day you visit the theme parks. The bottom line is that you can achieve the degree of connection and togetherness you desire with a little advance planning and a realistic awareness of the distractions you will encounter.

LIGHTEN UP

PREPARE YOURSELF MENTALLY to be a little less compulsive on vacation about correcting small behavioral deviations and pounding home the lessons of life. So what if Matt eats hamburgers for breakfast, lunch, and dinner every day? You can make him eat peas and broccoli when you get home and are in charge of meal preparation again. Roll with the little stuff, and remember when your children act out that they are wired to the max. At least some of that adrenaline is bound to spill out in undesirable ways. Coming down hard will send an already frayed little nervous system into orbit.

SOMETHING FOR EVERYONE

IF YOU TRAVEL WITH AN INFANT, toddler, or any child who requires a lot of special attention, make sure that you have some energy and time remaining for your other children. In the

LILIANE Try to schedule some time alone with each of your children—if not each day, then at least a couple of times during the trip.

course of your planning, invite each child to name something special to do or see at Walt Disney World with Mom or Dad alone. Work these special activities into your trip itinerary. If you commit to something, write it down so you don't forget. Also remember that a casually expressed willingness to do this or that may be perceived as a promise by your children.

LILIANE Short forays to the parks interspersed with naps, swimming, and quiet activities, such as reading to your children, will go a long way toward keeping things on an even keel.

WHOSE IDEA WAS THIS, ANYWAY?

THE DISCORD THAT MANY VACATIONING families experience arises from the kids being on a completely different wavelength from Mom and Dad. Parents and grandparents are often worse than children when it comes to conjuring up fantasy scenarios of what a Walt Disney World vacation will be like. A Disney vacation can be many things, but believe us when we tell you that there's a lot more to it than just riding Dumbo and seeing Mickey.

In our experience, most parents (and nearly all grandparents) expect children to enter a state of rapture at Walt Disney World, bouncing from attraction to attraction in wide-eyed wonder, appreciative beyond words of their adult benefactors. What they get, more often than not, is not even in the same ballpark. Preschoolers will, without a doubt, be wide-eyed, often with delight but also with a general sense of being overwhelmed by noise, crowds, and Disney characters as big as toolsheds. We have substantiated through thousands of interviews and surveys that the best part of a Disney vacation for a preschooler is the hotel swimming pool. With some grade-schoolers and pre-driving-age teens, you get near-manic hyperactivity coupled with periods of studied nonchalance. This last, which relates to the importance of being cool at all costs, translates into a maddening display of boredom and a "been there, done that" attitude. Older teens are frequently the exponential version of the younger teens and grade-schoolers, except without the manic behavior.

For preschoolers, keep things light and happy by limiting the time you spend in the theme parks. The most critical point is that the overstimulation of the parks must be balanced by adequate rest and more mellow activities. For grade-schoolers and early teens,

LILIANE The more information your children have before arriving at Walt Disney World, the less likely they will be to act out.

moderate the hyperactivity and false apathy by enlisting their help in planning the vacation, especially by allowing them to take a leading role in determining the itinerary for days at the theme parks. Being in charge of specific responsibilities that focus on the happiness of other family members also works well. One reader, for example, turned a 12-year-old liability into an asset by asking him to help guard against attractions that might frighten his 5-year-old sister.

Knowledge enhances anticipation and at the same time affords a level of comfort and control that helps kids understand the big picture. The more they feel in control, the less they will act out of control.

DISNEY, KIDS, AND SCARY STUFF

DISNEY ATTRACTIONS, both rides and shows, are adventures, and they focus on themes common to adventures: good and evil, life and death, beauty and the grotesque, fellowship and enmity. As you sample the attractions at Walt Disney World, you transcend the spinning and bouncing

BOB Before lining up for any attraction, check out our description of it and see our Small-Child Fright-Potential Table on pages 213–215.

of midway rides to thought-provoking and emotionally powerful entertainment. All of the endings are happy, but the adventures' impact, given Disney's gift for special effects, often intimidates and occasionally frightens young children.

There are rides with burning towns and ghouls popping out of their graves, all done with a sense of humor, provided you're old enough to understand the joke. And bones. There are bones everywhere: human bones, cattle bones, dinosaur bones, even whole skeletons. There's a stack of skulls at the headhunter's camp on the Jungle Cruise, a platoon of skeletons sailing ghost ships in Pirates of the Caribbean, and a haunting assemblage of skulls and skeletons in The Haunted Mansion. Skulls, skeletons, and bones punctuate Peter Pan's Flight and Big Thunder Mountain Railroad. And in the Animal Kingdom, an entire children's playground is made up exclusively of giant bones and skeletons.

A reader from Thibodaux, Louisiana, wrote to us about his experiences at the Magic Kingdom:

> *I found SO MANY of the rides to be dark and too spooky for my almost-3-year-old. She hated The Many Adventures of Winnie the Pooh and Peter Pan's Flight because they were dark. There's only so many times one can ride It's a Small World and the carousel before one starts to curse the Imagineers who created so many dark rides.*

On the other hand, the special effects at Disney's Hollywood Studios seem more real and sinister than those in the other theme parks. If your child has difficulty coping with the ghouls of The Haunted Mansion, think twice about exposing him or her to Star Tours. One reader tells of taking his preschool children on Star Tours:

LILIANE While there is no certain way to know what will scare your kids or what will garner a big smile, many rides are so intense that they can even affect adults. I make a huge detour around The Twilight Zone Tower of Terror and Space Mountain, but I can't get enough of Slinky Dog Dash and Kali River Rapids—and I've survived the Mad Tea Party and Expedition Everest. Parents know their children best. I remember braving the Tower of Terror once because I felt I couldn't deprive my then-10-year-old just because I was a chicken. I didn't let on that this was not my cup of tea. My prayers to exit the attraction were answered when he asked me shyly if we could ask a cast member to get out. The request was granted instantly by both me and the cast member.

> *We took a 4-year-old and a 5-year-old, and they had the *^%#! scared out of them at Star Tours. We did this first thing in the morning, and it took hours of Tom Sawyer Island and It's a Small World to get back to normal.*
>
> *Preschoolers should start with Dumbo and work up to the Jungle Cruise in late morning, after being revved up and before getting hungry, thirsty, or tired. Pirates of the Caribbean is out for preschoolers. You get the idea.*

At Walt Disney World, anticipate the almost inevitable emotional overload of your young children. Be sensitive, alert, and prepared for practically anything, even behavior that is out of character for your child at home. Most young children take Disney's macabre trappings in stride, and others are easily comforted by an arm around the shoulder or a squeeze of the hand. Parents who know their children tend to become upset should take it slow and easy, sampling more benign adventures, gauging reactions, and discussing with the children how they felt about what they saw.

Some Tips

1. START SLOW AND WARM UP Though each major theme park offers several fairly nonintimidating attractions that you can sample to determine your child's relative sensitivity, the Magic Kingdom is probably the best testing ground. There, try Buzz Lightyear's Space Ranger Spin in Tomorrowland, Peter Pan's Flight in Fantasyland, and the Jungle Cruise in Adventureland to measure your child's reaction to unfamiliar sights and sounds. If your child takes these in stride, try Pirates of the Caribbean. Try the Mad Tea Party or The Barnstormer, both in Fantasyland, or the Astro Orbiter in Tomorrowland to observe how your child tolerates certain ride speeds and motions.

Don't assume that because an attraction is a theater presentation, it will not frighten your child. Trust us on this one. An attraction does not have to be moving to trigger unmitigated, panic-induced hysteria. Rides such as Big Thunder Mountain Railroad and Splash Mountain may look scary, but they don't have even one-fiftieth the potential for terrorizing children as do theater attractions such as *It's Tough to be a Bug!*

LILIANE You know I scream a lot on roller coasters, but did you know that I don't leave my feet on the floor during *It's Tough to Be a Bug!* at the Animal Kingdom? Well, now you know I do not like bugs, and they sting too; they do, they do.

2. BE ATTUNED TO PEER AND PARENT PRESSURE Sometimes young children will rise above their anxiety in an effort to please parents or siblings. This doesn't necessarily indicate a mastery of fear, much less enjoyment. If children leave a ride in apparently good shape, ask if they would like to go on it again (not necessarily now, but sometime). The response usually will indicate how much they actually enjoyed the experience. There's a big difference between having a good time and just mustering the courage to get through.

3. ENCOURAGE AND EMPATHIZE Evaluating a child's capacity to handle the visual and tactile effects of Disney World requires patience, understanding, and experimentation. If a child balks at or is frightened by a ride, respond constructively. Let your children know that lots of people, adults and children, are scared by what they see and feel. Help them understand that it's OK if they get frightened and that their fear doesn't lessen your love or respect. Take pains not to compound the discomfort by making a child feel inadequate; try not to undermine self-esteem, impugn courage, or ridicule. Most of all, don't induce guilt by suggesting the child's trepidation might be ruining the family's fun. It's also sometimes necessary to restrain older siblings' taunting or teasing.

FELICITY Research the rides—watching the POV videos can help you know if you would like certain rides beforehand, so you don't waste your time in the parks or, even worse, get scared!

The Fright Factor

Of course, each youngster is different, but there are eight attraction elements that alone or combined can push a child's buttons:

SMALL-CHILD FRIGHT-POTENTIAL TABLE

THIS QUICK REFERENCE *identifies attractions to be wary of if you have kids ages 3–7. Younger children are more likely to be frightened than older ones. Attractions not listed aren't frightening in any respect. For details on Rider Switch, see page 260.*

The Magic Kingdom

ADVENTURELAND

- **JUNGLE CRUISE** Moderately intense with some macabre sights. A good test attraction.
- **THE MAGIC CARPETS OF ALADDIN** Could scare kids who don't like heights if you raise your ride vehicle high in the air.
- **PIRATES OF THE CARIBBEAN** Slightly intimidating queuing area; intense boat ride with gruesome (though humorously presented) sights and a short, unexpected slide.
- **SWISS FAMILY TREEHOUSE** Anyone who's afraid of heights may want to skip it.
- ***WALT DISNEY'S ENCHANTED TIKI ROOM*** A thunderstorm, loud volume level, and simulated explosions frighten some preschoolers.

FRONTIERLAND

- **BIG THUNDER MOUNTAIN RAILROAD** Visually intimidating from outside, with moderately intense visual effects. The roller coaster is wild enough to frighten many adults, particularly seniors. Rider Switch option provided.
- **FRONTIERLAND SHOOTIN' ARCADE** Frightening to kids who are scared of guns.
- **SPLASH MOUNTAIN** Visually intimidating from the outside, the ride culminates in a 52-foot plunge down a steep chute. Rider Switch option provided.
- **TOM SAWYER ISLAND AND FORT LANGHORN** Some very young children are intimidated by dark walk-through tunnels that can be easily avoided.

LIBERTY SQUARE

- **THE HAUNTED MANSION** The name raises anxiety, as do the sounds and sights of the waiting area. Intense attraction with humorously presented macabre sights. The ride itself is gentle.

FANTASYLAND

- **THE BARNSTORMER** May frighten some preschoolers.
- **DUMBO** Could scare kids who don't like heights if you raise your ride vehicle high in the air.
- **MAD TEA PARTY** Midway-type ride; can induce motion sickness in all ages.
- **THE MANY ADVENTURES OF WINNIE THE POOH** Frightens a few preschoolers.
- **SEVEN DWARFS MINE TRAIN** May frighten some preschoolers.
- **UNDER THE SEA: JOURNEY OF THE LITTLE MERMAID** Animatronic octopus frightens some preschoolers.

TOMORROWLAND

- **ASTRO ORBITER** Visually intimidating from the waiting area, but relatively tame.
- **BUZZ LIGHTYEAR'S SPACE RANGER SPIN** May frighten some preschoolers.
- ***MONSTERS, INC. LAUGH FLOOR*** May frighten some preschoolers.
- **SPACE MOUNTAIN** Very intense roller coaster in the dark; the Magic Kingdom's wildest ride and a scary coaster by any standard. Rider Switch option provided.
- **TOMORROWLAND SPEEDWAY** The noise of the waiting area slightly intimidates preschoolers; otherwise, not frightening.
- **TRON LIGHTCYCLE/RUN** *(opens 2023)* Intense outdoor coaster.

EPCOT

FUTURE WORLD

- **GUARDIANS OF THE GALAXY: COSMIC REWIND** Intense roller coaster in the dark.
- **JOURNEY INTO IMAGINATION WITH FIGMENT** Loud noises and unexpected flashing lights startle younger children. *continued on next page*

SMALL-CHILD FRIGHT-POTENTIAL TABLE

EPCOT *(continued)*

FUTURE WORLD *(continued)*

- **SOARIN' AROUND THE WORLD** May frighten kids age 7 and under, or anyone with a fear of heights. Otherwise mellow. Rider Switch option provided.
- **MISSION: SPACE** Extremely intense space-simulation ride that has been known to frighten guests of all ages. Rider Switch option provided.
- **THE SEAS WITH NEMO & FRIENDS** Sweet but may frighten toddlers.
- **SPACESHIP EARTH** Dark, imposing presentation intimidates a few preschoolers.
- **TEST TRACK** Intense thrill ride that may frighten guests of any age. Rider Switch option provided.

WORLD SHOWCASE

- **NORWAY: FROZEN EVER AFTER** Small drop at the end could scare little ones. Rider Switch option provided.
- **FRANCE: REMY'S RATATOUILLE ADVENTURE** May frighten some preschoolers.

Disney's Animal Kingdom

DISCOVERY ISLAND

- *AWAKENINGS* This nighttime show's shadows, sounds, and projections may frighten kids 5 years and younger.
- **THE TREE OF LIFE/*IT'S TOUGH TO BE A BUG!*** Intense and loud, with special effects that startle viewers of all ages and potentially terrify little kids.

AFRICA

- *FESTIVAL OF THE LION KING* A bit loud, but otherwise not frightening.
- **KILIMANJARO SAFARIS** The proximity of real animals makes a few young children anxious.

ASIA

- **EXPEDITION EVEREST** Can frighten guests of all ages. Rider Switch option provided.
- *FEATHERED FRIENDS IN FLIGHT* Swooping birds may frighten a few small children.
- **KALI RIVER RAPIDS** Potentially frightening and certainly wet for guests of all ages. Rider Switch option provided.
- **MAHARAJAH JUNGLE TREK** Some children may balk at the bat exhibit.

DINOLAND U.S.A.

- **DINOSAUR** High-tech thrill ride rattles riders of all ages. Rider Switch option provided.
- **TRICERATOP SPIN** This midway-type ride frightens only a handful of younger kids.

PANDORA—THE WORLD OF AVATAR

- **AVATAR FLIGHT OF PASSAGE** May frighten kids age 7 and younger, those with claustrophobia or a fear of heights, or those who are prone to motion sickness. Rider Switch option provided.
- **NA'VI RIVER JOURNEY** Dark ride with imposing animatronic figures frighten some preschoolers. Rider Switch option provided.

Disney's Hollywood Studios

ANIMATION COURTYARD

- **STAR WARS LAUNCH BAY** Small children may be scared when meeting Chewbacca because he is huge, and Kylo Ren is intimidating.

SUNSET BOULEVARD

- *FANTASMIC!* Terrifies some preschoolers.
- **ROCK 'N' ROLLER COASTER** The wildest coaster at Walt Disney World. May frighten guests of any age. Rider Switch option provided.

SMALL-CHILD FRIGHT-POTENTIAL TABLE
Disney's Hollywood Studios *(continued)*

SUNSET BOULEVARD *(continued)*

- **THE TWILIGHT ZONE TOWER OF TERROR** Visually intimidating to young kids; contains intense and realistic special effects. The plummeting elevator at the end frightens many adults as well as kids. Rider Switch option provided.

ECHO LAKE

- *INDIANA JONES EPIC STUNT SPECTACULAR!* An intense show with powerful special effects, including explosions, but young kids generally handle it well.
- **STAR TOURS—THE ADVENTURES CONTINUE** Extremely intense visually for all ages; too intense for kids under age 8. Rider Switch option provided.

GRAND AVENUE

- *MUPPET-VISION 3-D* Intense and loud, but not frightening.

HOLLYWOOD BOULEVARD

- **MICKEY & MINNIE'S RUNAWAY RAILWAY** Track ride with wild twists and turns but benign visuals. May scare kids 6 and under.

TOY STORY LAND

- **ALIEN SWIRLING SAUCERS** Can induce motion sickness in riders of all ages. Rider Switch option provided.
- **SLINKY DOG DASH** Mild first roller coaster for most kids. May frighten preschoolers. Rider Switch option provided.
- **TOY STORY MANIA!** Dark ride may frighten some preschoolers.

STAR WARS: GALAXY'S EDGE

- *MILLENNIUM FALCON:* SMUGGLERS RUN Intense visual effects and movement. Rider Switch option provided.
- **STAR WARS: RISE OF THE RESISTANCE** Intense visual effects and movement for all ages.

1. THE ATTRACTION'S NAME Young children will naturally be apprehensive about something called The Twilight Zone Tower of Terror.

2. THE VISUAL IMPACT FROM OUTSIDE Big Thunder Mountain Railroad and Splash Mountain look scary enough to give even adults second thoughts, and the two rides visually terrify many young children.

3. THE VISUAL IMPACT OF THE QUEUING AREA Pirates of the Caribbean's caves and dungeons, for instance can frighten kids.

4. THE INTENSITY OF THE ATTRACTION Some attractions are overwhelming, inundating the senses with sights, sounds, movement, and even smell. *It's Tough to Be a Bug!* at Animal Kingdom, for example, combines loud sounds, lights, smoke, animatronic insects, and 3-D cinematography to create a total sensory experience. For some preschoolers, this is two or three senses too many.

5. THE VISUAL IMPACT OF THE ATTRACTION ITSELF Sights in various attractions range from falling boulders to lurking buzzards, grazing dinosaurs, and waltzing ghosts. What one child calmly absorbs may scare the bejabbers out of another.

6. THE DARK Many Disney World attractions operate indoors in the dark. For some children, darkness alone triggers fear. A child who is frightened on one dark ride (The Haunted Mansion, for example) may be unwilling to try other indoor rides.

7. THE PHYSICAL EXPERIENCE Some rides are wild enough to cause motion sickness, wrench backs, and discombobulate patrons of any age.

8. THE VOLUME The sounds in some attractions and live shows are so loud that younger children flip out, even though the general content of the presentation is quite benign. For toddlers and preschoolers especially, it's good to have a pair of earplugs handy.

Disney Orientation Course

We receive many tips from parents telling how they prepared their young children for the Disney experience. A common strategy is to acquaint children with the characters and stories behind the attractions by reading Disney books and watching Disney videos at home. A more direct approach is to watch videos that show the attractions. A Lexington, Kentucky, mom reports:

> *My timid 7-year-old daughter and I watched rides and shows on YouTube, and we cut out all the ones that looked too scary.*

LILIANE My first roller-coaster experience ever was with my son. We rode The Barnstormer. I screamed his ears off. Next I took a ride with you-know-who: Bob. He tricked me into riding The Incredible Hulk Coaster at Universal's Islands of Adventure. One cannot print what I said to him. (*Editor's note:* Bob is still deaf in one ear.)

You can also view videos at disneyplanning.com. As a YouTube supplement, it gives your kids an adequate sense of what they'll see. You can also watch the **Travel Channel**'s Disney World specials streaming on Hulu, Netflix, and Disney+.

A MAGICAL TIME FOR MOM AND DAD

LILIANE WRITING HERE. Because Bob's idea of a romantic evening is watching *Monday Night Football* on the sofa with his honey instead of sitting in his La-Z-Boy, I'm going to tackle this subject solo.

Let's face it: We all know that moms and dads deserve some special time. But the reality on the ground is that the kids come first. And when the day is over, Mom and Dad are way too tired to think about having a special evening alone. It's difficult enough to catch a movie or go out for a romantic dinner in our hometowns, so how realistic is a romantic parents' night out while on vacation at Walt Disney World?

The answer is: no planning, no romance! With a little magic and some advance preparation, you can make it happen. Here we offer a few suggestions.

Staying at a hotel that offers great kids' programs is a big plus. Consider signing up small children for a half-day program with lunch or dinner while you enjoy your resort. Go to the pool and read a book, and then have a meal in calm and peace. Rent a bike, a boat, or just take off outside the World. This is also a great opportunity to enjoy the thrill rides you passed up when you were busy worshipping at the altar of Dumbo.

PREPARING YOUR CHILDREN TO MEET THE CHARACTERS

FELICITY Mickey didn't speak, but meeting him made me so happy that I cried. I got to hug the greatest sorcerer in the world!

ALMOST ALL THE DISNEY CHARACTERS are quite large; several, like Baloo, are huge! Young children don't expect this and can be intimidated, if not terrified. Discuss the characters with your children before you go. If there is a high school, college, or other sports team with a costumed mascot nearby, arrange to let your kids check it out. If not, then Santa Claus or the Easter Bunny will do.

On the first encounter, don't thrust your child at the character. Allow your little one to deal with this big thing from whatever distance feels safe to him or her. If two adults are present, one should stay near the youngster while the other approaches the character and demonstrates that it's safe and friendly. Some kids warm to the characters immediately; some never do. Most take a little time and several encounters.

There are two kinds of characters: furs, or those whose costumes include face-covering headpieces (including animal characters and humanlike characters such as Captain Hook), and face characters, or those for whom no mask or headpiece is necessary. These include Tiana, Anna, Elsa, Mary Poppins, Ariel, Jasmine, Aladdin, Cinderella, Belle, Snow White, Merida, and Prince Charming.

Only face characters speak. Headpiece characters don't make noises of any kind. Because cast members couldn't possibly imitate the distinctive cinema voice of the character, Disney has determined that it's more effective to keep them silent. Lack of speech notwithstanding, headpiece characters are very warm and responsive and communicate very effectively with gestures.

BOB If your child wants to collect character autographs, it's a good idea to carry a pen the width of a Magic Marker. Costumes make it exceedingly difficult for characters to wield a pen, so the bigger the writing instrument, the better. Unfortunately, a few characters, such as Buzz Lightyear, can't sign autographs at all but will gladly pose for photos.

Some character costumes are cumbersome and limit cast members' ability to see and maneuver. (Eyeholes frequently are in the mouth of the costume or even on the neck or chest.) Children who approach the character from the back or side may not be noticed. It's possible in this situation for the character to accidentally step on the child or knock him or her down. It's best for a child to approach a character from the front, but occasionally not even this works. Duck characters (such as Donald, Daisy, and Uncle Scrooge), for example, have to peer around their bills. Most characters will sign autographs or pose for pictures.

Another great way to show young children how the characters appear in the parks is to buy a *Disney SingAlong Songs* DVD. These programs show Disney characters interacting with real kids. At a minimum, the videos will give your kids a sense of how big the characters are. The best two are *Flik's Musical Adventure SingAlong Songs at Disney's Animal Kingdom* and *SingAlong Songs at Walt Disney*

World—Campout. SingAlong Songs: Disneyland Fun—It's a Small World is a third offering . . . but then there's THAT SONG. No sense turning your brain to mush before even leaving home.

See "Character Analysis," page 262 for an in-depth discussion of the Disney characters.

PHYSICAL PREPARATION

YOU'LL FIND THAT SOME PHYSICAL CONDITIONING, coupled with a realistic sense of the toll that Walt Disney World takes on your body, will preclude falling apart in the middle of your vacation. As one of our readers put it, "If you pay attention to eat, heat, feet, and sleep, you'll be OK."

As you contemplate your family's stamina, it's important to understand that somebody is going to run out of steam first, and when they do, the whole family will be affected. Sometimes a cold drink or a snack will revive the flagging member. Sometimes, however, no amount of cajoling or treats will work. In this situation it's crucial that you recognize that the child, grandparent, or spouse is at the end of his or her rope. The correct decision is to get them back to the hotel. Pushing the exhausted beyond their capacity will spoil the day for them—and you. Accept that stamina and energy levels vary, and be prepared to assist members of your family who poop out. One more thing: no guilt trips. "We've driven 1,000 miles to take you to Disney World and now you're going to ruin everything!" is not an appropriate response.

PREVENT BLISTERS IN FIVE EASY STEPS

1. PREPARE You can easily cover 5–12 miles a day at the parks, and the walking at Disney World is nothing like a 5-mile hike in the woods. At Disney you will be in direct sunlight and on hot pavement most of the time, will have to navigate through huge jostling crowds, and will have to endure waits in line between bursts of

 LILIANE Be sure to give your kids adequate recovery time between training walks (48 hours will usually be enough).

walking. Though most children are active, their normal play usually doesn't condition them for the exertion of touring a Disney theme park. We recommend starting a program of family walks six weeks or more before your trip. A Pennsylvania mom who did just that offers the following testimonial:

> We had our 6-year-old begin walking with us a bit every day one month before leaving. When we arrived [at Walt Disney World], her little legs could carry her, and she had a lot of stamina.

Start with short walks around the neighborhood, on pavement, and increase the distance about 0.25 mile on each outing. Increase your distance gradually until you can do 6 miles without needing

CPR. As you begin, remember that little people have little strides, and though your 6-year-old may create the appearance of running circles around you, consider that (1) he won't have the stamina to go at that pace very long, and (2) more to the point, he probably has to take two strides or so to every one of yours to keep up when you walk together.

2. PAY ATTENTION During your training program, your feet will tell you if you're wearing the right shoes. Choose well-constructed, broken-in running or hiking shoes. If you feel a "hot spot" coming on, chances are that a blister isn't far behind. The most common sites for blisters are heels, toes, and balls of feet. If you develop a hot spot in the same place every time you walk, cover it with a blister bandage or cushion before you set out.

BOB If your children (or you, for that matter) don't consider it cool to wear socks, get over it! Bare feet, whether encased in Nikes, Weejuns, Docksides, or Birkenstocks, will turn into lumps of throbbing red meat if you tackle a Disney park without socks.

Don't wear sandals, flip-flops, or slip-ons in the theme parks. Even if your feet don't blister, they'll get stepped on by other guests or run over by strollers.

3. SOCK IT UP Good socks are as important as good shoes. When you walk, your feet sweat like a mule in a peat bog, and the moisture only increases friction. To counteract this, wear socks made from materials that wick perspiration away from your feet, such as Smartwool or CoolMax. To further combat moisture, dust your feet with antifungal powder.

4. DON'T BE A HERO Take care of foot problems the minute you notice them. Carry a small foot-emergency kit with gauze, antibiotic ointment, disinfectant, and moleskin or blister bandages. Extra socks and foot powder are optional.

If carrying all of that sounds like too much, stop by a First Aid Center in the park as soon as you notice a hot spot on your foot.

BOB If your child is age 8 or younger, we recommend regular foot inspections, whether he or she understands the hot-spot idea or not. Even the brightest and most well-intentioned child will fail to sound off when distracted.

5. CHECK THE KIDS Young children might not say anything about blisters forming until it's too late. Stop several times a day and check their feet. Look for red spots and blisters, and ask if they have any places on their feet that hurt. If you find a blister, either treat it using the kit you're carrying, or stop by a First Aid Center.

A stroller will provide the child the option of walking or riding, and if he collapses, you won't have to carry him. Even if your child hardly uses the stroller at all, it serves as a convenient depository for water bottles and other stuff you may not feel like carrying. Strollers at Walt Disney World are covered in detail starting on page 275.

LILIANE If you have a child who will physically fit in a stroller, use one, no matter how well conditioned your family is.

THE IMPORTANCE OF REST

PHYSICAL CONDITIONING IS IMPORTANT but is *not* a substitute for adequate rest. Even marathon runners need recovery time. If you push too hard and try to do too much, you'll either crash or, at a minimum, turn what should be fun into an ordeal. Rest means plenty of sleep at night, naps during the afternoon on most days, and planned breaks in your vacation itinerary. And don't forget that the brain needs rest and relaxation as well as the body. The stimulation inherent in touring a theme park is enough to put many children and some adults into system overload. It's imperative that you remove your family from this unremitting assault on the senses, preferably for part of each day, and do something relaxing and quiet like swimming or reading.

The theme parks are huge; don't try to see everything in one day. Tour in the early morning and return to your hotel around 11:30 a.m. for lunch, a swim, and a nap. Even during the off-season, when the crowds are comparatively smaller and the temperature more pleasant, the size of the major theme parks will exhaust most children under age 8 by lunchtime. Return to the park in late afternoon or early evening and continue touring. A family from Texas underlines the importance of naps and rest:

> We visited a specific park in the morning, left midafternoon for either a nap in the room or a trip to the pool, and then returned to a park in the evening. On the few occasions we skipped your advice, I was muttering to myself by dinner. I can't tell you what I was muttering . . .

When it comes to naps, this mom does not mince words:

> For parents of small kids—take the book's advice and get out of the park and take the nap, take the nap, TAKE THE NAP! Never in my life have I seen so many parents screaming at, ridiculing, or slapping their kids. (What a vacation!) Disney World is overwhelming for kids and adults. Although the rental strollers recline for sleeping, we noticed most toddlers and preschoolers didn't give up and sleep until 5 p.m., several hours after the fun had worn off, and right about the time their parents wanted them to be awake and polite in a restaurant.

A mom from Rochester, New York, was equally adamant:

> You absolutely must rest during the day. Kids went 8 a.m.–9 p.m. in the Magic Kingdom. Kids did great that day, but we were all completely worthless the next day. Definitely must pace yourself. Don't ever try to do two full days of park sightseeing in a row. Rest during the day. Sleep in every other day.

If you plan to return to your hotel midday and would like your room made up by the time you come back, let housekeeping know before you leave in the morning.

DEVELOPING *a* GOOD PLAN

ALLOW YOUR CHILDREN to participate in the planning of your time at Disney World. Guide them diplomatically through the options, establishing advance decisions about what to do each day and how the day will be structured. Begin with your trip *to* Walt Disney World, deciding what time to depart, who sits by the window, whether to stop for meals or eat in the car, and so on. For the Disney World part of your vacation, build consensus for wake-up call, bedtime, and naps in the itinerary, and establish ground rules for eating, buying refreshments, and shopping. Determine the order for visiting the different theme parks and make a list of must-see attractions. To help you with filling in the blanks of your days, and especially to prevent you from spending most of your time standing in line, we offer a number of field-tested touring plans. The plans are designed to minimize your waiting time at each park by providing step-by-step itineraries that route you counter to the flow of traffic. The plans are explained in detail starting on page 247.

Generally it's better to just sketch in the broad strokes on the master plan. The detail of what to do when you actually arrive at the park can be decided the night before you go or with the help of one of our touring plans once you get there. Above all, be flexible. One important caveat, however: Make sure you keep any promises or agreements that you make when planning. They may not seem important to you, but they will to your children, who will remember for a long, long time if you let them down.

BOB To keep your thinking fresh and to adequately cover all bases, develop your plan in a series of family meetings no longer than 30 minutes each. You'll discover that all members of the family will devote a lot of thought to the plan both during and between meetings. Don't try to anticipate every conceivable contingency, or you'll end up with something as detailed and unworkable as the tax code.

The more you can agree to and nail down in advance, the less potential you'll have for disagreement and confrontation once you arrive. Because children are more comfortable with the tangible than the conceptual, and because they sometimes have short memories, we recommend typing up all of your decisions and agreements and giving a copy to each child. Create a fun document, not a legalistic one. You'll find that your children will review it in anticipation of all the things they will see and do, will consult it often, and will even read it to their younger siblings.

LOGISTICAL PREPARATION

WHEN WE LAUNCHED into our spiel about good logistical preparation for a Walt Disney World vacation, a friend from Indianapolis said, "Wait, what's the big deal? You pack clothes and a few games for the car, then go!" OK, we confess, that will work, but life can be sweeter and the vacation smoother (as well as less expensive) with the right gear.

CLOTHING

LET'S START WITH CLOTHES. We recommend springing for vacation uniforms. For each child buy several sets of matching jeans (or shorts) and T-shirts. For a one-week trip, as an example, get each child three or so pairs of khaki shorts, three or so light-yellow shirts, and three pairs of Smartwool or CoolMax hiking socks. What's the point? First, you don't have to play fashion designer, coordinating a week's worth of stylish combos. Each morning the kids put on their uniform. It's simple, it's time-saving, and there are no decisions to make or arguments about what to wear. Second, uniforms make your children easier to spot and keep together in the theme parks. Third, the uniforms give your family, as well as the vacation itself, some added identity. You might even go so far as to create a logo for the trip to be printed on the shirts.

LILIANE Give your teens the job of coming up with the logo for your shirts. They will love being the family designers.

When it comes to buying your uniforms, we have a few suggestions. Purchase well-made, durable shorts or jeans that will serve your children well beyond the vacation. Buy short-sleeve T-shirts in light colors for warm weather or long-sleeve, darker-colored T-shirts for cooler weather. If you have a big group, we suggest purchasing shirts from a local screen printing company; they offer a wide choice of colors not generally available in retail clothing stores, as well as various sizes. Plus, the shirts will cost a fraction of what a clothing retailer would charge. All-cotton shirts are a little cooler and more comfortable in hot, humid weather; polyester-cotton blends dry faster if they get wet.

LABELS A great idea, especially for younger children, is to attach labels with your family name, hometown, the name of your hotel, the dates of your stay, and your cell phone number inside the shirt. For example:

Carlton Family of Frankfort, KY; Port Orleans–Riverside
May 14–20; 502-555-2108

Instruct your smaller children to show the label to an adult if they get separated from you. Elimination of the child's first name (which most children of talking age can articulate in any event) allows you to order labels that are all the same, can be used by anyone in the family, and can also be affixed to such easily lost items as hats, jackets, hip packs, ponchos, and umbrellas. If fooling with labels sounds like too much of a hassle, check out "When Kids Get Lost" (see page 272) for some alternatives.

FELICITY In addition to our tips, find detailed packing lists online so you know exactly what to bring to the parks and what not to bring.

TEMPORARY TATTOOS An easier and trendier option is a temporary tattoo with your child's name and your phone number. Unlike labels, ID bracelets, or wristbands, the tattoos cannot fall off or be lost. Temporary tattoos last about two weeks, won't wash or sweat off, and are not irritating to the skin. They can be purchased online from **SafetyTat** (safetytat.com). Special tattoos are available for children with food allergies or a cognitive impairment such as autism.

DRESSING FOR COOLER WEATHER Central Florida experiences a wide range of temperatures from November to March, so it could be a bit chilly if you visit during those months. Our suggestion is to layer: For example, a breathable, waterproof or water-resistant windbreaker over a light, long-sleeved polypropylene shirt over a long-sleeved T-shirt. As with the baffles of a sleeping bag or down coat, it's the air trapped between the layers that keeps you warm. If all the layers are thin, you won't be left with something bulky to cart around if you want to pull one or more off. Later in this section, we'll advocate wearing a hip pack. Each layer should be sufficiently compressible to fit into that pack, along with whatever else is in it.

ACCESSORIES

BELTS We recommend pants with reinforced elastic waistbands for children so they don't need a belt (one less thing to find when you're trying to get out the door). If your children like belts or want to carry an item suspended from a belt, buy them military-style 1-inch-wide web belts, available at any Army/Navy surplus or outdoors store. The belts weigh less than half as much as leather, are cooler, and are washable.

SUNGLASSES The Florida sun is so bright and the glare so blinding that we recommend sunglasses for each family member. A good accessory item is an adjustable-length, polypropylene strap for eyewear. This allows your child to comfortably hang sunglasses from his or her neck when indoors or to secure them to his or her head while experiencing a fast ride outdoors.

HIP PACKS AND WALLETS Unless you're touring with an infant or toddler, the largest thing anyone in your family should carry is a hip pack, or fanny pack. Each adult and child should have one. They should be large enough to carry at least a half-day's worth of snacks, as well as other items deemed necessary (such as lip balm, a bandanna, or antibacterial hand gel), and still have enough room to stash a hat, a poncho, or a light windbreaker. We recommend buying full-size hip packs as opposed to small, child-size hip packs at outdoor retailers. The full-size packs are light; can be adjusted to fit any child large enough to tote a hip pack; have slip-resistant, comfortable, wide belting; and will last for years.

FELICITY Don't bring lots of stuff from home, except for clothes, of course. You'll need space in your suitcase for souvenirs. If you're coming from the UK, like me, you won't need to bring much warm clothing, as it is really hot there. You will definitely need lots of sunscreen, sunglasses, a water mister, and a fan, as it is so hot. You will be doing a lot of walking, so you need comfortable shoes. A backpack to wear in the park with comfortable straps is also important.

BOB Unless you advise the front desk to the contrary, all MagicBands (or park cards) can be used for park admission and as credit cards. They are definitely something you don't want to lose. Our advice is to void the charge privileges on preteens' bands or cards and to collect them and put them together someplace safe when not in use.

Do not stash wallets, car keys, park cards, or room keys in children's packs because children tend to inadvertently drop these items in the process of rummaging around for snacks and such.

Before your trip, weed through your billfold and remove to a safe place anything you won't need on your vacation (family photos, local library card, department store credit cards, business cards, and so on). In addition to having a lighter wallet to lug around, you will decrease your exposure in the event that your wallet is lost or stolen. When we're at Walt Disney World, we carry a slim-profile billfold with a driver's license, a credit card, our hotel room key (or MagicBand), and a small amount of cash. You don't need anything else.

LILIANE Equip each child with a big bandanna. Bandannas not only come in handy for wiping noses, scouring ice cream from chins and mouths, and dabbing sweat from the forehead, but they can also be tied around the neck to protect from sunburn.

DAY PACKS We see a lot of folks at Disney World carrying day packs (that is, small, frameless backpacks) and/or water-bottle belts that strap around the waist. Day packs might be a good choice if you plan to carry a lot of camera equipment or baby supplies on your person. Otherwise, try to travel as light as possible. Packs are hot, cumbersome, and not very secure, and they must be removed every time you get on a ride or sit down for a show. In contrast, hip packs can simply be rotated around the waist from your back to your abdomen if you need to sit down. Additionally, our observation has been that the contents of one day pack can usually be redistributed to two or so hip packs.

CAPS Caps protect young eyes from damaging ultraviolet rays, but the lifespan of a child's hat is usually pretty short. Simply put, kids pull caps on and off as they enter and exit attractions, restrooms, and restaurants, and—big surprise—they lose them.

If your children are partial to caps, purchase a short, light cord with little alligator clips on both ends, usually sold at outdoors stores. Hook one clip to the shirt collar and the other to the hat.

LILIANE If your kids are little and don't mind a hairdo change, consider getting them a short haircut before you leave home. Not only will they be cooler and more comfortable, but—especially with your girls—you'll save them (and yourself) the hassle of tangles and about 20 minutes of foo-fooing a day. Don't try this with your confident teen or preteen, though. Braids will do the trick for girls, and your Mick Jagger in the party will be grateful for the bandanna or sports headband, unless of course the hair is meant to keep the monsters and dinosaurs out of sight!

RAINGEAR Rain in Central Florida is a fact of life, though persistent rain day after day is unusual (it is the Sunshine State, after all!). Our suggestion is to check out The Weather Channel or weather forecasts online for three or so days before you leave home to see if there are any major storm systems heading for Central Florida. If it appears that you might see some rough weather during your visit, you're better off bringing raingear from home. If, however, nothing big is on the horizon weather-wise, you can take your chances.

At Disney World, ponchos are available in seemingly every retail shop for $12 (adults) and $10 (kids). If you opt to bring your own, however, any dollar store will usually have them.

If you do find yourself in a big storm, you'll want to have both a poncho and an umbrella. As one *Unofficial* reader put it:

Umbrellas make the rain much more bearable. When rain isn't beating down on your ponchoed head, it's easier to ignore.

Another advantage of buying ponchos before you leave home is that you can choose the color. At Disney World all the ponchos are clear, and it's quite a sight when 30,000 differently clad individuals suddenly transform themselves into what looks like an army of really big larvae. If your family is wearing blue ponchos, they'll be easier to spot.

And consider this tip from a Memphis, Tennessee, mom:

LUCY A poncho or an umbrella is a must when you visit in the summer. The weather changes quickly. A hat is also a must. I like to buy mine at the parks, but you can also bring your own. Get creative and decorate your hat.

Scotchgard your shoes. The difference is unbelievable.

MISCELLANEOUS ITEMS

MEDICATION Some parents of hyperactive children on medication discontinue or decrease the child's normal dosage at the end of the school year. If you have such a child, be aware that Disney World might overly stimulate him or her. Consult your physician before altering your child's medication regimen. Also, if your child has attention-deficit/hyperactivity disorder (ADHD), remember that especially loud sounds can drive him or her right up the wall. Unfortunately, some Disney theater attractions are almost unbearably loud.

SUNSCREEN Overheating and sunburn are among the most common problems of younger children at Disney World. Carry and use broad-spectrum sunscreen of SPF 30 or higher. Be sure to put some on children in strollers, even if the stroller has a canopy. Some of the worst cases of sunburn we've seen were on the exposed foreheads and feet of toddlers and infants in strollers. To avoid overheating, rest regularly in the shade or in an air-conditioned restaurant or show.

BOB Several companies, such as Neutrogena and California Baby, make sunscreens that won't burn your eyes. Look for a product *without* the active ingredient avobenzone, which is usually the culprit when it comes to stinging and burning.

WATER BOTTLES Don't count on keeping young children hydrated with soft drinks and stops at water fountains. Long lines may hamper buying refreshments, and fountains may not be handy. Furthermore, excited children may not realize or tell you they're thirsty or hot. We recommend using a stroller for children age 6 and younger and carrying plastic bottles of water. Bottles run about $3.50 in all major parks. You can save oodles of money by buying your own outside the parks (Disney allows you to bring water into the parks). If you're staying in a rental home, freeze the water and use it to keep sandwiches cool. By the time you're thirsty, the water should be just right. You can also refill the water bottles at any Disney counter-service restaurant by asking for free tap water.

RESPECT FOR THE SUN

Health and science writer **Avery Hurt** sheds some light on the often confusing products and methods for avoiding sunburn. Here's the basic advice from the medical experts.

- **Choose a sunscreen that is convenient for you to use.** Some prefer sprays, others lotions. The form doesn't matter, so choose the one you're most likely to apply.
- **Apply sunscreen a half-hour before going out,** and be sure to apply enough. For adults, 1 ounce per application is recommended—that means a full shot glass's worth each time you apply. An average 7-year-old will probably require two-thirds of an ounce (20 cc). Measure 1 ounce in your hands at home, so you'll be familiar with what an ounce looks like in your palms. It's far more sunscreen than you tend to think.
- **Generously coat all exposed skin.** Then reapply (another full shot glass) every 2 hours or after swimming or sweating. No matter what it says on the label, water resistance of sunscreen is limited. And none of them last all day.
- **There is very little difference in protection** between SPF 30 and SPF 45, 50, or greater. There is no need to spend more for a higher SPF. In fact, it's much safer to choose a lower (and typically less expensive) SPF (as long as it is at least 30) and apply it more often. However, be sure to choose a product that has broad-spectrum coverage, meaning that it filters out both UVA and UVB rays. There's no need to pay extra for special formulas made for children.
- **It's best to keep babies under 6 months old covered** and out of the sun altogether. However, the American Academy of Pediatrics condones a small amount of sunscreen on vulnerable areas, such as the nose and chin, when you have your baby out. Be very careful to monitor your baby even if he is wearing a hat and sitting under an umbrella.
- **Use a lip balm** with an SPF of 15 and reapply often, to your own lips and those of your kids.
- **Sunglasses are also a must.** Too much sun exposure can contribute to age-related macular degeneration (among other things). Not all sunglasses filter out damaging rays. Be sure to choose shades (for adults and kids) that have 99% UV protection. Large lenses and wraparound styles might not look as cool, but they offer better protection.
- **If you do get a sunburn,** cool baths, aloe gel, and ibuprofen (or for adults, aspirin) usually help ease the suffering. Occasionally, sunburns can be as dangerous in the short term as they are in the long term. If you or your child experiences nausea, vomiting, high fever, severe pain, confusion, or fainting, seek medical care immediately.

COOLERS If you drive to Walt Disney World, bring two coolers: a small one for drinks in the car and a large one for the hotel room. If you fly and rent a car, stop and purchase a large biodegradable cooler, which can be discarded at the end of the trip. Refrigerators in all Disney resort rooms are free of charge. If you arrive at your room and there is no refrigerator, call and request one.

Coolers allow you to have breakfast in your hotel room, store snacks and lunch supplies to take to the theme parks, and bypass the expensive vending machines at the hotel. To keep the contents of your cooler cold on a long drive, we suggest freezing two 1-gallon milk jugs full of water before you head out. In a good cooler, it will take the jugs a few days to thaw. If you buy a cooler in Florida or to supplement your frozen jugs, you can use bagged ice and ice from the ice machine at your hotel. You will save a bundle of cash, as well as significant time, by reducing dependence on restaurant meals and expensive snacks and drinks purchased from vendors.

Please note that Disney no longer allows guests to bring loose ice or dry ice into its theme parks and water parks. If you bring a cooler into the parks, use reusable ice packs, freeze water inside sealed bags or bottles, or request free ice from any quick-service restaurant. This change is intended to speed up security screenings.

FOOD-PREP KIT If you plan to make sandwiches or have cereal in your hotel room, bring your favorite condiments and seasonings from home. A good travel kit will include mayonnaise, ketchup, mustard, salt and pepper, and packets of sugar or artificial sweetener. Also bring plastic knives, spoons, bowls, and cups; paper napkins; and sandwich bags. Of course, you can buy this stuff in Florida, but you probably won't consume it all, so why waste the money? If you drink bottled beer or wine, bring a bottle opener and corkscrew. If you fly, make sure

LILIANE About one week before I arrive at WDW, I ship a box to my hotel containing food, plastic cutlery, and toiletries, plus pretty much any other consumables that might come in handy during my stay. If you fly, this helps avoid baggage fees and problems with liquid restrictions for carry-on luggage.

the corkscrew is in your checked baggage. Liliane has donated a few to the Transportation Security Administration by leaving them in her carry-on.

ENERGY BOOSTERS Kids get cranky when they're hungry, and when that happens, your entire group has a problem. Like many parents, you might, for nutritional reasons, keep a tight rein on snacks available to your children at home. At Walt Disney World, however, maintaining energy and equanimity trumps snack discipline. For maximum zip and contentedness, give your kids snacks containing complex carbohydrates (fruits, crackers, nonfat energy bars, and the like) *before* they get hungry or show signs of exhaustion. You should avoid snacks high in fats and proteins because these foods take a long time to digest and will tend to unsettle your stomach if it's a hot day.

Bob enthusiastically recommends **Clif Bloks,** chewable cubes that replace electrolytes in the body. They're light, come in several flavors (all tasty), and don't melt even on the hottest days.

ELECTRONICS Regardless of your children's ages, always bring a night-light. Flashlights are also handy for finding stuff in a dark hotel room after the kids are asleep. If you are a big coffee drinker and are traveling by car, bring along a coffee maker if it's not included in your room (all Disney resort rooms have them).

Smartphones, tablets, and electronic games with earbuds are often controversial gear for a family outing. We recommend compromise. Earbuds allow kids to create their own space even when they're with others, and that can be a safety valve. That said, try to agree before the trip on some earbud parameters, so you don't begin to feel as if they're being used to keep other family members and the trip itself at a distance.

POWERING UP Speaking of smart devices, their use has become standard in the parks. In addition to taking photos, guests also use apps to check on waiting times and score seats at restaurants. All that technology comes at a price: dead batteries. You spend all day using your phone to make ride reservations and post pictures on social media, but at the end of the day, you can't find the missing members of your party because you don't have enough power to place a call or even send a text. Having experienced the problem firsthand, Liliane has a few suggestions:

First, bring a portable phone charger and always, *always* bring the charging cable. You can purchase a portable phone charger at the theme parks for $30; the kit includes Android and iPhone cables. When it runs out of juice, simply go to one of the kiosks (available in all parks) and swap your empty battery for a charged one at no cost! Back at home, you can charge the battery via a USB cable plugged into your computer or any AC outlet. Liliane and Bob were instant fans.

You can recharge at the Baby Care Centers in the parks and at restrooms. Charging policies at restaurants vary—our experience has been that the upscale places will fuss about a request, while the counter-service places don't mind.

Here are a few good choices during lunch- or dinnertime: In the Magic Kingdom, several tables at the **Columbia Harbour House** (especially upstairs) are near electrical outlets. At **Pecos Bill Tall Tale Inn and Cafe,** a table opposite the condiments station is next to a power outlet. The tent at the back of Storybook Circus, next to **Pete's Silly Sideshow,** is set up with several charging stations and benches to rest. Another great station is in the rest area across from the *Tangled*–**themed restrooms;** outlets are located in fake tree stumps. At these stations you can charge via USB or a regular plug. Also try the shopping area at the exit to **Space Mountain.** At Disney's Hollywood Studios, don't count on the sit-down restaurants; rather, head for **Backlot Express,** which has lots of tables nestled next to power outlets. At EPCOT, you'll find outlets at **Sunshine Seasons.** At Animal Kingdom, try the outlets at **Pizzafari** or **Tusker House.** The bar at **Tiffins** is the mother of all charging stations.

DON'T FORGET THE TENT *Bob here:* When my daughter was preschool-age, I almost went crazy trying to get her to sleep in a shared hotel room. She was accustomed to having her own room at home and was hyper-stimulated whenever she traveled. I tried makeshift curtains and room dividers and even rearranged the furniture in a few hotel rooms to create the illusion of a more private, separate space for her. It wasn't until she was around 4 years old and I took her camping that I seized on an idea that had some promise. She liked the cozy, secure, womblike feel of a backpacking tent and quieted down much more readily than she ever had in hotel rooms. So the next time the family stayed in a hotel, I pitched my backpacking tent in the corner of the room. In she went, nested for a bit, and fell asleep.

Modern tents are self-contained, with floors and an entrance that can be zipped up (or not) for privacy but cannot be locked. Affordable and sturdy, many are as simple to put up as opening an umbrella. Some tents are even specifically made to turn a bed into a fort. Kids appreciate having their own space and enjoy the adventure of being in a tent, even one set up in the corner of a hotel room. Light and compact when stored, a two-person tent in its own storage bag (called a stuff sack) will take up about one-tenth or less of a standard overhead bin on a commercial airliner. Another option for infants and toddlers is to drape a sheet over a portable crib or playpen to make a tent.

"THE BOX" *Bob again:* On one memorable Disney World excursion when my kids were young, we started each morning with an involuntary scavenger hunt. Invariably, seconds before our scheduled departure to the theme park, we discovered that some combination of shoes, bill-folds, sunglasses, hip packs, or other necessity was missing. For the next 15 minutes we would root through the room like pigs hunting truffles in an attempt to locate the absent items. Finally, I swung by a liquor store and mooched a big empty box. From then on, every time we returned to the room, I had the kids deposit shoes, hip packs, and other potentially wayward items in the box. After that the box was off-limits until the next morning, when I doled out the contents.

PLASTIC GARBAGE BAGS On two attractions, **Kali River Rapids** in Animal Kingdom and **Splash Mountain** in the Magic Kingdom, you are certain to get wet and possibly soaked. If it's really hot and you don't care, then fine. But if it's cool or you're just not up for a soaking, bring a large plastic trash bag to the park. By cutting holes in the top and on the sides, you can fashion a sack poncho that will keep your clothes from getting wet. On the raft ride, you will also get your feet wet. If you're not up for walking around in squishy, soaked shoes, bring a second, smaller plastic bag to wear over your feet while riding.

LILIANE Often little ones fall asleep in their strollers (hallelujah!). Bring a large light-weight cloth to drape over the stroller to shield your child from the sun. A few clothespins will keep it in place.

SUPPLIES FOR INFANTS AND TODDLERS

BASED ON RECOMMENDATIONS from hundreds of *Unofficial Guide* readers, here's what we suggest you carry with you when touring with infants and toddlers:

- A disposable diaper for every hour you plan to be away from your hotel room
- A cloth diaper or kitchen towel to put over your shoulder for burping
- Two receiving blankets: one to wrap the baby and one to lay the baby on or to drape over you when you nurse. You can also use a blanket as a makeshift canopy to shelter a baby in a stroller from the sun.
- Ointment for diaper rash
- A box of baby wipes
- Prepared formula in bottles if you aren't breastfeeding
- A bib, a baby spoon, and baby food if your infant is eating solid foods
- For toddlers, a small toy for comfort and to keep them occupied

Baby Care Centers at the theme parks will sell you just about any-thing you forget or run out of. As with all things Disney, prices will be higher than elsewhere, but at least you won't need to detour to a drugstore in the middle of your touring day.

TIPS FOR EXPECTANT MOTHERS

A VISIT TO WALT DISNEY WORLD may not be the ideal vacation for an expectant mom, but even so, quite a lot of them visit the World every year. The most important advice for expectant moms is to take it easy. If you travel by car or plane, make sure you incorporate plenty of time for rest into your schedule. Don't stay on your feet all day; stick to a healthy, balanced diet (most of all, don't skip meals); and drink plenty of fluids. Keep the dining options flexible; morning sickness or sudden aversions to or preferences for food can be dealt with easily if you don't make reservations and go for whatever you feel like eating. Always carry some snacks and bottled water with you. A plastic bag folded in your pocket in case you feel unwell takes no space but gives peace of mind. You should also discuss your upcoming Walt Disney World visit with your physician, who will certainly have valuable tips. From a Branchburg, New Jersey, woman:

> Moms should be really mindful of the temperature. Stay hydrated, and have realistic expectations for how much you'll be able to do. We averaged 5–7 miles of walking per day, and this may have been a bit too much for me. A midday nap or swim break was required.

Comfortable clothes are a must, as are broken-in, supportive shoes. You might consider getting a maternity support belt to keep your back from hurting. If you're using a special pillow at night to support your belly, don't forget to bring it with you. If you don't have enough space in your suitcase, consider shipping one ahead. Of course, the hotel will provide you with extra pillows if needed.

While there have been no confirmed cases of the Zika virus in the Orlando area to date, there have been a small number of confirmed cases in other parts of Florida. Disney provides free insect repellent to all guests. Pregnant women, or those expecting to become pregnant, may want to take extra precautions.

If you don't own a maternity bathing suit, purchase one; you will be glad you did. A relaxing afternoon at the pool or a float down the lazy river in the water parks is wonderful.

At the parks, take frequent breaks; put your legs up! Expectant moms are welcome at the Baby Care Centers, where they can sit and relax in a pleasant atmosphere. Go back to the hotel for a nap during the day, or even plan a day away from the parks. Go splurge and have a massage; your back and feet will be grateful. Sleep is precious, so don't skimp on it; a good night of sleep is better than all the fireworks in the sky.

Heed the warnings! Here is a short list of **rides that are absolutely not suitable for expectant moms:** Alien Swirling Saucers, Avatar Flight of Passage, The Barnstormer, Big Thunder Mountain Railroad, Dinosaur, Expedition Everest, Guardians of the Galaxy: Cosmic Rewind, Kali River Rapids, Kilimanjaro Safaris, *Millennium Falcon:* Smugglers Run, Mission: Space, Remy's Ratatouille Adventure, Rock 'n' Roller Coaster, Seven Dwarfs Mine Train, Slinky Dog Dash, Space Mountain,

Splash Mountain, Star Tours, Star Wars: Rise of the Resistance, Test Track, Tomorrowland Speedway, The Twilight Zone Tower of Terror, and Tron Lightcycle/Run. Remember, this is just a short list; use your own best judgment.

A word about the water parks: Obviously, experiencing the offerings of **Crush 'n' Gusher** or **Miss Adventure Falls** at Typhoon Lagoon or barreling down **Summit Plummet** at Blizzard Beach is ill-advised if you're in the family way, but the water parks offer great lazy rivers and pools, as well as shady beaches where you can relax and let the rest of your group enjoy the wild things.

TIPS FOR NURSING MOTHERS

BABY CARE CENTERS are available at all Walt Disney World parks, and nursing mothers will not have difficulty finding a comfortable, clean, pleasant place to take care of their infants. In addition to breastfeeding rooms equipped with rocking chairs and love seats, the childcare facilities have sinks for washing and a room with toys and videos for your older children. Should you need diapers, baby clothes, children's medicines, and other small necessities, Disney has those items available right there for a fee.

Here are some tips to remember when visiting:

- Getting there by plane: Remember to nurse your child at takeoff and landing. It helps to open the baby's ears and eliminates discomfort due to pressure changes.

- Nurse your infant at the first sign of hunger. You and the baby will be calmer, and you will attract much less attention if you feed the baby before he or she gets fussy and screams at the top of his or her lungs.

- Wear comfortable clothes. While you can access the Baby Care Centers at any time, there is nothing wrong with nursing your infant in a calm, shady spot anywhere at Walt Disney World or at the pool of your hotel. A dress with buttons in the front and a small baby blanket to put over your shoulder will do the trick. A large T-shirt that allows the baby to nurse "from under" is another option. In case you feel self-conscious, remember that Florida was the first state to protect breastfeeding in public by law in 1993.

- Pick a quiet place to nurse your baby.

- Adequate rest is another must. Schedule several breaks into your day and go back to the hotel for a nap.

- Make sure you plan regular, healthy meals. A nursing mom, much like an expectant mother, has increased nutritional needs. In addition to eating a well-balanced diet and drinking plenty of fluids, it's always a good idea to take along some snacks.

- It is hot in Florida, and while it's important for all visitors to drink lots of water, it's crucial for nursing moms, so stay hydrated!

- Schedule a down day. If you have older children, let Dad take them to the park while you stay behind with the baby. A day of rest works wonders.

- If you plan on a parents' evening out, consider pumping milk for later use or supplementing breast milk with a bottle of formula.

- Nursing is exhausting, and so is touring Walt Disney World. Fatigue can reduce milk flow. Get enough rest and don't stay up past your bedtime. The night of a nursing mom is already short. Leave the park whenever you feel tired, and get enough sleep.

- A bath and a massage calm most fussy babies and are good for Mom as well. Bring along some Epsom salts for a relaxing bath, or stop at Basin at Disney Springs and splurge on bath bombs.

TRIAL RUN

AFTER GIVING THOUGHTFUL CONSIDERATION to all areas of mental, physical, organizational, and logistical preparation discussed in this chapter, what remains is to familiarize yourself with Walt Disney World itself and, of course, to conduct your field test. Yep, that's right; we want you to take the whole platoon on the road for a day to see if you are combat-ready. No joke; this is important. You'll learn who poops out first; who is prone to developing blisters; who has to pee every 11 seconds; and, given the proper forum, how compatible your family is in terms of what you like to see and do.

For the most informative trial run, choose a local venue that requires lots of walking, dealing with crowds, and making decisions on how to spend your time. Regional theme parks and state fairs are your best bets, followed by large zoos and museums. Devote the whole day. Kick off the morning with an early start, just like you will at Walt Disney World, paying attention to who's organized and ready to go and who's dragging their butt and holding up the group. If you have to drive an hour or two to get to your test venue, no big deal. You'll have to do some commuting at Disney World too. Spend the whole day, eat a couple meals, and stay late.

Don't bias the sample (that is, mess with the outcome) by telling everyone you're practicing for Walt Disney World. Everyone behaves differently when they know they're being tested or evaluated. Your objective is not to run a perfect drill but to find out as much as you can about how the individuals in your family, as well as the family as a group, respond to and deal with everything they experience during the day. Pay attention to who moves quickly and who is slow; who is adventuresome and who is reticent; who keeps going and who needs frequent rest breaks; who sets the agenda and who is content to follow; who is easily agitated and who stays cool; who tends to dawdle or wander off; who is curious and who is bored; who is demanding and who is accepting. You get the idea.

Evaluate the findings of the test run the next day. Don't be discouraged if your test day wasn't perfect; few (if any) are. Distinguish between problems that are remediable and problems that are intrinsic to your family's emotional or physical makeup (no amount of hiking, for example, will toughen up some people's feet).

Establish a plan for addressing fixable problems (further conditioning, setting limits before you go, trying harder to achieve family consensus, and so on), and develop strategies for minimizing or working around problems that are a fact of life (waking sleepyheads 15 minutes early, placing moleskin on likely blister sites before setting out, packing familiar food for the toddler who balks at restaurant fare). If you are an attentive observer, a fair diagnostician, and a creative problem solver, you'll be able to work out a significant percentage of the issues you're likely to encounter at Walt Disney World before you ever leave home.

WALT DISNEY WORLD *for* GUESTS *with* SPECIAL NEEDS

DISNEY WORLD IS EXCEPTIONALLY ACCOMMODATING to guests with physical challenges. If you have a disability, Disney is well prepared to meet your needs.

DISNEY RESORTS

IF YOU'LL BE STAYING AT A DISNEY RESORT, let the reservation agent know of any special needs you have when you book your room. The following equipment, services, and facilities are available at most Disney hotels; note that not all hotels offer all items.

Accessible vanities	Portable toilets
Bed and bathroom rails	Refrigerators
Braille on signs and elevators	Roll-in showers
Closed-captioned TVs	Rubber bed padding
Double peepholes in doors	Shower benches
Handheld showerheads	Strobe-light smoke detectors
Knock and phone alerts	TTYs
Lowered beds	Wheelchairs for temporary use
Phone amplifiers	Widened bathroom doors

SERVICE ANIMALS

DISNEY WELCOMES DOGS AND MINIATURE HORSES that are trained to assist guests with disabilities. Service animals are permitted in most locations in all Disney resorts and theme parks, although they may not be admitted on certain theme park rides. Check disneyworld .disney.go.com/guest-services/service-animals for more information.

IN THE THEME PARKS

EACH THEME PARK OFFERS a free booklet describing services and facilities for disabled guests at tinyurl.com/disabilitiesguide. You can also obtain these pamphlets when you enter the parks, at resort front desks, and at wheelchair-rental locations inside the parks.

For specific requests, call ☎ 407-560-2547 (voice). When the recorded menu begins, press 1. Limit your questions to those regarding services and accommodations for your disability (address other questions to ☎ 407-824-4321 or 407-827-5141 [TTY]).

DISNEY'S DISABILITY ACCESS SERVICE (DAS)

DISNEY'S DISABILITY ACCESS SERVICE is designed to accommodate guests who can't wait in regular standby lines. Among its benefits is the complimentary access to the (much shorter) Lightning Lane lines at popular attractions. We strongly suggest registering online (see tinyurl.com/wdw-das) between 2 and 30 days before your trip; you'll have a video chat with a Disney representative, who'll help get everything set up. Alternatively, you can register on the day of your visit at the **Guest Relations** window of the first theme park you enter.

You only need to sign up once every 60 days, and the service carries over to each subsequent park you visit. The process is explained below. For clarity, we'll refer to the person signing up for the DAS service as the DAS enrollee. *Note:* Guests whose disability requires only a wheelchair or mobility vehicle do not need the DAS.

PREPARATION Before you sign up, make sure you have either the MagicBands, park tickets, or My Disney Experience emails of everyone in your group. All your group's MagicBands/tickets will be linked to the DAS—this comes in handy in situations we'll describe below. The DAS is good for parties of up to six people. For parties of more than six, check with Guest Relations.

SIGNING UP FOR DAS At your video chat or Guest Relations, you'll be asked to present identification and describe the enrollee's limitations. You don't have to provide documentation of a specific condition; rather, what Disney is looking for is a description of how the condition affects the enrollee in the parks. The goal is to determine the right level of assistance, not to obligate you to prove that the enrollee qualifies. The enrollee must be present during this call or visit.

Be as detailed as possible in describing limitations. For instance, if your child has autism spectrum disorder and has trouble waiting in long lines or has sensory issues such as sensitivity to noise, let the cast member know each of these things specifically.

The DAS also requires a photograph. Pictures are taken with an iPad (the cast member will come to you if you can't make it up to the counter). If the DAS is for a child, you may use either the child's photo or substitute your own.

Finally, you must check a box that says you agree to be bound by Disney's DAS rules. While this seems like a formality, this Disney travel agent notes that nothing happens until you click:

> *Make sure readers know to follow down through the directions and click on "Accept Terms and Conditions." This is really important and they won't help you if you don't accept them, so do this before you start the chat.*

Once registered, the interview process gets rave reviews, such as this one from a reader from Greenwich, Connecticut:

> *I signed up for DAS this morning, and the process was really easy.*

The whole thing took less than an hour, and I was able to prebook all the rides I wanted.

DAS ADVANCE The DAS Advance feature allows you to select two attractions to visit on each day of your trip. For example, if you say you're visiting EPCOT on the Tuesday of your trip, then at some point before Tuesday, you'll be able to pick two attractions in EPCOT to visit using the Lightning Lane (see page 323). You'll see these DAS Advance reservations in My Disney Experience, too. Like Genie+, you'll get a 1-hour return window during which you can come back and ride those selected attractions. And unlike the regular Genie+ and Individual Lightning Lane programs (see page 254), guests using DAS can reride these attractions via Lightning Lane on the same day.

This dad loved the DAS Advance selections:

The DAS Advance selections are a lifesaver for those that need it. I don't know what we would have done without DAS and being able to effectively stay one ride ahead of the crowds. I was very impressed that all rides were available—we could have used DAS for Rise of the Resistance if we had wanted to.

USING DAS ON THE DAY OF YOUR VISIT The DAS may be used at any attraction or character-greeting venue with a queue. Anyone with a linked MagicBand or ticket can present it outside the attraction; if the standby wait time is less than 15 minutes, you'll usually be escorted through the standby entrance or the alternative-access/Lightning Lane entrance. If the standby time is higher, a cast member will provide a time for you to return to ride—again, this is entered into MDE.

The return time will be the current wait time minus 10 minutes—if, say, you get to Splash Mountain at 12:20 p.m. and the standby time is 40 minutes, your return time will be 30 minutes later, at 12:50 p.m. You may return at the specified time or anytime thereafter. The DAS enrollee must also return to ride. When you return, the enrollee will scan his or her MagicBand first, followed by the other members of your group. Everyone will be given access to the Lightning Lane or alternative-access line.

Make sure that everyone enrolled in the DAS wants to ride the same rides. Because they're effectively Genie+ or Individual Lightning Lane reservations, people in your group who want another reservation instead of DAS will still be constrained by the "when can I get a next reservation" rules of Genie+ and Individual Lightning Lane. Here's some advice from a large family with different tastes in rides:

A word of warning: Only add to your DAS selection for a ride those people that plan on riding that ride. If someone backs out, MDE doesn't easily let you cancel their inclusion immediately. MDE will think some of your party won't be eligible for a "next" DAS selection because they haven't used their most recent. And if you do book a future one with the eligible party members, there's no way of adding the remaining party later without going to Guest Relations. It made me think twice before booking so I wouldn't have to stop by Guest Relations every time I needed help clearing up the past ride they didn't use.

After your initial two DAS Advance selections, you can hold one DAS return time at a time. However, you can also use Genie+ (where offered), Individual Lightning Lane, boarding groups, and the DAS at the same time. Bring an extra battery for your phone.

WHEELCHAIRS AND ELECTRIC VEHICLES

GUESTS WITH LIMITED MOBILITY may rent wheelchairs, three-wheeled electric conveyance vehicles (ECVs, also known as scooters), and electric standing vehicles (ESVs). These give nonambulatory guests tremendous freedom and mobility. Most rides, shows, attractions, restrooms, and restaurants accommodate them. If you're in a park and you need assistance, go to Guest Relations.

Wheelchairs rent for $12 per day, or $10 per day for multiday rentals. Rentals are available at all Walt Disney World theme parks (see Parts 11–14 for specific locations) and at Disney Springs. ECVs and ESVs cost $50 per day, plus a $20 refundable deposit ($100 refundable deposit at Disney Springs and the water parks). Wheelchairs are available for rent at the water parks and Disney Springs for $12 per day with a refundable $100 deposit.

Your rental deposit slip is good for a replacement wheelchair in any park during the same day. You can rent a chair at the Magic Kingdom in the morning, return it, go to any other park, present your deposit slip, and get another chair at no additional charge.

Buena Vista Scooters (☎ 866-484-4797 or 407-331-9147, buenavistascooters.com) rents scooters with a wide variety of options, starting at around $33 per day for two to six days. **Apple Scooter** (☎ 321-726-6837, applescooter.com) also rents ECVs but is slightly more expensive for shorter rentals. Both companies include free delivery to and pickup from your Disney resort. You'll need to be present for delivery and pickup, however.

All Disney lots have close-in parking for disabled visitors; request directions when you pay your parking fee. Most (not all) rides, shows, restrooms, and restaurants accommodate wheelchairs, as do monorails and buses, as outlined below.

Even if an attraction doesn't accommodate wheelchairs, ECVs, or ESVs, nonambulatory guests may ride if they can transfer from their wheelchair to the ride vehicle. Disney staff, however, aren't trained or permitted to assist with transfers—guests must be able to board the ride unassisted or have a member of their party assist them. Either way, members of the nonambulatory guest's party will be permitted to ride with him or her.

Because the waiting areas of most attractions won't accommodate wheelchairs, nonambulatory guests and their parties should ask a cast member for boarding instructions as soon as they arrive at an attraction entrance.

Disabled guests and their families give Disney high marks for accessibility and sensitivity. An Arlington, Virginia, woman writes:

My mom has mobility problems, and she was worried about getting around. Disney supplied a free wheelchair, every bus had kneeling steps for wheelchair users, and the cast members sprang into action when they saw us coming.

Much of the Disney transportation system is disability accessible. Monorails can be accessed by ramp or elevator, the Skyliner has special gondolas for wheelchairs and scooters, and all bus routes are served by vehicles with wheelchair lifts, though unusually wide or long wheelchairs (or motorized chairs) may not fit the lift. Watercraft accommodations for wheelchairs are iffier.

A large number of Disney hotel guests use scooters (ECVs). This affects commuting times by bus, as each Disney bus can accommodate only two scooters or wheelchairs. A Minneapolis woman touring with her parents shared her experience:

I was stunned by the number of scooters this year. My parents each had one, and several times they had to wait to find a bus that had available space for scooters or wheelchairs. If people needing a scooter can make it to the bus stop on foot, they'd be better off waiting until they get to the park and renting a scooter there.

If you plan to use a wheelchair or scooter while visiting **Wilderness Lodge & Villas, Fort Wilderness Resort & Campground,** or an **EPCOT** resort, call ☎ 407-560-2547 (voice) for the latest information on watercraft accessibility.

Food and merchandise locations at theme parks, Disney Springs, and hotels are generally accessible, but some fast-food queues and shop aisles are too narrow for wheelchairs. At these locations, ask a cast member or member of your party for assistance.

A scooter user from Riverside, California, shares her experience:

Had a great time! It wasn't easy using a scooter, though. Stores and restaurants have little room for a scooter to maneuver—I kept getting boxed in by people or had to back out of areas that had no turnaround space.

DIETARY RESTRICTIONS AND ALLERGIES

WALT DISNEY WORLD RESTAURANTS work hard to accommodate guests' special dietary needs. When you make a dining reservation online or by phone, you'll be asked about food allergies and the like. When you arrive at table-service restaurants and buffets, alert the host or hostess and your server.

Almost all Walt Disney World restaurants have dedicated allergy-friendly menus available; ask any cast member for a menu when you arrive at the restaurant. Allergy-friendly menus cover most people and offer a variety of food as diverse as the standard menu. For example, the Magic Kingdom's **Cosmic Ray's Starlight Cafe** offers at least 14 entrées for guests with seafood, nut, grain, egg, dairy, and soy allergies, as well as for guests who keep kosher.

Also, Disney chefs at many sit-down restaurants have adapted their dishes so that almost anyone with a common allergy can order off the standard menu. At **Narcoossee's**, for example, every item on the standard menu has been adapted to the allergy menu. **TouringPlans.com** also maintains a list of Disney World restaurant menus, including most special offerings and prices—look for the words *allergy friendly* on the menu list at tinyurl.com/allergymenuswdw. For more information, email special.diets@disneyworld.com or visit tinyurl.com/wdw specialdiets.

An Idaho mom and her teenage daughter found Disney restaurants very responsive to their dietary needs:

> *My daughter and I both have a gluten allergy. I have never felt so well cared for and safe eating anywhere else in the world. From our resort (both the food court and Boatwright's) to every single quick-service or sit-down restaurant, we had several choices, and we never waited longer than 8 minutes for our special orders.*

To request kosher meals at table-service restaurants, call ☎ 407-824-1391 24 hours in advance. All Disney menus have vegetarian options; most can be made vegan without having to speak to the chef, but vegetarians, vegans, and pescatarians should still speak up when making dining reservations.

Those with special diets and a sweet tooth should try the vegan, gluten-free, and kosher treats from **Erin McKenna's Bakery NYC**, with locations at Disney Springs and many Disney hotel food courts (they also deliver to the Disney area). Besides sweets, the bakery does a tasty line of savory breads from time to time. You can also order special-occasion cakes and baked goods (☎ 407-938-9044 or 855-462-2292, erinmckennasbakery.com).

MEDICATIONS

FOR GUESTS WHO EXPERIENCE ALLERGIC REACTIONS that can be severe or life-threatening, Disney provides epinephrine injectors (**EpiPens**) at **First Aid Centers** and other locations throughout the parks (check your park guide maps for locations). Nurses and emergency responders are trained in EpiPen use, but guests with known conditions should always travel with their own supplies.

CBD PRODUCTS In 2019, a 69-year-old grandmother from Tennessee was arrested at a Magic Kingdom security checkpoint for possession of CBD (cannabidiol) oil, which her doctor had prescribed to treat arthritis pain. The charges against her were later dropped, but the incident highlighted a major discrepancy between federal and then-current Florida law. Federal law permits the production and sale of hemp-derived CBD products containing 0.3% THC or less, but at the time of the woman's arrest, these products were subject to the same restrictions as medical marijuana in Florida. A state law that removed these restrictions went into effect July 1, 2019. Disney guests should verify that their products' THC content falls within legal limits.

VISUALLY IMPAIRED, DEAF, OR HARD-OF-HEARING GUESTS

GUEST RELATIONS PROVIDES FREE **assistive-technology devices** to guests who are visually impaired, deaf, or hard of hearing ($25 refundable deposit, depending on the device). Visually impaired guests can customize the given information (such as architectural details, restroom locations, and descriptions of attractions and restaurants) through an interactive audio menu that is guided by a GPS in the device. For deaf or hard-of-hearing guests, amplified audio and closed-captioning for attractions can be loaded into the device.

Braille guidebooks are available from Guest Relations at all parks ($25 refundable deposit), and **Braille menus** are available at some theme park restaurants. Some rides provide **closed-captioning;** many theater attractions provide **reflective captioning.**

Disney provides **sign language interpretations** of live shows at the theme parks on certain designated days of the week:

- **Magic Kingdom** Mondays and Thursdays
- **EPCOT** Fridays
- **Disney's Animal Kingdom** Saturdays and Tuesdays
- **Disney's Hollywood Studios** Sundays and Wednesdays

Get confirmation of the interpreted-performance schedule a minimum of one week in advance by calling Disney World information at ☎ 407-824-4321 (voice) or 407-827-5141 (TTY). You'll be contacted before your visit with a schedule.

NONAPPARENT DISABILITIES

WE RECEIVE MANY LETTERS from readers whose traveling companion or child requires special assistance but who, unlike a person in a wheelchair, is not visibly disabled. Autism, for example, can make it very difficult or impossible for someone to wait in line for more than a few minutes or in queues surrounded by a crowd. A trip to Disney World can be nonetheless positive and rewarding for guests who are on the autism spectrum. And while any Disney vacation requires planning, a little extra effort to accommodate the affected person will pay large dividends. Disney's guide for guests with cognitive disabilities is available for download at tinyurl.com/wdwcognitiveguide.

If you have a family member with autism or another developmental disability, we recommend visiting autismattheparks.com, which was awarded the 2015 Sunshine Blog Award for Best Cause Blog. The creator, Maureen Deal, regularly shares with us her tips for navigating Orlando's theme parks and resorts with your autistic child. Make sure to visit her website.

REMEMBERING *Your* TRIP

1. Purchase a notebook for each child, and spend some time each evening recording the events of the day. If your children have trouble getting motivated or don't know what to write about, start a discussion; otherwise, let them write or draw whatever they want to remember from the day's events.

SABRINA I always collect extra park maps to remember my trip. They're also useful for scrapbooks.

2. Collect mementos along the way, and create a treasure box in a small tin or cigar box. Months or years later, it's fun to look at postcards, pins, or park cards to jump-start a memory.

3. Add inexpensive postcards to your photographs to create an album; then write a few words on each page to accompany the images.

4. Give each child a disposable camera to record their version of the trip. One 5-year-old snapped photos that never showed anyone above the waist—his view of the world—and they were priceless.

5. Many families take cameras or make videos with their smartphones and tablets, though we recommend using them sparingly so you don't end up viewing the trip through the lens rather than being in the moment. If you must, take your device along, but record only a few moments of major sights (too much is boring anyway). And let the kids record and narrate—be sure they speak loudly so as to be heard over the not-insignificant background noise of the parks. Use the lockers available at all the parks if the equipment becomes a burden or when you're going to experience an attraction on which it might get damaged or wet. Unless your device is waterproof, leave it behind on Splash Mountain, Kali River Rapids, and any other ride where water is involved. Selfie sticks are not allowed at any Walt Disney World theme park.

6. Polaroid cameras are back in fashion, and the instant pictures will become the stars of your scrapbook.

7. At the Magic Kingdom, collect any button that applies to your visit (such as First Visit, Birthday, Just Married, or Engaged); they are available for free at City Hall/Guest Relations.

8. At the Main Street Fire Station, you can get a free pack of the Sorcerers of the Magic Kingdom cards for each member of the family. Get the cards even if you don't play the game—they're great keepsakes. You can obtain one new pack every day you visit the Magic Kingdom.

Finally, when it comes to taking photos and collecting mementos, don't let the tail wag the dog. You're not going to Disney World to build the biggest scrapbook in history. Or as this Houston mom put it:

Tell your readers to get a grip on the photography thing. We were so busy shooting pictures that we kind of lost the thread.

HOW TO HAVE FUN BEFORE AND AFTER YOUR VISIT—OR, THINGS BOB WOULD NEVER DO

PREPARING FOR YOUR Walt Disney World vacation is important, but it's equally important to have a good time. Doing so before you leave is yet another way to get the whole family involved.

The weekend before your departure, plan a party for all who are going to Walt Disney World. Pick a Disney movie everyone will enjoy and plan a meal in front of the TV. A chocolate cake or cookies shaped like the famous mouse head will be a guaranteed success and add to the fun. This is the perfect time to go over the must-see list and reiterate the dos and don'ts.

LILIANE Don't forget to send Bob an invitation.

A similar event can be planned upon your return, when it's time to share pictures and maybe even the movie you made during your visit to Disney World.

BOB Liliane throws a party at the least provocation—Groundhog Day, National Tulip Day, Bless the Reptiles Day, you name it. But scheduling a wingding the weekend before you go to Disney World is to me like holding an Easter egg hunt in a cattle stampede—just a little too much going on to add one more thing.

Great Websites

ARTS AND CRAFTS AND PARTY TIPS: thefrugalsouth.com/easy-disney-crafts-for-kids

SOME SERIOUS COOKING: magicalkingdoms.com/wdw/recipes

TRY LILIANE'S RECIPE FOR THE MASTER'S CUPCAKE, or Grey Stuff, as Lumière calls it in *Beauty and the Beast*. These delicious cupcakes are served at Be Our Guest in Fantasyland at the Magic Kingdom: tinyurl.com/masterscupcake.

PART 6

READY, SET, TOUR!

▐ TOURING RECOMMENDATIONS

HOW MUCH TIME IS REQUIRED TO SEE EACH PARK?

THE MAGIC KINGDOM AND EPCOT offer such a large number of attractions and special live-entertainment options that it's impossible to see everything in a single day, with or without a midday break. For a reasonably thorough tour of each, allocate a minimum of a day and a half and preferably two days. The Animal Kingdom can be seen in a day, though planning on a day and a half allows for a more relaxed visit. If you're a *Star Wars* fan, be prepared to spend at least two days at Disney's Hollywood Studios (DHS).

WHICH PARK TO SEE FIRST?

THIS QUESTION IS LESS OBVIOUS than it appears, especially if your party includes children or teenagers. Children who see the Magic Kingdom first expect the same type of entertainment at the other parks. At EPCOT, they're often disappointed by the educational orientation (as are many adults). And children may not find Animal Kingdom as exciting as the Magic Kingdom or DHS—real animals, after all, can't be programmed to entertain on cue.

First-time visitors should see **EPCOT** first; you'll be able to enjoy it without having been preconditioned to think of Disney entertainment as solely fantasy or adventure. See **Animal Kingdom** second. Like EPCOT, it's educational, but its live animals provide a change of pace.

Next see **DHS,** which helps you make the transition from the educational EPCOT and Animal Kingdom to the fanciful Magic Kingdom. And, because DHS has fewer substantial attractions, you won't walk as much.

We recommend saving the **Magic Kingdom** for last, though we do recognize that, for many readers, the Magic Kingdom *is* Disney World. If you can't postpone the Magic Kingdom without a major revolt, at least see EPCOT first. Adult orientation notwithstanding, there's lots that children age 7 and up will love, younger children not so much. At EPCOT make sure to visit the Kidcot Fun Spot at each of the 11 international pavilions around World Showcase, described in Part 8. They'll be the highlight of your child's day. If seeing Mickey is your kid's top priority, be advised that you can see him in each of the major theme parks. Any cast member can tell you where to find him.

OPERATING HOURS

THE DISNEY WORLD WEBSITE publishes preliminary park hours in advance, but **schedule adjustments can happen at any time, including the day of your visit.** Check disneyworld.com or call ☎ 407-824-4321 for the exact hours before you arrive. Off-season, parks may be open as few as 9 hours (9 a.m.–6 p.m.). At busy times (particularly holidays), they may operate 8 a.m.–2 a.m.

When Disney launches new attractions or lands, that drives up demand and contributes to unbearably long lines, such as those seen at Pandora at Animal Kingdom, as well as at Star Wars: Galaxy's Edge and Toy Story Land at DHS. To be safe, call the number in the previous paragraph if you're going to Animal Kingdom or DHS and you want to be there at or before opening.

OFFICIAL OPENING VERSUS REAL OPENING

WHEN YOU CALL, you're given "official" hours. Sometimes parks open earlier. If the official hours are 9 a.m.–9 p.m., for example, Hollywood Boulevard at DHS might open at 8:30 a.m., and the remainder of the park at 9 a.m.

The Magic Kingdom is a special case: Main Street, U.S.A., opens a full hour before the park's official opening time on days without morning Early Theme Park Entry. If the listed opening time is 9 a.m., then most of Main Street and the Central Plaza will be open for photos, shopping, and getting in line for rides by 8 a.m. This significantly alters the Magic Kingdom's early-morning traffic patterns by dumping up to 500 people at Seven Dwarfs Mine Train the instant the park opens.

Disney surveys local hotel reservations, estimates how many visitors to expect on a given day, and opens the theme parks early to avoid bottlenecks at parking facilities and ticket windows, as well as to absorb crowds as they arrive.

Attractions shut down at approximately the official closing time. Main Street in the Magic Kingdom remains open 30 minutes to an hour after the rest of the park has closed, though as mentioned earlier, high-demand rides such as those in Star Wars: Galaxy's Edge and Avatar Flight of Passage in Pandora will stay open to serve those still waiting in line at closing.

THE RULES

SUCCESSFUL TOURING of the Magic Kingdom, EPCOT, Animal Kingdom, or DHS hinges on five rules:

1. Determine in Advance What You Really Want to See

What rides and attractions appeal most to you? Which additional rides and attractions would you like to experience if you have some time left? What are you willing to forgo?

To help you set your touring priorities, we describe each theme park and its attractions in subsequent chapters. In each description, we include the authors' evaluation of the attraction and the opinions of Walt Disney World guests, expressed as star ratings. Five stars is the best possible rating.

Finally, because attractions range from midway-type rides to high-tech extravaganzas, we've developed a hierarchy of categories to pinpoint an attraction's magnitude:

SUPER-HEADLINERS The best attractions the theme park has to offer. Mind-boggling in size, scope, and imagination, they represent the cutting edge of modern attraction technology and design.

HEADLINERS Full-blown, multimillion-dollar, full-scale themed adventures and theater presentations. These employ modern technology and design, along with a range of special effects.

MAJOR ATTRACTIONS Themed adventures on a more modest scale but incorporating state-of-the-art technologies. Or, larger-scale attractions of older design.

MINOR ATTRACTIONS Midway-type rides, small dark rides (cars on a track, zigzagging through the dark), small theater presentations, transportation rides, and elaborate walk-through attractions.

DIVERSIONS Exhibits, both passive and interactive. These include playgrounds, video arcades, and street theater.

Not every attraction fits neatly into these descriptions, but it's a handy way to compare any two. Remember that bigger and more elaborate doesn't always mean better. Peter Pan's Flight, a minor attraction in the Magic Kingdom, continues to be one of the park's most beloved rides. Likewise, for many young children, no attraction, regardless of size, surpasses Dumbo.

2. Arrive Early! Arrive Early! Arrive Early!

This is the single most important key to efficient touring and avoiding long lines. First thing in the morning, there are no lines for attractions, and there are fewer people. The same four rides you experience in 1 hour in the early morning can take as long as 3 hours after 10:30 a.m. Eat breakfast before you arrive at the park; don't waste prime touring time sitting in a restaurant.

The earlier a park opens, the greater your advantage. This is because most vacationers won't rise early and get to a park before it opens. Fewer people are willing to make an 8 a.m. opening than a 9 a.m. opening. If you visit during midsummer, arrive at the turnstile 30–40 minutes before opening. During holiday periods, arrive 45–60 minutes early. By arriving, we mean be at the turnstiles at the recommended time. Consider that you'll have to clear security before advancing to the turnstiles.

LILIANE You'll be able to see and do much more if you arrive early.

If getting the kids up earlier than usual makes for rough sailing, don't despair: You'll have a great time no matter when you get to the park. Many families with young children have found that it's better to accept the relative inefficiencies of arriving at the park a bit late than to jar the children out of their routine. We include a number of touring plans for sleepyheads in this guide.

3. Avoid Bottlenecks

Crowd concentrations and/or faulty crowd management cause bottlenecks. Avoiding bottlenecks involves being able to predict where, when, and why they occur. Concentrations of hungry people create bottlenecks at restaurants during lunch and dinner. Concentrations of people moving toward the exit at closing time create bottlenecks in gift shops en route to the gate. Concentrations of visitors at new and popular rides and at rides slow to load and unload create bottlenecks and long lines.

The best way to avoid bottlenecks is to use one of our field-tested touring plans available in clip-out form, complete with a map, on pages 487–518. The plans will save you as much as 4.5 hours of standing in line in a single day.

4. Go Back to Your Hotel for a Midday Rest

You may think we're beating a dead horse with this midday nap thing, but if you plug away all day at the theme parks, you'll understand how the dead horse feels. No joke; resign yourself to going back to the hotel in the middle of the day for swimming, reading, and a snooze.

LILIANE If you can't calm them—dunk them. Whenever my son was too wound up to nap or go to bed at night, I took him to the pool—water works wonders.

5. Let Off Steam

Time at a Disney theme park is extremely regimented for younger children. Often held close for fear of losing them, they are ushered from line to line and attraction to attraction throughout the day. After a couple of hours of being on such a short leash, it's not surprising that they're in need of some physical freedom and an opportunity to discharge pent-up energy. If you don't return to your hotel for a break, consider one of the creative play areas in the parks. At the Magic Kingdom, the best place for kids to let off steam is Tom Sawyer Island. At the Animal Kingdom, The Boneyard offers plenty of opportunity for exploration. Less contained but wonderful on a hot summer day are the splash zones at EPCOT, the Magic Kingdom, and Disney Springs. Just remember to bring a change of clothes, and keep footwear dry—touring the park in wet sneakers is a recipe for blisters. And please, parents, stay off your phone and keep an eye on your kids, as all play areas are fairly large, and it's pretty easy to lose sight of a child while he or she is playing.

YOUR DAILY ITINERARY

PLAN EACH DAY in three blocks:

1. Early-morning theme park touring
2. Midday break
3. Late-afternoon and evening theme park touring

BOB We strongly recommend deferring parades, stage shows, and other productions until the afternoon or evening.

Choose the attractions that interest you most, and check what time of day we recommend you visit. If your children are 8 years old or younger, review the attractions' fright-potential ratings (see table on pages 213–215). Use one of our touring plans, or work out a step-by-step plan of your own and write it down. Experience popular attractions as early as possible, transitioning to less popular attractions around midmorning. Plan on departing the park for your midday break by 11:30 a.m. or so.

For your late-afternoon and evening touring block, you don't necessarily have to return to the same theme park. If you purchased the Park Hopper option, you may opt to spend the afternoon/evening block somewhere different. In any event, as you start your afternoon/evening block, see less popular attractions until about 5 p.m. After 5 p.m., any attraction is fair game, but if you stay into the evening, try the most popular attractions during the hour just before closing, when they are likely to be less crowded.

In addition to attractions, each theme park offers a broad range of live entertainment. In the morning, concentrate on the attractions. For the record, we regard live shows that offer five or more daily performances (except street entertainment) as attractions. Thus, *Indiana Jones Epic Stunt Spectacular!* at Disney's Hollywood Studios is an attraction, as is *Festival of the Lion King* at the Animal Kingdom. The evening fireworks at EPCOT and the parades at the Magic Kingdom, on the other hand, are live-entertainment events. When planning your day, also be aware that major live events draw large numbers of guests from the attraction lines. Thus, a good time to see an especially popular attraction is during a parade or other similar event.

TOURING PLANS

OUR TOURING PLANS are step-by-step guides for seeing as much as possible with a minimum of standing in line. They're designed to help you avoid crowds and bottlenecks during times of moderate-to-heavy attendance. On days of lighter attendance (see "When to Go to Walt Disney World," page 42), the plans will still save time, but they won't be as critical to successful touring. *Unofficial Guide* touring plans, it seems, have side effects. As two readers attest, the plans can fan the embers of love and help you impress your friends. First from a 30-something mother of two from Oconomowoc, Wisconsin:

LILIANE Don't get obsessed with the touring plans. It's your vacation, after all. You can amend or even scrap the plans if you want.

> *My husband was a bit doubtful about using a touring plan, but on our first day at Magic Kingdom, when we had done all of the Fantasyland attractions and ridden Splash Mountain twice before lunch, he looked at me with amazement and said, "I've never been so attracted to you."*

And from a young Gardner, Massachusetts, reader:

> *I went with my school for Magic Music Days. I've been to Disney World before several times, and my parents have always used the guide. I looked crazy to my friends, with my book marked and well-worn and a stack of clip-out touring plans in my hand. The group that traveled around with me were amazed, commenting that it seemed like we were in front of a huge crowd. As soon as we left a ride that we had walked onto with no wait just minutes before, there would be a line! Thank you for helping me impress my friends!*

What You Can Realistically Expect from the Touring Plans

The best way to see as much as possible with the least amount of waiting is to arrive early. Several of our touring plans require that you be at the park when it opens. Because this is often difficult and sometimes impossible for families with young children or nocturnal teens, we've developed additional touring plans for families who get a late start. You won't see as much as with the early-morning plans, but you'll see significantly more than visitors without a plan.

Variables That Affect the Success of the Touring Plans

The touring plans' success will be affected by how quickly you move from ride to ride; when you take breaks and how many you take; when, where, and how (counter service or table service) you eat meals; and your ability, or lack thereof, to find your way around. Smaller groups almost always move faster than larger groups, and parties of adults generally cover more ground than families with young kids. Rider Switch, also known as baby swap or child swap, among other things (see page 260), inhibits families with little ones from moving expeditiously among attractions.

Many of the touring plans already include time for meeting the most popular characters at their dedicated venues. However, the spontaneous appearance of a Disney character strolling the park can stop a touring plan in its tracks. If your kids collect character autographs, anticipate these interruptions by including character greetings when creating your online touring plans, or else negotiate some understanding with your children about when you'll collect autographs. Note that queues for autographs are sometimes as long as the queues for major attractions. Early morning is the best time to experience popular attractions, so you may have some tough choices to make.

LILIANE Character meals are another way to collect autographs and might be something you could promise your avid collector in exchange for a full day of touring when the signature hunt is off.

While we realize that following the touring plans isn't always easy, we nevertheless recommend continuous, expeditious touring until around noon.

A multigenerational family from Aurora, Ohio, wonders how to know if you're on track or not, writing:

It seems like the touring plans were very time-dependent, yet there were no specific times attached to the plan outside of the early morning. On more than one day, I often had to guess as to whether we were on track. Having small children and a grandparent in our group, we couldn't move at a fast pace.

There is no objective measurement for being on track—each group's experience will differ to some degree. Nevertheless, the sequence of attractions in the touring plans will allow you to enjoy the most attractions in the least amount of time. Two quickly moving adults will probably take in more attractions in a specific time period than will a large group made up of children, parents, and grandparents. However, each will maximize their touring time and experience as many attractions as possible.

What To Do If You Lose the Thread

If unforeseen events interrupt a plan:

1. If you're following a touring plan in our **Lines** app (touringplans.com/lines), just press the Optimize button when you're ready to start touring again. Lines will figure out the best possible plan for the remainder of your day.

2. If you're following a printed touring plan, skip a step on the plan for every 20 minutes' delay. For example, if you lose your phone and spend an hour hunting for it, skip three steps and pick up from there.

3. Forget the plan and organize the remainder of the day using the standby wait times listed in Lines.

Because most touring plans are based on being present as soon as the theme park opens, you need to know about opening procedures. Disney transportation to the parks begins 1–2 hours before official opening. The parking lots open at around the same time.

Each park has an entrance plaza outside the turnstiles. Usually, you're held there until 30 minutes before the official opening time, when you're admitted. What happens next depends on the season, the day's crowds, and whether or not you are an on-site guest.

HOW TO FIND THE TOURING PLAN
THAT'S BEST FOR YOU

THE TOURING PLANS FOR EACH PARK are described in the parks' respective chapters. The descriptions will tell you for whom (for example, teens, parents with preschoolers, grandparents, and so on) or for what situation (such as sleeping late or enjoying the park at night) the plans are designed. The actual plans are on pages 487–518. Each plan includes a numbered map of the park to help you find your way around. Clip out the plan of your choice and take it with you to the park.

Our best touring plans are those provided in this guide. However, customized plans are available at TouringPlans.com; there you can create specific plans based on your family setup, your favorite attractions, restaurants, and more.

Will the Plans Continue to Work Once the Secret Is Out?

Yes! First, most of the plans require that a patron be there when a park opens. Many Disney World patrons simply won't get up early while on vacation. Second, less than 2% of any day's attendance has been exposed to the plans—too few to affect results. Last, most groups tailor the plans, skipping rides or shows according to taste.

How Frequently Are the Touring Plans Revised?

We revise them every year, and updates are always available at Touring Plans.com. Most complaints we receive come from readers using out-of-date editions of *The Unofficial Guide*. Even if you're up-to-date, though, be prepared for surprises. Opening procedures and showtimes may change, for example, and you can't predict when an attraction might break down.

"Bouncing Around"

Disney generally tries to place its popular rides on opposite sides of the park. In the Magic Kingdom, for example, the most popular attractions are positioned as far apart as possible—in the north, east, and west corners of the park—so that guests are more evenly distributed throughout the day.

It's often possible to save a lot of time in line by walking across the park to catch one of these rides when crowds are low. Some readers object to this crisscrossing. A woman from Decatur, Georgia, told us she "got dizzy from all the bouncing around." Believe us, we empathize.

In general, our touring plans recommend crossing the park only if you'll save more than 1 minute in line for every 1 minute of extra walking. We sometimes recommend crossing the park to see a newly opened ride, too; in these cases, a special trip to visit the attraction early avoids much longer waits later. Also, live shows, especially at the Studios, sometimes have performance schedules so at odds with each other (and the rest of the park's schedule) that orderly touring is impossible.

If you want to experience headliner attractions in one day without long waits, you can see those first (requires crisscrossing the park), use Genie+ or Individual Lightning Lane, or hope to squeeze in visits during parades and the last hour the park is open (may not work).

Touring Plans and the Type-A Reader

We suggest sticking to the plans religiously, especially in the mornings, if you're visiting during busy times. The consequence of touring spontaneity in peak season is hours of standing in line. When using the plans, however, relax and always be prepared for surprises and setbacks.

If you find your type-A brain doing cartwheels, reflect on the advice of a woman from Trappe, Pennsylvania:

> I had planned for this trip for two years and researched it using guidebooks, websites, and information received from WDW. On night three of our trip, I took an unscheduled trip to the emergency room. When the doctor asked what the problem was, I responded, "I don't know, but I can't stop shaking, and I can't stay here very long because I have to get up in a couple hours to go to Disney's Hollywood Studios." Diagnosis: an anxiety attack caused by my excessive itinerary.

However, a vet from Annandale, Virginia, warns:

> I'm retired Navy, and planning a Disney visit today is almost like planning an amphibious landing for the invasion! I pity any free spirit who blithely shows up at a Disney park for the first time without any advance planning and expects to flit from ride to ride without a care in the world. Disney World will eat you alive if you're not careful!

Touring Plan Rejection

Some folks don't respond well to the regimentation of a touring plan. If you encounter this problem with someone in your party, roll with the punches, as this Maryland couple did:

> The rest of the group was not receptive to the use of the touring plans. Rather than argue, I left the touring plans behind as we ventured off for the parks. You can guess the outcome. We recorded our trip and watched the movies when we returned home. About every 5 minutes or so, there's a shot of us all gathered around a park map trying to decide what to do next.

A reader from Royal Oak, Michigan, ran into trouble by not getting her family on board ahead of time:

> If one member of the family is doing most of the research and planning (like I did), communicate what the book/touring plans suggest. I failed to do this and it led to some, shall we say, tense moments between my husband and me on our first day. However, once he realized how much time we were saving, he understood why I was so bent on following the plans.

Finally, note that our mobile app, **Lines,** can be used to find attractions with low wait times, even if you're not using a touring plan.

Touring Plans for Low-Attendance Days

Each year we receive a number of letters similar to the following one from Lebanon, New Jersey:

> *The guide always assumed there would be large crowds. We had no lines. An alternate tour for low-traffic days would be helpful.*

There are, thankfully, still days on which crowds are low enough that a full-day touring plan isn't needed. However, some attractions in each park develop a bottleneck even if attendance is low:

- **MAGIC KINGDOM** *Enchanted Tales with Belle,* The Many Adventures of Winnie the Pooh, Peter Pan's Flight, Seven Dwarfs Mine Train, Space Mountain, Splash Mountain, and Tron Lightcycle/Run (once it opens)
- **EPCOT** Frozen Ever After, Meet Anna and Elsa at Royal Sommerhus, Test Track, Soarin', and the brand-new Guardians of the Galaxy: Cosmic Rewind
- **ANIMAL KINGDOM** Avatar Flight of Passage, Dinosaur, Expedition Everest, Kilimanjaro Safaris, and Na'vi River Journey
- **DISNEY'S HOLLYWOOD STUDIOS** Alien Swirling Saucers, Mickey & Minnie's Runaway Railway, *Millennium Falcon:* Smugglers Run, Rock 'n' Roller Coaster, Slinky Dog Dash, Star Wars: Rise of the Resistance, Toy Story Mania!, and The Twilight Zone Tower of Terror

For this reason, we recommend following a touring plan at least through the first five or six steps. If you're pretty much walking onto every attraction, scrap the remainder of the plan. Alternatively, you can see the aforementioned attractions immediately after the park opens.

Early Theme Park Entry and the Touring Plans

If you're a Disney resort guest you will be admitted to all four Disney theme parks 30 minutes before official park opening. Off-site resort guests who enter the parks at official opening will find thousands of on-site guests already ahead of them in lines.

In the **Magic Kingdom,** Early Entry attractions currently operate in Fantasyland and Tomorrowland. At **EPCOT,** they're *Beauty and the Beast Sing-Along,* Frozen Ever After, Mission: SPACE, Remy's Ratatouille Adventure, The Seas with Nemo & Friends, Soarin' Around the World, Spaceship Earth, and Test Track. At **Animal Kingdom,** they're Avatar Flight of Passage, Dinosaur, Expedition Everest, *It's Tough to Be a Bug!,* Na'vi River Journey, and TriceraTop Spin. At **Disney's Hollywood Studios:** Alien Swirling Saucers, Mickey & Minnie's Runaway Railway, *Millennium Falcon:* Smugglers Run, Rock 'n' Roller Coaster, Slinky Dog Dash, Star Tours—The Adventures Continue, Rise of the Resistance, Toy Story Mania!, and The Twilight Zone Tower of Terror.

Extended Evening Theme Park Hours and the Touring Plans

Extended Evening Theme Park Hours (EETPH) is the limited revival of the former Evening Extra Magic Hours program. Typically held on one night per week, and (for now) only for certain parks, EETPH allows guests staying at Disney's Deluxe and DVC resorts—and only those guests—two extra hours in that park after official closing. Thus, if the

Magic Kingdom closes at 9 p.m. to regular guests, the park will operate extended hours from 9 to 11 p.m. for guests at Disney Deluxe or DVC resorts only. Most attractions are open during extended hours, although new rides are often excluded, for maintenance. The advantage to extended hours is that so few guests qualify that those lines are exceptionally short. Crowds are so low that a touring plan isn't needed—just head to any attraction that interests you. The same is true for most special events, including the Halloween and Christmas parties.

WHO SUMMONED *the* GENIE?

PRIOR TO 2021, Disney ran a *free* ride reservation system called FastPass+, which allowed you to reserve a spot on an attraction for a specific day and time. You could book a reservation at a specific ride, for a specific 1-hour time window, up to two months before your trip. When your reservation arrived, you went to the attraction, got in a line separate from the regular ("standby") line, and were given priority access to get on the ride. In practice, the wait to use a FastPass+ was often around 20% of the wait in the standby line, all free of charge.

The original goal of FastPass+ was to increase guest satisfaction—Disney knew that guests who used it were more satisfied than guests who did not. The problem, from Disney management's perspective, was that it was hard to translate an increase in guest satisfaction—through shorter waits in line—into more money for shareholders.

In 2021 Disney's management decided to make this trade-off much clearer, by charging money to wait less. The result is an unprecedented, unpopular, unwieldy system for navigating Disney's theme parks. There are now at least four different Disney processes for waiting in line at rides. Each method has its own set of rules, and often those rules are put in place for Disney's benefit, not yours. We think this complexity is intentional—some guests will simply give up trying to figure out how it all works and throw money at Disney to make it simpler.

Here are the ways you can wait in line at Walt Disney World:

STANDBY QUEUES This is what most people are familiar with: You get in a line for a ride, and you wait some number of minutes until it's your turn to ride. It doesn't cost anything, and the wait-time sign in front of the attraction gives you some idea of how long you'll be waiting.

It's rare for any Walt Disney World ride not to operate a standby queue. The latest one not to do so was EPCOT's Guardians of the Galaxy: Cosmic Rewind, which uses boarding groups instead (see opposite page). We expect that the Tron Lightcycle/Run roller coaster will operate with boarding groups when it opens.

Standby queues are free with park admission.

SINGLE-RIDER LINE This time-saver is a line for individuals riding alone. It's available at **Test Track** at EPCOT; **Expedition Everest** at Animal Kingdom; and **Rock 'n' Roller Coaster** and *Millennium Falcon:* **Smugglers**

Run at the Studios. The objective is to fill odd spaces left by groups that don't quite fill the ride vehicle. Because there aren't many singles and most groups are unwilling to split up, single-rider lines are usually shorter. The only downside is you miss most of the queue theming or preshow entertainment.

BOARDING GROUPS/VIRTUAL QUEUES A boarding group, also known as a virtual queue, is a virtual line without a specific return time. Boarding groups are typically used at new, popular rides, so it's possible you'll see them at Tron Lightcycle/Run when it opens at the Magic Kingdom. Here's how it works: You first make a park reservation for whatever park has the ride you want to ride. At exactly 7 a.m. on the day of your visit, you'll use the My Disney Experience (MDE) app to request a boarding group for that ride. If you're successful, you'll get a boarding group number (e.g., boarding group 57) and a rough estimate of how long you must wait until your boarding group is called (e.g., 250 minutes).

You need to be fast and lucky: Boarding groups for Guardians of the Galaxy: Cosmic Rewind were often completely allocated for the entire day within 10 seconds of 7 a.m. So many people tried to get a boarding group that it was essentially a lottery as to who got in. And if anything went wrong, your chance to experience the ride was almost certainly gone. (A second group of reservations was available at 1 p.m., using the same process. These afternoon reservations were less likely to be called to ride, however.)

If the ride is running smoothly, boarding groups typically start getting called within 30 minutes of park opening, beginning with boarding group 1. The MDE app will display the current range of boarding groups that are able to ride now. When your group is called, the app will alert you so you can return.

Boarding groups are used at rides that Disney thinks are likely to break down often. Because new rides may not have worked out all their bugs, Disney isn't confident that it can give guests a specific time to return and ride. For example, suppose Disney gave you a specific time of 1–2 p.m. to ride Tron. If that ride breaks down and is unavailable between 1 and 2 p.m., then at 2 p.m., it must accommodate everyone who didn't get to ride between 1 and 2, plus everyone who was scheduled to ride between 2 and 3. There's not enough ride capacity to do that (and Disney doesn't want to run the ride at half capacity in anticipation of it, either). Boarding groups solve this problem by not attaching a specific return time to your virtual wait.

An issue with boarding groups is that you are not able to ride unless your first park of the day is where the attraction using boarding groups is located. You have to have a park reservation before you attempt to get a boarding group. So, if you plan to park-hop to the park where the boarding-group attraction is located, you have almost no chance of riding this parks' headliner for free. The same is likely to be true of any ride that uses boarding groups, in any park.

The good news is that you can also make an Individual Lightning Lane (ILL) reservation for Guardians of the Galaxy or other eligible rides that use boarding groups, even if you are park-hopping to its location later. It's exactly the same as the process for booking any other ILL (see opposite page).

Boarding groups are free with park admission and reservations.

GENIE+ AND LIGHTNING LANE (AKA PAID FASTPASS+) Genie+ is a paid version of FastPass+, built as a feature in the My Disney Experience app. For **$15.98 per person per day,** you'll have access to the **Lightning Lane**—a separate line that's shorter than the standby line—at participating attractions. As with FastPass+, guests in the Lightning Lane are given priority to board. Almost all the attractions and character greetings that offered FastPass+ now offer Lightning Lane.

Here's how it works: Genie+ will show you the next available 1-hour return-time window, such as 1–2 p.m., at each participating attraction. You'll pick the attraction whose return time works best for your day. You can make another Genie+ reservation when you redeem your first, or 2 hours after making the reservation, whichever comes first. If you plan on park-hopping, though, you won't be able to pick a Genie+ reservation at your second park until return times are being distributed for after 2 p.m.

When you return to ride, you'll use the Lightning Lane. You can use your pass up to 5 minutes before the stated return-time window, or up to 15 minutes after, but beyond that grace period, the reservation will be invalid.

Disney hasn't said how much of each ride's capacity is now for sale. In practice, Disney puts between four and nine people from the Lightning Lane on the ride for every one person it takes from the standby line. But even so, people often wait 20 minutes or more in the Lightning Lane line once they return to ride.

Note that you can only purchase Genie+ on a day-by-day basis, starting at midnight before each morning of your reserved park visit. That differs from FastPass+, where you could make a ride reservation up to 60 days in advance. Thus, it's possible for a ride to run out of Genie+ return times before you arrive at the park.

You do not need to purchase Genie+ on every day of your trip, or for every member of your party. You also do not need to be in the park to make a Lightning Lane reservation. Guests staying at Disney's resorts can make Individual Lightning Lane (ILL) purchases starting at 7 a.m., which is also the time at which you make your first Genie+ Lightning Lane reservation and (when offered) boarding group reservations. We're not sure why Disney has scheduled these critical, mutually exclusive tasks for the exact same time of day—we suspect it's that nobody who made the decision ever had to do this for themselves. It would be better if the start times for each were staggered slightly.

Speaking of boarding groups, Genie+ isn't available on rides that use boarding groups. For those, you'll need ILL.

INDIVIDUAL LIGHTNING LANE (ILL) The idea here is that you'll pay even more to get on a new or very popular ride. If, when it opens, Tron Lightcycle/Run offers boarding groups but you didn't get one, or if you want to avoid a 2-hour wait at Guardians of the Galaxy: Cosmic Rewind, Disney will offer you a chance to ride at a price, using Individual Lightning Lane. ILL is offered only at the most popular attractions. At press time, these were the ILL attractions in each park:

- **MAGIC KINGDOM** Seven Dwarfs Mine Train
- **EPCOT** Guardians of the Galaxy: Cosmic Rewind
- **HOLLYWOOD STUDIOS** Star Wars: Rise of the Resistance
- **ANIMAL KINGDOM** Avatar Flight of Passage

Individual Lightning Lane is separate from Genie+; you don't need to purchase Genie+ to purchase Individual Lightning Lane. Likewise, purchasing Individual Lightning Lane does not get you access to the attractions in the Genie+ portfolio.

Purchasing an ILL in MDE is straightforward. Passes are sold per-person, and guests are limited to two purchases per day. As mentioned previously, **guests staying at Disney's resorts can make ILL purchases starting at 7 a.m. Off-site guests must wait to make reservations until the park they're visiting opens officially.** Popular ILLs frequently sell out before park opening; if you're not eligible to book at 7 a.m., you shouldn't rely on getting one as part of your touring strategy. Unlike with Genie+ Lightning Lane, Individual Lightning Lane buyers are given several return times to choose from. When it's your time to ride, you'll be directed to the Lightning Lane to board.

Prices vary by attraction, day of year, and time of day. The lowest cost we've seen so far for an ILL is $7, at Space Mountain and Expedition Everest. The highest cost (so far) is $15 at Star Wars: Rise of the Resistance. We expect these prices to increase.

Is Genie+ Worth the Cost?

In general, yes. We recommend using Genie+ at the Magic Kingdom, Hollywood Studios, and Animal Kingdom, in conjunction with a touring plan. We're not ready to say that a family of four should spend $64 on Genie+ at EPCOT, though: It has fewer rides and they're spaced far apart, limiting the amount of time you'd save using Genie+ beyond what you'd get just by showing up early and hitting the key attractions first. For specific advice on how best to use Genie+ at each park, read the Genie+ section in that park's chapter.

Most reader comments we get on Genie+ are negative, focusing on the cost and the constant need to use smartphones:

Genie+ makes everyone miserable. If you don't have it, you resent all the people flying by you, the unpredictable wait times, and the feeling that you're somehow less than everyone else. If you have it, you sacrifice any sense of being "in the moment" because your face is constantly buried in your phone working to plan your next Lightning Lane. And when there's a wait in the LL line, you feel like you just wasted all your money. The whole system has added a level of sadness to the Happiest Place on Earth. You end up feeling like everyone's out for themselves and just gross.

—A reader from Cincinnati

Genie+ is a money shakedown and we refused to buy it. Everyone seemed angry and the crowds were awful.

—A reader from Vancouver, Washington

Disney is doing a lot to cause us to vacation elsewhere. The CEO's statements about Annual Pass holders [being less profitable than infrequent guests], the lack of [free] FastPass+, and Disney's taking away benefits and raising prices makes other bucket list trips more attractive. We will be selling our DVC and moving on. Raising prices and cutting amenities is a poor way to control crowds.

—A family from Port Jefferson, New York

Disney World is still magical but far less enjoyable with Genie+. We visited during a relatively off-peak time, and had we not bought Lightning Lane reservations, our waits for the popular rides would've been over an hour within 30–60 minutes of park opening on most days.

—A family from Missouri

And regarding phone usage, a visitor from North Wales, Pennsylvania, says:

Vacation was less than magical this time. I'm not entirely sure why, but I think it had something to do with working my phone so much. I am not high-tech, but I was able to do mobile ordering, Genie+, and ILL with few problems. But my phone became the focus too many times during the day instead of the park.

These folks from Cincinnati agree:

I don't need an app or map to know how to navigate the parks, and I still spent 22 hours MORE TIME on my phone during our VACATION. An entire day, staring at MDE and mobile ordering. Something's gotta give.

Remember that we're not printing just the negative comments— this is a representative sample of what we get every day. A reader from Charleston, South Carolina, adds:

I refuse to pay that much extra for something that was once included, so we just walked around and hung out at bars. It was still fun but very different.

And a reader from Erdenheim, Pennsylvania, declares:

Disney Genie+ and Lightning Lane purchases are another way for Disney to extract money from visitors who already pay plenty for park tickets.

The bad news: Disney is saying that 33%–50% of park guests are using these reservations, throwing tens of millions of dollars per year into its coffers. So prices aren't going down (or away) anytime soon.

Genie+ Guidelines

- Park tickets are required to obtain Lightning Lane return times.

- Before 2 p.m., you can make Genie+ reservations only for the park where you have a reservation. If you try to make a reservation at another park, Genie+ will only offer you return times after 2 p.m.

- Don't make a Genie+ reservation unless it can save you 30 minutes or more at an attraction or if the ride is distributing immediate return times.

- If you arrive after a park opens, obtain a return time for your preferred Genie+ attraction first thing.

- Always check the return period before obtaining your reservation. Keep an eye out for attractions whose return time is immediate, or at least sooner than the standby wait.

- Don't depend on Lightning Lane being available for popular attractions after noon during busier times of the year. This especially applies to Guardians of the Galaxy, Rise of the Resistance, Remy's Ratatouille Adventure, and Tron (when it opens).

- Make sure everyone in your party has their own return time. Reservations are tied to each individual admission pass and may not be transferred.

- You can obtain a second return time (1) as soon as you use your first, (2) 2 hours after you obtained your last reservation, or (3) when your unused return-time window has expired. You can maximize efficiency by always obtaining a new return time for the next attraction while waiting to board the previous one.

- Be mindful of your return time, and plan intervening activities accordingly. You may use your reservation 5 minutes before its start time and up to 15 minutes after its end time. This unadvertised grace period is typically the only exception to your return window.

- Attractions may not dispense Lightning Lane reservations while they are closed for technical difficulties or special events. If an attraction is unavailable due to technical difficulties during your return window, your Lightning Lane automatically converts to a Replacement Lightning Lane pass. Replacement passes remain valid for use until closing time at that attraction (if it reopens) or at selected other Lightning Lane attractions in the same park. If the original return window was near closing time, the Replacement pass may be valid the next day.

- You may hold only one Genie+ Lightning Lane reservation at a time (unless 2 hours have elapsed since you obtained a Genie+ reservation for a ride whose return-time window has not yet started) and/or up to two reservations for ILL attractions. The only other exceptions to this rule are that (1) there is no limit to the number of Replacement Lightning Lane reservations you can simultaneously hold and (2) users of Disney's Disability Access Service (DAS) can make two Genie+ reservations at the start of each day.

- You may want to pick one member of your party to handle everyone's tickets and Lightning Lane reservations on their phone. This gives your group the option of splitting up while retaining access to each other's plans; however, each person must still use their own ticket to enter the park or redeem Lightning Lane reservations.

DISNEY GENIE (MINUS THE PLUS)

DISNEY ANNOUNCED THE GENIE itinerary-planning feature of the MDE app in 2019 and said little more about it for the next two years. Originally, it sounded a lot like our computer-optimized touring plans: You'd tell Genie what rides you wanted to ride, and Genie would plan your day to minimize your wait in line. But that's not at all what it does. In fact, Genie is one of the worst products Disney has ever produced. Its real purpose isn't to plan your day—because it doesn't. It's to serve Disney's park-management needs.

To understand why requires some background: In the old FastPass+ system, in order to give each guest at least three FastPasses per day, Disney had to offer it at many attractions that guests wouldn't normally ride if they had to wait long. Making that many passes available, at rides located around the park, turned FastPass+ into an effective crowd-distribution tool; you had to move around the park to use the passes, and spreading guests throughout the park lessened waits at the head-liner rides. We considered FastPass+ to be one of the great industrial engineering achievements of its decade, and we still believe that.

In contrast, the Genie+ ride reservation system costs money, so far fewer people use it. That means Disney loses the all-important crowd-distribution mechanism. The risk to Disney's park operations is that guests will simply line up for Disney's best, most popular rides, resulting in long lines there, while other attractions sit underused.

That's where Genie comes in—it sends guests to lower-rated, less popular attractions that they wouldn't have otherwise visited and directs crowds away from the parks' most popular attractions.

That's a bold claim, but it has been borne out in our field-testing. When Len tested out the feature, it suggested exactly one ride in the first 3½ hours he was in the park, despite no lines at the headliners. Instead, it suggested three ways for him to spend money before noon, including purchasing Genie+ and Individual Lightning Lane and purchasing a $100 *Star Wars* droid. Readers have had similar unsatisfying experiences. A family from Chicago shared theirs:

> We only did one Disney park—Hollywood Studios—and it was such a train wreck with ride closures and a Genie system that never worked to offer a reservation slot all day, we cut our losses, ate the mistake of $140 each for tickets, and left at 4 p.m. having done only THREE rides. Never again would any of us give a single dollar to Disney parks.

In fact, we've heard that guest satisfaction survey results for Genie are terrible. One insider described them as "disastrous" and "far below even the lowest expectations." That's not surprising.

As we see it, Genie is part crowd control for Disney park operations, part upselling engine, and part itinerary-planning app. Genie is unlikely to get you to all of the park's highest-rated attractions. Needless to say, we don't think it's a substitute for our touring plans. We don't think it's good, period.

HEIGHT REQUIREMENTS

A NUMBER OF ATTRACTIONS require children to meet minimum height and age requirements; see the table below. If you have children too short or too young to ride, you have several options, including Rider Switch (see page 260). Though the alternatives may resolve some practical and logistical issues, be forewarned that your smaller children might be resentful of their older (or taller) siblings who qualify to ride. A mom from Virginia bumped into just such a situation, writing:

ATTRACTION AND RIDE RESTRICTIONS

THE MAGIC KINGDOM

The Barnstormer 35" minimum height

Big Thunder Mountain Railroad 40" minimum height

Seven Dwarfs Mine Train 38" minimum height

Space Mountain 44" minimum height

Splash Mountain 40" minimum height

Tomorrowland Speedway 32" minimum height to ride, 54" to drive unassisted

Tron Lightcycle/Run *(opens 2023)* 48" minimum height (estimated)

EPCOT

Guardians of the Galaxy: Cosmic Rewind 42" minimum height

Mission: Space 40" minimum height (Green); 44" minimum height (Orange)

Soarin' Around the World 40" minimum height

Test Track 40" minimum height

DISNEY'S ANIMAL KINGDOM

Avatar Flight of Passage 44" minimum height

Dinosaur 40" minimum height

Expedition Everest 44" minimum height

Kali River Rapids 38" minimum height

DISNEY'S HOLLYWOOD STUDIOS

Alien Swirling Saucers 32" minimum height

***Millennium Falcon:* Smugglers Run** 38" minimum height

Rock 'n' Roller Coaster 48" minimum height

Slinky Dog Dash 38" minimum height

Star Tours—The Adventures Continue 40" minimum height

Star Wars: Rise of the Resistance 40" minimum height

The Twilight Zone Tower of Terror 40" minimum height

You mention height requirements for rides but not the intense sibling jealousy this can generate. Frontierland was a real problem in that respect. Our very petite 5-year-old, to her outrage, was stuck hanging around while our 8-year-old went on Splash Mountain and Big Thunder Mountain with Grandma and Granddad, and the nearby alternatives weren't helpful (too long a line for rafts to Tom Sawyer Island, etc.). If we had thought ahead, we would have left the younger kid with one of the grown-ups for another roller coaster or two and then met up later at a designated point.

The reader makes a valid point, though in practical terms splitting the group and meeting up later can be more complicated than she might imagine. If you choose to split up, ask the Disney greeter at the entrance to the attraction how long the wait is. Tack on 5 minutes for riding, and then add 5 or so minutes to exit and reach the meeting point to get an idea of how long the younger kids (and their supervising adult) will have to do other stuff. Our guess is that even with a long line for the rafts, the reader would have had more than sufficient time to take her daughter to Tom Sawyer Island while the sibling rode Splash and Big Thunder with the grandparents. For sure she had time to tour the Swiss Family Treehouse in adjacent Adventureland.

WAITING-LINE STRATEGIES

CHILDREN HOLD UP BETTER through the day if you minimize the time they spend in lines. Besides arriving early and using our touring plans, here are some other ways to reduce stress for kids:

1. RIDER SWITCH Several attractions have minimum height and/or age requirements (see table on page 259). Some couples with children too small or too young forgo these attractions, while others take turns riding. Missing some of Disney's best rides is an unnecessary sacrifice, and waiting in line twice for the same ride is a tremendous waste of time.

Instead, take advantage of Rider Switch, also known as baby swap, rider swap, or switching off. To switch off, there must be at least two adults. Here's how it works: Adults and children wait in line together. When you reach a cast member, say you want to switch off. The cast member will divide the group into those riding first and those riding second—that is, the nonriding child and up to three supervising adults. The first group will enter the ride. The cast member will scan the MagicBands of the adults riding second, who then wait with the nonriding child in a designated spot near the ride entrance. When the first group returns, those adults take over watching the nonriding child while the other adults return to the alternate-access line. The cast member will scan the second group's MagicBands again, after which the group enters the alternate-access line. The entire group reunites after the second group finishes the ride.

Rider Switch passes (digital entitlements that are scanned into your MagicBand) must be used within 90 minutes of the same day they're issued. You can only hold one pass at a time, but it will not interfere with any other passes. There is no cost to use the switching-off option.

ATTRACTIONS WHERE RIDER SWITCH IS USED	
MAGIC KINGDOM	**DISNEY'S ANIMAL KINGDOM**
• The Barnstormer • Big Thunder Mountain Railroad • Seven Dwarfs Mine Train • Space Mountain • Splash Mountain • Tomorrowland Speedway • Tron Lightcycle/Run *(opens 2023)*	• Avatar Flight of Passage • Dinosaur • Expedition Everest • Kali River Rapids • Na'vi River Journey
EPCOT	**DISNEY'S HOLLYWOOD STUDIOS**
• Frozen Ever After • Guardians of the Galaxy: Cosmic Rewind • Mission: Space • Soarin' Around the World • Test Track	• Alien Swirling Saucers • *Millennium Falcon:* Smugglers Run • Rock 'n' Roller Coaster Starring Aerosmith • Slinky Dog Dash • Star Tours—The Adventures Continue • The Twilight Zone Tower of Terror

2. LINE GAMES Wise parents anticipate restlessness in line and plan activities to reduce the stress and boredom. In the morning, have waiting children discuss what they want to see and do during the day. Later, watch for and count Disney characters or play simple guessing games such as 20 Questions. Lines move continuously, so games requiring pen and paper are impractical. The holding area of a theater attraction, however, is a different story. Here, tic-tac-toe, hangman, drawing, and coloring make the time fly by. We've also provided a trivia game for each park at the end of each park chapter.

3. PHONE FUN Game apps are a great tool for staying entertained while waiting in a queue. In 2018 Disney rolled out the Play Disney Parks app, which offers trivia, games, and even music in all its parks. Note that in order to play certain games and earn badges, you must be in a specific location in the park or in the queue of a ride. The free app is available for both iOS and Android. Make sure you turn location services on.

For a good list of non-Disney games, see techradar.com/news/best -free-games-for-kids or learn4good.com/games/mobile_phone_games .htm. Some apps are free—make sure to check before downloading. Last but not least, bring lots of battery power.

4. LAST-MINUTE COLD FEET If your young child gets cold feet just before boarding a ride where there's no age or height requirement, you usually can arrange a switch-off with the loading attendant. (This happens frequently in Pirates of the Caribbean's dungeon waiting area.)

No law says you have to ride. If you reach the boarding area and someone is unhappy, tell an attendant you've changed your mind and you'll be shown the way out.

CHARACTER ANALYSIS

BOB Check your MDE app to find out where any character is in the parks.

THE LARGE, FRIENDLY COSTUMED versions of Mickey, Minnie, Donald, Goofy, and others provide a link between Disney animated films and the theme parks. To people emotionally invested, the characters in Disney films are as real as next-door neighbors, never mind that they're just cartoons. In recent years, theme park personifications of the characters have also become real to us. It's not just a person in a mouse costume we see; it's Mickey himself. Similarly, meeting Goofy or Snow White is an encounter with a celebrity, a memory to be treasured.

While Disney animated-film characters number in the hundreds, only about 250 have been brought to life in costume. Of these, fewer than a fifth mix with guests; the others perform in shows or parades. Disney usually updates the character schedules on Saturday nights or early Sunday mornings. The best website to check on who meets where is Kenny the Pirate's Character Locator (characterlocator.com). The small annual fee is well worth your investment if meeting characters is at the top of your list. Characters are found in all the major theme parks and at Disney Deluxe resorts that host character meals. They also often visit the Disney water parks and occasionally appear at Disney Springs.

See page 217 for tips on preparing your young children to meet the Disney characters for the first time.

CHARACTER-WATCHING

LILIANE The only way to meet The Beast at the Magic Kingdom is after dinner at Be Our Guest.

FAMILIES PURSUE CHARACTERS relentlessly, armed with autograph books and cameras. Some characters are only rarely seen, so character-watching has become character-collecting. (To cash in on character-collecting, Disney sells autograph books throughout the World.) Mickey, Minnie, and Goofy seem to be everywhere. But some characters, such as the Queen of Hearts and Friar Tuck, seldom come out, and quite a few appear only in parades or stage shows. Other characters appear only in a location consistent with their starring role. For instance, Buzz Lightyear, Winnie the Pooh, and Peter Pan appear close to their eponymous attractions.

A Brooklyn, New York, dad complains that character-collecting has gotten out of hand:

When we took our youngest child, he had already seen his siblings' collection and was determined to outdo them. Because the characters are available practically all day long at different locations, we spent more time standing in line for autographs than we did for the most popular rides!

A family from Birmingham, Alabama, found some benefit in their children's pursuit of characters:

> *After my daughters got Pocahontas to sign your guidebook (we had no blank paper), we quickly bought an autograph book and gave in. It was actually the highlight of their trip, and my son even got into the act by helping get places in line for his sisters. They LOVED looking for characters. It was an amazing, totally unexpected part of our visit.*

FROZEN FEVER

THERE IS NO DOUBT that the *Frozen* gals are here to stay. Cindy learned to reckon with the power of a nor'easter, vacated the castle during the holiday season, and learned to "let it go." Here are our recommendations on how to have the most *Frozen* fun while visiting Walt Disney World.

Magic Kingdom

The Festival of Fantasy Parade is a must, and you can see Anna and Elsa on their float without standing in line. Anna and Elsa are also part of *Mickey's Royal Friendship Faire,* the castle forecourt stage show. Cinderella Castle is home to one of three locations of Bibbidi Bobbidi Boutique, where you can give your princess a total Anna or Elsa makeover. A second location is at the Grand Floridian nearby. At press time, only the Magic Kingdom location was open for business.

EPCOT

Frozen Ever After is, of course, an absolute must. The ride's popularity draws long lines all day. For now, it is part of Genie+. Anna and Elsa meet their fans next door at the Royal Sommerhus.

Disney's Hollywood Studios

For the First Time in Forever: A Frozen Sing-Along Celebration at the Hyperion Theater is a fun and interactive show where Anna, Elsa, Kristoff, and the royal historians of Arendelle tell the story of their kingdom. Olaf takes up residence inside the Celebrity Spotlight at Echo Lake.

When All Elsa Fails

You won't find anything *Frozen* related at Animal Kingdom. But there is always Disney Springs, where you can visit the third location of Bibbidi Bobbidi Boutique, though at press time, it was temporarily closed. Until it reopens, there is only one thing to do: Let it go!

CHARACTER DINING: WHAT TO EXPECT

LILIANE Even with Advance Reservations, expect to wait 10-20 minutes to be seated.

BECAUSE OF THE INCREDIBLE POPULARITY of character dining, reservations can be hard to come by if you wait until a couple of months before your vacation to book your choices. What's more, you must provide Disney with a credit card number. Your card will be charged $10 per person if you don't show or you cancel your reservation less than 24 hours in advance; you may, however, reschedule with no penalty. See "Getting Advance Reservations at Popular Restaurants" (page 163) for the full story.

WDW CHARACTER-GREETING VENUES

*Indicates character has returned (we think all will return by the end of the year)

MAGIC KINGDOM

MICKEY AND HIS POSSE

- **Daisy, Donald, Goofy, Minnie, and Pluto** Pete's Silly Sideshow
- **Mickey*** Town Square Theater

DISNEY ROYALTY *(Princesses, Princes, Suitors, and Such)*

- **Aladdin and Jasmine** Adventureland • **Anna and Elsa** On float during the Festival of Fantasy Parade and in *Mickey's Royal Friendship Faire* stage show • **Ariel** Ariel's Grotto • **Belle** *Enchanted Tales with Belle* • **Cinderella, Elena of Avalor, Rapunzel, and Tiana*** Princess Fairytale Hall
- **Gaston** Fountain outside Gaston's Tavern • **Merida*** Fairytale Garden
- **Snow White** Next to City Hall
- **The Tremaines and Fairy Godmother*** In Fantasyland near Cinderella's Castle

FAIRIES

- **Tinker Bell** Town Square Theater

MISCELLANEOUS

- **Alice** (*Alice in Wonderland*) Mad Tea Party
- **Buzz Lightyear*** (*Toy Story*) Tomorrowland
- **Captain Jack Sparrow*** (*Pirates of the Caribbean*) Adventureland
- **Chip 'n' Dale*** Storybook Circus/Fantasyland
- **Country Bears*** Frontierland
- **Mary Poppins** Liberty Square
- **Peter Pan** Fantasyland next to Peter Pan's Flight
- **Pooh and Tigger** Fantasyland by The Many Adventures of Winnie the Pooh
- **Stitch*** (*Lilo & Stitch*) Tomorrowland

EPCOT

MICKEY AND HIS POSSE

- **Daisy** World Showcase Plaza • **Donald*** Mexico, at the Mexico Pavilion
- **Mickey*** Disney and Pixar Short Film Festival

DISNEY ROYALTY

- **Anna and Elsa*** Norway • **Aurora*** France gazebo • **Belle*** France
- **Jasmine*** Morocco • **Mulan*** China • **Snow White*** Germany

MISCELLANEOUS

- **Alice*, Mary Poppins*, and** (on rare occasions) **Bert** United Kingdom
- **Winnie the Pooh*** Lawn between the Imagination and Land Pavilions in Future World West • **Vanellope von Schweetz*** (*Wreck-It Ralph*), **Joy*** (*Inside Out*) Near the Imagination Pavilion

DISNEY'S ANIMAL KINGDOM

MICKEY AND HIS POSSE

- **Daisy** DinoLand U.S.A., Lower Cretaceous Trail
- **Donald** DinoLand U.S.A., Celebration Welcome Center
- **Goofy and Pluto** Near main entrance
- **Mickey and Minnie** Adventurers Outpost on Discovery Island

DISNEY ROYALTY

- **Pocahontas** Discovery Island at Character Landing

MISCELLANEOUS

- **Chip 'n' Dale** DinoLand U.S.A., Upper Cretaceous Trail
- **Flik** (*A Bug's Life*) Discovery Island across from Creature Comforts
- **Kevin** (*Up*) Discovery Island and near *Feathered Friends in Flight*
- **Launchpad McQuack** DinoLand U.S.A., Aerial Adventure Base
- **Russell** (*Up*) Discovery Island (**Dug** may appear randomly.)
- **Scrooge McDuck** DinoLand U.S.A., near Restaurantosaurus

DISNEY'S HOLLYWOOD STUDIOS

MICKEY AND HIS POSSE

- **Chip 'n' Dale** Grand Avenue
- **Daisy and Donald** Near park entrance
- **Goofy** Grand Avenue across from BaseLine Tap House
- **Minnie and Sorcerer Mickey** Red Carpet Dreams on Commissary Lane
- **Pluto** Animation Courtyard

DISNEY CHANNEL STARS

- **Doc McStuffins and Friends** Animation Courtyard near *Disney Junior Play and Dance*
- **Vampirina** Animation Courtyard

MISCELLANEOUS

- **Buzz, Jessie, Woody, and Green Army Men** (*Toy Story*) Toy Story Land
- **Chewbacca, Darth Vader, and BB-8** (*Star Wars*) Star Wars Launch Bay
- **Cruz Ramirez** (*Cars*) Lightning McQueen's Racing Academy
- **Edna Mode** (*The Incredibles*) Municiberg at Pixar Place
- **The Incredibles** Municiberg at Pixar Place
- **Mike and Sulley** (*Monsters, Inc.*) Walt Disney Presents
- **Olaf** (*Frozen*) Celebrity Spotlight in Echo Lake
- **Stormtroopers** (*Star Wars*) Animation Courtyard

BLIZZARD BEACH

- **Goofy** Appears seasonally, usually from spring break until Labor Day, at park entrance

TYPHOON LAGOON

- **Lilo and Stitch** Singapore Sal's near the park entrance. They meet in the spring and summer months on a rotational basis.

At very popular character meals like the breakfast at Cinderella's Royal Table (*temporarily unavailable*), you're required to make a for-real reservation and guarantee it with a for-real deposit.

Character meals are bustling affairs held in the hotels' or theme parks' largest full-service restaurants. Character breakfasts offer a fixed menu served individually, family-style, or on a buffet. The typical breakfast includes scrambled eggs; bacon, sausage, and ham; hash browns; waffles or French toast; biscuits, rolls, or pastries; and fruit. Family-style meals, such as at Akershus, are served in large skillets or platters at your table and are all-you-can-eat.

FELICITY Chef Mickey's is my favorite place to eat. I always have ice cream with lots of toppings and give Mickey and the gang a big hug. The napkin twirling is a lot of fun.

Character dinner buffets, such as those at 1900 Park Fare at the Grand Floridian (*temporarily unavailable*) and Chef Mickey's at the Contemporary Resort, separate the kids' fare from the grown-ups', though everyone is free to eat from both lines. Typically, the children's buffet includes hamburgers, hot dogs, pizza, fish sticks, chicken nuggets, macaroni and cheese, and peanut-butter-and-jelly sandwiches. Selections at the adult buffet usually include prime rib or other carved meat, baked or broiled seafood, pasta, chicken, an ethnic dish or two, vegetables, potatoes, and salad.

At all meals, characters circulate around the room while you eat. During your meal, each of the three to five characters present will visit your table, arriving one at a time to cuddle the kids (and sometimes the adults), pose for photos, and sign autographs. Keep autograph books (with pens) handy and cameras or phones at the ready.

LILIANE If you've secured Advance Reservations for a character meal, I say roll out the costume chest. Dress up your little one—from princess to pirate, anything goes.

For the best photos, adults should sit across the table from their children. Seat the children where characters can easily reach them. If a table is against a wall, for example, adults should sit with their backs to the wall and children on the aisle.

Servers generally don't rush you to leave after you've eaten—you can stay as long as you wish to enjoy the characters. Remember, however, that lots of eager kids and adults are waiting not so patiently to be admitted. When going to press, some of the character meals were not yet available. Always call the restaurant to make sure characters are indeed visiting.

When to Go

Attending a character breakfast usually prevents you from arriving at the theme parks in time for opening. Because early morning is best for touring and you don't want to burn daylight lingering over breakfast, we suggest the following:

1. Schedule your in-park character breakfast for the first seating if the park opens at 9 a.m. or later. You'll be admitted to the park before other guests through a special line at the turnstiles. Arrive early to be among the first parties seated. Be sure to have a park reservation for the park where the restaurant is located.

2. Go to a character dinner or lunch instead of breakfast. It will be a nice break.

3. Schedule the last seating for breakfast. Have a light snack such as cereal or bagels before you head to the parks for opening, hit the most popular attractions until 10:15 a.m. or so, and then head to brunch. The buffet should keep you fueled until dinner, especially if you eat another light snack in the afternoon.

4. Go on your arrival or departure day. The day you arrive and check in is usually a good time for a character dinner. Settle at your hotel, swim, and then dine with the characters. This strategy has the added benefit of exposing your children to the characters before the chance encounters they'll have at the parks. Moreover, some children won't settle down to enjoy the parks until they've seen Mickey. Departure day is also good for a character meal. Schedule a character breakfast on your checkout day before you head for the airport or begin your drive home.

5. Go on a rest day. If you plan to stay five or more days, you'll probably take a day or half-day from touring to rest or do something else.

How to Choose a Character Meal

Many readers ask for advice about character meals. This question from a Waterloo, Iowa, mom is typical:

Are all character breakfasts pretty much the same, or are some better than others? How should I go about choosing one?

In fact, some are better, sometimes much better. When we evaluate character meals, we look for these things:

1. **THE CHARACTERS** The meals offer a diverse assortment of characters. Select a meal that features your kids' favorites. Check out our **Character-Meal Hit Parade table** (see pages 270–271) to see which characters are assigned to each meal. Most restaurants stick with the same characters. Even so, check the lineup when you call to make Advance Reservations.

2. **ATTENTION FROM THE CHARACTERS** At all character meals, characters circulate among guests, hugging children, posing for pictures, and signing autographs. How much time a character spends with your children depends primarily on the ratio of characters to guests. The more characters and fewer guests, the better. Because many character meals never fill to capacity, the character-to-guest ratios found in our Character-Meal Hit Parade table reflect average attendance. Even so, there's quite a range. The best ratio is at Cinderella's Royal Table, where there's approximately one character to every 26 guests. However, Cindy does not circulate (though the other characters at the Royal Table do); rather, she sees her guests for a quick chat and photo opportunity upon arrival.

   The worst ratio is theoretically at the Swan hotel's Garden Grove, where there could be as few as one character for every 198 guests. We say *theoretically* because in practice there are far fewer guests at the Garden Grove than at character meals in Disney-owned resorts, and often more characters.

3. **THE SETTING** Some character meals are in exotic settings. We rate each meal's setting using the familiar scale of zero (worst) to five (best) stars. Two restaurants, Cinderella's Royal Table in the Magic Kingdom and Garden Grill Restaurant in The Land Pavilion at EPCOT, deserve special mention. Cinderella's Royal Table is on the first and second floors of Cinderella Castle in Fantasyland, offering guests a look inside the castle. The Garden Grill is a revolving restaurant overlooking several scenes from the Living with the Land boat ride. Also at EPCOT, the popular princess character meals are held in the castlelike Akershus Royal Banquet Hall. Though Chef Mickey's at the Contemporary Resort is rather sterile in appearance, it affords a great view of the monorail running through the hotel. Themes and settings of the remaining character-meal venues, while apparent to adults, will be lost on most children.

4. **THE FOOD** Though some food served at character meals is quite good, most is average (palatable but nothing to get excited about). In variety, consistency, and quality, restaurants generally do a better job with breakfast than with lunch or dinner (if served). Some restaurants offer a buffet, while others opt for one-skillet family-style service, in which all hot items are served from the same pot or skillet. To help you sort it out, we rate the food at each character meal using the five-star scale.

5. **THE PROGRAM** Some larger restaurants stage modest performances where the characters dance, lead a parade around the room, or lead songs and cheers. For some guests, these activities give the meal a celebratory air; for others, they

turn what was already mayhem into absolute chaos. Either way, the antics consume time the characters could spend with families at their tables.

6. **NOISE** If you want to eat in peace, character meals are a bad choice. That said, some are noisier than others. Check our table for what to expect at each.

7. **WHICH MEAL?** Though breakfasts seem to be most popular, character lunches and dinners are usually more practical because they don't interfere with early-morning touring. In hot weather, a character lunch can be heavenly.

8. **COST** Dinners cost more than lunches, and lunches cost more than breakfasts. Prices for meals vary considerably from the least expensive to the most. Breakfasts run $45–$65 for adults and $35–$40 for kids ages 3–9. For character lunches or dinners, expect to pay $65–$85 for adults and $35–$45 for kids. Little ones age 2 years and younger eat free. The meals at the high end of the price range are at Cinderella's Royal Table in the Magic Kingdom and Akershus Royal Banquet Hall at EPCOT.

9. **ADVANCE RESERVATIONS** You can make Advance Reservations for character meals 60 days before you wish to dine (Disney resort guests can reserve 60 days out for the entire length of their trip, up to 10 days). Advance Reservations for most character meals are easy to obtain even if you call only a couple of weeks before you leave home. Meals at Cinderella's Royal Table, Be Our Guest, and Story Book Dining at Artist Point are another story. For these three, you'll need our strategy (see Part 4), as well as help from Congress and the Pope.

10. **"FRIENDS"** For some venues, Disney has stopped specifying characters scheduled for a particular meal, instead listing a specific character "and friends"—for example, "Pooh and friends," meaning Eeyore, Piglet, and Tigger, or some combination thereof, or "Mickey and friends" with some assortment of Minnie, Goofy, Pluto, Donald, Daisy, Chip, and Dale.

11. **THE BUM'S RUSH** Most character meals are leisurely affairs, and you can usually stay as long as you want. An exception is Cinderella's Royal Table in the Magic Kingdom. Because Cindy's is in such high demand, the restaurant does everything short of prechewing your food to move you through, as this European mother of a 5-year-old can attest:

> We dined a lot, including three character meals and a few Signature restaurants, and every meal was awesome except for lunch with Cinderella in the castle. While I'd often read it wouldn't be a rushed affair, it was exactly that. We had barely sat down when the appetizers were thrown on our table, the princesses each spent just a few seconds with our daughter—almost no interaction—and the side dishes were cold. We were out of there within 40 minutes and felt very stressed. Considering the price for the meal, I cannot recommend it.

12. **BOYS** To answer a common reader question, most character meals featuring Disney princesses include some element to appeal to the young roughnecks. A Texas mom shares her experience:

> We ate at Cinderella's Royal Table for lunch, and my sons were made to feel very welcome. They loved the swords they received and have enjoyed "fighting off the dragons" with them.

Getting an Advance Reservation at Cinderella's Royal Table

NOTE: Character meals at Cinderella's Royal Table have not yet resumed.

Once upon a time, breakfast was the only character meal at Cinderella Castle in the Magic Kingdom, and all reservations were gone within minutes of becoming available each morning. Disney responded by adding character lunches and dinners—and jacking up the price. Now, it's now much easier to get in for a meal during your stay. Also, the opening of the wildly popular Be Our Guest Restaurant in Fantasyland has taken a lot of pressure off Cindy's.

There are two new kids on the block, and getting a reservation at either one of them takes a lot of pixie dust. Young kids will love Story Book Dining with Snow White at Artist Point (Wilderness Lodge), while the entire family will enjoy Breakfast à la Art with Mickey & Friends at Topolino's Terrace (Disney's Riviera Resort). Book as soon as your 60-day window opens.

LILIANE The character meals at Akershus are my all-time favorite. There are plenty of princesses, and I love the food.

DISNEY'S ROYAL ALTERNATIVES If you're unwilling to fund Cinderella's shoe habit or you simply weren't able to get an Advance Reservation before young Ariel graduates from college, rest assured there are other venues that will feed you in the company of princesses.

Akershus Royal Banquet Hall, in the Norway Pavilion of EPCOT's World Showcase, serves family-style breakfast, lunch, and dinner. Ariel, Cinderella, Snow White, and Belle are regulars. Entrées are a combination of traditional buffet fare and the occasional Scandinavian dish.

Dinner at the Grand Floridian's **1900 Park Fare** (*temporarily closed*) features the whole crew from *Cinderella*, including Lady Tremaine and the stepsisters (breakfast is a supercalifragilisticexpialidocious affair with Mary Poppins and friends, which currently include Alice in Wonderland, the Mad Hatter, Winnie the Pooh, and Tigger). This is a far more economical option for diners wishing to get their princess on, and the stepsisters are an absolute hoot. This meal is also a little more boy-friendly if you're entertaining a mixed crowd. Finally, remember that your princess may be feeding off your own excitement over eating in the castle—she might be just as happy with a plastic crown purchased in the gift shop and a burger from Cosmic Ray's. We recommend visiting 1900 Park Fare on a day when you're not visiting the parks.

If you were unable to get to the Frozen Ever After ride and your little Anna and Elsa really want to experience it without waiting at least an hour in line, consider breakfast at Akershus Royal Banquet Hall. Pick a day when the park opens early. Next, book the first breakfast seating available, probably 8 a.m. Enjoy the breakfast, and by 8:45 a.m. make your way outside to the ride, right next to the restaurant, and be the first in line to ride.

FELICITY The stepsisters at 1900 Park Fare are so much fun. We made ugly faces instead of posing for photos, and it was hilarious. I liked the food, and cast members were helpful when I had a problem with my autograph book.

Story Book Dining at **Artist Point** with Snow White is a character dinner at Wilderness Lodge.

continued on page 272

CHARACTER-MEAL HIT PARADE

1. CHEF MICKEY'S   CONTEMPORARY

- **MEALS SERVED** Breakfast, dinner • **SETTING** ★★★
- **CHARACTERS** Mickey, Minnie, Donald, Goofy, Pluto
- **TYPE OF SERVICE** Family-style • **FOOD VARIETY & QUALITY** ★★★½
- **NOISE LEVEL** Very loud • **CHARACTER–GUEST RATIO** 1:56

2. GARDEN GRILL RESTAURANT   EPCOT

- **MEAL SERVED** Lunch, dinner • **SETTING** ★★★★
- **CHARACTERS** Mickey, Pluto, Chip 'n' Dale • **TYPE OF SERVICE** Family-style
- **FOOD VARIETY & QUALITY** ★★★½ • **NOISE LEVEL** Very quiet
- **CHARACTER–GUEST RATIO** 1:46

3. HOLLYWOOD & VINE   DISNEY'S HOLLYWOOD STUDIOS

- **MEALS SERVED** Breakfast (seasonal lunch and dinner) • **SETTING** ★★½
- **CHARACTERS** *Breakfast:* Disney Junior characters
  Seasonal lunch and dinner: Minnie, Mickey, Goofy, Pluto, Donald (and sometimes Daisy)
- **TYPE OF SERVICE** Family-style • **FOOD VARIETY & QUALITY** ★★★
- **NOISE LEVEL** Moderate • **CHARACTER–GUEST RATIO** 1:71

4. TOPOLINO'S TERRACE   RIVIERA RESORT

- **MEALS SERVED** Breakfast • **SETTING** ★★★★
- **CHARACTERS** Mickey, Minnie, Donald, Daisy
- **TYPE OF SERVICE** Fixed menu • **FOOD VARIETY & QUALITY** ★★★★
- **NOISE LEVEL** Moderate • **CHARACTER–GUEST RATIO** 1:45

5. CINDERELLA'S ROYAL TABLE**   MAGIC KINGDOM

- **MEALS SERVED** Breakfast, lunch, dinner • **SETTING** ★★★★
- **CHARACTERS** Cinderella, Ariel, Aurora, Belle, Jasmine, Snow White, Fairy Godmother
- **TYPE OF SERVICE** Fixed menu • **FOOD VARIETY & QUALITY** ★★★
- **NOISE LEVEL** Quiet • **CHARACTER–GUEST RATIO** 1:26

6. THE CRYSTAL PALACE**   MAGIC KINGDOM

- **MEALS SERVED** Lunch, dinner • **SETTING** ★★★
- **CHARACTERS** Pooh, Eeyore, Piglet, Tigger • **TYPE OF SERVICE** Buffet
- **FOOD VARIETY & QUALITY** Breakfast ★★½ Lunch and dinner ★★★
- **NOISE LEVEL** Very loud
- **CHARACTER–GUEST RATIO** Breakfast, 1:67; lunch and dinner, 1:89

7. AKERSHUS ROYAL BANQUET HALL*   EPCOT

- **MEALS SERVED** Breakfast, lunch, dinner • **SETTING** ★★★★
- **CHARACTERS** 4–6 Disney princesses chosen from among Ariel, Belle, Jasmine, Snow White, Aurora, Mulan, and Cinderella
- **TYPE OF SERVICE** Family-style and menu (all you care to eat)
- **FOOD VARIETY & QUALITY** ★★★½ • **NOISE LEVEL** Loud
- **CHARACTER–GUEST RATIO** 1:54

Characters are subject to change, so check before you go.

 * Closed at press time
** Open, but no characters at press time

CHARACTER-MEAL HIT PARADE

8. 1900 PARK FARE* GRAND FLORIDIAN

- MEALS SERVED Breakfast, dinner • SETTING ★★★
- CHARACTERS *Breakfast:* Mary Poppins, Alice, Mad Hatter, Pooh, Tigger *Dinner:* Cinderella, Prince Charming, Lady Tremaine, the two stepsisters
- TYPE OF SERVICE Buffet
- FOOD VARIETY & QUALITY Breakfast ★★★ Dinner ★★★½
- NOISE LEVEL Moderate • CHARACTER-GUEST RATIO Breakfast, 1:54; dinner, 1:44

9. TUSKER HOUSE RESTAURANT DISNEY'S ANIMAL KINGDOM

- MEALS SERVED Breakfast, lunch, dinner • SETTING ★★★
- CHARACTERS Donald, Daisy, Mickey, Goofy, Pluto • TYPE OF SERVICE Fixed menu
- FOOD VARIETY & QUALITY ★★★ • NOISE LEVEL Very loud
- CHARACTER-GUEST RATIO 1:112

10. CAPE MAY CAFE** DISNEY'S BEACH CLUB

- MEAL SERVED Breakfast SETTING ★★★ • CHARACTERS Goofy, Donald, Minnie, Daisy
- TYPE OF SERVICE Buffet • FOOD VARIETY & QUALITY ★★½
- NOISE LEVEL Moderate • CHARACTER-GUEST RATIO 1:67

11. 'OHANA** POLYNESIAN VILLAGE

- MEAL SERVED Breakfast SETTING ★★
- CHARACTERS Lilo and Stitch, Mickey, Pluto • TYPE OF SERVICE Family-style
- FOOD VARIETY & QUALITY ★★½ • NOISE LEVEL Loud
- CHARACTER-GUEST RATIO 1:57

12. ARTIST POINT WILDERNESS LODGE

- MEAL SERVED Dinner • SETTING ★★★½
- CHARACTERS Snow White, Dopey, Grumpy, the Evil Queen
- TYPE OF SERVICE Fixed menu with several choices
- FOOD VARIETY & QUALITY ★★★★
- NOISE LEVEL Quiet • CHARACTER-GUEST RATIO 1:35

13. TRATTORIA AL FORNO** DISNEY'S BOARDWALK

- MEAL SERVED Breakfast • SETTING ★★★½
- CHARACTERS Rapunzel, Flynn Ryder, Ariel, Prince Eric
- TYPE OF SERVICE Fixed menu with several choices
- FOOD VARIETY & QUALITY ★★★½
- NOISE LEVEL Quiet • CHARACTER-GUEST RATIO 1:50

14. GARDEN GROVE** SWAN

- MEALS SERVED Breakfast (Sat. and Sun.) • SETTING ★★½
- CHARACTERS Chip 'n' Dale, Goofy, Pluto • TYPE OF SERVICE Buffet
- FOOD VARIETY & QUALITY ★★½ • NOISE LEVEL Moderate
- CHARACTER-GUEST RATIO 1:198, but frequently much better

Characters are subject to change, so check before you go.
 * Closed at press time
 ** Open, but no characters at press time

continued from page 269

The prix fixe dinner comes with shared appetizers and desserts, and guests choose their own entrée. Prime rib, roasted chicken, and braised veal shank are among the choices. One of the desserts comes in a smoking box called The Hunter's Gift to the Queen. You can't keep the box, but you can enjoy the maple popcorn and chocolate-ganache hearts inside. During the meal, Snow White, Dopey, and Grumpy entertain guests with sing-alongs and a mini parade around the restaurant to the tune of "Whistle While You Work." They also visit each table for pictures and autographs. At the end of the meal, guests can meet the Evil Queen in front of a themed backdrop.

The experience is pricey ($60 adults, $35 children ages 3–9), but the setting comes with above-average food and seldom-seen characters.

 LILIANE Interacting with characters is easy, and you can take it to another level by sporting a beret yourself when enjoying Breakfast à la Art with Mickey & Friends. Little ones wearing a tutu will be sure to get special attention from Daisy.

 BRENDAN Go to Topolino's for breakfast to get some great eats, and meet Mickey, Minnie, Daisy, and Donald.

Breakfast à la Art with Mickey & Friends takes place daily at **Topolino's Terrace** at Riviera Resort. The prix fixe menu comes with fresh pastries and a choice of entrées, including quiche, waffles, steak, smoked salmon, and eggs any style.

OTHER CHARACTER EVENTS

A CAMPFIRE AND SING-ALONG are held nightly (times vary with the season) near the Meadow Trading Post at **Fort Wilderness Resort & Campground.** Chip 'n' Dale lead the songs, and a Disney film is shown. The free program is open to Disney resort guests (☎ 407-824-2900).

WHEN KIDS GET LOST

 BOB We suggest that children younger than age 8 be dressed in vacation "uniforms" with distinctively colored T-shirts or equally eye-catching apparel.

IF YOUR CHILD gets separated from you, don't panic. All things considered, Walt Disney World is about the safest place we can think of to get lost. Because it happens so frequently in the theme parks, cast members are trained for the situation. If they encounter a lost child, they will take the child immediately to the park's Baby Care Center.

If you lose a child in the Magic Kingdom, report it to a Disney employee, then check at the Baby Care Center and City Hall, where lost-child logs are kept. At EPCOT, report the loss, then check at the Baby Care Center. At Animal Kingdom, go to the Baby Care Center in Discovery Island. At Hollywood Studios, report the loss at Guest Relations, at the entrance end of Hollywood Boulevard. Paging isn't used, but in an emergency, an all-points bulletin will be issued throughout the park(s) via internal communications.

As comforting as this knowledge is, however, it's still scary when a child goes missing. Fortunately, circumstances surrounding a child becoming lost are fairly predictable and, for the most part, preventable.

Iron on or sew a label into each child's shirt that states his or her name, your name, the name of your hotel, and, if you have one, your cell phone number. Accomplish the same thing by writing the information on a strip of masking tape or by attaching a MagicBand to the child's clothing (resist the urge to put it on like a dog collar).

Other than just blending in, children tend to become separated from their parents under remarkably similar circumstances:

1. PREOCCUPIED SOLO PARENT In this situation, the party's only adult is preoccupied with something like buying refreshments, taking pictures, or using the restroom. Junior is there one second and gone the next.

2. THE HIDDEN EXIT Sometimes parents wait on the sidelines while two or more young children experience a ride together. Parents expect the kids to exit in one place and, lo and behold, the youngsters pop out somewhere else. Exits from some attractions are distant from the entrances. Make sure you know exactly where your children will emerge before letting them ride by themselves. If in doubt, ask a cast member.

3. AFTER THE SHOW At the end of many shows and rides, a Disney staffer will announce, "Check for personal belongings and take small children by the hand." When dozens, if not hundreds, of people leave an attraction simultaneously, it's surprisingly easy for parents to lose contact with their children unless they have them directly in tow.

4. RESTROOM PROBLEMS Mom tells 6-year-old Tommy, "I'll be sitting on this bench when you come out of the restroom." Three possibilities: One, Tommy exits through a different door and becomes disoriented (Mom may not know there's another door). Two, Mom decides she will also use the restroom, and Tommy emerges to find her gone. Three, Mom pokes around in a shop while keeping an eye on the bench but misses Tommy when he comes out.

If you can't find a companion- or family-accessible restroom, make sure there's only one exit. The restroom on a passageway between Frontierland and Adventureland in the Magic Kingdom is the all-time worst for disorienting visitors. Children and adults alike have walked in from the Adventureland side and walked out on the Frontierland side (and vice versa). Adults realize quickly that something is wrong. Children, however, sometimes fail to recognize the problem. Designate a distinctive meeting spot and give clear instructions: "I'll meet you by this flagpole. If you get out first, stay right here." Have your child repeat the directions back to you.

5. PARADES There are many parades and shows at which the audience stands. Children tend to jockey for a better view. By moving a little this way and that, the child quickly puts distance between you before either of you notices.

6. MASS MOVEMENTS Be on guard when huge crowds disperse after fireworks or a parade, or at park closing. With 20,000–40,000 people in one area at the same time, it's very easy to get separated from a child or others in your party. Use extra caution after the evening fireworks or any other day-capping event. Have a specific plan for where to meet if your family gets separated.

7. CHARACTER GREETINGS Usually, there's a lot of activity around a character, with both adults and kids jockeying for a handshake or photo. Most commonly, Mom and Dad stand back while Junior approaches the character. In the excitement and with the character moving around, Junior heads in the wrong direction to look for Mom and Dad. In the words of a Salt Lake City mom: "Milo was shaking hands with Dopey one minute, then some confusion happened and Milo was gone."

BOB Our advice for parents with preschoolers is to stay with the kids when they meet characters, stepping back only to take a quick picture.

8. GETTING LOST AT ANIMAL KINGDOM It's especially easy to lose a child in Animal Kingdom, particularly at the Oasis entryway, on the Maharajah Jungle Trek, and on the Gorilla Falls Exploration Trail. Mom and Dad will stop to observe an animal. Junior stays close for a minute or so and then, losing patience, wanders to the exhibit's other side or to a different exhibit.

9. LOST . . . IN THE ZONE More often than you'd think, kids don't realize they're lost. They are so distracted that they sometimes wander around for quite a while before they notice their whole family has disappeared. Fortunately, Disney cast members are trained to look out for kids who have zoned out and will either help them find their family or deposit them at the Baby Care Center.

LILIANE'S TIPS FOR KEEPING TRACK OF YOUR BROOD

ON A GOOD DAY, it's possible for Liliane to lose a cantaloupe in her purse. Thus challenged, she works overtime developing ways to hang on to her possessions. Here's what she has to say:

I've seen parents write their cell phone numbers on a child's leg with a felt-tip marker . . . effective but crude. Before you resort to that, or perhaps a cattle brand, consider some of the tips I've dreamed up. My friends, some much ditzier than I, have used them with great success.

- On your very first day in the parks, teach your kids how to recognize a Disney cast member by pointing out the Disney name tags they wear. Instruct your children to find someone with such a name tag if they get separated from you.

- Same-colored shirts for the whole family will help you gather your troops in an easy and fun way. Opt for just a uniform color, or go the extra mile and have the shirts printed with a logo such as "The Brown Family's Assault on the Mouse." You might also include the date or the year of your visit.

- Clothing labels are great. If you don't sew, buy labels that you can iron on the garment. If you own a cell phone, be sure to include the number on the label. If you don't own a cell phone, put in the phone number of the hotel where you'll be staying. Another option is a custom-made temporary tattoo with all the pertinent info. They're cheap, last 2 weeks, don't wash off, and solve the problem of having to sew or iron a label on every garment. (They can be purchased online at safetytat.com.)

- In pet stores you can have name tags printed for a very reasonable price. These are great to add to necklaces and bracelets or attach to your child's shoelace or belt loop.

- When you check into the hotel, take a hotel business card for each member in your party, especially those old enough to carry wallets and purses.

- Agree on a meeting place before you see a parade or a fireworks show such as *Harmonious* at EPCOT and *Fantasmic!* at Disney's Hollywood Studios. Make sure the meeting place is in the park (as opposed to the car or outside the front gate).

- If you have a digital camera or phone camera, take a picture of your kids every morning. If they get lost, the picture will show what they look like and what they're wearing.

- If all the members of your party have cell phones, it's easy to locate each other. Be aware, however, that the ambient noise in the parks is so loud that you probably won't hear your phone ring. Your best bet is to carry your phone in a front pants pocket and to program the phone to vibrate. Even better, communicate via text messages. If any of your younger kids carry cell phones, secure the phones with a strap. To ensure your cell phone still has power at the end of the day, carry an extra battery or use mealtimes to recharge all phones (see page 228 for specific locations).

- Save key tags and luggage tags for use on items you bring to the parks, including your stroller, diaper bag, and backpack or hip pack.

- Don't underestimate the power of the permanent marker, such as a Sharpie. They are great for labeling pretty much anything. Mini-Sharpies are sold as clip-ons and are handy for collecting character autographs. The Sharpie also serves well for writing down the location of your car in the parking lot.

- Finally, a word about keeping track of your MagicBands: They're difficult, but not impossible, to lose. Most adults will be fine, but slender children without much articulation between the forearm and wrist need to wear the band more tightly. If you're worried about the band slipping off, ask for a park card instead (see page 68). Alternatively, have your child wear the MagicBand on a chain, like a necklace. For very young children, I strongly recommend having an adult hold on to the MagicBand—no need to put yourself through all that stress.

STROLLERS

STROLLERS CAN BE RENTED at all four theme parks and Disney Springs (single strollers are $15 per day with no deposit, $13 per day for multiday rentals; double strollers are $31 per day with no deposit, $27 per day for multiday rentals; stroller rentals at Disney Springs require a $100 credit card deposit).

LILIANE Rental strollers are too large for all infants and many toddlers. If you plan to rent a stroller for your infant or toddler, bring pillows, cushions, or rolled towels to buttress him in.

Strollers are welcome at Blizzard Beach and Typhoon Lagoon, but no rentals are available.

With multiday rentals, you can skip the rental line entirely after your first visit—just head to the stroller-handout area, show your receipt, and you'll be wheeling out in no time. If you rent a stroller at the Magic Kingdom and you decide to go to EPCOT, Animal Kingdom, or Disney's Hollywood Studios, turn in your Magic Kingdom stroller and present your receipt at the next park. You'll be issued another stroller at no additional charge.

You can rent a stroller in advance; this allows you to bypass the payment line and go straight to the pickup line. Disney resort guests can pay ahead at their resort's gift shop, so hang on to your receipts!

Several Orlando companies undercut Disney's prices, have more comfortable strollers, and deliver them to your hotel. Most of the larger companies offer the same stroller models, such as the City Mini, for example. The primary differences between the companies are price and service. Unlike in the past, Disney no longer allows third-party deliveries to be dropped off with their hotels' bell service. Instead, guests are required to meet the third-party vendors in person.

We had mom and TouringPlans.com writer Angela Dahlgren rent strollers from different companies, use them in the parks, and then return them. Her evaluations cover the overall experience, from the ease with which the stroller was rented to the delivery of the stroller, its condition on arrival, its usability in the parks, and the return process.

Kingdom Strollers (☎ 407-271-5301; kingdomstrollers.com) took first place on Angela's list, getting top marks for website ease of use, stroller selection, condition, and overall service. The stroller was also much easier to use, had more storage, and had an easier-to-use braking system than Disney's standard stroller. A rental of one to three nights costs $55, and four to seven nights is $75. Kingdom Strollers now also offers delivery and drop-off at Orlando International Airport (MCO).

Angela also recommends **Orlando Stroller Rentals, LLC** (☎ 800-281-0884; orlandostrollerrentals.com), which has similar prices, plus an excellent website that allows you to easily compare the features of different strollers.

Disney recommends **ScooterBug** (☎ 800-726-8284; scooterbug .com/orlando). If you use their service, you do not have to be present at your resort for the delivery or return of the stroller. Their rate starts at $65 for four days, with a minimum rental of four days.

In 2019 Disney introduced new rules regarding the maximum allowable dimensions for strollers, banning oversize strollers and stroller wagons from its parks. The new regulation requires strollers to be less than 31 inches (79 centimeters) wide and 52 inches (132 centimeters) long.

Another important matter is sun protection. Liliane always used a stroller with an adjustable canopy and also had lightweight pieces of cloth handy to protect her child from the sun. You can use anything for that purpose; a receiving blanket works well. Liliane used clothespins and safety pins to attach the pieces to the canopy. Don't overdo it, though. While it's important to protect your child from the sun, make sure there is enough air circulating—temperatures climb quickly in enclosed spaces.

Strollers are a must for infants and toddlers, but we've observed many sharp parents renting strollers for somewhat older children (up to age 5 or so). The stroller keeps parents from having to carry kids when they sag and provides a convenient place to carry water and snacks.

A family from Tulsa, Oklahoma, recommends springing for a double stroller:

> We rent a double for baggage room or in case the older child gets tired of walking.

If you go to your hotel for a break and intend to return to the park, leave your rental stroller by an attraction near the park entrance, marking it with something personal, such as a bandanna. When you return, your stroller will be waiting.

A Charleston, West Virginia, mom recommends a backup plan:

Strollers are not allowed in lines for rides, so if you have a small child (ours was 4) who needs to be held, you might end up holding him a long time. If I had it to do over, I'd bring along some kind of child carrier for when he was out of the stroller.

Bringing your own stroller is permitted. However, only collapsible strollers are allowed on monorails, parking lot trams, and buses. Your stroller is unlikely to be stolen, but mark it with your name. If you're bringing your own stroller to save money, you're flying, and you're checking the stroller as luggage, see if the airline's luggage fees outweigh the cost of renting or buying in Orlando.

BOB Don't try to lock your stroller to a fence, post, or anything else at WDW. You'll get in big trouble.

Having her own stroller was indispensable to a Mechanicsville, Virginia, mother of two toddlers:

How I was going to manage to get the kids from the parking lot to the park was a big worry for me before I made the trip. I didn't read anywhere that it was possible to walk to the entrance of the parks instead of taking the tram, so I wasn't sure I could do it.

I found that for me personally, since I have two kids aged 1 and 2, it was easier to walk to the entrance of the park from the parking lot with the kids in my own stroller than to take the kids out of the stroller, fold the stroller (while trying to control the two kids and associated gear), load the stroller and the kids onto the tram, etc. No matter where I was parked, I could always just walk to the entrance.

An Oklahoma mom, however, reports a bad experience with bringing her own stroller:

The first time we took our kids, we had a large stroller (big mistake). It is so much easier to rent one in the park. The large (personally owned) strollers are nearly impossible to get on the buses and are a hassle at the airport. I remember feeling dread when a bus pulled up that was even semifull of people. People look at you like you have a cage full of live chickens when you drag a heavy stroller onto the bus.

Liliane recommends that you bring your own stroller or rent a stroller for the entire duration of your stay. It is so much easier to get around with your child in a stroller, especially at the end of the day when you leave the park and have to return to your hotel via the parking lot or bus station. Once you are back at the hotel, you may also have quite a walk to your room.

STROLLER WARS Sometimes strollers disappear while you're enjoying a ride or show. Cast members often rearrange strollers parked outside an attraction. This may be done to tidy up or to clear a walkway. Don't assume that your stroller is stolen because it isn't where you left it. It may be neatly arranged a few feet away—or perhaps more than a few feet away.

Sometimes, however, strollers are taken by mistake or ripped off by people not wanting to spend time replacing one that's missing. Don't be alarmed if yours disappears. You won't have to buy it, and you'll be issued a new one.

You'd be surprised at how many people are injured by strollers pushed by parents who are aggressive or in a hurry. Given the number of strollers, pedestrians, and tight spaces, mishaps are inevitable on both sides. A simple apology and a smile are usually the best remedy.

A mom from New Hampshire reports:

If you're at park opening going toward a headliner attraction with a stroller, think of the stroller as a tractor-trailer during rush hour traffic—everyone cuts in front of you, and they get mad if you run into them. ABANDON the stroller and proceed on foot!

A mom from Arkansas reports:

When we exited Spaceship Earth, we were so turned around the first time we parked our stroller that it took us quite a while to find it. Find a central location to a few of the rides you want to explore, and park your stroller strategically. You will save time and steps that way.

While waiting at rope drop to head to the Frozen Ever After ride at EPCOT, Bob and Liliane were horrified to see an expectant mom being run over by a stroller. Please look out for your fellow guests. The ride will still be there, and it's not worth the injuries or the remorse.

PART 7

The MAGIC KINGDOM

OPENED IN 1971, THE MAGIC KINGDOM was the first of Walt Disney World's four theme parks to be built. Many of the attractions found here are originals from that park opening, and a few—including **Cinderella Castle, Pirates of the Caribbean,** and **Splash Mountain**—have helped define the basic elements of theme park attractions the world over. Indeed, the Magic Kingdom is undoubtedly what most people think of when they think of Walt Disney World.

But the Magic Kingdom is also welcoming the future, with the **Tron Lightcycle/Run** roller coaster slated to open in Tomorrowland in 2023. In celebration of Walt Disney World's 50th anniversary, Cinderella Castle got a royal makeover. After being painted a bolder pink color, with lots of gold and shimmery accents, Cindy's home now shines prettier than ever before. We are sure that she, like us, is breathing a sigh of relief that her castle wasn't turned into a golden birthday cake.

Wheelchair and **ECV/ESV rentals** are to the right of the train station, as are **lockers.** The lockers operate with a digital keypad system; they accept cash but can only give a maximum of $15 change, so don't try to pay with a $100! Prices are $10 (small), $12 (medium), and $15 (large) per day. Stroller rentals are now located under the railway arcs. On your left as you enter Main Street is **City Hall,** the center for information, Guest Relations, lost and found, guided tours, and entertainment information. **ATMs** are near the Transportation and Ticket Center (TTC), City Hall, near Pinocchio Village Haus in Fantasyland, and at the Tomorrowland Light & Power Company. Down Main Street and left around the Central Plaza (toward Adventureland) are the **Baby Care Center** and **First Aid.** Across from Disney's Port Orleans Resorts, **Best Friends Pet Care** provides a comfortable home away from home for Fido, Fluffy, and all their pet pals.

Get a **park map** as you enter the park underneath the Main Street Railroad Station or at City Hall. The map lists all attractions, shops, and eateries; provides helpful information about first aid, baby care, and assistance for disabled guests; and gives tips for good photos. Additionally, it tells where to find Disney characters.

It also identifies attractions closed for refurbishment and what Disney calls **Special Hours**, or operating hours for attractions and restaurants that open late or close early, as well as which quick-service locations offer mobile ordering. The entertainment schedule formerly known as the *Times Guide* has not returned to the parks, and we doubt it will, as Disney is driving guests to find all that information on the My Disney Experience app.

Main Street, U.S.A., ends at the **Central Plaza**, from which branch the entrances to the other five sections of the Magic Kingdom: **Adventureland, Frontierland, Liberty Square, Fantasyland**, and **Tomorrowland**.

In this and the following four chapters, we rate the individual attractions at each of the four major Disney theme parks and the two Universal theme parks. The **authors' rating**, which uses the same scale as the Appeal by Age ratings, is from the perspective of an adult. The authors, for example, might rate a ride such as Dumbo much lower than the age group for which the ride is intended—in this case, children. The authors' star rating is located next to the attraction's name. **Appeal by Age ratings** are expressed on a scale of one to five stars—the more stars, the better the attraction.

When entering any park, no matter what the occasion is, get a free pin at Guest Relations so you can show everyone what you are celebrating.

Brendan

OPENING PROCEDURES (ROPE DROP)

ARRIVING AT THE MAGIC KINGDOM **30–60 minutes before official opening** ensures the shortest possible waits for rides.

On-site guests who want to take advantage of Early Theme Park Entry should arrive at the park entrance 60 minutes before official opening (that is, 30 minutes before Early Entry) on all days. Off-site guests (who aren't eligible for Early Theme Park Entry) should arrive 30 minutes before official opening on all days.

Once in the park, you'll find most of the rides in Fantasyland and Tomorrowland running. Rides in Adventureland, Frontierland, and Liberty Square may start operating closer to the park's official opening time.

Main Street's larger shops, such as the **Emporium**, will be open when you're admitted into the park, in case you need sunscreen, ponchos, or aspirin. **Main Street Bakery (Starbucks)** will also be open for coffee and breakfast items.

Upon entering the park, most guests head for one of the headliner attractions: Seven Dwarfs Mine Train in Fantasyland gets the biggest crowds, followed by Space Mountain in Tomorrowland, with Big Thunder Mountain Railroad in Frontierland in third place. When

continued on page 284

The Magic Kingdom

G+ Attraction Offers Genie+

ILL Attraction Offers Individual Lightning Lane

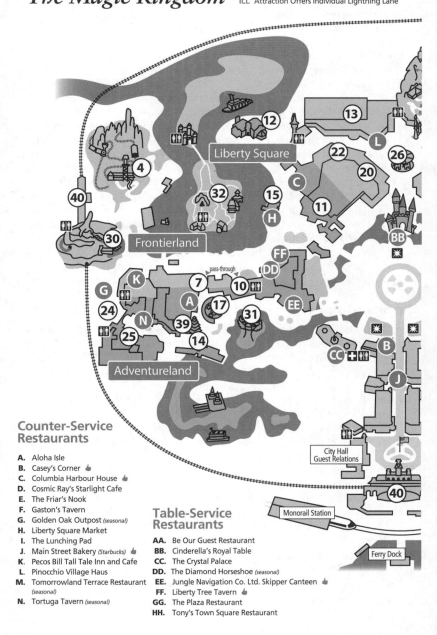

Liberty Square

Frontierland

pass-through

Adventureland

City Hall
Guest Relations

Monorail Station

Ferry Dock

Counter-Service Restaurants

A. Aloha Isle
B. Casey's Corner 👍
C. Columbia Harbour House 👍
D. Cosmic Ray's Starlight Cafe
E. The Friar's Nook
F. Gaston's Tavern
G. Golden Oak Outpost *(seasonal)*
H. Liberty Square Market
I. The Lunching Pad
J. Main Street Bakery *(Starbucks)* 👍
K. Pecos Bill Tall Tale Inn and Cafe
L. Pinocchio Village Haus
M. Tomorrowland Terrace Restaurant *(seasonal)*
N. Tortuga Tavern *(seasonal)*

Table-Service Restaurants

AA. Be Our Guest Restaurant
BB. Cinderella's Royal Table
CC. The Crystal Palace
DD. The Diamond Horseshoe *(seasonal)*
EE. Jungle Navigation Co. Ltd. Skipper Canteen 👍
FF. Liberty Tree Tavern 👍
GG. The Plaza Restaurant
HH. Tony's Town Square Restaurant

First Aid Center ✶ *Enchantment* Viewing Area

Restrooms 👍 Recommended Dining ☑ Not To Be Missed

Fantasyland

Tomorrowland

11. *The Hall of Presidents*
12. The Haunted Mansion ☑ G+
13. It's a Small World G+
14. Jungle Cruise G+
15. *Liberty Belle* Riverboat
16. Mad Tea Party G+
17. The Magic Carpets of Aladdin G+
18. The Many Adventures of Winnie the Pooh G+
19. Meet Merida at Fairytale Garden ☑

20. *Mickey's PhilharMagic* ☑ G+
21. *Monsters, Inc. Laugh Floor* G+
22. Peter Pan's Flight ☑ G+
23. Pete's Silly Sideshow *(temporarily closed)*
24. A Pirate's Adventure: Treasures of the Seven Seas ☑
25. Pirates of the Caribbean ☑ G+
26. Prince Charming Regal Carrousel
27. Princess Fairytale Hall Meet and Greets ☑ G+
28. Seven Dwarfs Mine Train ☑ ILL
29. Space Mountain ☑ G+
30. Splash Mountain ☑ G+
31. Swiss Family Treehouse
32. Tom Sawyer Island and Fort Langhorn
33. Tomorrowland Speedway G+
34. Tomorrowland Transit Authority PeopleMover ☑
35. Town Square Theater Meet and Greets ☑ G+
36. Tron Lightcycle/Run *(opens 2023)* ☑ ILL *(probable)*
37. Under the Sea: Journey of the Little Mermaid G+
38. *Walt Disney's Carousel of Progress*
39. *Walt Disney's Enchanted Tiki Room*
40. WDW Railroad *(multiple stations; temporarily closed)*

Walkway to Resort Buses

Attractions

1. Ariel's Grotto
2. Astro Orbiter
3. The Barnstormer G+
4. Big Thunder Mountain Railroad ☑ G+
5. Buzz Lightyear's Space Ranger Spin ☑ G+
6. Casey Jr. Splash 'N' Soak Station
7. *Country Bear Jamboree*
8. Dumbo the Flying Elephant G+
9. *Enchanted Tales with Belle*
10. Frontierland Shootin' Arcade

continued from page 281

Tron Lightcycle/Run opens in Tomorrowland, it should be the biggest draw in the park for teens and adults.

GENIE+ AND INDIVIDUAL LIGHTNING LANE SELECTIONS AND THE TOURING PLANS

Is Genie+ Worth Paying For at the Magic Kingdom?

The Magic Kingdom might be the easiest park to recommend using Genie+. It's Disney World's busiest theme park and has the most rides that offer Genie+ (see table below).

GENIE+ AND INDIVIDUAL LIGHTNING LANE (ILL) RESERVATIONS AT THE MAGIC KINGDOM
ADVENTURELAND
• Jungle Cruise   • Pirates of the Caribbean   • The Magic Carpets of Aladdin
FANTASYLAND
• The Barnstormer   • *Mickey's PhilharMagic*   • Peter Pan's Flight • Mad Tea Party • Dumbo the Flying Elephant   • It's a Small World   • Seven Dwarfs Mine Train *(ILL)* • Both princesses at Princess Fairytale Hall   • The Many Adventures of Winnie the Pooh • Under the Sea: Journey of the Little Mermaid
FRONTIERLAND
• Big Thunder Mountain Railroad   • Splash Mountain
LIBERTY SQUARE   • The Haunted Mansion
MAIN STREET, U.S.A.   • Meet Mickey Mouse at Town Square Theater
TOMORROWLAND
• Buzz Lightyear's Space Ranger Spin   • Tomorrowland Speedway • *Monsters, Inc. Laugh Floor*   • Tron Lightcycle/Run *(opens 2023)* • Space Mountain

Note: Character greetings were not operating when Genie+ was introduced, but we think they'll be added in the near future. We also think Tron will be Individual Lightning Lane when it opens.

We think Genie+ is worth the cost at the Magic Kingdom if you meet any of these criteria:

- You'll arrive at the park after Early Theme Park Entry begins (that is, you won't be at the park as soon as it opens). This includes off-site guests, who aren't eligible for Early Theme Park Entry, and on-site guests who want to sleep in.
- You won't be using a touring plan.
- You're visiting during a holiday, spring break, or other day of moderate to busy crowds.

The other consideration with Genie+ is the number of Genie+ ride reservations you'll be able to get in a given day. Under the old FastPass+ system, we think the vast majority of guests used five or fewer Fast-Passes per day at the Magic Kingdom. Here is how much time we think it's possible to save using Genie+ with a touring plan, using different

	ESTIMATED TIME SAVINGS USING A TOURING PLAN WITH GENIE+ FOR VARIOUS CROWD LEVELS		
CROWD LEVEL	TYPICAL USE (5 RESERVATIONS PER DAY)	OPTIMISTIC USE (9 RESERVATIONS PER DAY)	PERFECT USE (16 RESERVATIONS PER DAY)
Low	20 minutes saved	40 minutes saved	65 minutes saved
Medium	40 minutes saved	80 minutes saved	130 minutes saved
High	60 minutes saved	100 minutes saved	170 minutes saved

assumptions about how many Genie+ reservations it's possible to obtain in a day.

The **Typical Use** scenario assumes that you'll be able to obtain Genie+ reservations for five attractions in your touring plan, where you haven't already experienced those rides, the reservations don't conflict with any meals or breaks you've already planned, and the standby lines are long enough to justify obtaining the reservation. The **Optimistic Use** scenario assumes all the preceding, plus that Genie+ reservations are available at almost exactly the pace at which you're going to visit the attractions. The **Perfect Use** scenario assumes that you're able to get Genie+ reservations, one-by-one, with an immediate return time, for every eligible ride on your touring plan. We think that's exceedingly unlikely to happen; we present it here to estimate the upper limit on what might be possible. Finally, remember that Seven Dwarfs Mine Train is not part of Genie+; there's a separate cost to use Individual Lightning Lane with this ride.

Which Attractions Benefit Most from Genie+ or Individual Lightning Lane?

For Genie+, the table on page 286 shows the top attractions that might benefit most from using Genie+, based on the data we've collected since its launch. The chart goes in descending order of priority and does not assume use of a touring plan.

Regarding Individual Lightning Lane (ILL), Seven Dwarfs Mine Train is currently the only ILL attraction. Whether it is worth the cost will depend on what Disney's charging for it, and how that lines up with your personal time-versus-money spectrum.

Which Attractions Run Out of Genie+ or Individual Lightning Lane First?

The table on page 287 shows the approximate time at which the Magic Kingdom's attractions run out of Genie+ or Individual Lightning Lane capacity, by crowd level. Use this table in conjunction with the "Which Attractions Benefit Most" table on page 286 to determine which reservations to get first.

How Can You Avoid Paying for Individual Lightning Lane Attractions?

There are a few strategies to avoid paying for ILL attractions. Each of them involves another cost:

MAGIC KINGDOM ATTRACTIONS THAT BENEFIT MOST FROM GENIE+ AND INDIVIDUAL LIGHTNING LANE (ILL) *(Highest Priority to Lowest)*	
ATTRACTION	**AVERAGE TIME IN LINE SAVED (in minutes)**
Seven Dwarfs Mine Train (ILL)	51
Peter Pan's Flight	49
Jungle Cruise	48
Space Mountain	26
Splash Mountain	25
Big Thunder Mountain	19
The Magic Carpets of Aladdin	18
Buzz Lightyear's Space Ranger Spin	18
The Many Adventures of Winnie the Pooh	18
The Haunted Mansion	17
Pirates of the Caribbean	16
It's a Small World	15
Mad Tea Party	12
Under the Sea: Journey of the Little Mermaid	11
Meet Mickey Mouse at Town Square Theater	11
Dumbo the Flying Elephant	10
Princess Fairytale Hall	10
Tomorrowland Speedway	9
Monsters, Inc. Laugh Floor	2
Mickey's PhilharMagic	0

Tron was not open at press time; we think it will also be an Individual Lightning Lane. Some character greetings, including *Enchanted Tales with Belle,* Meet Ariel at Her Grotto, and Pete's Silly Sideshow (Donald, Goofy, Minnie, and Daisy) were also not open at press time. Meet Merida at Princess Fairytale Garden is now open but does not offer Genie+.

1. Stay at a Disney resort, use Early Theme Park Entry over multiple days, and head to one of the ILL attractions as soon as the park opens. For new attractions, such as Tron, this will likely be the strategy recommended by our touring plan software.

2. Stay at a Disney Deluxe or DVC resort and visit the ILL attractions during Extended Theme Park Hours.

3. Visit the ILL attraction during an After Hours event, such as the Mickey's Not-So-Scary Halloween Party.

Clearly, Disney has thought hard about how to force consumers into an explicit time-versus-money calculation with these attractions.

How Do Genie+ and Individual Lightning Lane Work with the Touring Plans?

FOR INDIVIDUAL LIGHTNING LANE ATTRACTIONS First obtain an ILL attraction return time from My Disney Experience. Next: If you're using one of our touring plans, follow the plan step by step until it's time to use your reservation. Deviate from the touring plan to ride the ILL attraction, and then resume the plan where you left off. If the touring

WHEN GENIE+ AND INDIVIDUAL LIGHTNING LANE RESERVATIONS RUN OUT BY ATTENDANCE LEVEL			
ATTRACTION	LOW ATTENDANCE	MODERATE ATTENDANCE	HIGH ATTENDANCE
The Barnstormer	9 p.m.	9 p.m.	9 p.m.
Big Thunder Mountain Railroad	8 p.m.	6 p.m.	5 p.m.
Buzz Lightyear's Space Ranger Spin	9 p.m.	9 p.m.	9 p.m.
Dumbo the Flying Elephant	9 p.m.	8 p.m.	10 p.m.
The Haunted Mansion	8 p.m.	6 p.m.	6 p.m.
It's a Small World	9 p.m.	8 p.m.	8 p.m.
Jungle Cruise	6 p.m.	2 p.m.	2 p.m.
Mad Tea Party	9 p.m.	9 p.m.	7-8 p.m.
The Magic Carpets of Aladdin	9 p.m.	9 p.m.	9 p.m.
The Many Adventures of Winnie the Pooh	8 p.m.	6 p.m.	6 p.m.
Meet Cinderella at Princess Fairytale Hall	8 p.m.	6 p.m.	6 p.m.
Meet Mickey Mouse	8 p.m.	6 p.m.	6 p.m.
Meet Tiana at Princess Fairytale Hall	8 p.m.	6 p.m.	6 p.m.
Mickey's PhilharMagic	8 p.m.	8 p.m.	9 p.m.
Monsters, Inc. Laugh Floor	7 p.m.	6 p.m.	7 p.m.
Peter Pan's Flight	8 p.m.	5 p.m.	4 p.m.
Pirates of the Caribbean	9 p.m.	8 p.m.	9 p.m.
Seven Dwarfs Mine Train	8 p.m.	5 p.m.	11:30 a.m.
Space Mountain	8 p.m.	6 p.m.	6 p.m.
Splash Mountain	8 p.m.	7 p.m.	9 p.m.
Tomorrowland Speedway	9 p.m.	8 p.m.	9 p.m.
Under the Sea: Journey of the Little Mermaid	9 p.m.	9 p.m.	10 p.m.

LOW ATTENDANCE Crowd levels 1–3 on the TouringPlans crowd calendar
MODERATE ATTENDANCE Crowd levels 4–7
HIGH ATTENDANCE Crowd levels 8–10
Attractions closed for more than two years are not shown.

plan recommends visiting the attraction before or after your return time, skip that step.

If you're using our free touring plan software, enter the reservation return time into the touring plan software. The software will organize your touring plan so that you return to the attraction at your designated return time.

FOR GENIE+ If you're using one of our touring plans, keep track of the next two or three steps in your touring plan as you go through the park. In Genie+, get the first available reservation for any of those three attractions, and fit that return-time window into the plan. For example, suppose the next three steps in your touring plan are Jungle Cruise, Pirates of the Caribbean, and Big Thunder Mountain Railroad. You check Genie+ for the next available return time for those three attractions, and the return times are 11 a.m. for Jungle Cruise, 11:30 a.m. for

Pirates, and 10:45 a.m. for Big Thunder. You'd select Big Thunder because it's the next available return time from among those three. Once in line for Big Thunder, scan Genie+ availability for the next three attractions in your plan. If none of the next three steps in your plan participate in Genie+, then get a reservation for the next attraction in your plan that participates in Genie+.

If you're using our touring plan software, it will recommend which attraction to obtain a Genie+ reservation for next by analyzing your touring plan, the current Genie+ reservation distribution rate, and likely wait times for the rest of the day. When you obtain that reservation, simply enter the return time into the software, and the software will redo your touring plan to use it.

MAIN STREET, U.S.A.

YOU'LL BEGIN AND END YOUR VISIT ON MAIN STREET, which closes 30 minutes–1 hour after the rest of the park. Trolleys and buses ride up and down Main Street. While they save you a walk to Central Plaza in front of Cinderella Castle, they are not worth a wait. It's easy to get sidetracked when entering Main Street: This Disney-fied turn-of-the-19th-century small-town street is lovely, with exceptional attention to detail. But remember, time is of the essence, and the rest of the park is waiting to be discovered. The same goes for the one and only **Cinderella Castle.** Stick with your touring plan and return to the castle and Main Street after you've experienced the must-dos on your list.

KEY TO ABBREVIATIONS In the attraction profiles that follow, each star rating is accompanied by a category label in parentheses. **E** means **Exceptional, MAA** means **Much Above Average, AA** means **Above Average, A** means **Average, BA** means **Below Average,** and **MBA** means **Much Below Average.**

AVERAGE WAIT-IN-LINE TIMES This generally uses the attractions' maximum hourly capacity as a fixed reference, as capacity is subject to change.

Town Square Theater Meet and Greets: Mickey Mouse and Tinker Bell and Friends ★★★★

PRESCHOOL ★★★★★ (MAA)   GRADE SCHOOL, TEENS, AND OVER 30 ★★★★½ (MAA) YOUNG ADULTS ★★★★½ (AA)   SENIORS ★★★★½ (AA)

What it is Character-greeting venue. **Scope and scale** Minor attraction. **When to go** Before 10 a.m. or after 4 p.m. **Comments** Mickey and the fairies have 2 separate queues, requiring 2 separate waits in line. It all started with this mouse; not to be missed. **Duration of experience** 2 minutes per character. **Probable waiting time** 30 minutes. **Queue speed** Slow. **ECV/wheelchair access** May remain in wheelchair. **Participates in Genie+** Yes. **Early Theme Park Entry** No. **Extended Evening Hours** No.

Children and teenagers rate character greetings among the highest of any Disney attractions, and there's no bigger celebrity than Mickey Mouse. Meet Mickey, along with Tinker Bell and her Pixie Hollow friends, throughout the day at the

Town Square Theater, to your right as you enter the park. Lines usually recede after dinner. If Genie+ isn't available, our touring plans frequently put meeting Mickey as the first step in the day. He usually starts greeting guests at the park's official opening time, even if you're let into the park early.

Walt Disney World Railroad† *(temporarily unavailable)*

PRESCHOOL ★★★½ (MAA)   **GRADE SCHOOL** ★★★★½ (AA)   **TEENS** ★★★★ (BA)
YOUNG ADULTS ★★★★ (A)   **OVER 30** ★★★★½ (AA)   **SENIORS** ★★★★½ (AA)

†*Closed due to construction of the new Tron Lightcycle/Run roller coaster in Tomorrowland. At press time, no reopening date had been announced.*

Thumbs Up for the Whole Family

What it is Scenic railroad ride around the perimeter of the Magic Kingdom; provides transportation to Frontierland and Fantasyland. **Scope and scale** Minor attraction. **When to go** Anytime. **Comments** Main Street is usually the least congested station. **Duration of ride** About 20 minutes for a complete circuit. **Average wait in line per 100 people ahead of you** 8 minutes; assumes 2 or more trains operating. **Loading speed** Moderate. **ECV/wheelchair access** Guests must transfer from ECV to provided wheelchair. **Participates in Genie+** No. **Early Theme Park Entry** No. **Extended Evening Hours** No.

Later in the day, when you need a break, this full-circuit ride will give you and your feet 20 minutes of rest. Only folded strollers are permitted on the train, so you can't board with your rented Disney stroller. You can, however, obtain a replacement at your destination. Be advised that the railroad shuts down for the night immediately preceding the evening parade. If you're in Frontierland and headed out of the park, it's a nice way to end your visit.

ADVENTURELAND

THE FIRST LAND to the left of Main Street, Adventureland combines an African-safari theme with a tropical-island atmosphere.

Jungle Cruise ★★★½

PRESCHOOL ★★★★ (MBA)   **GRADE SCHOOL** ★★★★ (MBA)   **TEENS** ★★★★ (BA)
YOUNG ADULTS ★★★★ (A)   **OVER 30** ★★★★ (AA)   **SENIORS** ★★★★ (AA)

What it is Outdoor safari-themed boat ride adventure. **Scope and scale** Major attraction. **When to go** Before 10:30 a.m., the last 2 hours before closing, or use Genie+. **Duration of ride** 8–9 minutes. **Average wait in line per 100 people ahead of you** 3½ minutes; assumes 10 boats operating. **Loading speed** Moderate. **ECV/wheelchair access** May remain in EVC/wheelchair and wait for specially configured boats. **Participates in Genie+** Yes. **Early Theme Park Entry** Yes. **Extended Evening Hours** No.

Isabelle

During the holiday season the Jungle Cruise turns into the Jingle Cruise. Jingle Bells, Jingle Cruise—do you get it?

You have to put things into perspective to truly enjoy this ride and realize that it was once a super-headliner at the Magic Kingdom—it's fun and relaxing but far from high-tech. We think the ride is better at night. During the Christmas season it gets an overlay and turns into the Jingle Cruise with seasonal touches of holiday decorations.

I didn't really like this ride. The animals weren't real, but it was scary in the dark cave, and the big spider was absolutely terrifying.

Felicity

The Magic Carpets of Aladdin ★★

PRESCHOOL ★★★★½ (MAA) **GRADE SCHOOL** ★★★★ (BA) **TEENS** ★★★ (BA)
YOUNG ADULTS ★★★ (MBA) **OVER 30** ★★★ (MBA) **SENIORS** ★★★ (MBA)

What it is Elaborate midway ride. **Scope and scale** Minor attraction. **When to go**
Before 11 a.m. or after 7 p.m. **Duration of ride** 1½ minutes. **Average wait in line per
100 people ahead of you** 16 minutes. **Loading speed** Slow. **ECV/wheelchair access**
Must transfer from ECV to provided wheelchair. **Participates in Genie+** Yes. **Early
Theme Park Entry** Yes. **Extended Evening Hours** Yes.

> Keep your guard up when you're near this ride.
> The golden camel spits water randomly. I was struck in the ear
> and also got a glob of water in my eye. Don't say I didn't warn you.

A. J.

Like Dumbo, Aladdin is a must for parents with preschoolers. Try to get
your kids on in the first 30 minutes the park is open or just before park
closing. Beware of the spitting camel positioned to spray jets of water on riders. The front-seat control moves your "carpet" up and down, while the back-
seat control pitches it forward or backward. Sweet, but oh-so-slow loading.

This ride is inspired by the 1992 Disney movie Aladdin.
Did you know that Robin Williams was the voice of the genie?

A Pirate's Adventure: Treasures of the Seven Seas ★★★½

PRESCHOOL ★★★★½ (A) **GRADE SCHOOL** ★★★★½ (A) **TEENS** ★★★★½ (A)
YOUNG ADULTS ★★★★ (A) **OVER 30** ★★★★½ (A) **SENIORS** ★★★★ (A)

What it is Interactive game. **Scope and scale** Diversion. **When to go** Noon–6 p.m.
Comment Simple, fast, and fun. **Duration of experience** About 25 minutes to play
entire game. **ECV/wheelchair access** May remain in EVC/wheelchair. **Participates in
Genie+** No. **Early Theme Park Entry** No. **Extended Evening Hours** No.

A Pirate's Adventure features interactive areas with physical props and narra-
tions that lead guests through a quest to find lost treasure.

Guests begin their journey at The Crow's Nest near Golden Oak Outpost—
this is the central hub for adventurers helping to locate missing treasure. Your
group of up to six people chooses a leader; the leader's MagicBand (or ticket
or talisman) activates a video screen that assigns the group to one of five mis-
sions. The group is given a map and sent off to the first location.

Once at the location, the leader of the party touches the talisman to the
symbol at the station, and the animation begins. Each adventure has four or
five stops throughout Adventureland; each stop contains 30–45 seconds of
activity. No strategy or action is required; simply watch what unfolds on the
screen, get your next destination, and head off.

We like how well each station integrates into its surroundings and how the
stations' artifacts and props tie together the attraction and movie story lines.
If you're not yet convinced to play, stand in Adventureland and watch the
faces of the kids playing when they do something that triggers smoke, noise,
or other effects.

A Maryland mom writes:

*The very best thing we did with our 4-year-old was A Pirate's Adventure. It
was incredible. We did all five scavenger hunts, and it took 2 hours—our most
fun 2 hours at the park! It's high-tech, magical, imaginative, active, and individualized. And you can keep the beautiful maps!*

Pirates of the Caribbean ★★★★

PRESCHOOL ★★★½ (MBA) **GRADE SCHOOL** ★★★★ (A) **TEENS** ★★★★½ (MAA)
YOUNG ADULTS ★★★★½ (MAA) **OVER 30** ★★★★½ (MAA) **SENIORS** ★★★★½ (MAA)

What it is Indoor pirate-themed boat ride. **Scope and scale** Headliner. **When to go** Before 11 a.m., after 7 p.m., or use Genie+. **Comment** Frightens some children. **Duration of ride** About 7½ minutes. **Average wait in line per 100 people ahead of you** 3 minutes; assumes 1 Genie+ line and 1 standby line. **Loading speed** Fast. **ECV/wheelchair access** Must transfer from ECV to provided wheelchair and then from wheelchair to boat. **Participates in Genie+** Yes. **Early Theme Park Entry** Yes. **Extended Evening Hours** Yes.

This ride cruises through sets depicting a pirate raid on a Caribbean port. It's been a favorite attraction for decades, but with the release of five *Pirates of the Caribbean* movies since 2003, its popularity has soared to new heights.

The ride starts off scary because it's very dark and there are skeletons and loud voices. But it's great fun to try to spot Jack Sparrow. It was very silly of him to hide behind a lady's dress. I loved the boat ride and the music.

Felicity

See the movies before you go to Walt Disney World. They're a blast.

Swiss Family Treehouse ★★★

PRESCHOOL ★★★★ (BA) **GRADE SCHOOL** ★★★½ (MBA) **TEENS** ★★★ (MBA)
YOUNG ADULTS ★★★½ (MBA) **OVER 30** ★★★½ (MBA) **SENIORS** ★★★ (MBA)

Thumbs Up for the Whole Family

What it is Outdoor walk-through treehouse. **Scope and scale** Minor attraction. **When to go** Anytime. **Comments** Requires climbing a lot of stairs. **Duration of tour** 10–15 minutes. **Probable waiting time** None most days, 10 minutes tops. **ECV/wheelchair access** Must be ambulatory. **Participates in Genie+** No. **Early Theme Park Entry** Yes. **Extended Evening Hours** Yes.

This king of all tree houses is perfect for the 10-and-under crowd. Though a minor attraction, it's a great place to expend pent-up energy. Parents might be inclined to sit across the walkway and watch their aspiring Tarzans, but in truth the tree house is fun for adults too.

Swiss Family Robinson is a 1960 film adaptation of the Johann David Wyss novel and was the inspiration for the Swiss Family Treehouse.

Walt Disney's Enchanted Tiki Room ★★★

PRESCHOOL ★★★★ (MBA) **GRADE SCHOOL** ★★★½ (MBA) **TEENS** ★★★½ (MBA)
YOUNG ADULTS ★★★½ (MBA) **OVER 30** ★★★★ (BA) **SENIORS** ★★★★ (A)

What it is Audio-Animatronic Pacific Island musical-theater show. **Scope and scale** Minor attraction. **When to go** Before 11 a.m. or after 3:30 p.m. **Comment** Young children might be frightened by the thunder-and-lightning storm, plus the theater is at times plunged into utter darkness. **Duration of show** 15½ minutes. **Preshow entertainment** Talking birds. **Probable waiting time** 15 minutes. **ECV/wheelchair access** May remain in EVC/wheelchair. **Participates in Genie+** No. **Early Theme Park Entry** No. **Extended Evening Hours** Yes.

The tiki birds are a great favorite of the 8-and-under set. The outright absurdity of the whole concept saves the show for older patrons—if you can look beyond the cheese, it's actually hilarious. The air-conditioned theater is a great place to cool off and rest your feet.

> We always seem to end up here because it's raining, but it's actually good fun. The singing birds are really clever, and the songs get stuck in your head.

Felicity

FRONTIERLAND

THIS LAND ADJOINS ADVENTURELAND as you move clockwise around the Magic Kingdom. Frontierland's focus is on the Old West, with stockade-type structures and pioneer trappings.

Big Thunder Mountain Railroad   ★★★★

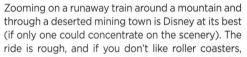

PRESCHOOL ★★★★ (BA)	GRADE SCHOOL ★★★★½ (MAA)	TEENS ★★★★½ (MAA)
YOUNG ADULTS ★★★★½ (MAA)	OVER 30 ★★★★½ (MAA)	SENIORS ★★★★½ (A)

What it is Western mining–themed roller coaster. **Scope and scale** Headliner. **When to go** Before 10 a.m. or in the hour before closing. **Comments** Must be 40″ tall to ride; Rider Switch option provided (see page 260). **Duration of ride** About 3½ minutes. **Average wait in line per 100 people ahead of you** 2½ minutes; assumes 5 trains operating. **Loading speed** Moderate–fast. **ECV/wheelchair access** Must transfer to the ride vehicle. **Participates in Genie+** Yes. **Early Theme Park Entry** Yes. **Extended Evening Hours** Yes.

Lose Things   **Rough**   **Scary**

Zooming on a runaway train around a mountain and through a deserted mining town is Disney at its best (if only one could concentrate on the scenery). The ride is rough, and if you don't like roller coasters, this will remind you why. The air-conditioned queue features first-rate examples of Disney creativity; a realistic mining town, geysers, swinging possums, petulant buzzards, and the like will keep kids busy while waiting in line. Ride after dark if you can. Seats in the back offer a better experience.

Country Bear Jamboree   ★★★★½

PRESCHOOL ★★★★ (BA)	GRADE SCHOOL ★★★½ (MBA)	TEENS ★★★ (MBA)
YOUNG ADULTS ★★★½ (MBA)	OVER 30 ★★★½ (MBA)	SENIORS ★★★★ (BA)

What it is Corny Audio-Animatronic hoedown. **Scope and scale** Minor attraction. **When to go** Anytime. **Duration of show** 11 minutes. **Preshow entertainment** None. **Probable waiting time** Not terribly popular but has a comparatively small capacity. Waiting time between noon and 5:30 p.m. on a busy day will average 11–22 minutes. **ECV/wheelchair access** May remain in wheelchair. **Participates in Genie+** No. **Early Theme Park Entry** No. **Extended Evening Hours** Yes.

A charming cast of Audio-Animatronic bears sings and stomps in a Western-style hoedown. *Country Bear Jamboree* has run for so long that the geriatric bears are a step away from assisted living. Reader comments tend to echo the need for something new. From a Sandy Hook, Connecticut, mom:

> *I know they consider it a classic, and kids always seem to love it, but could they PLEASE update it after half a century?*

Check out Liliane's review of the show at theunofficialguides.com/2022/04 /28/country-bear-jamboree-show-still-going-strong-at-walt-disney-world.

Frontierland Shootin' Arcade ★½

PRESCHOOL ★★★ (MBA)   **GRADE SCHOOL ★★★★** (BA)   **TEENS ★★★½** (BA)
YOUNG ADULTS ★★★ (MBA)   **OVER 30 ★★★½** (MBA)   **SENIORS ★★★★** (A)

What it is Electronic shooting gallery. **Scope and scale** Diversion. **When to go** Anytime. **ECV/wheelchair access** May remain in EVC/wheelchair. **Participates in Genie+** No. **Early Theme Park Entry** No. **Extended Evening Hours** No.

For years one had to come armed with lots of quarters to play this game, but lo and behold, it is now free. Yes, you read that right: free!

Splash Mountain ★★★★★

PRESCHOOL ★★★★† (BA)   **ALL OTHER AGE GROUPS ★★★★½** (MAA)

†*Many preschoolers are too short to ride; others freak out when they see it from the waiting line. Among preschoolers who actually ride, however, most love it.*

What it is Indoor-outdoor water-flume adventure. **Scope and scale** Super-headliner. **When to go** During warm weather: as soon as the park opens, during afternoon or evening parades, just before closing, or use Genie+. **Comments** Must be 40" to ride; Rider Switch option provided (see page 260). **Duration of ride** About 10 minutes. **Average wait in line per 100 people ahead of you** 3½ minutes; assumes ride is operating at full capacity. **Loading speed** Moderate. **ECV/wheelchair access** Must transfer to the ride vehicle; transfer device available. **Participates in Genie+** Yes. **Early Theme Park Entry** Yes. **Extended Evening Hours** No.

The first time I rode Splash Mountain, I spent the entire time worrying about every drop to come until the big one. Don't make the same mistake. Yes, there are multiple drops, but you'll know when the big one is coming. So in the meantime, enjoy the ride.

A. J.

Lose Things   Wet   Scary

Zip-a-dee-doo-dah, having fun yet? My, oh, my, will you get wet! This 0.5-mile ride through swamps, caves, and backwoods bayous is wonderful. Based on the 1946 Disney film *Song of the South,* the log flume ride takes you through Uncle Remus's tales of Br'er Rabbit. Three small drops lead up to the big one—a five-story plunge at 40 miles per hour! In 2020 Disney announced that the ride would be rethemed to the animated feature *The Princess and the Frog.* More than two years after the announcement we still do not know if Tiana will indeed take over Splash Mountain and what exactly the overhaul of Splash Mountain will look like. At press time, we did not have a date as to when Disney will be fully rolling out these changes both at Walt Disney World and Disneyland. But changes will be coming.

Bring a change of clothes, or wear a bathing suit or a poncho, because you might get very wet.

Sabrina

Movie Tip

Unavailable in the United States, Song of the South *will become public domain in 2039, and Disney might rerelease the movie before it loses the rights to it. If you're interested in the history of this controversial movie, visit songofthesouth.net.*

I liked going through Br'er Bear's village, but the big drop made me feel very woozy. We also got really wet.

Felicity

Tom Sawyer Island and Fort Langhorn ★★★

PRESCHOOL ★★★★½ (AA) **GRADE SCHOOL** ★★★★½ (AA) **TEENS** ★★★½ (BA)
YOUNG ADULTS ★★★½ (MBA) **OVER 30** ★★★½ (MBA) **SENIORS** ★★★½ (MBA)

Thumbs Up for the Whole Family

What it is Outdoor walk-through exhibit and rustic playground. **Scope and scale** Minor attraction. **When to go** Midmorning–late afternoon. **Comments** Closes at dusk. Great for rambunctious kids. **ECV/wheelchair access** Must be ambulatory. **Participates in Genie+** No. **Early Theme Park Entry** No. **Extended Evening Hours** No.

This is a great place for kids age 5 and up to unwind. The wildest and most uncooperative youngster will relax after exploring caves and climbing around in an old fort. It's also a great place for a picnic, but there is no food, so bring your own. Access is by raft with a (usually short) wait both coming and going. Plan to give your kids at least 40 minutes on the island—left to their own devices, they would likely stay all day.

Liliane

I love Tom Sawyer Island. It's the perfect place to take a break or have a picnic; plus, it's a great place for nursing moms to find a quiet spot. Be aware, though, that raft transportation to the island stops at sunset.

▌ LIBERTY SQUARE

THIS LAND RE-CREATES AMERICA at the time of the American Revolution. The architecture is Federal or Colonial. The **Liberty Tree,** a live oak more than 150 years old, lends dignity and grace to the setting.

The Hall of Presidents ★★★

PRESCHOOL ★★★† (MBA) **GRADE SCHOOL** ★★★† (MBA) **TEENS** ★★★½† (MBA)
YOUNG ADULTS ★★★★ (BA) **OVER 30** ★★★★ (A) **SENIORS** ★★★★½ (MAA)

† This is the lowest-rated Magic Kingdom attraction among preschoolers, grade-schoolers, and teens.

What it is Audio-Animatronic historical theater presentation. **Scope and scale** Minor attraction. **When to go** Anytime. **Duration of show** Almost 23 minutes. **Preshow entertainment** None. **Probable waiting time** About 15 minutes. It would be exceptionally unusual not to be admitted to the next show. **ECV/wheelchair access** May remain in wheelchair. **Participates in Genie+** No. **Early Theme Park Entry** No. **Extended Evening Hours** No.

Thumbs Up for the Whole Family

The Hall of Presidents combines a wide-screen theater presentation of the highlights and milestones in the United States' political history with a short stage show, including life-size animatronic replicas of every US president. In addition to Abraham Lincoln and George Washington, all presidents since Teddy Roosevelt, except George H. W. Bush, have small speaking roles in the show, either in the film or onstage. *The Hall of Presidents* is definitely a must-see for adults, but kids are likely to fidget or fall asleep.

Liliane

Did you know that famous Western actor Royal Dano is the voice of President Lincoln? He also was the voice of Lincoln for Disneyland's *Great Moments with Mr. Lincoln* program, first presented at the 1964–65 World's Fair in New York.

The attractions' latest addition is President Joseph R. Biden, who recites the oath of office. Over the last decade or so, it's become commonplace for some members of the audience to cheer or jeer, according to their political affiliation, as the current president and his contemporaries are named. These partisan displays are divisive and not in keeping with the show's positive message, but they aren't likely to go away—so skip The Hall of Presidents if you'd rather not be reminded of politics on vacation.

The Haunted Mansion ★★★★½

PRESCHOOL ★★★ (MBA) **GRADE SCHOOL ★★★★** (MBA) **TEENS ★★★★½** (MAA)
YOUNG ADULTS ★★★★½ (MAA) **OVER 30 ★★★★½** (MAA) **SENIORS ★★★★½** (MAA)

What it is Haunted-house dark ride. **Scope and scale** Major attraction. **When to go** Before 11 a.m. or the last 2 hours before closing. **Comment** Frightens some very young children. **Duration of ride** 7-minute ride plus a 1½-minute preshow. **Average wait in line per 100 people ahead of you** 2½ minutes; assumes both "stretch rooms" operating. **Loading speed** Fast. **ECV/wheelchair access** Must transfer to the ride vehicle. **Participates in Genie+** Yes. **Early Theme Park Entry** Yes. **Extended Evening Hours** Yes.

Don't let the apparent spookiness of the old-fashioned Haunted Mansion put you off. This is one of the best attractions in the Magic Kingdom. It's not scary, except in the sweetest of ways, but it will remind you of the days before ghost stories gave way to slasher flicks. The Haunted Mansion takes less than 10 minutes to ride, preshow included, but you may have to do it more than once—it's jam-packed with visual puns, special effects, hidden Mickeys, and really lovely Victorian-spooky sets. The Haunted Mansion also has a photo opportunity. As your Doom Buggy journeys through the haunted chambers, watch out for ghosts and smile for the camera.

Liberty Belle Riverboat ★★½

PRESCHOOL ★★★½ (BA) **GRADE SCHOOL ★★★½** (BA) **TEENS ★★★** (BA)
YOUNG ADULTS ★★★½ (BA) **OVER 30 ★★★½** (MBA) **SENIORS ★★★★** (A)

What it is Scenic boat ride. **Scope and scale** Minor attraction. **When to go** Anytime. **Duration of ride** About 16 minutes. **Average wait to board** 10–14 minutes. **ECV/wheelchair access** May remain in EVC/wheelchair. **Participates in Genie+** No. **Early Theme Park Entry** No. **Extended Evening Hours** No.

Thumbs Up for the Whole Family

This fully narrated 16-minute trip is relaxing and offers great photo ops. It's also a good choice at night, when the boat and the attractions along the waterfront are lighted. Did you know that the *Liberty Belle* runs on a track hidden just below the water?

FANTASYLAND

THE HEART OF THE MAGIC KINGDOM, Fantasyland is a truly enchanting place spread gracefully like a miniature alpine village beneath the steepled towers of Cinderella Castle.

Fantasyland is divided into three distinct sections. Directly behind Cinderella Castle and set on a snowcapped mountain is Beast's Castle, part of a ***Beauty and the Beast*-themed area.** Most of this section holds dining and shopping. Outside Beast's Castle is Belle's Village. Nestled inside lush, beautifully decorated grounds, with gardens, meadows, and waterfalls, is Maurice's cottage, home of *Enchanted Tales with Belle* (*temporarily closed*).

LILIANE The only way to visit Beast's Castle is by eating at Be Our Guest, which is booked months in advance.

The far-right corner of Fantasyland, including Dumbo, The Barnstormer kiddie coaster, and the Fantasyland Train Station, is called **Storybook Circus** as an homage to the *Dumbo* films. These are low-capacity amusement park rides appropriate for younger children. Also located here is Pete's Silly Sideshow, a character-greeting venue (*temporarily closed*).

The middle of Fantasyland holds the headliners, including Under the Sea: Journey of the Little Mermaid and Seven Dwarfs Mine Train. The **original part of Fantasyland,** behind Cinderella Castle, contains classic attractions, such as Peter Pan's Flight and The Many Adventures of Winnie the Pooh. It also hosts the popular Princess Fairytale Hall meet and greet.

Finally, when nature calls, don't miss the *Tangled*-themed restrooms and outdoor seating, near Peter Pan's Flight and It's a Small World. Outlets for charging your phone are hidden in the faux tree trunks. And no, you can't visit Rapunzel's Tower. Sometimes a restroom is just that, a restroom.

Ariel's Grotto *(temporarily unavailable)* ★★★

PRESCHOOL ★★★★½ (MAA) GRADE SCHOOL ★★★★½ (MAA) TEENS ★★★½ (BA) YOUNG ADULTS ★★★★ (A) OVER 30 ★★★★ (MBA) SENIORS ★★★½ (MBA)

What it is Character-greeting venue. **Scope and scale** Minor attraction. **When to go** Before 10:30 a.m. or during the last 2 hours before closing. **Duration of experience** Maybe 30–90 seconds. **Probable waiting time** 45 minutes. **Queue speed** Slow. **ECV/wheelchair access** May remain in wheelchair. **Participates in Genie+** No. **Early Theme Park Entry** No. **Extended Evening Hours** No.

Ariel's home base is next to Under the Sea: Journey of the Little Mermaid. In the base of the seaside cliffs under Prince Eric's Castle, Ariel (in mermaid form) greets guests from a seashell throne. The queue (not air-conditioned) isn't as detailed as other character-greeting venues in the park.

The Barnstormer ★★

PRESCHOOL ★★★★ (A) GRADE SCHOOL ★★★★ (MBA) TEENS ★★★ (MBA) YOUNG ADULTS ★★★ (MBA) OVER 30 ★★★ (MBA) SENIORS ★★★ (MBA)

What it is Small roller coaster. **Scope and scale** Minor attraction. **When to go** Before 11 a.m., during parades, or the last 2 hours the park is open. **Comments** Must be 35" to ride. **Duration of ride** About 53 seconds. **Average wait in line per 100 people ahead of you** 7 minutes. **Loading speed** Slow. **ECV/wheelchair access** Must transfer to the ride vehicle. **Participates in Genie+** Yes. **Early Theme Park Entry** Yes. **Extended Evening Hours** No.

Note the height requirement for this ride. If you want to see how your child handles riding coasters, The Barnstormer is the perfect testing ground (Seven Dwarfs Mine Train is next).

Liliane

Yours truly screamed big-time from start to end (thankfully it only lasted a minute), and no way would I let the apple of my eye ride alone unless he or she were 6 years or older.

Bob

Liliane is a gentle and sensitive soul. Most kids experience rides wilder than The Barnstormer on their tricycles. When I heard Liliane wailing like a banshee on this dinky coaster, I thought her appendix must have ruptured.

Casey Jr. Splash 'N' Soak Station ★★★

PRESCHOOL ★★★★½ (MAA)   **GRADE SCHOOL** ★★★★ (AA)   **TEENS** ★★ (MBA)
YOUNG ADULTS ★½ (MBA)   **OVER 30** ★★ (MBA)   **SENIORS** ★★ (MBA)

What it is Elaborate water-play area. **Scope and scale** Diversion. **When to go** When it's hot. **ECV/wheelchair access** May remain in wheelchair. **Participates in Genie+** No. **Early Theme Park Entry** No. **Extended Evening Hours** No.

Wet

Casey Jr., the circus train from *Dumbo,* hosts an absolutely drenching experience outside the Fantasyland Train Station in the Storybook Circus area. Expect a cadre of captive circus beasts to spray water on you in this elaborate water-play area. It's a marvel to watch. Be sure to bring a change of clothes and a big towel.

Dumbo the Flying Elephant ★★½

PRESCHOOL ★★★★½ (MAA)   **GRADE SCHOOL** ★★★★ (MBA)   **TEENS** ★★★ (MBA)
YOUNG ADULTS ★★★ (MBA)   **OVER 30** ★★★½ (MBA)   **SENIORS** ★★★★ (BA)

What it is Disney-fied midway ride. **Scope and scale** Minor attraction. **When to go** Before 11 a.m. or after 6 p.m. **Duration of ride** 1½ minutes. **Average wait in line per 100 people ahead of you** 10 minutes. **Loading speed** Slow. **ECV/wheelchair access** Must transfer to the ride vehicle. **Participates in Genie+** Yes. **Early Theme Park Entry** Yes. **Extended Evening Hours** Yes.

Thumbs Up for the Whole Family

Making sure your kids get their fill of this tame, happy children's ride is what a mother's love is all about. The 90-second ride is hardly worth waiting in line for, unless, of course, you're under 7 years old.

Movie Tip

If you haven't seen Dumbo *(first released in 1941 and winner of an Academy Award for original music score), you have an elephant-size gap in your Disney education. Watch the movie, fun for all ages, when you get home. In 2019, Disney released the live-action adaptation of* Dumbo. *The film is directed by Tim Burton, who has worked on many memorable films, including* Edward Scissorhands *(1990),* The Nightmare Before Christmas *(1993),* Charlie and the Chocolate Factory *(2005),* Alice in Wonderland *(2010), and* Alice Through the Looking Glass *(2016), just to name a few.*

Enchanted Tales with Belle *(temporarily unavailable)* ★★★★

PRESCHOOL ★★★★½ (MAA)   **GRADE SCHOOL** ★★★★½ (AA)   **TEENS** ★★★ (MBA)
YOUNG ADULTS ★★★½ (MBA)   **OVER 30** ★★★★ (MBA)   **SENIORS** ★★★★ (BA)

What it is Interactive live character show. **Scope and scale** Minor attraction. **When to go** As soon as the park opens or during the last 2 hours before closing. **Duration of presentation** About 20 minutes. **Preshow entertainment** A walk through Maurice's cottage and workshop. **Probable waiting time** 30 minutes. **ECV/wheelchair access** Must transfer from ECV to provided wheelchair. **Participates in Genie+** Probably upon return. **Early Theme Park Entry** No. **Extended Evening Hours** No.

A multiscene *Beauty and the Beast* experience takes guests into Maurice's workshop, through a magic mirror, and into Beast's library, where the audience shares a story with Belle.

This is so much fun, especially if you get chosen to play one of the characters. I did, and even my parents got a part. It's a great way to meet Belle and have your photo taken with her.

Felicity

You enter the attraction by walking through Maurice's cottage, where you see mementos tracing Belle's childhood, including her favorite books, and lines drawn on one wall showing how fast Belle grew every year.

Then you go into Maurice's workshop at the back of the cottage. An assortment of Maurice's odd wood gadgets covers every inch of the floor, walls, and ceiling. Take a moment to peruse the gadgets, and then focus your attention on the mirror on the wall to the left of the entry door.

Soon enough, the room gets dark and the mirror begins to sparkle. With magic and some really good carpentry skills, the mirror turns into a full-size doorway, through which guests enter into a wardrobe room. Once you reach the wardrobe room, the attraction's premise is explained: You're supposed to reenact the story of *Beauty and the Beast* for Belle on her birthday, and guests are chosen to act out key parts in the play.

After the parts are cast, everyone walks into the castle's library and takes a seat. Cast members explain how the play will take place and introduce Belle, who gives a short speech about how thrilled she is for everyone to be there. The play is acted out within a few minutes, and the actors get a photo op with Belle and receive a small bookmark as a memento.

Enchanted Tales with Belle is surely the prettiest and most elaborate meet and greet in Disney World. For the relative few who get to act in the play, it's also a chance to interact with Belle in a way that isn't possible in other character encounters.

It's a Small World ★★★½

PRESCHOOL ★★★★½ (MAA)   **GRADE SCHOOL** ★★★★ (MBA)   **TEENS** ★★★ (MBA)
YOUNG ADULTS ★★★½ (MBA)   **OVER 30** ★★★★ (BA)   **SENIORS** ★★★★ (BA)

What it is World unity–themed indoor boat ride. **Scope and scale** Major attraction. **When to go** Before 11 a.m. or after 7 p.m. **Duration of ride** About 11 minutes. **Average wait in line per 100 people ahead of you** 3½ minutes; assumes busy conditions with 30 or more boats operating. **Loading speed** Fast. **ECV/wheelchair access** Must transfer from ECV to provided wheelchair. **Participates in Genie+** Yes. **Early Theme Park Entry** Yes. **Extended Evening Hours** Yes.

It's such a happy ride, and it was so cool to see our names at the end.

Felicity

Small boats carry visitors on a tour around the world, with singing and dancing dolls showcasing the dress and culture of each nation. At the end of the ride, look for the panel bidding you (and your MagicBand) a personal goodbye. The ride, which debuted at the 1964 New York World's Fair, is one of Disney's oldest entertainment offerings; the original exhibit was moved to Disneyland after the fair, and a duplicate was created for Disney World when it opened in 1971. Of course, there's no escaping the brain-numbing tune. Just when you think you've repressed it, the song will resurface without warning to torture you some more.

Mad Tea Party   ★★

PRESCHOOL ★★★★½ (MAA)   **GRADE SCHOOL** ★★★★½ (AA)   **TEENS** ★★★★ (AA)
YOUNG ADULTS ★★★★ (BA)   **OVER 30** ★★★½ (MBA)   **SENIORS** ★★★ (MBA)

What it is Midway-style spinning ride. **Scope and scale** Minor attraction. **When to go** Before 11 a.m. or after 5 p.m. **Comments** The teacup spins faster when you turn the wheel in the center. We're not sure if that's a good thing or not. **Duration of ride** 1½ minutes. **Average wait in line per 100 people ahead of you** 7½ minutes. **Loading speed** Slow. **ECV/wheelchair access** Must transfer to the ride vehicle; transfer device available. **Participates in Genie+** Yes. **Early Theme Park Entry** Yes. **Extended Evening Hours** Yes.

Teenagers love to lure unsuspecting adults into the spinning teacups and then turn the wheel in the middle (making the cup spin faster) until the grown-ups are plastered against the sides and on the verge of throwing up. Unless you aspire to be a living physics experiment, don't even *consider* getting on this one with anyone younger than 21.

This ride is notoriously slow-loading. Ride the morning of your second day if your schedule is more relaxed. Characters from *Alice in Wonderland,* including Alice herself, meet intermittently in front of the ride.

Did you know that the voice of Alice, British voice actress and schoolteacher Kathryn Beaumont, is also the voice of Wendy in Peter Pan?

The Many Adventures of Winnie the Pooh   ★★★½

PRESCHOOL ★★★★½ (MAA)   **GRADE SCHOOL** ★★★★ (MBA)   **TEENS** ★★★ (MBA)
YOUNG ADULTS ★★★½ (MBA)   **OVER 30** ★★★½ (MBA)   **SENIORS** ★★★★ (MBA)

What it is Indoor track ride. **Scope and scale** Minor attraction. **When to go** Before 10 a.m. or in the last hour the park is open. It is also a good option if you're touring over 2 days or more. **Comment** Cute as the Pooh bear himself. **Duration of ride** About 4 minutes. **Average wait in line per 100 people ahead of you** 4 minutes. **Loading speed** Moderate. **ECV/wheelchair access** Must transfer from EVC to provided wheelchair. **Participates in Genie+** Yes. **Early Theme Park Entry** Yes. **Extended Evening Hours** Yes.

Thumbs Up for the Whole Family

This attraction is sunny, upbeat, and charming without being saccharine. You ride a "hunny pot" through the pages of a huge picture book into the Hundred Acre Wood, where you encounter Pooh, Piglet, Eeyore, Owl, Rabbit, Tigger, Kanga, and Roo as they contend with a blustery day. The ride is a perfect test to assess how your very young children will react to indoor (dark) rides. Nearby, Winnie the Pooh and Tigger meet little fans throughout the day.

Did you know Paul Winchell won a Grammy for his voicing of Tigger? He also voiced a Chinese cat in The Aristocats *and Boomer the woodpecker in* The Fox and the Hound; *plus, he provided the voice of the evil Gargamel in the animated TV series* The Smurfs.

Meet Merida at Fairytale Garden
★★★½

PRESCHOOL ★★★★½ (MAA)   GRADE SCHOOL ★★★★ (A)   TEENS ★★★½ (MBA)
YOUNG ADULTS ★★★½ (MBA)   OVER 30 ★★★½ (MBA)   SENIORS ★★★★ (A)

What it is Storytelling session plus character meet and greet. **Scope and scale** Diversion. **When to go** Check My Disney Experience app for schedule. **Duration of experience** About 10 minutes. **Probable waiting time** 30 minutes. **Queue speed** Slow. **ECV/wheelchair access** May remain in wheelchair. **Participates in Genie+** No. **Early Theme Park Entry** No. **Extended Evening Hours** No.

Merida, the flame-haired Scottish princess from *Brave,* greets guests in Fairytale Garden, next to Cinderella Castle on the Tomorrowland side, between the castle and Cosmic Ray's Starlight Cafe. Princess meet and greets tend to be popular, so expect lines.

Mickey's PhilharMagic   ★★★★

PRESCHOOL ★★★★ (A)   GRADE SCHOOL ★★★★½ (AA)   TEENS ★★★★ (A)
YOUNG ADULTS ★★★★ (A)   OVER 30 ★★★★ (A)   SENIORS ★★★★½ (AA)

What it is 3-D movie. **Scope and scale** Major attraction. **When to go** Anytime. **Duration of presentation** About 12 minutes. **Probable waiting time** 20–30 minutes. **ECV/wheelchair access** May remain in wheelchair. **Participates in Genie+** Yes. **Early Theme Park Entry** Yes. **Extended Evening Hours** Yes.

Mickey's PhilharMagic combines three fabulous ideas: Mickey and Donald mix and meet with Disney stars such as Aladdin, Jasmine, Ariel, the Beast's pantry servants (such as Lumière and Mrs. Potts), and Simba; it uses a form of computer-enhanced 3-D video technology that is truly impressive; and the whole shebang is projected on a 150-foot-wide, 180-degree screen. *Mickey's PhilharMagic* even employs some of those famous Disney scent effects and turns the old sorcerer's apprentice trick back on Mickey. However, we think the attraction would benefit from a digital-quality upgrade. Adding a few new musical numbers and experiences wouldn't hurt either.

Where other Disney 3-D movies are loud, in-your-face affairs, this one is softer and cuddlier. Things pop out of the screen, but they're really not scary. It's the rare child who is frightened—but there are always exceptions, as was the case with the 3-year-old child of this North Carolina mom:

> Our family found PhilharMagic *way too violent (minutes on end of Donald getting the crap kicked out of him by musical instruments). I had to haul my screaming child out of the theater and submit to a therapeutic carousel ride afterward.*

Happily, an Oregon mom has an easy way to nip the willies in the bud:

> *My advice to parents is simply to have their kids not wear the 3-D glasses. We took my daughter's off right away, and then she began giggling and having a good time watching the movie.*

Peter Pan's Flight   ★★★★

PRESCHOOL ★★★★½ (AA)   GRADE SCHOOL ★★★★ (A)   TEENS ★★½ (MBA)
YOUNG ADULTS ★★★★ (MBA)   OVER 30 ★★★★ (A)   SENIORS ★★★★½ (AA)

What it is Indoor track ride. **Scope and scale** Minor attraction. **When to go** First or last 30 minutes the park is open. Along with Jungle Cruise, Peter Pan's Flight is one of the most helpful Genie+ reservations you can get in the Magic Kingdom. **Duration of ride** A little more than 3 minutes. **Average wait in line per 100 people ahead of you** 5½ minutes. **Loading speed** Moderate–slow. **ECV/wheelchair access** Must be ambulatory. **Participates in Genie+** Yes. **Early Theme Park Entry** Yes. **Extended Evening Hours** Yes.

Thumbs Up for the Whole Family

Peter Pan's Flight is superbly designed and absolutely delightful, with a happy theme uniting some favorite Disney characters, beautiful effects, and charming music. This dark (indoor) ride takes you on a relaxing trip in a "flying pirate ship" over old London and then to Never Land, where Peter saves Wendy from walking the plank and Captain Hook rehearses for *Dancing with the Stars* on the snout of the ubiquitous crocodile. There's nothing here that will jump out at you or frighten young children. An interactive queuing area alleviates the pain of waiting in line as guests go through the Darlings' house before boarding their ride to Never Land.

Because Peter Pan's Flight is very popular, count on long lines all day. You can meet the boy who never grew up, and at times Wendy, next to the ride.

Isabelle

There are many little details to discover when riding Peter Pan's Flight. Be on the lookout for Ariel in the mermaid lagoon.

It was brilliant! I felt like I was flying, and I got to see Tink.

Movie Tip

Disney's animated film version of Peter Pan *is, of course, the inspiration for this wonderful ride. While the original is easy to find, the sequel,* Return to Never Land, *is not. Try to get a copy at a library or find a used one at amazon.com, and reunite with Peter, Wendy, Tinker Bell, Mr. Smee, the Lost Boys, and Captain Hook. But most of all: Never grow up.*

Felicity

Pete's Silly Sideshow *(temporarily unavailable)* ★★★½

PRESCHOOL ★★★★★ (E) **GRADE SCHOOL** ★★★★★ (E) **TEENS** ★★★★ (A)
YOUNG ADULTS ★★★★ (A) **OVER 30** ★★★★ (A) **SENIORS** ★★★★ (A)

What it is Character-greeting venue. **Scope and scale** Minor attraction. **When to go** Before 11 a.m. or in the last 2 hours before closing. **Duration of experience** 3 minutes per character. **Probable waiting time** Under 30 minutes each side. **Queue speed** Slow. **ECV/wheelchair access** May remain in wheelchair. **Participates in Genie+** Likely upon return. **Early Theme Park Entry** No. **Extended Evening Hours** No.

In this circus-themed character-greeting area in the Storybook Circus part of Fantasyland, the costumes are distinct from the ones normally used around the parks. Characters include Goofy as The Great Goofini, Donald Duck as The Astounding Donaldo, Daisy Duck as Madame Daisy Fortuna, and Minnie Mouse as Minnie Magnifique. The queue is indoors and air-conditioned. There is one queue for Goofy and Donald and another for Minnie and Daisy. You can meet two characters at once but must line up twice to meet all four.

Prince Charming Regal Carrousel ★★★

PRESCHOOL ★★★½ (MAA) **GRADE SCHOOL** ★★★★ (BA) **TEENS** ★★★½ (MBA)
YOUNG ADULTS ★★★½ (MBA) **OVER 30** ★★★½ (MBA) **SENIORS** ★★★½ (MBA)

What it is Merry-go-round. **Scope and scale** Minor attraction. **When to go** Anytime. **Duration of ride** About 2 minutes. **Average wait in line per 100 people ahead of you** 5 minutes. **Loading speed** Slow. **ECV/wheelchair access** Must transfer from EVC to provided wheelchair. **Participates in Genie+** No. **Early Theme Park Entry** Yes. **Extended Evening Hours** Yes.

You'll have a long wait, but the beauty of the carousel (formerly known as Cinderella's Golden Carrousel) captures everyone. The carousel, built in 1917, was discovered in New Jersey, where it was once part of an amusement park. It is beautifully maintained and especially magical at night when all the lights are on. Check out your children's delighted expressions as the painted ponies go up and down.

A shy 9-year-old girl from Rockaway, New Jersey, thinks our rating of the carousel should be higher:

> *I want to complain. I went on the Prince Charming Regal Carrousel four times, and I loved it! Raise those stars right now!*

> It was so enjoyable riding up and down on a lovely horse. I felt like a princess.

Felicity

Princess Fairytale Hall ★★★

PRESCHOOL ★★★★★ (MAA) GRADE SCHOOL ★★★★½ (MAA) TEENS ★★★★ (A)
YOUNG ADULTS ★★★★ (A) OVER 30 ★★★½ (A) SENIORS ★★★★ (A)

What it is Character-greeting venue. **Scope and scale** Minor attraction. **When to go** Before 10:30 a.m. or after 4 p.m. **Duration of experience** 7–10 minutes (estimated). **Probable waiting time** Under 50 minutes (estimated). **Queue speed** Slow. **ECV/wheelchair access** May remain in wheelchair. **Participates in Genie+** Yes. **Early Theme Park Entry** No. **Extended Evening Hours** No.

Princess Fairytale Hall is royalty central in the Magic Kingdom. Inside are two greeting venues, each with a small reception area for two royals. Thus, there are four royals meeting and greeting at any time, and you can see two of them at once. Signs outside tell you which line leads to which royal pair and how long the wait will be. Rapunzel usually leads one side with Tiana, and Cinderella is typically joined by Elena of Avalor, Disney's first Latina princess, on the other side. About 5–10 guests are admitted to each greeting area, where there's plenty of time for small talk, a photo, and a hug from each princess.

Seven Dwarfs Mine Train ★★★

PRESCHOOL ★★★★ (A) GRADE SCHOOL ★★★★½ (MAA) TEENS ★★★★½ (MAA)
YOUNG ADULTS ★★★★½ (MAA) OVER 30 ★★★★½ (MAA) SENIORS ★★★★ (AA)

What it is Indoor-outdoor roller coaster.. **Scope and scale** Headliner. **When to go** As soon as the park opens. **Comments** Must be 38″ to ride. **Duration of ride** About 2 minutes. **Average wait in line per 100 people ahead of you** About 4½ minutes. **Loading speed** Fast. **ECV/wheelchair access** Must transfer to the ride vehicle. **Participates in Genie+** No (it's an Individual Lightning Lane attraction). **Early Theme Park Entry** Yes. **Extended Evening Hours** Yes.

Thumbs Up for the Whole Family

Scary

Seven Dwarfs Mine Train is geared to older grade-school kids who have been on amusement park rides before. There are no loops, inversions, or rolls in the track and no massive hills or steep drops; the Mine Train's trick is that the ride vehicle's seats swing side to side as you go through turns. And—what a coincidence!—Disney has designed a curvy track with steep turns. An elaborate indoor section shows the dwarfs' underground operation. The exterior design includes waterfalls, forests, and landscaping.

While it's a charming ride in a lovely setting, Liliane isn't smitten. This mom from Utah concurs:

> *Seven Dwarfs Mine Train is the most overrated ride EVER. My kids (ages 6 and 7) were completely bored standing in line and unimpressed with the ride.*

Seven Dwarfs Mine Train is an Individual Lightning Lane attraction, but your chances of grabbing one of these paid spots is slim if you are not staying at a Disney resort: On-site guests can book Individual Lightning Lane attractions as of 7 a.m., while guests staying off-site can do so only at official park opening time, when very often most spots are gone.

The Seven Dwarfs Mine Train was a total and utter disappointment. No sharp turns, no drops, and not much speed. Don't waste your time if you like thrills. It's a good test coaster for small children though.

A. J.

To get any momentum going downhill, try to sit in the back of the Seven Dwarfs Mine Train.

Brendan

Under the Sea: Journey of the Little Mermaid ★★★½

PRESCHOOL ★★★★½ (MAA)   **GRADE SCHOOL** ★★★★ (MBA)   **TEENS** ★★★½ (MBA)
YOUNG ADULTS ★★★★ (MBA)   **OVER 30** ★★★★ (MBA)   **SENIORS** ★★★★ (MBA)

What it is Dark ride retelling the film's story. **Scope and scale** Major attraction. **When to go** Before 10:30 a.m. or during the last 2 hours before closing. **Duration of ride** About 5½ minutes. **Average wait in line per 100 people ahead of you** 3 minutes. **Loading speed** Fast. **ECV/wheelchair access** Must transfer from EVC to provided wheelchair. **Participates in Genie+** Yes. **Early Theme Park Entry** Yes. **Extended Evening Hours** Yes.

Under The Sea takes riders through almost a dozen scenes retelling the story of *The Little Mermaid,* with Audio-Animatronics, video effects, and a vibrant 3-D set the size of a small theater. Guests board a clamshell-shaped ride vehicle running along a continuously moving track (similar to The Haunted Mansion's). Once you're on board, the ride descends "under water," past Ariel's grotto, and to King Triton's undersea kingdom. The most detailed animatronic is Ursula the octopus, and she's a beauty. Other scenes hit the film's highlights, including Ariel meeting Prince Eric, her deal with Ursula to become human, and, of course, the happy couple at the end.

I was disappointed! The ride feels very much like a clone of The Seas with Nemo & Friends at EPCOT. The queuing area is whimsical, but who wants to be stuck in a queuing area?

Liliane

TOMORROWLAND

AT VARIOUS POINTS IN ITS HISTORY, Tomorrowland's attractions presented life's possibilities in adventures ranging from the modern day (If You Had Wings, a 'round-the-world travel ride in the 1970s) to the distant future (Mission to Mars, which opened as Rocket to the Moon in 1955 but received a name change in 1975 following the first moon landing in 1969). The problem that stymied Disney repeatedly: The future came faster and looked different than they'd envisioned.

Today, Tomorrowland's theme makes the least sense of any area in any Disney park. Its current attractions are based on gas-powered race cars; rocket travel (two rides); a look back at 20th-century technology; a ride with aliens; a comedy show with monsters; and, when Tron Lightcycle/Run opens, a motorcycle race inside a computer. It's not so much a vision of the future as it is a collection of attractions that don't fit anywhere else in the park.

The new roller coaster themed to Disney's *Tron* movie franchise is expected to open in 2023 (no official opening date had been announced as we went to press). It sits mostly behind the Tomorrowland Speedway and outside the current park boundary. Parts of the ride building extend over the WDW Railroad, which required the railroad to close in 2018; Disney is using the closure for a full refurbishment of this iconic attraction.

The semi-enclosed attraction will be a super-headliner; make sure you join a boarding group, if available, or purchase an Individual Lightning Lane pass.

Astro Orbiter ★★

PRESCHOOL ★★★★ (BA)   **GRADE SCHOOL ★★★★** (MBA)   **TEENS ★★★½** (BA)
YOUNG ADULTS ★★★ (MBA)   **OVER 30 ★★★** (MBA)   **SENIORS ★★½** (MBA)

What it is Retro-style rockets revolving around a central axis. **Scope and scale** Minor attraction. **When to go** Before 11 a.m. or the last hour the park is open. **Comments** Not as innocuous as it appears. **Average wait in line per 100 people ahead of you** 13½ minutes. **Loading speed** Slow. **ECV/wheelchair access** Must transfer to the ride vehicle. **Participates in Genie+** No. **Early Theme Park Entry** Yes. **Extended Evening Hours** Yes.

Parents, beware! If you're prone to motion sickness, this ride spins round and round and is faster than Dumbo; for added "fun," a joystick lets you raise and lower the rocket throughout your 1½-minute journey. We like to ride it at night. The combination of lighting and the view is spectacular. Though visually appealing, the Astro Orbiter is at heart a slow-loading carnival ride: The fat little rocket ships simply fly in circles, albeit circles on a three-story platform above Tomorrowland. The best thing about the Astro Orbiter is the nice view when you're aloft.

Buzz Lightyear's Space Ranger Spin ★★★★

PRESCHOOL ★★★★½ (A)   **GRADE SCHOOL ★★★★½** (MAA)   **TEENS ★★★★** (MAA)
YOUNG ADULTS ★★★★ (A)   **OVER 30 ★★★★** (BA)   **SENIORS ★★★★** (A)

What it is Whimsical space-themed indoor ride. **Scope and scale** Minor attraction. **When to go** First or last hour the park is open. **Duration of ride** About 4½ minutes. **Average wait in line per 100 people ahead of you** 3 minutes. **Loading speed** Fast. **ECV/wheelchair access** Must transfer from EVC to provided wheelchair. **Participates in Genie+** Yes. **Early Theme Park Entry** Yes. **Extended Evening Hours** Yes.

This indoor attraction, based on the space-commando character Buzz Lightyear from the *Toy Story* film series, has you and Buzz spinning your car and shooting simulated laser cannons at evil Emperor Zurg and his minions. Each time you pull the trigger, you release a red laser beam that you can see hitting or missing the target. Most folks spend their first ride learning how to use the equipment, but once you get the hang of it, you'll come back for more, to infinity and beyond!

> *The ride is based on the space-commando character Buzz Lightyear from the 1995 Disney-Pixar feature* Toy Story. *Did you know that Tom Hanks and Tim Allen are the voices of Woody and Buzz?*

Monsters, Inc. Laugh Floor ★★★½

PRESCHOOL ★★★★ (MBA)   GRADE SCHOOL ★★★★½ (AA)   TEENS ★★★★ (AA)
YOUNG ADULTS ★★★★ (AA)   OVER 30 ★★★★ (AA)   SENIORS ★★★★ (A)

What it is Interactive animated comedy routines. **Scope and scale** Major attraction. **When to go** Anytime. **Comments** Audience members may be asked to participate in skits. **Duration of presentation** About 15 minutes. **ECV/wheelchair access** May remain in wheelchair. **Participates in Genie+** Yes. **Early Theme Park Entry** No. **Extended Evening Hours** Yes.

> *The show is based on the 2001 Pixar film* Monsters, Inc., *starring Billy Crystal (voice) in the role of Mike Wazowski. It won an Oscar for best song.*

In Disney-Pixar's *Monsters, Inc.,* children's screams are converted into electricity used to power a town inhabited by monsters. During the film, the monsters discover that children's laughter is an even better source of energy. In this attraction, the monsters have set up a comedy club to capture as many laughs as possible. Mike Wazowski, the one-eyed character from the film, emcees the club's three comedy acts. Each consists of an animated monster (most not seen in the film) trying out various bad puns, knock-knock jokes, and comedy routines. Using the same cutting-edge technology as EPCOT's *Turtle Talk with Crush,* behind-the-scenes Disney employees voice the characters and often interact with audience members during the skits. As with any comedy set, some performers are funny and some are not, but Disney has shown a willingness to experiment with new routines and jokes. A Sioux Falls, South Dakota, mom is a big fan:

> Laugh Floor *was great. It's amazing how the characters interact with the audience. I got picked on twice without trying. Plus, kids can text jokes to Roz.*

Space Mountain ★★★★

PRESCHOOL ★★½† (MBA)   GRADE SCHOOL ★★★★½ (MAA)   TEENS ★★★★★ (E)
YOUNG ADULTS ★★★★½ (MAA)   OVER 30 ★★★★½ (MAA)   SENIORS ★★★½ (MBA)

†*Some preschoolers love Space Mountain; others are frightened by it.*

What it is Roller coaster in the dark. **Scope and scale** Super-headliner. **When to go** When the park opens or in the last hour the park is open. **Comments** Great fun—much wilder than Big Thunder Mountain Railroad. Must be 44" to ride; Rider Switch option provided (see page 260). **Duration of ride** Almost 3 minutes. **Average wait in line per 100 people ahead of you** 3 minutes; assumes two tracks, dispatching at 21-second intervals. **Loading speed** Moderate–fast. **ECV/wheelchair access** Must transfer from EVC to provided wheelchair and then from wheelchair to the ride vehicle. **Participates in Genie+** Yes. **Early Theme Park Entry** Yes. **Extended Evening Hours** Yes.

Space Mountain is one of Walt Disney World's zippiest (and darkest) rides, lasting a little less than 3 minutes and featuring numerous abrupt turns and plummets.

However, the top speed is only about 28 miles per hour, a leisurely pace by 21st-century standards.

Space Mountain involves sudden blackouts. Those who suffer from claustrophobia (Liliane), who tend to panic in the dark (Liliane), or who have vision problems with extremes of light and darkness (Liliane) should avoid this attraction, as should those with neck or back problems or vertigo. Plunged into darkness and bouncing around like a marble in a spittoon, many warmly recall Space Mountain as the longest 3 minutes of their lives. Your kids will love it. There are no long drops or swooping hills as there are on a traditional roller coaster—only quick, unexpected turns and small drops.

Periodic refurbishments have added new lighting and effects and an improved sound system and soundtrack. Look for special effects during Halloween. If you don't catch Space Mountain first thing in the morning, use Genie+ or try again during the 30 minutes before closing.

> I dream of riding Space Mountain at the pace of Spaceship Earth
> in EPCOT. At last, I would be able to enjoy the twinkling lights.

Liliane

Tomorrowland Speedway ★★

PRESCHOOL ★★★★½ (AA)   GRADE SCHOOL ★★★★ (A)   TEENS ★★★½ (MBA)
YOUNG ADULTS ★★★ (MBA)   OVER 30 ★★½ (MBA)   SENIORS ★★½ (MBA)

What it is Drive-'em-yourself minicars. **Scope and scale** Major children's attraction. **When to go** Before 10 a.m. or in the last 2 hours the park is open. **Comments** Kids must be 54" to drive unassisted, 32" with person age 14 or older. **Duration of ride** About 4¼ minutes. **Average wait in line per 100 people ahead of you** 4½ minutes; assumes 285-car turnover every 20 minutes. **Loading speed** Slow. **ECV/wheelchair access** Must transfer to the ride vehicle; transfer device available. **Participates in Genie+** Yes. **Early Theme Park Entry** Yes. **Extended Evening Hours** Yes.

The sleek cars and racetrack noise will get your younger kids hopped up to ride this extremely prosaic attraction. The younger (or shorter) set will have to ride with an adult. After getting into the car, shift your child over behind the steering wheel. From your position, you will still be able to control the foot pedals. Children will feel like they're really driving, and because the car travels on a self-guiding track, there's no way they can make a mistake while steering. The loading and unloading speeds are excruciatingly slow, and the attraction offers hardly any protection from the sun.

Tomorrowland Transit Authority PeopleMover ★★★½

PRESCHOOL ★★★★ (A)   GRADE SCHOOL ★★★★ (BA)   TEENS ★★★★ (A)
YOUNG ADULTS ★★★★½ (A)   OVER 30 ★★★★½ (MAA)   SENIORS ★★★★½ (MAA)

Thumbs Up for the Whole Family

What it is Scenic tour of Tomorrowland. **Scope and scale** Minor attraction. **When to go** Anytime, but especially during hot, crowded times of day (11:30 a.m.–4:30 p.m.). **Comments** A good way to check out the lines at Space Mountain and Tomorrowland Speedway. **Duration of ride** 10 minutes. **Average wait in line per 100 people ahead of you** 1½ minutes; assumes 39 trains operating. **Loading speed** Fast. **ECV/wheelchair access** Must be ambulatory. **Participates in Genie+** No. **Early Theme Park Entry** Yes. **Extended Evening Hours** No.

The ride is ideal for taking a break. It's also a great way to see Tomorrowland all aglow at night. The route gives a sneak preview of Buzz Lightyear's Space

Ranger Spin, and you can check on those screams emanating from Space Mountain. Most of the time cast members will let you ride several times in a row without having to get off. This, according to many moms, makes the ride a great option for nursing.

Tron Lightcycle/Run *(opens 2023)*

What it is Indoor-outdoor roller coaster. **Scope and scale** Super-headliner. **When to go** As soon as the park opens, using Early Theme Park Entry if possible, or the last hour the park is open. **Comments** Estimated 48″ minimum height requirement. **Duration of ride** About 2 minutes. **Average wait in line per 100 people ahead of you** About 3½ minutes; assumes 39 trains operating. **Loading speed** Fast. **ECV/wheelchair access** Must transfer from wheelchair. **Participates in Genie+** No (it will probably be an Individual Lightning Lane attraction). **Early Theme Park Entry** Yes. **Extended Evening Hours** Yes.

Tron Lightcycle/Run is an elevated, high-speed, indoor-outdoor roller coaster. Riders sit as if on a motorcycle while they rocket past scenes that simulate being inside a computer (and one with neon lighting at that).

The ride vehicles are set up as 14 semidetached light cycles, with seven rows of two cycles each. Riders must lean forward slightly to hold onto the cycle's handlebars. Once seated and out of the ride's loading zone, riders are launched catapult-style into the ride's first set of turns. An impressive set of video effects surrounds you through most of the journey.

Tron is most similar to the Rock 'n' Roller Coaster at Hollywood Studios, which is also a catapult-launched, indoor coaster. Tron is by far the most intense coaster in the Magic Kingdom, although it doesn't have any loops or inversions. If Seven Dwarfs Mine Train, Splash Mountain, or Big Thunder Mountain give you pause, skip Tron.

Tron Lightcycle/Run will be one of the Magic Kingdom's hottest rides once it opens. Expect hundreds of theme park guests to head straight for it as soon as the park opens. If you're an off-site guest, it's possible that 1,000 or more guests will already be in line ahead of you before you arrive at the attraction. Individual Lightning Line reservations for Tron will sell out daily within minutes of being offered.

If you're staying on-site, your best bet for riding with minimal waits is to arrive at the Magic Kingdom at least an hour before official opening. As soon as you're admitted into the park for Early Theme Park Entry, head for Tomorrowland and ride Tron. Once you're done, ride Space Mountain nearby if the wait is 15 minutes or less. If Early Theme Park Entry isn't an option, try Tron in the last hour the park is open, or during lunch or dinner. Expect long waits at almost any time of day.

Tron Lightcycle/Run is definitely not for the faint of heart, and the 48″ height restriction will not allow younglings to experience the ride.

Liliane

Walt Disney's Carousel of Progress ★★★

PRESCHOOL ★★★ (MBA) **GRADE SCHOOL** ★★★½ (MBA) **TEENS** ★★★½ (MBA)
YOUNG ADULTS ★★★★ (BA) **OVER 30** ★★★★ (A) **SENIORS** ★★★★½ (AA)

What it is Audio-Animatronic theater production. **Scope and scale** Major attraction. **When to go** Anytime. **Duration of show** 21 minutes. **Preshow Entertainment** Documentary on the attraction's long history. **Probable waiting time** Less than 10 minutes.

ECV/wheelchair access May remain in wheelchair. **Participates in Genie+** No. **Early Theme Park Entry** Yes. **Extended Evening Hours** No.

Walt Disney's Carousel of Progress offers a nostalgic look at how technology and electricity have changed the lives of an animatronic family over several generations from circa 1900 to 1990. The family is easy to identify with, and a cheerful, sentimental tune bridges the generations. Adults will be amused at the references to laser discs and car phones as examples of modern technology; kids will be confused.

Though dated, *Carousel of Progress* was almost entirely conceived and guided by Walt Disney himself, rare among Magic Kingdom attractions. It's the only Magic Kingdom attraction to display Walt's optimistic vision of a better future through technology and industry. If you're interested in the man behind the mouse, this show is a must-see.

Carousel handles big crowds effectively and is a good choice during busier times of day. Because of its age, this attraction seems to have more minor operational glitches than most attractions, so you may be subjected to the same dialog and songs several times.

LIVE ENTERTAINMENT *and* PARADES *in the* MAGIC KINGDOM

IT'S IMPOSSIBLE TO TAKE IN all the many live-entertainment offerings at the Magic Kingdom in a single day. To experience both the attractions and the live entertainment, we recommend you allocate at least two days to this park. In addition to parades, stage shows, and fireworks, check the daily entertainment schedule via the My Disney Experience app or ask a cast member about the Flag Retreat at Town Square and the appearances of the various bands, singers, and street performers who roam the park daily. WDW live-entertainment guru Steve Soares usually posts the Magic Kingdom's performance schedule about a week in advance at wdwent.com.

The **Dapper Dans** sing soulful Americana a cappella; be sure to see them as they put on a show for whomever is wandering the street. The **Casey's Corner pianist** plays tunes from a bygone era next to the eatery of the same name. He even takes requests! The legendary **Main Street Philharmonic** performs tunes from classic Disney films, mixed with ragtime and swing, at several locations in the park.

Parades at the Magic Kingdom are full-fledged spectaculars with dozens of Disney characters and amazing special effects. Remember that parades disrupt traffic, making it nearly impossible to move around the park when one is going on. Parades also draw thousands of guests away from the attractions, making parade time the perfect moment to catch your favorite attraction with a shorter line. Finally, be advised that the Walt Disney World Railroad (when operating) shuts down for the night prior to the parades.

The best place to view a parade is the upper platform of the **Walt Disney Railroad station,** but you'll have to stake out your position

FAVORITE EATS IN THE MAGIC KINGDOM
MAIN STREET **Casey's Corner** | Hot Dogs every which way | **Main Street Bakery** Sandwiches and salads; pretty much anything that Starbucks has
ADVENTURELAND **Tortuga Tavern** (*seasonal*) | Teriyaki Burger
FANTASYLAND **Friar's Nook** | Hot dogs and tots | **Gaston's Tavern** | Turkey Legs and LeFou's Brew | **Pinocchio Village Haus** | Flatbreads
FRONTIERLAND **Pecos Bill Tall Tale Inn & Cafe** | Tacos three ways and a fajita platter
LIBERTY SQUARE **Columbia Harbour House** | Lobster roll and New England clam chowder | **Sleepy Hollow** | Funnel cake
TOMORROWLAND **Cosmic Ray's Starlight Cafe** | Greek Salad with chicken; kosher choices | **The Lunching Pad** | Hot dogs and frozen soda

30–45 minutes before the event. Try also, especially on rainy days, the **covered walkway between Liberty Tree Tavern and The Diamond Horseshoe,** on the border of Liberty Square and Frontierland.

Following is a short list of daily events with special appeal for families with children:

FESTIVAL OF FANTASY ★★★★ The afternoon parade, usually staged at 3 p.m., features floats and marching Disney characters. (During busy times it's held twice a day, usually at noon and 3 p.m.) It has an original score and floats paying tribute to *The Little Mermaid*, *Brave*, and *Frozen*, among other Disney films. Many of the floats' pieces spin and swing to extremes not normally found in Disney parades: The *Tangled* platform has characters swinging wood hammers from one side of the street to the other. The most talked-about float is Maleficent (the villain from *Sleeping Beauty*) in dragon form—she spits fire at a couple of points along the route. Evening parades, so far, only take place during Mickey's Not-So-Scary Halloween Party and Mickey's Very Merry Christmas Party.

LILIANE The afternoon parade is a must-see—great music, outstanding costumes, and more than 100 live performers. The 26-foot-tall Maleficent is awe-inspiring. Disney really went big with this one.

LUCY If you've already seen Festival of Fantasy, you can use that time to get on rides, as they are less crowded then.

BAY LAKE AND SEVEN SEAS LAGOON ELECTRICAL WATER PAGEANT ★★★★ Performed at nightfall most of the year on Seven Seas Lagoon and Bay Lake, this pageant is the perfect culmination of a wonderful day. You have to leave the Magic Kingdom to see the show—take the monorail to the Polynesian Village Resort, get the kids a snack and yourself a drink, and walk to the end of the pier to watch—pure magic, minus the crowds. The pageant floats past Disney's Grand Floridian Resort at approximately 8:15 p.m., Disney's Polynesian Village Resort around 8:30 p.m, Wilderness Lodge around 9:30 p.m., Fort Wilderness Resort & Campground around 9:45 p.m., and the Contemporary Resort around 10:05 p.m., ending in front of the Magic Kingdom at 10:30 p.m. Note that the times can fluctuate due to the operating hours of the Magic Kingdom. On the day of your visit, check the My Disney Experience app.

CASTLE FORECOURT STAGE ★★★½ *Mickey's Royal Friendship Faire* brings to life beloved Disney stories, both classic and contemporary. Tiana, Naveen, and Louis from *The Princess and the Frog* have traveled from New Orleans to be with their friends; Rapunzel and Flynn Rider from *Tangled* are the special guests of Daisy Duck; and Olaf, Anna, and Elsa from *Frozen* bring some icy magic to the party.

CHARACTER SHOWS AND APPEARANCES A number of characters are usually on hand to greet guests when the park opens. Because they snarl pedestrian traffic and stop most kids dead in their tracks, this is sort of a mixed blessing. Check the My Disney Experience app for character-greeting locations and times, or see our table on pages 264–265.

FIREWORKS SHOWS The 15-minute *Disney Enchantment* presentation (★★★★★) combines memorable vignettes from popular animated films with a stellar fireworks display. New for this show is the extension of projection images down Main Street, U.S.A., allowing more guests to see these fantastic animations. We still think that the show projected on the castle is best viewed right in front of it. If you only want to see the fireworks and intend to remain in the park, our two favorite spots are in Fantasyland, between Seven Dwarfs Mine Train and *Enchanted Tales with Belle,* or on the bridge between the Central Plaza and Tomorrowland. Anywhere along Main Street is also a good viewing location, especially if you plan to leave the park immediately afterward. When the park is open late, be on the lookout for **Tinker Bell's Flight.** This quintessentially Disney special effect takes place in the sky above Cinderella Castle during *Enchantment.*

LUCY Watching the fireworks is simply the best. Make sure you get a good spot before they start.

The Magic Kingdom offers five **Fireworks Dessert Parties.** Each includes a viewing of the *Enchantment* fireworks.

Disney reserves the **Plaza Gardens** and **Tomorrowland Terrace** restaurant for paid fireworks viewing. Three options are available:

The **Disney Enchantment Pre-Party** ($99 per adult and $59 per child, tax included) includes all-you-care-to-eat desserts in the Plaza Gardens while you watch the fireworks. This option requires you to stand while watching the show. However, the view and the audio is better than the more expensive Treats & Seats offering (see below).

Held at Tomorrowland Terrace, the **Disney Enchantment After-Party** ($99 per adult and $59 per child, tax included) includes use of the restaurant's terrace to view the show and offers post-show desserts, wine, and beer.

Disney Enchantment Treats & Seats ($114 per adult and $69 per child, tax included) runs before, during, and after the show at Tomorrowland Terrace. Note that the view of the castle is blocked at many seats, and the sound quality is poor inside the

LILIANE If all you want is a serene spot to watch the fireworks or the Bay Lake and Seven Seas Lagoon Electrical Water Pageant, you don't need to spend big bucks. The gardens of the Grand Floridian are perfect for the fireworks, and the beach of the Polynesian Village Resort does the trick for the pageant.

all-concrete echo chamber of the restaurant. The big advantage here is, as the title suggests, actual seats for the show.

A St. Louis reader who went to the party pronounced it "meh":

We did the fireworks dessert party at Tomorrowland Terrace against my better judgment. While the vantage point was pretty good and the desserts were tasty, it was definitely not worth the price.

Reservations can be made 60 days in advance online or by calling ☎ 407-WDW-DINE (939-3463).

For a different view, you can take the **Fireworks Cruise** aboard a pontoon boat on Seven Seas Lagoon. The cost is $399, plus tax, for up to 10 people. Snacks, soda, and water are provided. Your Disney captain will take you for a little cruise and then position the boat in a perfect place to watch the fireworks. (A major indirect benefit of the charter is that you can enjoy the fireworks without fighting the mob afterward. Because this is a private charter, only your group will be aboard. Life jackets are provided, but wearing them is at your discretion. To reserve a fireworks cruise, call 60 days in advance at ☎ 407-WDW-PLAY (939-7529).

Ferrytale Fireworks: A Sparkling Dessert Cruise ($99 for adults and $69 for children, tax and gratuity included) is another option for seeing the evening fireworks at an extra cost. Guests board a ferry at the TTC for desserts, souvenir glasses, and a view of the fireworks. This event includes alcoholic beverages for the adults. Unlike the pontoon cruise, it's not a private charter. Reserve at ☎ 407-939-3463 or online at disneyworld.disney.go.com (search for Ferrytale Fireworks).

On July 3–4, the Magic Kingdom celebrates our nation's independence in red, white, and blue with *Disney's Celebrate America! A Fourth of July Concert in the Sky* at 9:15 p.m. The New Year is welcomed on December 30–31 with *Fantasy in the Sky Fireworks.*

FLAG RETREAT Takes place daily at 5 p.m. at Town Square (the railroad station end of Main Street). It's sometimes performed with great fanfare and college marching bands, sometimes with a smaller Disney band.

LET THE MAGIC BEGIN This 5-minute show on the Castle Forecourt Stage starts each day at the Magic Kingdom. It's a diversion at best and not worth veering from your touring plans.

MAGIC KINGDOM BANDS Several bands, including the Main Street Philharmonic, perform on Main Street, U.S.A. Guest bands partake at the start of the daily parade.

MOVE IT! SHAKE IT! MOUSEKEDANCE IT! STREET PARTY ★★★ (*temporarily unavailable*) Starting at the railroad station end of Main Street, U.S.A., and working toward the Central Plaza, this small parade incorporates about a dozen floats, Disney characters (including Nick Wilde and Judy Hopps from *Zootopia)*, and entertainers. An original tune called "It's a Good Time!" serves as the theme song, and there's a good amount of interaction between the entertainers and the crowd.

TOMORROWLAND STAGE Located behind the Astro Orbiter, the stage occasionally hosts DJ-led dance parties. They are fun at Halloween and Christmas but totally skippable. Little tykes will like shaking their sillies out though.

VIEWING (AND EXIT) STRATEGIES FOR PARADES AND FIREWORKS

MAGIC KINGDOM PARADES circle **Town Square,** head down **Main Street,** go around the **Central Plaza,** and cross the bridge to **Liberty Square.** In Liberty Square, they follow the waterfront and end in Frontierland. Sometimes they begin in Frontierland and run the route in the opposite direction.

BOB Digital displays at the Magic Kingdom exit show the wait to board the monorails and ferry. Take the one with the shorter line.

Because most spectators pack Main Street and the Central Plaza, we recommend watching the parade from **Liberty Square** or **Frontierland** instead. Great vantage points that are frequently overlooked are

1. **Sleepy Hollow snack-and-beverage shop,** immediately to your right as you cross the bridge into Liberty Square. If you arrive early, buy refreshments, and claim a table closest to the rail. You'll have a perfect view of the parade as it crosses Liberty Square Bridge, but only when the parade begins on Main Street.

2. **The pathway on the Liberty Square side of the moat from Sleepy Hollow snack-and-beverage shop to Cinderella Castle.** Any point along the way offers an unobstructed view as the parade crosses Liberty Square Bridge. Once again, this spot works only for parades coming from Main Street.

3. **The covered walkway between Liberty Tree Tavern and the Diamond Horseshoe Saloon.** This elevated vantage point is perfect (particularly on rainy days) and usually goes unnoticed until just before the parade starts.

4. **Elevated platforms in front of Frontierland Shootin' Arcade, Frontier Trading Post, and the building with the sign reading** FRONTIER MERCANTILE. These spots usually get picked off 10–12 minutes before parade time.

5. **Benches on the perimeter of the Central Plaza, between the entrances to Liberty Square and Adventureland,** offer a comfortable places to sit down and an unobstructed (though somewhat distant) view of the parade as it crosses Liberty Square Bridge.

6. **Liberty Square and Frontierland dockside areas.** Spots here usually go early.

7. **The porch of Tony's Town Square Restaurant, on Main Street,** offers an elevated viewing platform and an easy exit path when the fireworks are over.

Assuming it starts on Main Street (evening parades usually do), the parade takes 16–20 minutes to reach Liberty Square or Frontierland. On evenings when the parade runs twice, the first parade draws a huge crowd, siphoning guests from the attractions. Many guests leave the park after the early parade, and many more depart following the fireworks, which are scheduled on the hour between the two parades.

Vantage Points for Fireworks

The nightly fireworks show includes a dazzling video-projection display on the front of Cinderella Castle and down Main Street, U.S.A. The best viewing spots for the entire presentation are **between the Central Plaza and Cinderella Castle**, offering up-close views of the castle projections.

The next-best spots are in **Plaza Gardens East and West** nearest the castle. These gardens are specifically constructed for fireworks viewing. We prefer Plaza Gardens East (the same side of the park as Tomorrowland) because the configuration of light/audio poles is slightly less obtrusive when you're viewing the castle.

If those spots are already taken, your next-best alternatives are on Main Street, where you'll get to see the (smaller) projections closer. Watching from the train-station end of Main Street is the easiest way to facilitate a quick departure, but you won't recognize most of the castle's images.

If we're staying in the park and trying to avoid the crowds on Main Street, our two favorite spots to see just the fireworks are

1. **In Fantasyland between Seven Dwarfs Mine Train and** *Enchanted Tales with Belle.* Some of the minor fireworks that float above the castle will be behind you, but all of the major effects will be right in front of you.

2. **On the bridge between the Central Plaza and Tomorrowland.** A few trees block some of the castle, but if Tinker Bell does her fireworks flight from the castle, she'll fly directly over this area.

Leaving the Park After Evening Parades and Fireworks

With armies of guests leaving the park after evening parades and fireworks, the Disney transportation system (buses, ferries, and monorail) gets overwhelmed, causing long waits in boarding areas. (Similar situations often occur during the special holiday parades and fireworks, when they're offered.)

A mom from Kresgeville, Pennsylvania, recounts:

> *Our family of five made the mistake of going to the Magic Kingdom the Saturday night before Columbus Day to watch the parade and fireworks. Afterwards, we lingered at The Crystal Palace to wait for the crowds to lessen, but it was no use. We started walking toward the gates and soon became trapped by the throng, not able to go forward or back. Our group became separated, and it became a nightmare. We left the park at 10:30 p.m. and didn't get back to the Polynesian Village (less than a mile away) until after midnight. Even if they were to raise Walt Disney himself from cryogenic sleep and parade him down Main Street, I'll never go to the Magic Kingdom on a Saturday night again!*

Be aware that the railroad (when it reopens) doesn't run during parades because the floats must cross the tracks when entering or exiting the parade route in Frontierland.

An Oklahoma City dad offers this advice:

Never leave the Magic Kingdom just after the evening fireworks. Go for another ride—no lines because everyone else is trying to get out!

Congestion persists from the end of the early evening parade (if it's performed) until closing time. Most folks watch the early parade and then the fireworks a few minutes later. If you're parked at the Transportation and Ticket Center (TTC) and are intent on beating the crowd, view the early parade from the Town Square end of Main Street, leaving the park as soon as the parade ends.

Here's what happened to a family from Cape Coral, Florida:

We tried to leave the park before the parade began, but Main Street was already packed and we didn't see any way to get out of the park—we were stuck. In addition, it was impossible to move across the street, and even the shops were so crowded it was virtually impossible to maneuver a stroller through them to get close to the entrance.

If you don't have a stroller (or are willing to forgo the return refund for rental strollers), catch the Walt Disney World Railroad (when it's operating) in Frontierland and ride to the park exit at Main Street. Again, don't cut it too close—the train stops running for the parade.

LILIANE Instead of walking outside, you can cut through the Main Street shops—they have interior doors that let you pass from one shop to the next.

The Magic Kingdom has two pedestrian walkways behind the shops on either side of Main Street, U.S.A., specifically for guests who want to get out of the park without walking down Main Street. If you're on the Tomorrowland side, look for a passageway that runs from between **The Plaza Restaurant** and **Tomorrowland Terrace**, back behind the east side of Main Street, to **Tony's Town Square Restaurant** near the park exit. If you're on the Adventureland side, the passageway runs from the **First Aid** area to the **Main Street Fire Station** near the park exit. However, these passageways aren't used every night, so there's no guarantee they'll be available.

If the passageways aren't open and you're on the Tomorrowland side of the park, here's how to exit during a parade: Cut through Tomorrowland Terrace and then work your way down Main Street until you're past the Main Street Bakery (Starbucks) and have crossed a small cul-de-sac. Bear left into the side door of that corner shop. Work your way from shop to shop until you reach Town Square—easy, because people will be outside watching the parade. Then, at Town Square, bear left to reach the train station and park exit. *Note:* This won't work if you're on the Adventureland side of the park. You can make your way through **Casey's Corner** to Main Street and then work your way through the shops, but when you pop out of the **Emporium** at Town Square, you'll be trapped by the parade. As soon as the last float passes, however, you can bolt for the exit.

If your car is parked at the TTC lot, you could also just watch the early parade and then leave before the fireworks show. Line up for the ferry; one will depart about every 8–10 minutes. Try to catch the one that will be crossing Seven Seas Lagoon while the fireworks show is in progress. The best vantage point is on the top deck to the right of the pilothouse as you face the Magic Kingdom—the sight of fireworks silhouetting the castle and reflecting off the lagoon is unforgettable.

While there's no guarantee that a ferry will load and depart within 3 or 4 minutes of the fireworks, your chances are about 50–50 of timing it just right. If you're in the front of the line for the ferry and don't want to board the boat that's loading, stop at the gate and let people pass you. You'll be the first to board the next boat.

Strollers, wheelchairs, and ECVs make navigating crowds even more difficult. If you have one of these, or if you're staying at a Disney hotel that is not served by the monorail and you have to depend on Disney transportation, watch the early parade and fireworks; then enjoy the attractions until about 20–25 minutes before the late parade is scheduled to begin. Then leave the park using one of the strategies listed previously and catch the Disney bus or boat back to your hotel.

MAGIC KINGDOM HARD-TICKET EVENTS

FROM MID-AUGUST THROUGH DECEMBER, the Magic Kingdom hosts several after-hours events celebrating Halloween and Christmas. They require separate paid admission and can sell out.

DISNEY VILLAINS AFTER HOURS This event offers guests unique, wicked experiences from 10 p.m. to 1 a.m., after the park officially closes. More than 20 popular Magic Kingdom attractions are open with low wait times, and a villain show takes place in front of Cinderella Castle. Ice-cream novelties, popcorn, and bottled beverages are included in the cost of admission. Ticket holders may enter the park at 7 p.m. At press time Disney had not yet announced the new dates or prices for the event.

SABRINA You can meet Santa Claus at the Magic Kingdom too. I do, and I tell him what's on my list.

MICKEY'S NOT-SO-SCARY HALLOWEEN PARTY Aimed primarily at younger children, this event is happy and upbeat rather than spooky and frightening. We recommend arriving at least an hour before the beginning of the party. Once admitted, go straight to the rides on your must-do list, and then just enjoy the party. This year's villain show, the **Hocus Pocus Villain Spelltacular,** is absolutely spectacular! We suggest attending the last showing to avoid losing too much time claiming an unobstructed spot in front of the stage. An absolute must-ride is **The Haunted Mansion,** which is spooky but only in the sweetest way. Look for the ghost in the garden when you're queuing up; his hilarious tales and interaction with the guests will make you forget you're standing in line. Characters are out in full force all over the park, and the **Boo-to-You Parade** is pretty amazing. Our favorite parts are the Headless Horseman riding at full speed and The Haunted Mansion's groundskeeper, with his dim lantern and his bloodhound, followed by a large group of ghosts and gravediggers. If trick-or-treating is a priority, do that first thing after you arrive or toward the end of the night, when crowds thin out and there are no long lines in front of the trick-or-treating stations. For more on the party, see page 48.

MICKEY'S VERY MERRY CHRISTMAS PARTY See page 49.

MAGIC KINGDOM TOURING PLANS

OUR STEP-BY-STEP TOURING PLANS are field-tested, independently verified itineraries that will keep you moving counter to the crowd flow and allow you to see as much as possible in a single day with minimal time in line.

> **BOB** Don't worry that other people will be following the plans and render them useless. Fewer than 2 in every 100 people in the park have been exposed to this info.

Some plans offer a midday break of at least 3 hours back at your hotel. It's debatable whether the kids will need the nap more than you, but you'll thank us later, we promise.

If you have just one day to spend, our one-day plans allow you to see the best attractions for kids while avoiding crowds and long waits. If you're looking for a more relaxed, less structured tour of the park, try the one-and-a-half-day, two-day, or sleepyhead plan. These alternatives have less backtracking. The sleepyhead plan assumes you'll get to the park around 11 a.m., so it's great for mornings when you don't feel like rising early.

In the Magic Kingdom, the 19 attractions rated highest by kids age 12 and under are character greetings, parades, or fireworks. The Mad Tea Party is the ride kids rate highest. The same is true when teens are included: 20 of the top 25 attractions aren't rides at all. Our touring plans for kids, therefore, include more character greetings, along with the parades and fireworks we've always recommended. Tweens and teens will, of course, be eager to experience the new Tron Lightcycle/ Run roller coaster as soon as it opens.

We recommend eating lunch outside the Magic Kingdom, but if you decide to have lunch in the park, we recommend **Columbia Harbour House** in Liberty Square, **Pecos Bill Tall Tale Inn and Cafe** in Frontierland, and **Cosmic Ray's Starlight Cafe** in Tomorrowland.

The different Magic Kingdom touring plans are described on the opposite page. The descriptions will tell you for whom (for example, tweens, parents with preschoolers, grandparents, and so on) or for what situation (such as sleeping late) the plans are designed. The actual touring plans are located on pages 487–495. Each plan includes a numbered map of the park to help you find your way around.

Each plan lists the attractions most likely to need Genie+ or Individual Lightning Lane (ILL) and the approximate return times for which you should try to make reservations. Visit TouringPlans.com if any attractions, Genie+ reservations, or times need changing, either while planning or in the parks.

EARLY-ENTRY 2-DAY TOURING PLAN FOR PARENTS WITH SMALL CHILDREN This plan, designed to eliminate extra walking and backtracking, is a comprehensive touring plan of the Magic Kingdom and includes nearly every child-friendly attraction in the park. The plan features long midday breaks for lunch and naps outside the park.

2-DAY SLEEPYHEAD TOURING PLAN FOR PARENTS WITH SMALL CHILDREN Another version of the plan described above, this plan allows families with young children to sleep in, arrive at the park in the late morning, and still see the very best attractions in the Magic Kingdom over two days.

PARENTS' TOURING PLAN—1 AFTERNOON AND 1 FULL DAY This day-and-a-half plan works perfectly if you're arriving in Orlando late in the morning of your first vacation day and can't wait to start touring. It also works great for families who want to sleep in one morning after spending a full day in the Magic Kingdom the day before.

The plan employs Genie+ and takes advantage of lower evening crowds to visit other popular attractions. It should work well during the more crowded times of the year.

HAPPY FAMILY 1-DAY TOURING PLAN This touring plan includes something for everyone in the family: small children, tweens (ages 8–12), teenagers, parents, and seniors. It keeps everyone together for most of the day, including dinner. A midday break is integrated into the parents' part of the plan; teens can visit the park's thrill rides at this time, using Genie+/ILL to minimize their waits in line.

1-DAY EARLY-ENTRY TOURING PLAN FOR TWEENS AND THEIR PARENTS This plan for parents with children ages 8–12 sets aside ample time for lunch and dinner and includes about 2 hours of free time in the late afternoon to explore. If time permits, consider meeting Mickey at Town Square Theater or more princesses at Fairytale Hall.

1-DAY EARLY-ENTRY TOURING PLAN FOR GRANDPARENTS WITH SMALL CHILDREN This plan allows for a slightly slower walking speed between attractions and features a long midday break for lunch and a nap outside the park. The result should be more fun with less effort.

PRELIMINARY INSTRUCTIONS FOR ALL MAGIC KINGDOM TOURING PLANS

ON DAYS OF MODERATE TO HEAVY ATTENDANCE, follow your chosen touring plan exactly, deviating only when

1. You aren't interested in an attraction it lists. In this case, simply skip it and proceed to the next step.

2. You encounter a very long line at an attraction the touring plan calls for. Crowds ebb and flow at the park, and an unusually long line may have gathered at an attraction to which you're directed. It's possible that this is a temporary situation caused by several hundred people arriving en masse from a recently concluded performance of a nearby show. If this is the case, skip it and go to the next step, returning later to retry.

BEFORE YOU GO

1. Call ☎ 407-824-4321 or check disneyworld.com for operating hours.
2. Purchase admission and make park reservations.
3. Familiarize yourself with park-opening procedures and reread the touring plan you've chosen.

MAGIC KINGDOM TRIVIA QUIZ

1. On which movie series is Tomorrowland's next new attraction based?
   - **a.** *Star Wars*
   - **b.** *Avengers*
   - **c.** *Tron*
   - **d.** *Avatar*

2. Which princess does *not* meet guests at the Magic Kingdom?
   - **a.** Belle
   - **b.** Ariel
   - **c.** Rapunzel
   - **d.** Elsa

3. Who does Princess Tiana marry in *The Princess and the Frog*?
   - **a.** Prince Eric
   - **b.** Prince Naveen
   - **c.** Prince Charming
   - **d.** Prince Philip

4. What body of water does the *Liberty Belle* riverboat travel?
   - **a.** The Sassagoula River
   - **b.** Seven Seas Lagoon
   - **c.** The Rivers of America
   - **d.** Echo Lake

5. Which character does *not* meet guests at Pete's Silly Sideshow?
   - **a.** Mickey
   - **b.** Minnie
   - **c.** Donald
   - **d.** Daisy

6. What was the Prince Charming Regal Carrousel formerly called?
   - **a.** Merida's Wild Ride
   - **c.** Cinderella's Golden Carrousel
   - **b.** Ariel's Carrousel Under the Sea
   - **d.** Prince Eric's Royal Carrousel

7. Who plays Madame Leota in the *Haunted Mansion* movie?
   - **a.** Jennifer Tilly
   - **b.** Demi Moore
   - **c.** Raquel Alessi
   - **d.** Eva Mendes

8. What is inside Beast's Castle?
   - **a.** A store
   - **b.** A ride
   - **c.** A restaurant
   - **d.** A show

9. In which land can you ride Walt Disney's Carousel of Progress?
   - **a.** Adventureland
   - **b.** Tomorrowland
   - **c.** Frontierland
   - **d.** Fantasyland

10. What is the name of the attraction that opened in 2014 at Fantasyland?
    - **a.** Pete's Silly Sideshow
    - **b.** Ariel's Grotto
    - **c.** Seven Dwarfs Mine Train
    - **d.** Casey Jr. Splash 'N' Soak Station

Answers can be found on page 458.

PART 8

EPCOT

EPCOT IS THE MOST ADULT of the Walt Disney World theme parks. What it gains in taking a technological, educational look at the world, it loses, just a bit, in warmth, happiness, and charm. Some people find the attempts at education to be superficial; others want more entertainment and less education. Most visitors, however, are in between, finding plenty of amusement *and* information.

EPCOT is divided into two main sections: The back half, known as **World Showcase,** features landmarks, cuisine, and culture from almost a dozen nations. Until 2019, the front half of EPCOT was known as **Future World,** with attractions presenting a futuristic, semi-educational, "better living through technology" view of the world. In 2019, Disney announced that Future World would be subdivided into three "lands": **World Discovery** covers the east side (formerly Future World East) and includes the Test Track, Mission: Space, Play!, and Guardians of the Galaxy Pavilions. **World Nature** incorporates attractions in what was Future World West, such as the Imagination!, Land, and Seas Pavilions. The central part, including Spaceship Earth, is now known as **World Celebration.** For simplicity's sake, we'll use the older term *Future World* to broadly refer to the half of the park that isn't World Showcase, and we'll use the new land names when discussing those specific sections.

After years of neglect, much-needed updates and new experiences have been introduced at EPCOT. Two headliners—**Remy's Ratatouille Adventure,** a family-friendly ride in France based on the Pixar film *Ratatouille,* and **Guardians of the Galaxy: Cosmic Rewind,** an indoor roller coaster themed to the *Guardians of the Galaxy* movie series and opened in time for the 50th anniversary of Walt Disney World—are the first completely new attractions in EPCOT in almost 16 years.

Other construction projects are moving more slowly. **The Play! Pavilion,** "devoted to playful fun," on the site of the old Wonders of Life Pavilion, has been announced but at press time had neither a

continued on page 322

EPCOT

Attractions

1. *The American Adventure* ☑
2. *Awesome Planet*
3. *Canada Far and Wide*
4. Club Cool
5. Disney and Pixar Short Film Festival G+
6. Frozen Ever After ☑ G+
7. Gran Fiesta Tour Starring the Three Caballeros
8. Guardians of the Galaxy: Cosmic Rewind ☑ ILL
9. *Impressions de France/ Beauty and the Beast Sing-Along*
10. Journey into Imagination with Figment G+
11. Living with the Land ☑ G+
12. Mission: Space ☑ G+
13. *Reflections of China*
14. Remy's Ratatouille Adventure ☑ G+
15. SeaBase ☑
16. The Seas with Nemo & Friends G+
17. See Anna and Elsa at Royal Sommerhus
18. Soarin' Around the World ☑ G+
19. Spaceship Earth ☑ G+
20. Test Track ☑ G+
21. *Turtle Talk with Crush* ☑ G+

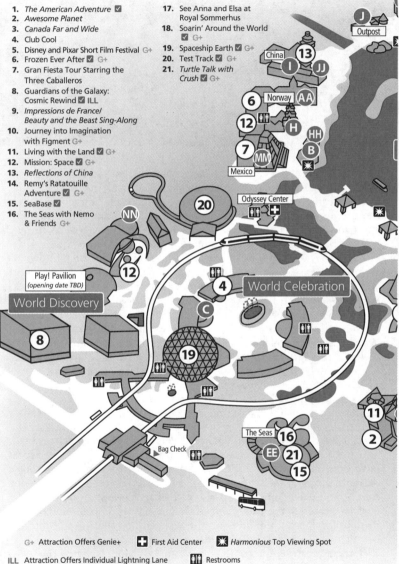

G+ **Attraction Offers Genie+**   ✚ **First Aid Center**   ✹ *Harmonious* Top Viewing Spot

ILL **Attraction Offers Individual Lightning Lane**   🚻 **Restrooms**

👍 **Recommended Dining**   ☑ **Not To Be Missed**

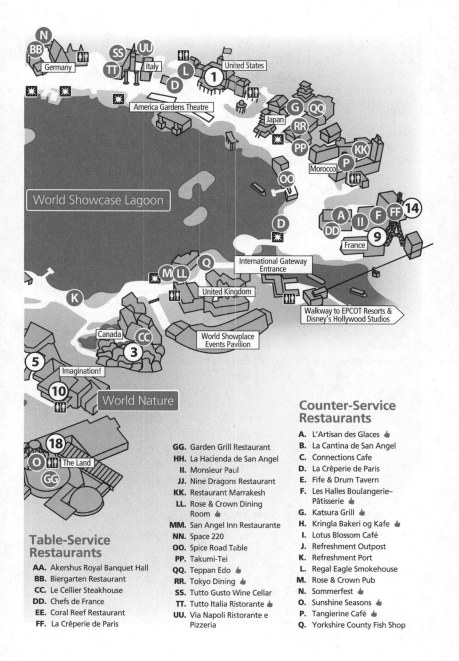

Counter-Service Restaurants

A. L'Artisan des Glaces 👍
B. La Cantina de San Angel
C. Connections Cafe
D. La Crêperie de Paris
E. Fife & Drum Tavern
F. Les Halles Boulangerie–Pâtisserie 👍
G. Katsura Grill 👍
H. Kringla Bakeri og Kafe 👍
I. Lotus Blossom Café
J. Refreshment Outpost
K. Refreshment Port
L. Regal Eagle Smokehouse
M. Rose & Crown Pub
N. Sommerfest 👍
O. Sunshine Seasons 👍
P. Tangierine Café 👍
Q. Yorkshire County Fish Shop

GG. Garden Grill Restaurant
HH. La Hacienda de San Angel
II. Monsieur Paul
JJ. Nine Dragons Restaurant
KK. Restaurant Marrakesh
LL. Rose & Crown Dining Room 👍
MM. San Angel Inn Restaurante
NN. Space 220
OO. Spice Road Table
PP. Takumi-Tei
QQ. Teppan Edo 👍
RR. Tokyo Dining 👍
SS. Tutto Gusto Wine Cellar
TT. Tutto Italia Ristorante 👍
UU. Via Napoli Ristorante e Pizzeria

Table-Service Restaurants

AA. Akershus Royal Banquet Hall
BB. Biergarten Restaurant
CC. Le Cellier Steakhouse
DD. Chefs de France
EE. Coral Reef Restaurant
FF. La Crêperie de Paris

continued from page 319

well-defined description nor an opening date. The **Journey of Water** attraction, inspired by the Walt Disney Animation Studios flick *Moana,* is still under construction. A few other already-announced projects, including a *Mary Poppins*–themed attraction in the UK Pavilion, an update to Spaceship Earth, and a new festival center, have been canceled, put on hold, or scaled back.

Disney should finish the major remodel of Future World by the end of 2023. Until then, expect construction in the areas around and behind Spaceship Earth and on many of the walking paths between the east and west sides of Future World.

A brand-new fireworks show, **Harmonious,** replaced EPCOT's long-running classic fireworks show *IllumiNations.*

Space 220, a space–themed table-service restaurant operated by the same group that runs Tutto Italia and Via Napoli at EPCOT and Morimoto Asia at Disney Springs, opened in World Discovery between Mission: Space and Test Track. Near Remy's Ratatouille Adventure, Disney opened **La Crêperie de Paris**—featuring the cuisine of celebrity chef Jérôme Bocuse and offering both table service and quick service.

At the France Pavilion, a new **Beauty and the Beast Sing-Along** plays in rotation with *Impressions de France.* The *O Canada!* attraction was replaced with *Canada Far and Wide,* a brand-new Circle-Vision 360 film. **Wondrous China** is to replace the *Reflections of China* film in the China Pavilion; at press time, no opening date had been announced. **Awesome Planet** plays at the Harvest Theater inside the Land Pavilion; the theater was formerly the home of the film *Circle of Life: An Environmental Fable.*

EPCOT is more than twice as large as the Magic Kingdom, so unless one day is all you have, plan on spending two days to savor all it has to offer. Unlike the Magic Kingdom, EPCOT may not seem to be a natural for kids at face value, but rest assured that families can have as much fun here as at any of the theme parks. Consider staying at a Disney hotel, so that you can take advantage of Early Theme Park Entry, which will help maximize your time in the parks.

OPENING PROCEDURE (ROPE DROP)

FUTURE WORLD AND WORLD SHOWCASE both typically open at 9 a.m. and close at 9 p.m., except in spring and summer, when they commonly open at 8:30 a.m. Make sure to check the Disney Monthly Calendar (disneyworld.disney.go.com/calendars/month) to plan your visit, and check the park hours again once you arrive in Orlando.

EPCOT has two entrances. The larger one is in Future World, at the front of the park, and it's the one you will use if you arrive by car, bus, or monorail. The other entrance, the **International Gateway (IG),** is located in the rear of the park, between the France and United Kingdom Pavilions in World Showcase.

The Future World entrance can handle more people and is closer to headliner rides such as Soarin' Around the World, Test Track, and Guardians of the Galaxy: Cosmic Rewind. However, the IG entrance will put you closer to Remy's Ratatouille Adventure, which is important if you're touring with small children.

Once you arrive, pick up a park map. Navigating EPCOT is unlike getting around at the Magic Kingdom, where nearly every "land" is discrete and visually distinct from its neighbors—for example, Liberty Square and Main Street, U.S.A. EPCOT, by contrast, is visually open. And while it might seem odd to see a Japanese pagoda and the Eiffel Tower on the same horizon, getting around is simple. An exception is Future World, where construction walls hide (for now) everything on its east and west sides.

Stroller, wheelchair, and **ECV/ESV rentals** are available inside the main entrance to the left, toward the rear of the Entrance Plaza, and at the International Gateway entrance. **Storage lockers** are near the Camera Center at the main entrance; there are also lockers at the International Gateway. The **Baby Care Center** is on the World Showcase side of the Odyssey Center complex. At the same location are the **First Aid Center** and the **Lost Persons** meeting place. There are three **Guest Relations** locations: one at EPCOT's main entrance, inside the park; one in World Celebration to the left of Spaceship Earth; and a third at International Gateway near the Disney Skyliner. **Lost and found** is located at the main entrance and at Guest Relations. **ATMs** are available at the main entrance, The American Adventure, and at the International Gateway. Across from Disney's Port Orleans Resorts, **Best Friends Pet Care** provides a comfortable home away from home for Fido, Fluffy, and all their pet pals.

GENIE+ AND INDIVIDUAL LIGHTNING LANE AND THE TOURING PLANS

DISNEY'S GENIE+ ride reservation system is offered at 11 EPCOT attractions. One attraction, Guardians of the Galaxy, is designated as Individual Lightning Lane:

GENIE+ AND INDIVIDUAL LIGHTNING LANE (ILL) SELECTIONS AT EPCOT
FUTURE WORLD
• Disney and Pixar Short Film Festival • Guardians of the Galaxy: Cosmic Rewind *(ILL)*   • Journey into Imagination with Figment • Living with the Land • Mission: Space   • The Seas with Nemo & Friends • Soarin' Around the World • Spaceship Earth   • Test Track • Turtle Talk with Crush
WORLD SHOWCASE
• Frozen Ever After • Remy's Ratatouille Adventure

Character greetings weren't being offered with Genie+ or ILL at press time, but we think they'll be added soon.

It was easy for us to recommend using Disney's old FastPass+ system with our touring plans, because it was free to use, had plenty of historical data to analyze, and behaved predictably. None of that is true with Genie+. So the four big questions for this edition are

1. Is Genie+ worth paying for at EPCOT?
2. If it's worth the cost, which attractions benefit most from Genie+ or Individual Lightning Lane?
3. How can you avoid paying for Individual Lightning Lane?
4. How do Genie+ and Individual Lightning Lane work with the touring plans?

Is Genie+ Worth Paying For at EPCOT?

We think so, provided you meet any of these three criteria:

- You'll be arriving at EPCOT after Early Theme Park Entry begins (that is, you won't be at the park as soon as it opens). This includes off-site guests who aren't eligible for Early Entry and on-site guests who want to sleep in.
- You won't be using a touring plan.
- You're visiting during a holiday, spring break, or another peak season.

Regardless of the time of year you visit, arriving at park opening should allow you to see at least one of EPCOT's headliner attractions without significant waits.

The table below shows how much time we estimate you'll be able to save using Genie+ with one of our EPCOT touring plans, at three different crowd and Genie+ usage levels (see page 285 for an explanation of the different usage levels):

	ESTIMATED TIME SAVINGS USING A TOURING PLAN WITH GENIE+ FOR VARIOUS CROWD LEVELS		
CROWD LEVEL	**TYPICAL USE (3 GENIE+ RESERVATIONS PER DAY)**	**OPTIMISTIC USE (3 GENIE+ RESERVATIONS PER DAY)**	**PERFECT USE (7 GENIE+ RESERVATIONS PER DAY)**
Low	52 minutes saved	56 minutes saved	63 minutes saved
Moderate	66 minutes saved	79 minutes saved	91 minutes saved
High	84 minutes saved	102 minutes saved	102 minutes saved

Which EPCOT Attractions Benefit Most from Genie+?

The table on the opposite page shows the attractions that might benefit most from using Genie+, based on current wait times and historical Genie+ data. The table goes in descending order of priority. At press time, we didn't have enough data for Guardians of the Galaxy, which is currently the only EPCOT attraction offering ILL; we expect the use of ILL to save at least 75 minutes in line on average there, making it worth the cost.

When Do Genie+ and Individual Lightning Lane Reservations Run Out at EPCOT?

The table on the opposite page shows the approximate time at which EPCOT attractions run out of Genie+ or ILL capacity, by crowd level. Use this table along with the "Which Attractions Benefit Most" table to determine which reservations to get first.

EPCOT ATTRACTIONS THAT BENEFIT MOST FROM GENIE+ AND INDIVIDUAL LIGHTNING LANE *(Highest Priority to Lowest)*	
ATTRACTION	**AVERAGE TIME IN LINE SAVED (IN MINUTES)**
Remy's Ratatouille Adventure	77
Frozen Ever After	64
Test Track	33
Soarin' Around the World	16
Spaceship Earth	11
Mission: Space	9
Living with the Land	7
Journey into Imagination with Figment	7
The Seas with Nemo and Friends	5
Turtle Talk with Crush	2

WHEN GENIE+ AND INDIVIDUAL LIGHTNING LANE RESERVATIONS RUN OUT BY ATTENDANCE LEVEL			
ATTRACTION	**LOW ATTENDANCE**	**MODERATE ATTENDANCE**	**HIGH ATTENDANCE**
Disney and Pixar Short Film Festival	10 p.m.	10 p.m.	10 p.m.
Frozen Ever After	1 p.m.	12 p.m.	12 p.m.
Guardians of the Galaxy: Cosmic Rewind	Not available at press time but likely before 10 a.m.		
Journey into Imagination with Figment	10 p.m.	9 p.m.	10 p.m.
Living with the Land	10 p.m.	9 p.m.	9 p.m.
Mission: Space	10 p.m.	9 p.m.	8 p.m.
Remy's Ratatouille Adventure	10 p.m.	9 p.m.	9 p.m.
The Seas with Nemo and Friends	10 p.m.	9 p.m.	9 p.m.
Soarin' Around the World	10 p.m.	9 p.m.	7 p.m.
Spaceship Earth	10 p.m.	9 p.m.	9 p.m.
Test Track	4 p.m.	12 p.m.	10 am
Turtle Talk with Crush	9 p.m.	8 p.m.	9 p.m.

AVAILABLE Attractions rarely run out of reservations at this crowd level.
LOW ATTENDANCE Crowd levels 1–3 on the TouringPlans crowd calendar
MODERATE ATTENDANCE Crowd levels 4-7   HIGH ATTENDANCE Crowd levels 8-10
Attractions closed for more than two years are not shown.

How Do Genie+ and Individual Lightning Lane Work with the Touring Plans?

See our corresponding advice for the Magic Kingdom on page 286.

FUTURE WORLD

IMMENSE, GLEAMING FUTURISTIC STRUCTURES define the first themed area just beyond EPCOT's main entrance. The new headliner at the park is Guardians of the Galaxy: Cosmic Rewind, a brand-new roller coaster in the space that once was *Universe of Energy: Ellen's Energy Adventure*. Note that the new attraction is NOT a version of the Guardians of the Galaxy—Mission: Breakout! ride at

Disney California Adventure Park. We lead off this section with the pavilions and attractions in World Discovery, then World Celebration, and then World Nature.

KEY TO ABBREVIATIONS In the attraction profiles that follow, each star rating is accompanied by a category label in parentheses. E means Exceptional, MAA means **Much Above Average**, AA means **Above Average**, A means **Average**, BA means **Below Average**, and MBA means **Much Below Average**.

AVERAGE WAIT-IN-LINE TIME This generally uses the attraction's maximum hourly capacity as a fixed reference, as ride capacity is subject to change throughout the year.

Guardians of the Galaxy: Cosmic Rewind *(World Discovery)*

TOO NEW TO RATE

What it is Massive indoor roller coaster. **Scope and scale** Super-headliner. **When to go** As soon as the park opens, using Early Theme Park Entry if possible. **Comment** 42" minimum height requirement. **Participates in Genie+** No (it's an Individual Lightning Lane attraction). **Early Theme Park Entry** No. **Extended Evening Hours** Yes.

A roller coaster with cars capable of rotating 360 degrees, Guardians of the Galaxy: Cosmic Rewind is a new style of ride for Disney World. Guests begin in the Galaxarium, a planetarium-like exhibition that explores the similarities and mysteries of the formation of Earth's galaxy and the planet Xandar. The Guardians of the Galaxy arrive, and everything goes haywire. Cosmic Rewind includes the first reverse launch on a Disney coaster. Check out Liliane's review of the ride at tinyurl.com/gotgcosmicrewindreview.

Cosmic Rewind is the highest-priority attraction for most guests once the park opens. Your best bet to ride without a long wait in line is to (1) stay at a Disney resort to take advantage of Early Theme Park Entry, (2) arrive at EPCOT's main entrance at least an hour before official opening, and (3) head for Cosmic Rewind as soon as you're admitted into the park.

Club Cool *(World Celebration)*

PRESCHOOL ★★★ (BA)   GRADE SCHOOL ★★★★ (A)   TEENS ★★★★½ (AA)
YOUNG ADULTS ★★★★ (A)   OVER 30 ★★★★ (A)   SENIORS ★★★★ (A)

This Coca Cola–sponsored exhibit provides free unlimited samples of soft drinks from around the world. Kids will love to fill their own tasting cups and move from sampling to sampling. In China, Smart Sour Plum is in; in Korea, Maid Joy Apple Lychee is popular. And the Italian favorite Beverly is back. Club Cool used to be part of the old Innoventions West structure and is now located in World Celebration, sharing a building with Creations Shop.

I admit that Beverly is an acquired taste, but it is my favorite Club Cool drink!

Liliane

Mission: Space *(World Discovery)* ★★★★

PRESCHOOL ★★★½ (BA/GREEN)   GRADE SCHOOL ★★★★ (A/BOTH)
TEENS ★★★★½ (MAA/ORANGE)   YOUNG ADULTS ★★★★½ (AA/ORANGE)
OVER 30 ★★★★ (A/ORANGE)   SENIORS ★★★½ (BA/BOTH)

What it is Space-flight simulator ride. **Scope and scale** Super-headliner. **When to go** First or last hour the park is open. **Comments** Orange version not recommended for pregnant women or anyone prone to motion sickness or claustrophobia; must be 40" to ride Green (the gentler nonspinning version) and 44" to ride the Orange version. **Duration of ride** About 5 minutes plus preshow. **Average wait in line per 100 people ahead of you** 4 minutes. **Loading speed** Moderate–fast. **EVC/wheelchair access** Must transfer to the ride vehicle. **Participates in Genie+** Yes. **Early Theme Park Entry** Yes. **Extended Evening Hours** Yes.

Rough   Queasy

In this attraction, you join three other guests in a four-person crew to fly a space mission. Each guest plays a role (commander, pilot, navigator, or engineer) and is required to perform certain functions during the flight. Mission: Space has an Orange Mission to Mars, where guests experience g-forces. A less intense Green Mission takes guests on an orbital adventure around our planet, with visuals similar to Soarin' Around the World.

Follow the Orange brick road; it's much more fun. The ride is too intense for little ones and people prone to motion sickness, but grade-schoolers, teens, and brave moms and dads will love it!

Lillane

The host during your expedition is Gary Sinise, known for his roles in the space flicks Apollo 13 *and* Mission to Mars.

A space-themed restaurant, Space 220, opened between Mission: Space and Test Track in 2021. The restaurant's theme is "dine on a space station" and features video displays of Earth from orbit. Find out more on page 173.

PLAY! PAVILION *(World Discovery; opening date not yet announced)*

Disney hasn't said much about this new pavilion since the pandemic put a hold on indoor entertainment spaces. The concept art seems to show a futuristic cityscape whose storefronts are entrances to mini attractions. All of these should be themed around the idea of play and feature (and promote) Disney characters and films. It's supposed to open in 2023, which seems awfully soon for a major attraction.

TEST TRACK PAVILION *(World Discovery)*

SPONSORED BY CHEVROLET, this pavilion consists of the Test Track attraction and Inside Track, a collection of transportation-themed exhibits and multimedia presentations. The pavilion is the last one on the left before World Showcase.

Test Track *(World Discovery)* ★★★★

PRESCHOOL ★★★★ (A) GRADE SCHOOL ★★★★½ (MAA) TEENS ★★★★½ (MAA)
YOUNG ADULTS ★★★★½ (MAA) OVER 30 ★★★★½ (MAA) SENIORS ★★★★ (AA)

What it is Auto-test-track simulator ride. **Scope and scale** Super-headliner. **When to go** The first 30 minutes the park is open or just before closing, or use the single-rider line (if offered). **Comments** Must be 40" to ride. **Duration of ride** About 4 minutes. **Average wait in line per 100 people ahead of you** 4½ minutes. **Loading speed** Moderate–fast. **EVC/wheelchair access** Must transfer to the ride vehicle. **Participates in Genie+** Yes. **Early Theme Park Entry** Yes. **Extended Evening Hours** Yes.

Rough

Scary

Test Track takes you through the process of designing a new vehicle and then "testing" your car in a high-speed drive through and around the pavilion. After hearing about auto design, you enter the Chevrolet Design Center to create your own concept car. Using a large touch-screen interface (like a giant iPad), groups of up to three guests design their car's body, engine, wheels, trim, and color. Next, you board a six-seat ride vehicle, attached to a track on the ground, for an actual drive through Chevrolet's test track. The vehicle's tests include braking maneuvers, cornering, and acceleration, culminating in a spin around the outside of the pavilion at speeds of up to 65 miles per hour.

Test Track is a favorite attraction of teens. If nobody in your family wants to join you on the ride and you don't have Genie+ reservations, join the single-rider line, which moves much faster (but skips the auto-design preshow). Test Track breaks down more often than any other ride in Walt Disney World, experiencing an outage roughly 4 out of every 10 days of operation. The attraction is often offline even at park opening. Check with a cast member to determine whether the ride is operating before you make the trek to this corner of Future World.

Felicity

I was super nervous going on Test Track. Seeing the design room and the big posh cars calmed my nerves, but the ride was too dark, too fast, too high, and way too twisty! Way too scary for me to go on again.

A. J.

Test Track breaks down a lot, especially when it rains, and my family and I found ourselves not being able to ride it at all. If you can, plan on visiting it on a sunny day.

Spaceship Earth *(World Celebration)* ★★★★

PRESCHOOL ★★★½ (MBA)	**GRADE SCHOOL** ★★★★ (A)	**TEENS** ★★★★ (A)
YOUNG ADULTS ★★★★ (AA)	**OVER 30** ★★★★ (MAA)	**SENIORS** ★★★★½ (AA)

Thumbs Up for the Whole Family

What it is Educational dark ride through past, present, and future. **Scope and scale** Headliner. **When to go** Before 10 a.m. or after 4 p.m. **Comments** If lines are long when you arrive, try again after 4 p.m. **Duration of ride** About 16 minutes. **Average wait in line per 100 people ahead of you** 3 minutes. **Loading speed** Fast. **EVC/ wheelchair access** Must transfer from ECV to provided wheelchair and then from wheelchair to the ride vehicle. **Participates in Genie+** Yes. **Early Theme Park Entry** Yes. **Extended Evening Hours** Yes.

This ride spirals through the 18-story interior of EPCOT's premier landmark, taking guests through Audio-Animatronic scenes depicting mankind's development in communications, from cave painting to the internet. It's actually more fun than it sounds and is carried off with a lot of humor. Spaceship Earth draws crowds like a magnet first thing in the morning because it's so close to the park entrance.

IMAGINATION! PAVILION *(World Celebration)*

THIS MULTIATTRACTION PAVILION is on the south side of World Nature. Outside are an "upside-down" waterfall and "jumping" water, a fountain that hops over the heads of unsuspecting passersby.

Disney and Pixar Short Film Festival *(World Celebration)* ★★

PRESCHOOL ★★★★ (A)	**GRADE SCHOOL** ★★★★½ (AA)	**TEENS** ★★★★ (AA)
YOUNG ADULTS ★★★★ (AA)	**OVER 30** ★★★★ (AA)	**SENIORS** ★★★★ (AA)

What it is Short movies and trailers for Disney and Pixar films. **Scope and scale** Diversion. **When to go** Hardly ever. **Duration of presentation** About 20 minutes. **Probable waiting time** About 13 minutes. **EVC/wheelchair access** May remain in wheelchair. **Participates in Genie+** Yes. **Early Theme Park Entry** No. **Extended Evening Hours** No.

The air-conditioned space shows Disney and Pixar animated 4-D short movies (10–15 minutes long). The short films are fun and enjoyable even for young viewers but are in no way a headliner. Enjoy the attraction on a second day at EPCOT, during inclement weather, or when it's hot and your feet need a break. These are the same movie previews that you can see online for free, on Apple TV, or before actual movies in actual theaters.

Don't waste Genie+ for this experience, as lines are never long.

Liliane

Journey into Imagination with Figment
(World Celebration) ★★½

| PRESCHOOL ★★★★ (A) | GRADE SCHOOL ★★★★ (MBA) | TEENS ★★★ (MBA) |
| YOUNG ADULTS ★★★ (MBA) | OVER 30 ★★★ (MBA) | SENIORS ★★★½ (MBA) |

What it is Dark fantasy-adventure ride. **Scope and scale** Major-attraction wannabe. **When to go** Anytime. **Duration of ride** About 6 minutes. **Average wait in line per 100 people ahead of you** 2 minutes. **Loading speed** Fast. **EVC/wheelchair access** May remain in wheelchair. **Participates in Genie+** Yes. **Early Theme Park Entry** No. **Extended Evening Hours** No.

"One little spark of inspiration is at the heart of all creation," croons the ever-popular Figment as he takes you on a tour of the Imagination Institute with the

help of your five senses. Young children will love the little purple dragon, but grown-ups and teens will be only mildly amused (and probably bored).

Felicity

This ride was special. I have never been on a ride that features a dragon. Figment is too funny. I loved all the interactive stuff at the end.

At the end of Journey into Imagination with Figment, make sure to play the fun games. There is also a cool gift shop.

Isabelle

Journey of Water, Inspired by *Moana*
(World Nature; still under construction at press time)

This walk-through attraction, built to simulate the lush landscapes of natural waterfalls and streams, sits—appropriately—on the walk from the center of Future World to The Seas Pavilion. Because it's walk-through, it can be toured at any time.

The attraction is themed on the 2016 flick produced by Walt Disney Animation Studios. If you haven't seen it, do so! The heartwarming tale of the strong-willed Moana is based on Polynesian myths with the feature song "How Far I'll Go," written by Lin-Manuel Miranda.

THE LAND *(World Nature)*

THIS HUGE PAVILION contains two attractions and two restaurants. When the pavilion was originally built, its emphasis was on farming, but now it focuses on environmental concerns. Dry as that sounds, kids really enjoy The Land's attractions. Note that The Land gets super crowded during mealtimes. Strollers aren't allowed in the pavilion—those with babies too young to walk might want to bring an infant carrier.

Awesome Planet (World Nature) ★★½

PRESCHOOL ★★★ (MBA)　**GRADE SCHOOL ★★★½** (MBA)　**TEENS ★★★½** (MBA)
YOUNG ADULTS ★★★½ (BA)　**OVER 30 ★★★½** (MBA)　**SENIORS ★★★★** (BA)

What it is Indoor film about the environment. **Scope and scale** Minor attraction. **When to go** Anytime, but save it for later in the day. **Comments** The film is shown on the pavilion's upper level. **Duration of presentation** About 15 minutes. **Probable waiting time** 10 minutes. **EVC/wheelchair access** May remain in wheelchair. **Participates in Genie+** No. **Early Theme Park Entry** No. **Extended Evening Hours** No.

Awesome Planet is a movie that highlights Earth's geography, animals, and people. The theater is large enough to accommodate everyone who wants to see the film, at almost any time of year. The theater once housed the film *Circle of Life: An Environmental Fable,* which closed in 2018 after a 22-year run.

Living with the Land *(World Nature)* ★★★★

PRESCHOOL ★★★½ (MBA)　**GRADE SCHOOL ★★★½** (MBA)　**TEENS ★★★½** (MBA)
YOUNG ADULTS ★★★★ (A)　**OVER 30 ★★★★** (MAA)　**SENIORS ★★★★½** (MAA)

Thumbs Up for the Whole Family

What it is Indoor boat-ride adventure through the past, present, and future of farming and agriculture in the US. **Scope and scale** Major attraction. **When to go** Before noon or after 3 p.m. **Comments** Go early and save other Land attractions (except for Soarin' Around the World) for later in the day. The ride is on the pavilion's lower level. **Duration of ride** About 14 minutes. **Average wait in line per 100 people ahead of you** 3 minutes; assumes 15 boats operating. **Loading speed** Moderate. **EVC/wheelchair access** Must transfer from EVC to provided wheelchair. **Participates in Genie+** Yes. **Early Theme Park Entry** No. **Extended Evening Hours** No.

This boat ride through four experimental growing areas is inspiring and educational. Kids like seeing the giant fruits and vegetables. Teens will be fascinated by the imaginative ways to grow crops—without soil, hanging in the air, and even on a space station. A lot of the produce grown here is served in the restaurants at EPCOT.

Soarin' Around the World *(World Nature)* ★★★★½

PRESCHOOL ★★★★ (A)　**GRADE SCHOOL ★★★★½** (MAA)　**TEENS ★★★★½** (MAA)
YOUNG ADULTS ★★★★½ (MAA)　**OVER 30 ★★★★½** (MAA)　**SENIORS ★★★★★** (E)

What it is Flight simulator ride. **Scope and scale** Super-headliner. **When to go** First hour the park is open or after 4 p.m. **Comments** Entrance is on the lower level of the pavilion. May induce motion sickness; must be 40″ to ride; Rider Switch option provided (see page 260). **Duration of ride** 5½ minutes. **Average wait in line per 100 people ahead of you** 4 minutes; assumes 3 concourses operating. **Loading speed** Moderate. **EVC/wheelchair access** Must transfer to the ride vehicle. **Participates in Genie+** Yes. **Early Theme Park Entry** Yes. **Extended Evening Hours** Yes.

Queasy

This attraction is the closest you'll come to hang gliding without trying the real thing. Once you're "airborne," IMAX-quality aerial images of the world are projected all around you, and the flight simulator moves in sync with the movie. In 2016 a new version of the film debuted, taking guests on an epic journey that spans six continents and shows some of the greatest wonders of the world, such as the Great Wall of China and the Sydney Opera House. A third ride theater and a 4-D projection system were added to the attraction, increasing the ride's capacity by 50%. The images are well chosen and drop-dead beautiful. Special effects include wind, sound, and even smell. The ride itself is thrilling but perfectly smooth. Any child (or adult) who meets the 40-inch minimum height requirement will love Soarin'. Landmarks such as the Eiffel Tower look distorted from seats on the far ends. For an ideal viewing experience, we recommend politely asking a cast member to seat you in row B1.

I loved Soarin', especially since this was the first time I went on the ride with my eyes open! It was exquisite and very realistic. Make sure you put all your belongings under your seat, so you don't have to worry about dropping anything during the flight. **Felicity**

Soarin' is my favorite ride at EPCOT. I didn't expect it to be so good. You literally feel like you're soaring. **A. J.**

THE SEAS PAVILION *(World Nature)*

FEATURING CHARACTERS from Disney/Pixar's *Finding Nemo* and *Finding Dory,* this pavilion in World Nature encompasses what was once one of America's top marine aquariums, a ride that tunnels through the aquarium, an interactive animated film, and several walk-through exhibits. Those exhibits need updating, but the tank alone makes this pavilion a must-visit. Little kids will love *Turtle Talk with Crush* and The Seas with Nemo & Friends.

SeaBase *(World Nature)* ★★★½

PRESCHOOL ★★★★½ (MAA) GRADE SCHOOL ★★★★½ (MAA) TEENS ★★★★ (A)
YOUNG ADULTS ★★★★ (A) OVER 30 ★★★★ (A) SENIORS ★★★★ (A)

What it is A huge saltwater aquarium, plus exhibits on oceanography, ocean ecology, and sea life. **Scope and scale** Major attraction. **When to go** Before 12:30 p.m. or after 5 p.m., especially when it gets dark early. **Comments** Watch for tank feeding times at 10 a.m. and 3:30 p.m. **Loading speed** Fast. **EVC/wheelchair access** May remain in wheelchair. **Participates in Genie+** No. **Early Theme Park Entry** No. **Extended Evening Hours** No.

Thumbs Up for the Whole Family

Take a *Finding Nemo*–themed ride (see next profile) to SeaBase Alpha to start your discovery of The Seas' main tank and exhibits, which feature fish, mammals, and crustaceans in a simulation of an ocean ecosystem. Visitors can observe the activity through windows below the surface (including inside the Coral Reef Restaurant). Children will be enchanted to discover the substantial fish population and the many exhibits offered. While we think the exhibits need updating and reimagining, the tank alone makes this pavilion not to be missed. Save the exhibits for later, after experiencing the ride and *Turtle Talk.*

The Seas with Nemo & Friends *(World Nature)* ★★★

PRESCHOOL ★★★★½ (MAA) GRADE SCHOOL ★★★★ (BA) TEENS ★★★½ (MBA)
YOUNG ADULTS ★★★½ (MBA) OVER 30 ★★★½ (MBA) SENIORS ★★★½ (MBA)

What it is A ride through a tunnel in SeaBase's main tank. **Scope and scale** Major attraction. **When to go** After 2 p.m. **Duration of ride** 4 minutes. **Average wait in line per 100 people ahead of you** 3½ minutes. **Loading speed** Fast. **EVC/wheelchair access** Must transfer to the ride vehicle. **Participates in Genie+** Yes. **Early Theme Park Entry** Yes. **Extended Evening Hours** Yes.

Upon entering The Seas, you proceed to the loading area, where you'll be made comfortable in a "clamobile" for your journey through the aquarium. The technology used makes it seem as if the animated characters are swimming with the live fish. Meet characters from *Finding Nemo,* such as Mr. Ray, and help Dory, Bruce, Marlin, Squirt, and Crush find Nemo. This cool ride attracts lots of the lovable clown fish's fans, so ride early.

See Finding Nemo *before your visit if you haven't already. You won't soon forget this superb family movie, which won the 2004 Oscar for Best Animated Feature. In 2016,* Finding Dory, *a sequel to* Finding Nemo, *brought back Ellen DeGeneres as the voice of the adorably forgetful blue tang.*

Turtle Talk with Crush *(World Nature)* ★★★★

PRESCHOOL ★★★★½ (MAA)   **GRADE SCHOOL** ★★★★½ (MAA)   **TEENS** ★★★½ (BA)
YOUNG ADULTS ★★★½ (BA)   **OVER 30** ★★★★ (A)   **SENIORS** ★★★★ (A)

What it is Interactive animated film. **Scope and scale** Minor attraction. **When to go** After 3 p.m. **Duration of presentation** 15 minutes. **Preshow** None. **Probable waiting time** 10–20 minutes. **EVC/wheelchair access** May remain in wheelchair. **Participates in Genie+** Yes. **Early Theme Park Entry** No. **Extended Evening Hours** No.

This interactive theater show starring the 150-year-old surfer-dude turtle from *Finding Nemo* starts like a typical theme park movie but quickly turns into an interactive encounter, as Crush begins conversing with audience members. With the release of *Finding Dory,* Dory the blue tang, Destiny the whale shark, Bailey the beluga whale, and Hank the seven-legged octopus joined Crush in his "Human Tank," providing lots of *awesome,* fun interactions for little dudes. It's unusual to wait more than one or two shows to get in. If you find long lines in the morning, come back after 3 p.m., when more of the crowd has moved on to World Showcase, or use Genie+.

WORLD SHOWCASE

EPCOT'S OTHER THEMED AREA, World Showcase, is an ongoing world's fair encircling a picturesque 40-acre lagoon. The cuisine, culture, history, and architecture of almost a dozen countries are permanently displayed in individual pavilions spaced out along a 1.2-mile promenade. The pavilions replicate familiar landmarks and depict representative street scenes from the host countries.

World Showcase's live entertainers are among the most highly rated attractions in EPCOT. World Showcase also offers some of the most diverse and interesting shopping in Walt Disney World.

If you have a sweet tooth like me, you can play a sweet game by trying a treat or candy from each of the 11 countries in World Showcase.

Lucy

KIDCOT FUN STOPS AND PASSPORT KITS

This program is designed to make EPCOT more interesting for younger visitors. At each pavilion in World Showcase, cast members discuss their native country with the children and give them stickers and cards. The traveler cards have fun facts about the country on one side and a picture for coloring on the other. Kids also receive a Ziploc bag that looks like a suitcase in which to carry their cards. Look for the brightly colored Kidcot signs.

Shops in EPCOT also sell Passport Kits for about $14. Each kit contains a blank "passport" and stamps for every World Showcase country. As kids visit each country, they tear out the appropriate stamp and stick it in the passport. Disney has built a lot of profit into this little product, but parents don't seem to mind the cost. Liliane feels that the free Kidcot activities are just as much fun.

An adult version of collecting traveler cards, known as Drinking Around the World, has been the base of many complaints we received in the past year. Complaints have also come from guests visiting the Animal Kingdom. While Bob loves his wine, and Liliane her margaritas, we sincerely hope that Disney will curb the bad behavior that ruins the experience of all guests, not just those visiting with young ones. As a dad from New Hampshire wrote:

Though Disney might not be actively pushing alcohol consumption, they were very obviously not policing it either. If it gets any worse than it was this year, I can see where families might start taking their vacations elsewhere—there was nothing fun or relaxing about it. Folks were either way too drunk or having to do battle to protect their families from those who were.

Now, moving clockwise around the World Showcase promenade, here are the nations represented and their attractions:

MEXICO PAVILION

SPANISH 101	
HELLO: Hola	**Pronunciation:** *Oh-la*
GOODBYE: Adios	**Pronunciation:** *Ah-dee-ohs*
THANK YOU: Gracias	**Pronunciation:** *Grah-see-ahs*
MICKEY MOUSE: El Ratón Miguelito	**Pronunciation:** *El Rah-tone Mee-gel-lee-toe*

A PRE-COLUMBIAN PYRAMID dominates the architecture of this exhibit. Inside you'll find authentic and valuable artifacts, a village scene complete with restaurant, and the **Gran Fiesta Tour** boat ride. The meet and greet for **Donald Duck** is outside on the right side of the pavilion. Several times a day, **Mariachi Cobre** delights EPCOT guests with performances of traditional mariachi music—as they've done since 1982.

Mexico's Kidcot Fun Stop is in the first entryway inside the pyramid. On the first floor, you will also find exhibits about *Coco*.

The award-winning 2017 animated Pixar Studios film Coco *centers around Dia de los Muertos (Day of the Dead) and the respect owed to our elders.* Coco *won two Academy Awards (Best Animated Feature and Best Song, for "Remember Me"). It also won Best Animated Film at the BAFTA Awards, Golden Globes, and more. If you haven't seen it, do so—don't forget a box of tissues. Liliane cries every time.*

Gran Fiesta Tour Starring the Three Caballeros ★★½

PRESCHOOL ★★★★ (AA)	GRADE SCHOOL ★★★★ (BA)	TEENS ★★★½ (BA)
YOUNG ADULTS ★★★½ (MBA)	OVER 30 ★★★½ (MBA)	SENIORS ★★★½ (MBA)

Thumbs Up for the Whole Family

What it is Scenic indoor boat ride. **Scope and scale** Minor attraction. **When to go** Before noon or after 5 p.m. **Duration of ride** About 7 minutes (plus 1½-minute wait to disembark). **Average wait in line per 100 people ahead of you** 4½ minutes; assumes 16 boats in operation. **Loading speed** Moderate. **EVC/wheelchair access** Must transfer to provided wheelchair. **Participates in Genie+** No. **Early Theme Park Entry** No. **Extended Evening Hours** Yes.

Gran Fiesta Tour's story line features Donald Duck, José Carioca (a parrot), and Panchito (a Mexican charro rooster) from the 1944 Disney film *The Three Caballeros.* The story has our heroes racing to Mexico City for a gala reunion performance. Guests are treated to detailed scenes in eye-catching colors.

I would love to see the Gran Fiesta Tour ride get a Coco *overlay. It would be a fitting use of the boat ride on El Rio del Tiempo. Who's with me?*

Liliane

NORWAY PAVILION

NORWEGIAN 101	
HELLO: God dag	**Pronunciation:** *Good dagh*
GOODBYE: Ha det	**Pronunciation:** *Hah deh*
THANK YOU: Takk	**Pronunciation:** *Tahk*
MICKEY MOUSE: Mikke Mus	**Pronunciation:** *Mikeh Moose*

SURROUNDING A COURTYARD is an assortment of traditional Scandinavian buildings, including a replica of the late 13th-century **Akershus Castle,** now home to princess-hosted character meals. The major attraction is the boat ride **Frozen Ever After.** Make sure to visit the replica of a Norwegian stave church. The church currently displays *Gods of the Vikings,* an exhibit showcasing the Norse gods and goddesses that Scandinavian Vikings celebrated in their day. Learn about the original Thor, Odin, Freya, and Loki through authentic artifacts.

It's hard to say no to the mouthwatering pastries at Kringla Bakeri Og Kafe in Norway. This is one of my favorite stops at the end of the day to pick up the next day's breakfast.

Liliane

Frozen Ever After ★★★★

PRESCHOOL ★★★★½ (MAA)	GRADE SCHOOL ★★★★½ (MAA)	TEENS ★★★★ (A)
YOUNG ADULTS ★★★★ (AA)	OVER 30 ★★★★ (A)	SENIORS ★★★★ (A)

What it is Indoor boat ride. **Scope and scale** Major attraction. **When to go** Before noon, after 7 p.m., or use Genie+. **Comment** Breaks down fairly often, so check if it's running before you head over. **Duration of ride** Almost 5 minutes. **Average wait in line per 100 people ahead of you** 4 minutes; assumes 12 or 13 boats operating. **Loading speed** Fast. **EVC/wheelchair access** Must transfer to the ride vehicle. **Participates in Genie+** Yes. **Early Theme Park Entry** Yes. **Extended Evening Hours** Yes.

Frozen Ever After is a boat ride through Arendelle, the fictional kingdom from the movie *Frozen.* The ride's queue features the Wandering Oaken's Trading Post. While waiting, you'll hear Oaken call, "Yoo-hoo!" while steam pours from his sauna's windows.

Next you board the boats formerly used in the Maelstrom ride, and following the same path, you are off to Arendelle to celebrate the Winter in Summer Festival, where Elsa uses her magical powers to make it snow during the hottest part of the year.

The ride features Anna, Elsa, Olaf, Kristoff, Sven, and Marshmallow (the snowman Elsa created with the adorable Snowgies from the *Frozen Fever* short) singing songs from the movie.

Halfway through the ride, the boat moves backward for a few seconds; this is followed by a short downhill and a small splash that most kids take in stride. Frozen Ever After experiences more breakdowns than most Walt Disney World attractions. If you're planning to experience it first thing in the morning, ask a cast member if it's running before you hike all the way to Norway.

Along with Guardians of the Galaxy, Remy's Ratatouille Adventure, Soarin' Around the World, and Test Track, Frozen Ever After is one of the attractions that guests head to first. Its popularity, coupled with its frequent breakdowns and relatively low capacity (around 900 riders per hour versus 2,200 at Remy's, for example), makes it one of the biggest bottlenecks in EPCOT. The good news is that the opening of Remy's Ratatouille Adventure and Guardians of the Galaxy: Cosmic Rewind took much of the park-opening crowd away from Frozen.

Frozen Ever After is the BEST ride at EPCOT. I loved everything—
the ice palace, Elsa singing, and the amazing Olaf.

Felicity

Meet Anna and Elsa at Royal Sommerhus ★★★★

**PRESCHOOL ★★★★★ (E)   GRADE SCHOOL ★★★★½ (MAA)   TEENS ★★★½ (A)
YOUNG ADULTS ★★★★ (AA)   OVER 30 ★★★★ (A)   SENIORS ★★★½ (BA)**

What it is Meet and greet with the *Frozen* royalty. **Scope and scale** Minor attraction. **When to go** At opening, at lunch or dinner, or in the last hour the park is open. **Duration of experience** About 3 minutes. **Average wait in line per 100 people ahead of you** 15–25 minutes. **EVC/wheelchair access** May remain in wheelchair. **Participates in Genie+** No. **Early Theme Park Entry** No. **Extended Evening Hours** No.

Norway's Royal Sommerhus is a character meet and greet set inside Anna and Elsa's summerhouse. The house is nicely decorated with tokens of the *Frozen* gals' childhood and attempts to give the look and feel of Norwegian architecture and crafts. Inside the house, a tapestry pays tribute to the three-headed troll from the now-extinct Maelstrom attraction. This meet and greet has multiple rooms, with Anna and Elsa operating simultaneously, so waits are usually manageable to see these princesses.

The best meet and greet I ever had.
Anna and Elsa are my heroes!

Felicity

CHINA PAVILION

CHINESE (MANDARIN) 101	
HELLO: Ni hao	**Pronunciation:** *Knee how*
GOODBYE: Zai jian	**Pronunciation:** *Zy jehn*
THANK YOU: Xiè xie	**Pronunciation:** *Chi-eh chi-eh*
MICKEY MOUSE: Mi Lao Shu	**Pronunciation:** *Me Lah-oh Su*

THERE IS NO RIDE at the China Pavilion, but the majestic half-size replica of the **Temple of Heaven** in Beijing will surely make it into your photo album. See *Reflections of China,* an impressive film about the people and natural beauty of China. Don't dismiss this beautiful pavilion. Kids love meeting **Mulan,** who holds court outside most of the time or inside the Temple of Heaven during inclement weather. Disney has announced an updated film for the theater, *Wondrous China*. The film had not yet been replaced at press time.

Reflections of China ★★★½

PRESCHOOL ★★½ (MBA)　GRADE SCHOOL ★★★ (MBA)　TEENS ★★★½ (MBA)
YOUNG ADULTS ★★★½ (A)　OVER 30 ★★★★ (AA)　SENIORS ★★★★ (MAA)

What it is Film about the Chinese people and culture. **Scope and scale** Major attraction. **When to go** Anytime. **Comments** Audience stands throughout performance. **Duration of show** About 14 minutes. **Preshow entertainment** None. **Probable waiting time** 10 minutes. **EVC/wheelchair access** May remain in wheelchair. **Participates in Genie+** No. **Early Theme Park Entry** No. **Extended Evening Hours** No.

Warm and appealing, *Reflections of China* is a brilliant (albeit politically sanitized) introduction to the people and natural beauty of China.

GERMANY PAVILION

GERMAN 101	
HELLO: Hallo	**Pronunciation:** *Hall-o*
GOODBYE: Auf wiedersehen	**Pronunciation:** *Owf veeh-der-zain*
THANK YOU: Danke	**Pronunciation:** *Dan-keh*
MICKEY MOUSE: Micky Maus	**Pronunciation:** *Me-key Mouse*

THE MAIN FOCUS in the Germany Pavilion, which has no rides, is **Biergarten,** a full-service (reservations recommended) restaurant serving German food and beer. Yodeling and oompah band music are regularly performed during mealtimes. Be sure to check out the large, elaborate model railroad just beyond the restrooms as you walk from Germany toward Italy. **Snow White** signs autographs at the well just as you reach the Germany Pavilion.

The Germany Pavilion is the perfect place to introduce your kids to a great snack: Gummibärchen (gummy bears), my favorite candy.

Lillane

ITALY PAVILION

ITALIAN 101	
HELLO: Buon giorno	**Pronunciation:** *Bon jor-no*
GOODBYE: Ciao (informal)	**Pronunciation:** *Chow*
THANK YOU: Grazie	**Pronunciation:** *Grah-zee-eh*
MICKEY MOUSE: Topolino	**Pronunciation:** *To-po-lee-no*

THE ENTRANCE TO ITALY is marked by an 83-foot-tall **campanile (bell tower)** intended to mirror the one in St. Mark's Square in Venice. Left of the campanile is a replica of the 14th-century **Doge's Palace.**

Streets and courtyards in the Italy Pavilion are among the most realistic in the World Showcase. You really do feel as if you're in Italy. Because there's no film or ride, you can tour anytime. **Sergio,** an Italian mime and juggler, performs five days a week.

UNITED STATES PAVILION

THIS IMPOSING BRICK STRUCTURE—home to a patriotic, albeit sanitized, retrospective of US history—is reminiscent of Colonial Philadelphia. The American Heritage Gallery currently hosts rotating exhibits well worth seeing.

Don't miss the performances of Voices of Liberty, an a cappella choir that performs regularly either in the rotunda of the US Pavilion or across the plaza in the America Gardens Theatre, EPCOT's premier venue for concerts and stage shows.

Liliane

The American Adventure ★★★★

PRESCHOOL ★★½ (MBA)	GRADE SCHOOL ★★★ (MBA)	TEENS ★★★½ (MBA)
YOUNG ADULTS ★★★★ (A)	OVER 30 ★★★★ (AA)	SENIORS ★★★★½ (MAA)

What it is Patriotic mixed-media and Audio-Animatronic theater presentation on US history. **Scope and scale** Headliner. **When to go** Anytime. **Duration of presentation** About 29 minutes. **Preshow entertainment** Voices of Liberty vocal group. **Probable waiting time** 25 minutes. **EVC/wheelchair access** May remain in wheelchair. **Participates in Genie+** No. **Early Theme Park Entry** No. **Extended Evening Hours** No.

Thumbs Up for the Whole Family

Narrated by animatronic Mark Twain and Ben Franklin, the show reminds you of a contest: Tell us everything you love about America in 30 minutes or less. Opened 40 years ago, it has not been updated and unfortunately hasn't kept pace with topics such as racism, gender equality, and the environment, for example, as they are treated as solved problems instead of ongoing challenges.

JAPAN PAVILION

JAPANESE 101	
HELLO: Konnichiwa	**Pronunciation:** *Ko-nee-chee-wah*
GOODBYE: Sayonara	**Pronunciation:** *Sigh-yo-nah-ra*
THANK YOU: Arigato	**Pronunciation:** *Ah-ree-gah-toe*
MICKEY MOUSE: Mikki Mausu	**Pronunciation:** *Mikkee Mou-su*

Brendan

Did you know you can get great Pokémon merchandise at the Japan Pavilion?!

THE FIVE-STORY, BLUE-ROOFED PAGODA, inspired by an eighth-century shrine in Nara, sets this pavilion apart. A hill garden behind it encompasses waterfalls, rocks, flowers, lanterns, paths, and rustic bridges. There are no attractions, unless you count the huge Japanese retail venue. Not to be missed, though, are the **Matsuriza Taiko drummers.** The drums can often be heard throughout the World Showcase, but you need to be up close to see the graceful way they're played.

MOROCCO PAVILION

ARABIC 101	
HELLO: Salaam alekoum	**Pronunciation:** *Sah-lahm ah-leh-koom*
GOODBYE: Ma'salama	**Pronunciation:** *Mah sah-lah-mah*
THANK YOU: Shoukran	**Pronunciation:** *Shoe-krahn*
MICKEY MOUSE: Mujallad Miki	**Pronunciation:** *Muh-jahl-lahd Me-key*

THE BUSTLING MARKET, winding streets, a lofty minaret, and stuccoed archways re-create the romance and intrigue of Marrakesh and Casablanca. Attention to detail makes Morocco one of the most exciting World Showcase pavilions. It is also home to **Jasmine** and **Aladdin.** **Spice Road Table** serves up tasty tapas-style Mediterranean dishes and good views of the fireworks—along with high prices. For a quick lunch, try **Tangierine Café,** one of EPCOT's highest-rated eateries.

FRANCE PAVILION

FRENCH 101	
HELLO: Bonjour	**Pronunciation:** *Bon-jure*
GOODBYE: Au revoir	**Pronunciation:** *Oh reh-vwa*
THANK YOU: Merci	**Pronunciation:** *Maer-si*
MICKEY MOUSE: Mickey	**Pronunciation:** *Mee-keh*

BIENVENUE À PARIS, the Eiffel Tower, and more. The restaurants, along with the bakery, **Les Halles Boulangerie-Patisserie,** and the ice-cream shop **L'Artisan des Glaces,** are very popular. The new kid in the arrondissement is **La Crêperie de Paris,** a sit-down restaurant that also offers a takeout window. **Givenchy,** the French fashion and beauty house, has a shop at the pavilion and is the only retail location in the United States that offers the full line of Givenchy makeup and skin-care products, as well as a large selection of fragrances. **Remy's Ratatouille Adventure,** a 3-D dark ride based on the 2007 Disney/Pixar animated film *Ratatouille,* took the French Pavilion by storm. The ride resembles the one currently delighting guests at Disneyland Paris.

Don't miss **Serveur Amusant,** an acrobatic comedy team performing several times a day at the pavilion. If you're looking for **Belle,** she meets fans at the pavilion. **Aurora** meets at the gazebo. Note that

EPCOT entertainers and characters are coming back to the parks but might not be available during your visit.

Try some of the many handmade ice creams or sorbets at L'Artisan des Glaces. So many flavors to choose from!

Isabelle

The France Pavilion hosts two films alternating performances in the same theater: a *Beauty and the Beast*–themed sing-along show, which plays 11 a.m.–6 p.m., and *Impressions de France*, which plays from 6:30 p.m. to park closing.

Beauty and the Beast Sing-Along ★★

PRESCHOOL ★★★★ (A)   **GRADE SCHOOL ★★★★** (A)   **TEENS ★★★** (MBA)
YOUNG ADULTS ★★★½ (MBA)   **OVER 30 ★★★½** (BA)   **SENIORS ★★★½** (BA)

What it is Film retelling of the story of *Beauty and the Beast,* with singing. **Scope and scale** Minor attraction. **When to go** 11 a.m.–6 p.m. **Duration of presentation** About 15 minutes. **Preshow entertainment** None. **Probable waiting time** 15 minutes. **Participates in Genie+** No. **Early Theme Park Entry** Yes. **Extended Evening Hours** Yes.

This is the third current Walt Disney World attraction to tell the *Beauty and the Beast* story, along with the Magic Kingdom's *Enchanted Tales with Belle* and Hollywood Studios' *Beauty and the Beast Live on Stage*. It's also the lowest-rated version, lacking the intimate charm of *Enchanted Tales* and the production value of *Live on Stage.*

I was not impressed.

Liliane

Impressions de France ★★★½

PRESCHOOL ★★½ (MBA)   **GRADE SCHOOL ★★★** (MBA)   **TEENS ★★★** (MBA)
YOUNG ADULTS ★★★★ (A)   **OVER 30 ★★★★** (A)   **SENIORS ★★★★½** (AA)

What it is Film essay on France and its people. **Scope and scale** Major attraction. **When to go** 6:30 p.m.–park closing. **Duration of presentation** About 18 minutes. **Preshow entertainment** None. **Probable waiting time** 15 minutes (at suggested times). **Participates in Genie+** No. **Early Theme Park Entry** No. **Extended Evening Hours** No.

France, here we come! This truly lovely 18-minute movie will make you want to pack your suitcase. An added bonus is that the showing is *très civilisé,* as you get to sit down and rest your weary feet. The movie is outdated, and we wouldn't be surprised to see another film commissioned soon.

Remy's Ratatouille Adventure ★★★★

Thumbs Up for the Whole Family

ALL AGE GROUPS ★★★★½ (MAA)

What it is Indoor dark ride. **Scope and scale** Major attraction. **When to go** As soon as the park opens. **Duration of ride** About 4½ minutes. **Average wait in line per 100 people ahead of you** About 3 minutes; assumes hourly capacity of around 2,200 riders. **Loading speed** Moderate. **EVC/wheelchair access** Must transfer to ride vehicle. **Participates in Genie+** Yes. **Early Theme Park Entry** Yes. **Extended Evening Hours** Yes.

Brendan

Request the front row on Remy's Ratatouille Adventure for an even better experience.

On this ride, modeled after the original Ratatouille: L'Aventure Totalement Toquée de Rémy ride at Disneyland Paris, you're shrunk down to the size of a rat and whisked through Paris for a quick retelling of the *Ratatouille* film. As one of Remy's rat friends, you watch his ascent from a rodent with a dream to one of Paris's celebrated chefs.

The storytelling combines 3-D films shown on room-size screens with large, detailed ride-through sets, including water and heat effects. A couple of frenetic scenes, including one in which Remy is chased with a meat cleaver, may frighten small children.

This is the first all-new major attraction in EPCOT in more than a decade, and the first in World Showcase since 1988. It's also family-friendly, with good theming and a well-liked lead character. Lines form as soon as the park opens.

Your best bet to ride Remy is to arrive at EPCOT's International Gateway entrance about an hour before opening. (If you're driving, park at one of the EPCOT resorts—the Swan and Dolphin are the closest; parking is $35 a day. That gives you a 10-minute head start on folks walking from the park's front entrance. Ride as soon as the park opens. If you have small children, head next to Frozen Ever After in Norway, about 0.5 mile either way around World Showcase. After that, you'll have completed two of the park's five headliner rides, with Guardians of the Galaxy, Test Track, and Soarin' remaining.

The ride is based on the 2007 Pixar Animation Studios flick featuring a rat that aspires to become a great chef. Remy's hilarious adventures are a delight. In 2008 Ratatouille *won the Academy Award for Best Animated Feature.*

UNITED KINGDOM PAVILION

A BLEND OF ARCHITECTURE attempts to capture Britain's city, town, and rural atmospheres. One street alone has a thatched-roof cottage, a four-story timber-and-plaster building, a pre-Georgian plaster building, a formal Palladian exterior of dressed stone, and a city square with a Hyde Park bandstand (whew!). There are no attractions. **Alice in Wonderland** and **Mary Poppins** greet their fans outside the little English cottage.

If your child loves Mary Poppins, your best chance to meet her is here.

Liliane

CANADA PAVILION

THE CULTURAL, NATURAL, AND ARCHITECTURAL diversity of Canada are reflected in this large, impressive pavilion. Older kids will be interested in the 30-foot-tall totem poles that embellish a Canadian Indian village. The Canada Pavilion is also home to the famous **Le Cellier** steakhouse.

Canada Far and Wide ★★★½

PRESCHOOL ★★★ (MBA)	GRADE SCHOOL ★★★ (MBA)	TEENS ★★★ (MBA)
YOUNG ADULTS ★★★½ (BA)	OVER 30 ★★★★ (BA)	SENIORS ★★★★ (A)

What it is Film essay on Canada and its people. **Scope and scale** Major attraction. **When to go** Anytime. **Comments** Audience stands. **Duration of show** About 14 minutes. **Preshow entertainment** None. **Probable waiting time** 9 minutes. **EVC/wheelchair access** May remain in wheelchair. **Participates in Genie+** No. **Early Theme Park Entry** No. **Extended Evening Hours** No.

The third film shown in this pavilion since EPCOT opened, *Canada Far and Wide* is the best one yet. It combines all the visual majesty that you'd want in a 360-degree film with a faster, more modern script that works its way from one end of the country to the other. As in the previous films, Montreal, Calgary, and Vancouver get their own segments (some of which have been repurposed from the old films). *Canada Far and Wide* has additional clips of Canada's capital, Ottawa, and specifically mentions its three territories—Yukon, Northwest Territories, and Nunavut—highlighting their Indigenous peoples and cultures.

LIVE ENTERTAINMENT *at* EPCOT

LIVE ENTERTAINMENT AT EPCOT is more diverse than at the Magic Kingdom. Kids will love the crew of drumming janitors (**The JAMMitors**), as well as **Sergio** the mime and juggler.

Street performances in and around World Showcase are what set live entertainment at EPCOT apart from the other Disney theme parks. A mariachi group can be found in Mexico; street actors in France; the **Voices of Liberty** in the United States; traditional drummers in Japan; and the raucous Oktoberfest entertainment at Germany's **Biergarten.**

The street entertainment at EPCOT frequently undergoes changes, and limited-time musical acts come and go throughout World Showcase. While we don't mind change, our major complaint is that the frequency of the performances has been substantially reduced.

Liliane

WDW live-entertainment guru Steve Soares usually posts the EPCOT performance schedule about a week in advance at wdwent.com.

AMERICA GARDENS THEATRE

THIS AMPHITHEATER ON THE LAGOON across from the United States Pavilion features pop (and oldies pop) musical acts throughout

FAVORITE EATS IN EPCOT	
WORLD NATURE Coral Reef Restaurant*	Food with a view—fish menu. The aquarium will keep the kids happy for quite some time.	**Sunshine Seasons**	Healthy choices—our all-time favorite
MEXICO La Cantina de San Angel	Kids' plate with empanada, tortilla chips, and drink
NORWAY Kringla Bakeri Og Kafe	Lefse and School Bread.
CHINA Lotus Blossom Café	Sweet-and-sour chicken, pot stickers, and egg rolls
GERMANY Sommerfest	Bratwurst with sauerkraut
ITALY Tutto Italia*	Good pasta and kids' menu	**Via Napoli**	Best pizza in WDW	*Table service only*
UNITED STATES Regal Eagle Smokehouse	If you're craving smoked barbecue
JAPAN Katsura Grill	Beef and chicken teriyaki
MOROCCO Tangierine Café	Grilled kebabs with couscous, stone-baked Moroccan bread with dips; outdoor seating
FRANCE Les Halles Boulangerie–Patisserie	Croissants, chocolate mousse, and yummy sandwiches on baguettes	**L'Artisan des Glaces**	The place to go for ice cream
UNITED KINGDOM Yorkshire County Fish Shop	Fish-and-chips

* Table service only—Advance Reservations highly recommended

much of the year, as well as EPCOT's popular **Candlelight Processional** for the Christmas holidays. Showtimes are posted outside the theater.

Harmonious ★★★

PRESCHOOL ★★★★ (A)	GRADE SCHOOL ★★★★½ (AA)	TEENS ★★★★½ (AA)
YOUNG ADULTS ★★★★ (BA)	OVER 30 ★★★★ (BA)	SENIORS ★★★★ (A)

Harmonious is the replacement for EPCOT's long-running classic fireworks show *IllumiNations: Reflections of Earth*. It's also the lowest-rated of any current Disney nighttime spectacular. We think *Harmonious* has at least three significant problems.

The first is the show's hideous projection barges, which project a screen of water at night on which various Disney film clips are shown. Besides having absolutely no aesthetic appeal whatsoever, these floating, black warts are an abomination on the picturesque views of World Showcase. They should never have been approved for use in the park.

The second problem with *Harmonious* is that the show's main visual elements are only visible in two relatively narrow slices around World Showcase lagoon, whereas *IllumiNations* was visible at almost any point around the lagoon. Again, this is a design decision that's baffling to anyone who's ever set foot in World Showcase. It makes us think the people who designed the show never considered the needs of paying customers.

The third problem is that the vast majority of its soundtrack comes from films that are also featured in the Magic Kingdom's nighttime fireworks show *Happily Ever After*. Of *Harmonious*'s approximately 14 songs, we counted 11 that either came directly from *Happily Ever After* or were from the same film as another song in *Happily Ever After*. It's as if the writers for both shows had exactly one CD of music between them. We honestly believe that the only reason Disney hastily replaced *Happily Ever After* with *Enchantment* at the Magic Kingdom in 2021 is because they knew *Harmonious* was the same show.

IllumiNations was a good fireworks show. I am sad that it's gone.

I really don't want to be in the shoes of those who created the new permanent show. *IllumiNations* had a powerful soundtrack. And those hideous projection barges ruin the view of World Showcase.

Liliane

Sabrina

Harmonious dining packages are available to see the show at either of two lagoon-side venues: the **Rose & Crown Dining Room** in the United Kingdom and **Spice Road Table** in Morocco. Check-in for dinner starts 45 minutes before the show begins, meaning your meal should end around the same time the show ends. Both restaurants feature fixed-price dinners: $89 per adult and $39 per child at Rose & Crown, and $72 per adult and $31 per child at Spice Road Table. Reservations are strongly encouraged.

VIEWING (AND EXIT) STRATEGIES FOR *HARMONIOUS*

THE BEST VIEWING LOCATIONS for *Harmonious* are in **Showcase Plaza**—the area where Future World meets World Showcase—between the Disney Traders and Port of Entry shops.

The best place on World Showcase Lagoon for *Harmonious* is around Japan. Come early—at least 90 minutes before the show—and relax with a cold drink or snack while you wait for the show.

La Hacienda de San Angel in Mexico, the **Rose & Crown Pub** in the United Kingdom, and **Spice Road Table** in Morocco also offer lagoon views. The views at Spice Road Table are better than those at the other two restaurants. If you want to combine dinner at these sit-down locations with viewing the show, make a reservation for about 1 hour and 15 minutes before showtime. Report a few minutes early for your seating and tell the host that you want a table outside where you can watch the show. Our experience is that the staff will bend over backward to accommodate you.

Because most guests run for the exits after a presentation and islands in the southern (US Pavilion) half of the lagoon block the view from some places, the most popular spectator positions are along the **northern waterfront**, from Norway and Mexico to Canada and the United Kingdom. Although the northern half of the lagoon offers good views, you must usually claim a spot 60–100 minutes before the show begins.

For those who are late finishing dinner or don't want to spend an hour or more standing by a rail, here are some good viewing spots along the **southern perimeter** (moving counterclockwise from the United Kingdom to Germany) that often go unnoticed until 10–30 minutes before showtime:

1. **International Gateway Island** The pedestrian bridge across the canal near the International Gateway spans an island that offers great viewing. This island normally fills 30 minutes or more before showtime.

2. **Second-floor (restaurant-level) deck of the Mitsukoshi building in Japan** An Asian arch slightly blocks your sight line, but this covered deck offers a great vantage point, especially if the weather is iffy. Only La Hacienda de San Angel in Mexico is more protected. If you take up a position on the Mitsukoshi deck and find the wind blowing directly at you, you can be reasonably sure that the smoke from the fireworks won't be far behind. May be reserved by Disney for private viewings.

3. **Gondola landing at Italy** An elaborate waterfront promenade offers decent viewing of all but the central barge images. Claim a spot at least 30 minutes before showtime. May be reserved by Disney for private viewings.

4. **Boat dock opposite Germany** Another good vantage point, the dock generally fills 30 minutes before the show. Note that this area may be exposed to more smoke from the fireworks because of EPCOT's prevailing winds.

5. **Waterfront Promenade by Germany** Views are good from the 90-foot-long lagoon-side walkway between Germany and China.

None of these viewing locations are reservable (except by Disney), and the best spots get snapped up early on busy nights. Most nights, you can still find an acceptable vantage point 15–30 minutes before the show. Don't position yourself under a tree, an awning, or anything that blocks your overhead view.

Getting Out of EPCOT After *Harmonious*

Harmonious ends the day at EPCOT—when it's over, everyone leaves at once. It's important, then, not only to decide how quickly you want to flee the park after the show but also to pick a vantage point that will help you do that most efficiently.

The **Skyliner** gondola system connects EPCOT with Disney's Hollywood Studios as well as the **Caribbean Beach, Riviera, Pop Century, and Art of Animation Resorts**. EPCOT's Skyliner station is just beyond the International Gateway (IG) exit. Waits for the Skyliner can be half an hour or more on busy nights.

If you're staying at (or you parked at) an EPCOT resort (**Swan, Dolphin, Swan Reserve, Yacht & Beach Club Resorts**, or **BoardWalk Inn & Villas**), watch the show from somewhere on the southern (**United States Pavilion**) half of World Showcase Lagoon; then leave through the **IG,** between France and the United Kingdom. You can walk or take a boat back to your hotel from the IG.

If you're staying at any other Disney hotel and you don't have a car, the fastest way home is to join the mass exodus through **the main EPCOT gate** after the show and catch a bus or the monorail.

Those who've left a car parked in the EPCOT lot have a stickier situation. To beat the crowds, find a viewing spot at **the end of World Showcase Lagoon** (nearest the exit). Leave as soon as the show wraps up, trying to exit ahead of the crowd (noting that thousands of people will be doing the same thing).

If you want a good vantage point **between Mexico and Canada** on the northern end of the lagoon, stake out your spot 60–100 minutes before the show (45–90 minutes during less-busy periods). Otherwise, you may squander more time holding your spot before the show than you would if you watched from the less congested southern end of the lagoon and took your chances with the crowd upon departure.

More groups get separated and more kids get lost following the evening fireworks than at any other time. In summer, you'll be walking in a throng of up to 30,000 people. If you're heading for the parking lot, anticipate this congestion and pick a spot in the main EPCOT entrance area where you can meet if someone gets separated from the group. Wherever you decide to meet, **do NOT leave the park,** and make sure your cell phones are charged.

For those with a car, the hardest part is reaching the parking lot: Once you've made it there, you're more or less home. If you've paid close attention to where you parked, consider skipping the tram and walking. But if you do, watch your children closely and hang on to them for all they're worth—the parking lot can get dicey at this time of night, with hundreds of moving cars.

If you did not come by car, we strongly recommend you use the IG exit (next to the United Kingdom Pavilion), skip the gondola and the boat, walk to the BoardWalk Inn, and get a Lyft or Uber ride to your hotel. This Salt Lake City mom did just that:

We watched the fireworks from the bridge at the International Gateway; then we just walked straight to the BoardWalk Inn and got a ride from Lyft. It took us 10 minutes from leaving the fireworks to getting to our ride to getting dropped off at our hotel. Super convenient, and we didn't have to leave with the 30,000 people exiting EPCOT in the front of the park!

EPCOT TOURING PLANS

OUR STEP-BY-STEP TOURING PLANS are field-tested, independently verified itineraries that will keep you moving counter to the crowd flow and allow you to see as much as possible in a single day with minimum time wasted in line.

Touring EPCOT is much more strenuous and demanding than touring the other theme parks. EPCOT requires about twice as much walking and has no effective in-park transportation. Our plans will help you avoid crowds and bottlenecks on days of moderate to heavy attendance, but they can't shorten the distance you have to walk. (Wear comfortable shoes.) On days of lighter attendance, when crowd conditions aren't a critical factor, the plans will help you organize your tour.

We love EPCOT, and we really want small children to enjoy it too. The key is to brief children on what they are likely to see in each attraction and tie it back to something they can relate to. During the tour of the greenhouse in Living with the Land, for example, make a game finding foods they like. (They have cocoa beans—chocolate—so we think that covers almost everyone.) While riding Test Track, ask which parent's driving was most like the ride's.

The different touring plans are described below. The descriptions will tell you for whom or for what situation the plans are designed. The actual touring plans are located on pages 496–500. Each plan includes a numbered map of the park to help you find your way around.

Last but not least, getting through security at EPCOT's main entrance is much more time-consuming than at the other parks. Take this delay into consideration when using one of our EPCOT plans.

1-DAY TOURING PLAN FOR PARENTS WITH SMALL CHILDREN This plan is designed for parents of children ages 3–8 who wish to see the very best age-appropriate attractions in EPCOT. Every attraction has a rating of at least three-and-a-half stars (out of five) from preschool and grade-school children surveyed by *The Unofficial Guide*. Special advice is provided for touring the park with small children. The plan keeps walking and backtracking to a minimum.

1-DAY SLEEPYHEAD TOURING PLAN FOR PARENTS WITH SMALL CHILDREN A relaxed plan that allows families with small children to sleep late and still see the highlights of EPCOT. The plan begins around 11 a.m., sets aside ample time for lunch, and includes the very best child-friendly attractions in the park.

PARENTS' TOURING PLAN—1 AFTERNOON AND 1 FULL DAY This touring plan is for families who want to tour EPCOT comprehensively over two days. Day one uses early-morning touring opportunities. Day two begins in the afternoon and continues until closing. The afternoon plan also works great if you're arriving in Orlando in the morning and want to tour a park after you've checked in.

1-DAY TOURING PLAN FOR TWEENS AND THEIR PARENTS A plan for parents with children ages 8–12. It includes attractions rated three-and-a-half stars and higher by this age group, and it sets aside ample time for lunch and dinner.

BEFORE YOU GO

1. Call ☎ 407-824-4321 or check disneyworld.com for operating hours.
2. Purchase admission and make park reservations.
3. Familiarize yourself with park-opening procedures and reread the touring plan you've chosen.

EPCOT TRIVIA QUIZ

1. Who is no longer performing at World Showcase?

   a. Mariachi Cobre
   b. *Serveur Amusant*
   c. Off Kilter
   d. Voices of Liberty

2. What is the newest attraction at EPCOT?

   a. Soarin' Around the World
   b. Remy's Ratatouille Adventure
   c. Mission: Space
   d. Spaceship Earth

3. Which Disney princess is *not* found at EPCOT?

   a. Belle
   b. Mulan
   c. Merida
   d. Snow White

4. Which character's meet and greet do you encounter at the Mexico Pavilion?

   a. Donald Duck
   b. Goofy
   c. Mickey
   d. Pluto

5. Which country do you find between France and Canada?

   a. Germany
   b. United Kingdom
   c. Morocco
   d. Japan

6. Where can you find the Frozen Ever After ride?

   a. Canada
   b. China
   c. Norway
   d. Italy

7. Which team do you join if you want to experience the spinning version of Mission: Space?

   a. The Red team
   b. The Green team
   c. The Orange team
   d. The Blue team

8. What drink is available free of charge at Club Cool?

   a. Mello Yello
   b. Beverly
   c. Orangina
   d. Mountain Dew

9. What kind of ride is Living with the Land?

   a. A simulation ride
   b. A boat ride
   c. A water-flume ride
   d. A roller coaster

10. What event does *not* take place at EPCOT?

    a. Candlelight Processional
    b. International Food & Wine Festival
    c. International Flower & Garden Festival
    d. Mickey's Very Merry Christmas Party

Answers can be found on page 458.

PART 9

DISNEY'S ANIMAL KINGDOM

WITH ITS LUSH FLORA, winding streams, meandering paths, and exotic setting, Disney's Animal Kingdom is a stunningly beautiful theme park. Add a population of more than 1,700 animals, replicas of Africa's and Asia's most intriguing architecture, and a diverse array of attractions, and you have the most distinctive of all Disney World theme parks.

The park is arranged somewhat like the Magic Kingdom. The lush, tropical **Oasis** serves as Main Street, funneling visitors to **Discovery Island**, the park's retail and dining center. From Discovery Island, guests can access the respective theme areas: **Africa, Asia, DinoLand U.S.A.,** and **Pandora: World of Avatar,** which brings the flora and fauna of James Cameron's *Avatar* to the park.

On Discovery Island, on your left just before you cross the bridge to Africa, are the **Baby Care Center** and **First Aid.** An ATM is located in DinoLand U.S.A. near the Chester & Hester's Dinosaur Treasures. As you pass through the turnstiles, **ECV, wheelchair, and stroller rentals** (at Garden Gate Gifts) are to your right. **Guest Relations**—headquarters for information, park maps, missing persons, and lost and found—is to the left. **Lockers** are just inside the main entrance to the left; a second set is located at Kali River Rapids Expedition Storage. Across from Disney's Port Orleans Resorts, **Best Friends Pet Care** provides a comfortable home away from home for Fido, Fluffy, and all their pet pals.

OPENING PROCEDURES (ROPE DROP)

ANIMAL KINGDOM IS usually the first Disney World park to open in the morning and the first to close. Expect it to open at 8 a.m. daily, possibly earlier during holidays and other times of peak attendance.

On-site guests, who are eligible for Early Theme Park Entry, should arrive at the entrance 60 minutes before official opening (30 minutes before Early Entry) on all days. Off-site guests should arrive 30 minutes before official opening on all days.

continued on page 350

Disney's Animal Kingdom

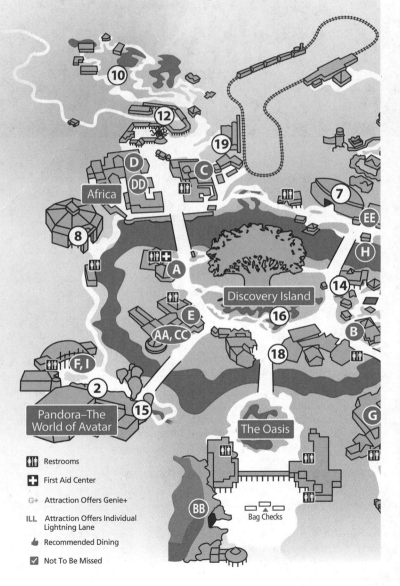

Restrooms

First Aid Center

G+ Attraction Offers Genie+

ILL Attraction Offers Individual
Lightning Lane

Recommended Dining

☑ Not To Be Missed

Attractions

1. The Animation Experience at Conservation Station G+
2. Avatar Flight of Passage ☑ ILL
3. The Boneyard
4. Conservation Station and Affection Section
5. Dinosaur ☑ G+
6. Expedition Everest ☑ G+
7. *Feathered Friends in Flight* ☑ G+
8. *Festival of the Lion King* ☑ G+
9. *Finding Nemo: The Big Blue . . . and Beyond!* ☑ G+
10. Gorilla Falls Exploration Trail
11. Kali River Rapids G+
12. Kilimanjaro Safaris ☑ G+
13. Maharajah Jungle Trek
14. Meet Favorite Disney Pals at Adventurers Outpost G+
15. Na'vi River Journey ☑ G+
16. Tree of Life ☑ / *Awakenings/ It's Tough to Be a Bug!* G+
17. TriceraTop Spin
18. Wilderness Explorers ☑
19. Wildlife Express Train

Rafiki's Planet Watch

DinoLand U.S.A.

Table-Service Restaurants

AA. Nomad Lounge
BB. Rainforest Cafe
CC. Tiffins 👍
DD. Tusker House Restaurant 👍
EE. Yak & Yeti Restaurant 👍

Counter-Service Restaurants

A. Creature Comforts *(Starbucks)* 👍
B. Flame Tree Barbecue 👍
C. Harambe Market 👍
D. Kusafiri Coffee Shop & Bakery 👍
E. Pizzafari
F. Pongu Pongu
G. Restaurantosaurus
H. Royal Anandapur Tea Company 👍
I. Satu'li Canteen 👍
J. Thirsty River Bar & Trek Snacks
K. Yak & Yeti Local Food Cafes 👍

continued from page 347

Once you're in the park, you'll usually find all of Pandora, along with *It's Tough to be a Bug!,* Expedition Everest, Dinosaur, and Tricera-Top Spin, already open.

Because Avatar Flight of Passage is among the hottest tickets in all of Walt Disney World, Animal Kingdom adjusts its opening procedures based on crowd levels, catching some guests by surprise. Here's what a Fort Wayne, Indiana, reader experienced while trying to beat the morning crush:

> If you plan to tour Animal Kingdom, arrive as early as possible, then 30 minutes earlier. We arrived at 7:20 expecting to be in the crowd for rope drop, but the crowd had already been admitted and we immediately had a 90-minute wait—before 7:40 a.m.—for Avatar Flight of Passage.

Because the park has relatively few attractions, most guests who arrive at park opening have left the park by midafternoon. The lack of attractions also means Animal Kingdom can get swamped from midmorning to early afternoon during holidays.

During slower or colder times of year, Disney may delay the daily opening of the several attractions: Kali River Rapids and Maharajah Jungle Trek in Asia, as well as the Boneyard playground and Dinosaur in DinoLand U.S.A. The Wildlife Express Train and Conservation Station may have a delayed opening as well.

We cannot reiterate enough to remember to confirm the official park-opening time—check online the night before you go. To stay abreast of ride closures, delays, and the like, also check the MDE app.

Animal Kingdom's best features are its animals, nature trails, and cast members. The **Wilderness Explorers** scavenger hunt (see page 355) ties together all of the park's best elements.

You can experience a nighttime version of Kilimanjaro Safaris. Live entertainment brings music and lively performances to Discovery Island and Harambe Village in Africa. The theme park's symbol, the **Tree of Life,** is brought to life by magical "fireflies" (twinkling lights) when the sun sets.

GENIE+ AND INDIVIDUAL LIGHTNING LANE AND THE TOURING PLANS

GENIE+ IS OFFERED AT 10 Animal Kingdom attractions and one character greeting. Avatar Flight of Passage is designated as ILL. As a reminder, the big questions for Genie+ and ILL are

1. Is Genie+ worth paying for at Animal Kingdom?
2. If worth the cost, which attractions benefit most from Genie+ or Individual Lightning Lane?
3. How can you avoid paying for Individual Lightning Lane?
4. How do Genie+ and Individual Lightning Lane work with the touring plans?

GENIE+ AND INDIVIDUAL LIGHTNING LANE (ILL) SELECTIONS AT ANIMAL KINGDOM		
AFRICA		
• The Animation Experience at Conservation Station • *Festival of the Lion King* • Kilimanjaro Safaris		
ASIA		
• Expedition Everest • *Feathered Friends in Flight* • Kali River Rapids		
DINOLAND U.S.A.		
• Dinosaur • *Finding Nemo: The Big Blue . . . and Beyond!*		
DISCOVERY ISLAND		
• *It's Tough to Be a Bug!* • Meet Favorite Disney Pals at Adventurers Outpost		
PANDORA—THE WORLD OF AVATAR		
• Avatar Flight of Passage *(ILL)* • Na'vi River Journey		

Note: Except for Adventurers Outpost, character greetings were not part of Genie+ at press time, but we expect them to return and be part of the Genie+ lineup.

Is Genie+ Worth Paying For at Animal Kingdom?

We think Genie+ is worth the cost at Animal Kingdom if you meet any of these criteria:

- You'll arrive at the park after Early Theme Park Entry begins (that is, you won't be at the park as soon as it opens). This includes off-site guests, who aren't eligible for Early Theme Park Entry, and on-site guests who want to sleep in.
- You won't be using a touring plan.
- You're visiting during a holiday, spring break, or other peak season.

Regardless of the time of year you visit, arriving at park opening should allow you to see at least two of the Animal Kingdom's headliner attractions without significant waits. Since only a few attractions participate in the Genie+ program, it's unlikely that you'd need more than two or three Genie+ reservations per day. On days of heavy attendance, though, the lack of attractions at Animal Kingdom means you'll be competing with lots of other people for Genie+ reservations, pushing out return times, and limiting how many you can obtain.

The table below shows how much time we estimate you'll be able to save using Genie+ with one of our Animal Kingdom touring plans, at three different crowd and Genie+ usage levels (see page 285 for an explanation of the different usage levels):

ESTIMATED TIME SAVINGS USING A TOURING PLAN WITH GENIE+ FOR VARIOUS CROWD LEVELS			
CROWD LEVEL	**TYPICAL USE (5 RESERVATIONS PER DAY)**	**OPTIMISTIC USE (9 RESERVATIONS PER DAY)**	**PERFECT USE (16 RESERVATIONS PER DAY)**
Low	20 minutes saved	40 minutes saved	65 minutes saved
Medium	40 minutes saved	80 minutes saved	130 minutes saved
High	60 minutes saved	100 minutes saved	170 minutes saved

Which Animal Kingdom Attractions Benefit Most from Genie+ or Individual Lightning Lane?

The table below shows the top attractions that might benefit most from using Genie+, based on current and historical wait times.

ANIMAL KINGDOM ATTRACTIONS THAT BENEFIT MOST FROM GENIE+ AND INDIVIDUAL LIGHTNING LANE (ILL) *(Highest Priority to Lowest)*	
ATTRACTION	**AVERAGE TIME IN LINE SAVED (IN MINUTES)**
Avatar Flight of Passage (ILL)	66
Na'vi River Journey	44
Kilimanjaro Safaris	42
Expedition Everest	18
Dinosaur	15
Kali River Rapids	10 (spring, fall, winter); 20 (summer)

Note: We haven't observed any time savings using Genie+ at the Animal Kingdom's live shows, *It's Tough to Be a Bug!,* or The Animation Experience at Conservation Station.

When Do Genie+ and Individual Lightning Lane Reservations Run Out at Animal Kingdom?

The table below shows the approximate times at which the Animal Kingdom's attractions run out of Genie+ or ILL capacity, by attendance level. Use this table in conjunction with the "Which Attractions Benefit Most" table to determine which reservations to get first.

WHEN GENIE+ AND INDIVIDUAL LIGHTNING LANE (ILL) RESERVATIONS RUN OUT BY ATTENDANCE LEVEL			
ATTRACTION	**LOW ATTENDANCE**	**MODERATE ATTENDANCE**	**HIGH ATTENDANCE**
The Animation Experience	Available	Available	Available
Avatar Flight of Passage (ILL)	2 p.m.	10 a.m.	8 a.m.
Festival of the Lion King	Available	Available	Available
Dinosaur	7–8 p.m.	7–8 p.m.	3–5 p.m.
Expedition Everest	Available	8 p.m.	6–8 p.m.
Feathered Friends in Flight	Available	Available	Available
Finding Nemo	Last show	Last show	Last show
It's Tough to Be a Bug!	7 p.m.	7 p.m.	8 p.m.
Kali River Rapids	8 p.m.	7–8 p.m.	7–8 p.m.
Kilimanjaro Safaris	5–6 p.m.	4–5 p.m.	Noon–1 p.m.
Meet Favorite Disney Pals	1 hour to close	4 p.m.	2 p.m.
Na'vi River Journey	7–8 p.m.	5–6 p.m.	1–2 p.m.

AVAILABLE Attractions rarely run out of reservations at this crowd level.
LAST SHOW Reservations are almost always available until the start of the day's last show.
1 HOUR TO CLOSE Reservations are available until an hour before the park closes.
LOW ATTENDANCE Crowd levels 1–3 on the TouringPlans.com crowd calendar
MODERATE ATTENDANCE Crowd levels 4–7 **HIGH ATTENDANCE** Crowd levels 8–10
Attractions closed for more than two years are not shown.

How Can You Avoid Paying for Individual Lightning Lane?

Our touring plans do a good job of getting you to Expedition Everest without long lines, so that's half the battle. Animal Kingdom doesn't participate in Extended Evening Theme Park Hours, so your best option to see Flight of Passage is to stay at a Disney resort and use Early Theme Park Entry. Head to Flight of Passage as soon as the park opens.

How Do Genie+ and Individual Lightning Lane Work with the Touring Plans?

See our advice for the Magic Kingdom on page 286.

The OASIS

THOUGH THE FUNCTIONAL PURPOSE of The Oasis is to funnel guests to the center of the park, it also sets the stage and gets you into the right mood to enjoy Animal Kingdom. There's no one broad thoroughfare but rather multiple paths; each delivers you to Discovery Island at the center of the park, but the path you choose and what you see along the way are up to you. The natural-habitat zoological exhibits are primarily designed for the comfort and well-being of the animals. A sign will identify the animal(s) in each exhibit, but there's no guarantee that the animals will be immediately visible. Because most habitats are large and provide ample places for the occupants to hide, you must concentrate, looking for small movements in the vegetation. The Oasis is a place to linger and appreciate—if you're a blitzer in the morning, definitely set aside some time here on your way out of the park. The Oasis usually closes 30–60 minutes after the rest of the park.

DISCOVERY ISLAND

THIS ISLAND OF TROPICAL GREENERY and whimsical equatorial African architecture connects to the other lands by bridges. Discovery Island is the hub from which guests can access the park's various themed areas; it's also the park's central shopping and services headquarters. For the best selection of Disney merchandise, try **Island Mercantile.** Counter-service food and snacks are available, as is the **Tiffins** sit-down restaurant. In addition to several wildlife exhibits, Discovery Island's **Tree of Life** hosts the film *It's Tough to Be a Bug!* The indoor **Adventurers Outpost** character meet and greet is just before the bridge to Asia.

Walking trails winding behind the Tree of Life offer several animal-viewing opportunities, from otters and kangaroos to lemurs, storks, and porcupines. Besides the animals, you'll find verdant landscaping, waterfalls, and quiet spots to sit and reflect on your relationship with nature.

During the evening hours, the Tree of Life awakens with thousands of lights, as a sound-and-light show is projected onto its branches. **Flik,** your favorite ant from *A Bug's Life,* meets near the entrance to

It's Tough to Be a Bug! Discovery Island is also home to **Pocahontas,** as well as **Russell** and **Dug** from *Up!* The latest addition from the *Up!* gang is **Kevin.** This free-roaming bird loves surprising guests anywhere between the Anandapur Theater in Asia and Discovery Island. Kevin is huge, measuring 10 feet tall from the plumage adorning her head to her feet! Chip 'n' Dale, Daisy Duck, Donald Duck, Goofy, Launchpad McQuack, and Scrooge McDuck can all be found at DinoLand U.S.A. Make sure to check the My Disney Experience app to see which character meet and greets are available.

KEY TO ABBREVIATIONS In the attraction profiles that follow, each star rating is accompanied by a category label in parentheses. **E** means **Exceptional, MAA** means **Much Above Average, AA** means **Above Average, A** means **Average, BA** means **Below Average,** and **MBA** means **Much Below Average.**

AVERAGE WAIT-IN-LINE TIMES This generally uses the attractions' maximum hourly capacity as a fixed reference, as ride capacity is subject to change throughout the year.

Meet Favorite Disney Pals at Adventurers Outpost ★★★½

PRESCHOOL ★★★★★ (E)　**GRADE SCHOOL ★★★★½** (AA)　**TEENS ★★★★** (A)
YOUNG ADULTS ★★★★ (A)　**OVER 30 ★★★★½** (AA)　**SENIORS ★★★★½** (AA)

What it is Character-greeting venue. **Scope and scale** Minor attraction. **When to go** First thing in the morning or after 5 p.m. **Duration of experience** About 2 minutes. **Probable waiting time** About 20 minutes. **Queue speed** Fast. **EVC/wheelchair access** May remain in wheelchair. **Participates in Genie+** Yes. **Early Theme Park Entry** No. **Extended Evening Hours** No.

An indoor, air-conditioned character-greeting location for Mickey and Minnie, Adventurers Outpost is decorated with photos, memorabilia, and souvenirs from the Mouses' world travels. Two greeting rooms house two identical sets of characters, so lines move fairly quickly. Good use of Genie+ if you have kids too small to ride Expedition Everest or Dinosaur.

> You can meet quite a few characters in the park, but my favorite place to meet lots of them is during breakfast at Tusker House.

Lucy

Tree of Life
It's Tough to Be a Bug! ★★★

PRESCHOOL ★★★ (MBA)　**GRADE SCHOOL ★★★½** (MBA)　**TEENS ★★★½** (MBA)
YOUNG ADULTS ★★★½ (MBA)　**OVER 30 ★★★★** (MBA)　**SENIORS ★★★★** (BA)

Awakenings ★★★★

PRESCHOOL ★★★★ (A)　**GRADE SCHOOL ★★★★** (A)　**TEENS ★★★★** (A)
YOUNG ADULTS ★★★★½ (A)　**OVER 30 ★★★★½** (A)　**SENIORS ★★★★½** (AA)

What it is 3-D theater show/nighttime projection show. **Scope and scale** Major attraction. **When to go** Anytime. **Comments** The theater is inside the tree. **Duration of presentation** Approximately 8 minutes. **Probable waiting time** Under 20 minutes. **EVC/wheelchair access** May remain in wheelchair. **Participates in Genie+** Yes (*It's Tough To Be a Bug!* only). **Early Theme Park Entry** Yes. **Extended Evening Hours** No.

Dark   Loud   Scary

Before entering the show, take a close look at the Tree of Life, the remarkable home of the 3-D movie *It's Tough to Be a Bug!* and *Awakenings*, a child-friendly nighttime show projected onto the tree's trunk and canopy. The primary icon and focal point of Animal Kingdom, the tree features a trunk with high-relief carvings depicting 325 animals.

It's Tough to Be a Bug! is cleverly conceived but very intense. For starters, the show is about bugs, and bugs always rank high on the ick-factor scale. That, coupled with some startling special effects and a very loud soundtrack, makes *It's Tough to Be a Bug!* a potential horror show for kids age 7 and under, but you can prepare them by watching *A Bug's Life* before you leave home—many of the characters are the same.

Awakenings, shown several times a night (when the park is open that late), combines digital video projections with music and special effects. We've seen four different 3-minute shows; in each, special projection effects make it appear that some of the animals carved into the tree trunk have come alive. Other special effects happen in the leaves and branches. We rate *Awakenings* as not to be missed.

If you don't like bugs crawling on you, even simulated ones, keep your feet off the floor. The closing line of the show tipped me off when it announced that "honorary bugs [audience members] remain seated while all the lice, bedbugs, maggots, and cockroaches exit first."

Liliane

Wilderness Explorers ★★★★

PRESCHOOL ★★★★½ (A)   GRADE SCHOOL ★★★★½ (AA)   TEENS ★★★½ (BA)
YOUNG ADULTS ★★★★ (A)   OVER 30 ★★★★ (BA)   SENIORS ★★★½ (BA)

What it is Park-wide scavenger hunt and puzzle-solving adventure game. **Scope and scale** Diversion. **When to go** Sign up first thing in the morning, and complete activities throughout the day. **Comments** Collecting all 32 badges takes 3–5 hours and can be done over several days. **EVC/wheelchair access** May remain in wheelchair. **Participates in Genie+** No. **Early Theme Park Entry** No. **Extended Evening Hours** No.

Wilderness Explorers is a scavenger hunt based on Russell's Boy Scout–esque troop from the movie *Up!* Players earn "badges"—stickers given out by cast members—for completing certain activities throughout the park. For example, to earn the Gorilla Badge, you walk the Gorilla Falls Exploration Trail to observe how the primates behave, and then mimic that behavior to a cast member to show what you've seen. Register for the game near the bridge from The Oasis to Discovery Island. You'll be given an instruction book and a map showing the location for each badge to be earned. It's tons of fun for kids and adults; we play it every time we're in the park. Activities are spread throughout the park, including Pandora and some areas where many guests never venture. You have to ride specific attractions to earn certain badges, so visiting those at our suggested times will save you precious touring time.

I love Wilderness Explorers! The interaction between the field guides (cast members) and the young explorers is absolutely fabulous. Make sure to meet Russell and Dug from *Up!* near the entrance to *It's Tough to be a Bug!* It's a great opportunity to get your Wilderness Explorers handbook autographed. Wilderness must be explored!

Liliane

PANDORA:
The World of Avatar

INSPIRED BY JAMES CAMERON'S MOVIE *Avatar,* this land consists of lush flora, winding streams, and meandering paths—an exotic destination that will keep you busy from sunrise to sunset, and beyond!

The Valley of Mo'ara is the port of entry to Pandora. Beautiful during the day, the valley is even more mesmerizing at night, as a mixture of real and artificial plants creates a host of special effects.

The ultimate discovery, however, is the view of the floating mountains of Pandora. Waterfalls seem to float in midair, and a combination of sparkling creeks and canopied paths creates a soothing atmosphere.

LILIANE The inhabitants of Pandora communicate in the Na'vi language, a constructed language such as Sindarin and Quenya, J. R. R. Tolkien's elvish tongues. I love languages, and even though I'm still learning, here are the basics: "Please" is *rutxe,* "thank you" is *irayo,* and "hello" is *kaltxì.*

LILIANE I am not charmed. What ever happened to the Na'vi? I want blue people!

There is much to see, and you will certainly want to return at nightfall, when the exotic, bioluminescent-like plants of Pandora come to life.

If exploring Pandora makes you hungry, the globally inspired **Satu'li Canteen** is the perfect place to sit and enjoy a meal. The snack stand **Pongu Pongu** serves Pandora-inspired specialty drinks.

BRENDAN To enjoy Pandora more, you may want to watch *Avatar* before your visit.

At **Windtraders,** the gift shop, you can find T-shirts, plush toys, and other collectibles. The big hit, however, is the mechanical pet banshee on a leash. The banshee is connected to a small hand unit, allowing you to control your pet by making his head move and his wings flap.

Pandora is a beautifully executed addition to Animal Kingdom, and you don't have to have seen *Avatar* to enjoy the land and its rides. Lines for the rides will be long for the foreseeable future, but simply walking around the immersive themed area is worth your while.

Avatar Flight of Passage   ★★★★½

| PRESCHOOL ★★★ (MBA) | GRADE SCHOOL ★★★★½ (MAA) | TEENS ★★★★★ (E) |
| YOUNG ADULTS ★★★★★ (E) | OVER 30 ★★★★★ (E) | SENIORS ★★★★½ (MAA) |

What it is Flight simulator. **Scope and scale** Super-headliner. **When to go** As soon as the park opens or after 3 p.m. **Comments** One of Disney's most advanced rides; must be 44″ to ride. **Duration of ride** About 6 minutes. **Average wait in line per 100 people ahead of you** About 5 minutes. **Loading speed** Moderate. **EVC/wheelchair access** Must transfer from EVC to provided wheelchair, and then from wheelchair to the ride vehicle; transfer device available. **Participates in Genie+** No (it's an Individual Lightning Lane attraction). **Early Theme Park Entry** Yes. **Extended Evening Hours** No.

Queasy

The queue and preshow of this ride take you through caves covered with petroglyphs and paintings, nocturnal jungle scenes, and the Alpha Centauri Expedition (ACE) research center. The laboratory displays experiments and studies about the planet's wildlife. Nothing, however, is as mesmerizing as the sight of the sleeping Na'vi avatar floating inside a huge water-filled tube. The avatar moves only so slightly, never awakening, yet it's difficult to take your eyes away from him.

At the end of the queue, guests are taken, 16 at a time, into a room where they are "decontaminated" in preparation for their flight and watch a video. In the next room, guests are handed 3-D glasses and mount what looks like 16 bicycles; restraints are deployed along your calves and lower back, ensuring that you don't fall off during your flight.

The Flight of Passage line is boring, and so is the video you watch, especially if you haven't seen the movie. The ride is scary-fun. Fun because you get to see Pandora, and scary when you go through caves, really high up in the sky, and underwater. Next time I will ride it with my eyes open longer. **Felicity**

Now connected with your banshee, the room goes dark, and with a flash of light similar to going into hyperspace on Star Tours, guests are off on a simulated flight. As you fly over Pandora's plains, soar through its mountains, and skim its sea, you can hear and feel the banshee breathing beneath you.

The banshee vibrates like it's breathing. It's so cool.

Sabrina The ride is just a tad wilder than EPCOT's Soarin' Around the World, and most guests will be able to tolerate the movements and special effects. Unlike Soarin' you will not have other guests' feet dangling overhead, but you can still see other riders next to you. Depending on where you are seated, you will see all of the riders when you divert your attention from the screen. The flight over Pandora is absolutely amazing and the visuals stunning, so keep your eyes on that screen and enjoy what is the most exciting simulated ride we have ever experienced.

Flight of Passage is super intense and so much fun.

Note that the bikes do not accommodate riders of all body shapes; they are not suitable for larger riders. A tall Oklahoman experienced this issue: **Brendan**

I am 6'6", and I was too tall to ride. Two others from my pod were also too tall/large.

The snug restraint system, coupled with the confined space of the room, may cause some claustrophobic guests to exit before riding.

Last but not least, while the ride's queue is absolutely stunning, you don't want to be stuck in it—the queue can absorb 3-4 hours of waiting guests inside the attraction itself. At times cast members direct the queue all the way along the path toward Africa and back before you reach the actual queue of the attraction.

Flight of Passage remains one of the most popular rides at Disney World, and it can be difficult to figure out how to ride without devoting half a day to standing in line.

The other primary complicating factor is how variable the park's opening procedure is. A reader from Napa, California, shares this typical experience:

We did rope drop at Animal Kingdom during spring break on a day with park opening at 7 a.m. for resort guests. By 6:30 a.m., the line to get in was out in the parking lot. It's also kind of stressful with everyone bumping into each other trying to get to Flight of Passage.

There are several reasons for the erratic park-opening procedures, but it's primarily a matter of safety and traffic control. To forestall a huge mob at the park entrance and an ensuing (and possibly dangerous) stampede to Pandora, Disney elects to absorb the crowd as it arrives and usher guests safely into a queue. But Animal Kingdom's walkways are the narrowest in all the Disney theme parks, which creates choke points. This makes getting guests out of the rushing current and into a calm eddy even more critical.

The tide of arrivals is stunning every morning, when buses disgorge hordes of resort guests at the park entrance.

If your intent is to be among the first in the park:

1. Check online or call the night before to confirm official park-opening time.

2. On-site guests should arrive 60 minutes before official opening; off-site guests should arrive 30 minutes before official opening.

3. Don't depend on Disney transportation. Use a cab or ride service rather than your own car, so you don't get stuck waiting to pay for parking.

4. Have your admission in hand, thus avoiding the ticket booth.

5. Look for a turnstile that seems to be processing people smoothly. (We got hung up for 15 minutes because of an erratic finger scanner.)

6. There are restrooms to the left of the entrance. If you need to use them, Disney has a process for letting you go and rejoin your party, but it involves everyone waiting to reunite at the first Genie+ checkpoint.

7. Walk briskly to Pandora. Once there (or at some point before), a cast member will place you in the queue for Flight of Passage.

8. If you can't arrive at park opening or stay until closing, we think purchasing Individual Lightning Lane for Flight of Passage is worth the cost.

Na'vi River Journey ★★★★

PRESCHOOL ★★★★ (A)   **GRADE SCHOOL ★★★★** (BA)   **TEENS ★★★½** (MBA)
YOUNG ADULTS ★★★½ (MBA)   **OVER 30 ★★★★** (BA)   **SENIORS ★★★★** (BA)

What it is Boat ride. **Scope and scale** Headliner. **When to go** Before 9:30 a.m. or in the last 2 hours before closing. **Duration of ride** 5 minutes. **Average wait in line per 100 people ahead of you** About 5 minutes. **Loading speed** Moderate. **EVC/wheelchair access** Must transfer from EVC to the ride vehicle; transfer device available. **Participates in Genie+** Yes. **Early Theme Park Entry** Yes. **Extended Evening Hours** No.

A less exciting but absolutely charming experience awaits you at the family-friendly Na'vi River Journey boat ride. Travel through the nighttime jungle on a sacred river, discover the creatures of the rainforest, and meet the Na'vi shaman of songs. She is the most sophisticated animatronic we have ever seen, and it's impossible not to fall under her spell.

There is no height restriction for the ride; while it is a dark ride, it's not scary at all. We think of the ride as It's a Small World on steroids.

The queue of the ride, while filled with beautiful details, is not built to handle huge crowds. Ride before 9:30 a.m. or in the last 2 hours before closing if the lines are not long.

Eywa ngahu, a popular greeting in the Na'vi language, means "May Eywa be with you." It sure feels as if Eywa is with you on this ride, as Eywa keeps the ecosystem of Pandora in perfect equilibrium.

Liliane

The first Avatar *movie was released in 2009 and was the world's top-grossing film for a decade, earning $2.8 billion. Four more sequels are scheduled to be released, with* Avatar 2 *hitting screens December 16, 2022. As for the other three movies, not even James Cameron knows.*

The Na'vi River Journey is a beautiful ride, but it really is just another boat ride. Don't stand in line for it too long.

Isabelle

The Na'vi River Journey makes you feel like you're visiting a different world. It's quite dark, but that's OK because it's all lit up with lights from another planet. The music and the realistic shaman at the end are amazing.

Felicity

AFRICA

GUESTS ENTER THE LARGEST of Animal Kingdom's lands through **Harambe,** Disney's idealized and sanitized version of a modern rural African town, with shops, a sit-down buffet, limited counter service, and snack stands. It serves as the gateway to the African veld habitat, Animal Kingdom's largest zoological exhibit. Access the veld via **Kilimanjaro Safaris.** Harambe is also the departure point for the train to **Rafiki's Planet Watch** and **Conservation Station** (the park's veterinary headquarters), and it's home to *Festival of the Lion King,* a long-running live show. A walkway by *Lion King* connects Africa to Pandora.

Festival of the Lion King   ★★★★

TEENS ★★★★ (AA)   ALL OTHER AGE GROUPS ★★★★½ (MAA)

What it is Theater-in-the-round stage show. **Scope and scale** Major attraction. **When to go** Before 11 a.m. or after 4 p.m. Check My Disney Experience app for showtimes. **Duration of presentation** 30 minutes. **Preshow entertainment** None. **Probable waiting time** 20-30 minutes. **EVC/wheelchair access** May remain in wheelchair. **Participates in Genie+** Yes. **Early Theme Park Entry** No. **Extended Evening Hours** No.

Fantastic pageantry, dazzling costumes, a mini Broadway show, and air-conditioning too. *Festival of the Lion King* was the precursor to the Broadway production of *The Lion King.*

Try to score front-row seats. Kids are invited to play musical instruments and join the performance. (Your chances are best if you're celebrating a special day.) Ask a cast member if a cast meet and greet will occur after the performance.

Liliane

The show is based on the animated feature The Lion King, *a must-see movie. Did you know that James Earl Jones, the voice of Mufasa (father of Simba), was also the voice of Darth Vader in several of the* Star Wars *movies?*

I love the movie and the show. I was picked to shake maracas and walk around with the performers—that was very cool.

Felicity

If you do not like to go on a fast ride, go see the *Lion King* show.

Sabrina

One of my favorite shows at the Animal Kingdom is *The Festival of the Lion King.* It gets a 10 out of 10 and is not to be missed.

Lucy

Gorilla Falls Exploration Trail ★★★★

PRESCHOOL ★★★★ (A)   GRADE SCHOOL ★★★★ (A)   TEENS ★★★★ (A)
YOUNG ADULTS ★★★★½ (AA) OVER 30 ★★★★½ (A) SENIORS ★★★★½ (AA)

What it is Walk-through zoological exhibit. **Scope and scale** Major attraction. **When to go** Before or after Kilimanjaro Safaris. Also check the My Disney Experience app for early off-season closures. **Duration of tour** About 20–25 minutes. **EVC/wheelchair access** May remain in wheelchair. **Participates in Genie+** No. **Early Theme Park Entry** No. **Extended Evening Hours** No.

The Gorilla Falls Exploration Trail is lush, beautiful, and filled with people much of the time—particularly unpleasant if you have to wiggle your way through with a stroller. Walk the trail before 10 a.m. or after 4:30 p.m., or get a Genie+ return time for Kilimanjaro Safaris for 60–90 minutes after the park opens. That's long enough for an uncrowded, leisurely tour of the trail and a quick snack before you go on safari.

Kilimanjaro Safaris ★★★★★

SENIORS ★★★★★ (E)   ALL OTHER AGE GROUPS ★★★★½ (MAA)

What it is Ride through a simulated African wildlife reservation. **Scope and scale** Super-headliner. **When to go** As soon as the park opens or after 3 p.m **Duration of ride** About 20 minutes. **Average wait in line per 100 people ahead of you** 4 minutes; assumes full-capacity operation with 18-second dispatch interval. **Loading speed** Fast. **EVC/wheelchair access** Must transfer from EVC to provided wheelchair. **Participates in Genie+** Yes. **Early Theme Park Entry** No. **Extended Evening Hours** No.

Off you go in an open safari vehicle through a simulated African savanna, looking for hippos, zebras, giraffes, lions, and rhinos. Many readers have asked us whether fewer animals are visible from Kilimanjaro Safaris around lunchtime than at park opening, out of concern that the animals might be less active in the midday heat. To help answer that question, we sent a team of researchers to ride continuously during one week in the summer and had them count the number and type of animals visible at different times of day. Our results indicate that you'll probably see the same number of animals regardless of when you visit. This finding is almost certainly due to Disney's deliberate placement of water, food, and shade near the safari vehicles. Animal Kingdom also offers a nighttime version of Kilimanjaro Safaris. Here are the details: The path through the African savanna is adjusted during these sunset tours, and the trucks make longer stops, allowing guests more time to spot animals. The start time for the nighttime tours depends on what time the sun sets. Some amazing technology ensures that the magical sunset lasts about 4–5 hours every night. To give the animals the rest they need, different animals are in the savanna at night.

I absolutely love Kilimanjaro Safaris, day and night. Remember, flash photography is NOT allowed during the nighttime safari.

Liliane

I liked seeing the animals up close. It was very funny to see an elephant doing a poo and a wee.

Felicity

If you want to see lots of animals on Kilimanjaro Safaris, it's best to go early in the morning. I think the animals are more awake and active because they're being fed.

Lucy

RAFIKI'S PLANET WATCH

THIS AREA ISN'T REALLY A LAND. Disney uses the name as an umbrella for Conservation Station, the petting zoo, and the environmental exhibits accessible from Harambe via the Wildlife Express Train. The educational area features a few new enhancements, experiences based on Disney's animated feature *The Lion King*, and **The Animation Experience.** Check the My Disney Experience app before you trek out there; the area opens later than the rest of the park.

The Animation Experience at Conservation Station ★★★

PRESCHOOL ★★½ (MBA)   **GRADE SCHOOL** ★★★★ (A)   **TEENS** ★★★★½ (MAA)
YOUNG ADULTS ★★★★ (AA)   **OVER 30** ★★★★½ (MAA)   **SENIORS** ★★★★½ (MAA)

What it is Character-drawing class. **Scope and scale** Minor attraction.
When to go Check the My Disney Experience app for hours. **Comments** Accessible only by the Wildlife Express Train. Fun but out of place in this theme park. **Participates in Genie+** Yes. **Early Theme Park Entry** No. **Extended Evening Hours** No.

Thumbs Up for the Whole Family

In this 25-minute class, guests learn to draw some of Disney's most famous animal characters. The Animation Experience is in a remote section of the park, so crowds shouldn't be large during the early and late parts of the day. Only use Genie+ here if you're out of other things to use it on.

Conservation Station and Affection Section ★★★

PRESCHOOL ★★★½ (A)   **GRADE SCHOOL** ★★★★ (A)   **TEENS** ★★★ (MBA)
YOUNG ADULTS ★★★ (MBA)   **OVER 30** ★★★½ (BA)   **SENIORS** ★★★½ (BA)

What it is Behind-the-scenes educational exhibit and petting zoo. **Scope and scale** Minor attraction. **When to go** Anytime. **Comments** Opens later and closes earlier than the rest of the park. Check My Disney Experience for hours. Accessible only by the Wildlife Express Train. **Probable waiting time** None. **EVC/wheelchair access** May remain in wheelchair. **Participates in Genie+** No. **Early Theme Park Entry** No. **Extended Evening Hours** No.

This is the Animal Kingdom's veterinary and conservation headquarters, where guests can meet wildlife experts, observe ongoing projects, and learn about park operations. It includes a rehabilitation area for injured animals, a nursery for recently born (or hatched) critters, and a petting zoo (Affection Section).

What you see will largely depend on what's going on when you arrive. Some readers think there isn't enough happening to warrant waiting in line twice (coming and going) for the train, but others, such as this university biologist from Springfield, Missouri, have had better luck:

If you get to Conservation Station between 10 a.m. and noon, you can see the vet techs actually doing some routine procedures as they maintain the health of the animals. Our 7-year-old aspiring vet LOVED visiting with the technician. She spent 20 minutes asking her all kinds of questions.

Conservation Station is interesting, but you have to invest a little effort, and it helps to be inquisitive. Because it's so removed from the rest of the park, you'll never bump into Conservation Station unless you take the train round-trip from Harambe.

Wildlife Express Train ★★

PRESCHOOL ★★★★ (A) **GRADE SCHOOL ★★★★** (A) **TEENS ★★★** (MBA)
YOUNG ADULTS ★★★ (MBA) **OVER 30 ★★★½** (BA) **SENIORS ★★★½** (BA)

Thumbs Up for the Whole Family

What it is Scenic railroad ride to Rafiki's Planet Watch and Conservation Station. **When to go** Anytime. **Comments** Opens 90 minutes after rest of park; last train departs at 4:30 p.m. **Duration of ride** About 7 minutes one-way. **Average wait in line per 100 people ahead of you** 9 minutes. **Loading speed** Moderate. **EVC/wheelchair access** May remain in wheelchair. **Participates in Genie+** No. **Early Theme Park Entry** No. **Extended Evening Hours** No.

Take the train only if you have small kids who would really enjoy the Affection Section petting zoo. If you have a future veterinarian in your family, it's also worth checking out the behind-the-scenes exhibits at Conservation Station. All ages will enjoy The Animation Experience.

◼ ASIA

CROSSING THE BRIDGE FROM DISCOVERY ISLAND, you enter this land through the village of **Anandapur**, a veritable collage of Asian themes inspired by the architecture and ruins of India, Thailand, Indonesia, and Nepal. Anandapur provides access to an animal exhibit and to Asia's two feature attractions, the **Kali River Rapids** whitewater raft ride and **Expedition Everest**. Also in Asia is *Feathered Friends in Flight*, an educational production about birds, and **Kite Tales**, a set of inflated balloon-kites pulled around a lagoon by performers on Jet Skis.

Expedition Everest ★★★★½

PRESCHOOL ★★½ (MBA) **GRADE SCHOOL ★★★★½** (MAA) **TEENS ★★★★★** (E)
YOUNG ADULTS ★★★★★ (E) **OVER 30 ★★★★½** (MAA) **SENIORS ★★★½** (AA)

What it is High-speed outdoor roller coaster through a Nepalese mountain village. **Scope and scale** Super-headliner. **When to go** First or last hour the park is open. **Comments** Must be 44″ to ride; Rider Switch option provided (see page 260); single-rider line available. Not to be missed. **Duration of ride** 4 minutes. **Average wait in line per 100 people ahead of you** 4 minutes; assumes 2 tracks operating. **Loading speed** Moderate-fast. **EVC/wheelchair access** Must transfer to the ride vehicle. **Participates in Genie+** Yes. **Early Theme Park Entry** Yes. **Extended Evening Hours** No.

Lose Things Scary

As you enjoy one of the most spectacular panoramas in Walt Disney World, you wish this expedition would never end. But you get over that in a hurry as the train starts whirring through the guts of Disney's largest man-made mountain. After a high-speed encounter with a large, smelly (and often AWOL) yeti and a dead stop at the base camp of Mount Everest, the 50-mile-per-hour chase continues backward. The ride is very smooth and is rich in both visuals and special effects. The backward segment is one of the most creative and exciting 20 seconds in the annals of roller coasters.

Felicity

I didn't like this ride, not one bit. It made me feel really sick.

Be on the lookout for the yeti toward the end of Expedition Everest.

Isabelle

Kali River Rapids ★★★½

PRESCHOOL, YOUNG ADULTS, AND OVER 30 ★★★★ (A)
GRADE SCHOOL ★★★★½ (MAA)   TEENS ★★★★½ (AA)   SENIORS ★★★★ (BA)

What it is Whitewater raft ride. **Scope and scale** Headliner. **When to go** Before 11 a.m. or in the last hour the park is open. **Comments** You're likely to get wet; may open 30 minutes after the rest of the park and close early on off-peak or cold days; must be 38″ tall to ride; Rider Switch option provided (see page 260). **Duration of ride** About 5 minutes. **Average wait in line per 100 people ahead of you** 5 minutes. **Loading speed** Moderate. **EVC/wheelchair access** Must transfer to the ride vehicle; transfer device available. **Participates in Genie+** Yes. **Early Theme Park Entry** No. **Extended Evening Hours** No.

 This tame raft ride lets you take in the outstanding scenery as you drift through a dense rainforest, past waterfalls and temple ruins. There are neither big drops nor terrifying rapids; nevertheless, Disney still manages to drench you. Nonriding park guests, especially those who don't meet the height requirement, will take great pleasure in squirting water at the rafters from above.

If you ride early in the morning or on a cool day, use raingear and make sure your shoes stay dry. Touring in wet clothes is no fun, and walking all day in soaked sneakers is a recipe for blisters.

Liliane

 Kali River Rapids can get you anywhere from sprinkled with water to soaking wet. Make sure your possessions are protected. A wet wallet and a soaked cell phone are no fun.

A. J.

Oh my goodness, this ride is trouble. I rode it with my dad, and we got drenched. The line is fun, like a nature walk. Watch out for people squirting you with water! If you don't want to walk around in dripping wet clothes, wear a poncho.

Felicity

Maharajah Jungle Trek ★★★★

PRESCHOOL ★★★★ (A)   **GRADE SCHOOL ★★★★** (A)   **TEENS ★★★★** (A)
YOUNG ADULTS ★★★★½ (AA)   OVER 30 ★★★★ (A)   **SENIORS ★★★★½ (A)**

What it is Walk-through zoological exhibit. **Scope and scale** Headliner. **When to go** Anytime it's open. **Comment** May open later and close earlier than rest of park. **Duration of tour** About 20–30 minutes. **EVC/wheelchair access** May remain in wheelchair. **Participates in Genie+** No. **Early Theme Park Entry** No. **Extended Evening Hours** No.

The Jungle Trek is less congested than the Gorilla Falls Exploration Trail and is a good choice for midday touring. Tigers, water buffalo, and birds are waiting to be discovered along a path winding through the fabulous ruins of the maharajah's palace.

Feathered Friends in Flight ★★★★

ALL AGE GROUPS ★★★★½ (MAA)

What it is Stadium show about birds. **Scope and scale** Major attraction. **When to go** Anytime. **Special comment** Performance times listed in park map or the My Disney Experience app. **Duration of presentation** 30 minutes. **Preshow entertainment** None. **When to arrive** 10–15 minutes before showtime. **EVC/wheelchair access** May remain in wheelchair. **Participates in Genie+** Yes. **Early Theme Park Entry** No. **Extended Evening Hours** No.

Thumbs Up for the Whole Family

Feathered Friends in Flight debuted in summer 2020. Hosted by some of Disney's animal trainers, who explain different bird species' habitats and characteristics. Several species are represented, with plenty more flying overhead. The show is fast-paced, informative, and entertaining for everyone. In many ways, the show is a model of how other shows in the park might work. We rate it as not to be missed.

Like its predecessor, *Feathered Friends in Flight* focuses on the birds' natural talents and characteristics, which far surpass any tricks learned from humans—don't expect parrots riding bikes or cockatoos playing tiny pianos. A Brattleboro, Vermont, reader found the birds extremely compelling:

> *The birds are thrilling, and we especially appreciated the fact that their antics were not the results of training against the grain but actual survival techniques that the birds use in the wild.*

Feathered Friends plays at the stadium near the bridge on the walkway into Asia. Although the stadium is covered, it is not air-conditioned; thus, early-morning and late-afternoon performances are more comfortable. To play it safe, get to the stadium about 10–15 minutes before showtime.

▌ DINOLAND U.S.A.

THIS MOST TYPICALLY DISNEY of Animal Kingdom's lands is a cross between an anthropological dig and a quirky roadside attraction. Accessible via the bridge from Discovery Island, DinoLand U.S.A. is home to a children's play area, a nature trail, and a thrill ride (Dinosaur). It's also home to *Finding Nemo—The Big Blue . . . and Beyond!* shown at The Theater in the Wild. **Donald, Daisy, Goofy, Chip 'n' Dale, Launchpad McQuack,** and **Scrooge McDuck** all make appearances here.

We think that DinoLand U.S.A. needs some major TLC. With the Primeval Whirl coaster demolished, the land is lacking rides and in need of refurbishments. Whether this is in the form of an overhaul or a retheming remains to be seen.

The Boneyard ★★★½

PRESCHOOL ★★★★½ (MAA)   GRADE SCHOOL ★★★★½ (MAA)   TEENS ★★★ (MBA)
YOUNG ADULTS ★★ (MBA)   OVER 30 ★★★ (MBA)   SENIORS ★★ (MBA)

What it is Elaborate playground. **Scope and scale** Diversion. **When to go** Anytime. **Comments** Opens 1 hour after rest of park. **Duration of experience** Varies. **Probable waiting time** None. **EVC/wheelchair access** May remain in wheelchair. **Participates in Genie+** No. **Early Theme Park Entry** No. **Extended Evening Hours** No.

Time to play! This elaborate playground for kids age 12 and younger is a great place for them to let off steam and get dirty (or at least sandy). The playground equipment consists of skeletal replicas of *Triceratops, Tyrannosaurus rex, Brachiosaurus,* and the like. In addition, there are climbing mazes, as well as sandpits where little ones can scrounge for bones and fossils.

The Boneyard can get very hot in the scorching Florida sun, so make sure your kids are properly hydrated and protected against sunburn. The playground is huge, and parents might lose sight of a small child. Fortunately, however, there's only one entrance and exit. Your little ones are going to love The Boneyard, so resign yourself to staying awhile.

Dinosaur ★★★★

PRESCHOOL ★★½ (MBA) **GRADE SCHOOL** ★★★½ (BA) **TEENS** ★★★★ (A)
YOUNG ADULTS ★★★★ (A) **OVER 30** ★★★★ (A) **SENIORS** ★★★½ (MBA)

What it is Motion-simulator dark ride. **Scope and scale** Headliner. **When to go** Before 10:30 a.m. or after 4 p.m. **Comments** Must be 40" tall to ride; Rider Switch option provided (see page 260). **Duration of ride** 3½ minutes. **Average wait in line per 100 people ahead of you** 3 minutes; assumes full-capacity operation with 18-second dispatch interval. **Loading speed** Fast. **EVC/wheelchair access** Must transfer to the ride vehicle. **Participates in Genie+** Yes. **Early Theme Park Entry** Yes. **Extended Evening Hours** No.

Here you board a time capsule to return to the Jurassic age in an effort to bring back a live dinosaur before a meteor hits Earth and wipes them out. The bad guy in this epic is the little-known *Carnotaurus*, an evil-eyed, long-in-the-tooth, *Tyrannosaurus rex*-type fellow. A combination track ride and motion simulator, Dinosaur is not for the faint of heart—you get tossed and pitched around in the dark, with pesky dinosaurs jumping out at you. Dinosaur has left many an adult weak-kneed. Most kids under age 9 find it terrifying.

Dinosaur is one of my favorite rides at Animal Kingdom, but it might scare the poop out of little kids. Make sure you warn them before going on the ride.

A. J.

Theater in the Wild /
Finding Nemo—The Big Blue . . . and Beyond! ★★★★

TOO NEW TO RATE

Thumbs Up for the Whole Family

What it is Enclosed venue for live stage shows. **Scope and scale** Major attraction. **When to go** Anytime. **Comment** Check your park map or My Disney Experience for showtimes. **Duration of presentation** 25 minutes. **Probable waiting time** 30 minutes. **When to arrive** 30 minutes before showtime. **EVC/wheelchair access** May remain in wheelchair. **Participates in Genie+** Yes. **Early Theme Park Entry** No. **Extended Evening Hours** No.

Before the pandemic, *Finding Nemo—The Musical* was arguably the most elaborate live show in any Disney World theme park. Incorporating dancing, special effects, and sophisticated digital backdrops of the undersea world, it featured human performers retelling Nemo's story with colorful, larger-than-life puppets.

While the new, updated show is 15 minutes shorter than the original, it is still Broadway-quality and an absolute must-see.

To get a seat, show up 20–25 minutes in advance for morning and late-afternoon shows and 30–35 minutes early for shows scheduled noon–4:30 p.m. Access to the theater is via a relatively narrow pedestrian path; if you arrive as the previous show is letting out, you'll feel like a salmon swimming upstream.

When the line is very long, don't assume that you'll get into the next show just by queuing up. Ask a cast member whether you're likely to get into the next show.

Liliane

TriceraTop Spin ★★

PRESCHOOL ★★★★½ (MAA) **GRADE SCHOOL ★★★★ (BA)** **TEENS ★★★ (MBA)**
YOUNG ADULTS ★★½ (MBA) **OVER 30 ★★★ (MBA)** **SENIORS ★★★½ (MBA)**

What it is Hub-and-spoke midway ride. **Scope and scale** Minor attraction. **When to go** Before noon or after 3 p.m. **Duration of ride** 1½ minutes. **Average wait in line per 100 people ahead of you** 10 minutes. **Loading speed** Slow. **EVC/wheelchair access** Must transfer from EVC to provided wheelchair. **Participates in Genie+** No. **Early Theme Park Entry** Yes. **Extended Evening Hours** No.

Instead of Dumbo, you get Dino spinning around a central axis. It's fun for little ones, but this slow-loader is infamous for inefficiency and long waits.

Kite Tales ★★

PRESCHOOL ★★★★ (BA) **GRADE SCHOOL ★★★★ (BA)** **TEENS ★★★½ (MBA)**
YOUNG ADULTS ★★★½ (MBA) **OVER 30 ★★★½ (BA)** **SENIORS ★★★½ (BA)**

What it is Water-based kite show. **Scope and scale** Diversion. **When to go** See performance schedule. **Comment** Subject to cancellation due to inclement weather. **Duration of show** About 8 minutes. **EVC/wheelchair access** May remain in wheelchair. **Participates in Genie+** No. **Early Theme Park Entry** No. **Extended Evening Hours** No.

Designed as entertainment for the Animal Kingdom during Disney World's 50th anniversary, Kite Tales opened to mixed reviews. The premise is about as simple as it gets: A set of inflated balloon-kites are pulled by performers on Jet Skis around the lagoon formed by the Discovery River, all set to music. There's no plot, story, or dialog, and the audience sits in the direct sun.

Kite Tales is rated below average by every age group, so getting in isn't difficult. If it's not too hot outside, try to find a seat where the sun is partially blocked by trees. The outdoor show may not run in the event of high winds or poor weather.

LIVE ENTERTAINMENT
at ANIMAL KINGDOM

NOTE THAT NOT ALL MUSICAL ACTS or character meetings are available every day, so check the My Disney Experience app for showtimes. Also, WDW live-entertainment guru Steve Soares usually posts the Animal Kingdom performance schedule about a week in advance at wdwent.com.

ANIMAL ENCOUNTERS Throughout the day, Disney staff conduct short, impromptu lectures on specific animals at the park. Look for a cast member in safari garb holding a bird, reptile, or small mammal.

CHARACTER CAVALCADES In place of parades and other live entertainment that has not yet returned, small boats whisk Disney characters on the waterway around Discovery Island, each to its own soundtrack. Characters include Chip 'n' Dale, Donald and other characters from *DuckTales,* Pocahontas and friends, the *Lion King* cast, and Mickey and

Minnie Mouse. Characters appear regularly starting about an hour after park opening, but not at specific times. The spot where you can see the characters the closest is under the bridge on the walkway between Pandora and Africa.

DONALD'S DINO-BASH (*temporarily unavailable*) Donald Duck takes over DinoLand U.S.A. to celebrate his recent discovery that ducks are descendants of dinosaurs. Characters usually appear intermittently starting at 10 a.m., as follows: **Chip 'n' Dale,** across from TriceraTop Spin until 4:30 p.m.; **Daisy, Donald, and Goofy** until 5:30 p.m. at Chester and Hester's Dino-Rama; and **Launchpad McQuack and Scrooge McDuck** at The Boneyard until 4 p.m.

HOLIDAY EVENTS Holiday decorations in the form of animal-inspired luminaries are found at Discovery Island, and during the day, life-size puppets of winter animals, such as reindeers, foxes, polar bears, and penguins, interact with guests. The Tree of Life's *Awakenings* show gets an overlay of a series of wintry tales.

Africa's village of Harambe offers holiday presentations, and diners at Tusker House will be treated to much holiday cheer by Mickey and friends.

Expats living on Pandora display kitschy holiday decor, mixing vintage Earth pieces with handcrafted items made from materials native to Pandora.

STREET PERFORMERS Far and away the most intriguing is the performer you can't see—at least not at first. A perfect fusion between fantasy and reality, **DiVine** (★★★★) is an artist best described as half vine and half creeping plant. She blends perfectly with the foliage at Animal Kingdom and is noticeable only when she moves—which can be quite startling if you're not aware of her presence. DiVine is most often found at The Oasis; if you don't encounter her, ask a cast member when and where she can be found. Videos of her are available on YouTube (go to youtube.com and search for "DiVine Disney's Animal Kingdom").

FAVORITE EATS AT ANIMAL KINGDOM

DISCOVERY ISLAND **Flame Tree Barbecue** | Ribs and chicken with baked beans **Pizzafari** | Pizza, Romaine salad with chicken, and garlic knots.

AFRICA **Tamu Tamu Eats & Refreshments** | Dole Whips and sundaes **Tusker House Restaurant** | Moroccan-spiced beef, spit-roasted herb chicken, and berbere-marinated pork; animal-inspired mini cakes for dessert. Tusker House has a character breakfast, lunch, and dinner featuring Donald, Daisy, Goofy, and Mickey. | *Buffet*

ASIA **Yak & Yeti Restaurant** | Korean beef and coconut shrimp | *Table service only*

DINOLAND U.S.A. **Restaurantosaurus** | All-beef foot-long hot dog, Cobb salad with chicken, and angus cheeseburger; kid's cheeseburger or chicken nuggets served in a sand pail, complete with a shovel

OUTSIDE ENTRANCE **Rainforest Cafe** | Beef lava nachos; ribs, steak, and shrimp trio. Breakfast, lunch, and dinner in a tropical rainforest setting with a huge saltwater aquarium, gorillas going wild once in a while, and simulated thunderstorms. The place to take the kids if you want to sit down! They'll love you for it. | *Table service only*

But DiVine isn't the only performer worth seeing. The park's most popular live performers are found in Africa, including the **Tam Tam Drummers of Harambe** (★★★★) and a harp-playing act called **Kora Tinga Tinga** (★★★★). The **Viva Gaia Street Band** (★★★★) plays high-energy sets across from Flame Tree Barbecue on Discovery Island.

TREE OF LIFE/*AWAKENINGS* This nighttime show plays several times per night at the Tree of Life. It combines digital video projections with music; special projection effects make it appear that some animals carved into the tree trunk have come alive. Each show lasts about 3 minutes and features an original musical score. It's a must-see.

WINGED ENCOUNTERS—THE KINGDOM TAKES FLIGHT This outdoor show features macaws and their handlers in front of the Tree of Life. Guests can talk to the trainers and see the birds fly around the middle of the park. The show occurs several times throughout the day. Check the My Disney Experience app for times.

ANIMAL KINGDOM TOURING PLANS

OUR STEP-BY-STEP TOURING PLANS are field-tested, independently verified itineraries that will keep you moving counter to the crowd flow. The plans will also allow you to see as much as possible in a day with minimal time waiting in line. Because Animal Kingdom has fewer attractions than the other parks, it's possible to experience them all in a single day, even when traveling with young children.

The different touring plans are described below. The descriptions will tell you for whom or for what situation the plans are designed. The actual touring plans are located on pages 501–504. Each plan includes a numbered map of the park to help you find your way around.

Each plan lists the attractions most likely to need Genie+ or Individual Lightning Lane and the approximate return times for which you should try to make reservations. Visit TouringPlans.com if any attractions or times need changing, either while planning or in the parks.

1-DAY TOURING PLAN FOR PARENTS WITH SMALL CHILDREN This plan is designed for parents of children ages 3–8 who wish to see the very best age-appropriate attractions in the Animal Kingdom. Every attraction has a rating of at least three-and-a-half stars (out of five) from preschool and grade-school children surveyed by *The Unofficial Guide*. Special advice is provided for touring the park with small children, including restaurant recommendations. The plan keeps walking and backtracking to a minimum.

1-DAY SLEEPYHEAD TOURING PLAN FOR PARENTS WITH SMALL CHILDREN A relaxed plan that allows families with small children to sleep late and still see the highlights of the Animal Kingdom. The plan begins around 11 a.m., sets aside ample time for lunch, and includes the best child-friendly attractions in the park.

1-DAY TOURING PLAN FOR TWEENS AND THEIR PARENTS This plan for parents with kids ages 8–12 includes every attraction rated three stars and higher by this age group and sets aside ample time for lunch.

1-DAY HAPPY FAMILY TOURING PLAN This plan for families of all ages includes time-saving tips for teens and adults visiting the park's thrill rides, as well as age-appropriate attractions for parents with small children. The entire family stays together as much as possible (including for lunch), but this plan allows groups with different interests to explore their favorite attractions without everyone having to wait around.

BEFORE YOU GO

1. Call ☎ 407-824-4321 or check disneyworld.com for operating hours.
2. Purchase admission and make park reservations.
3. Familiarize yourself with park-opening procedures, and reread the touring plan you've chosen.

DISNEY'S ANIMAL KINGDOM TRIVIA QUIZ

1. Which attraction is inside the iconic Tree of Life?
   - **a.** Pocahontas and Her Forest Friends
   - **b.** *It's Tough to Be a Bug!*
   - **c.** Wilderness Explorers
   - **d.** *Feathered Friends in Flight*

2. What parade ran for 14 years at Animal Kingdom?
   - **a.** Festival of Fantasy Parade
   - **b.** Festival of the Lion King Parade
   - **c.** Mickey's Jammin' Jungle Parade
   - **d.** Mickey's Soundsational Parade

3. In which land do you find Kali River Rapids?
   - **a.** Africa
   - **b.** India
   - **c.** Thailand
   - **d.** Asia

4. What show plays at Theater in the Wild?
   - **a.** *Indiana Jones Epic Stunt Spectacular!*
   - **b.** *Voyage of the Little Mermaid*
   - **c.** *Finding Nemo—The Big Blue . . . and Beyond!*
   - **d.** *Beauty and the Beast Live on Stage!*

5. Which restaurant can be accessed without paying for admission to Animal Kingdom?
   - **a.** Tusker House
   - **b.** Rainforest Cafe
   - **c.** Flame Tree Barbecue
   - **d.** Yak & Yeti

6. The newest land in Animal Kingdom is based on which movie?
   - **a.** *The Jungle Book*
   - **b.** *Avatar*
   - **c.** *Tarzan*
   - **d.** *A Bug's Life*

7. Which one of the following attractions can only be experienced in a vehicle?
   - **a.** Gorilla Falls Exploration Trail
   - **b.** Wilderness Explorers
   - **c.** Kilimanjaro Safaris
   - **d.** Maharajah Jungle Trek

8. What is the closest water park to Animal Kingdom?

    a. Volcano Bay   **c.** Blizzard Beach

    b. Typhoon Lagoon   **d.** Aquatica

9. What is Animal Kingdom's interactive adventure game?

    a. Kids' Discovery Club   **c.** Finding Nemo

    b. Wilderness Explorers   **d.** Expedition Everest

10. What was the first animal to be born in Animal Kingdom?

    a. A black rhino   **c.** A Masai giraffe

    b. A Micronesian kingfisher chick   **d.** A kudu (a large African antelope)

Answers can be found on page 458.

PART 10

DISNEY'S HOLLYWOOD STUDIOS

THE "STUDIOS" IN "DISNEY'S HOLLYWOOD STUDIOS" is of little significance today: Movie and TV production ceased here long ago, and nothing remains that offers a peek behind the scenes. About half of Disney's Hollywood Studios (DHS) is set up as a theme park; the other half is off-limits to guests. Though modest in size, the Studios' open-access areas are confusingly arranged (a product of the park's hurried expansion in the early 1990s).

As at the Magic Kingdom, you enter the park and head down a main street, only this time it's the **Hollywood Boulevard** of the 1920s and 1930s. The boulevard leads to a magnificent replica of **Grauman's Chinese Theatre,** home of the **Mickey & Minnie's Runaway Railway** ride. The 11-acre **Toy Story Land** opened in the summer of 2018; see page 387 for a full description.

In August 2019 the eagerly awaited 14-acre **Star Wars: Galaxy's Edge** opened. The land is themed to a small town on the planet of Batuu, a remote outpost on the galaxy's edge. The *Star Wars*–inspired landscape is a collection of squat, sand-colored buildings set amid rock outcrops and surrounded by a green forest. The land first opened with only the *Millennium Falcon:* **Smugglers Run** operating. **Star Wars: Rise of the Resistance** opened later that year. In addition to the two main rides, Galaxy's Edge has several shops and eateries.

Guest Relations, on your left as you enter, serves as the park headquarters and information center. Go there for general information, park maps, first aid, a schedule of live performances, and lost persons, or in an emergency. To the right are **locker, stroller, ECV, and wheelchair rentals,** as well as package pickup and **lost and found.**

The **Baby Care Center** is located at Guest Relations, and **Oscar's** sells baby food and other necessities. Camera supplies for those precious moments can be purchased at **The Darkroom,** on the right side of Hollywood Boulevard just past Oscar's. The closest **ATMs** are just inside the

continued on page 374

Disney's Hollywood Studios

G+ Attraction Offers Genie+

ILL Attraction Offers Individual Lightning Lane

☑ Not To Be Missed

👍 Recommended Dining

🚻 Restrooms

✚ First Aid Center

Counter-Service Restaurants

A. ABC Commissary

B. Backlot Express 👍

C. Catalina Eddie's

D. Docking Bay 7 Food and Cargo 👍

E. Dockside Diner

F. Fairfax Fare

G. Milk Stand

H. Oga's Cantina

I. PizzeRizzo

J. Ronto Roasters 👍

K. Rosie's All-American Café

L. The Trolley Car Café *(Starbucks)* 👍

M. Woody's Lunch Box 👍

Table-Service Restaurants

AA. 50's Prime Time Café 👍

BB. Hollywood & Vine

CC. The Hollywood Brown Derby 👍

DD. Mama Melrose's Ristorante Italiano

EE. Roundup Rodeo BBQ *(opens 2022)*

FF. Sci-Fi Dine-In Theater Restaurant

Attractions

1. Alien Swirling Saucers G+
2. *Beauty and the Beast Live on Stage/ Theater of the Stars* G+
3. *Disney Junior Play and Dance!* G+
4. *Fantasmic! (temporarily suspended)* ☑
5. *For the First Time in Forever: A Frozen Sing-Along Celebration* G+
6. *Indiana Jones Epic Stunt Spectacular!* G+
7. *Lightning McQueen's Racing Academy*

8. Meet Olaf at Celebrity Spotlight ☑ G+
9. Mickey & Minnie's Runaway Railway ☑ G+
10. *Millennium Falcon:* Smugglers Run ☑ G+
11. *Muppet-Vision 3-D* G+
12. Rock 'n' Roller Coaster Starring Aerosmith ☑ G+
13. See Disney Stars at *Red Carpet Dreams* ☑
14. Slinky Dog Dash ☑ G+
15. Star Tours—The Adventures Continue ☑ G+
16. Star Wars Launch Bay
17. Star Wars: Rise of the Resistance ☑ ILL
18. Toy Story Mania! ☑ G+
19. The Twilight Zone Tower of Terror ☑ G+
20. *Vacation Fun* at Mickey Shorts Theater
21. *Walt Disney Presents*

continued from page 371

park, to the right of the turnstiles, and Sunset Boulevard. Across from Disney's Port Orleans Resorts, **Best Friends Pet Care** provides a comfortable home away from home for Fido, Fluffy, and all their pet pals.

OPENING PROCEDURES AT DHS

VIRTUALLY ALL RIDES will begin operation as soon as guests are admitted into the park. Shows normally begin running an hour or more after the rest of the park opens. On-site guests wishing to use Early Theme Park Entry should arrive at the Studios entrance 60 minutes before official opening on off-peak days and 90 minutes before official opening on days with high attendance. Off-site guests should arrive 30 minutes before official opening on all days.

Depending on when you arrive, the time of year you tour, and how big a *Star Wars* fan you are, a comprehensive tour of the park takes 7–8 hours with lunch and breaks. Allow more time if you want to enjoy the lightsaber- or droid-building experiences in Galaxy's Edge.

GENIE+ AND INDIVIDUAL LIGHTNING LANE AND THE TOURING PLANS

GENIE+ IS OFFERED AT 13 DHS ATTRACTIONS. Only Rise of the Resistance is designated as Individual Lightning Lane.

GENIE+ AND INDIVIDUAL LIGHTNING LANE (ILL) SELECTIONS IN DHS	
ANIMATION COURTYARD	
• *Disney Junior Play and Dance!*	
ECHO LAKE	
• *For the First Time in Forever—A Frozen Sing-Along Celebration* • *Indiana Jones Epic Stunt Spectacular* • Meet Olaf at Celebrity Spotlight • Star Tours—The Adventures Continue	
GALAXY'S EDGE	
• Millennium Falcon: Smugglers Run • Star Wars: Rise of the Resistance *(ILL)*	
GRAND AVENUE	**HOLLYWOOD BOULEVARD**
• *Muppet-Vision 3-D*	• Mickey & Minnie's Runaway Railway
SUNSET BOULEVARD	
• *Beauty and the Beast Live on Stage* • Rock 'n' Roller Coaster • The Twilight Zone Tower of Terror	
TOY STORY LAND	
• Alien Swirling Saucers • Slinky Dog Dash • Toy Story Mania!	

As a reminder, the big questions for Genie+ and Individual Lightning Lane are

1. Is Genie+ worth paying for at Disney's Hollywood Studios?
2. If worth the cost, which attractions benefit most from Genie+ or Individual Lightning Lane?
3. How can you avoid paying for Individual Lightning Lane?
4. How do Genie+ and Individual Lightning Lane work with the touring plans?

Is Genie+ Worth Paying For at Disney's Hollywood Studios?

Along with the Magic Kingdom, the Studios might be the easiest park to recommend Genie+, especially if you meet any of these criteria:

- You'll arrive at the park after Early Theme Park Entry begins (that is, you won't be at the park as soon as it opens). This includes off-site guests, who aren't eligible for Early Theme Park Entry, and on-site guests who want to sleep in.
- You won't be using a touring plan.
- You're visiting during a day of moderate or high crowds.

Regardless of the time of year you visit, arriving at park opening should allow you to see one or two headliners without significant waits. On days of heavy attendance, you'll be competing with lots of other people for reservations, pushing out the return times and limiting how many you can obtain per day.

The table below shows how much time we estimate you'll be able to save using Genie+ with one of our DHS touring plans, at three different crowd and Genie+ usage levels (see page 285 for an explanation of the different usage levels).

ESTIMATED TIME SAVINGS USING A TOURING PLAN WITH GENIE+ FOR VARIOUS CROWD LEVELS			
CROWD LEVEL	TYPICAL USE (3 RESERVATIONS PER DAY)	OPTIMISTIC USE (5 RESERVATIONS PER DAY)	PERFECT USE (8 RESERVATIONS PER DAY)
Low	30 minutes saved	50 minutes saved	90 minutes saved
Medium	70 minutes saved	100 minutes saved	140 minutes saved
High	90 minutes saved	150 minutes saved	200 minutes saved

Which Attractions Benefit Most from Genie+ or Individual Lightning Lane?

For Genie+, the table below shows the attractions that might benefit most from using Genie+, based on current wait times and historical Genie+/Individual Lightning Lane data. The chart goes in descending order of priority. At press time, we had not seen evidence that Genie+ reduces waits at shows. Nor had we collected enough data on character greetings to make those calculations.

DHS ATTRACTIONS THAT BENEFIT MOST FROM GENIE+ AND INDIVIDUAL LIGHTNING LANE (ILL) *(Highest Priority to Lowest)*	
ATTRACTION	AVERAGE TIME IN LINE SAVED *(in minutes)*
Star Wars: Rise of the Resistance (ILL)	91
Slinky Dog Dash	51
Millennium Falcon: Smugglers Run	38
Mickey & Minnie's Runaway Railway	34
Rock 'n' Roller Coaster	32
Toy Story Mania!	31
Alien Swirling Saucers	15
Star Tours—The Adventures Continue	9

Which Attractions Run Out of Genie+ or Individual Lightning Lane First?

The table below shows the approximate times at which the Studios' attractions run out of Genie+ or Individual Lightning Lane capacity, by crowd level. Use this chart in conjunction with the "Which Attractions Benefit Most" table on the previous page to determine which reservations to get first.

WHEN GENIE+ AND INDIVIDUAL LIGHTNING LANE (ILL) RESERVATIONS RUN OUT BY ATTENDANCE LEVEL			
ATTRACTION	**LOW ATTENDANCE**	**MODERATE ATTENDANCE**	**HIGH ATTENDANCE**
Alien Swirling Saucers	8 p.m.	6–8 p.m.	4–5 p.m.
Beauty and the Beast Live on Stage	Available	5 p.m.	5 p.m.
Disney Junior Play and Dance!	Available	6 p.m.	7 p.m.
For the First Time in Forever	Available	8 p.m.	7 p.m.
Indiana Jones Epic Stunt Spectacular	Available	6 p.m.	5 p.m.
Meet Olaf at Celebrity Spotlight	Available	4–5 p.m.	2–3 p.m.
Mickey & Minnie's Runaway Railway	Available	2–3 p.m.	1–2 p.m.
Millennium Falcon: Smugglers Run	4–5 p.m.	1–2 p.m.	11 a.m.–noon
Muppet-Vision 3-D	8 p.m.	8 p.m.	8 p.m.
Star Wars: Rise of the Resistance (ILL)	8 a.m.	7 a.m.	7 a.m.
Rock 'n' Roller Coaster	8 p.m.	3–4 p.m.	1–2 p.m.
Slinky Dog Dash	10 a.m.–1 p.m.	8–10 a.m.	8 a.m.
Star Tours—The Adventures Continue	9 p.m.	9 p.m.	9 p.m.
Toy Story Mania!	8 p.m.	5–6 p.m.	2–3 p.m.
The Twilight Zone Tower of Terror	8 p.m.	4–5 p.m.	1–2 p.m.

AVAILABLE Attractions rarely run out of reservations at this crowd level.
LOW ATTENDANCE Crowd levels 1–3 on the TouringPlans crowd calendar
MODERATE ATTENDANCE Crowd levels 4–7 **HIGH ATTENDANCE** Crowd levels 8–10
Attractions closed for more than two years are not shown.

How Can You Avoid Paying for Individual Lightning Lane?

The easiest way to avoid paying for Individual Lightning Lane at Star Wars: Rise of the Resistance is to be at the park for Early Theme Park Entry, then head for Rise as soon as you enter the park.

How Do Genie+ and Individual Lightning Lane Work with the Touring Plans?

See our advice for the Magic Kingdom on page 286.

HOLLYWOOD *and* SUNSET BOULEVARDS

WITH ITS ART DECO AND MODERN ARCHITECTURE, Hollywood Boulevard is reminiscent of Tinseltown's yesteryear. Most of the

Studios' service facilities are housed here, interspersed with eateries and shops. The famous **Hollywood Brown Derby** restaurant is also located here. The boulevard leads straight to the iconic replica of Grauman's Chinese Theatre, home of **Mickey & Minnie's Runaway Railway.**

The first right off Hollywood Boulevard brings you onto the palm-lined Sunset Boulevard, evoking the glamour of the 1940s. It's home to **The Twilight Zone Tower of Terror, Rock 'n' Roll Coaster Starring Aerosmith,** the *Beauty and the Beast Live on Stage* show, and the incredible, not-to-be-missed *Fantasmic!* fireworks. There are plenty of shopping opportunities and small eateries on Sunset Boulevard. Roving Hollywood characters perform on both boulevards.

KEY TO ABBREVIATIONS In the attraction profiles that follow, each star rating is accompanied by a category label in parentheses. **E** means **Exceptional, MAA** means **Much Above Average, AA** means **Above Average, A** means **Average, BA** means **Below Average,** and **MBA** means **Much Below Average.**

AVERAGE WAIT-IN-LINE TIMES This is the attractions' maximum hourly capacity in passengers per hour.

Beauty and the Beast Live on Stage/Theater of the Stars
★★★★

PRESCHOOL ★★★★½ (AA) **GRADE SCHOOL** ★★★★ (BA) **TEENS** ★★★★ (MBA)
YOUNG ADULTS ★★★★ (BA) **OVER 30** ★★★★ (A) **SENIORS** ★★★★½ (AA)

What it is Live Hollywood-style musical with Disney characters, performed in an open-air theater. **Scope and scale** Major attraction. **When to go** Anytime, but it's not as hot after sunset. **Comment** Check the My Disney Experience app for showtimes. **Duration of show** 25 minutes. **Preshow entertainment** None. **When to arrive** 25–35 minutes in advance. **EVC/wheelchair access** May remain in wheelchair. **Participates in Genie+** Yes. **Early Theme Park Entry** No. **Extended Evening Hours** No.

Join Cogsworth, Lumière, Chip, and Mrs. Potts as they help Belle break the spell. This musical stage show of Disney's *Beauty and the Beast* will charm everybody. The show is popular, so arrive 30 minutes early to get a seat.

Lillane

The decor, the costumes, the actors, the music: Everything is in perfect harmony. Little girls fond of Belle will want that ball gown, and young boys will be eager to teach that mean Gaston a lesson.

Lucy

Shows are a great way to take a break. My favorite shows are *Beauty and the Beast* and *Fantasmic!*

Lightning McQueen's Racing Academy ★★½

PRESCHOOL ★★★★½ (AA) **GRADE SCHOOL** ★★★★ (BA) **TEENS** ★★★ (BA)
YOUNG ADULTS ★★★½ (BA) **OVER 30** ★★★ (MBA) **SENIORS** ★★★ (MBA)

What it is Wide-screen movie of Lightning McQueen's racing tips. **Scope and scale** Minor attraction. **When to go** Anytime. **Duration of show** 10 minutes. **Preshow entertainment** None. **EVC/wheelchair access** May remain in wheelchair. **Participates in Genie+** No. **Early Theme Park Entry** No. **Extended Evening Hours** No.

This *Cars*-themed show, which opened in early 2019, is held inside Sunset Showcase Theater, adjacent to Rock 'n' Roller Coaster. The all-new show stars Lightning McQueen, a full-size Audio Animatronic, interacting in a humorous way with Cruz Ramirez and Tow Mater, who appear on a wraparound screen. After the show, guests get a chance to snap a photo with trainer-turned-racer Cruz Ramirez just outside the academy. *Ka-chow!*

Mickey & Minnie's Runaway Railway ★★★★

ALL AGE GROUPS ★★★½ (AA)

Thumbs Up for the Whole Family

What it is Indoor dark ride through the new Mickey Mouse cartoon universe. **Scope and scale** Headliner. **When to go** As soon as the park is open or in the last hour before closing. **Duration of ride** 5 minutes. **Average wait in line per 100 people ahead of you** 4 minutes; assumes all trains operating. **Loading speed** Moderate. **EVC/wheelchair access** Must transfer to the ride vehicle. **Participates in Genie+** Yes (for now, but it may join the Individual Lightning Lane list). **Early Theme Park Entry** Yes. **Extended Evening Hours** Yes.

Disney restarted regular production of Mickey Mouse cartoons in 2013. Mostly written and directed by Paul Rudish, these 7-minute vignettes—more than 100 have been made so far—are minor masterpieces of storytelling, animation, and humor; Mickey and Minnie sport a retro-1930s look, complete with "pie eyes." In settings across the world, and sometimes entirely in languages other than English, the Mouses, Goofy, Donald, and the rest of the gang embark on crazy adventures that always seem to end up just fine. If you haven't seen them yet, plan on binge-watching them with your kids (they're on YouTube and Disney+).

Runaway Railway places you in the center of one of those cartoons. The premise is that you're on an out-of-control railroad car, courtesy of Goofy. You careen, gently, through 10 large cartoon show scenes, from tropical islands to cities to out-of-control factories. In each scene, Mickey and Minnie attempt to save you from disaster, with mixed results.

Disney uses a mix of traditional, three-dimensional painted sets and the latest in video projection technology to show movement and special effects. It's all done very well, and there are so many things to see on either side of the ride that it's impossible to catch everything in one or two rides.

I enjoyed Mickey & Minnie's Runaway Railway, even though the song will not go out of your head. If you want a different experience, try to follow the story of Pluto trying to bring back the picnic basket to Mickey and Minnie.

Brendan

Lillane

The ride is cute, but I personally was not impressed. Little tykes, however, will love it.

Runaway Railway is the Studios' sleeper hit of the decade, so expect long lines throughout the day. Your best bet is to get in line as soon as the park opens or late in the afternoon. An Individual Lightning Lane purchase (if offered) saves about 34 minutes in line here on average but might be worth the cost on days of high attendance, especially if you can't ride early or late.

Rock 'n' Roller Coaster Starring Aerosmith ★★★★

PRESCHOOL ★½ (MBA) **GRADE SCHOOL ★★★★½ (MAA)** **TEENS ★★★★★ (E)**
YOUNG ADULTS ★★★★★ (E) **OVER 30 ★★★★½ (MAA)** **SENIORS ★★★★ (BA)**

What it is Rock music–themed roller coaster. **Scope and scale** Headliner. **When to go** First 30 minutes the park is open or after 4 p.m. **Comments** Must be 48″ to ride; Rider Switch option provided (see page 260). **Duration of ride** Almost 1½ minutes. **Average wait in line per 100 people ahead of you** 2½ minutes; assumes all trains operating. **Loading speed** Moderate–fast. **EVC/wheelchair access** Must transfer from EVC to provided wheelchair and then from wheelchair to the ride vehicle; transfer device available. **Participates in Genie+** Yes. **Early Theme Park Entry** Yes. **Extended Evening Hours** Yes.

Dark   Lose Things   Rough   Queasy   Scary

Aerosmith once did a tour called Route of All Evil, and this notorious ride at the Studios makes good on fans' expectations. Expect loops, corkscrews, and drops that make Space Mountain seem like the Jungle Cruise. You are launched from 0 to 57 miles per hour in less than 3 seconds, and by the time you enter the first loop, you'll be pulling five g's—two more than astronauts experience at liftoff on a space shuttle. If Space Mountain or Big Thunder Mountain Railroad pushes your limits, stay away from this coaster.

If you can't ride first thing in the morning, waits should be manageable during *Fantasmic!* Alternatively, consider using the single-rider line or Genie+.

Aerosmith describes this ride best in one of their songs: "Livin' on the Edge."

My parents told me I would like the Rock 'n' Roller Coaster, and I was excited when the limo pulled up, but as soon as we shot off, I felt really sick. I kept my eyes closed the whole time and just wished it was over soon. I hated being in the dark and going upside down. I don't want to do this ride again.

Liliane

Felicity

The Twilight Zone Tower of Terror ★★★★★

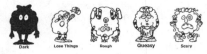

PRESCHOOL ★★½ (MBA)   GRADE SCHOOL ★★★★ (MBA)   TEENS ★★★★★ (MAA)
YOUNG ADULTS ★★★★★ (MAA)   OVER 30 ★★★★½ (MAA)   SENIORS ★★★★ (AA)

What it is Sci-fi-themed indoor thrill ride. **Scope and scale** Super-headliner. **When to go** First 30 minutes the park is open or after 4 p.m. **Comments** Must be 40" to ride; Rider Switch option provided (see page 260). **Duration of ride** About 4 minutes plus preshow. **Average wait in line per 100 people ahead of you** 4 minutes; assumes all elevators operating at full capacity. **Loading speed** Moderate. **EVC/wheelchair access** Must transfer from EVC to provided wheelchair and then from wheelchair to the ride vehicle. **Participates in Genie+** Yes. **Early Theme Park Entry** Yes. **Extended Evening Hours** No.

Dark   Rough   Scary

And suddenly the cable went *snap.* If riding a capricious elevator in a haunted hotel sounds like fun to you, this is your ride. Erratic yet thrilling, the Tower of Terror is an experience to savor. The Tower has great potential for terrifying young children and rattling more mature visitors. Random ride-and-drop sequences keep you guessing about when, how far, and how many times the elevator will drop.

We suggest using teenagers in your party as experimental probes. If they report back that they really, really liked the Tower of Terror, run in the opposite direction.

Sabrina

My favorite part of the Tower of Terror is when you go down and you get pulled off your seat.

Tower of Terror is too scary. I had to leave the line via the chicken exit.

Felicity

Little kids will feel like they're flying out of their seats when riding Tower of Terror and may be frightened by this.

Isabelle

The attractions in Galaxy's Edge, along with Slinky Dog Dash and Mickey & Minnie's Runaway Railway, draw crowds away from Tower of Terror. If you can't ride first thing in the morning, waits should be shorter in the last hour the park is open.

Save time once you're inside the queuing area: When you enter the library waiting room, stand in the far back corner across from the door where you entered and at the opposite end of the room from the TV. When the doors to the loading area open, you'll be the first admitted.

ECHO LAKE

TOWERING OVER ECHO LAKE is Gertie the dinosaur, a tribute to one of the first popular animated characters in the history of film. Echo Lake has several quick-service eateries and two sit-down restaurants, including **50's Prime Time Café,** where servers treat you like family (including scolding you if you put your elbows on the table), and **Hollywood & Vine,** home of the Disney Junior Play and Dine character breakfast and Minnie's Seasonal Dining at dinner. Echo Lake has one attraction, **Star Tours,** and two shows, *Indiana Jones Epic Stunt Spectacular!* and the musical *For the First Time in Forever,* based on *Frozen.*

For the First Time in Forever: A Frozen Sing-Along Celebration ★★★★

**PRESCHOOL ★★★★½ (MAA) GRADE SCHOOL ★★★★½ (AA) TEENS ★★★★ (BA)
YOUNG ADULTS ★★★★ (BA) OVER 30 ★★★★½ (AA) SENIORS ★★★★½ (A)**

What it is Sing-along stage show retelling the story of *Frozen,* with appearances by Anna and Elsa. **Scope and scale** Minor attraction. **When to go** Check the My Disney Experience app for showtimes. **Duration of presentation** 30 minutes. **When to arrive** 25 minutes before showtime. **EVC/wheelchair access** May remain in wheelchair. **Participates in Genie+** Yes. **Early Theme Park Entry** No. **Extended Evening Hours** No.

Scenes from the movie *Frozen,* projected on a drive-in-movie-size screen in the background, provide continuity and familiarize those who haven't seen the film with the characters and story line. Live performers, including two "royal historians" and several characters from *Frozen,* lay down a stand-up comedy shtick to facilitate the narrative and add some corny and occasionally punchy humor. Most of the story is related at a leisurely pace, but the ending is presented in a nanosecond, leaving much of the audience stupefied. Of course, the finale features another rousing round of "Let It Go." Even if you're not a fan, you'll enjoy the show's spirit, as well as that of a theater full of enraptured children—it's contagious. Using Genie+ grants you access to a preferred-seating section closer to the stage, while standby guests are seated in whatever seats are left.

> Everything in the theater was so sparkly, and I loved singing along with all the other children. I was so surprised and excited when the real Elsa appeared at the end of the show.

Felicity

Indiana Jones Epic Stunt Spectacular! ★★★½

**PRESCHOOL ★★★½ (MBA) GRADE SCHOOL ★★★★½ (A) TEENS ★★★★ (BA)
YOUNG ADULTS ★★★★ (BA) OVER 30 ★★★★ (MBA) SENIORS ★★★★½ (A)**

What it is Movie-stunt demonstration and action show. **Scope and scale** Headliner. **When to go** First two shows or last show. **Comment** Performance times posted at the

Thumbs Up for the Whole Family

entrance to the theater. **Duration of show** 30 minutes. **When to arrive** 20-30 minutes before showtime. **EVC/ wheelchair access** May remain in wheelchair. **Participates in Genie+** Yes. **Early Theme Park Entry** No. **Extended Evening Hours** No.

Professional stuntmen and -women demonstrate dangerous stunts with a behind-the-scenes look at how they're done. Most kids handle the show well. The indoor theater is one of Disney's largest and most comfortable, with excellent sight lines from every seat. Crowd management when entering the theater is a little confusing, but once you're inside, it sorts itself out.

This is an amazing show with fiery explosions and nonstop action. Did you know that the folks at Disney have a vault filled with sound effects ranging from gunshots to magical twinkles? When a show is created, they pick and choose from this treasure chest and upload the sounds into their state-of-the-art computerized mixing table.

Liliane

Bob

Huh? What's a magical twinkle sound like? But now that I think about it, I sure remember the noise my innards made after eating about a dozen magical twinkles.

Those were Twinkies, Mr. Tiki-Birdbrain!

Liliane

Star Tours—The Adventures Continue ★★★½

| PRESCHOOL ★★★½ (BA) | GRADE SCHOOL ★★★★½ (AA) | TEENS ★★★★½ (AA) |
| YOUNG ADULTS ★★★★ (A) | OVER 30 ★★★★ (A) | SENIORS ★★★★½ (AA) |

What it is Indoor space-flight-simulation ride. **Scope and scale** Major attraction. **When to go** During lunch or after 4 p.m. **Comments** Expectant mothers and anyone prone to motion sickness should not ride. Too intense for many children younger than 8; must be 40" to ride; Rider Switch option available (see page 260). **Duration of ride** About 7 minutes. **Average wait in line per 100 people ahead of you** 5 minutes; assumes all simulators operating. **Loading speed** Moderate-fast. **EVC/wheelchair access** Must transfer from ECV to provided wheelchair and then from wheelchair to the ride vehicle. **Participates in Genie+** Yes. **Early Theme Park Entry** Yes. **Extended Evening Hours** Yes.

Rough   Queasy   Scary

Based on the *Star Wars* movies, the ride is a 3-D motion simulator with more than 50 combinations of opening and ending scenes. Hold on tight as you experience dips, turns, twists, and light speed, only to exit hyperspace above Coruscant; on Naboo, Tatooine, or Endor; or inside the dreaded Death Star. You could ride Star Tours all day without seeing the same film segment twice. Despite having the same theme as the rides in Galaxy's Edge, Star Tours is located in Echo Lake.

Oh, no! We're caught in a tractor beam!

Liliane

Vacation Fun at Mickey Shorts Theater ★★★½

| PRESCHOOL ★★★★ (A) | GRADE SCHOOL ★★★★½ (AA) | TEENS ★★★★ (A) |
| YOUNG ADULTS ★★★★ (A) | OVER 30 ★★★★ (A) | SENIORS ★★★★ (A) |

What it is Cartoon featuring Mickey Mouse. **Scope and scale** Diversion. **When to go** Anytime. **Duration of presentation** 10 minutes. **Preshow entertainment** None.

Probable waiting time 9 minutes. **EVC/wheelchair access** May remain in wheelchair. **Participates in Genie+** No. **Early Theme Park Entry** No. **Extended Evening Hours** No.

The Mickey Shorts Theater shows a new 10-minute Mickey Mouse cartoon called *Vacation Fun,* which pastes together clips from several of the best newer Mickey Mouse cartoons into one. If you've seen *Couple Sweaters, O Sole Minnie, Amore Motore,* or *Potatoland,* you'll recognize the scenes.

If you loved Mickey & Minnie's Runaway Railway, here's your chance to see more of the new-style cartoons. And if you've not yet seen the new cartoons, this is the place to get familiar with them. Even if you've seen them, the air-conditioned theater is the perfect short break in the middle of a hot day.

GRAND AVENUE

THE FORMER STREETS OF AMERICA, which incorporates what was once Muppet Courtyard, now portrays present-day downtown Los Angeles and serves as a pedestrian thoroughfare to Galaxy's Edge. Here you'll find **Muppet-Vision 3-D,** **PizzeRizzo,** **Mama Melrose's Ristorante Italiano,** and **BaseLine Tap House,** a pub specializing in beer and wines from California.

Muppet-Vision 3-D ★★★★

PRESCHOOL ★★★★ (A)   **GRADE SCHOOL ★★★★** (MBA)   **TEENS ★★★½** (MBA)
YOUNG ADULTS ★★★★ (MBA)   **OVER 30 ★★★★** (MBA)   **SENIORS ★★★★½** (A)

What it is 3-D movie starring the Muppets. **Scope and scale** Major attraction. **When to go** Anytime. **Comment** Uproarious; not to be missed. **Duration of show** 17 minutes. **Preshow** Muppets on television. **Probable waiting time** 12 minutes. **EVC/wheelchair access** May remain in wheelchair. **Participates in Genie+** Yes. **Early Theme Park Entry** No. **Extended Evening Hours** No.

Kermit, Miss Piggy, and the gang will lift your spirits as they unleash their hilarious mayhem. Because adults tend to associate Muppets with *Sesame Street,* many bypass this attraction. Big mistake. *Muppet-Vision 3-D* operates on several planes, and there's as much here for oldsters as for youngsters. The show is intense and sometimes loud, but most preschoolers handle it well. If your child is a little scared, encourage him to watch without the 3-D glasses at first. A New Brunswick, Canada, reader thinks the Muppets are heaven-sent:

> Muppet-Vision 3-D *is a godsend: 1) It NEVER has a line (even on our visit on New Year's Day). 2) Everyone ages 1–100 gives the show high marks. 3) Between the preshow and the movie, it's half an hour seated comfortably in an air-conditioned theater. 4) Between the live actors and animatronics, it's so much more than just another silly 3-D movie. 5) IT'S THE MUPPETS! Who doesn't love these hysterical creatures and their 3-D shenanigans?*

Waits generally peak around lunchtime, and it's unusual to find a wait of more than 20 minutes. Because it's near one of the main pathways to Galaxy's Edge, *Muppet-Vision* may get more traffic. Watch for throngs waiting to enter or coming from Galaxy's Edge; if you do encounter a long line, try again later.

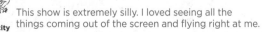 This show is extremely silly. I loved seeing all the things coming out of the screen and flying right at me.

Felicity

STAR WARS: *Galaxy's Edge*

STAR WARS: GALAXY'S EDGE is an outpost in the village of Black Spire, on the planet of Batuu. Formerly a busy trading port and way-point before the invention of light speed–capable transportation, it's now a dusty backwater filled with bounty hunters, smugglers, and those who make a living by not being recognized. As if that wasn't enough, members of the Resistance and First Order live in and around Black Spire in an uneasy coexistence.

Galaxy's Edge has two access points, via Grand Avenue and Toy Story Land. Entering through Grand Avenue puts you in the middle of the Resistance's encampment, while the entrance at Toy Story Land is controlled by the First Order. When the land is crowded, the Toy Story Land entrance may be designated as exit-only, for crowd control.

In the Resistance section of the park, guests complete a critical mission on the *Millennium Falcon:* **Smugglers Run** ride. How you do on the mission has high stakes: Perform with skill, and you may earn extra galactic credits, while bringing the ship back banged up could put you on bounty hunter Harkos's list, and you may face a problem if you show up at the local cantina.

On the First Order side of the land, **Star Wars: Rise of the Resistance** makes guests feel like they're inside a hangar bay in the middle of a fight between the First Order and the Resistance. The ride has a large amount of animatronics and scenes with almost life-size AT-ATs.

SHOPPING Between the two sections is a merchant's alley with shops and stalls. A stall selling playthings and dolls is overseen by a **Toydarian,** a creature fans first encountered on the planet Tatooine in *Star Wars: The Phantom Menace.* **Dok-Ondar's Den of Antiquities** sells ancient artifacts (memorabilia) from the movies and prebuilt legacy lightsabers. **Creature Stall** has unique companions, such as cackling Kowakian monkey-lizards, for you to take home. The biggest hits, however, are **The Droid Depot,** where you can build a droid, and **Savi's Workshop,** where you design your own one-of-a-kind lightsaber. Costumes and Galaxy's Edge–related clothes are available at **Black Spire Outfitters**. Hats, pins, badges, and souvenirs are sold at **Resistance Supply,** for those who are with the Force, and at **First Order Cargo,** for those who have crossed to the dark side. **Jewels of Bith** has pins, patches, and trinkets from across the Outer Rim.

If your heart is set on building a lightsaber and/or droid of your own, make sure to do the following:

- Make a park reservation as soon as you can.
- Make a reservation for Savi's Workshop and/or The Droid Depot 60 days in advance. These reservations must be for the same day as your park reservation. You will be asked for a valid credit card but won't be charged until you are at the shop(s).

The cost for the droid unit is $99 plus tax and includes a carrying box and instructions. The experience is limited to one builder and one guest. Only the builder is allowed to build a droid. For an additional charge, chips and accessories are available. If you do not show up for your appointment, a no-show fee of the full cost of the experience will be charged to your credit card.

BUILD A LIGHTSABER! I used my own money—worth every penny! Make your reservations for the end of the day and you get an empty park to take pictures in afterward, and you're not rushed out at all.

Brendan

At Savi's, small groups (up to 14 builders per session) are led by "Gatherers" through the process of building the lightsabers, from picking a colorful kyber crystal to selecting customizable handles. The cost of the experience is $219 plus tax and includes a carrying case. The experience is limited to one builder and one guest. Only the builder is allowed to build the lightsaber. Additional customization is available for a cost. As with The Droid Depot, the no-show fee is the cost of the experience—a whopping $219 per builder will show up on your credit card!

DINING The main eatery in the land is the quick-service **Docking Bay 7 Food and Cargo.** According to Disney lore, it's the home of chef Strono "Cookie" Tuggs, former chef at Maz Kanata's castle on Takodana from *The Force Awakens.* The restaurant, housed in a working hangar bay, serves beef, chicken, fish, and vegetarian dishes.

At **Oga's Cantina,** the galaxy's most infamous watering hole, join smugglers, rogue traders, and bounty hunters for Bespin Fizz, Bloody Rancor, Dagobah Slug Slinger, Jedi Mind Trick, and T-16 Skyhopper, to name just a few. Nonalcoholic drinks are also available. Oga's is super popular, and we strongly recommend you make reservations 60 days in advance. Spots for walk-ins are rarely available. A credit card guarantee is required, and a no-show fee of $10 per person will be charged if you decide not to use your reservation. Oga's is very small and mostly standing room. There is a maximum of two drinks per guest, and your visit is limited to 45 minutes. The cantina also serves two snack plates. And yes, you have to have a park reservation AND a reservation for Oga's Cantina.

Ronto Roasters serves meats roasted over an old pod racer's engine (wraps with roasted pork and spicy grilled sausage; plant-based options available). For breakfast, there's an egg-and-pork-sausage wrap and yogurt with oats and fruit. At **The Milk Stand** try the famous blue or green milk. A popcorn stand dubbed **Kat Saka's Kettle** sells a sweet-and-spicy popcorn snack.

LILIANE The Milk Stand's blue and green milk are an acquired taste, to say the least. I strongly recommend that you purchase one drink for all to taste before ordering one for each member of your party.

INTERACTIVITY IN GALAXY'S EDGE Throughout the land, guests encounter familiar characters from the movies, including Chewbacca, members of the First Order, and—among many others—Captain Rex, the RX-series droid pilot of Star Tours fame, who takes on a new role as a DJ at Oga's Cantina.

On Batuu, cast members interact with visitors, staying in character at all times. Stormtroopers and Kylo Ren roam the land on the lookout for guests suspected of helping the Resistance. Rey and

Chewbacca also engage with visitors. It's a treat to watch Chewie trying to fix ships of the Resistance's fleet.

Make sure to download the **Play Disney Parks** app before you get to the park. Once inside Galaxy's Edge, the app turns into a "datapad" and allows you to interact with the land's many control panels and droids. It's up to you to pledge your alliance to the Resistance or the First Order. Be aware that if you play the game, there will be consequences. If you survive an encounter with Kylo Ren, you'll be hailed as a hero and get extra points from the Resistance, but bang up the *Millennium Falcon,* and you'll see your score go down.

GALAXY'S EDGE TOURING TIPS Be sure to make park reservations for the Studios as soon as your travel dates are known. Obtain Individual Lightning Lane reservations for Rise of the Resistance at 7 a.m. on the day of your visit. Ride *Millennium Falcon:* Smugglers Run early in the morning, after you've experienced Slinky Dog Dash, or try riding in the last hour the park is open. Save shopping and dining for after you've done the rides.

LILIANE Much to my chagrin, costumes are forbidden at Galaxy's Edge for guests age 14 and older.

If you're not staying at a Disney resort, consider booking a room at a Value resort the night before your Galaxy's Edge visit, so you can take advantage of Early Theme Park Entry. Disney resort guests can purchase access to Individual Lightning Lane attractions every day at 7 a.m. If you are staying off-property, you cannot purchase an Individual Lightning Lane until official park opening.

In 1977 George Lucas released the first Star Wars *movie, and fans eagerly followed him to a galaxy far, far away. Now, 40 years and 12 movies later,* Star Wars *has found a home at Disney's Hollywood Studios. With a recently opened* Star Wars*–themed hotel and more movies scheduled over the next two years, there is no doubt that the Force is very strong indeed.*

IT'S A HOTEL, IT'S AN EXPERIENCE—AND IT WILL COST YOU! Disney has built a *Star Wars*–themed hotel, called Star Wars: Galactic Starcruiser, adjacent and connected to Galaxy's Edge. It's a separate, fully immersive, two-day live-action role-playing experience. It starts at around $5,000 for two people (that's not a typo)! Find out more on page 111.

Millennium Falcon: Smugglers Run   ★★★★★

PRESCHOOL ★★★½ (BA) **GRADE SCHOOL** ★★★★½ (AA) **TEENS** ★★★★½ (AA)
YOUNG ADULTS ★★★★½ (AA) **OVER 30** ★★★★½ (AA) **SENIORS** ★★★★ (A)

What it is Interactive simulator ride. **Scope and scale** Super-headliner. **When to go** As soon as it opens or after 6 p.m. **Comments** Could've been great; 38" height requirement; Rider Switch option available (see page 260). **Duration of ride** 4½ minutes. **Average wait in line per 100 people ahead of you** 3½ minutes. **Loading speed** Moderate-fast. **ECV/wheelchair access** Must transfer to the ride vehicle. **Participates in Genie+** Yes. **Early Theme Park Entry** Yes. **Extended Evening Hours** Yes.

Riding in the cockpit of the fabled *Millennium Falcon* fulfills the dreams of many *Star Wars* fans, including coauthor Liliane. Hondo Ohnaka, a well-known businessman (also known as a smuggler), has cut a deal with Chewbacca to use the *Falcon,* and he's recruiting a flight crew to help him deliver hard-to-find items to his clientele. This is where you come in. As you wait in the ride's queue, you are handed boarding cards, which break riders into groups of six: two pilots, two engineers, and two gunners. Before getting into the cockpit, riders are led into the lounge of the *Millennium Falcon,* complete with the famous Dejarik (holochess) table. Once the boarding call comes, riders board the exceptionally detailed cockpit of the ship. With the jobs assigned, it's time to jump into hyperspace.

The motion-simulator ride is similar to Star Tours, except that you and the rest of the crew are given partial control of the *Millennium Falcon,* and what happens next depends on the actions of the six people controlling the ship. Furthermore, your actions in the cockpit have consequences and will follow you throughout your time at Galaxy's Edge. Be prepared to do your best, because who wants to be known throughout the galaxy as the one who wrecked the *Millennium Falcon*?

There are more than 100 buttons, switches, and levers in the cockpit, and each one does something when activated; watch for indicator rings to illuminate around certain controls, clueing you into the correct moment to punch them. Two stationary simulators allow disabled guests to experience the attraction without interrupting operations for other guests.

After experiencing the entire *Millennium Falcon* queue once, see if the single-rider line is operating. The experience is not much diminished.

Liliane

Star Wars: Rise of the Resistance ★★★★★

PRESCHOOL ★★½ (BA)   **GRADE SCHOOL ★★★½** (E)
ALL OTHER AGE GROUPS ★★★★★ (E)

What it is Next-generation dark ride. **Scope and scale** Super-headliner. **When to go** When your boarding group is called. **Comments** Not to be missed; get a boarding group on the My Disney Experience app at exactly 7 a.m. or 1 p.m. on the day of your visit; 40" height requirement; Rider Switch option available (see page 260). **Duration of ride** About 25 minutes with all preshows; about 5 minutes for ride. **Average wait in line per 100 people ahead of you** 4 minutes. **Loading speed** Moderate–fast. **ECV/wheelchair access** Must transfer to the ride vehicle. **Participates in Genie+** No (it's an Individual Lightning Lane attraction). **Early Theme Park Entry** Yes. **Extended Evening Hours** Yes.

Dark   Queasy   Loud   Scary

A mobile Resistance gun turret tucked into a scrubland forest marks the entrance of the most epic indoor dark ride in Disney theme park history. Rise of the Resistance is an innovative attempt to integrate at least four different ride experiences— including trackless vehicles, a motion simulator, walk-through environments, and even an elevator drop—into Disney's longest attraction ever.

The adventure begins as you explore the Resistance military outpost, which has been laser-carved out of ancient stone. An animatronic BB-8 rolls in, accompanied by a hologram of Rey, who recruits you to strike a blow against the First Order. Fifty guests at a time exit the briefing room to board a standing-room-only shuttle craft piloted by Nien Nunb from *Return of the Jedi.* You can feel the rumble as the ship breaks orbit and you see Poe Dameron accompanying you in his X-Wing, until a Star Destroyer snags you in its tractor beam and sucks you into its belly.

When the doors to your shuttle craft reopen, you've been convincingly transported into an enormous hangar, complete with 50 Stormtroopers, TIE Fighters, and a 100-foot-wide bay window looking into outer space. Cast members clad as First Order officers brusquely herd captive guests into holding rooms to await their interrogation by helmet-headed baddie Kylo Ren.

Before long, you make a break for it in an eight-passenger troop transport with an animatronic astromech droid as your driver; the car is capable of traveling without a fixed track. The ride blends dozens of robotic characters and enormous sets with video projections to create some of the most overwhelming environments ever seen in an indoor ride. One sequence sends you between the legs of two towering AT-ATs as you dodge laser fire from legions of Stormtroopers, while another puts you face-to-face with the Solo-slaying Ren. In the epic finale (spoiler alert), you'll survive an escape pod's dramatic crash back to Batuu, a heart-stopping multistory plunge enhanced by digital projections.

Rise of the Resistance is the second-most popular ride in the park, right behind *Millennium Falcon: Smugglers Run.* Make it your first destination of the day or your very last. And while the drop at the end isn't quite as intense as The Twilight Zone Tower of Terror, we recommend that you don't underestimate its ability to loosen your lunch.

A. J. The potato barrels at Woody's Lunch Box were good. I also liked the grilled cheese, though it could've been cooked a little longer.

TOY STORY LAND

THE 11-ACRE TOY STORY LAND opened in 2018. The idea behind it is that you've been shrunk to the size of a toy and placed in Andy's backyard, where you get to play with other toys he's set up.

The land has three rides (**Alien Swirling Saucers** and **Slinky Dog Dash,** plus the preexisting **Toy Story Mania!**) and a quick-service restaurant, **Woody's Lunch Box,** serving American fare and soda floats (see page 188). Two stands offer plenty of *Toy Story* merchandise, including headbands inspired by aliens, Slinky Dog toys, fashion accessories, and T-shirts. Disney has also added an inside toy shop, **Jessie's Trading Post,** located in the exit queue of Toy Story Mania!

SABRINA Toy Story Land is so much fun, and Slinky Dog Dash is awesome! The ride takes you through Andy's room, and you get to see all his toys.

Roundup Rodeo BBQ, a much-needed table-service restaurant, is scheduled to open sometime this year. The restaurant is decorated with Andy's Toys and even has two children's play areas.

Woody, Buzz, and **Jessie** greet guests throughout the land. **Sarge** and the **Green Army Men Drum Corps** proudly march through several times daily. They play "Sarge Says" and are on the lookout for willing cadets for their interactive boot camp. Are you ready to become an official recruit in Andy's Backyard?

BRENDAN
Toy Story Land is so detailed. I love the giant characters.

In 1995 Pixar debuted Toy Story, *a movie where all toys are secretly alive (unbeknownst to humans). This feature-length film was followed by three more successful installments. Now Woody and his friends also have a land to welcome honorary toys. Go ahead and join them, to infinity and beyond!*

Movie Tip

Alien Swirling Saucers   ★★½

PRESCHOOL ★★★★½ (MAA)   GRADE SCHOOL ★★★★ (MBA)   TEENS ★★★½ (MBA) YOUNG ADULTS ★★★½ (MBA)   OVER 30 ★★★½ (MBA)   SENIORS ★★★½ (MBA)

What it is Spinning car ride. **Scope and scale** Minor attraction. **When to go** First 30 minutes the park is open or after 3 p.m. **Comment** Must be 32" to ride. **Duration of ride** 3 minutes. **Average wait in line per 100 people ahead of you** 10 minutes. **Loading speed** Slow. **ECV/wheelchair access** Must transfer to the ride vehicle. **Participates in Genie+** Yes. **Early Theme Park Entry** Yes. **Extended Evening Hours** Yes.

Queasy

Alien Swirling Saucers is themed around *Toy Story*'s vending machine aliens and their obsession with The Claw. The ride features an electronic space music soundtrack with eight songs that may sound familiar. For the shortest waits, ride during the first 30 minutes or last hour the park is open. Consider skipping the Saucers if the wait exceeds 20 minutes.

Brendan

Alien Swirling Saucers is wilder than it looks. You really get tossed around.

Felicity

I instantly loved Alien Swirling Saucers. It's quite wobbly and you dash all over the place. The music is loud but fun.

Alien Swirling Saucers is not worth the wait. It is slow moving and dull. One of its only highlights is the techno music.

A. J.

Slinky Dog Dash   ★★★★

PRESCHOOL ★★★★½ (AA)   GRADE SCHOOL ★★★★★ (E) ALL OTHER AGE GROUPS ★★★★½ (MAA)

What it is Outdoor roller coaster. **Scope and scale** Major attraction. **When to go** As soon as the park opens or just before closing. **Comment** Must be 38" to ride. **Duration of ride** 2 minutes. **Average wait in line per 100 people ahead of you** 4 minutes. **Loading speed** Moderate. **ECV/wheelchair access** Must transfer from ECV to provided wheelchair and then from wheelchair to the ride vehicle. **Participates in Genie+** Yes. **Early Theme Park Entry** Yes. **Extended Evening Hours** Yes.

Scary

Slinky Dog Dash is a long, outdoor roller coaster designed to look like Andy built it out of Tinker Toys. The trains are themed (naturally) to *Toy Story*'s Slinky Dog. The ride is more intense than the Magic Kingdom's Barnstormer and Seven Dwarfs Mine Train—lots of hills but no loops or high-speed curves—but not as forceful as Big Thunder Mountain Railroad. Slinky Dog Dash is likely to be inundated as soon as the park opens and to stay that way all day. Visit at park opening or right before closing.

Brendan

I rode Slinky Dog Dash twice. It's intense!

A. J.

Slinky Dog Dash is my favorite ride at the Studios. You won't want to miss it, and it's a good ride to do at night. The lines are a little shorter than during the day, and the park looks amazing, as everything is lit up with neon lights.

Toy Story Mania!   ★★★★½

ALL AGE GROUPS ★★★★½ (MAA)

What it is 3-D ride through indoor shooting gallery. **Scope and scale** Headliner. **When to go** At park opening or after 4:30 p.m. **Duration of ride** About 6½ minutes. **Average**

wait in line per 100 people ahead of you 4½ minutes. **Loading speed** Fast. **ECV/ wheelchair access** Must transfer from ECV to provided wheelchair. **Participates in Genie+** Yes. **Early Theme Park Entry** Yes. **Extended Evening Hours** Yes.

This ride is an interactive shooting gallery, much like Buzz Lightyear's Space Ranger Spin at the Magic Kingdom, but here your vehicle passes through a totally virtual midway, with booths offering such games as ring toss and ball throw. The pull-string cannon on your ride vehicle uses computer-generated imagery to toss rings, shoot balls, and even throw eggs and pies. Each game booth is manned by a *Toy Story* character who is right beside you in 3-D glory, cheering you on. You also experience vehicle motion, wind, and water spray.

The ride begins with a training round to familiarize you with the nature of the games and then continues through a number of games in which you compete against your riding mate for a higher score. The technology has the ability to self-adjust the level of difficulty, and there are plenty of easy targets for young children to reach. *Tip:* Let the pull-string retract all the way back into the cannon before pulling it again.

Toy Story Mania!, Slinky Dog Dash, and Alien Swirling Saucers are hot tickets. Ride as soon as the park opens.

> This ride was absolutely awesome. I wanted to ride it again and again.

Felicity

ANIMATION COURTYARD

THIS AREA IS TO THE RIGHT of Grauman's Chinese Theatre and contains *Disney Junior Play and Dance!, Star Wars Launch Bay,* and *Walt Disney Presents.* Disney Junior characters meet their fans right next to the attractions.

> If you love Disney Junior characters, bring your autograph book. You can meet them in Animation Courtyard.

Lucy

Disney Junior Play and Dance! ★★★★

PRESCHOOL ★★★★½ (MAA)   **GRADE SCHOOL** ★★★★½ (AA)   **TEENS** ★★ (MBA)
YOUNG ADULTS ★★½ (MBA)   **OVER 30** ★★★ (MBA)   **SENIORS** ★★½ (MBA)

What it is Live show for preschool children. **Scope and scale** Minor attraction. **When to go** Check My Disney Experience for showtimes. **Comment** Audience sits on the floor. **Duration of presentation** 25 minutes. **When to arrive** 20–30 minutes before showtime. **ECV/wheelchair access** May remain in wheelchair. **Participates in Genie+** Yes. **Early Theme Park Entry** No. **Extended Evening Hours** No.

This high-energy music-and-video show features Disney Junior characters and music. In addition to Doc McStuffins, Vampirina, Mickey, and Timon, a DJ rallies the kids to jump and dance. The audience sits on the floor so that kids can spontaneously erupt into motion when the mood strikes—and they do! Get there around 25 minutes before showtime, pick a spot on the floor, and chill until the action begins. Even for adults without children, it's a treat to watch the tykes rev up. For preschoolers, *Disney Junior* will be the highlight of their day, as a Thomasville, North Carolina, mom attests:

> *The show was fantastic! My 3-year-old loved it. The children danced, sang, and had a great time.*

The Florida mother of a 4-year-old agrees:

My daughter absolutely LOVED the show! If you have preschoolers, this is a MUST!

Disney Junior Play and Dance! is the fourth iteration of the stage show since 2007. The show is staged in a huge building to the right of Star Wars Launch Bay. Show up at least 25 minutes before showtime. Once inside, pick a spot on the floor and take a breather until the performance begins. Outside, little ones can meet the stars of the show, including Doc McStuffins.

Star Wars Launch Bay ★★★
Exhibits

**PRESCHOOL ★★★½ (BA)   GRADE SCHOOL ★★★★ (MBA)   TEENS ★★★★ (BA)
YOUNG ADULTS ★★★★ (BA)   OVER 30 ★★★★ (MBA)   SENIORS ★★★★ (BA)**

Character Greetings

**PRESCHOOL ★★★★ (AA)   GRADE SCHOOL ★★★★½ (A)   TEENS ★★★★½ (A)
YOUNG ADULTS ★★★★½ (AA) OVER 30 ★★★★½ (A) SENIORS ★★★★½ (AA)**

What it is Displays of a few *Star Wars* movie models and props, a movie trailer, and character greetings. **Scope and scale** Diversion. **When to go** Anytime. **Comment** The movie trailer includes plot spoilers from the entire *Star Wars* oeuvre. **Probable waiting time** 20–30 minutes each for the movie trailer and character greetings. **ECV/wheelchair access** May remain in wheelchair. **Participates in Genie+** No. **Early Theme Park Entry** No. **Extended Evening Hours** No.

Located in the back of Animation Courtyard, Star Wars Launch Bay is home to a walk-through exhibit, three meet-and-greet areas, a theater showing movies (featuring interviews with some of the creators of the new *Star Wars* films), a small mock-up of the Mos Eisley cantina, and the Launch Bay Cargo shop.

If you're a die-hard *Star Wars* fan, you'll want to see it all and you won't mind the huge amount of time it will take. But if meeting Chewie, BB-8, and Kylo Ren are your priorities, get there at park opening and head right away to the meet and greets.

Each character has a separate queuing area, and lines move slowly. Once you exit one, head right away to the next.

Walt Disney Presents ★★★

**PRESCHOOL ★★½ (MBA)   GRADE SCHOOL ★★★½ (MBA)   TEENS ★★★½ (MBA)
YOUNG ADULTS ★★★★ (BA)   OVER 30 ★★★★ (BA)   SENIORS ★★★★½ (A)**

What it is Disney-memorabilia collection plus a short film about Walt Disney. **Scope and scale** Minor attraction. **When to go** Anytime. **Duration of presentation** 25 minutes. **Preshow entertainment** Disney memorabilia. **Probable waiting time** For the film, 7 minutes. **ECV/wheelchair access** May remain in wheelchair. **Participates in Genie+** No. **Early Theme Park Entry** No. **Extended Evening Hours** No.

Walt Disney Presents consists of an exhibit area showcasing Disney memorabilia and recordings, followed by a film about Walt Disney's life and achievements, narrated by Julie Andrews. On display are various innovations in animation developed by Disney, along with models and plans for Disney World and other Disney theme parks. The standard film is sometimes replaced with previews of current Disney or Pixar movies.

LIVE ENTERTAINMENT *at* DISNEY'S HOLLYWOOD STUDIOS

THE STUDIOS' LIVE ENTERTAINMENT is generally as good as that at the other Disney theme parks. Shows, musical acts, street performers, and fireworks are all part of the offerings. Read on for details.

BEACONS OF MAGIC This new projection show started in 2021 on Sunset Boulevard's Twilight Zone Tower of Terror. It runs approximately every 15 minutes starting at dusk. When it starts, the Tower's exterior walls are bathed in bright, shimmering projections. Look closely; the best views are on Sunset and by the Tower of Terror entrance, and you'll see hotel guests dancing in the windows. The event might not return once the 50th anniversary celebrations are over.

DISNEY CHARACTERS *Toy Story*'s Buzz, Woody, Jessie, and Green Army Men meet in Toy Story Land, while Minnie and Mickey Mouse can be found on Commissary Lane in an indoor venue dubbed Mickey and Minnie Starring in *Red Carpet Dreams*. Chip 'n' Dale meet right outside this venue. The star of Echo Lake is Olaf, the quirky snowman from *Frozen*. Disney Junior stars appear inside Animation Courtyard

DISNEY MOVIE MAGIC A 12-minute nighttime projection show displayed on the front of Grauman's Chinese Theatre (home of Mickey & Minnie's Runaway Railway), *Movie Magic* shows classic clips from Disney and the studios it has acquired. It's not the best Disney projection show, but it's a nice way to end the evening if you're around. Check your My Disney Experience app for showtimes.

HOLIDAY EVENTS During the Christmas season, the **Jingle Bell, Jingle BAM!** nighttime show is projected on Grauman's Chinese Theatre. This nighttime holiday spectacular has projections, seasonal music, fireworks, and even a snowfall. Hosted by Wayne and Lanny, the comical elves from ABC's *Prep & Landing*, the show also features holiday scenes from *Mickey's Christmas Carol, Beauty and the Beast, Pluto's Christmas Tree, Bambi,* and *The Nightmare Before Christmas*. On Sunset Boulevard, **Sunset Seasons Greetings**—a sound-and-light show projected on The Twilight Zone Tower of Terror—is performed about every 20 minutes nightly. As on Main Street, U.S.A., the show comes with lots of magical snow. Even **Echo Lake** gets a holiday overhaul, and Gertie the giant dinosaur wears a Santa hat!

STREET ENTERTAINMENT ★★★½ Appearing mainly on Hollywood and Sunset Boulevards, the Citizens of Hollywood, also known as Streetmosphere, portray old-time Tinseltown characters. The Citizens have been absent from the park since 2020 but made a surprise appearance in January 2022 cheering the runDisney marathon runners as they entered the Studios. As we went to print, Disney still had them listed as "temporarily unavailable." As other characters have returned to the park, we hope that they, too, will return soon.

THE WONDERFUL WORLD OF ANIMATION The new laser light and projection show takes viewers on a tour of 90 years of Disney animation. The 12-minute show features animated Pixar and Disney releases and is projected on Grauman's Chinese Theatre. The show takes place right after *Disney Movie Magic.*

Check the My Disney Experience app for schedule changes, as Disney adds or removes performances according to park occupancy.

Fantasmic! (temporarily unavailable)   ★★★★½

PRESCHOOL ★★★★ (A)   **GRADE SCHOOL** ★★★★½ (AA)   **TEENS** ★★★★½ (AA)
YOUNG ADULTS ★★★★½ (AA)   **OVER 30** ★★★★½ (AA)   **SENIORS** ★★★★½ (AA)

What it is Mixed-media nighttime spectacular. **Scope and scale** Super-headliner.
When to go Check the My Disney Experience app for schedule; if 2 shows are offered, the second is less crowded. **Comment** Not to be missed. **Duration of show** 25 minutes.
Probable waiting time 50–90 minutes for a seat; 35–40 minutes for standing room.

Loud   Scary

A must-see for the whole family. Starring Mickey Mouse in his role as the sorcerer's apprentice from *Fantasia,* the production uses lasers, images projected on a shroud of mist, dazzling fireworks, lighting effects, and powerful music. *Fantasmic!* has the potential to frighten young children. Prepare your children for the show, and make sure that they know that, in addition to all the favorite Disney characters, the Maleficent dragon and the evil Jafar will make appearances. To give you an idea, picture the evil Jafar turning into a cobra 100 feet long and 16 feet high. Rest assured, however, that during the final parade, your kids will cheer on Cinderella and Prince Charming, Belle, Snow White, Ariel and Prince Eric, Jasmine and Aladdin, Donald Duck, Minnie, and Mickey. You can alleviate the fright factor somewhat by sitting back a bit. Also, if you are seated in the first 12 rows, you will get sprayed with water at times.

The theater is huge, but so is the popularity of the show. If there are two performances, the second show will almost always be less crowded. If you attend the first (or only) scheduled performance, show up at least 1 hour in advance. If you opt for the second show, arrive at least 40 minutes early. Plan to use that time for a picnic. If you forget to bring munchies, not to worry; there are concessions in the theater.

Unless you buy a *Fantasmic!* dining package, you will not have reserved seats, so arrive early for best choice. Try to sit in the middle three or four

---

FAVORITE EATS AT DISNEY'S HOLLYWOOD STUDIOS

COMMISSARY LANE   ABC Commissary | Mediterranean salad with or without chicken, both served with hummus and flatbread.

ECHO LAKE   Backlot Express | Great burgers | **Sci-Fi Dine-In Theater** | It's not about the food (dismal) but about eating in a vintage convertible car watching old sci-fi movie previews. Teens love it! Great place to cool off. *Table service only*

GRAND AVENUE   PizzeRizzo | Pizza and meatball sub

SUNSET BOULEVARD   Fairfax Fare | Hot dogs

TOY STORY LAND   Woody's Lunch Box | Shredded smoked brisket sandwich and "Totchos," aka tater tots served like nachos

sections, a bit off-center. No refunds are given if *Fantasmic!* is canceled due to weather or other circumstances.

Brendan

> The number one show in my opinion is *Fantasmic!* You can't miss it.

Fantasmic! Dining Packages

Three restaurants offer a ticket voucher for the members of your dining party to enter *Fantasmic!* via a special entrance and sit in a reserved section of seats. The package consists of a buffet at **Hollywood & Vine** or a fixed-price dinner at **Mama Melrose's Ristorante Italiano** or **The Hollywood Brown Derby**. Call ☎ 407-WDW-DINE (939-3463) up to 60 days in advance to request the package. This is a real reservation and must be guaranteed by a credit card at the time of booking. There's a 48-hour cancellation policy.

Prices fluctuate according to season, so call to find out the exact dinner charge for a particular date. If there are two scheduled performances in one night, the lunch package will only grant you reserved seating for the first performance.

LILIANE If there are two *Fantasmic!* performances during the time of your visit, you really have no reason to spend extra money on the dining package. Just grab some food, enter the theater at least 40 minutes prior to the show, and relax!

Allow at least 2 hours to eat. You will receive the ticket vouchers at the restaurant. After dinner, report to the *Fantasmic!* sign on Hollywood Boulevard next to Oscar's (just inside the front entrance to the park) no later than 35 minutes prior to showtime. A cast member will escort you to the reserved section. If *Fantasmic!* is canceled for any reason, you will not receive a refund. However, you can go to Guest Relations to receive a voucher for a performance within the next five days. This only works if you're still in town and if you're willing to pay for another admission to the Studios. If you're still around and you have a Park Hopper, go for it!

EXIT STRATEGIES

EXITING THE STUDIOS at the end of the day following *Fantasmic!* is not nearly as difficult as leaving after the EPCOT fireworks. We recommend that you take it easy and make your way out of the park after the first wave of guests has departed. Pick a spot inside the park and instruct your group not to go through the turnstiles before everyone is reunited. Most important, latch onto your kids.

DISNEY'S HOLLYWOOD STUDIOS TOURING PLANS

OUR STEP-BY-STEP TOURING PLANS are field-tested, independently verified itineraries that will keep you moving counter to the crowd flow and allow you to see as much as possible in a single day with minimal time wasted in line. You can take in all the attractions at DHS in one day, even when traveling with young children. If you aren't interested in an attraction on the touring plan, simply skip it and proceed to the next step. Likewise, if you encounter a very long line at an attraction, skip it.

The different touring plans are described below. The descriptions will tell you for whom or for what situation the plans are designed. The actual touring plans are on pages 505–509 and each includes a numbered map of the park to help you find your way around.

1-DAY EVERYTHING *STAR WARS* TOURING PLAN   An itinerary for families who love *Star Wars*, this plan includes rides, shopping, and general exploration of Star Wars: Galaxy's Edge. Be sure to try the interactive games in the Play Disney Parks app as you wait in the attraction queues and wander around the land. On busy days, Disney may restrict access to Galaxy's Edge and only give guests a limited amount of time (usually 4 hours). If that's the case, you may need to forgo some steps of the plan because there won't be enough time to experience everything. If you're limited on time, consider skipping Savi's Workshop and Droid Depot. They're very cool but also extremely popular and expensive, and waiting for them will take valuable time you could be using to explore all the beautiful details of the land. The plan also includes *Star Wars* attractions outside the land, including Star Wars Launch Bay and Star Tours–The Adventures Continue.

1-DAY TOURING PLAN FOR PARENTS WITH SMALL CHILDREN   This plan is for parents of children ages 3–8 who wish to see the very best age-appropriate attractions and shows in Hollywood Studios. Every attraction has a rating of at least three-and-a-half stars (out of five) from preschool and grade-school children surveyed by *The Unofficial Guide*. The plan includes a midday break outside the park, so families can rest and regroup. The plan keeps walking and backtracking to a minimum.

1-DAY SLEEPYHEAD TOURING PLAN FOR PARENTS WITH SMALL CHILDREN   A relaxed plan that allows families with young children to sleep late and still see the highlights of DHS. The plan begins around 11 a.m., sets aside ample time for lunch and dinner, and includes the very best child-friendly attractions and shows in the park. Special advice is provided for touring the park with small kids.

1-DAY TOURING PLAN FOR TWEENS AND THEIR PARENTS   This plan for parents with children ages 8–12 includes every attraction rated three-and-a-half stars and higher by this age group and sets aside ample time for lunch and dinner.

1-DAY HAPPY FAMILY TOURING PLAN   An itinerary for multigenerational families, this plan allows teens and older children to experience the Studios' thrill rides while parents and young children visit more age-appropriate attractions. The family stays together most of the day, including lunch and dinner, and each attraction in the plan is rated three-and-a-half stars or higher.

BEFORE YOU GO

1. Call ☎ 407-824-4321 or check disneyworld.com for operating hours.
2. Purchase admission and make park reservations.
3. Familiarize yourself with park-opening procedures and reread the touring plan you've chosen.

DISNEY'S HOLLYWOOD STUDIOS TRIVIA QUIZ

1. In *Toy Story,* Rex is Andy's dinosaur. What is the name of Bonnie's dinosaur?

a. Baby Bob   **c.** Barney
b. Riff   **d.** Trixie

2. Which famous rock band stars in Rock 'n' Roller Coaster?

a. The Rolling Stones   **c.** The Who
b. Aerosmith   **d.** Queen

3. The Tower of Terror is based on which TV series?

a. *The Tower of Terror*   **c.** *The Twilight Hotel*
b. *Hotel California*   **d.** *The Twilight Zone*

4. What is the name of the lake at Disney's Hollywood Studios?

a. Echo Lake   **c.** Studio Lake
b. Bay Lake   **d.** Lake Buena Vista

5. What was the original name of Disney's Hollywood Studios?

a. Pixar Studios   **c.** DreamWorks
b. Paramount Studios   **d.** Disney-MGM Studios

6. Where does *Beauty and the Beast Live on Stage* take place?

a. Theater of the Stars   **c.** Castle Forecourt Stage
b. American Gardens Theatre   **d.** Hollywood Hills Amphitheater

7. What is the name of the roller coaster at Toy Story Land?

a. Alien Swirling Saucers   **c.** Woody's Lunch Box
b. Slinky Dog Dash   **d.** Andy's Toy Box

8. What restaurant is not located in Disney's Hollywood Studios?

a. Hollywood & Vine   **c.** Mama Melrose's Ristorante
b. Cosmic Ray's Starlight Cafe   **d.** Hollywood Brown Derby

9. What is the name of the nighttime spectacular held at Disney's Hollywood Studios?

a. *Happily Ever After*   **c.** *IllumiNations: Reflections of Earth*
b. *Cinematic Spectacular*   **d.** *Fantasmic!*

10. What is the current name of the former Pizza Planet?

a. PizzeRizzo   **c.** The Flying Zucchini Brothers
b. The Great Gonzo's Pandemonium Pizza Parlor   **d.** The Swedish Chef

Answers can be found on page 458.

Things Universal Might Split Up And "Wizard-ify" To Make More Money

Water Fountains

Changing Tables

Valet Parking

Buses

Park Maps

UNIVERSAL ORLANDO

UNIVERSAL ORLANDO

UNIVERSAL ORLANDO is a complete destination resort, with two theme parks; a water park (covered on pages 428–432); soon-to-be-eight hotels; and **CityWalk,** a shopping, dining, and entertainment complex (see page 445). A system of roads and two multistory parking facilities are connected by moving sidewalks to CityWalk, which also serves as a gateway to **Universal Studios Florida (USF)** and **Universal's Islands of Adventure (IOA)** theme parks.

And Universal isn't done. Over the last few years, it has acquired hundreds of acres of land along Destination Parkway to Sand Lake Road, more land than Universal Orlando currently sits on. In August 2019, Universal officially announced construction of its second resort campus, **Universal's Epic Universe.** Roads and other infrastructure are already being constructed on more than 750 acres acquired by Universal near the Orange County Convention Center, about a 12-minute drive south of the current resort. Early concept art depicted a central hub with fountain-filled lagoons, surrounded by hotels, restaurants, and at least four highly themed "lands."

The first featured franchise officially confirmed for the new park is **Super Nintendo World,** featuring an interactive dark ride based on the Mario Kart video games; a Donkey Kong Country–themed roller coaster; and a family-friendly Yoshi attraction. NBCUniversal CEO Jeff Shell has said that Epic Universe will be Universal's largest in the US and that characters from **DreamWorks** (likely from *How to Train Your Dragon*) and **Illumination** (creators of *Despicable Me*) will be included. The park's other rumored intellectual properties are from **J. K. Rowling's Wizarding World** universe (specifically, the Ministries of Magic from Harry Potter's London and/or *Fantastic Beasts'* Paris), along with classic Universal monsters, such as Dracula and Frankenstein. Of course, all these plans are subject to change.

continued on page 400

Universal Orlando

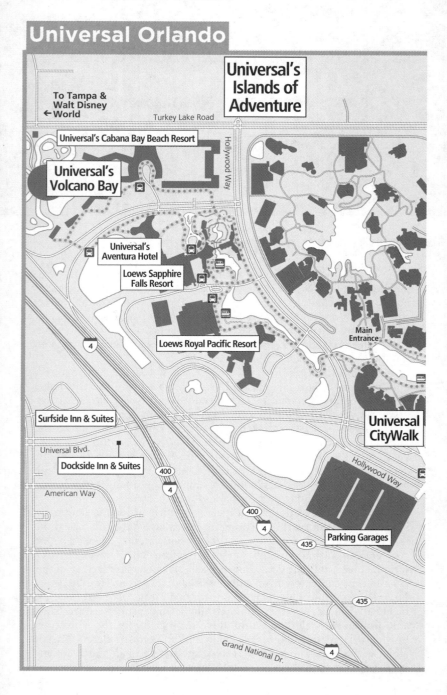

Universal's
Islands of
Adventure

To Tampa &
Walt Disney
← World

Turkey Lake Road

Hollywood Way

Universal's Cabana Bay Beach Resort

Universal's
Volcano Bay

Universal's
Aventura Hotel

Loews Sapphire
Falls Resort

Loews Royal Pacific Resort

Main
Entrance

Surfside Inn & Suites

Universal Blvd.

Dockside Inn & Suites

American Way

Universal
CityWalk

Hollywood Way

400

400

4

435

Parking Garages

435

Grand National Dr.

4

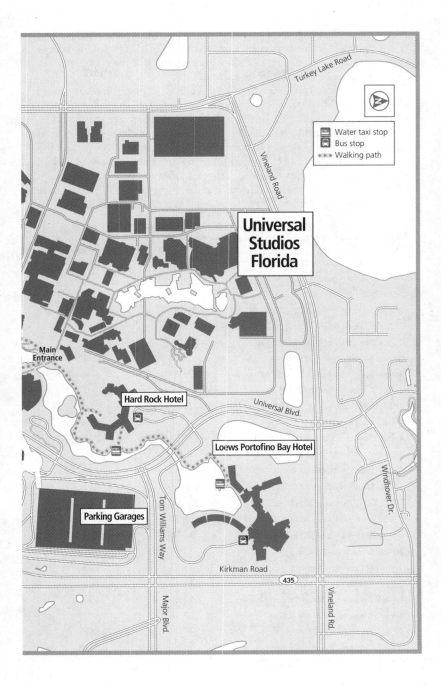

Water taxi stop
Bus stop
Walking path

Turkey Lake Road

Vineland Road

Universal Studios Florida

Main Entrance

Hard Rock Hotel

Universal Blvd.

Loews Portofino Bay Hotel

Parking Garages

Tom Williams Way

Windhover Dr.

Kirkman Road

435

Major Blvd.

Vineland Rd.

continued from page 397

Originally anticipated to open in 2023, Epic Universe was delayed by the pandemic, but construction resumed in March 2021; a new opening date has not been officially announced, but the theme park is anticipated to be completed by early 2025.

Both existing Universal theme parks are accessed via CityWalk. Crossing CityWalk from the parking garages, you can bear right to Universal Studios Florida or left to Islands of Adventure.

Universal Orlando has developed into a world-class, multifaceted resort destination—one we can no longer adequately cover in the pages allocated here. For in-depth coverage of the Universal parks, consider *The Unofficial Guide to Universal Orlando,* by Seth Kubersky with Bob Sehlinger and Len Testa. It is the most comprehensive guide to Universal Orlando in print, with more than 400 pages devoted to

UNIVERSAL ORLANDO ADMISSIONS		
TICKET TYPE	**ADULTS**	**CHILDREN (ages 3–9)**
1-Day Single-Park (USF/IOA)	$109–$159	$104–$154
1-Day Volcano Bay	$70–$85	$65–$80
1-Day Park-to-Park (USF/IOA)	$164–$214	$159–$209
2-Day Single-Park (USF/IOA)	$213–$291	$203–$281
2-Day Park-to-Park (USF/IOA)	$273–$361	$263–$341
2-Day Park-to-Park (USF/IOA/VB)	$313–$386	$303–$376
3-Day Single-Park (USF/IOA)	$233–$316	$223–$306
3-Day Single-Park (USF/IOA/VB)	$273–$351	$263–$341
3-Day Park-to-Park (USF/IOA)	$293–$376	$283–$366
3-Day Park-to-Park (USF/IOA/VB)	$333–$411	$323–$401
4-Day Single-Park (USF/IOA)	$247–$328	$237–$318
4-Day Single-Park (USF/IOA/VB)	$297–$373	$287–$363
4-Day Park-to-Park (USF/IOA)	$312–$393	$302–$323
4-Day Park-to-Park (USF/IOA/VB)	$362–$438	$352–$428
5-Day Single-Park (USF/IOA)	$259–$340	$249–$330
5-Day Single-Park (USF/IOA/VB)	$319–$395	$309–$385
5-Day Park-to-Park (USF/IOA)	$329–$410	$319–$400
5-Day Park-to-Park (USF/IOA/VB)	$389–$465	$379–$455
2-Park Seasonal Annual Pass	$350	$350
2-Park Power Annual Pass	$400	$400
2-Park Preferred Annual Pass	$450	$450
2-Park Premier Annual Pass	$625	$625
3-Park Seasonal Annual Pass	$450	$450
3-Park Power Annual Pass	$510	$510
3-Park Preferred Annual Pass	$560	$560
3-Park Premier Annual Pass	$815	$815

the subject. Though we'll continue to cover Universal Orlando in this book, we strongly recommend the Universal-specific guide for all the tips, insights, elaborations, and details needed to plan your visit.

The main Universal information number is ☎ 407-363-8000 or visit universalorlando.com. **Guest Services** is at ☎ 407-224-4233. **ATMs** are available at several locations in both parks. For **Lost and Found,** first go to Guests Services or call ☎ 407-224-4233.

LODGING AT UNIVERSAL ORLANDO

LILIANE If your kids are *Despicable Me* fans, check out the Minion-themed Kids' Suites at Portofino Bay.

THE 750-ROOM **Portofino Bay Hotel** is a gorgeous property set on an artificial bay and themed like an Italian coastal town. The 650-room **Hard Rock Hotel** is an ultracool "Hotel California" replica, and the 1,000-room, Polynesian-themed **Royal Pacific Resort** is sumptuously decorated and richly appointed. These three resorts are on the pricey side, but guests get free unlimited Universal Express Passes for the length of their stay. For a fun night outside the parks, check out the **Wantilan Luau** at Royal Pacific. Enjoy island music and a great feast. Prices are $89 for adults, $39 for kids (includes gratuity but not tax). For an extra $20 per person, Premium Seating gets you a souvenir tiki mug and a reserved table near the stage.

The retro-style **Cabana Bay Beach Resort,** Universal's largest hotel, has 2,200 moderate- and value-priced rooms, plus amenities not seen at comparable Disney resorts (bowling alley, lazy river). **Sapphire Falls Resort** has a Caribbean theme and is priced between the Royal Pacific and Cabana Bay Beach Resorts. The 16-story **Aventura Hotel,** a moderately priced 600-room hotel, also features 13 kids' suites, a food hall showcasing five distinct cuisine options, and a rooftop bar and grill. Located adjacent to Sapphire Falls Resort and across from Cabana Bay Beach Resort, Aventura Hotel is within walking distance of USF, IOA, and Universal's water park, Volcano Bay. Cabana Bay, Sapphire Falls, and Aventura *do not* offer complimentary Universal Express Passes to any of the three parks.

The latest addition to the Universal hotel portfolio is the **Endless Summer Resorts,** which encompasses two hotel towers: **Surfside Inn and Suites** and **Dockside Inn and Suites.**

When **Epic Universe** opens, it will have a 500-room hotel attached to the rear of the new theme park's central hub, as well as a 750-room hotel across the street from its main entrance, adding a total of 1,250 rooms to Universal's inventory. See pages 132–140 for more details on all Universal Orlando hotels.

PARK PASSES

UNIVERSAL ORLANDO OFFERS one- to five-day passes for one or two theme parks; adding Volcano Bay to a multiday ticket costs $40–$61 plus tax, depending on length. Be sure to check the website (universal orlando.com) for seasonal deals and specials. You can save as much as $20 off the gate prices by buying your tickets online.

UNIVERSAL EXPRESS

THIS SYSTEM ALLOWS ANY GUEST to "skip the line" and experience an attraction via a special queue with little or no waiting. Universal Express involves no advance planning; simply visit any eligible operating attraction whenever you choose, no return-time windows required. Universal Express is not free for everyone.

Unlimited Universal Express access at the two theme parks is a complimentary perk for guests at **Portofino Bay Hotel, Hard Rock Hotel,** and **Royal Pacific Resort;** these guests may use the Express lines all day long simply by flashing the pass they get at check-in. This perk far surpasses any benefit accorded to guests of Disney resorts and is especially valuable during peak season.

Day guests or guests staying at hotels not listed above can purchase Universal Express Passes starting at $79.99 plus tax for a single theme park or $109.99 plus tax for both parks (depending on the season); passes allow you to jump the line once at each Universal Express attraction at a given park. Unlimited Universal Express Passes, which allow unlimited line-jumping, start at $89.99 plus tax for one park or $119.99 plus tax for both parks. The number of Express Passes is limited each day, and they can sell out, so increase your chances of securing passes by buying and printing them at home off Universal's website. You'll need to know when you plan on using it, though, because prices vary depending on the date. More than 90% of attractions are covered by Universal Express.

UNIVERSAL, KIDS, AND SCARY STUFF

THOUGH THERE IS PLENTY FOR CHILDREN to see and do at the Universal parks, most major attractions can potentially make kids under age 8 wig out. To be frank, they freak out a fairly large percentage of adults as well. On average, Universal's rides move more aggressively and feature more intense experiences. See table at right for details on the fright potential of each attraction at USF, IOA, and Volcano Bay.

CHARACTERS AT UNIVERSAL ORLANDO

LIKE WALT DISNEY WORLD, Universal Orlando also has a stable of characters to call its own. There are two kinds of characters: animated, or those whose costumes include face-covering headpieces (including animal characters and humanlike cartoon characters, such as the Simpsons), and celebrities or face characters, those for whom no mask or headpiece is necessary. The latter include Marilyn Monroe, Doc Brown, and the Knight Bus and Hogwarts express conductors.

CHARACTER DINING

AT PRESS TIME, character dining had not returned.

continued on page 406

SMALL-CHILD FRIGHT-POTENTIAL TABLE

This table provides a quick reference to identify attractions to be wary of, and why. It relates specifically to kids ages 3–7 and represents a generalization, as all kids are different. Children at the younger end of the range are more likely to be frightened than children in their sixth or seventh year. For more information about ride elements that may induce sensory overload, download Universal's planning guide for cognitive accessibility at tinyurl.com/uocognitive.

UNIVERSAL STUDIOS FLORIDA

PRODUCTION CENTRAL

- **Despicable Me Minion Mayhem** Universal's mildest simulator motion-wise, but the huge images and loud soundtrack may startle preschoolers. Stationary benches are available in the front row to avoid the moving seats. Child swap available (see page 260).
- **Hollywood Rip Ride Rockit** The tallest roller coaster at Universal, with loud music to cover your screams. May terrify guests of any age. Child swap available (see page 260).
- **Transformers: The Ride—3D** Intense, bloodlessly violent virtual reality simulator may frighten younger children and deafen guests of any age. Child swap available (see page 260).

NEW YORK

- **Race Through New York Starring Jimmy Fallon** Moderate simulator motion, intense 3-D imagery, loud sounds, and the comedy stylings of Jimmy Fallon may disturb younger kids (and adults who remember Johnny Carson). Child swap available (see page 260).
- **Revenge of the Mummy** Very intense roller coaster in the dark with angry mummies, bugs, and fireballs. May frighten guests of any age. Child swap available (see page 260).

SAN FRANCISCO

- **Fast & Furious: Supercharged** Parental guidance suggested for intense simulated street-racing action with blasts of fog, loud noises, and improper use of turn signals. The actual motion of the vehicle is very mild. Child swap available (see page 260).

THE WIZARDING WORLD OF HARRY POTTER—DIAGON ALLEY

- **Harry Potter and the Escape from Gringotts** Visually intimidating with intense 3-D effects and brief moments of moderately fast roller-coaster motion. Less frightening than Harry Potter and the Forbidden Journey but may still rattle some riders. Child swap available (see page 260).
- **Hogwarts Express: King's Cross Station** Brief encounter with Dementors may scare some preschoolers; otherwise, not frightening.
- **Ollivanders** Not frightening in any respect.

WORLD EXPO

- **Men in Black Alien Attack** Dark ride with spinning cars and comical aliens may frighten some preschoolers. Child swap available (see page 260).

SPRINGFIELD: HOME OF THE SIMPSONS

- **Kang & Kodos' Twirl 'n' Hurl** Dumbo-style midway ride. A favorite of many young children. Child swap available (see page 260).
- **The Simpsons Ride** Extremely intense visually, with USF's strongest simulated motion. May frighten many adults as well as kids. Child swap available (see page 260).

WOODY WOODPECKER'S KIDZONE

- *Animal Actors on Location!* Not frightening in any respect, unless you have a phobia of animals.
- **Curious George Goes to Town** Not frightening in any respect, but your kid may get soaked.
- **DreamWorks Destination** Not frightening in any respect.
- **E.T. Adventure** Dark ride with simulated flight and psychedelic creatures. A little intense for a few preschoolers, but the end is all happiness and harmony. Child swap available (see page 260).
- **Fievel's Playland** Not frightening in any respect, except for the big slide that may scare some preschoolers.
- **Woody Woodpecker's Nuthouse Coaster** A beginner's roller coaster; safe for all but the most timid tykes. Child swap available (see page 260).

HOLLYWOOD

- *The Bourne Stuntacular* Intense action-movie fight choreography, including live gunfire and loud explosions, may startle viewers of all ages.

SMALL-CHILD FRIGHT-POTENTIAL TABLE *(continued)*

HOLLYWOOD *(continued)*

- *Universal Orlando's Cinematic Celebration* Oversize images of dinosaurs and Dementors, accompanied by loud fireworks, may startle small children.
- *Universal Orlando's Horror Make-Up Show* Gory props and film clips, presented educationally and humorously, may wig out wee ones, but most children seem to handle it disturbingly well. Interestingly, very few families report problems with this show.

ISLANDS OF ADVENTURE

MARVEL SUPER HERO ISLAND

- **The Amazing Adventures of Spider-Man** Immersive 3-D effects and spinning simulator movement may frighten younger kids, but most take the comic book mayhem in stride. Technically similar to Transformers at USF but significantly less intense. Child swap available (see page 260).
- **Doctor Doom's Fearfall** Visually intimidating to all guests, with an intense launch and brief weightlessness. The actual plummeting is less protracted than on WDW's Twilight Zone Tower of Terror. Child swap available (see page 260).
- **The Incredible Hulk Coaster** Very intense looping roller coaster with a high-speed launch. This is a scary coaster by any standard. Child swap available (see page 260).
- **Storm Force Accelatron** Teacups-type midway ride can induce motion sickness in all ages, though most kids seem to love it. Child swap available (see page 260).

TOON LAGOON

- **Dudley Do-Right's Ripsaw Falls** Visually intimidating from outside, with several intense, potentially drenching plunges. A toss-up, to be considered only if your kids like water-flume rides. Child swap available (see page 260).
- **Me Ship, *The Olive*** Not frightening in any respect.
- **Popeye & Bluto's Bilge-Rat Barges** Potentially frightening and certainly soaking for guests of all ages. Most younger children handle it well. Child swap available (see page 260).

SKULL ISLAND

- **Skull Island: Reign of Kong** The ride vehicle's motion is fairly mild, but don't let the low minimum height (36″) fool you: The 3-D visuals of mutant bugs are pretty gross, and the queue is even more frightening, with sections that resemble a haunted house. Child swap available (see page 260).

JURASSIC PARK

- **Camp Jurassic** Some preschoolers may be spooked by the dark caves and dinosaur sounds; guests who are afraid of heights should avoid the net climb.
- **Jurassic Park Discovery Center** Not frightening in any respect.
- **Jurassic Park River Adventure** Visually intimidating boat ride with life-size dinosaurs and an intense flume finale. May frighten and dampen guests of any age. Child swap available (see page 260).
- **Jurassic World VelociCoaster** An extremely intense roller coaster featuring multiple high-speed launches, stomach-lurching loops, and close encounters with rapacious raptors. Child swap available (see page 260).
- **Pteranodon Flyers** A short, slow suspended roller coaster. Frightens some children who are scared of heights.
- **Raptor Encounter** The velociraptor makes loud, growling noises and sudden, snapping movements that startle even some adults.

THE WIZARDING WORLD OF HARRY POTTER—HOGSMEADE

- **Flight of the Hippogriff** Another beginner coaster, comparable to The Barnstormer at the Magic Kingdom. May frighten some preschoolers. Child swap available (see page 260).
- **Hagrid's Magical Creatures Motorbike Adventure** A moderately intense outdoor coaster with no loops, but with forward and backward launches, dramatic drops, and close encounters with magical creatures. This ride may intimidate younger Muggles. Child swap available (see page 260).
- **Harry Potter and the Forbidden Journey** Extremely intense special effects and macabre visuals with wild simulated movement that may frighten and discombobulate guests of any age. Child swap available (see page 260).
- **Hogwarts Express: Hogsmeade Station** Not frightening in any respect.

THE LOST CONTINENT

- *Poseidon's Fury* Loud explosions, water effects, and brief periods of pitch darkness may scare younger children. You must remain standing through the entire attraction.

SEUSS LANDING

- **Caro-Seuss-el** Not frightening in any respect. Child swap available (see page 260).
- **The Cat in the Hat** Mild spinning motion and modest visual effects may frighten a small percentage of preschoolers. Child swap available (see page 260).
- **The High in the Sky Seuss Trolley Train Ride!** May scare kids who are afraid of heights; otherwise, not frightening in any respect. Child swap available (see page 260).
- **If I Ran the Zoo** Not frightening in any respect.
- **One Fish, Two Fish, Red Fish, Blue Fish** A tame midway ride that's a great favorite of most young children, though they will likely get wet. Child swap available (see page 260).

VOLCANO BAY *(see pages 428–432)*

THE VOLCANO

- **Vol's Caverns** Dark pathways may spook sensitive toddlers; otherwise, not frightening.

RAINFOREST VILLAGE

- **Kala & Tai Nui Serpentine Body Slides** Even more terrifying than the Ko'okiri Body Plunge (see below), with twisting enclosed tubes and extreme g-forces.
- **Maku Round Raft Ride** Maku is one of the milder family raft rides in the park, with mostly open troughs and gentle curves. Don't mix it up with the Puihi Round Raft Ride!
- **Ohyah and Ohno Drop Slides** The shortest twisting tube slides in the park, but the final drop of 4–6 feet can knock the wind out of weak swimmers.
- **Puihi Round Raft Ride** Puihi is among the scariest family raft rides in the park, with sharp turns that seem to nearly toss you onto the interstate.
- **Puka Uli Lagoon** Not frightening in any respect.
- **Punga Racers** Enclosed tubes may upset claustrophobes; otherwise, not frightening.
- **Taniwha Tubes** A moderately fast-moving raft slide with some surprising twists and drops. Each of the four tubes has a different configuration. Accompany smaller kids on a two-seater raft, and ask for a green Tonga slide with more open-air sections if you get claustrophobic.
- **TeAwa the Fearless River** Swift current can swamp smaller swimmers; mandatory life jackets are available in all sizes.

RIVER VILLAGE

- **Honu Slide** Honu's hair-raising high-banked walls will wig out almost anyone. Don't confuse it with its sibling, ika Moana.
- **ika Moana Slide** ika Moana is a mild raft ride that most kids can handle.
- **Kopiko Wai Winding River** A brief segment floats through a dark, foggy cave; otherwise, not frightening in any respect.
- **Krakatau Aqua Coaster** Roller coaster–style dips and brief enclosed tunnels may scare younger kids, but most find it thrilling.
- **Runamukka Reef** Not frightening in any respect.
- **Tot Tiki Reef** Not frightening in any respect.

WAVE VILLAGE

- **Ko'okiri Body Plunge** High-speed vertical drop slide that will scare anyone silly.
- **The Reef** Not frightening in any respect.
- **Waturi Beach** Larger waves may overwhelm little ones; otherwise, not frightening in any respect.

continued from page 402

UNIVERSAL'S
ISLANDS *of* ADVENTURE

IOA IS ARRANGED IN A LARGE CIRCLE surrounding a lake. You first encounter the Moroccan-style **Port of Entry,** where you'll find **Guest Services, lockers, stroller and ECV rentals,** and shopping. The **First Aid Station** is located next to the park entrance and is staffed with registered nurses and paramedics. **ATMs** are located at several locations throughout the park. Loose items are not permitted on select attractions; free single-time-use lockers are available at the following IOA rides: The Incredible Hulk Coaster, Harry Potter and the Forbidden Journey, Hagrid's Magical Creatures Motorbike Adventure, and the Jurassic World VelociCoaster.

From Port of Entry, moving counterclockwise around the lagoon, you access **Marvel Super Hero Island, Toon Lagoon, Skull Island, Jurassic Park, The Wizarding World of Harry Potter–Hogsmeade, The Lost Continent,** and **Seuss Landing.** For families, there are three interactive playgrounds as well as six rides or shows without height restrictions that young children can enjoy.

BOB Roller coasters at Islands of Adventure are the real deal— not for the timid or for little ones.

BEWARE OF THE WET AND WILD

ISLANDS OF ADVENTURE OFFERS MANY wet and wild rides. Eight out of the top 10 attractions at IOA are thrill rides; of these, three will not only scare the crap out of you but will also drench you with water. If you get soaked during warm weather, you're better off just air-drying; when it's cool, pack a change of clothes.

THE WIZARDING WORLD OF
HARRY POTTER–HOGSMEADE

PASSING BENEATH A STONE ARCHWAY, you enter the village of **Hogsmeade.** Depicted in winter, the village setting is rendered in exquisite detail: Stone cottages and shops have steeply pitched slate roofs; bowed multipaned windows; gables; and tall, crooked chimneys. In keeping with

ISABELLE Listen for Moaning Myrtle, the female ghost who appears in many of the *Harry Potter* movies, in the ladies' restroom.

Isabelle

the stores depicted in the films, the shopping venues in The Wizarding World of Harry Potter–Hogsmeade are small and intimate—so intimate, in fact, that they feel congested when they're serving only 12–20 shoppers. With so many avid Potter fans, lines for the shops develop most days by 9:30 or 10 a.m. The lines are frequently longer than the wait for the rides.

continued on page 411

ATTRACTION HEIGHT REQUIREMENTS

UNIVERSAL STUDIOS FLORIDA

Despicable Me Minion Mayhem	40" minimum height
E.T. Adventure	34" minimum height
Fast & Furious: Supercharged	40" minimum height
Harry Potter and the Escape from Gringotts	42" minimum height
Hollywood Rip Ride Rockit	51" minimum height; 79" maximum height
Men in Black Alien Attack	42" minimum height
Race Through New York Starring Jimmy Fallon	40" minimum height
Revenge of the Mummy	48" minimum height
The Simpsons Ride	40" minimum height
Transformers: The Ride—3D	40" minimum height
Woody Woodpecker's Nuthouse Coaster	36" minimum height

ISLANDS OF ADVENTURE

The Amazing Adventures of Spider-Man	40" minimum height
The Cat in the Hat	36" minimum height
Doctor Doom's Fearfall	52" minimum height
Dudley Do-Right's Ripsaw Falls	44" minimum height
Flight of the Hippogriff	36" minimum height
Hagrid's Magical Creatures Motorbike Adventure	48" minimum height
Harry Potter and the Forbidden Journey	48" minimum height
The High in the Sky Seuss Trolley Train Ride!	36" minimum height
The Incredible Hulk Coaster	54" minimum height
Jurassic Park River Adventure	42" minimum height
Jurassic World VelociCoaster	51" minimum height
Popeye & Bluto's Bilge-Rat Barges	42" minimum height
Pteranodon Flyers *(Guests taller than 56" must be accompanied by a guest 36"–56".)*	36" minimum height; 56" maximum height
Skull Island: Reign of Kong	36" minimum height

VOLCANO BAY *(see pages 428–432)*

Honu Raft Slide	48" minimum height
ika Moana Raft Slide	42" minimum height
Kala & Tai Nui Serpentine Body Slides	48" minimum height
Ko'okiri Body Plunge	48" minimum height
Krakatau Aqua Coaster	42" minimum height
Maku Round Raft Ride	42" minimum height
Ohyah and Ohno Drop Slides	48" minimum height
Puihi Round Raft Ride	42" minimum height
Puka Uli Lagoon	under 48" must wear life vest
Punga Racers	42" minimum height
The Reef	under 48" must wear life vest
Taniwha Tubes: Tonga and Raki	42" minimum height
TeAwa the Fearless River	42" minimum height
Waturi Beach	under 48" must wear life vest

Universal's Islands of Adventure

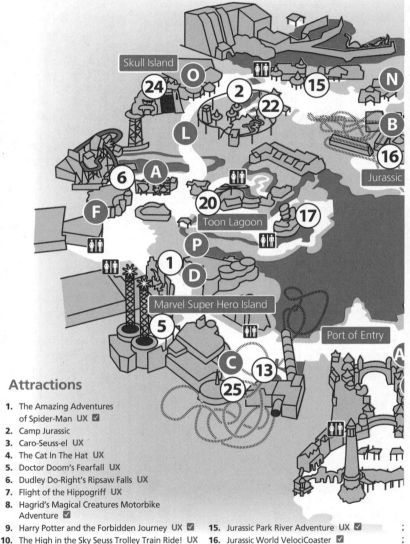

Attractions

1. The Amazing Adventures of Spider-Man UX ☑
2. Camp Jurassic
3. Caro-Seuss-el UX
4. The Cat In The Hat UX
5. Doctor Doom's Fearfall UX
6. Dudley Do-Right's Ripsaw Falls UX
7. Flight of the Hippogriff UX
8. Hagrid's Magical Creatures Motorbike Adventure ☑
9. Harry Potter and the Forbidden Journey UX ☑
10. The High in the Sky Seuss Trolley Train Ride! UX
11. Hogwarts Express: Hogsmeade Station UX ☑
12. If I Ran The Zoo
13. The Incredible Hulk Coaster UX ☑
14. Jurassic Park Discovery Center
15. Jurassic Park River Adventure UX ☑
16. Jurassic World VelociCoaster ☑
17. Me Ship, *The Olive*
18. Ollivanders
19. One Fish, Two Fish, Red Fish, Blue Fish UX
20. Popeye & Bluto's Bilge-Rat Barges UX ☑

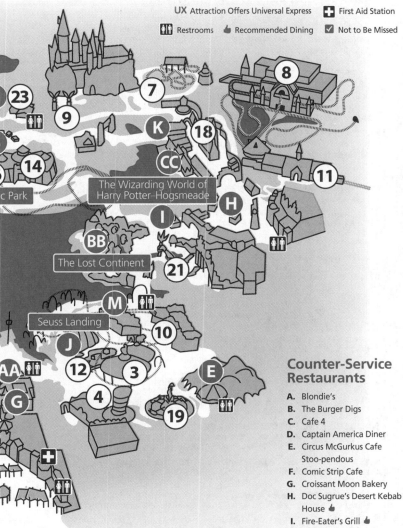

UX Attraction Offers Universal Express   First Aid Station

Restrooms   Recommended Dining   Not to Be Missed

The Wizarding World of Harry Potter–Hogsmeade

c Park

The Lost Continent

Seuss Landing

Counter-Service Restaurants

A. Blondie's
B. The Burger Digs
C. Cafe 4
D. Captain America Diner
E. Circus McGurkus Cafe Stoo-pendous
F. Comic Strip Cafe
G. Croissant Moon Bakery
H. Doc Sugrue's Desert Kebab House
I. Fire-Eater's Grill
J. Green Eggs and Ham Cafe
K. Hog's Head
L. The Mess Tent
M. Moose Juice, Goose Juice
N. Pizza Predattoria
O. Thunder Falls Terrace
P. Wimpy's

21. *Poseidon's Fury* UX
22. Pteranodon Flyers
23. Raptor Encounter
24. Skull Island: Reign of Kong UX
25. Storm Force Accelatron UX

Table-Service Restaurants

AA. Confisco Grille
BB. Mythos Restaurant
CC. Three Broomsticks (counter service)

ISLANDS OF ADVENTURE ATTRACTIONS

ATTRACTION | STAR RATING | HEIGHT REQUIREMENT | WHAT TO EXPECT

THE AMAZING ADVENTURES OF SPIDER-MAN | ★★★★★ | 40" | Indoor adventure 3-D simulator ride. One of the best attractions anywhere; not to be missed.

CAMP JURASSIC | ★★★½ | None | Camp Jurassic is the most elaborate kid's play area at Universal, and one of the best theme park playgrounds you'll find anywhere. Camp Jurassic will fire the imaginations of the under-13 set. If you don't impose a time limit on the exploration, you could be here awhile.

CARO-SEUSS-EL | ★★★ | None | This full-scale, 56-mount merry-go-round is made up entirely of Dr. Seuss characters, each of which has an interactive effect (wagging tongues, blinking eyes) that the rider can control. While you turn, a Seussian orchestra of ridiculous instruments plays like a cacophonous calliope. A gentle ride, even for the youngest children.

THE CAT IN THE HAT | ★★★½ | 36" | This indoor, sit-down attraction recounts the entire *Cat in the Hat* story from beginning to end in a little less than 4 minutes. Of course, mayhem ensues when Cat brings Thing 1 and Thing 2 over to play, as the beleaguered goldfish tries to maintain order in the midst of bedlam, but the entire mess is cleaned up just before Mom gets home. This is fun for all ages.

DOCTOR DOOM'S FEARFALL | ★★★ | 52" | Tower launch and free fall. Riders are strapped in a seat with feet dangling, blasted 300 feet up in the air, and then allowed to partially free-fall back down.

DUDLEY DO-RIGHT'S RIPSAW FALLS | ★★★½ | 44" | There are several medium-size drops during this 5-minute log-flume ride, and a heart-stopping 75-foot one near the end. This ride will get you wet.

FLIGHT OF THE HIPPOGRIFF | ★★★ | 36" | Kiddie roller coaster that affords excel- lent views of Hogwarts and the area within the Wizarding World. *Harry Potter* fans will want to see two gorgeous items in this attraction: The first is a faithful re-creation of Hagrid's Hut in the queue (complete with the sound of Fang howling), and the second is an incredible animatronic of Buckbeak that you pass while on the ride. Remember that when Muggles encounter hippogriffs such as Buckbeak, proper etiquette must be main-tained to avoid any danger. Hippogriffs are extremely proud creatures; show them the proper respect by bowing to them and waiting for them to bow in return.

HAGRID'S MAGICAL CREATURES MOTORBIKE ADVENTURE | ★★★½ | 48" | Indoor– outdoor roller coaster. A super-headliner and must-ride! Meet centaurs, Cornish pixies, and the iconic three-headed dog Fluffy.

HARRY POTTER AND THE FORBIDDEN JOURNEY | ★★★★★ | 48" | This ride pro- vides the only opportunity at Universal Orlando to come close to Harry, Ron, Hermione, and Dumbledore as portrayed by the original actors. Half the attraction is a series of pre-shows, setting the stage for the main event, a thrilling dark ride. Marvelous for Muggles; not to be missed.

THE HIGH IN THE SKY SEUSS TROLLEY TRAIN RIDE! | ★★★½ | 36" | An elevated train ride through and around the buildings in Seuss Landing, the Trolley Train putters along elevated tracks while a voice reads a Dr. Seuss story over the train's speakers.

HOGWARTS EXPRESS: HOGSMEADE STATION | ★★★★½ | None | Transportation attraction with special effects connecting Hogsmeade Station (IOA) to King's Cross Sta-tion (USF).

IF I RAN THE ZOO | ★★★ | None | Themed to Dr. Seuss rhymes, this interactive play area and outdoor maze is filled with fantastic animals and gizmos from the stories.

THE INCREDIBLE HULK COASTER | ★★★★½ | 54" | A 3,700-foot-long track roller coaster with a total of seven upside-down experiences in a little more than 2 minutes.

JURASSIC PARK DISCOVERY CENTER | ★★½ | This educational exhibit mixes fiction from the *Jurassic Park* movies, such as using fossil DNA to bring dinosaurs to life, with skeletal remains and other paleontological displays. The best exhibit lets guests watch an animatronic raptor being hatched, with a young witness getting to name the newborn.

JURASSIC PARK RIVER ADVENTURE | ★★★★ | 42" | On this indoor–outdoor river- raft adventure, the boats make a huge splash at the bottom of the 85-foot drop, but you can stay relatively dry if you're sitting in an interior seat. Young children must endure a double whammy on this ride. First, they're stalked by giant, salivating (sometimes spit-ting) reptiles, and then sent catapulting over the falls. Unless your children are fairly hardy, wait a year or two before you spring the River Adventure on them.

JURASSIC WORLD VELOCICOASTER | ★★★★★ | 51" | Riders board 24-passenger trains to experience two high-speed launches, an 80-degree dive down a towering 155-foot-tall "top hat" and close encounters with realistic rockwork and sculpted dinosaurs, all while secured by nothing more than a lap bar (and Newtonian physics). With a top speed of 70 mph and an astounding 12 moments of out-of-your-seat air time (including a first-of-its-kind zero-g inverted stall), VelociCoaster boasts the kind of statistics that make coaster nerds salivate. Not for the faint at heart, and do not spring this coaster on a first-time roller-coaster rider—child or adult!

ME SHIP, *THE OLIVE* | ★★★ | None | *The Olive* is Popeye's beloved boat coming to life as a three-floor interactive playground. A separate play area, called Swee'Pea's Playpen, is available for younger children.

OLLIVANDERS | ★★★★ | None | Every few minutes a wand-selection show takes place, where a random customer (often a child dressed in Potter regalia) is selected to take part in a wand-choosing ceremony. This enchanting wizarding demonstration is followed by a wand-shopping opportunity. Note that the store here is much smaller than its counterpart at USF.

ONE FISH, TWO FISH, RED FISH, BLUE FISH | ★★★ | None | Imagine a mild spinning ride similar to Disney's Magic Carpets of Aladdin, TriceraTop Spin, and Dumbo, only with Seuss-style fish for ride vehicles, and you have half the story. The other half involves yet another opportunity to get soaked.

POPEYE & BLUTO'S BILGE-RAT BARGES | ★★★★ | 42" | Hands-down our favorite whitewater raft ride on the East Coast. If you didn't drown on Dudley Do-Right, here's a second chance. You'll get a lot wetter from the knees down on this ride, so use your poncho or a garbage bag or you will get soaked. You've been warned! If your child is apprehensive about riding, take them to any of the platforms overlooking the ride to see how much fun everyone is having.

POSEIDON'S FURY | ★★★½ | None | High-tech theater attraction during which the audience stands throughout. While most of the action takes place on movie screens, Poseidon's Fury can frighten many young children. The entire theater is thrown into total darkness many times during the show, and several of the special effects involve fire, loud noises, and flashing lights.

PTERANODON FLYERS | ★★★ | 36" min./56" max. | This two-seater kiddie coaster dangles you on a swing below a track that passes over a small part of Jurassic Park. (Guests taller than 56" must be accompanied by a guest 36"–56").

RAPTOR ENCOUNTER | ★★★½ | None | Blue, *Jurassic World*'s semitame saurian star, makes regular appearances in her paddock next to the River Adventure. A Universal photographer will take your picture, and selfies are also encouraged—just don't be surprised if the dino snaps when you say, "Smile!" When the full-grown Blue needs a break, an adorable (but equally deadly) handheld baby velociraptor may take her place.

SKULL ISLAND: REIGN OF KONG | ★★★★ | 36" | Indoor–outdoor truck safari with 3-D effects. The ride is not wild; however, on a sensory and psychological level, it's extremely intense. The standby queue alone is enough to reduce fearful kids to tears, though the Express line bypasses most of the scares. If you or your little one has a fear of darkness, insects, or man-eating monsters, you may want to forgo the experience. And you don't have to be a small fry for Skull Island to leave you shaken.

STORM FORCE ACCELATRON | ★★½ | None | Storm Force Accelatron is a spiffed-up version of Disney's nausea-inducing Mad Tea Party. If you're prone to motion sickness, keep your distance.

continued from page 406

Hogwarts Express: Hogsmeade Station ★★★★½

Because the Hogsmeade Station doesn't include the cool Platform 9¾ effect found at the King's Cross end, expect waits for the one-way trip to be shorter here. If you wish to experience the train going from IOA to USF, do so before midafternoon, when lines can build.

Nearly every retail space sports some sort of animatronic or special effects surprise. At **Dervish and Banges,** the fearsome *Monster Book of Monsters* rattles and snarls at you as Nimbus 2001 brooms strain at their tethers overhead. At the **Hog's Head** pub, the titular porcine part, mounted behind the bar, similarly thrashes and growls. (The pub also serves The Wizarding World's signature nonalcoholic brew, Butterbeer. Outdoor vendors also sell it, but the wait at Hog's Head is generally 10 minutes or less, versus half an hour or more in the lines outside. Also, the outdoor vendors charge a few cents more and don't honor Annual Pass discounts.)

Roughly across the street from the pub, you'll find shaded benches at the **Owlery**, where animatronic owls (complete with lifelike poop) ruffle and hoot from the rafters. Next to the Owlery is the **Owl Post**, where you can have mail stamped with a Hogsmeade postmark before dropping it off for delivery (an Orlando postmark will also be applied by the real USPS). You can't enter through the Owl Post's front door on busy days, when it serves exclusively as an exit. Because it's so difficult to get into the Owl Post, IOA sometimes stations a team member outside to stamp your postcards with the Hogsmeade postmark.

Live Entertainment in The Wizarding World—Hogsmeade

Street entertainment at the Forbidden Journey end of Hogsmeade includes the **_Frog Choir_** (★★★), composed of four singers, two of whom hold large amphibian puppets sitting on pillows, and the **_Triwizard Spirit Rally_** (★★★), showcasing dancing and martial arts. Performances run about 6–15 minutes.

Don't miss the *Harry Potter*–themed Christmas event, held at both Wizarding Worlds (the other is Diagon Alley; see page 415) mid-November–January 5. Expect holiday decor and food adapted from the novels, as well as an amazing sound-and-light show (see below).

LIVE ENTERTAINMENT *at* ISLANDS *of* ADVENTURE

ISLANDS OF ADVENTURE is home to two not-to-be-missed acts: a song-and-dance show that brings to life characters from Dr. Seuss books a music-and-light show projected onto Hogwarts Castle.

OH! THE STORIES YOU'LL HEAR! (★★★) Featuring many of Dr. Seuss's most beloved characters (including The Lorax, The Grinch, Thing 1 and Thing 2, Sam I Am, and the Cat in the Hat), *Oh! The Stories You'll Hear!* is a fun singing and dancing show staged in an outdoor area between the One Fish, Two Fish, Red Fish, Blue Fish and Cat in the Hat rides. After each show, the characters separate for individual meet and greets and autographs. Shows run multiple times daily, usually starting by 10:30 a.m. During inclement weather, the performance takes place within the Circus McGurkus Cafe Stoo-pendous restaurant nearby.

THE NIGHTTIME LIGHTS AT HOGWARTS CASTLE (★★★½) On select nights, Hogwarts Castle, home of the Harry Potter and the Forbidden Journey ride, is the backdrop for a dazzling digital projection show.

Video-mapping effects are synchronized to the music of John Williams in an absolute must-see show. There are no fireworks, but the music and spectacular lighting effects make it simply magical. The show repeats every 15–20 minutes after sunset. Check park map for times.

Christmas at Universal Orlando starts mid-November and lasts through the first week of January. Seasonal decorations adorn the attractions, holiday songs are broadcast from speakers in the streets, and each park has a headliner holiday event. Universal transforms Seuss Landing into the whimsical world of Grinchmas. Be sure to explore every nook and cranny of this wintry wonderland, as it's filled with special touches that Dr. Seuss fans are sure to adore.

You won't want to miss the *Grinchmas Who-liday Spectacular Show,* a live retelling of Dr. Seuss's classic holiday tale, starring The Grinch, with music recorded by Mannheim Steamroller. The half-hour musical is performed six to eight times daily through January 1 at the soundstage behind Circus McGurkus Cafe Stoo-pendous.

Throughout the day, Whos from Whoville stroll through Seuss Landing, and The Grinch himself holds court inside the All the Books You Can Read store. The Grinch takes time to interact before each photograph, which is a lot of fun but results in a long, slow-moving line. If meeting the Grinch is a priority, make this your first stop in the morning. Check the park map for showtimes and character meet and greets.

On select days in November and December, feast with the Grinch and enjoy meeting Thing 1 and Thing 2 during **The Grinch & Friends Character Breakfast,** held in Circus McGurkus Cafe Stoo-pendous. Call 407-503-DINE (3463) for more information. *Note:* The breakfast was not confirmed to return as we went to press.

FAVORITE EATS AT UNIVERSAL'S ISLANDS OF ADVENTURE
PORT OF ENTRY Croissant Moon Bakery	Croissants and sandwiches
TOON LAGOON Blondie's	Hot dogs
JURASSIC PARK Pizza Predattoria	Pizza	**Thunder Falls Terrace**	Chicken, roasted pernil, smoked turkey legs
THE WIZARDING WORLD OF HARRY POTTER—HOGSMEADE Three Broomsticks	Shepherd's pie, fish-and-chips
LOST CONTINENT Fire Eater's Grill	Gyros	**Mythos Restaurant**	Risotto, souvlaki couscous bowl, lamb burger, mezze platter	*Table service only*
SEUSS LANDING Circus McGurkus Cafe Stoo-pendous	Fried chicken, burgers, pizza

ISLANDS *of* ADVENTURE TOURING PLANS

1-DAY TOURING PLAN (TWO VERSIONS) These touring plans (one for tweens and one for families with small children) are for guests without Park-to-Park tickets. They include thrill rides that may induce motion sickness or get you wet. If the plan calls for you to experience an attraction that doesn't interest you, simply skip it and go to the next step. Be aware that the plans call for some backtracking.

Because there are so many attractions with the potential to frighten children, be prepared to skip a few things. For the most part, attractions designed especially for young children, such as playgrounds, can be enjoyed anytime. Work them into the plan at your convenience. Be aware that in this park, there are an inordinate number of attractions that will get you wet. If you want to experience them, come armed with ponchos, large plastic garbage bags, or other rainwear. Failure to follow this prescription will make for a squishy, sodden day.

Hagrid's Magical Creatures Motorbike Adventure is super fun, but if you don't like roller coasters at all, you might want to skip it. If coasters are your thing, try to ride on the motorcycle seat for a better experience.
If you don't care who you ride with, using the single-rider line on Hagrid's and VelociCoaster can shorten your wait time drastically.

Brendan

1-DAY/2-PARK TOURING PLAN (TWO VERSIONS) These touring plans are for guests with 1-Day Park-to-Park tickets who wish to see the highlights of USF and IOA in a single day. See page 423 for more details. See pages 511–518 for the actual Universal touring plans.

UNIVERSAL STUDIOS FLORIDA

BEGINNING AT THE PARK ENTRANCE, you'll find to the left **stroller, wheelchair, and ECV rentals,** as well as **lockers** (for a fee). Loose items are not permitted on select attractions; free, single-time-use lockers are available at the following rides: Revenge of the Mummy, Men in Black: Alien Attack, Hollywood Rip Ride Rockit, and Harry Potter and the Escape from Gringotts. The **First Aid Station** is located at Family Services, near the Studio Audience Center at the front of the park. **ATMs** are located at several locations throughout the park.

USF is laid out in a *P* configuration, with the rounded part of the *P* sticking out disproportionately from the stem. Beyond the main entrance, a wide boulevard stretches past several shows and rides toward the park's New York area. Branching off this pedestrian thoroughfare to the right are four streets that access other areas of the park and intersect a promenade circling a large lake. The area of USF open to visitors is a bit smaller than EPCOT.

BOB Get to the park turnstiles with your admission already purchased about 30–45 minutes before official opening time. Arrive 45–60 minutes before official opening time if you need to buy admission. **Be aware that you can't do a comprehensive tour of both Universal parks in a single day.**

Going clockwise, the first area you'll encounter is **Production Central**, which includes Despicable Me Minion Mayhem, Hollywood Rip Ride Rockit, and Transformers: The Ride—3D. In the **New York** area you'll find Race Through New York Starring Jimmy Fallon and Revenge of the Mummy. Next is **San Francisco**, the home of **Fast & Furious: Supercharged; The Wizarding World of**

Harry Potter—Diagon Alley, with Hogwarts Express: King's Cross Station and Harry Potter and the Escape from Gringotts; **World Expo,** with Men in Black Alien Attack; **Springfield: Home of the Simpsons,** featuring, of course, the Simpsons ride; and **Woody Woodpecker's KidZone,** containing E.T. Adventure, an animal show, and several play areas. The last themed area, back near the front of the park, is **Hollywood,** featuring *Universal Orlando's Horror Make-Up Show* and *The Bourne Stuntacular.*

THE WIZARDING WORLD OF HARRY POTTER—DIAGON ALLEY

LILIANE I want to sneak into the Wizarding World through the Leaky Cauldron pub. OK, I'll take the Hogwarts Express.

SECRETED BEHIND A LONDON STREET SCENE that features **Grimmauld Place** and **Wyndham's Theatre, Diagon Alley** is accessed through a secluded entrance in the middle of the facade. As in the books and films, the unmarked portal is concealed within a magical brick wall that's ordinarily reserved for wizards and the like. (Unfortunately, the wall doesn't actually move, due to safety concerns.) The endless queue of Muggles (plain old humans) in shorts and flip-flops will leave little doubt where that entryway is.

When **Early Park Admission** is offered, USF admits eligible on-site resort guests 1 hour before the general public, with the turnstiles opening up to 90 minutes before the official opening time. Arrive at least 30 minutes before early entry starts; during peak season, we recommend showing up on the very first boat or bus from your hotel. If you're a day guest visiting on an Early Park Admission day, Diagon Alley will already be packed when you arrive. Even when Early Park Admission isn't offered, all guests may enter Diagon Alley from the front gates up to 30 minutes before park opening, and hotel guests in IOA will arrive via Hogwarts Express a little after that, though Harry Potter and the Escape from Gringotts doesn't begin operating until close to official opening time.

Hogwarts Express: King's Cross Station ★★★★½

Diagon Alley at USF is connected to Hogsmeade at Islands of Adventure (IOA) by the Hogwarts Express, just as in the novels and films. The counterpart to Hogsmeade Station in IOA is USF's King's Cross Station, a landmark London train depot that has been re-created a few doors down from Diagon Alley's hidden entrance. (Note that King's Cross has a separate entrance and exit from Diagon Alley: You can't go directly between them without crossing through the London Waterfront.)

The passage to Platform 9¾, from which Hogwarts students depart on their way to school, is concealed from Muggles by a seemingly solid brick wall, through which guests ahead of you dematerialize. (Spoiler alert: The Pepper's Ghost effect creates a clever but congestion-prone

continued on page 419

Universal Studios Florida

Attractions

1. *Animal Actors on Location!* UX
2. *The Bourne Stuntacular* UX ☑
3. Curious George Goes to Town
4. Despicable Me Minion Mayhem UX
5. DreamWorks Destination
6. E.T. Adventure UX
7. Fast & Furious: Supercharged UX
8. Fievel's Playland
9. Harry Potter and the Escape from Gringotts UX ☑
10. Hogwarts Express: King's Cross Station UX ☑
11. Hollywood Rip Ride Rockit UX
12. Kang & Kodos' Twirl 'n' Hurl UX
13. Men in Black Alien Attack UX ☑
14. Ollivanders
15. Race Through New York Starring Jimmy Fallon UX

16. Revenge of the Mummy UX ☑
17. The Simpsons Ride UX ☑
18. Transformers: The Ride–3-D UX ☑
19. *Universal Orlando's Horror Make-Up Show* UX ☑

Counter-Service Re

A. Bumblebee Man's Taco Truck
B. Central Park Crepes
C. Chez Alcatraz
D. Duff Brewery
E. Fast Food Boulevard 👍
F. Florean Fortescue's Ice-Cream Parlour 👍
G. Fountain of Fair Fortune

20. *Universal Orlando's Cinematic Celebration* (seasonal)

21. Woody Woodpecker's Nuthouse Coaster UX

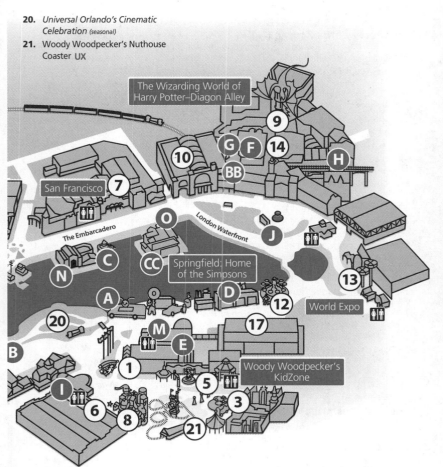

The Wizarding World of Harry Potter–Diagon Alley

San Francisco

The Embarcadero

London Waterfront

Springfield: Home of the Simpsons

World Expo

Woody Woodpecker's KidZone

Restaurants

- **H.** The Hopping Pot
- **I.** KidZone Pizza Company *(seasonal)*
- **J.** London Taxi Hut
- **K.** Louie's Italian Restaurant
- **L.** Mel's Drive-In
- **M.** Moe's Tavern
- **N.** Richter's Burger Co.
- **O.** San Francisco Pastry Company
- **P.** Schwab's Pharmacy *(seasonal)*
- **Q.** Today Cafe 👍

Table-Service Restaurants

- **AA.** Finnegan's Bar & Grill
- **BB.** Leaky Cauldron (counter service) 👍
- **CC.** Lombard's Seafood Grille

UX Attraction Offers Universal Express ✚ First Aid Station 👥 Restrooms

👍 Recommended Dining ☑ Not to Be Missed • • • Parade Route

UNIVERSAL STUDIOS ATTRACTIONS

ATTRACTION | STAR RATING | HEIGHT REQUIREMENT | WHAT TO EXPECT

ANIMAL ACTORS ON LOCATION! | ★★★½ | None | Live show featuring performing dogs, birds, pigs, and a menagerie of other animals. Don't miss these cute li'l critters.

THE BOURNE STUNTACULAR | ★★★★½ | None | Live-action stunt show. Fast-paced, faithful to the film franchise, and filled with show-stopping special effects, this is easily the best stunt show in Orlando. Not to be missed. Loud noises might unsettle some kids.

CURIOUS GEORGE GOES TO TOWN | ★★½ | None| This interactive playground exemplifies the Universal obsession with wet stuff. In addition to innumerable spigots, pipes, and spray guns, two giant roof-mounted buckets periodically dump 1,000 gallons of water on unsuspecting visitors below.

DESPICABLE ME MINION MAYHEM | ★★★½ | 40" | Motion-simulator ride. Expect long lines.

E.T. ADVENTURE | ★★★½ | 34" | An indoor adventure dark ride inspired by Steven Spielberg's movie.

FAST & FURIOUS: SUPERCHARGED | ★★★ | 40" | Car-chase motion simulator. The dialogue and visual effects are shockingly cheesy even by theme park standards. The ride takes up a lot of real estate that could be better used for an attraction more worthy of Universal Studios.

FIEVEL'S PLAYLAND | ★★★ | None | Children's play area with waterslide. A great place for the little ones to blow off some steam.

HARRY POTTER AND THE ESCAPE FROM GRINGOTTS | ★★★★★ | 42" | Superhigh-tech 3-D dark ride with roller-coaster elements. Escape from Gringotts incorporates a substantial part of the overall experience into its elaborate queue, which even nonriders should experience. Not to be missed.

HOGWARTS EXPRESS: KING'S CROSS STATION | ★★★★½ | None | Hogwarts Express transports guests between Diagon Alley at Universal Studios and Hogsmeade at Islands of Adventure. The ride isn't an adrenaline rush, but for those invested in Potter lore, it is thrilling. Unlike most Potter attractions, it can be experienced by the whole family, regardless of size.

HOLLYWOOD RIP RIDE ROCKIT | ★★★★ | 51" min./79" max. | High-tech roller coaster that runs on a 3,800-foot steel track, with a maximum height of 167 feet and a top speed of 65 mph.

KANG & KONDO'S TWIRL 'N' HURL | ★★★ | None | Think of this spinning ride as the Dumbo ride with Bart Simpson's sense of humor.

MEN IN BLACK ALIEN ATTACK | ★★★★ | 42" | Interactive dark thrill ride based on science fiction action comedy films also known as MIB. If you are prone to motion sickness, do not ride.

OLLIVANDERS | ★★★★ | None | Every few minutes, a random customer (often a child dressed in Potter regalia) is selected to take part a wand-selection ceremony. This enchanting wizarding demonstration is followed by a wand-shopping opportunity.

RACE THROUGH NEW YORK STARRING JIMMY FALLON | ★★★½ | 40" | Comedic 3-D simulator ride inspired by *The Tonight Show Starring Jimmy Fallon.* The main attractions, however, are live appearances by some *Tonight Show* regulars: the Ragtime Gals (a male vocal quintet that performs tongue-in-cheek barbershop interpretations of pop hits) and Hashtag the Panda.

REVENGE OF THE MUMMY | ★★★★½ | 48" | A high-tech hybrid indoor roller coaster/dark ride based on the *Mummy* flicks. Killer! Not to be missed. Will scare younglings and a few grown-ups.

THE SIMPSONS RIDE ★★★★ | 40" | Mega-simulator ride. There will be jokes and visuals that you'll get but will fly over your children's heads—and most assuredly vice versa. Skip it if you're an expectant mom or prone to motion sickness. Some parents may find the humor too coarse for younger kids.

TRANSFORMERS: THE RIDE—3D | ★★★★ | 40" | Multisensory 3-D dark ride. A breathtaking, deafening blur; not to be missed.

UNIVERSAL ORLANDO'S HORROR MAKE-UP SHOW | ★★★★½ | The *Horror Make-Up Show* is a brief but humorous look at how basic monster-movie special effects are done. May frighten young children. A gory knee-slapper; not to be missed.

WOODY WOODPECKER'S NUTHOUSE COASTER | ★★½ | 36" (riders 36"–48" must be accompanied by a supervising companion) | Kids' roller coaster.

continued from page 415

photo op, but you experience only a dark corridor with whooshing sound effects when crossing over yourself.)

Once on the platform, you'll pass a pile of luggage before being assigned to one of the three train cars' seven compartments. The train itself looks exactly authentic, from the billowing steam to the brass fixtures and the upholstery in your eight-passenger private cabin. Along your one-way Hogwarts Express journey, you'll see moving images projected beyond the windows of the car, with the streets of London and the Scottish countryside (rather than the park's backstage areas) rolling past outside your window. You experience a different presentation coming and going, and in addition to pastoral scenery, there are surprise appearances by secondary characters (Fred and George Weasley, Hagrid) and threats en route (bone-chilling Dementors, licorice spiders), augmented by sound effects in the cars.

To board the train, passengers need a valid Park-to-Park ticket; you can upgrade your 1-Park Base Ticket at the station entrance. Disembarking passengers must enter the second park and, if desired, queue again for their return trip. Park-to-Park ticket holders should make the train their second stop after Escape from Gringotts if going from Diagon Alley to Hogsmeade. Or, if Diagon Alley is your top priority of the day, enter IOA as early as possible and line up at the Hogsmeade Station for the train to London King's Cross. If the posted wait is 15 minutes or less, it's typically quicker to take the train than to walk to the other Wizarding World.

Wizarding World Entertainment

Take a moment to spot Kreacher (the house elf regularly peers from a second-story window above 12 Grimmauld Place) and chat with the Knight Bus conductor and his Caribbean-accented shrunken head. Look down the alley to the rounded facade of **Gringotts Wizarding Bank,** where a 40-foot fire-breathing Ukrainian Ironbelly dragon (as seen in *Harry Potter and the Deathly Hallows: Part 2*) perches atop the dome.

To the right of Escape from Gringotts is **Carkitt Market,** a canopy-covered plaza where live shows are staged every half hour or so. *Celestina Warbeck and the Banshees* (★★★★) showcases the singing sorceress swinging to jazzy tunes titled and inspired by J. K. Rowling herself, and *Tales of Beedle the Bard* (★★★½) recounts the Three Brothers fable from *Deathly Hallows* with puppets crafted by Michael Curry (*Festival of the Lion King, Finding Nemo: The Big Blue . . . and Beyond*).

Intersecting Diagon Alley near the Leaky Cauldron is **Knockturn Alley,** a labyrinth of twisting passageways where the *Harry Potter* bad guys hang out. A covered walk-through area with a projected sky creating perpetual night, it features spooky special effects in the faux shop windows (don't miss the creeping tattoos and crawling spiders).

Visit Knockturn Alley in Diagon Alley for a quieter but very spooky place.

Brendan

The *Harry Potter*–themed Christmas events held at both Wizarding Worlds mid-November–January 5 are an absolute must. Even Celestina Warbeck and the Banshees have a special yuletide program. Hearing Celestina perform "My Baby Gave Me a Hippogriff for Christmas" is a hoot. Expect holiday decor and food adapted from the *Harry Potter* novels.

LIVE ENTERTAINMENT *at* UNIVERSAL STUDIOS

UNIVERSAL STUDIOS OFFERS two major outdoor performances, along with a wide range of smaller ones, and special entertainment inside The Wizarding World of Harry Potter—Diagon Alley.

UNIVERSAL ORLANDO'S CINEMATIC CELEBRATION (seasonal; ★★★★) is Universal's Studios' big nighttime event, shown on the lagoon in the middle of the Studios. The presentation pays tribute to favorite franchises featured around Universal's parks, including *Jurassic World, Despicable Me, Transformers,* and *Fast & Furious.* The scenes are projected onto multiple enormous "screens" made by spraying water from the lagoon into the air; these are augmented by more than 120 illuminated fountains. Highlights include Harry Potter defeating a pack of Dementors with his Patronus, E.T.'s spaceship blasting into space, and a joyful Justin Timberlake tune from *Trolls.* Cinematic Celebration is a great way to end your day in the park. Try to claim a good spot 45 minutes ahead of time on peak attendance days, or 5–10 minutes prior to the show during slower seasons. Central Park, a three-tiered seating and viewing area, is located across the lagoon from San Francisco.

If you didn't manage to claim a spot in Central Park, try to see the show directly across the lagoon from Richter's Burger Co., where the sidewalk makes a small protrusion overlooking the water, or between Mel's Diner and Transformers.

THE BLUES BROTHERS SHOW (★★★½) Held on the corner of the New York area, Jake and Elwood perform a few of the hit songs from the classic 1980 movie musical, including "Soul Man "and "Sweet Home Chicago." The brothers are joined onstage by Jazz the saxophone player and his girlfriend, Mabel the waitress, who covers an Aretha Franklin song to start the show. The concert is a great pick-me-up, and the short run time (12 minutes) keeps the energy high. During the holiday season, a special Blues Brothers Holiday Show is performed, featuring songs such as "Blue Christmas" and "Run Rudolph Run," sung around a festive tree festooned with beer cans and cigarette packs. It's even better than the regular show. **Marilyn Monroe and the Diamond Bellas** (★★½) perform a 4-minute song-and-dance routine (anachronistically lip-synched to the *Moulin Rouge* cover of her signature song), followed by a photo op; during the holiday season, "Santa Baby" joins the set list. The **Beat Builders** (★★★) are a quartet of beefy guys who hang out on the scaffolding outside Louie's Italian restaurant and turn their construction equipment into percussion instruments, in the tradition of *Stomp*. During peak periods, you may hear the **City Tones** (★★½), an a cappella group, harmonizing to Motown hits or holiday classics in New York; it's impossible to say what kind of act Universal will pull out when the parks get packed.

In addition to the live performances, costumed comic-book and cartoon characters (SpongeBob SquarePants and Scooby-Doo and the gang), along with movie star look-alikes, roam the park for photo ops. Meet characters like Homer, Bart, Marge, Lisa, and Maggie from *The Simpsons*, as well as the penguins of *Madagascar*. Optimus Prime, Bumblebee, and Megatron meet outside Transformers: The Ride—3D.

SPECIAL EVENTS AT UNIVERSAL STUDIOS

BEYOND ITS YEAR-ROUND OFFERINGS, USF also hosts some of the best seasonal events in the theme park industry, and most of them are included with any regular admission (including Annual Passes). For those events that aren't—Rock the Universe and Halloween Horror Nights—you'll need to purchase a separate ticket, and daytime Universal Express Passes (those offered with hotel rooms) won't be honored.

MARDI GRAS At Universal Studios, this celebration lasts 50 nights! From early February through the end of March, the park brings a family-friendly version of the New Orleans celebration to Florida, where guests excitedly collect generously distributed beads.

The Mardi Gras parade at Universal is remarkable and a fun experience. The floats are so colorful and very detailed, and they change the floats every year!

Isabelle

Prior to the parade at the French Quarter Courtyard, guests can enjoy authentic New Orleans bands and amazing food, such as jambalaya, gumbo, and beignets. On select nights you can also enjoy free Mardi Gras concerts.

Mardi Gras Parade

Universal engages Kern Studios, the same company that's been building floats for the real deal since 1932, to create the park's parade platforms.

Floats are updated every year with new themes, but you can always count on the massive king gator float and multistory riverboat to roll down Universal's boulevards. The floats are each accompanied by dozens of strolling performers and stilt walkers, while costumed revelers ride upon them and toss colorful plastic beads to the crowds below.

Special reserved viewing areas are available to guests with disabilities (near Macy's in New York) and young Little Jesters and their families (in front of the Brown Derby Hat Shop). This section allows parents to exit the park speedily once the parade is over. For more information, visit tinyurl.com/unimardigras.

UNIVERSAL'S HOLIDAY PARADE FEATURING MACY'S Once the legendary Macy's Thanksgiving Day Parade ends in New York City, some of the balloons are sent to USF to become the star of the Universal Studios Christmas celebration. The parade, held daily, early December–January 1, features marching bands and, of course, an appearance by Santa.

USF has been bringing elements of Macy's famous New York parade down to Orlando for a post-Thanksgiving encore every December for two decades. Macy's balloons are still a big part of the fun: While the largest balloons you've seen sailing through Manhattan on TV can't make it down the narrower streets of USF, several of the smaller ones join the parade, and more of the classic king-size inflatables (such as Garfield and Grover) are on stationary display around the park.

Universal's Holiday Parade begins each evening around 5 p.m. (subject to change; check the show schedule in the Universal smartphone app) near the *Horror Make-Up Show,* continues down Hollywood Boulevard toward the park entrance, travels past Despicable Me Minion Mayhem toward New York, and then turns near Revenge of the Mummy and again past Transformers, exiting through the gate it originally entered.

You can get a good view of the parade from anywhere along the route, but ideal viewing spots are near Mel's Drive-In at the beginning of the route and near the large tree in New York toward the end. Reserved viewing areas are available for guests with disabilities (in front of Macy's in New York), for Annual Pass holders (near Mel's Drive-In), and for young Little Stars and their families (near Hollywood's Brown Derby Hat Shop).

After the parade, on select nights, USF's Music Plaza stage hosts live concerts by **Mannheim Steamroller**.

HALLOWEEN HORROR NIGHTS (early September–early November) the godfather (or is that gorefather?) of all Universal Orlando seasonal events, Halloween Horror Nights (or HHN, as it's known to its legions of bloodthirsty fans) is recognized as the nation's most popular and industry-awarded haunted theme park event.

HHN is a gory, gruesome bacchanalia of simulated violence and tasteless satire, marinated with a liberal dose of alcohol and rock and roll. In other words, it's a heck of a party as long as you know what you're getting into. If the idea of copious blood, guts, and booze doesn't appeal to you, we advise staying far, far away. It's not appropriate for young children, though you will likely see many there.

For more information, check out *The Unofficial Guide to Universal Orlando 2023,* which dedicates several pages to the event.

FAVORITE EATS AT UNIVERSAL STUDIOS
PRODUCTION CENTRAL Today Cafe | Sandwiches, salad, pastries
NEW YORK Finnegan's Bar and Grill | Irish pub with fish-and-chips; frequently features live music | *Table service only* | **Louie's Italian Restaurant** | Pizza
SAN FRANCISCO Richter's Burger Co. | Burgers
THE WIZARDING WORLD OF HARRY POTTER—DIAGON ALLEY **Leaky Cauldron** | Bangers and mash, fish-and-chips, cottage pie
SPRINGFIELD Fast Food Boulevard | Several eateries with food inspired by *The Simpsons.* We love the tacos at **Bumblebee Man's Taco Truck.**
WOODY WOODPECKER'S KIDZONE Kidzone Pizza Company | Pizza
HOLLYWOOD Mel's Drive-In | Old-fashioned root beer float, BLT, burgers

UNIVERSAL STUDIOS TOURING PLANS

1-DAY TOURING PLAN (TWO VERSIONS) These touring plans are for guests without Park-to-Park tickets and includes every recommended attraction at USF. If you don't want to experience a ride on the list, skip that step and proceed to the next. Move quickly from attraction to attraction, and if possible, hold off on lunch until after experiencing at least six rides. One version is for families with small children, and one version is geared toward tweens (ages 8–12).

1-DAY/2-PARK TOURING PLAN (TWO VERSIONS) These touring plans are for guests with 1-Day Park-to-Park tickets who wish to see the highlights of USF and IOA in a single day. The plan uses Hogwarts Express to get from one park to the other and then back again; you can walk back to the first park for the return leg if the line is too long. The plan includes counter-service meals for lunch and dinner. One version is for families with small children, and one version is geared toward tweens (ages 8–12). See pages 511–518 for the actual Universal touring plans.

PART 12

THE BEST
of the REST

The WATER PARKS (DISNEY *and* UNIVERSAL ORLANDO)

DISNEY AND UNIVERSAL ORLANDO operate water parks alongside their Orlando theme parks. Disney's water parks are **Blizzard Beach** (*temporarily closed for refurbishment*) and **Typhoon Lagoon,** and Universal's is **Volcano Bay.**

Disney's and Universal's water parks are much larger and more elaborately themed than the local or regional water parks you may have visited. Almost all the waterslides, wave pools, and lazy rivers at these parks are larger and longer than those at local and regional water parks as well. Blizzard Beach takes the prize for the most slides and most bizarre theme (a ski resort in meltdown), but Typhoon Lagoon has a surf pool where you can bodysurf. Both parks have excellent and elaborate themed areas for toddlers and preschoolers.

 BOB During summer and holiday periods, Typhoon Lagoon and Blizzard Beach fill to capacity on weekdays and close their gates before 11 a.m.

One day of admission to either of Disney's water parks costs around $73 for adults and $68 for kids, including tax. Peak season is late May–late September. If you visit outside of that window, Disney offers a discount of around $5 per ticket. Admission to Volcano Bay (including tax) costs $75–$91 per adult ($69–$85 for kids ages 3–9).

GETTING THERE Disney provides regular daily bus service between its resorts and water parks. Likewise, Universal runs shuttle buses between most of its resort hotels and Volcano Bay; Universal's Aventura and Cabana Bay hotels are adjacent to Volcano Bay, so walking is usually faster. Disney's bus service might route you through other hotels or Disney Springs, though, and it does take a while to get there.

If you're staying at a Disney hotel and you don't have a car, a ride service or taxi is the best way to get to Disney's water parks.

The best way to get to these parks from off-site is to drive if you have a car. Parking is free and close by at Disney's water parks; Universal's parking fee is $28 (including tax), and you'll take a shuttle bus from the parking structure to the water park. If you don't have a car, then a ride service, taxi, or shuttle can drop you off at the entrance.

DISNEY'S WATER PARKS

NOTE: AT PRESS TIME, Blizzard Beach was temporarily closed for refurbishment. A reopening date had not been announced.

Blizzard Beach and Typhoon Lagoon are almost as large and elaborate as the major theme parks. You must be prepared for a lot of walking, exercise, sun, and jostling crowds.

TOURING STRATEGIES

JUST AS AT THE THEME PARKS, the key to a successful visit to the water parks is to get up early, have breakfast, and **arrive at the park 30 minutes before opening.** Though Typhoon Lagoon and Blizzard Beach are huge parks with many slides, armies of guests overwhelm them almost daily. If your main reason for going is the slides and you hate long lines, try to be among the first guests to enter the park. Go directly to the slides and ride as many times as you can before the park fills.

WHAT TO BRING Wear your swimsuit under clothes so you don't have to bother with lockers or dressing rooms. Wear shoes—paths are relatively easy on bare feet, but there's a lot of ground to cover.

Guests are permitted to take coolers with food and drinks into the parks, but alcoholic beverages, glass containers, and loose ice and dry ice are prohibited; reusable ice packs are permitted. Only one cooler per family is allowed. The in-park food is comparable to fast food, but the prices are a bit high.

Personal swim gear (fins, masks, rafts, and the like) isn't allowed. Everything you need is provided or available to rent. If you forgot your swimsuit, you can buy one. If you don't have towels, they can be rented for $2 each. Sunscreen is available in all park shops.

A limited number of wheelchairs and ECVs can be rented at Typhoon Lagoon from **Singapore Sal's** and at Blizzard Beach from **Beach Haus.** The cost is $12 with a $100 refundable deposit. Life jacket rentals are free. Strollers are welcome but unavailable for rent.

Carry enough money for the day and your Disney resort ID (if you have one), or use your MagicBand to pay for things.

WHERE TO STASH YOUR STUFF Though no location is completely safe, we've felt comfortable hiding our money in our cooler—nobody disturbed our stuff, and our cash was easy to access. If, however, you're

BLIZZARD BEACH ATTRACTIONS*

CHAIRLIFT UP MOUNT GUSHMORE Height requirement: 32". Great ride even if you go up just for the view. When the park is packed, use the singles line.

CROSS COUNTRY CREEK No height requirement. Lazy river circling the park; grab a tube and float away.

DOWNHILL DOUBLE DIPPER Height requirement: 48". Side-by-side tube-racing slides. The tube zooms through water curtains and free falls. It's a lot of fun, but it's rough.

MELT-AWAY BAY No height requirement. Wave pool with gentle, bobbing waves. Great for younger swimmers.

RUNOFF RAPIDS No height requirement. Three corkscrew tube slides to choose from. The center slide is for solo raft rides; the other two slides offer one- or two-person tubes. The dark, enclosed tube gives you the feeling of being flushed down a toilet.

SKI PATROL TRAINING CAMP Height requirement: 60" for T-Bar. Place for preteens to train for the big rides.

SLUSH GUSHER Height requirement: 48". 90-foot double-humped slide. Ladies, cling to those tops—all others, hang on for your lives.

SNOW STORMERS No height requirement. Consists of three mat-slide flumes; down you go on your belly.

SUMMIT PLUMMET Height requirement: 48". 120-foot free fall at 60 mph. Needless to say, this ride is very intense. Make sure your child knows what to expect; being over 48 inches tall doesn't guarantee an enjoyable experience. If you think you'd enjoy being washed out of a 12th-floor window during a heavy rain, then this slide is for you.

TEAMBOAT SPRINGS No height requirement. 1,200-foot group whitewater raft flume. Wonderful ride for the whole family.

TIKE'S PEAK Height requirement: 48" and under only. Kid-size version of Blizzard Beach. This is the place for little ones.

TOBOGGAN RACERS No height requirement. Eight-lane race course. You go down the flume on a mat. Less intense than Snow Stormers.

* Blizzard Beach is currently closed for refurbishment.

carrying a wad or you're simply a worrywart when it comes to money, rent a locker. Another great device is a water-resistant case with a lanyard to hold park tickets, a credit card, some cash, and your hotel key/card. You can buy these cases at the water parks; more-sophisticated versions are available at any good outdoors or sporting-goods shop.

Rental lockers are $10 per day for a standard size and $15 per day for a large (lockers are keyless). Standard-size lockers are roomy enough for one person or a couple, but a family will generally need a large locker. Though you can access your locker freely all day, not all lockers are conveniently located.

WHERE TO SET UP CAMP Once you're in the park, you'll want to establish your base for the day. Beautiful sunning and lounging spots are plentiful throughout both water parks; arrive early so you can have your pick. The breeze is best along the beaches of the lagoon at Blizzard Beach and the surf pool at Typhoon Lagoon. At Typhoon Lagoon, if children younger than age 6 are in your party, choose a spot to the left of Mount Mayday near the children's swimming area.

TYPHOON LAGOON ATTRACTIONS

BAY SLIDES Height requirement: 60″ and under only. Miniature two-slide version of Storm Slides, specifically designed for small children. The kids splash down into a far corner of the Surf Pool.

CASTAWAY CREEK No height requirement. Half-mile lazy river in a tropical setting with cool mists, waterfalls, and a tunnel through Mount Mayday. Wonderful!

CRUSH 'N' GUSHER Height requirement: 48″. Water roller coaster where you can choose from three slides—Banana Blaster, Coconut Crusher, and Pineapple Plunger—ranging from 410 to 420 feet long. This thriller leaves you wondering what exactly happened, if you make it down in one piece, that is; it's not for the faint of heart. If your kids are new to water-park rides, this is not the place to break them in, even if they're tall enough to ride.

GANGPLANK FALLS No height requirement. Whitewater raft flume in a 4-person tube.

HUMUNGA KOWABUNGA Height requirement: 48″. Speed slides that hit 30 mph. A five-story drop in the dark rattles even the most courageous rider. Women should ride this one in a one-piece swimsuit.

KEELHAUL FALLS No height requirement. Fast whitewater ride in a single-person tube.

KETCHAKIDDEE CREEK Height requirement: 48″ and under only. Toddlers and preschoolers love this area reserved only for them. Say "splish-splash" and have lots of fun.

MAYDAY FALLS No height requirement. Wild single-person tube ride. *Hang on!*

MISS ADVENTURE FALLS No height requirement. Gentle family raft ride down a well-themed slide.

STORM SLIDES No height requirement. Three body slides plunge down and through Mount Mayday.

SURF POOL No height requirement. World's largest inland surf facility, with waves up to 6 feet high. Adult supervision required. Surfing lessons may be offered.

Blizzard Beach and Typhoon Lagoon offer premium cabana/patio spaces for rental that can accommodate up to 12 people (6 at Blizzard Beach). Four premium spaces in each water park include the personalized services of an attendant, private lockers, all-day drink mugs, a cooler with bottled water, lounge furniture, tables, and rental towels. You can also rent a premium beach-chair space at both parks. The deal includes two lounge chairs, an umbrella, a cocktail table, and two towels. Limit for this setup is 4 people; if you have more than 4 people in your party, a second reservation is needed. Both options should be reserved in advance but may be available on a same-day basis if any locations are left (check at **Shade Shack** in Blizzard Beach and at **High and Dry Rentals** in Typhoon Lagoon). Cost for either setup varies by season and must be paid at the time of reservation. Reserve by calling 407-WDW-PLAY (939-7529). The cabanas run from around $225 to $450 (including tax), depending on the season.

BRENDAN Summit Plummet is a rough ride and can give you bad skin chafing. It happened to my dad.

THE SLIDES Waterslides come in many shapes and sizes. Some are steep and vertical, and some are long and undulating. Some resemble corkscrews, while others imitate the pool-and-drop nature of whitewater streams. Depending on the slide, swimmers ride mats, inner tubes, or rafts. With body slides, swimmers slosh to the bottom on the seat of their pants. Ladies may think twice about wearing a two-piece bathing suit. Some slides and rapids have a minimum height requirement. Riders for **Humunga Kowabunga** at Typhoon Lagoon and for **Slush Gusher** and **Summit Plummet** at Blizzard Beach, for example, must be 4 feet tall. Pregnant women and people with back problems or other health difficulties shouldn't ride.

LILIANE While I don't feel any better on a water roller coaster than I do on a dry one, I love the water parks. My all-time favorite water ride is Teamboat Springs, the 1,200-foot whitewater raft flume at Blizzard Beach.

OTHER ACTIVITIES When lines for the slides become intolerable, head for the surf or wave pool or the lazy rivers. The lazy rivers at both parks are perfect for relaxation. Float on inner tubes through caves, beneath waterfalls, past gardens, and under bridges. Also available (for free) are flat lounges (nonadjustable) and chairs (better for reading), shelters for guests who prefer shade, picnic tables, and a few hammocks.

PRECAUTIONS It's as easy to lose a child or become separated from your party at one of the water parks as it is at a major theme park. On arrival, pick a very specific place to meet in the event you are separated. If you split up on purpose, establish times for checking in. Children under age 14 must be accompanied by an adult.

Keep in mind that the water parks are great fun for the whole family, but if you have very young children or if you aren't a thrill-seeking water puppy, the pool of your hotel might serve just as well.

LILIANE Lost-children stations at the water parks are so out of the way that neither you nor your child will find them without help from a Disney cast member. Explain to your children how to recognize cast members (by their distinctive name tags) and how to ask for help.

BEFORE YOU GO

1. Call ☎ 407-560-3400 (Blizzard Beach) or 407-560-4120 (Typhoon Lagoon) before you go to get the official park opening time.
2. Purchase admission tickets online before you arrive.
3. Decide if you want to picnic or not, and then plan or pack accordingly (see restrictions on page 425). Pets are not allowed at the water parks.

VOLCANO BAY *at* UNIVERSAL ORLANDO

VOLCANO BAY IS UNIVERSAL'S first highly themed water park, designed to directly compete with Disney's Blizzard Beach and Typhoon Lagoon. At just under 30 acres, it's the same size as Disney's water parks, excluding parking lots. The park opens at 9 or 10 a.m.

FAVORITE EATS AT BLIZZARD BEACH AND TYPHOON LAGOON

BLIZZARD BEACH* Avalunch | Hot dogs and turkey sandwiches for kids Cooling Hut | Popcorn, fresh fruit cups. | Lottawatta Lodge | Flatbreads, burgers, and (for kids) chicken wrap in your own sand pail with shovel, served with a mandarin orange, strawberry-flavored yogurt smoothie, and choice of small low-fat milk or small Dasani water. | Warming Hut | Chicken or tuna sandwich, shrimp wrap; churro, pineapple or vanilla soft-serve ice cream for dessert. * *Currently closed*

TYPHOON LAGOON Happy Landings | Ice cream, cookies, waffle cones, Garbage Pail (chocolate and vanilla soft-serve ice cream with waffle cone pieces, Oreo pieces, sprinkles, hot fudge, caramel sauce, whipped cream, and a cherry served in a sand pail with a shovel). | Leaning Palms | Caribbean-inspired rice bowls and salads, flatbreads, a hot dog, burgers; ham sandwich, cheese pizza, or chicken rice bowl for kids. | Lowtide Lou's | Chicken and shrimp wraps, cauliflower tabbouleh, soft pretzels; turkey sandwich or PB&J for kids. | Typhoon Tilly's | Fish, barbecue pork, and kids' meals; great beer

---

(with early admission an hour earlier for all on-site hotel guests) and stays open as late as 9 p.m. during the summer.

Volcano Bay is located directly south of Universal's Cabana Bay Beach Resort and accessible via a walking path. It is a short walk from Universal's Royal Pacific, Aventura, and Sapphire Falls hotels. The park's four areas are based on the story of the fabled Waturi, an ancient tribe from Polynesia. The tribe set out on outrigger canoes to find a new home, believing that Kunuku, a golden-finned fish, would show them the way. The Waturi visited many Polynesian islands without encountering the elusive fish until they caught sight of Kunuku playing in the waves of Volcano Bay, where the Waturi settled. The park is themed to the islands of the South Pacific, with lush palm trees, tiki carvings, and thatched cabanas.

The heart of the park is **Krakatau,** a 200-foot volcano rising above a pristine beach, its majestic waterfalls transforming into blazing lava by night. The volcano is home to the **Krakatau Aqua Coaster. Wave Village** includes two huge pools and a beautiful beach; **River Village** holds activities for little tykes and the winding river experience; and **Rainforest Village** is home to several raft and speed slides, a pool, and a whitewater rafting experience.

Another novelty for Orlando water parks is that Volcano Bay offers a leisure pool. **The Reef** is to the right of the volcano, and most of the pool is meant for swimmers. Swim up to the edge of the pool overlooking **Waturi Beach** and get a glimpse of the brave souls shooting down Ko'okiri Body Plunge.

TOURING STRATEGIES

UNIVERSAL USES VIRTUAL LINES instead of a traditional queuing system. Each visitor is issued a wristband called **TapuTapu,** which, in addition to claiming your place in the virtual line, can also be used to reserve and open lockers ($12–$16) and make payments throughout the park when linked to

ISABELLE Inside the volcano, there are some interactive touch points you can activate with your TapuTapu, but beware—you might get wet!

a credit card via the Universal Orlando website or app. Guests tap the band against a totem outside a ride, and the device alerts them when it's time to return to experience the attraction. In the meantime, you can explore other areas of the park. The bands also trigger special effects throughout Volcano Bay, such as controlling streams of water in **Tot Tiki Reef** or shooting water cannons at other guests who are enjoying the **Kopiko Wai Winding River.**

As with standby queues, you can wait in only one virtual line at a time. Early in the day, the virtual wait system works very well, and guests can often ride a few slides immediately and reserve short waits at others. The problems start as the crowds grow. By lunchtime, the virtual waits for many slides are 60 minutes or more. **Universal Express** is available for Volcano Bay starting at $21 per person for one use per ride; it can be purchased online or inside the park on select days.

If possible, try staying at Aventura, Cabana Bay Beach, or Sapphire Falls Resort, which are connected to the park by a walking path, and take advantage of early entry for Universal hotel guests. During the extra hour, most of the slides are kept at "Ride Now," resulting in relatively short lines.

LILIANE I could spend an entire day at Volcano Bay just enjoying the amazing view of the volcano, the beach, and the lazy river. It is my favorite water park.

Some Volcano Bay attractions might be frightening for kids under age 8 and even some adults as well. The table on page 217 provides a quick reference to help you identify which attractions to be wary of, and why.

RESTAURANTS AND AMENITIES

THE THEMED RESTAURANTS AND BARS throughout Volcano Bay are particularly noteworthy, far exceeding what we've come to expect from water-park grub, with light, refreshing meals perfect for a day at the beach. Caribbean- and island-inspired foods are on the menu, and even less-adventurous fare like pizza and hot dogs has been upgraded with flatbread crusts and pretzel buns.

At **Bambu,** in Rainforest Village, we love the quinoa-edamame burger, topped with roasted shiitake mushrooms and Sriracha mayo, with a side of fries. Also at Rainforest Village is **The Feasting Frog;** try the tacos or poke tuna, both served with plantain chips. At River Village, **Whakawaiwai Eats** offers a Hawaiian pizza with caramelized pineapple, diced ham, and pickled jalapeños. In Wave Village, at **Kohola Reef Restaurant and Social Club,** the slow-smoked glazed chicken, served with mango slaw and fries, doesn't disappoint. For dessert, try the chocolate lava cake. **Dancing Dragons Boat Bar** (Rainforest Village) and **Kunuku Boat Bar** (Wave Village) serve a variety of exotic signature cocktails, but these are far too sugary for our taste. Stick with the locally brewed Volcano Blossom beer instead.

Each area of the park offers amenities such as concierge locations and lockers ($10–$17 for all-day access). You can upgrade your visit with reserved padded loungers ($32–$159 per pair), 6-person cabanas ($170 and up), or 16-person Family Suite cabanas ($320–$640); all

VOLCANO BAY ATTRACTIONS

Rainforest Village

KALA AND TA NUI SERPENTINE BODY SLIDES **Height requirement: 48".** After falling through a drop door, two riders go down 124-foot body slides simultaneously. Their paths cross several times as they hurtle down translucent, intertwining tubes. The green side is like the Incredible Hulk Coaster of slides: It starts fast and somehow gets faster as it goes.

MAKU AND PUIHI ROUND RAFT RIDES **Height requirement: 42", 48" if riding alone.** *Maku* and *Puihi* mean "wet" and "wild," and that's no exaggeration. North America's first "saucer ride," the 6-person Maku raft plunges riders through bowl-like formations before landing them in a pool surrounded by erupting geysers. Puihi is the far more frightening slide of the pair: A 6-person raft launches down into a dark, winding tunnel before shooting up a banked curve; riders glimpse the highway below and momentarily experience zero gravity prior to sliding back down.

OHYAH AND OHNO DROP SLIDES **Height requirement: 48".** Two short but intense twisting slides that launch you 4 and 6 feet above the water at the end; Ohno is taller.

PUKA ULI LAGOON **No height requirement.** Tranquil leisure pool.

PUNGA RACERS **Height requirement: 42".** Guests go feet-first down 4 side-by-side body slides, passing through "underwater sea caves" (enclosed plastic tubes).

TANIWHA TUBES **Height requirement: 42", 48" if riding alone.** One tower sports 4 Easter Island–inspired waterslides with rafts for single or double riders. Along the way, tiki statues make sure you don't stay dry. The slides are similar but not identical—bear left to the green Tonga slides with more-open sections if you get claustrophobic.

TEAWA THE FEARLESS RIVER **Height requirement: 42", 48" if riding alone.** Guests hang tight in their flotation vests amid roaring whitewater rapids as they surf beneath the slides inside Krakatau. If you're looking for a lazy river, this ain't it!

River Village

HONU AND IKA MOANA SLIDES **Height requirement: ika Moana 42"; Honu 42", 48" if riding alone.** Honu and ika Moana are separate slides attached to the same tower, where guests board multiperson, animal-themed rafts (a sea turtle and a whale) before speeding down into a pool. Honu is a blue raft slide that sends you vertically up 2 giant sloped walls before sliding back down—it's the scariest group ride in the park. ika Moana is a much gentler journey in and out of twisting green tunnels.

KO'OKIRI BODY PLUNGE **Height requirement: 48".** Hop on this 125-foot slide, featuring a drop door with a 70-degree-angle descent, straight through the heart of the mountain. Drumbeats building up to the drop get your heart pounding, but the plunge itself is over before you have time to scream.

KOPIKO WAI WINDING RIVER **No height requirement.** A gentle lazy river that passes through the park's landscape and into the volcano's hidden caves.

KRAKATAU AQUA COASTER **Height requirement: 42", 48" if riding alone.** Guests board a specially designed canoe that seats up to 4. The ride uses linear induction motor technology, which launches the canoe uphill as well as downhill as you twist and turn around the volcano's blown-out interior. It's similar to Crush 'n' Gusher at Typhoon Lagoon, but far longer and more thrilling. Krakatau is the park's most popular ride, so get your TapuTapu reservation as early as possible.

RUNAMUKKA REEF **For children under 54" tall.** A 3-story water playground for older children inspired by the coral reef, featuring twisting slides, sprinklers, and more.

TOT TIKI REEF **For children under 48" tall.** Toddler play area with spraying Maori fountains, slides, and a kid-size volcano.

Wave Village

THE REEF **No height requirement.** Leisure pool with calm waters and its own waterfall. Relax and watch braver souls shoot down the Ko'okiri Body Plunge.

WATURI BEACH **Children under 48" must wear a life vest.** Features a multidirectional wave pool, situated at the foot of Krakatau Lagoon and fed by waterfalls cascading off the volcano's peak.

See page 405 for the Small-Child Fright Potential Table for Volcano Bay.

FAVORITE EATS AT VOLCANO BAY
RAINFOREST VILLAGE **Bambu** | Quinoa edamame burger topped with roasted shiitake mushroom and Sriracha mayo | **Dancing Dragons Boat Bar** | Volcano Blossom on tap brewed especially for the park by the Orange Blossom Brewery | **The Feasting Frog** | Tacos served with plantain chips and salsa
RIVER VILLAGE **Whakawaiwai Eats** | Hawaiian pizza with caramelized pineapple, diced ham, and pickled jalapeños
WAVE VILLAGE **Kohola Reef Restaurant & Social Club** | Slow-smoked glazed chicken, served with mango slaw and fries, and coconut curry chicken, served with rice and sweet plantains, chocolate lava cake for dessert. | **Kunuku Boat Bar** | Kona Big Wave on draft, imported from Kailua-Kona, Hawaii

prices depend on the date. While they're not a necessity, we recommend the private loungers for their included shade canopy, locking storage box, and attendant to deliver food and drink orders. The cabanas get all that, plus towel service, free fruit and bottled water, and a private kiosk for making TapuTapu reservations.

BEFORE YOU GO

1. Call ☎ 407-363-8000, or visit universalorlando.com/volcanobay, the day before you go to find out the official park opening time.

2. Purchase admission tickets online before you arrive.

3. Visit the website to determine which attractions are appropriate for the kids in your party.

4. Familiarize yourself with the TapuTapu system before you arrive.

AQUATICA *by* SEAWORLD

AQUATICA IS LOCATED across International Drive from the back side of SeaWorld. From Kissimmee, Disney World, and Lake Buena Vista, take I-4 East, exit onto the Central Florida Parkway, and then bear left on International Drive. From Universal Studios, take I-4 West and exit onto FL 528; then exit onto I-Drive. Admission starts at $45.99, plus tax, online. A two-park ticket for Aquatica and SeaWorld starts at $124.99 (to be used within 14 days). A three-park ticket (any combination of SeaWorld, Aquatica, Busch Gardens Tampa Bay, or Adventure Island) starts at $134.99. Packages are available year-round and some include an all-day dining deal. See aquatica.com/orlando/tickets.

Aquatica is comparable in size to other water parks in the area. Landscaped with palms, ferns, and tropical flowers, it's far less themed than Typhoon Lagoon, Blizzard Beach, or Volcano Bay. You can take in all the attractions in one day, but remember that an entire day of action in the Florida sun will wear out even the most active kids, and most grown-ups too.

There are lockers, towels, wheelchairs, scooters, and strollers to rent; gift shops to browse; and places to eat. The three restaurants at Aquatica are **WaterStone Grill,** offering burgers, wraps, and salads;

AQUATICA ATTRACTIONS

CUTBACK COVE AND BIG SURF SHORES No height requirement. One cove serves up bodysurfing waves, while the other puts out gently bobbing floating waves. A spacious beach arrayed around the coves is the park's primary sunning venue. Shady spots under beach umbrellas ring the perimeter of the area.

IHU'S BREAKAWAY FALL Height requirement: 48". Orlando's steepest multidrop tower slide. Brace yourself, and make sure your swimsuit is securely fastened!

KAREKARE CURL Height requirement: 48"; maximum 2 people, with a combined weight not exceeding 400 pounds; individual riders must not exceed 250 pounds; single riders not allowed. Thrill seekers will love Aquatica's newest ride, opened in April 2019. This high-adrenaline ride on a 2-person raft is only 361 feet long, lasts about 20 seconds, and includes a 35-foot drop down an enclosed tube.

KATA'S KOOKABURRA COVE Height requirement: 48" maximum. Wading pool and slides for the preschool crowd.

LOGGERHEAD LANE Must be in a single or double tube. Take a tube and enjoy this lazy river, which at one point passes through the Fish Grotto, a tank populated by hundreds of exotic tropical fish.

OMAKA ROCKA Height requirement: 48". A wide-diameter, enclosed, 1-person tube ride. The name is derived from the wave action inside the tube, which washes you alternately up one side of the tube and then the other.

RAY RUSH Height requirement: 42". A multiperson raft ride with enclosed spirals and manta ray–inspired elements.

REEF PLUNGE Height requirement: 42". Twist and turn through more than 330 feet of translucent cutouts and rings, past a vibrant habitat housing an array of marine life, including Commerson's dolphins, leopard sharks, sardines, and other cold-water fish.

RIPTIDE RACE Height requirement: 42". The world's tallest dueling racer, Riptide Race is an adrenaline-pumping waterslide that pits teams against each other in a splash to the finish line. It all starts atop a 68-foot tower, where you'll grab a 2-person raft before racing through 650 feet of slide.

ROA'S RAPIDS Height requirement: 51" and under must wear a life vest. Floating stream with a very swift current but no rapids. There is only one place to get in and out.

TASSIE'S TWISTERS Must be able to maintain proper riding position while holding onto both handles unassisted. An enclosed slide tube spits you into an open bowl, where you careen around the edge like a ball in a roulette wheel.

TAUMATA RACER Height requirement: 42"; must be able to maintain proper riding position unassisted. A high-speed mat ride down a steep hill.

WALHALLA WAVE Height requirement: 42"; must be able to maintain proper riding position unassisted. Circular raft that can accommodate up to 4 people and splashes down a 6-story enclosed twisting tube.

WALKABOUT WATERS Height requirement: 36"–42" for slides into the main pool and over 42" for larger slides. 15,000-square-foot children's adventure area. If your children are under the age of 10, this alone may be worth the admission price. It's impossible not to get wet and impossible not to have fun!

WHANAU WAY Must be able to maintain the proper riding position while holding onto both handles unassisted. Tubes carry 1 or 2 passengers down one of 4 slides with a few twists and a corkscrew.

*Guests under 48" must wear a life vest.

Banana Beach Cook-Out, dishing up pizza, pulled pork, and chicken; and **Mango Market,** a diminutive eatery serving loaded fries and chicken tenders. WaterStone Grill and Mango Market serve beer. If food is important to you, you are out of luck. The eateries at Aquatica are dismal at best; unfortunately, the park does not allow you to bring in your own food.

BEFORE YOU GO

1. Call ☎ 407-545-5550, or visit aquatica.com, the day before you go to find out the official park opening time.

2. Purchase admission tickets online before you arrive.

3. Visit the website to determine which attractions are appropriate for the kids in your party.

A WORD FROM THE WEATHERMAN

THUNDERSTORMS ARE COMMON IN FLORIDA. On summer afternoons, such storms often occur daily, forcing the water parks to close temporarily while the threatening weather passes. If the storm is severe and prolonged, it can cause a great deal of inconvenience. The park may actually close for the day, launching a legion of guests through the turnstiles to compete for space on the Disney resort buses. If you depend on Disney buses, leave the park earlier, rather than later, when you see a storm moving in. Most important, though, instruct your children to immediately return to home base (see page 428) at the first sight of lightning or the first rumble of thunder.

We recommend monitoring the weather forecast the day before you go, and checking again in the morning before leaving for the park. Scattered thunderstorms are to be expected and usually cause no more than a temporary inconvenience, but avoid the parks when the forecast indicates a moving storm front.

We get a lot of questions about whether to go to the water parks during cold-weather months. Did you know that Disney actually heats all the water-park pools in the winter? Orlando-area temperatures can vary from the high 30s to the low 80s during December, January, and February. When it's warm, though, these months can serve up a dandy water-park experience, as this Batavia, Ohio, woman recounts:

> Going to Blizzard Beach in December was the best decision ever! They told us that if the park didn't reach 100 people by noon, they would be closing. . . . There was no wait for anything all day! In June we waited in line for an hour for Summit Plummet. In December it took us only the amount of time to walk up the stairs. We had the enormous wave pool to ourselves. We did everything in the entire park and had lunch in less than 3 hours. The weather was slightly chilly at 71°F and overcast with very light rain, but the water is heated, so we were fine.

SAFETY FIRST

FUN IN THE SUN is no longer fun if you get sunburned or dehydrated. Drink lots of fluids, use a broad-spectrum sunscreen with an SPF of at least 30 (reapply every 2 hours), and bring a T-shirt and a hat for extra protection. Lifeguards are on duty throughout the parks.

SEAWORLD

MANY DOZENS OF READERS have written to extol the virtues of SeaWorld. The following are representative. An English family writes:

> The best-organized park is SeaWorld. The park map included a show schedule and told us which areas were temporarily closed. Best of all, there was almost no queuing. Overall, we rated this day so highly that it's the park we would most like to visit again.

A woman in Alberta, Canada, gives her opinion:

> We chose SeaWorld as our fifth day at the World. What a pleasant surprise! It was every bit as good (and in some ways better) than WDW itself. Well worth the admission, an excellent entertainment value, educational, well run, and better value for the dollar in food services. Perhaps expand your coverage to give them their due!

Here's what you need to know. SeaWorld (☎ 407-545-5550; sea world.com/orlando) is a world-class marine-life theme park near the intersection of I-4 and the Beachline Expressway. It's about 10 miles east of Disney World. It opens daily at 9 or 10 a.m. and closes between 6 and 10 p.m., depending on the season. Admission starts at $64.99, plus tax. Several multipark tickets are available as well. A two-day pass to SeaWorld and Aquatica starts at $89.99, plus tax. A three-day park ticket allowing visits to three of the following four parks (SeaWorld Orlando, Aquatica Orlando, Busch Gardens Tampa Bay, and Adventure Island) starts at $149.99, plus tax. A four-day ticket with

BOB Be forewarned that you can't take food or drinks into SeaWorld or its swimming park, Aquatica.

admission to all four parks starts at $219.99, plus tax. For a fee you can purchase add-ons such as dining plans, quick views (front-of-line access), and reserved seating.

SeaWorld offers an all-day dining plan ($49.59 for adults and $29.29 for kids ages 3–9). Guests can eat at participating restaurants as often as once every 90 minutes. SeaWorld also offers behind-the-scenes tours, such as **Dolphin Encounter** and **Penguins Up-Close.** To book a tour, visit seaworld.com/orlando/upgrades/animal-experiences.

Strollers, wheelchairs, and electric scooters are available for rent. The general parking fee is $30; VIP parking is $45. The one-day Photo Key pass costs $70.

Figure 8–9 hours or more to see everything, 6 or so if you stick to the big deals. SeaWorld is about the size of the Magic Kingdom and requires about the same amount of walking. In terms of size, quality, and creativity, it's unequivocally on par with Disney's major theme parks. Unlike Walt Disney World, SeaWorld primarily features stadium shows and walk-through exhibits. This means you'll spend about 80% less time waiting in line during 8 hours at SeaWorld than you would for the same-length visit at a Disney park.

But you'll notice immediately as you check the performance times that the shows are scheduled so that it's almost impossible to see them back-to-back. A Cherry Hill, New Jersey, visitor confirms this rather major problem, complaining:

> *The shows were timed so we could not catch all the major ones in a 7-hour visit.*

Much of the year, you can get a seat for the stadium shows by showing up 10 or so minutes in advance. When the park is crowded, however, you need to be at the stadiums at least 20 minutes in advance (30 minutes for a good seat).

All the stadiums have splash zones, or specified areas where you're likely to be drenched with ice-cold salt water by whales, dolphins, and sea lions. Finally, SeaWorld has some of the best roller coasters— **Mako, Manta, Kraken,** and the brand-new **Ice Breaker**—in Florida. If you're a coaster lover, be on hand before park opening and ride all three rides as soon as the park opens.

Sesame Street Land replaced Shamu's Happy Harbor playground. The 6-acre environment, which re-creates iconic locations from the beloved TV show, includes both wet and dry play areas, a kid-size roller coaster, and a daily parade featuring Big Bird and friends.

On select days from May through September, SeaWorld puts on *Electric Ocean,* a nighttime show with music and fireworks. The fireworks can be seen from all around SeaWorld's large central lake.

The **Seven Seas Food Festival** takes place on weekends from mid-February to early May. It offers delightful Asian, Latin, Polynesian, European, and Mediterranean flavors at food kiosks throughout the park. In addition, concerts feature well-known artists such as Lynyrd Skynyrd, Styx, the Village People, Alabama, Daughtry, the Commodores, and Grupo Manía. Prices range from $3.75 to $6.50 per dish with the option to buy a sampling lanyard for $65 (10 items) or $80 (15 items), plus tax. The quality and variety of the food is topped only by the generous serving sizes. Check out our review of the 2021 festival at tinyurl.com/sevenseasfestreview.

Mid-November–December 31, SeaWorld has special events to celebrate the holidays. The park sparkles with over 3 million lights, and

FAVORITE EATS AT SEAWORLD		
KEY WEST AT SEAWORLD	**Captain Pete's Island Eats**	Nathan's hot dogs, waffle fries with chili and cheese
THE WATERFRONT	**Voyager's Smokehouse**	Barbecue ribs, chicken, brisket	**Seafire Grill**	Grilled chicken salad, buffalo wings, chicken tenders
SHARK ENCOUNTER	**Sharks Underwater Grill**	Lobster, lamb chops, filet mignon, tempura shrimp, Kobe beef sliders. Kids menu includes hot dogs, chicken tenders, grilled fish. Floor-to-ceiling glass allows guests to observe some 50 sharks and fish.	*Table service only*
WILD ARCTIC	**Mango Joe's**	Pizza, kids' meals
FRONT GATE PLAZA	**Sweet Sailin' Candy Shop**	Candy, chocolate turtles

SEAWORLD ATTRACTIONS

ANTARCTICA: EMPIRE OF THE PENGUIN Height requirement: 42". Motion-based trackless dark ride; you exit in a real penguin habitat. The ride part of this attraction was closed at press time, but guests can still visit the penguin exhibit.

DOLPHIN ADVENTURE No height requirement. Educational show with bottlenose dolphins in the Dolphin Stadium.

DOLPHIN COVE No height requirement. 2-acre outdoor dolphin habitat.

DOLPHIN NURSERY No height requirement. Outdoor pool for expectant dolphins or mothers and calves.

FLAMINGO PADDLE BOATS Height requirement: 56" to ride alone; no height requirement to ride with an adult. Babes in arms not permitted. Flamingo-themed boat ride on SeaWorld's lake. A separate fee of $6 is charged for the 20-minute voyage.

ICE BREAKER Height requirement: 54". Intense roller coaster featuring 4 airtime launches, both backward and forward, culminating in a reverse launch into the steepest vertical drop in Florida—a 93-foot tall spike with a 100-degree angle.

INFINITY FALLS Height requirement: 42". 4-minute rainforest-themed river rapids ride; a vertical lift raises rafts 40 feet then launches them into the river; you will get soaked!

JEWEL OF THE SEA AQUARIUM No height requirement. Located under Journey to Atlantis. The jellyfish exhibit is amazing.

JOURNEY TO ATLANTIS Height requirement: 42"; 42"–48" must be accompanied by a supervising companion at least 14 years old. Combination roller coaster/flume ride.

KRAKEN Height requirement: 54". Roller coaster.

MAKO Height requirement: 54". In SeaWorld's own words: the tallest, longest, fastest coaster in Orlando.

MANATEE REHABILITATION AREA No height requirement. Manatee-viewing area.

MANTA Height requirement: 54". Roller coaster.

MANTA AQUARIUM No height requirement. More than 3,000 marine animals; the pop-up aquarium lets kids feel like they're in the aquarium.

OCEAN DISCOVERY **No height requirement.** An educational killer whale show that occurs on certain days at the earliest Shamu show.

ORCA UNDERWATER VIEWING No height requirement. Whale-viewing area.

PACIFIC POINT PRESERVE No height requirement. Sea lion– and seal-viewing area.

PELICAN PRESERVE No height requirement. Pelican-viewing area.

PETS AHOY **No height requirement.** Show with performing birds, cats, dogs, and a pig. *Temporarily closed.*

SEA LION & OTTER SPOTLIGHT No height requirement. Fun and educational show about marine mammals.

SESAME STREET Height requirements: Abby's Flower Tower: 42"; Big Bird's Twirl 'n' Whirl: 36"; Cookie Drop!: 42"; Elmo's Choo Choo Train: 36"; Slimey's Slider: 42"; Sunny Day Carousel 42"; Super Grover's Box Car Derby: 38". Iconic locations from the beloved TV show, 7 *Sesame Street*–themed attractions, wet and dry play areas, and a daily parade with Big Bird and friends.

SHARK ENCOUNTER No height requirement. Shark-viewing area.

SKY TOWER Height requirement: 48" unless accompanied by a supervising companion at least 14 years old (babes in arms allowed). A 400-foot tower with a bird's-eye view of Orlando; rarely open.

STINGRAY LAGOON No height requirement. Stingray-viewing area.

TURTLETREK **No height requirement.** 3-D film about sea turtles; animal habitats.

WILD ARCTIC No height requirement. Come close to walruses and beluga whales in this walk-through exhibit.

guests can enjoy Elmo's Christmas Wish, a Sesame Street Christmas Parade, and a Winter Wonderland on Ice show. Guests can ice-skate at the Bayside Stadium. The Nautilus Theater stage will be the home of Sound of the Season concerts, and in addition to snow flurries, there will be fireworks illuminating the sky when the park closes.

DISCOVERY COVE

ALSO OWNED BY SEAWORLD, this intimate park is a welcome departure from the hustle and bustle of other Orlando parks. Its slower pace could be the overstimulated family's ticket back to mental health.

LILIANE With a focus on personal guest service and one-on-one animal encounters, Discovery Cove admits only 1,300 guests per day.

The main draw at Discovery Cove is the chance to **swim with an Atlantic bottlenose dolphin.** The 50-minute experience (30 minutes in the water) is open to visitors age 6 and up who are comfortable in the water. Trainers lead an orientation and allow participants to ask questions. Next, small groups wade into shallow water to get an introduction to the dolphin in its habitat. The experience culminates with guests swimming into deeper water for closer interaction with the dolphin before being towed back to shore by the mammal.

 LILIANE The price is high, but the prize is right. Swimming with a dolphin across the bay was one of the most amazing things I've ever done.

Snorkel or swim in the **Grand Reef,** which houses thousands of exotic fish and rays, as well as an underwater shipwreck and hidden grottoes. The **Freshwater Oasis** is a swimming and wading experience, where you can get up close and personal with otters and marmosets. In the **Explorer's Aviary,** you can touch and feed gorgeous tropical birds. The **Wind-Away River,** in which you can float or swim, threads through the park, with multiple beaches serving as pathways to the attractions.

All guests are required to wear flotation vests when swimming, and lifeguards are omnipresent. You'll need your swimsuit, pool shoes, and a cover-up. On rare days when it's too cold to swim in Orlando, wet suits are provided to guests for free. Discovery Cove also provides fish-friendly sunscreen samples; guests may not use their own sunscreen.

Discovery Cove is open daily, 9 a.m.–5 p.m.; check-in begins at 7:15 a.m. Admission is limited, so purchase tickets well in advance; call ☎ 877-557-7404 or visit discoverycove.com. Prices vary seasonally and start at $324 per person (no children's discount). Prices for Florida residents start at $259.20, if bought in advance. Admission includes the dolphin swim; self-parking; Continental breakfast; a substantial lunch; snacks and drinks; and use of beach umbrellas, lounge chairs, towels, lockers, and swim and snorkel gear. If you're not interested in the dolphin swim, you can visit Discovery Cove for the day starting at $224 per person, depending on the season. You can add admission to SeaWorld, Aquatica, Busch Gardens Tampa Bay, and/or Adventure Island for an additional fee.

For an additional $49–$69 per person, depending on the season, you can experience **SeaVenture,** a 25-minute underwater stroll on the bottom of the Grand Reef aquarium. Participants wear diving helmets (large enough to accommodate eyeglasses), and no experience or scuba certification is necessary. Minimum age is 10 years. Starting at $169, guests can swim freely alongside several species of sharks. And for $59 and up, depending on the season, guests can help feed stingrays and tropical fish and take a private, guided swim through The Grand Reef.

DISNEY SPRINGS

THIS SPRAWLING DINING, SHOPPING, and entertainment complex is strung along the banks of Lake Buena Vista, on the east side of Walt Disney World. It consists of the **Marketplace, The Landing, Town Center,** and the **West Side.** You can roam, shop, and eat without paying any sort of entrance fee.

If you have a car, use it. There are three parking garages and four surface lots. The **Lime** garage serves The Landing, Town Center, and Marketplace areas of Disney Springs. The **Orange** garage is closest to the West Side, the AMC 16 movie theater, and Planet Hollywood. The third garage, **Grapefruit,** sits opposite the Lime garage on the other side of Buena Vista Drive. It is connected to Disney Springs via a raised walkway. There is no charge to park in the garages.

An LED display on each level of the garages indicates how many open spaces there are on each level. As a rule, the lower levels fill up first, with more open spaces available on each successive level up. The Orange garage can be reached directly from westbound I-4 via Exit 67. All three garage entrances are accessed from Buena Vista Drive.

There is **bus transportation** from all the Disney resorts to Disney Springs, and some resorts offer boat transportation. All guests using bus transportation to Disney Springs are dropped off at The Gateway, which is centrally located at Town Center. The Gateway also has all the loading zones for your return trip to your Disney resort.

There are several **ATMs** throughout Disney Springs. All major **credit cards** are accepted, and if you're a Disney resort guest, you can have your **purchases delivered to your hotel** (if you're not checking out the next day). **Pets** are not allowed at Disney Springs. **Guest Services** is located in Town Center, near D-Luxe Burger, and there are two **Starbucks** locations—one on the West Side and one in the Marketplace. **Strollers, wheelchairs, and ECVs** are available for rent at Sundries in Town Center near Wolfgang Puck Bar & Grill.

When it comes to food, Disney Springs has plenty to offer, and we share some of our favorites for each area with you. All stores, entertainment offerings, and eateries are listed on the map on pages 442–443. For a more thorough rundown of all restaurants at Walt Disney World, including Disney Springs, check out *The Unofficial Guide to Walt Disney World 2023* by Bob Sehlinger and Len Testa, which provides complete reviews, ratings, insights, and additional details that we can't accommodate in the space of these pages.

MARKETPLACE

WITH WORLD OF DISNEY and many activities for children, the Marketplace is the most kid-friendly of the shopping and dining areas. It has a small carousel and minitrain rides for a nominal fee. Free, kid-oriented dance parties take place in the lakeside amphitheater, and a fountain splash area is great for cooling down. The centerpiece of shopping is the 50,000-square-foot **World of Disney,** the largest store in the country selling Disney-trademarked merchandise. Kids will particularly enjoy the **Lego Store**. You'll know you're there when you see Brickley, the 30-foot sea serpent, made out of more than a million Lego blocks, that lives in the lake in front of the store.

Once Upon a Toy is a joy. The biggest draws at this 16,000-square-foot store are classic toys with a Disney twist. Here you can find Mr. Potato Head with Mickey ears or a sorcerer's hat and the classic game Clue set in The Haunted Mansion. One of the most exciting shopping options is found at **Marketplace Co-Op,** a retail space such as **Disney Centerpiece** (home and kitchen items), **D-Tech on Demand** (custom electronics accessories), **WonderGround Gallery** (Disney-inspired original art), **Disney Tails** (Disney-themed accessories for your fur babies), and Liliane's favorite—**The Dress Shop on Cherry Tree Lane**—which has the most amazing dresses and accessories, of which even Mary Poppins would approve.

Bibbidi Bobbidi Boutique (*temporarily closed*), located at the far eastern end of the Disney Springs Marketplace next to Once Upon a Toy, transforms your child into a princess or a knight, albeit for a price. Fairy Godmother's Apprentices (as the shop's cast members are called) offer salon services for kids

LILIANE Save money by getting just the hairstyle and makeup at Bibbidi Bobbidi and taking your own pictures.

age 3 and up. Packages vary from $70 to $480, plus tip. Reservations can be made up to 60 days in advance. Call ☎ 407-939-7895 for information or reservations. Allow 30 minutes–1 hour for the whole makeover.

Disney's Days of Christmas This shop is just plain fun, with hundreds of holiday decorations, from ornaments to stockings to stuffed animals wearing their Christmas best. We especially like the station for ornament personalization. There's also a section dedicated to *The Nightmare Before Christmas*.

Goofy's Candy Co. An interactive show kitchen where you can enjoy create-your-own pretzel rods, marshmallows, and candy apples. At **Ghirardelli Soda Fountain & Chocolate Shop,** you can smell the chocolate when you walk in. Chocolate souvenirs abound, but treat yourself to a "world famous" sundae topped with hot fudge made daily at the shop. The line for ice cream often winds out the door—it's that good.

The Spice and Tea Exchange carries flavored salts and sugars, teas, and spice mixes. You can also purchase wines and cookbooks.

Tren-D is a fun, hip, urban-inspired boutique for women, with fashion apparel and accessories, plus exclusive items from cutting-edge designers and Disney merchandise you won't find anywhere else.

The Earl of Sandwich is still the best deal in the Marketplace. Kids will want to go to the **Rainforest Café** or **T-REX**. For a taste of Californian cuisine, parents will enjoy **Wolfgang Puck** (table service only).

THE LANDING AND TOWN CENTER

THE LANDING is the waterfront section of Disney Springs. Open, winding paths offer sweeping views of the water and Saratoga Springs resort as you walk between the Marketplace and the West Side.

Here, too, are lots of shopping opportunities, such as **The Art of Shaving** (high-end grooming essentials for Dad), **Sanuk** (casual footwear), and **Oakley** (sunglasses). **Havaianas** is the place for cool flip-flops, with options to design your own. Liliane's favorite stores are **Chapel Hats** and **The Ganachery**.

 LILIANE At Chapel Hats, I really had to control myself to keep from buying a fascinator for the next Kentucky Derby.

The Landing offers lots of eateries to choose from. At **Chef Art Smith's Homecomin'**, enjoy Southern food and drinks; **Paddlefish** is great for seafood and offers spectacular sunset views over Disney Springs from its top deck; **The Boathouse** is upscale waterfront dining and the launching pad for the *Venezia,* a 40-foot wooden Italian water taxi. Kids will enjoy the guided **Amphicar** rides, which take guests on a 20-minute tour of the landmarks of Disney Springs, albeit at an exorbitant price.

Kids will love the more informal **Jock Lindsey's Hangar Bar,** with great outdoor seating overlooking the lake. **Morimoto Asia** is Iron Chef Masaharu Morimoto's Pan-Asian restaurant. The setting is fabulous, and his take on Chinese, Japanese, and Korean dishes is really something for Mom and Dad's night out.

One of our all-time favorites is **Raglan Road.** Full table service is available indoors with Irish music and dancers. If you can't get a table inside, try the **Hole in the Wall** outside, which has a bar and several tables. You can order food from Raglan's main menu. Next door is **Cookes of Dublin,** serving over-the-counter fish-and-chips.

The Edison is an industrial Gothic-themed restaurant, bar, and entertainment destination. We are not impressed by **Maria & Enzo's Ristorante** (the food is nothing special, and the place is extremely noisy). **Enzo's Hideaway,** with a 1920s-speakeasy vibe, is a much better choice.

And, yes, we know there is a new cookie store in town. **Gideon's Bakehouse** opened in January 2021, and the last time Liliane walked

continued on page 444

Disney Springs

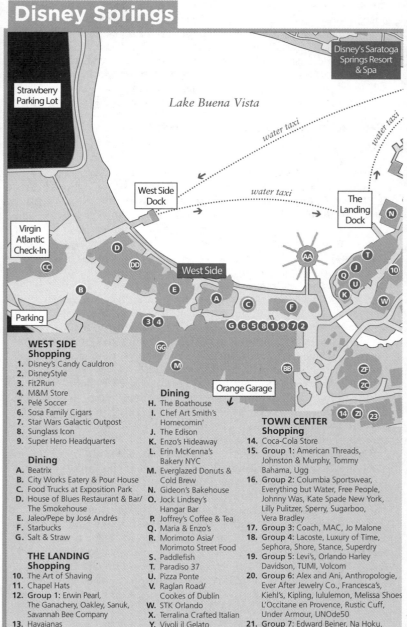

Disney's Saratoga Springs Resort & Spa

Strawberry Parking Lot

Lake Buena Vista

water taxi

water taxi

West Side Dock

water taxi

The Landing Dock

N

Virgin Atlantic Check-In

CC

D

DD

West Side

E

A

C

F

AA

T

Q J

U

K

W

10

Parking

B

3 4

GG

G 6 5 8 1 9 7 2

M

BB

Orange Garage

ZF

ZC

14 ZI 23

WEST SIDE
Shopping
1. Disney's Candy Cauldron
2. DisneyStyle
3. Fit2Run
4. M&M Store
5. Pelé Soccer
6. Sosa Family Cigars
7. Star Wars Galactic Outpost
8. Sunglass Icon
9. Super Hero Headquarters

Dining
A. Beatrix
B. City Works Eatery & Pour House
C. Food Trucks at Exposition Park
D. House of Blues Restaurant & Bar/ The Smokehouse
E. Jaleo/Pepe by José Andrés
F. Starbucks
G. Salt & Straw

THE LANDING
Shopping
10. The Art of Shaving
11. Chapel Hats
12. **Group 1:** Erwin Pearl, The Ganachery, Oakley, Sanuk, Savannah Bee Company
13. Havaianas

Dining
H. The Boathouse
I. Chef Art Smith's Homecomin'
J. The Edison
K. Enzo's Hideaway
L. Erin McKenna's Bakery NYC
M. Everglazed Donuts & Cold Brew
N. Gideon's Bakehouse
O. Jock Lindsey's Hangar Bar
P. Joffrey's Coffee & Tea
Q. Maria & Enzo's
R. Morimoto Asia/ Morimoto Street Food
S. Paddlefish
T. Paradiso 37
U. Pizza Ponte
V. Raglan Road/ Cookes of Dublin
W. STK Orlando
X. Terralina Crafted Italian
Y. Vivoli il Gelato
Z. Wine Bar George

TOWN CENTER
Shopping
14. Coca-Cola Store
15. **Group 1:** American Threads, Johnston & Murphy, Tommy Bahama, Ugg
16. **Group 2:** Columbia Sportswear, Everything but Water, Free People, Johnny Was, Kate Spade New York, Lilly Pulitzer, Sperry, Sugarboo, Vera Bradley
17. **Group 3:** Coach, MAC, Jo Malone
18. **Group 4:** Lacoste, Luxury of Time, Sephora, Shore, Stance, Superdry
19. **Group 5:** Levi's, Orlando Harley Davidson, TUMI, Volcom
20. **Group 6:** Alex and Ani, Anthropologie, Ever After Jewelry Co., Francesca's, Kiehl's, Kipling, lululemon, Melissa Shoes, L'Occitane en Provence, Rustic Cuff, Under Armour, UNOde50
21. **Group 7:** Edward Beiner, Na Hoku, Pandora

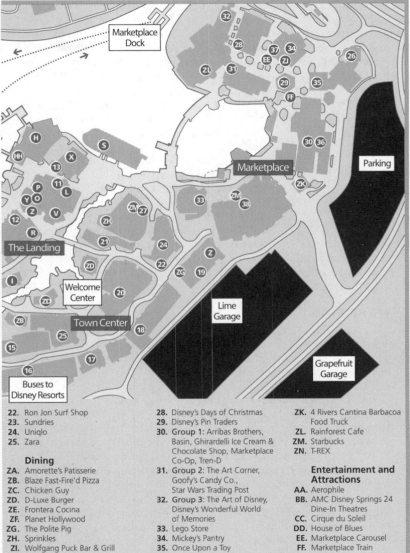

22. Ron Jon Surf Shop
23. Sundries
24. Uniqlo
25. Zara

Dining
ZA. Amorette's Patisserie
ZB. Blaze Fast-Fire'd Pizza
ZC. Chicken Guy
ZD. D-Luxe Burger
ZE. Frontera Cocina
ZF. Planet Hollywood
ZG. The Polite Pig
ZH. Sprinkles
ZI. Wolfgang Puck Bar & Grill

MARKETPLACE Shopping
26. Bibbidi Bobbidi Boutique
27. Build-A-Dino/Dino Store

28. Disney's Days of Christmas
29. Disney's Pin Traders
30. Group 1: Arribas Brothers, Basin, Ghirardelli Ice Cream & Chocolate Shop, Marketplace Co-Op, Tren-D
31. Group 2: The Art Corner, Goofy's Candy Co., Star Wars Trading Post
32. Group 3: The Art of Disney, Disney's Wonderful World of Memories
33. Lego Store
34. Mickey's Pantry
35. Once Upon a Toy
36. PhotoPass Studio
37. The Spice & Tea Exchange
38. World of Disney

Dining
ZJ. Earl of Sandwich

ZK. 4 Rivers Cantina Barbacoa Food Truck
ZL. Rainforest Cafe
ZM. Starbucks
ZN. T-REX

Entertainment and Attractions
AA. Aerophile
BB. AMC Disney Springs 24 Dine-In Theatres
CC. Cirque du Soleil
DD. House of Blues
EE. Marketplace Carousel
FF. Marketplace Train Express
GG. Splitsville Luxury Lanes
HH. Vintage Amphicar & Italian Water Taxi Tours

continued from page 441

by (June 2022), the line was so long she thought they were giving them away. Seriously? Queuing up for a $6 cookie?

The third area is the Old Florida–style **Town Center.** It offers plenty of well-known retail outposts, including **Anthropologie, L'Occitane en Provence** (Liliane's favorite store), **Zara, Vera Bradley, Tommy Bahama,** and **Uniqlo.** If you've ever found yourself at Pirates of the Caribbean and thought, "What this place needs is a Wetzel's Pretzels," you'll love shopping here. Town Center sits between The Landing and the parking lot.

Also at Town Center are the gourmet food kiosks **Aristocrepes, Daily Poutine,** and **B.B. Wolf's Sausage Co.,** as well as **Sprinkles.**

When hunger strikes, there is plenty to choose from at Town Center. We like **The Polite Pig, Blaze Fast-Fire'd Pizza,** and, for dessert, **Amorette's Patisserie.** While Amorette's does not deliver outside of Disney Springs, they will deliver a cake to your Disney Springs restaurant for special occasions with 72 hours' notice. For Liliane, Amorette's is the ne plus ultra of cakes. Make sure to at least have a look, or, even better, buy one of the Petit Cakes, and judge for yourself!

LILIANE You can still get your Sprinkles cupcake even if the store is closed or terribly busy. The cupcake ATM operates daily, 8 a.m.–3 a.m., and a menu tells you what choices are available. $5 cupcake, anyone?

WEST SIDE

ON THE WEST SIDE, the new Disney-themed **Cirque du Soleil** production, *Drawn to Life,* opened in 2021. It is the first collaboration between Cirque du Soleil, Walt Disney Animation Studios, and Walt Disney Imagineering, and it's a must-see! Shown Tuesday–Saturday, the show is 90 minutes long, with no intermission. Tickets start at $85. Read Liliane's review at tinyurl.com/drawntolifereview.

Catch the latest flick at the state-of-the art **AMC Dine-In Disney Springs 24,** showing movies and serving food in an Art Deco setting. For showtimes and ticket sales, go to tinyurl.com/amcorlandoshowtimes.

For a bird's-eye view of the Disney Springs area, try **Aerophile,** where you ascend up to 400 feet in a tethered helium balloon. The weather-dependent ride is about 8 minutes long and costs $25 for adults and $20 for children ages 3–9. Aerophile operates daily, 9 a.m.–11 p.m. The balloon is filled with 210,000 cubic feet of helium, and the basket holds 29 guests plus one pilot who is certified by French company Aérophile S.A., which builds and operates the balloons. For more information, visit disneysprings.com/attractions/aerophile-balloon-flight.

If you are looking to shade your eyes from the Florida sun, **Sunglass Icon** sports the latest frames from the world's top designers. Runners and walkers can find new gear at **Fit2Run.**

Sweet memories are made at **Disney's Candy Cauldron.** It's a very small store, but it's packed with goodies, most notably candy apples for all seasons. Check out Liliane's review at tinyurl.com/disneycaramel apples. More candy can be found at the **M&M's** store.

The place to be for parents' night out is **Jaleo by José Andrés,** by award-winning chef and Nobel Peace Prize nominee José Andrés. It features an extensive tapas menu reflecting the regional diversity of Spanish cuisine with a modern twist. See Liliane's review at tinyurl .com/jaleodisneysprings. Many readers may know the incredible work Andrés and his team do via **World Central Kitchen (WCK),** which he founded in 2010. Since then, the NGO has organized meals in the Bahamas, Cambodia, Cuba, the Dominican Republic, Nicaragua, Peru, Uganda, Ukraine, the United States, and Zambia. In late February 2022, Andrés and WCK began providing food for Ukrainian refugees, including in border areas and hard-hit Kharkiv. By March, the organization had opened eight kitchens on the Ukraine–Poland border.

Live concerts with an emphasis on rock and blues take place at the **House of Blues.** Developed by Blues Brother Dan Aykroyd, it consists of a restaurant and blues bar and a concert hall. The restaurant and bar are open daily, 10 a.m.–11:30 p.m. The music hall next door features concerts by an eclectic array of musicians and groups. Genres have included gospel, blues, funk, ska, dance, salsa, rap, zydeco, hard rock, groove rock, and reggae. For more information call ☎ 407-934-BLUE (2583), or visit houseofblues.com/orlando/concert-events.

The **NBA Experience,** opened in August 2019, closed permanently in 2021. Disney has not announced what will replace it. On a positive note, the West Side is home to one of Disney Springs' two **Starbucks**.

UNIVERSAL ORLANDO CITYWALK

HERE YOU'LL FIND RESTAURANTS, nightlife, and shopping. For date night, great entertainment is available at **Bob Marley—A Tribute to Freedom,** which has reggae; **Pat O'Brien's** dueling-pianos club; **Fat Tuesday,** specializing in New Orleans–style daiquiris; **Bigfire,** which cooks food over a wood fire at the center of the eatery; a **Hard Rock Cafe** and a **Hard Rock Live** concert venue; **Jimmy Buffett's Margaritaville;** the **Red Coconut Club,** a two-story upscale cocktail lounge with live music and dancing; and **Citywalk's Rising Star,** a karaoke club with a live backup band. In late 2022, **Universal's Great Movie Escape,** two escape rooms inspired by *Jurassic World* and *Back to the Future,* will replace the space formerly occupied by The Groove.

Kids will enjoy the **Toothsome Chocolate Emporium & Savory Feast Kitchen,** a full-service restaurant, bar, and confectionery that is well worth a visit for the confections alone, even if you don't stay to dine. The 19th-century-inspired steampunk chocolate factory is funky, and while all things chocolate are fabulous, the rest of the menu is also a

continued on page 448

Universal Orlando CityWalk

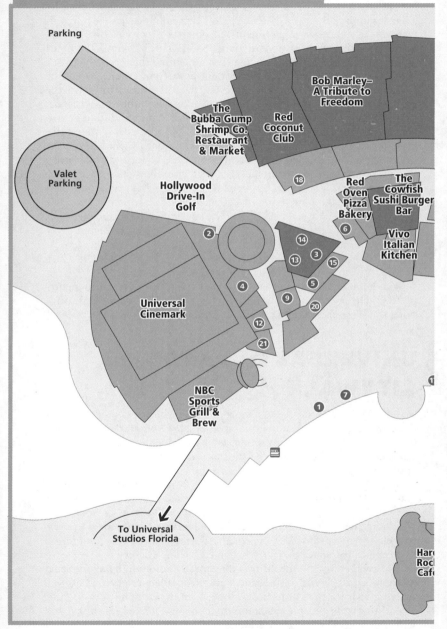

Parking

Valet
Parking

The
Bubba Gump
Shrimp Co.
Restaurant
& Market

Red
Coconut
Club

Bob Marley–
A Tribute to
Freedom

Hollywood
Drive-In
Golf

18

Red
Oven
Pizza
Bakery

The
Cowfish
Sushi Burger
Bar

Vivo
Italian
Kitchen

2

6

14

13   3

15

Universal
Cinemark

4

5

9

20

12

21

NBC
Sports
Grill &
Brew

7

1

To Universal
Studios Florida

Har
Roc
Caf

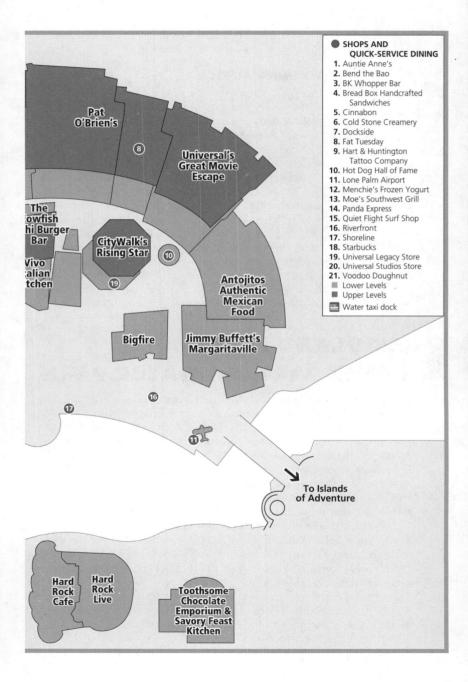

SHOPS AND QUICK-SERVICE DINING

1. Auntie Anne's
2. Bend the Bao
3. BK Whopper Bar
4. Bread Box Handcrafted Sandwiches
5. Cinnabon
6. Cold Stone Creamery
7. Dockside
8. Fat Tuesday
9. Hart & Huntington Tattoo Company
10. Hot Dog Hall of Fame
11. Lone Palm Airport
12. Menchie's Frozen Yogurt
13. Moe's Southwest Grill
14. Panda Express
15. Quiet Flight Surf Shop
16. Riverfront
17. Shoreline
18. Starbucks
19. Universal Legacy Store
20. Universal Studios Store
21. Voodoo Doughnut
- Lower Levels
- Upper Levels
- Water taxi dock

Pat O'Brien's

Universal's Great Movie Escape

The Cowfish Sushi Burger Bar

Vivo Italian Kitchen

CityWalk's Rising Star

Antojitos Authentic Mexican Food

Bigfire

Jimmy Buffett's Margaritaville

To Islands of Adventure

Hard Rock Cafe

Hard Rock Live

Toothsome Chocolate Emporium & Savory Feast Kitchen

continued from page 441

winner. And what could possibly not be good at **Voodoo Doughnut**? These one-of-a-kind doughnuts are sure to be a hit.

LILIANE I dream of a chocolate-coconut doughnut, while Bob thinks anything by the dozen in the pink box will be just fine!

TOURING ADVICE

CityWalk is open daily, 8 a.m.–2 a.m. (until midnight during slower seasons). As of August 2022, unaccompanied minors under age 18 must leave CityWalk by 9 p.m. Friday–Sunday, unless they are staying on-site; are attending a movie; or have a special event ticket, such as for Halloween Horror Nights (HHN).

Guest Services, restrooms, an **ATM,** and **First Aid** are all to your left, immediately past Cold Stone Creamery. Parking is available in the same garages that serve the theme parks. The regular parking fee is $27, Prime Upgrade is $32, and Prime Parking is $60. Self-parking is free after 6 p.m. (except during HHN and special events). If you stay at one of the Universal resorts, it's a short walk; water taxi and bus transportation are also available. For added fun, try one of the pedicabs that will take you from CityWalk to your resort for a modest tip. Call ☎ 407-224-FOOD (3663) for dinner reservations or visit universalorlando.com/web/en/us/theme-parks/citywalk.

LEGOLAND FLORIDA THEME PARK *and* WATER PARK

UNLIKE THE MASSIVE PARKS that emphasize cartoon heroes, action movies, or living creatures, Legoland Florida, which encompasses a theme park and a water park, has no similar competition. The lure is, of course, the models of real-life buildings, vehicles, and people, all made from the tiny plastic bricks. Among its more than 55 attractions is **Miniland,** an entire area filled with these models. Legoland Florida also has four roller coasters, but although the coasters launch and plunge their riders at various speeds, none are the whipsaw attractions that draw adrenaline junkies to the larger theme parks.

Legoland Theme Park is designed for the chief users of the plastic blocks, kids 2–12 years old. Thus, the pint-size rides will be the most enjoyable, and comfortable, for that age group. Several rides require a "responsible" person to accompany the shortest guests to ensure their safety (as noted in table at right).

Meet and greets with Lego characters, including familiar faces from *The Lego Ninjago Movie,* are available daily. Download the Legoland Florida Resort mobile app for times. You can even trade mini Lego figures with cast members!

Legoland Water Park includes various slides and a wave pool, and some attractions have minimum heights of 36–48 inches. It's open 365

LEGOLAND FLORIDA ATTRACTIONS

THE BEGINNING

THE LEGOLAND EXPERIENCE No height requirement. Immersive exhibit brings the history of Lego to life.

REBUILD THE WORLD No height requirement. Indoor building experience.

CYPRESS GARDENS

BOTANICAL GARDENS No height requirement. Cypress Gardens is home to exotic plants from all over the world. There are 30 kinds of palms, 10 varieties of banana trees, 15 types of azaleas, 10 kinds of camellias, and much more. The gardens are well kept and quiet. They are also home to a giant banyan tree that was planted as a seedling in 1939!

DUPLO VALLEY

DUPLO SPLASH AND PLAY No height requirement. Splash area amidst giant farm animals.

DUPLO TRACTOR Guests under 42" must ride with a responsible person 48" or taller and age 14 or older. | Kids can ride a tractor around Duplo farm animals.

DUPLO TRAIN Guests under 34" must ride with a responsible person 48" or taller. Train ride exploring countryside-themed Duplo Valley, which features farms, fishing holes, and campgrounds.

DUPLO TOT SPOT No height requirement. Play area for children under age 2.

FLORIDA PREPAID SCHOOLHOUSE No height requirement. Indoor play area for little tykes. Interactive touchscreens for kids to practice numbers and letters on. The schoolhouse houses a quiet area and the Baby Care Center.

FUN TOWN

BUILD-YOUR-ART GALLERY BY LEGO DOTS No height requirement. Kids can create their own masterpiece on the gallery wall using Lego Dots.

THE GRAND CAROUSEL Guests under 48" must ride with a responsible person 48" or taller and age 14 or older. Double-decker carousel.

HEARTLAKE CITY

HEARTLAKE STEPPING TONES FOUNTAIN No height requirement. Kids can create music by stepping on stones surrounding a heart-shaped fountain.

MIA'S RIDING ADVENTURE Height requirement: 48". Spin on a disk and travel up and down a U-shaped track, all while seated on a horse.

IMAGINATION ZONE

IMAGINATION ZONE No height requirement. Indoor space filled with thousands of Legos waiting to be assembled!

KID POWER TOWERS Height requirement: 38"; guests under 48" must be accompanied by a responsible rider age 14 or older. Kids pull themselves up to the top of a tower for an aerial view of the park before dropping "free-fall" back to the bottom.

LAND OF ADVENTURE

BEETLE BOUNCE Height requirement: 36". Small drop tower rising 15 feet.

COASTERSAURUS Height requirement: 42". Wooden roller coaster. Super-headliner!

LOST KINGDOM ADVENTURE Height requirement: 30"; guests under 48" must ride with a responsible person 48" or taller and age 14 or older. Indoor dark ride with laser guns used to shoot at objects throughout the ride and gain points.

PHARAOH'S REVENGE No height requirement. Outdoor play maze.

SAFARI TREK Height requirement: 34"; guests under 48" must be accompanied by a responsible rider age 14 or older. Track ride through a jungle of Lego animals.

LEGO CITY

COAST GUARD ACADEMY | Height requirement: 34"; guests under 48" must be accompanied by a responsible rider age 14 or older in the same boat. | Kids can navigate the waters in Lego-themed boats.

LEGOLAND FLORIDA ATTRACTIONS *(continued)*

LEGO CITY *(continued)*

FLYING SCHOOL Height requirement: 44". Guests under 52" must be accompanied by a responsible rider 52" or taller. Maximum rider height is 6'5". Suspended roller coaster.

FORD DRIVING SCHOOL For kids 6-13. Little brick fans learn the rules of the road while pretending to be police officers, firefighters, taxi drivers, or any driver they choose.

FORD JR. DRIVING SCHOOL For kids ages 3-5. Younglings can practice their driving skills and earn a Legoland driver's license.

NFPA RESCUE ACADEMY | 34" Guests below 48" must be accompanied by a responsible rider age 14 older | Guests board toy fire trucks and work to put out the "flames" on a building. There is a lot of water involved, and the truck that puts out the fire and gets back first to the starting point wins.

TOT SPOT No height requirement. Indoor airplane-themed toddler playground.

LEGO KINGDOMS

THE DRAGON Height requirement: 40" Guests under 48 inches must be accompanied by a responsible rider 14 years or older. Indoor/outdoor steel roller coaster.

THE FORESTMEN'S HIDEOUT No height requirement. Outdoor playground.

MERLIN'S CHALLENGE Height requirement: 36"; guests under 48" must be accompanied by a responsible rider age 14 older. Kid-friendly ride powered the wizard Merlin. A small wooden train spins around the wizard.

ROYAL JOUST Height requirement: 36". For kids ages 4-12. Weight limit: 170 lbs. Kids ride life-size Lego-themed horses on a track around a jousting ground.

THE LEGO MOVIE WORLD

BATTLE OF BRICKSBURG Guests under 48" must ride with an adult. Water ride. The idea is to defend Bricksburg from the evil Duplo alien invaders and stop them from stealing bricks. Beware, you will get soaked.

BENNY'S PLAY SHIP No height requirement. Space-themed playground.

EMMET'S SUPER SUITE No height requirement. Guests can visit Emmet's apartment in downtown Bricksburg. Emmet and his friends are available for photos.

THE LEGO MOVIE MASTERS OF FLIGHT Height requirement: 40" Riders less than 52" must be accompanied by a responsible rider 14 years or older. Flying theater experience with special effects, similar to Soarin' Around the World at EPCOT.

UNIKITTY'S DISCO DROP Height requirement: 48"; guests 40"–47" and ages 3–6 must be accompanied by a supervising companion age 14 or older. Guests under 40" or under age 3 are not permitted to ride. Drop tower ride.

LEGO NINJAGO WORLD

LEGO NINJAGO THE RIDE Children under age 6 or under 48" must ride with a responsible person 48" or taller. 4D attraction ride where children can interact with their favorite Ninja and work together to defeat the Great Devourer.

LEGO TECHNIC

AQUAZONE WAVE RACERS Height requirement: 52" Guests between 40"–52" must be accompanied by a responsible rider 14 years of age or older in the same vehicle. Make-believe flying boats skim the water as they move in a circle.

THE GREAT LEGO RACE Height requirement: 42" to ride without virtual reality headset; 48" to ride with virtual reality headset. Riders 42"–47" must be accompanied by a responsible rider age 14 or older and at least 48". Thrill roller coaster.

TECHNIC TOT SPOT No height requirement. Shaded playground for toddlers.

TECHNICYCLE Height requirement: 36"; guests between 36" and 48" must be accompanied by a responsible rider age 14 or older in the same ride unit. Rider-powered carousel ride that launches guests into the air as they pedal. The faster you pedal, the higher you will go!

LEGOLAND FLORIDA ATTRACTIONS *(continued)*

MINILAND USA

MINILAND USA No height requirement. Miniature themed areas made from Legos. The most famous landmarks of New York, Las Vegas, California, and Washington, D.C.; Florida's Kennedy Space Center; and even some *Star Wars* scenes are represented.

WATER PARK

BUILD-A-BOAT No height requirement. Here kids create their own Lego watercraft and race it through a fast-flowing river.

BUILD-A-RAFT RIVER Children under 42" must be accompanied by a responsible adult. Families can build their own unique Lego vessel and float around in a 1,000-foot-long lazy river.

JOKER SOAKER Height requirement: 36" to ride the 3 lower-level slides; 40" to ride the 4 upper-level slides. This interactive water playground has slides of various lengths and heights. With plenty of water spouts and a wading pool, there is something for the entire family. And don't forget the 300-gallon bucket of water providing you with refreshing spills!

LEGO WAVE POOL Children under 42" must be accompanied by a responsible adult and are advised not to go past the bright-red line across the pool at approximately 3' 4" deep. Wave pool for the entire family to enjoy. The waves go in increments of 8 minutes on and 10 minutes off.

SPLASH OUT Height requirement: 48". Water park thrill seekers will enjoy this attraction. You have a choice between 3 slides and will speed down a 60-foot drop before you splash in the water below the slide.

TWIN RACERS Height requirement: 42" to ride; guests under 48" must be accompanied by a rider at least 48", wear a life vest, and ride in a double tube. Tube ride 375 feet down an intertwining pair of enclosed slides.

days a year but can close due to inclement weather and on select dates. Like the theme park, the water park is specifically designed for kids ages 2–12. Featuring more than 4 million Lego bricks, it is a great trip down memory lane for parents who grew up with Legos. At **Surf Shop,** you can shop for swimwear, footwear, sunscreen, towels, and more.

In addition to the impressive models and kiddie-size rides, Legoland Florida boasts shaded areas and benches. Tables holding Legos are thoughtfully placed by the queues to occupy the younger guests.

The walkways are *very* narrow and can be tricky to navigate with strollers, especially double strollers. There is a minimum height requirement for almost every ride. We suggest measuring your child once and stopping at Guest Relations for a free color-coded height indicator to avoid disappointment.

Most shopping at Legoland is about, you guessed it, Legos. They come in an incredible range of colors, sizes, and shapes. Check out **The Big Shop, Driving School Store, Heartlake Mall,** the **Lego Factory Experience,** and **Wu's Warehouse.** Some stores specialize in Lego logo apparel, character costumes, and tchotchkes.

Hotels

Three Lego-themed hotels will make the heart of every toddler beat faster. The three hotels (**Pirate Island Hotel, Legoland Hotel,** and **Legoland Beach Retreat**) all come with a king bed in the adult sleeping area; little tykes have their own sleeping area with bunk bed, pull-out trundle bed, and entertainment unit. A free daily breakfast is included in the

FAVORITE EATS AT LEGOLAND FLORIDA
LEGO CITY | **Burger Kitchen** | Cheeseburgers, pizza, fried chicken, salads | **Kick'n Chicken Co.** | Chicken tenders with fries
LEGO KINGDOMS | **Dragon's Den** | Smoked turkey legs, bratwurst, honey-battered mini corn dogs, locally brewed beer. For dessert, ice cream at **Fire House Ice Cream** or soft-serve ice cream from **Kingdom Cones.**
FUN TOWN | **Fun Town Pizza & Pasta Buffet** | Pizza and pasta buffet. For dessert, Fun Town Slushies or Granny's Apple Fries, dusted with cinnamon and sugar and served with a sweet whipped cream.
LEGO TECHNIC | **Funnel Cake Factory** | Made-to-order funnel cakes
LEGO NINJAGO WORLD | **Ninja Kitchen Food Truck** | Egg rolls, spring rolls, bao buns
THE BEGINNING | **Pepper & Roni's Pizza Stop** | Personal-size cheese, pepperoni, and veggie pizzas | **The Legoland Coffee Co.** | Coffee, breakfast croissants, sandwiches
THE LEGO MOVIE WORLD | Taco Everyday | Tacos
LAND OF ADVENTURE | **Ultimate Sandwich Builder** | Food truck offering grilled cheese sandwich and loaded mac and cheese bowls
HEARTLAKE CITY | **Heartlake Ice Cream Parlor** | Traditional ice-cream shop
WATER PARK | **Beach-n-Brick Grill** | Fresh burgers, hot dogs, chicken tenders, salads | **Beach Street Tacos** | Tex-Mex style tacos

room rate, and each hotel has a pool. A standard room at any of the hotels starts at $163.74 per night. All-inclusive packages include admission tickets to Legoland Theme Park, Legoland Water Park, and Peppa Pig Theme Park for every day of your stay, from check-in to checkout, along with three meals (breakfast and dinner at your hotel and lunch at the park). Package prices start at $216 per person, per day. For a full description of all that's included, visit legoland.com/florida/places-to-stay/vacation-packages.

Pirate Island Hotel has an attractive resort-style heated pool with fun floating foam bricks to build with. There is nightly entertainment in the lobby, including PJ parties. The free Master Model Builder Workshops are very popular—reserve a spot as soon as you check in.

Legoland Hotel was the first hotel to open. It features 152 rooms and suites, each with its own immersive Lego theme designed just for kids. Six themes are available: Lego Ninjago, Adventure, Pirate, Kingdom, Lego Friends, and *The Lego Movie*. Nightly entertainment for the kiddos is also offered, and there is even a sound-and-light show in the elevator! It is the only hotel that has character appearances. Master Model Builder workshops are available here too. The resort-style heated pool and splash areas are lots of fun, complete with floating foam bricks. Parents can enjoy waterside bar service.

Legoland Beach Retreat is the latest addition to Legoland Resort. Here, guests can stay in bungalows that look like they're made of Legos. Check-in is done via a drive-through window when entering.

The village-style resort consists of 83 brightly colored, beach-themed bungalows grouped into 13 sections, each named after a popular Lego Minifigure, including Shark Suit Guy, Ocean King, and Sea

Captain. Each section has an outdoor play area that's within view of the bungalows' shaded patios so that parents can put their feet up and relax while kids play.

The layout of the rooms is like that at the other two hotels (king bed in the parents' room with a separate sleeping and play area for the kids), but here all the rooms are decorated the same. The decor is very playful and everywhere!

The resort has a giant heated pool and outdoor playground with views of Lake Dexter. While the resort is in walking distance (0.8 mile) from the Legoland park entrance, a free shuttle service is offered.

At The Lighthouse, the center of the resort, you'll find an ATM, guest services, vending and ice machines, and the restaurants. The Lighthouse is also home to the **Palm Tree Traders** shop, where snacks, drinks, and sundries are available. Nighttime entertainment starts at 5:30 p.m. at The Lighthouse.

For an additional fee, guests at all three hotels can enjoy s'mores around a campfire, a nine-hole minigolf course, or pontoon boat rides on Lake Eloise.

Dining

Pirate Island Hotel and Legoland Hotel offer the following dining options: Breakfast is served family-style (all-you-can-eat) at **Bricks Restaurant** and **Shipwreck Restaurant**. At Pirate Island, Bricks serves an all-you-can-eat buffet at dinner. Seating is first come, first served. At the Legoland Hotel, no dinner is offered at Bricks. Dinner at Shipwreck (Pirate Island Hotel) features a three-course family-style menu. Lunch and dinner are served at **Skyline Lounge** with an à la carte menu. Reservations are required for dinner at Shipwreck and Skyline Lounge. Both also have a kids' play area.

Legoland Beach Retreat has very limited eateries. All are located at The Lighthouse. **Sandy's Castle Restaurant** is open for breakfast and dinner. An all-you-can-eat breakfast is served family-style, while dinner is Latin American fare. At **Bricks Beach Bar** you can order food, drinks, and cocktails to-go; the bar has a full dinner menu.

Seasonal Events

Special seasonal events, including holiday celebrations and fireworks, happen throughout the year. For all the happenings, check legoland .com/florida/things-to-do/seasonal-events.

Admission and Touring Advice

Legoland Florida is roughly 35 miles (about 45 minutes) west of Walt Disney World. Strollers, wheelchairs, and electric conveyance vehicles (ECVs) are available for rent. Lockers are available; prices depend on the size. Parking is $25 per car.

Admission prices are available for one-, two-, and three-day tickets. There are also annual passes and combo tickets for the Legoland theme and water parks and Peppa Pig Theme Park. Buying online is a good option to save a few dollars on most of the ticket options. Prices start at $84.99 for one day at Legoland Theme Park only; $109.99 for one day at Legoland Theme Park and Water Park; and $109.99 for Legoland Theme Park and Peppa Pig Theme Park. A one-day ticket for Peppa Pig starts at only $34.99. Ticket prices are the same for all guests ages 2 and older; infants under 24 months are free. For more information, visit legoland.com/florida/tickets-passes/tickets.

For more information, visit florida.legoland.com, where you can also book vacation packages that include hotel stays as well. For general Legoland information, call ☎ 877-350-LEGO (5346).

PEPPA PIG THEME PARK

IF YOU'VE PARENTED A TODDLER over the past couple of decades, you're probably well aware of Peppa Pig's popularity among the preschool set. The series of UK cartoon shorts has attracted a worldwide following, with Peppa Pig–themed attractions, created by Merlin Entertainments, found from Shanghai to Chicago. Peppa Pig Theme Park Florida is billed as the first and only theme park in the world solely dedicated to the precocious porcine superstar.

Located about an hour southwest of Disney World in Winter Haven, Peppa Pig Theme Park is just steps away from Legoland Florida. It's far more compact than your average theme park, making it the perfect proportion for its pint-size target audience. After passing through the entry plaza, you'll find all the park's indoor amenities to your left, while all the outdoor attractions are spread out ahead of you.

Food and Merchandise

It wouldn't be a theme park without things to eat and buy, but the commercial offerings are surprisingly low-key at Peppa Pig Theme Park.

Mrs. Rabbit's Diner, the park's lone dining establishment, offers kid-friendly standards like grilled cheese and mac and cheese, alongside adult entrées like smoked brisket sandwiches and a yummy bowl of grains and greens.

Before you head out the exit, be sure to stop by **Mr. Fox's Shop** for a wide selection of Peppa Pig–branded toys and souvenirs. While most of the items currently in stock can be purchased elsewhere, the store will soon be home to exclusive Peppa Pig Theme Park merchandise.

Admission and Touring Advice

Single-day tickets to Peppa Pig Theme Park cost $34.99. Ticket prices are the same for all guests ages 2 and older; infants under 24 months are free. Admission to Peppa Pig can also be bundled with admission to Legoland Florida Theme Park as a Two-Park, One-Day Ticket.

Because the park is only open 10 a.m. to 5 p.m., you'll probably want to arrive at opening, especially if driving from the Disney area along the often-congested I-4 and US 27. The rides all have very low

PEPPA PIG THEME PARK ATTRACTIONS

CINEMA No height requirement. Indoor movie theater with a big screen where kids can watch *Peppa Pig* episodes. Seating is on beanbags.

DADDY PIG'S ROLLER COASTER Height requirement: 36"; guests less than 42" must be accompanied by a responsible rider age 14 or older. Family-friendly coaster.

FUN FAIR No height requirement. Fairground with free games for the entire family.

GEORGE'S FORT No height requirement. | Outdoor maze in Granny Pig's Garden.

GRAMPY RABBIT'S DINOSAUR ADVENTURE Height requirement: 34"; guests less than 42" must be accompanied by a responsible rider age 14 or older. Straddle dinos while shuffling past volcanoes and prehistoric mountains.

GRANDAD DOG'S PIRATE RIDE No height requirement, but guests 43" and under OR under age 4 must be accompanied by a responsible rider age 14 or older. Pirate-themed boat ride.

GRANDPA PIG'S GREENHOUSE No height requirement. Interactive playground.

MADAME GAZELLE'S NATURE TRAIL No height requirement. Nature trail for the entire family.

MR. BULL'S HIGH STRIKER Height requirement: 34"; guests less than 43" must be accompanied by a responsible rider age 14 or older. Kid-friendly drop ride.

MR. POTATO'S SHOWTIME ARENA No height requirement. Live show with Peppa and her family. Lots of songs, games, snorts, and giggles!

MUDDY PUDDLES SPLASH PAD No height requirement. Kids will love this splash pad, especially on a hot day. Getting wet has never been so much fun! Parents: Make sure to bring a change of clothes!

PEPPA'S PEDAL BIKE TOUR AND GEORGE'S TRICYCLE TRAIL No height requirement. Biking trail for kids. Smaller cyclists will enjoy the shorter pedal-path adventure on tricycles.

PEPPA PIG'S BALLOON RIDE No height requirement, but guests less than 51" must be accompanied by a responsible rider age 14 or older. Family-friendly aerial carousel ride.

PEPPA PIG'S TREEHOUSE No height requirement. Kids can climb up the treehouse and slide down to the bottom of this outdoor play structure.

PIRATE ISLAND SAND PLAY No height requirement. Pirate-themed sand beach.

REBECCA RABBIT'S PLAYGROUND No height requirement. Outdoor play area.

carrying capacity, so let your kids knock themselves out on the roller coaster and dinosaur adventure until the queues build. Then let them run rampant over the playgrounds, which don't require any waiting, and take them to the live shows or the cinema when they inevitably crash. Better yet, book a night at one of Legoland's well-themed hotels—located within a short stroller-push of the park gates—which will reduce the stress of returning to your room when nap time arrives.

SPECIAL NEEDS AT LEGOLAND FLORIDA AND PEPPA PIG THEME PARK

LEGOLAND FLORIDA AND PEPPA PIG THEME PARK have gone above and beyond in making their attractions accessible to all kids, regardless of physical or nonapparent disability, earning the parks accreditation as Certified Autism Centers by the International Board of Credentialing and Continuing Education Standards (IBCCES).

In addition to publishing comprehensive accessibility information on the parks' websites, you can also download a Sensory Guide, which contains ratings for every attraction that indicate how intensely stimulating they may be for each of the five senses.

BEYOND *the* THEME PARKS

KENNEDY SPACE CENTER

HISTORY CONTINUES TO BE MADE at the Kennedy Space Center. Since the summer of 1963, the center has been the training area and launch site for most major US space programs, including Project Apollo's voyages to the moon and the space shuttle program.

Visiting the Kennedy Space Center is most enjoyable for those with a serious interest in the space program, but the educational tour of the facility is memorable for all kids, especially age 6 and up. The Visitor Complex is thoroughly modern and offers some of the attractions and amenities of a contemporary theme park. The complex does a wonderful job of capturing the spirit of adventure. It also offers a unique glimpse into the latest NASA advancements and some interesting visions of where the future of space exploration may lead. The complex also is home to the U.S. Astronaut Hall of Fame, honoring American astronauts. It features the largest collection of their personal memorabilia.

Don't miss the Rocket Garden, an outdoor display of historical rockets, and the Space Mirror Memorial, dedicated to those who died in pursuit of space exploration. The most jaw-dropping—and—inspiring—exhibit is "Space Shuttle *Atlantis.*" For devotees, this alone might be worth the price of admission. Orbit Café and Moon Rock Café are the main eateries at Kennedy Space Center.

The center also gives visitors the opportunity to witness rocket launches on its premises. All the viewing locations are within a few miles of the launchpads. Check tinyurl.com/kennedyspacelaunches for information on upcoming launches, viewing opportunities, and tickets.

One-day admission tickets start at $60.99 when purchased online. A ticket including an exclusive meet and greet with an astronaut and much more starts at $139. For more information and all there is to see and do, visit kennedyspacecenter.com or call ☎ 321-867-5000. The center is open daily, 9 a.m.–5 p.m. It's located at Space Commerce Way, Merritt Island, Florida.

OUTDOOR RECREATION

WALT DISNEY WORLD OFFERS a wealth of fun stuff for families besides theme parks, water parks, eating, and shopping. You can fish, canoe, hike, bike, boat, play tennis and golf, ride horses, work out, or take cooking lessons.

Your kids will go nuts for the **Wilderness Lodge Resort,** and so will you. While you're there, have a family-style meal at the kid-friendly **Whispering Canyon Cafe,** and rent bikes for a ride on the paved paths of adjacent **Fort Wilderness Resort & Campground.** The outing will be a great change of pace. The only downside is that your kids might not want to go back to their own hotel.

At **ESPN Wide World of Sports Complex,** a 220-acre competition and training center, Disney guests are welcome as paying spectators, but none of the facilities are available for guests to use. For tickets and a schedule of events (including Major League Baseball exhibition games), call ☎ 407-939-1500, or visit espnwwos.com.

Located 40–60 minutes south of Walt Disney World is the **Disney Wilderness Preserve,** a wetlands-restoration area with hiking trails and an interpretive center, operated by The Nature Conservancy in partnership with Disney. The preserve is open Wednesday–Friday, 9 a.m.–4:30 p.m, and Saturday–Sunday, 9:30 a.m.–4:30 p.m. It's closed Monday–Tuesday.

Trail access and conditions are occasionally limited due to inclement weather or restoration activities. Check the weather before your visit, and call ahead to check trail access. Admission is free, though donations are appreciated. To confirm operating hours, call ☎ 407-935-0002, or visit tinyurl.com/disneywildernesspreserve.

GOLF AND MINIGOLF

IF GOLF IS YOUR THING, call ☎ 407-WDW-GOLF (939-4653) or visit golfwdw.com for information, tee times, and greens fees at **Palm Golf Course, Magnolia Golf Course, Lake Buena Vista Golf Course,** or **Oak Trail Golf Course.**

Fun for the whole family abounds at **Fantasia Gardens Miniature Golf,** across the street from the Walt Disney World Swan, and **Winter Summerland,** next to Blizzard Beach. Fantasia Gardens is a beautifully landscaped course with fountains, animated statues, topiaries, and flower beds. Winter Summerland offers two 18-hole courses—one has a "blizzard in Florida" theme, while the other sports a tropical-holiday theme, with Christmas ornaments hanging from palm trees.

Fantasia Gardens is quite demanding and not nearly as whimsical as Winter Summerland. Adults and older teens will enjoy the challenge of Fantasia Gardens, but if your group includes children younger than 12, head to Winter Summerland.

Admission to both courses is $14 for adults and $12 for children ages 3–9, plus tax. They are open daily, 10 a.m.–10 p.m. For more information, call ☎ 407-WDW-PLAY (939-7529).

One of our favorite family activities is located on one edge of the CityWalk entertainment complex: **Hollywood Drive-In Golf.** Courses are awash in elaborate settings, props, and even audio. The theme is a drive-in movie showing two features: *Invaders from Planet Putt* and

The Haunting of Ghostly Greens. Players can choose a single (18-hole) or double (36-hole) feature.

The course is open daily, 9 a.m.–midnight. For 18 holes, it costs $18.99 for adults and $16.99 for children ages 3–9. For 36 holes, it costs $34.98 for adults and $30.98 for children ages 3–9. For more information, visit hollywooddriveingolf.com or call ☎ 407-802-4848.

THEME PARK TRIVIA QUIZ ANSWERS

MAGIC KINGDOM

1. (C) **2.** (D) **3.** (B) **4.** (C) **5.** (A) **6.** (C) **7.** (A) **8.** (C) **9.** (B) **10.** (C)

EPCOT

1. (C) **2.** (B) **3.** (C) **4.** (A) **5.** (B) **6.** (C) **7.** (C) **8.** (B) **9.** (B) **10.** (D)

DISNEY'S ANIMAL KINGDOM

1. (B) **2.** (C) **3.** (D) **4.** (C) **5.** (B) **6.** (B) **7.** (C) **8.** (C) **9.** (B) **10.** (D)

DISNEY'S HOLLYWOOD STUDIOS

1. (D) **2.** (B) **3.** (A) **4.** (A) **5.** (D) **6.** (A) **7.** (B) **8.** (B) **9.** (D) **10.** (A)

INDEX

The Magic Kingdom

MAGIC KINGDOM EARLY-ENTRY 2-DAY TOURING PLAN FOR PARENTS WITH SMALL CHILDREN: DAY 1

Make park reservations for the Magic Kingdom as soon as you know your travel dates.

1. Arrive at the Magic Kingdom entrance 40 minutes before official opening (1 hour during holidays and busy times). Get guide maps while waiting to enter the park. Stroller rentals are just past the turnstiles at the park entrance.
2. As soon as the park opens, ride Seven Dwarfs Mine Train in Fantasyland.
3. Take Peter Pan's Flight.
4. Meet princesses at Princess Fairytale Hall.
5. Ride Under the Sea—Journey of the Little Mermaid.
6. Take the It's a Small World boat ride.
7. See *Mickey's PhilharMagic*.
8. Take a spin on the Prince Charming Regal Carrousel. Walk through Cinderella Castle to admire the art on your way to Main Street, U.S.A.

9. Meet Mickey Mouse at Town Square Theater.
10. Eat lunch and return to your hotel for a midday break of around 4 hours.
11. Return to the park and ride Splash Mountain in Frontierland.
12. See The Haunted Mansion in Liberty Square.
13. Ride The Many Adventures of Winnie the Pooh in Fantasyland.
14. Ride Dumbo the Flying Elephant.
15. Take a spin on The Barnstormer.
16. Eat dinner.
17. See the *Enchantment* fireworks. The best viewing spots are in front of the castle, between the castle itself and the central hub.
18. Circle back to any skipped attractions, or revisit favorites.

To use Genie+ with this plan: The most useful reservations are for Peter Pan's Flight, Splash Mountain, and The Haunted Mansion. Get the first available reservation for those (in that order), and fit that return-time window into the plan. Once you're able to get your next Genie+ reservation, look for the earliest return time for any of the next few attractions in the plan. **ILL** reservations shouldn't be needed for Seven Dwarfs Mine Train. If using ILL, try to make a reservation for around the park's official opening time.

See tinyurl.com/free-tplans to customize this plan at no charge, including your arrival time, attractions you'll see, and your walking speed, plus real-time updates while you're in the park.

The Magic Kingdom

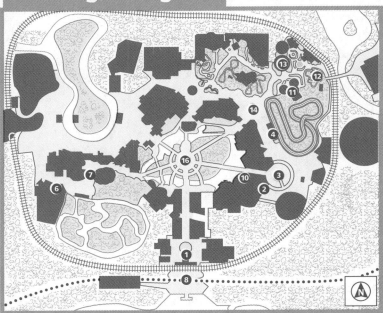

MAGIC KINGDOM EARLY-ENTRY 2-DAY TOURING PLAN
FOR PARENTS WITH SMALL CHILDREN: DAY 2

Make park reservations for the Magic Kingdom as soon as you know your travel dates.

1. Arrive at the Magic Kingdom entrance 40 minutes before official opening (1 hour during holidays and busy times). Get guide maps while waiting to enter the park. Stroller rentals are just past the turnstiles at the park entrance.

2. As soon as the park opens, ride Buzz Lightyear's Space Ranger Spin in Tomorrowland. Ride twice, if desired.

3. Take a spin on the Astro Orbiter.

4. Ride the Tomorrowland Speedway.

5. Using the MDE app, find the times and locations of any character greetings that interest you, and work in those visits around the next few steps.

6. Ride Pirates of the Caribbean.

7. Ride The Magic Carpets of Aladdin.

8. Leave the park for a midday break. Allow at least 4 hours. If you want to play in the Casey Jr.

Splash 'N' Soak Station this afternoon, bring a towel and a change of clothes when you return.

9. Return to the park. If you'd like to meet more characters, check the MDE app for times and locations, and work in those visits around the next few steps.

10. See *Monsters, Inc. Laugh Floor* in Tomorrowland.

11. Ride Dumbo the Flying Elephant in Fantasyland.

12. Ride The Barnstormer.

13. Try the Casey Jr. Splash 'N' Soak Station.

14. Take a spin on the Mad Tea Party.

15. Eat dinner.

16. If you haven't already, see the *Enchantment* fireworks. The best viewing spots are in front of the castle, between the castle itself and the central hub.

17. Circle back to any skipped attractions, or revisit favorites.

To use Genie+ with this plan: The most useful reservations are for Pirates of the Caribbean, The Magic Carpets of Aladdin, and Dumbo. Get the first available reservation for those (in that order), and fit that return-time window into the plan. Once you're able to get your next Genie+ reservation, look for the earliest return time for any of the next few attractions in the plan. **ILL** reservations shouldn't be needed for this plan.

See tinyurl.com/free-tplans to customize this plan at no charge, including your arrival time, attractions you'll see, and your walking speed, plus real-time updates while you're in the park.

The Magic Kingdom

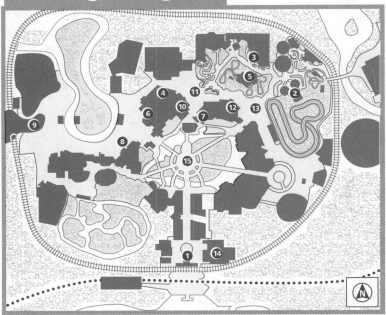

MAGIC KINGDOM 2-DAY SLEEPYHEAD TOURING PLAN
FOR PARENTS WITH SMALL CHILDREN: DAY 1

Review the Small-Child Fright-Potential Table on pages 213–215. Make park reservations for the Magic Kingdom as soon as you know your travel dates. Interrupt the plan for meals and rest.

1. Arrive before 11 a.m. Get guide maps. Stroller rentals are just past the turnstiles at the park entrance.
2. In Fantasyland, ride Dumbo the Flying Elephant.
3. Ride Under the Sea—Journey of the Little Mermaid.
4. Ride Peter Pan's Flight.
5. Ride Seven Dwarfs Mine Train. If using mobile ordering for lunch, place your order while in line, so it's ready as you're exiting the ride.
6. Eat lunch. The best nearby spot is Columbia Harbour House in Liberty Square.
7. Meet princesses at Princess Fairytale Hall.
8. See the *Festival of Fantasy* parade.
9. Ride Splash Mountain in Frontierland.
10. In Fantasyland, see *Mickey's PhilharMagic*.
11. Ride the Prince Charming Regal Carrousel.
12. See *The Many Adventures of Winnie the Pooh.*
13. Try the Mad Tea Party.
14. Meet Mickey Mouse at Town Square Theater on Main Street, U.S.A.
15. See the *Enchantment* fireworks. The best viewing spots are in front of the castle, between the castle itself and the central hub.
16. Circle back to any skipped attractions, or revisit favorites.

To use Genie+ with this plan: The most useful reservations are for Peter Pan's Flight (by a wide margin), Splash Mountain, and meeting Mickey Mouse. Get the first available reservation for those (in that order), and fit that return-time window into the plan. Once you're able to get your next Genie+ reservation, look for the earliest return time for any of the next few attractions in the plan. If using **ILL** for Seven Dwarfs Mine Train, try to make a reservation for after noon.

See tinyurl.com/free-tplans to customize this plan at no charge, including your arrival time, attractions you'll see, and your walking speed, plus real-time updates while you're in the park.

The Magic Kingdom

MAGIC KINGDOM 2-DAY SLEEPYHEAD TOURING PLAN
FOR PARENTS WITH SMALL CHILDREN: DAY 2

Review the Small-Child Fright-Potential Table on pages 213–215. Make park reservations for the Magic Kingdom as soon as you know your travel dates. Interrupt the plan for meals and rest.

1. Arrive before 11 a.m. Get guide maps. Stroller rentals are just past the turnstiles at the park entrance.
2. Using the MDE app, find the times and locations of any character greetings that interest you, and work in those visits around the next few steps.
3. In Fantasyland, ride The Barnstormer.
4. Ride Dumbo the Flying Elephant.
5. In Tomorrowland, see *Monsters, Inc. Laugh Floor*.
6. Try Buzz Lightyear's Space Ranger Spin in Tomorrowland.
7. Take a spin on the Tomorrowland Speedway.

8. If time permits, meet more princesses or Disney characters. Check the MDE app for locations and schedule.
9. Eat dinner.
10. Ride The Magic Carpets of Aladdin in Adventureland.
11. Ride Pirates of the Caribbean.
12. See the *Enchantment* fireworks. The best viewing spots are in front of the castle, between the castle itself and the central hub.
13. Circle back to any skipped attractions, or revisit favorites.

To use Genie+ with this plan: The most useful reservations are for Buzz Lightyear, Pirates of the Caribbean, and The Magic Carpets of Aladdin. Get the first available reservation for those (in that order), and fit that return-time window into the plan. Once you're able to get your next Genie+ reservation, look for the earliest return time for any of the next few attractions in the plan.

See tinyurl.com/free-tplans to customize this plan at no charge, including your arrival time, attractions you'll see, and your walking speed, plus real-time updates while you're in the park.

The Magic Kingdom

PARENTS' MAGIC KINGDOM PLAN:
1 AFTERNOON AND 1 FULL DAY: AFTERNOON

Review the Small-Child Fright-Potential Table on pages 213–215. Make park reservations for the Magic Kingdom as soon as you know your travel dates. Interrupt the plan for meals and rest.

1. Arrive at the Magic Kingdom around lunchtime. Get guide maps. Stroller rentals are just past the turnstiles at the park entrance.

2. Using the MDE app, find the times and locations of any character greetings that interest you, and work in those visits around the next few steps. You'll be spending most of your time in Adventureland and Frontierland today. Use the app to find times to meet characters nearby.

3. Ride Splash Mountain in Frontierland.

4. Ride Magic Carpets of Aladdin in Adventureland.

5. Ride Pirates of the Caribbean in Adventureland.

6. See The Haunted Mansion in Liberty Square.

7. See the *Enchantment* fireworks. The best viewing spots are in front of the castle, between the castle itself and the central hub.

8. If time permits, meet Mickey Mouse at Town Square Theater on Main Street, U.S.A.

9. Circle back to any skipped attractions, or revisit favorites.

To use Genie+ with this plan: The most useful reservations are for Splash Mountain, Pirates of the Caribbean, and The Magic Carpets of Aladdin. Get the first available reservation for those (in that order), and fit that return-time window into the plan. Once you're able to get your next Genie+ reservation, look for the earliest return time for any of the next few attractions in the plan.

See tinyurl.com/free-tplans to customize this plan at no charge, including your arrival time, attractions you'll see, and your walking speed, plus real-time updates while you're in the park.

The Magic Kingdom

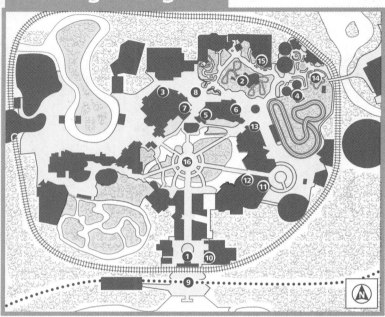

PARENTS' MAGIC KINGDOM PLAN:
1 AFTERNOON AND 1 FULL DAY: FULL DAY

Review the Small-Child Fright-Potential Table on pages 213–215. Make park reservations for the Magic Kingdom as soon as you know your travel dates. Interrupt the plan for meals and rest.

1. Arrive at the Magic Kingdom entrance 40 minutes before official opening (1 hour during holidays and busy times). Get guide maps while waiting to enter the park. Stroller rentals are just past the turnstiles at the park entrance.
2. In Fantasyland, ride the Seven Dwarfs Mine Train.
3. Ride Peter Pan's Flight.
4. Experience Dumbo the Flying Elephant.
5. Meet princesses at Princess Fairytale Hall.
6. Ride The Many Adventures of Winnie the Pooh.
7. See *Mickey's PhilharMagic*.
8. Ride the Prince Charming Regal Carrousel.
9. Eat lunch and return to your hotel for a midday break of 3–4 hours.

10. Return to the park and meet Mickey Mouse at Town Square Theater on Main Street, U.S.A., if you've not already done so.
11. Ride Buzz Lightyear's Space Ranger Spin in Tomorrowland.
12. See *Monsters, Inc. Laugh Floor*.
13. Eat dinner. Cosmic Ray's Starlight Café in Tomorrowland is a good choice.
14. Ride The Barnstormer in Fantasyland.
15. Ride Under the Sea—Journey of the Little Mermaid.
16. See the *Enchantment* fireworks. The best viewing spots are in front of the castle, between the castle itself and the central hub.
17. If time permits, circle back to any skipped attractions, or revisit favorites.

To use Genie+ with this plan: The most useful reservations are for Peter Pan's Flight (by a wide margin), then Buzz Lightyear, then Princess Fairytale Hall. Get the first available reservation for any of those (in that order), and fit that return-time window into the plan. Once you're able to get your next Genie+ reservation, look for the earliest return time for any of the next few attractions in the plan. ILL reservations shouldn't be needed for Seven Dwarfs Mine Train. If you arrive after park opening, however, get the earliest time available for it.

See tinyurl.com/free-tplans to customize this plan at no charge, including your arrival time, attractions you'll see, and your walking speed, plus real-time updates while you're in the park.

The Magic Kingdom

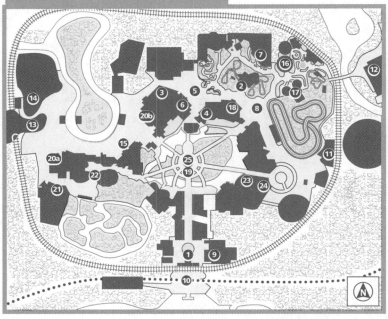

MAGIC KINGDOM HAPPY FAMILY 1-DAY TOURING PLAN

Review the Small-Child Fright-Potential Table on pages 213–215. Make park reservations for the Magic Kingdom as soon as you know your travel dates. Interrupt the plan for meals and rest.
Assumes: *Tron Lightcycle/Run is open*

1. Arrive at the Magic Kingdom entrance 40 minutes before official opening (1 hour during holidays and busy times). Get guide maps while waiting to enter. Stroller rentals are just past the turnstiles at the entrance.
2. As soon as the park opens, ride Seven Dwarfs Mine Train in Fantasyland.
3. Ride Peter Pan's Flight.
4. Meet princesses at Princess Fairytale Hall.
5. Ride the Prince Charming Regal Carrousel.
6. See *Mickey's PhilharMagic*.
7. Ride Under the Sea—Journey of the Little Mermaid.
8. Take a spin on the Mad Tea Party.
9. Meet Mickey Mouse at Town Square Theater.
10. **PARENTS:** Take a 4-hour break for lunch and a nap.
11. **TEENS:** Ride Space Mountain in Tomorrowland during the parents' break. If you're using Genie+ or ILL, choose the earliest available reservation for steps 11–13.
12. **TEENS:** Ride Tron Lightcycle/Run.
13. **TEENS:** Ride Splash Mountain in Frontierland.

14. **TEENS:** Ride Big Thunder Mountain Railroad.
15. **TEENS:** See the afternoon parade from Frontierland.
16. **PARENTS:** Return to the park. If it's warm enough, pack extra clothes and a towel for the Casey Jr. Splash 'N' Soak Station in Fantasyland.
17. **PARENTS:** Ride Dumbo the Flying Elephant.
18. Ride The Many Adventures of Winnie the Pooh.
19. Work in a viewing of *Mickey's Magical Friendship Faire* or a character greeting, around dinner.
20. Eat dinner. Good nearby choices are Pecos Bill Tall Tale Inn (**20a**) and Columbia Harbour House (**20b**).
21. Ride Pirates of the Caribbean in Adventureland.
22. Ride The Magic Carpets of Aladdin.
23. See *Monsters, Inc. Laugh Floor* in Tomorrowland.
24. Ride Buzz Lightyear's Space Ranger Spin.
25. See the *Enchantment* fireworks. The best viewing spots are in front of the castle, between the castle itself and the central hub.

To use Genie+ with this plan: The most useful reservations are for Peter Pan's Flight (by a wide margin), then Buzz Lightyear, then Magic Carpets of Aladdin. Get the first available reservation for any of those (in that order), and fit that return-time window into the plan. Once you're able to get your next Genie+ reservation, look for the earliest return time for any of the next few attractions in the plan. **ILL** reservations shouldn't be needed for Seven Dwarfs Mine Train but will probably be necessary for Tron. If using ILL, try to make a reservation for around 1 p.m.

See tinyurl.com/free-tplans to customize this plan at no charge, including your arrival time, attractions you'll see, and your walking speed, plus real-time updates while you're in the park.

The Magic Kingdom

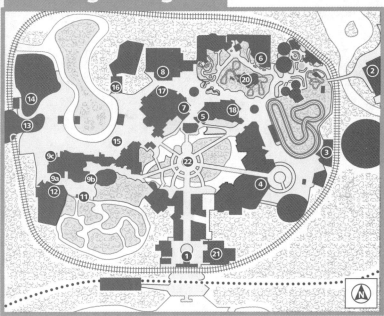

MAGIC KINGDOM EARLY-ENTRY 1-DAY TOURING PLAN FOR TWEENS AND THEIR PARENTS

Make park reservations for the Magic Kingdom as soon as you know your travel dates.
Assumes: Tron Lightcycle/Run is open

1. Arrive at the Magic Kingdom entrance 40 minutes before official opening (1 hour during peak times). Get guide maps while waiting to enter the park.
2. As soon as the park opens, ride Tron in Tomorrowland.
3. Ride Space Mountain.
4. Try Buzz Lightyear's Space Ranger Spin.
5. Meet princesses at Princess Fairytale Hall.
6. Ride Under the Sea—Journey of the Little Mermaid in Fantasyland.
7. See *Mickey's PhilharMagic*.
8. Take the It's a Small World boat ride in Fantasyland.
9. Walk through Cinderella Castle to get to Adventureland, and work in either *Captain Jack Sparrow's Pirate Tutorial* (**9a**) or a meeting with Jasmine and Aladdin (**9b**). Order lunch using mobile ordering while waiting for the characters. The closest, best spot nearby is Pecos Bill's (**9c**).
10. Eat lunch.

11. In Adventureland, take the Jungle Cruise.
12. Experience Pirates of the Caribbean.
13. Ride Splash Mountain in Frontierland.
14. Ride Big Thunder Mountain Railroad.
15. Watch the *Festival of Fantasy* parade.
16. Tour The Haunted Mansion in Liberty Square.
17. Take Peter Pan's Flight in Fantasyland. If eating dinner at a counter-service location, use mobile ordering to place your order now.
18. Ride The Many Adventures of Winnie the Pooh.
19. Eat dinner.
20. Ride Seven Dwarfs Mine Train.
21. If time permits, meet Mickey at Town Square Theater.
22. See the *Enchantment* fireworks show. The best viewing spots are in front of the castle, between the castle itself and the central hub.
23. Circle back to any skipped attractions, or revisit favorites.

To use Genie+ with this plan: The most useful reservations are for Peter Pan's Flight and Jungle Cruise. Get the first available reservation for either of those, and fit that return-time window into the plan. Once you're able to get your next Genie+ reservation, look for the earliest return time for any of the next few attractions in the plan. If using **ILL**, try to get a reservation for Tron with a return time for as close to park opening as possible, and a Seven Dwarfs Mine Train reservation for anytime after 5 p.m.

See tinyurl.com/free-tplans to customize this plan at no charge, including your arrival time, attractions you'll see, and your walking speed, plus real-time updates while you're in the park.

The Magic Kingdom

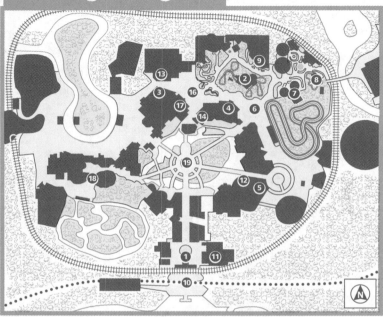

MAGIC KINGDOM EARLY-ENTRY 1-DAY TOURING PLAN
FOR GRANDPARENTS WITH SMALL CHILDREN

Review the Small-Child Fright-Potential Table on pages 213–215. Make park reservations for the Magic Kingdom as soon as you know your travel dates. Interrupt the plan for meals, rest, and a cocktail or two.

1. Arrive at the Magic Kingdom entrance 40 minutes before official opening (1 hour during peak times). Get guide maps while waiting to enter the park.
2. As soon as the park opens, head toward the right-hand side of Cinderella Castle and follow the path to Seven Dwarfs Mine Train in Fantasyland. Ride.
3. Take Peter Pan's Flight.
4. Ride The Many Adventures of Winnie the Pooh. On your way to Tomorrowland, take the route through Cinderella Castle to see the artwork in the walkway.
5. Ride Buzz Lightyear's Space Ranger Spin in Tomorrowland.
6. Give the Mad Tea Party a whirl in Fantasyland.
7. Ride Dumbo the Flying Elephant.
8. Try The Barnstormer.
9. Ride Under the Sea: Journey of the Little Mermaid.
10. Leave for lunch and a break of around 4 hours.

11. Meet Mickey Mouse at Town Square Theater.
12. See the *Monsters Inc. Laugh Floor* in Tomorrowland.
13. Try the It's a Small World boat ride in Fantasyland.
14. Meet princesses at Princess Fairytale Hall. Use mobile ordering to order dinner while in line. The best nearby location is Columbia Harbour House in Liberty Square.
15. Eat dinner.
16. Ride the Prince Charming Regal Carrousel.
17. See *Mickey's PhilharMagic*.
18. Ride The Magic Carpets of Aladdin in Adventureland.
19. See the *Enchantment* fireworks show. The best viewing spots are in front of the castle, between the castle itself and the central hub.
20. Circle back to any skipped attractions, or revisit favorites.

To use Genie+ with this plan: The most useful reservations are for Peter Pan's Flight (by far), then Buzz Lightyear, then Magic Carpets of Aladdin. Get the first available reservation for any of those (in that order), and fit that return-time window into the plan. Once you're able to get your next Genie+ reservation, look for the earliest return time for any of the next few attractions in the plan. ILL shouldn't be needed for Seven Dwarfs. If using it, make a reservation for around the park's official opening time.

See tinyurl.com/free-tplans to customize this plan at no charge, including your arrival time, attractions you'll see, and your walking speed, plus real-time updates while you're in the park.

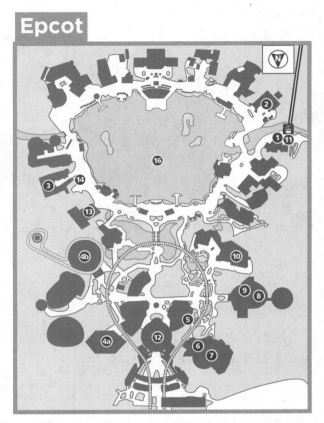

EPCOT 1-DAY TOURING PLAN FOR PARENTS WITH SMALL CHILDREN

Make park reservations as soon as you know your travel dates. If Guardians is using a virtual queue (see page 253), obtain a reservation at 7 a.m. or 1 p.m. on the day of your visit; interrupt the plan when it's time to ride.

1. Arrive at the International Gateway entrance 50 minutes before official opening (70 minutes on busy days and holidays). Get guide maps while waiting to enter.
2. As soon as the park opens, ride Remy's Ratatouille Adventure in World Showcase's France Pavilion.
3. Head to Norway, and ride Frozen Ever After. Save the Anna and Elsa character greeting for later.
4. If your kids are tall enough, try Guardians of the Galaxy (**4a**) or Test Track (**4b**) in World Discovery.
5. Walk through the Journey of Water exhibit, if it's open, on your way to The Seas pavilion in World Nature.
6. Ride The Seas with Nemo & Friends.
7. See *Turtle Talk with Crush* and tour the main tank and exhibits.

8. Take the Living with the Land boat ride at The Land.
9. If your kids are tall enough, try Soarin' Around the World.
10. Ride Journey into Imagination with Figment at the Imagination! Pavilion.
11. Eat lunch and take a break back at your hotel.
12. Return to the park and ride Spaceship Earth.
13. Begin a clockwise tour of World Showcase with the Mexico Pavilion, and take the Gran Fiesta Tour. Also check the MDE app for live performances, and visit the Kidcot Fun Stops as you tour.
14. Meet Anna and Elsa at Royal Sommerhus in Norway.
15. Eat dinner in World Showcase.
16. See *Harmonious*. Good viewing spots are around Mexico and between Canada and France.

To use Genie+ with this plan: The most useful reservations are for Remy's, Test Track, and Soarin' (in that order). Get the first available reservation for one of those, and fit that return-time window into the plan. Once you're able to get your next Genie+ reservation, look for the earliest return time for any of the next few attractions in the plan. If using **ILL**, try to get a Guardians reservation for around 10 a.m.

See tinyurl.com/free-tplans to customize this plan at no charge, including the attractions and your walking speed, plus real-time updates while you're in the park.

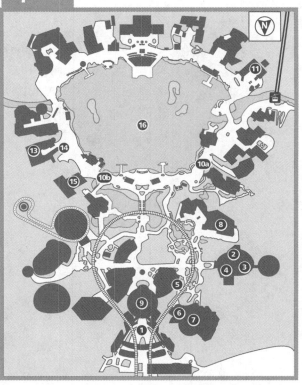

Epcot

EPCOT 1-DAY SLEEPYHEAD TOURING PLAN FOR PARENTS WITH SMALL CHILDREN

Make park reservations as soon as you know your travel dates.

1. Arrive at the main entrance around 11 a.m. Rent strollers if needed. Get guide maps.
2. Ride Soarin' Around the World at The Land Pavilion.
3. Take the Living with the Land boat ride, also at The Land Pavilion.
4. Eat lunch at Sunshine Seasons.
5. Walk through the Journey of Water exhibit, if open.
6. See The Seas with Nemo & Friends and tour the main tank and exhibits.
7. Experience *Turtle Talk with Crush*.
8. Ride Journey into Imagination with Figment at the Imagination! Pavilion.
9. Ride Spaceship Earth in World Celebration.

10. Begin a tour of World Showcase. If you were able to get Genie+ reservations for Remy's, start in Canada (**10a**) and follow steps 11–15 in order; if you got reservations for Frozen Ever After, start in Mexico (**10b**) and follow the steps in reverse order. Check the MDE app for performances, and visit the Kidcot Fun Stops as you tour.
11. Ride Remy's Ratatouille Adventure in France.
12. Eat dinner in World Showcase.
13. Tour Norway, and ride Frozen Ever After.
14. If time permits, meet Anna and Elsa at Royal Sommerhus.
15. Take the Gran Fiesta Tour boat ride in Mexico.
16. See *Harmonious*. Good viewing spots are available around Mexico and between Canada and France.

To use Genie+ with this plan: The most useful reservations are for Remy's, Frozen Ever After, and Soarin'. Get the first available reservation for one of those, and fit that return-time window into the plan. Once you're able to get your next Genie+ reservation, look for the earliest return time for any of the next few attractions in the plan. **ILL** selections aren't necessary for this plan.

See tinyurl.com/free-tplans to customize this plan at no charge, including the attractions and your walking speed, plus real-time updates while you're in the park.

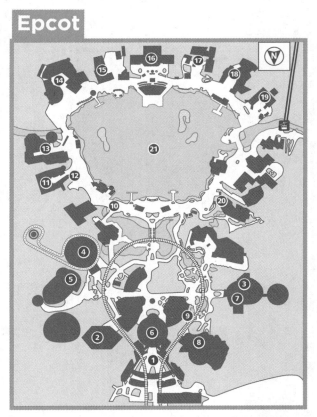

Epcot

EPCOT 1-DAY TOURING PLAN FOR TWEENS AND THEIR PARENTS

Make park reservations as soon as you know your travel dates. If Guardians is using a virtual queue (see page 253), obtain a reservation at 7 a.m. or 1 p.m. on the day of your visit; interrupt the plan when it's time to ride.

1. Arrive at the main entrance 50 minutes before official opening (70 minutes during peak times). Get guide maps.
2. If Guardians of the Galaxy is not using a virtual queue, ride it in World Discovery as soon as the park opens.
3. Ride Soarin' Around the World at The Land Pavilion.
4. Ask a cast member if Test Track is operating. If yes, ride.
5. Ride Mission: Space in World Discovery.
6. Ride Spaceship Earth in World Celebration.
7. Eat a light, late lunch. We like Sunshine Seasons.
8. Tour The Seas main tank and exhibits.
9. Visit Journey of Water exhibit, if it's open.
10. Begin a tour of World Showcase at Mexico. Skip the boat ride to save time. Also check the MDE app for live performances or character greetings.
11. Tour the Norway Pavilion and ride *Frozen Ever After*.
12. Meet Anna and Elsa at the Royal Sommerhus.
13. See the China Pavilion. Skip the film.
14. Check out the Germany Pavilion.
15. Tour the Italy Pavilion.
16. See *The American Adventure*.
17. Tour the Japan Pavilion and exhibits.
18. Tour the Morocco Pavilion and exhibits.
19. In France, ride Remy's. Skip either film being shown.
20. Tour the Canada Pavilion, and see *Canada Far and Wide*.
21. See *Harmonious*. Good viewing locations are around the Mexico Pavilion; in front of World Showcase where it meets Future World; and between Canada and France.

To use Genie+ with this plan: The most useful reservations are for Remy's, Test Track, and Soarin' (in that order). Get the first available reservation for one of those, and fit that return-time window into the plan. Once you're able to get your next Genie+ reservation, look for the earliest return time for any of the next few attractions in the plan. If using **ILL,** try to get a Guardians reservation for as close to park opening as possible, and a Frozen Ever After reservation (if it's not Genie+) for around 3 p.m.

See tinyurl.com/free-tplans to customize this plan at no charge, including the attractions and your walking speed, plus real-time updates while you're in the park.

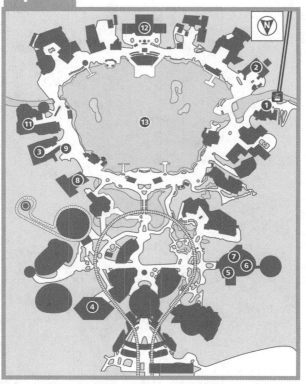

Epcot

PARENTS' EPCOT TOURING PLAN:
1 AFTERNOON AND 1 FULL DAY: FULL DAY

Make park reservations as soon as you know your travel dates. If Guardians is using a virtual queue (see page 253), obtain a reservation at 7 a.m. or 1 p.m. on the day of your visit, and interrupt the plan when it's time to ride.

1. Arrive at the International Gateway entrance 40 minutes before official opening (1 hour during peak times). Get guide maps while waiting to enter the park.

2. As soon as the park opens, ride Remy's Ratatouille Adventure in France.

3. In Norway, take the Frozen Ever After boat ride. Save the character greeting for later.

4. Head to World Discovery and ride Guardians of the Galaxy: Cosmic Rewind.

5. Eat lunch at Sunshine Seasons in The Land Pavilion.

6. Take the Living with the Land boat ride.

7. Ride Soarin' Around the World.

8. Begin a clockwise tour of World Showcase at Mexico, and take the Gran Fiesta Tour boat ride.

9. Tour Norway, and meet Anna and Elsa at Royal Sommerhus.

10. Check the MDE app for times of World Showcase live performances in the next three steps. Work these in around dinner in World Showcase.

11. See China and the acrobatics act.

12. See *The Voices of Liberty* at the United States Pavilion.

13. See *Harmonious*. Good viewing spots are available around Mexico and between Canada and France.

To use Genie+ with this plan: The most useful reservations are for Remy's, Frozen Ever After, and Soarin'. Get the first available reservation for one of those, and fit that return-time window into the plan. Once you're able to get your next Genie+ reservation, look for the earliest return time for any of the next few attractions in the plan. If using **ILL,** try to get a Guardians reservation for around 10:30 a.m.

See tinyurl.com/free-tplans to customize this plan at no charge, including the attractions and your walking speed, plus real-time updates while you're in the park.

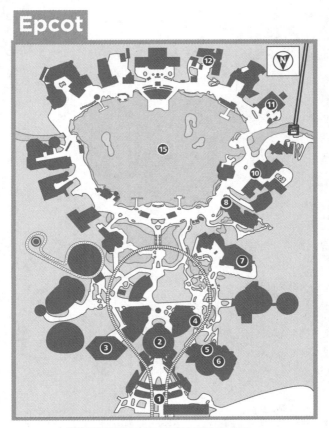

Epcot

PARENTS' EPCOT TOURING PLAN:
1 AFTERNOON AND 1 FULL DAY: AFTERNOON

Make park reservations as soon as you know your travel dates. If Guardians is using a virtual queue (see page 253), obtain a reservation at 7 a.m. or 1 p.m. on the day of your visit; interrupt the plan when it's time to ride.

1. Arrive at the main entrance around noon, and get guide maps.
2. Ride Spaceship Earth at the front of the park.
3. Ride Guardians of the Galaxy in World Discovery.
4. Walk through the Journey of Water exhibit, if open, on the way to The Seas in World Nature.
5. In World Nature, see The Seas with Nemo & Friends and tour the main tank and exhibits.
6. See *Turtle Talk with Crush.*
7. Ride Journey into Imagination with Figment. If time permits, meet characters at the Imagination! Pavilion.
8. Begin a counterclockwise tour of World Showcase at Canada, and see *Canada Far and Wide.*
9. Check the MDE app for performance times of live entertainment in World Showcase.
10. Tour the UK Pavilion, and see the band if it's playing.
11. See *Serveur Amusant* in France.
12. Tour Japan and the Mitsukoshi department store.
13. Eat dinner in World Showcase.
14. Tour any remaining pavilions you like.
15. See *Harmonious.* Good viewing spots are around Mexico and between Canada and France.

To use Genie+ with this plan: The most useful reservations are for Spaceship Earth, The Seas with Nemo & Friends, and Journey into Imagination. Get the first available reservation for one of those, and fit that return-time window into the plan. Once you're able to get your next Genie+ reservation, look for the earliest return time for any of the next few attractions in the plan. If using **ILL**, try to get a Guardians reservation for around 12:30 p.m.

See tinyurl.com/free-tplans to customize this plan at no charge, including the attractions and your walking speed, plus real-time updates while you're in the park.

Disney's Animal Kingdom

ANIMAL KINGDOM 1-DAY TOURING PLAN
FOR PARENTS WITH SMALL CHILDREN

Make park reservations for the Animal Kingdom as soon as you know your travel dates.

1. Arrive at the Animal Kingdom main entrance 50 minutes before official opening (70 minutes during holidays and busy times). Follow cast member instructions to line up for Flight of Passage. Get guide maps while waiting to enter.
2. Ride Avatar Flight of Passage (**2a**), then Na'vi River Journey (**2b**) in Pandora.
3. Sign up for Wilderness Explorers on the bridge from Discovery Island to The Oasis, on your way to Asia. Play a few games as you tour the park.
4. Ride Expedition Everest in Asia.
5. Ride Dinosaur in Dinoland U.S.A.
6. Walk the Maharajah Jungle Trek. Use mobile ordering to order lunch. The best restaurants in the park are Satu'li Canteen (**6a**) in Pandora and Flame Tree Barbecue (**6b**) on Discovery Island.
7. Eat lunch.

8. Work in the next showing of *Festival of the Lion King* in Africa around the next two steps.
9. Take the Kilimanjaro Safaris tour in Africa.
10. Walk the Gorilla Falls Exploration Trail.
11. See *Feathered Friends in Flight* in Asia.
12. Get wet on Kali River Rapids in Asia, if temperatures permit.
13. Tour the Discovery Island Trails and any other animal exhibits that interest you.
14. See *Finding Nemo: The Big Blue . . . and Beyond!* in Dinoland, U.S.A.

If the park is open past dark:
15. Eat dinner in the park.
16. See *Awakenings* at the Tree of Life. Check the MDE app for start time.
17. Tour the Valley of Mo'ara in Pandora.

To use Genie+ with this plan: The most useful reservations are for Na'vi River Journey and Kilimanjaro Safaris. Get the first available reservation for one of those, and fit that return-time window into the plan. Once you're able to get your next Genie+ reservation, look for the earliest return time for any of the next few attractions in the plan. If using **ILL**, you shouldn't need one for Flight of Passage. If Expedition Everest is offered as an ILL, try to get a return time of around 9 a.m.

See tinyurl.com/free-tplans to customize this plan at no charge, including the attractions and your walking speed, plus real-time updates while you're in the park.

Disney's Animal Kingdom

ANIMAL KINGDOM 1-DAY SLEEPYHEAD TOURING PLAN
FOR PARENTS WITH SMALL CHILDREN

Make park reservations for the Animal Kingdom as soon as you know your travel dates.

1. Arrive at the main entrance around 11 a.m., and get guide maps.
2. Sign up for Wilderness Explorers, on the bridge from The Oasis to Discovery Island. Work in this quick, fun game as you finish the tour.
3. Walk the Maharajah Jungle Trek in Asia.
4. See *Feathered Friends in Flight*.
5. Eat lunch at Flame Tree Barbecue (**5a**) on Discovery Island or Harambe Market (**5b**) in Africa.
6. Experience Kilimanjaro Safaris in Africa.
7. Work in a showing of *Festival of the Lion King* around the next two steps.
8. Ride Kali River Rapids in Asia.
9. Play in The Boneyard in DinoLand U.S.A.
10. Try TriceraTop Spin.
11. Meet Mickey and Minnie at Adventurers Outpost on Discovery Island.
12. See *Finding Nemo—The Big Blue . . . and Beyond* in DinoLand U.S.A.
13. Take the Na'vi River Journey in Pandora.
14. See *Awakenings* at the Tree of Life on Discovery Island.
15. Eat dinner.
16. Walk the Gorilla Falls Exploration Trail in Africa.
17. Experience Avatar Flight of Passage in Pandora if your kids are tall enough.
18. Tour the rest of Pandora, revisit any favorite attractions, or meet characters.

To use Genie+ with this plan: The most useful reservations are for Na'vi River Journey, Kilimanjaro Safaris, and meeting Mickey Mouse. Get the first available reservation for one of those, and fit that return-time window into the plan. Once you're able to get your next Genie+ reservation, look for the earliest return time for any of the next few attractions in the plan. If using **ILL**, try to get one for Flight of Passage around 7 p.m.

See tinyurl.com/free-tplans to customize this plan at no charge, including the attractions and your walking speed, plus real-time updates while you're in the park.

Disney's Animal Kingdom

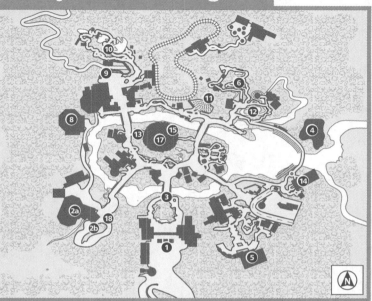

ANIMAL KINGDOM 1-DAY TOURING PLAN
FOR TWEENS AND THEIR PARENTS

Make park reservations for the Animal Kingdom as soon as you know your travel dates.

1. Arrive at the main entrance 50 minutes before official opening (70 minutes during holidays and busy times). Follow cast member instructions to line up for Flight of Passage. Get guide maps while waiting to enter.
2. Ride Avatar Flight of Passage (**2a**), then Na'vi River Journey (**2b**) in Pandora.
3. Sign up for Wilderness Explorers on the bridge from Discovery Island to The Oasis, on your way to Asia. Play the game as you tour the park.
4. Ride Expedition Everest in Asia. Use the single-rider line if your party is willing.
5. Ride Dinosaur in Dinoland U.S.A.
6. Walk the Maharajah Jungle Trek. Use mobile ordering to order lunch in advance. The best restaurants in the park are Satu'li Canteen in Pandora and Flame Tree Barbecue on Discovery Island.
7. Eat lunch.

8. Work in *Festival of the Lion King* in Africa around the next two steps.
9. Take the Kilimanjaro Safaris tour in Africa.
10. Walk the Gorilla Falls Exploration Trail.
11. See *Feathered Friends in Flight* in Asia.
12. Get wet on Kali River Rapids in Asia, if temperatures permit.
13. Tour the Discovery Island Trails and any other animal exhibits that interest you.
14. See *Finding Nemo: The Big Blue . . . and Beyond!* in Dinoland, U.S.A.
15. Meet Mickey and Minnie at Adventurers Outpost on Discovery Island.
    If the park is open past dark:
16. Eat dinner in the park.
17. See *Awakenings* at the Tree of Life. Check the MDE app for start time.
18. Tour the Valley of Mo'ara in Pandora.

To use Genie+ with this plan: The most useful reservations are for Na'vi River Journey, Kilimanjaro Safaris, and Adventurers Outpost. Get the first available reservation for one of those, and fit that return-time window into the plan. Once you're able to get your next Genie+ reservation, look for the earliest return time for any of the next few attractions in the plan. If using **ILL,** you shouldn't need one for Flight of Passage. If Expedition Everest is offered as an ILL, try to get a return time of around 10 a.m.

See tinyurl.com/free-tplans to customize this plan at no charge, including the attractions and your walking speed, plus real-time updates while you're in the park.

Disney's Animal Kingdom

ANIMAL KINGDOM 1-DAY HAPPY FAMILY TOURING PLAN

Make park reservations for the Animal Kingdom as soon as you know your travel dates.

1. Arrive at the main entrance 50 minutes before official opening (70 minutes during holidays and busy times). Follow cast member instructions to line up for Flight of Passage. Get guide maps while waiting to enter.
2. Ride Avatar Flight of Passage (**2a**), then Na'vi River Journey (**2b**) in Pandora.
3. Sign up for Wilderness Explorers on the bridge from Discovery Island to The Oasis, on your way to Dinoland, U.S.A. Play a few games as you tour the park.
4. **PARENTS:** Ride TriceraTop Spin in Dinoland, U.S.A.
5. **TEENS:** Ride Dinosaur.
6. **PARENTS:** Stop at The Boneyard while the teens finish up at Dinosaur.
7. Meet Mickey and Minnie at Adventurers Outpost on Discovery Island.
8. Take a ride on Kali River Rapids in Asia. You will get wet, so use ponchos or plastic bags to keep dry.
9. Walk the Maharajah Jungle Trek.

10. Eat lunch. The best spots nearby are Flame Tree Barbecue (**10a**) on Discovery Island, and Harambe Market (**10b**) in Africa.
11. Work in *Festival of the Lion King* in Africa around the next few steps.
12. Experience Kilimanjaro Safaris.
13. Walk the Gorilla Falls Exploration Trail.
14. Tour the Discovery Island Trails. One entrance is just over the bridge from Africa to Discovery Island, on the left. You'll end up on Discovery Island near the bridge to Asia.
15. See *Feathered Friends in Flight* in Asia.
16. See *Finding Nemo—The Big Blue . . . and Beyond* in DinoLand U.S.A.
17. Eat dinner. A good choice is Restaurantosaurus.
18. **PARENTS:** Tour any remaining animal exhibits at Discovery Island (**18a**) or The Oasis (**18b**).
19. **TEENS:** Ride Expedition Everest in Asia using the single-rider line.
20. Tour the rest of Pandora.
21. See *Awakenings* at the Tree of Life.

To use Genie+ with this plan: The most useful reservations are for Na'vi River Journey, Kilimanjaro Safaris, and Adventurers Outpost. Get the first available reservation for one of those, and fit that return-time window into the plan. Once you're able to get your next Genie+ reservation, look for the earliest return time for any of the next few attractions in the plan. If using **ILL**, you shouldn't need one for Flight of Passage. If Expedition Everest is offered as an ILL, try to get a return time of around 6 p.m.

See tinyurl.com/free-tplans to customize this plan at no charge, including the attractions and your walking speed, plus real-time updates while you're in the park.

Disney's Hollywood Studios

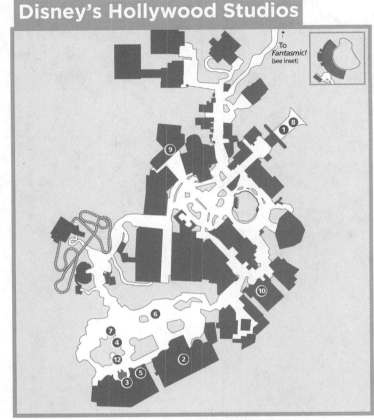

DISNEY'S HOLLYWOOD STUDIOS
1-DAY EVERYTHING *STAR WARS* TOURING PLAN

Make park reservations for the Studios as soon as you know your travel dates. Make reservations 60 days in advance for Savi's Workshop, the Droid Depot, and Oga's Cantina. Check tinyurl.com/dhs-swge before your trip for the latest information on Star Wars: Galaxy's Edge.

1. Check park hours the night before your visit. Arrive 50 minutes before official opening (70 minutes during peak times). Rent strollers, if needed, at the gas station on the right side of the park entrance, just beyond the turnstiles.
2. Enter Galaxy's Edge and ride Rise of the Resistance.
3. Ride *Millennium Falcon:* Smugglers Run.
4. Get in line for Savi's Workshop* if you want to build a lightsaber (or reserve a spot, if possible).
5. Eat lunch at Docking Bay 7 Food and Cargo.
6. As you tour the land, be on the lookout for Rey, Kylo Ren, and the Stormtroopers.

7. Get in line at the Droid Depot* if you want to build a droid.
8. Return to your hotel for lunch and a midday break.
9. Return to the park. Work in the Star Wars Launch Bay character greetings around the next few steps.
10. Ride Star Tours—The Adventures Continue in Echo Lake.
11. Eat dinner.
12. Pop in for a drink at Oga's Cantina.
13. Visit any other attractions or shows of interest, do some shopping, and explore the park.

* *This experience has a substantial, nonrefundable cost.*

To use Genie+ with this plan: The most useful reservations are for *Millennium Falcon:* Smugglers Run and Star Tours. Get the first available reservation for one of those, and fit that return-time window into the plan. Once you're able to get your next Genie+ reservation, look for the earliest return time for any of the next few attractions in the plan. You shouldn't need an **ILL** for Rise of the Resistance. If you're not sure you'll be at the park for opening, however, it's worth purchasing.

See tinyurl.com/free-tplans to customize this plan at no charge, including the attractions and your walking speed, plus real-time updates while you're in the park.

Disney's Hollywood Studios

DISNEY'S HOLLYWOOD STUDIOS 1-DAY TOURING PLAN
FOR PARENTS WITH SMALL CHILDREN

Make park reservations for the Studios as soon as you know your travel dates.

1. Check official park hours the night before your visit. Arrive 50 minutes before official opening (70 minutes during peak times). Rent strollers at the gas station on the right side of the park entrance, just beyond the turnstiles.
2. Ride Rise of the Resistance in Galaxy's Edge.
3. Ride *Millennium Falcon: Smugglers Run*.
4. Ride Toy Story Mania!
5. See *Muppet-Vision 3-D*.
6. Experience Star Tours in Echo Lake.
7. Work in a showing of *For the First Time in Forever* around the next two steps. Use mobile ordering to order lunch. The best nearby spot is Docking Bay 7 in Galaxy's Edge.
8. Eat lunch.
9. Try Mickey & Minnie's Runaway Railway.
10. Work in *Beauty and The Beast Live on Stage* on Sunset Boulevard and *Disney Junior Play and Dance!* in Animation Courtyard around the next two steps.
11. Ride Slinky Dog Dash in Toy Story Land.
12. Meet Mickey and Minnie at *Red Carpet Dreams*.
13. Meet Olaf at Celebrity Spotlight.
14. See the Mickey Mouse film *Vacation Fun* in Echo Lake.
15. Meet *Star Wars* characters at Star Wars Launch Bay in Animation Courtyard.
16. Revisit any favorite attractions, or tour the rest of the park.
17. See the fireworks (**17a**) and/or *Fantasmic!* (**17b**) (if they're performed).

To use Genie+ with this plan: The most useful reservations are for Slinky Dog Dash (by a wide margin), *Millennium Falcon: Smugglers Run*, and Mickey & Minnie's Runaway Railway. Get the first available reservation for one of those, and fit that return-time window into the plan. Once you're able to get your next Genie+ reservation, look for the earliest return time for any of the next few attractions in the plan. If using **ILL**, you shouldn't need one for Rise of the Resistance.

See tinyurl.com/free-tplans to customize this plan at no charge, including the attractions and your walking speed, plus real-time updates while you're in the park.

Disney's Hollywood Studios

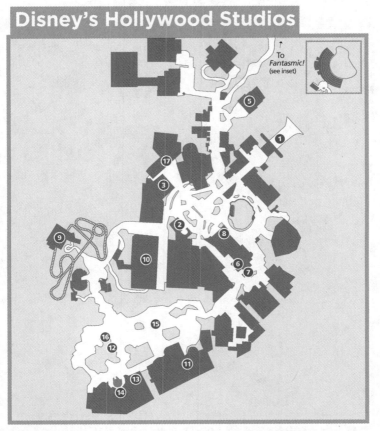

To
Fantasmic!
(see inset)

DISNEY'S HOLLYWOOD STUDIOS 1-DAY SLEEPYHEAD TOURING PLAN FOR PARENTS WITH SMALL CHILDREN

Make park reservations for the Studios as soon as you know your travel dates.

1. Arrive around 11 a.m. Grab a park map. Rent strollers, if needed, at the gas station on the right side of the park entrance, just beyond the turnstiles.
2. Ride Mickey & Minnie's Runaway Railway.
3. Join in the *Disney Junior Play and Dance!* show at Animation Courtyard.
4. Eat lunch.
5. See *Beauty and the Beast Live on Stage* on Sunset Boulevard. Check the MDE app for showtimes.
6. See Mickey and Minnie at *Red Carpet Dreams* on Commissary Lane.
7. Meet Olaf at Celebrity Spotlight in Echo Lake.
8. See *For the First Time in Forever*.
9. Ride Slinky Dog Dash in Toy Story Land.
10. Ride Toy Story Mania!
11. Enter Galaxy's Edge and ride Rise of the Resistance.
12. Get in line for Savi's Workshop* if you want to build a lightsaber (or reserve a spot, if possible).
13. Eat dinner at Docking Bay 7 Food and Cargo.
14. Ride *Millennium Falcon: Smuggler's Run.*
15. As you tour the land, be on the lookout for Rey, Kylo Ren, and the Stormtroopers.
16. Get in line at Droid Depot* if you want to build a droid.
17. Exit Galaxy's Edge and meet more *Star Wars* characters at Star Wars Launch Bay in Animation Courtyard.
18. See the fireworks (**18a**) and/or *Fantasmic!* (**18b**) (if they're performed).

* This experience has a substantial, nonrefundable cost.

To use Genie+ with this plan: The most useful reservations are for Slinky Dog Dash (by a wide margin), *Millennium Falcon: Smugglers Run,* and Mickey & Minnie's Runaway Railway. Get the first available reservation for one of those, and fit that return-time window into the plan. Once you're able to get your next Genie+ reservation, look for the earliest return time for any of the next few attractions in the plan. If using **ILL,** try to get one for Rise of the Resistance for around 3 p.m.

See tinyurl.com/free-tplans to customize this plan at no charge, including the attractions and your walking speed, plus real-time updates while you're in the park.

Disney's Hollywood Studios

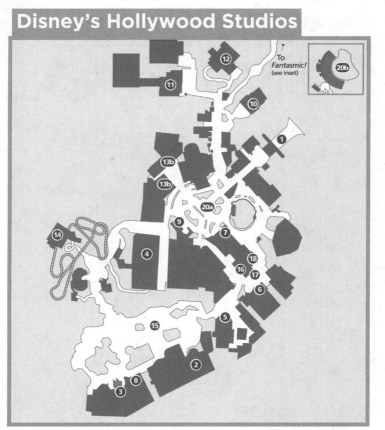

DHS 1-DAY TOURING PLAN FOR TWEENS AND THEIR PARENTS

Make park reservations for the Studios as soon as you know your travel dates. Make reservations 60 days in advance for Savi's Workshop, the Droid Depot, and Oga's Cantina. Visit tinyurl.com/dhs-swge for the latest information on Galaxy's Edge.

1. Check official park hours the night before your visit. Arrive 50 minutes before official opening (70 minutes during peak times). Rent strollers if needed.
2. Ride Rise of the Resistance in Galaxy's Edge.
3. Ride *Millennium Falcon:* Smugglers Run.
4. Ride Toy Story Mania!
5. See *Muppet-Vision 3-D.*
6. Experience Star Tours in Echo Lake.
7. Work in *For the First Time in Forever* around the next two steps. Use mobile ordering to order from Docking Bay 7.
8. Eat lunch.
9. Try Mickey & Minnie's Runaway Railway on Hollywood Blvd.
10. Work in a showing of *Beauty and The Beast Live on Stage* around the next two steps.

11. Ride the Rock 'n' Roller Coaster on Sunset Boulevard.
12. Experience The Twilight Zone Tower of Terror.
13. Meet the *Star Wars* characters at Star Wars Launch Bay (**13a**) in Animation Courtyard. If you have young children, try *Disney Junior Play and Dance!* (**13b**), also in Animation Courtyard, instead.
14. Ride Slinky Dog Dash in Toy Story Land.
15. Explore the rest of Galaxy's Edge.
16. Meet Mickey and Minnie at *Red Carpet Dreams.*
17. Meet Olaf at Celebrity Spotlight.
18. See the Mickey Mouse film *Vacation Fun* in Echo Lake.
19. Revisit any favorite attractions or tour the rest of the park.
20. See the fireworks (**20a**) and/or *Fantasmic!* (**20b**) (if they're performed).

To use Genie+ with this plan: The most useful reservations are for Slinky Dog Dash (by a wide margin), *Millennium Falcon:* Smugglers Run, and Rock 'n' Roller Coaster. Get the first available reservation for one of those, and fit that return-time window into the plan. Once you're able to get your next Genie+ reservation, look for the earliest return time for any of the next few attractions in the plan. If using **ILL,** you shouldn't need one for Rise of the Resistance.

See tinyurl.com/free-tplans to customize this plan at no charge, including the attractions and your walking speed, plus real-time updates while you're in the park.

Disney's Hollywood Studios

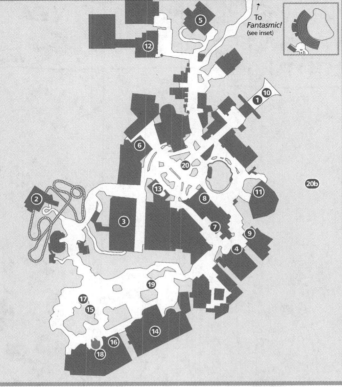

To
Fantasmic!
(see inset)

DHS 1-DAY HAPPY FAMILY TOURING PLAN

Make park reservations for the Studios as soon as you know your travel dates. Make reservations 60 days in advance for Savi's Workshop, the Droid Depot, and Oga's Cantina. Visit tinyurl.com/dhs-swge before your trip for the latest information on Galaxy's Edge.

1. Check official park hours the night before. Arrive 50 minutes before official opening (70 minutes during peak times). Rent strollers, if needed.
2. Ride Slinky Dog Dash in Toy Story Land.
3. Ride Toy Story Mania!
4. Ride Star Tours—The Adventures Continue in Echo Lake.
5. **TEENS:** Ride The Twilight Zone Tower of Terror.
6. **PARENTS:** See *Disney Junior Play and Dance!* in Animation Courtyard. Check the MDE app for showtimes.
7. Meet Mickey and Minnie at *Red Carpet Dreams*.
8. See *For the First Time in Forever* in Echo Lake.
9. Eat lunch. Try Backlot Express.
10. **PARENTS:** Go back to the hotel for a break of 3–4 hours.
11. **TEENS:** See *Indiana Jones Epic Stunt Spectacular!* Check the MDE app for times.

12. **TEENS:** Ride Rock 'n' Roller Coaster on Sunset Boulevard. Use the single-rider line if the wait exceeds 25 minutes.
13. Meet Mickey & Minnie's Runaway Railway on Hollywood Boulevard.
14. In Galaxy's Edge, ride Rise of the Resistance.
15. Get in line for Savi's Workshop* if you want to build a light-saber (or reserve a spot, if possible).
16. Eat dinner at Docking Bay 7 Food and Cargo.
17. If you want to build a droid, visit the Droid Depot.*
18. Ride *Millennium Falcon:* Smuggler's Run.
19. As you tour the land, be on the lookout for Rey, Kylo Ren, and the Stormtroopers.
20. See the evening fireworks and shows (if performed).
* *This experience has a substantial, nonrefundable cost.*

To use Genie+ with this plan: The most useful reservations are for *Millennium Falcon*, Mickey & Minnie's Runaway Railway, and Rock 'n' Roller Coaster. Get the first available reservation for one of those, and fit that return-time window into the plan. Once you're able to get your next Genie+ reservation, look for the earliest return time for any of the next few attractions in the plan. If using **ILL,** try to obtain one for Rise of the Resistance for around 5 p.m. See tinyurl.com/free-tplans to customize this plan at no charge, including the attractions and your walking speed, plus real-time updates while you're in the park.

Universal Studios Florida

UNIVERSAL STUDIOS FLORIDA 1-DAY TOURING PLAN
FOR FAMILIES WITH SMALL CHILDREN

1. Buy admission in advance. Call ☎ 407-363-8000 or visit universalorlando.com the day before for the official opening time.

2. Arrive 90–120 minutes before official opening time if Early Park Admission is offered and you're eligible (30–45 minutes if you're a day guest). Check Universal's app for daily showtimes. Rent a stroller if needed.

3. Early-entry guests should visit Ollivanders (**3a**), and experience Harry Potter and the Escape from Gringotts (**3b**). Use child swap or exit after the elevators if your kid is under 42″, or just enjoy Diagon Alley.

4. Before early entry ends, ride Despicable Me Minion Mayhem. Day guests should wait in the Front Lot until permitted to ride Despicable Me.

5. Experience Transformers: The Ride-3D if your kid can handle the noise and explosions.

6. Ride Race Through New York Starring Jimmy Fallon.

7. Ride E.T. Adventure.

8. Ride The Simpsons Ride in Springfield.

9. Try Kang & Kodos' Twirl 'n' Hurl.

10. See *Animal Actors on Location!* according to the schedule. Get a snack on Fast Food Boulevard while you're waiting for the show to start.

11. Between shows, work in Woody's Nuthouse Coaster (**11a**) and time in Fievel's Playland (**11b**) and Curious George Goes to Town (**11c**).

12. Take a break for at least 2 hours, depending on how late the park is open. If staying nearby, return to your room for a nap. Otherwise, take a rest at CityWalk or a resort hotel.

13. Return to the park. If your kids are brave, see *Universal Orlando's Horror Make-Up Show* (**13a**) and/or *The Bourne Stuntacular* (**13b**) according to the daily entertainment schedule.

14. Greet characters such as Shrek, SpongeBob, and the Transformers at locations shown on the map.

15. On your way into Diagon Alley, chat with the Knight Bus conductor and his shrunken head. Also look for Kreacher in the window of 12 Grimmauld Place, and dial MAGIC (62442) in the red phone booth.

16. See the *Celestina Warbeck and the Banshees* and *Tales of Beedle the Bard* shows.

17. See the wand ceremony at Ollivanders, and buy a wand if you wish.

18. Tour Diagon Alley. If you're hungry, try the Leaky Cauldron or Florean Fortescue's Ice-Cream Parlour.

19. Ride Harry Potter and the Escape from Gringotts from the standby queue (if you didn't earlier). If your kid is under 42″, use child swap or exit after the elevators.

20. Revisit favorite attractions, and (if scheduled) watch *Universal Orlando's Cinematic Celebration* from Central Park.

Universal's Islands of Adventure

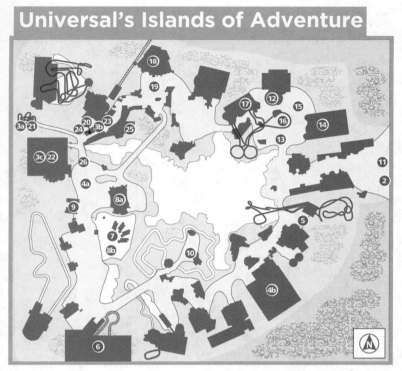

UNIVERSAL'S ISLANDS OF ADVENTURE 1-DAY TOURING PLAN FOR FAMILIES WITH SMALL CHILDREN

1. Buy admission in advance. Call ☎ 407-363-8000 or visit universalorlando.com the day before for the official opening time.

2. Arrive 90–120 minutes before opening if Early Park Admission is offered and you're eligible (30–45 minutes if you're a day guest). Check Universal's app for daily showtimes. Rent a stroller if needed.

3. Early-entry guests should ride Flight of the Hippogriff (**3a**), see the wand ceremony at Ollivanders (**3b**), and tour the queue (but exit before boarding) at Harry Potter and the Forbidden Journey (**3c**).

4. *Early-entry guests:* Exit Hogsmeade into Jurassic Park as early entry ends (**4a**) and ride Skull Island: Reign of Kong as soon as it opens (if your kids are brave enough), then continue to Marvel Super Hero Island to ride The Amazing Adventures of Spider-Man (**4b**). *Guests without early entry:* Start at this step with Spider-Man.

5. Ride Storm Force Accelatron.

6. Experience Skull Island: Reign of Kong if you dare (and haven't already).

7. Continue to Jurassic Park and get in line for Pteranodon Flyers if your child is 36"–56".

8. Let the kids explore the Jurassic Park Discovery Center (**8a**) and play in Camp Jurassic (**8b**).

9. Meet Blue at the Raptor Encounter.

10. Explore Me Ship, *The Olive* in Toon Lagoon.

11. Take a break for at least 2 hours, depending on how late the park is open. If staying nearby, return to your room for lunch and a nap. Otherwise, take a rest at CityWalk or a resort hotel.

12. Return to the park. See the next scheduled show of *Oh! The Stories You'll Hear!* in Seuss Landing.

13. Explore If I Ran the Zoo while waiting for the show.

14. Ride The Cat in the Hat.

15. Ride One Fish, Two Fish, Red Fish, Blue Fish.

16. Enjoy the Caro-Seuss-el.

17. Ride The High in the Sky Seuss Trolley Train Ride.

18. See *Poseidon's Fury* in The Lost Continent.

19. Chat with the Mystic Fountain.

20. Enter The Wizarding World of Harry Potter—Hogsmeade, and see the *Frog Choir* or *Triwizard Spirit Rally* perform outside Hogwarts.

21. Ride Flight of the Hippogriff (if you didn't earlier).

22. If you didn't already, walk through the queue of Harry Potter and the Forbidden Journey.

23. See the wand ceremony at Ollivanders if you didn't earlier, and buy a wand if you wish.

24. See the stage show you didn't see earlier. Snap a picture of the Hogwarts Express conductor, and explore the shops and interactive windows around Hogsmeade.

25. Have dinner at Three Broomsticks.

26. Watch the Hogwarts Castle light show (if scheduled), or revisit any favorite attractions.

Universal's Islands of Adventure

UNIVERSAL ORLANDO HIGHLIGHTS 1-DAY/2-PARK TOURING PLAN
FOR FAMILIES WITH SMALL CHILDREN: PART 1
Assumes: 1-Day Park-To-Park Ticket

1. Buy admission in advance. Call ☎ 407-363-8000 or visit universalorlando.com the day before for the official opening time.

2. Arrive at Islands of Adventure 90–120 minutes before the official opening time if Early Park Admission is offered and you're eligible (30–45 minutes if you're a day guest). Check Universal's app for daily showtimes. Rent a stroller if needed.

3. Early-entry guests should ride Flight of the Hippogriff (**3a**), see the wand ceremony at Ollivanders (**3b**), and tour the queue (but exit before boarding) at Harry Potter and the Forbidden Journey (**3c**).

4. Ride The Amazing Adventures of Spider-Man. *Day guests:* Start with Spider-Man (**4a**), followed by Skull Island: Reign of Kong (**4b**). *Early-entry guests:* Ride Reign of Kong (**4b**) on your way to Spider-Man (**4a**) while walking from Jurassic Park. All guests continue as follows.

5. Continue to Jurassic Park and get in line for Pteranodon Flyers if your child is 36"–56".

6. Meet Blue at the Raptor Encounter.

7. Let the kids explore the Jurassic Park Discovery Center (**7a**) and play in Camp Jurassic (**7b**).

8. Ride Hogwarts Express to USF. Have your park-to-park ticket ready.

Tour Universal Studios Florida using Part 2 of this plan (see next page); then return to IOA and resume at step 20 below.

20. Chat with the Mystic Fountain.

21. See *Poseidon's Fury* in The Lost Continent.

22. Experience The High in the Sky Seuss Trolley Train Ride! in Seuss Landing.

23. Enjoy the Caro-Seuss-el.

24. Ride One Fish, Two Fish, Red Fish, Blue Fish.

25. Experience The Cat in the Hat.

26. In Marvel Super Hero Island, ride Storm Force Accelatron.

27. Explore Me Ship, *The Olive* in Toon Lagoon.

28. Eat dinner at Thunder Falls Terrace (**28a**) in Jurassic Park or Three Broomsticks (**28b**) in Hogsmeade.

29. See the *Frog Choir* or *Triwizard Spirit Rally* perform on the small stage outside Hogwarts Castle.

30. See the wand ceremony at Ollivanders, and buy a wand if you wish.

31. Ride Flight of the Hippogriff if you haven't already.

32. If you haven't already, walk through the queue of Harry Potter and the Forbidden Journey.

33. Watch the Hogwarts Castle light show (if scheduled), or revisit any favorite attractions.

(continued on next page)

Universal Studios Florida

UNIVERSAL ORLANDO HIGHLIGHTS 1-DAY/2-PARK TOURING PLAN FOR FAMILIES WITH SMALL CHILDREN: PART 2

(continued from previous page)

9. Enter Diagon Alley and experience Harry Potter and the Escape from Gringotts. If your kid is under 42″, use child swap or exit after the elevators, or just enjoy Diagon Alley.

10. Experience The Simpsons Ride in Springfield.

11. Try Kang & Kodos' Twirl 'n' Hurl.

12. Ride E.T. Adventure in Woody Woodpecker's KidZone.

13. Break for lunch at Fast Food Boulevard in Springfield (**13a**) or Today Cafe (**13b**) near the front of the park.

14. See *Universal Orlando's Horror Make-Up Show* (**14a**) or *The Bourne Stuntacular* (**14b**) according to the daily entertainment schedule.

15. Between shows, work in Woody's Nuthouse Coaster (**15a**) and time in Fievel's Playland (**15b**) and Curious George Goes to Town (**15c**).

16. Ride Despicable Me Minion Mayhem.

17. Experience Transformers: The Ride—3D in Production Central if your kid can handle the noise and explosions.

18. Ride Race Through New York Starring Jimmy Fallon if the standby wait is short.

19. Return to IOA via Hogwarts Express, or walk back if the posted wait exceeds 20 minutes.

Resume Part 1 starting with step 20 (see previous page).

Universal Studios Florida

7th Ave.

UNIVERSAL STUDIOS FLORIDA 1-DAY TOURING PLAN FOR TWEENS

1. Buy admission in advance. Call ☎ 407-363-8000 or visit universalorlando.com the day before for the official opening time.

2. Arrive 90–120 minutes before official opening time if Early Park Admission is offered and you're eligible (30–45 minutes if you're a day guest). Check Universal's app for daily showtimes.

3. *Early-entry guests* should visit Ollivanders (**3a**) and ride Harry Potter and the Escape from Gringotts (**3b**). If Gringotts isn't operating, enjoy the rest of Diagon Alley, but don't get in line.

4. Before early entry ends, ride Despicable Me Minion Mayhem. *Day guests* should begin their tour here.

5. Ride Hollywood Rip Ride Rockit if your tween is brave and at least 51".

6. Experience Transformers: The Ride—3D.

7. Ride Revenge of the Mummy in New York.

8. Ride Race Through New York Starring Jimmy Fallon.

9. Experience Men in Black Alien Attack in World Expo.

10. Ride The Simpsons Ride in Springfield.

11. Ride E.T. Adventure in Woody Woodpecker's KidZone.

12. Eat lunch at Fast Food Boulevard.

13. Work in *Animal Actors on Location!* around lunch according to the daily entertainment schedule.

14. See *Universal Orlando's Horror Make-Up Show* (**14a**) and *The Bourne Stuntacular* (**14b**) according to the daily entertainment schedule.

15. Chat with the Knight Bus conductor and his shrunken head outside of Diagon Alley. Also look for Kreacher in the window of 12 Grimmauld Place, and dial MAGIC (62442) in the red phone booth.

16. See the *Celestina Warbeck and the Banshees* and *Tales of Beedle the Bard* shows.

17. See the wand ceremony at Ollivanders, and buy a wand if you wish.

18. Tour Diagon Alley. Browse the shops, explore the dark recesses of Knockturn Alley, and discover the interactive effects. If you're hungry, try the Leaky Cauldron or Florean Fortescue's Ice-Cream Parlour.

19. Ride Harry Potter and the Escape from Gringotts.

20. Revisit favorite attractions, if time permits.

21. If it's scheduled, watch *Universal Orlando's Cinematic Celebration* from Central Park (between Hollywood and Woody Woodpecker's KidZone).

Universal's Islands of Adventure

UNIVERSAL'S ISLANDS OF ADVENTURE 1-DAY TOURING PLAN
FOR TWEENS

1. Buy admission in advance. Call ☎ 407-363-8000 or visit universalorlando.com the day before for the official opening time.

2. Arrive at IOA 90–120 minutes before the official opening time if Early Park Admission is offered and you're eligible (30–45 minutes if you're a day guest). Check Universal's app for daily showtimes.

3. *Early-entry guests* should ride Hagrid's Magical Creatures Motorbike Adventure in Hogsmeade, but only if they are at the front of the pack.

4. *Early-entry guests* may ride the Jurassic World VelociCoaster (**4a**) if 51" or taller, or Flight of the Hippogriff (**4b**), followed by Harry Potter and the Forbidden Journey (**4c**), if at least 15 minutes remain in early entry.

5. *Guests without early entry* who are hardy and at least 54" tall should ride The Incredible Hulk Coaster first.

6. Ride The Amazing Adventures of Spider-Man. *Day guests:* Start with Spider-Man (**6a**), followed by Skull Island: Reign of Kong (**6b**). *Early-entry guests:* Ride Reign of Kong (**6b**) on your way to Spider-Man (**6a**) while walking from Jurassic Park. All guests continue as follows.

7. Take the Jurassic Park River Adventure. Put your belongings in a pay locker here, and leave them through the next two rides.

8. Ride Dudley Do-Right's Ripsaw Falls in Toon Lagoon.

9. Ride Popeye & Bluto's Bilge-Rat Barges. Retrieve your property from Jurassic Park.

10. Eat lunch. A good quick-service choice is Thunder Falls Terrace.

11. Meet Blue at the Raptor Encounter.

12. See the *Frog Choir* or *Triwizard Spirit Rally* perform on the small stage outside Hogwarts Castle.

13. See the wand ceremony at Ollivanders, and buy a wand if you wish.

14. Chat with the Mystic Fountain.

15. In Lost Continent, see *Poseidon's Fury.*

16. Experience The High in the Sky Seuss Trolley Train Ride! in Seuss Landing.

17. Experience The Cat in the Hat.

18. In Marvel Super Hero Island, ride Doctor Doom's Fearfall if 52" or taller.

19. Ride Storm Force Accelatron.

20. Ride The Incredible Hulk Coaster (**20a**) or Jurassic World VelociCoaster (**20b**), whichever you didn't ride earlier.

21. Have dinner at Three Broomsticks in Hogsmeade.

22. Ride Flight of the Hippogriff if you haven't already.

23. Ride Harry Potter and the Forbidden Journey.

24. Ride Hagrid's Magical Creatures Motorbike Adventure after sunset, if possible.

25. Watch the last Hogwarts Castle light show of the evening (if scheduled), or revisit any favorite attractions.

Universal's Islands of Adventure

UNIVERSAL ORLANDO HIGHLIGHTS 1-DAY/2-PARK TOURING PLAN
FOR TWEENS: PART 1
Assumes: *1-Day Park-To-Park Ticket*

1. Buy admission in advance. Call ☎ 407-363-8000 or visit universalorlando.com the day before for the official opening time.
2. Arrive at IOA 90–120 minutes before the official opening time if Early Park Admission is offered and you're eligible (30–45 minutes if you're a day guest). Check Universal's app for daily showtimes.
3. *Early-entry guests* should ride Hagrid's Magical Creatures Motorbike Adventure in Hogsmeade, but only if they are at the front of the pack.
4. *Early-entry guests* may ride the Jurassic World VelociCoaster (**4a**) if 51″ or taller or Flight of the Hippogriff (**4b**), followed by Harry Potter and the Forbidden Journey (**4c**), if at least 15 minutes remain in early entry.
5. *Guests without early entry* who are hardy and at least 54″ should first ride The Incredible Hulk Coaster.
6. Ride The Amazing Adventures of Spider-Man. *Day guests:* Start with Spider-Man (**6a**), followed by Skull Island: Reign of Kong (**6b**). *Early-entry guests:* Ride Reign of Kong (**6b**) on your way to Spider-Man (**6a**) while walking from Jurassic Park. All guests continue as follows.
7. Take the Jurassic Park River Adventure.
8. Meet Blue at the Raptor Encounter.
9. Ride Hogwarts Express to USF. Have your park-to-park ticket ready.

Tour Universal Studios Florida using Part 2 of this plan (see next page); then return to IOA and resume at step 21 below.

21. Chat with the Mystic Fountain.
22. Experience The High in the Sky Seuss Trolley Train Ride! in Seuss Landing.
23. Experience The Cat in the Hat.
24. In Marvel Super Hero Island, ride Doctor Doom's Fearfall if 52″ or taller.
25. Ride Storm Force Accelatron.
26. Ride The Incredible Hulk Coaster (**26a**) or Jurassic World VelociCoaster (**26b**), whichever one you didn't ride earlier.
27. Eat dinner at Thunder Falls Terrace (**27a**) in Jurassic Park or Three Broomsticks (**27b**) in Hogsmeade.
28. See the *Frog Choir* or *Triwizard Spirit Rally* perform on the small stage outside Hogwarts Castle.
29. See the wand ceremony at Ollivanders, and buy a wand if you wish.
30. Ride Flight of the Hippogriff if you haven't already.
31. Ride Harry Potter and the Forbidden Journey.
32. Ride Hagrid's Magical Creatures Motorbike Adventure in Hogsmeade after sunset, if possible.
33. Watch the last Hogwarts Castle light show of the night (if scheduled), or revisit favorite attractions.

(continued on next page)

Universal Studios Florida

UNIVERSAL ORLANDO HIGHLIGHTS 1-DAY/2-PARK TOURING PLAN FOR TWEENS: PART 2

(continued from previous page)

10. Enter Diagon Alley and ride Harry Potter and the Escape from Gringotts.

11. Ride Men in Black Alien Attack in World Expo.

12. Experience The Simpsons Ride in Springfield.

13. Ride E.T. Adventure in Woody Woodpecker's KidZone.

14. Break for lunch at Fast Food Boulevard (**14a**) in Springfield or Today Cafe (**14b**) near the front of the park.

15. See *Universal Orlando's Horror Make-Up Show* (**15a**) or *The Bourne Stuntacular* (**15b**) according to the daily entertainment schedule.

16. Experience Transformers: The Ride—3D.

17. Ride Hollywood Rip Ride Rockit if your tween is brave and at least 51".

18. Ride Race Through New York Starring Jimmy Fallon if the standby wait is short.

19. Ride Revenge of the Mummy in New York.

20. Take a look around Diagon Alley before returning to IOA via Hogwarts Express, or walk back if the posted wait exceeds 20 minutes.

Resume Part 1 starting with step 21 (see previous page).